Lecture Notes in Computer Science

Lecture Notes in Artificial Intelligence 16136

Founding Editor

Jörg Siekmann

The series Lecture Notes in Artificial Intelligence (LNAI) was established in 1988 as a topical subseries of LNCS devoted to artificial intelligence.

The series publishes state-of-the-art research results at a high level. As with the LNCS mother series, the mission of the series is to serve the international R & D community by providing an invaluable service, mainly focused on the publication of conference and workshop proceedings and postproceedings.

Valeria de Paiva · Peter Koepke
Editors

Intelligent Computer Mathematics

18th International Conference, CICM 2025 Brasilia, Brazil, October 6–10, 2025 Proceedings

Springer

Editors
Valeria de Paiva
Topos Institute
Shattuck Ave Berkeley, CA, USA

Peter Koepke
University of Bonn
Bonn, Germany

ISSN 0302-9743 ISSN 1611-3349 (electronic)
Lecture Notes in Artificial Intelligence
ISBN 978-3-032-07020-3 ISBN 978-3-032-07021-0 (eBook)
https://doi.org/10.1007/978-3-032-07021-0

LNCS Sublibrary: SL7 – Artificial Intelligence

This Springer imprint is published by the registered company Springer Nature Switzerland AG
The registered company address is: Gewerbestrasse 11, 6330 Cham, Switzerland

Preface

This volume contains the papers presented at the 18th Conference on Intelligent Computer Mathematics (CICM 2025), held in person from October 6–10, 2025, at the University of Brasilia, Federal District, Brazil.

The Conference on Intelligent Computer Mathematics (CICM) brings together a wide spectrum of research communities in **computational mathematics** whose interests range from formalization and mechanization of mathematical knowledge to the development of intelligent tools that support mathematical discovery, reasoning, and communication. These communities contribute theoretical foundations and practical solutions in areas such as artificial intelligence, symbolic computation, automated deduction, mathematical knowledge management, and advanced user interfaces for mathematical work. CICM serves as a meeting point where these diverse approaches can be integrated, fostering innovations that advance both the automation and the human understanding of mathematics.

In recent years, the field of Computer Mathematics has attracted growing attention, spurred in part by the remarkable advances in Large Language Models (LLMs) and their contributions to the autoformalization and informalization of mathematics.

Since its inception in 2008, CICM has provided a unique venue for addressing the challenges of integrating these areas, with a particular focus on theorem proving and computer algebra, mathematical knowledge management, and digital mathematical libraries. While each of these domains has its own strengths, their integration continues to generate powerful synergies and added value. The conference has been held annually in: Birmingham, UK (2008); Grand Bend, Canada (2009); Paris, France (2010); Bertinoro, Italy (2011); Bremen, Germany (2012); Bath, UK (2013); Coimbra, Portugal (2014); Washington, D.C., USA (2015); Białystok, Poland (2016); Edinburgh, UK (2017); Hagenberg, Austria (2018); Prague, Czech Republic (2019); Bertinoro, Italy (2020, online); Timişoara, Romania (2021, online); Tbilisi, Georgia (2022, hybrid); Cambridge, UK (2023, hybrid); and Montreal, Canada (2024).

CICM 2025 continued this tradition while placing particular emphasis on the interplay between AI techniques—especially LLMs—and the conference's established focus areas: proof assistants, logical frameworks and transformations, knowledge representation, proof certification, and proof search strategies.

This year, CICM received 34 full submissions, of which 24 research papers were accepted and published in this volume. Each submission underwent a single-blind review process, with evaluation by at least three Program Committee (PC) members and, when appropriate, additional input from subreviewers. A rebuttal phase allowed authors to address reviewer comments before the PC's final deliberations. In addition to the accepted research papers, the proceedings also contains a paper version of the invited talk by Fabian Huch.

The **Best Paper Award** was presented to the paper *Automated Symmetric Constructions in Discrete Geometry*, by Bernardo Subercaseaux, Ethan Mackey, Long Qian, and Marijn Heule.

The scientific program was enriched by keynote talks from:

- **Josef Urban** (Czech Institute of Informatics, Robotics and Cybernetics), *Alien Codes and Their Automated and Human Explanations*;
- **Assia Mahboubi** (INRIA, Nantes), *Formal Proofs: Computer Science at the Service of Rigour and Creativity in Mathematics*;
- **Fabian Huch** (Technische Universität München), *Supporting Maintenance of Formal Mathematics with Similarity Search*;
- **Daniele Nantes Sobrinho** (University of Brasilia), *Equational Reasoning in Program Verification*and
- **Temur Kutsia** (Research Institute for Symbolic Computation, Johannes Kepler University Linz), *Solving Symbolic Constraints* as a joint invited speaker with the Logical and Semantic Frameworks with Applications (LSFA 2025) conference.

Alongside the main track, CICM 2025 hosted a Doctoral Programme, offering PhD students a forum to present early research results and receive feedback. The conference also featured three workshops — *Math Datasets and Libraries: Alignments and Comparisons* (Align2025), the *Workshop on Natural Formal Mathematics* (NatFoM), and *Open Science and Digital Curation* (OSDC) — as well as four tutorials: *SAT-solving for Discrete Mathematics, Machine Learning for the Isabelle Proof Assistant, Interactive Theorem Proving in Lean*, and *Formal Proofs in PVS*.

We gratefully acknowledge the many people and institutions who contributed to the success of CICM 2025:

- the authors, for their submissions and presentations;
- the PC members and additional reviewers, for their detailed reports and thoughtful discussions;
- the steering committee and former PC chairs, for their guidance;
- the Doctoral Programme Chairs, **Claudia Nalon** (UnB) and **Marcelo Finger** (USP);
- the Workshop Chairs, **Thaynara Arielly de Lima** (University of Goiás) and **Edward Herman Haeusler** (PUC-Rio), and all workshop and tutorial organizers;
- the Publicity Chair, **Serge Autexier** (German Research Center for Artificial Intelligence – DFKI, Bremen); and
- above all, the Conference Chair, **Mauricio Ayala-Rincón** (University of Brasilia), and his local team, for their tireless efforts in hosting this event.

We also thank our institutional supporters: the University of Brasília, CAPES, CNPq, FINATEC, FAPDF, SBM, SBL, and ASL for their generous support.

August 2025

Valeria de Paiva
Peter Koepke

Organization

Programme Committee Chairs

Valeria de Paiva	Topos Institute, USA
Peter Koepke	University of Bonn, Germany

Programme Committee

Thaynara Arielly de Lima	Universidade Federal de Goiás, Brazil
Mauricio Ayala-Rincón	Universidade de Brasilía, Brazil
Haniel Barbosa	Universidade Federal de Minas Gerais, Brazil
Katja Berčič	University of Ljubljana and Institute of Mathematics, Physics and Mechanics, Slovenia
Ana Bove	Chalmers University of Technology and University of Gothenburg, Sweden
Kevin Buzzard	Imperial College London, UK
Mario Carneiro	Chalmers University of Technology and University of Gothenburg, Sweden
Flavio L. C. De Moura	Universidade de Brasilia, Brazil
Silvia De Toffoli	University of Pavia, Italy
María Inés de Frutos-Fernández	University of Bonn, Germany
Catherine Dubois	ENSIIE-Samovar, France
William Farmer	McMaster University, Canada
Yannick Forster	Inria Paris, France
Herman Geuvers	Radboud University, The Netherlands
Moa Johansson	Chalmers University of Technology, Sweden
Andrea Kohlhase	Neu-Ulm University of Applied Sciences, Germany
Michael Kohlhase	FAU Erlangen-Nürnberg, Germany
Angeliki Koutsoukou-Argyraki	Royal Holloway, University of London, UK
Heather Macbeth	Fordham University, USA
João Marcos	Universidade Federal de Santa Catarina, Brazil
Paul-André Melliès	CNRS, Université Paris Cité, France
Pedro Quaresma	University of Coimbra, Portugal
Florian Rabe	FAU Erlangen-Nürnberg, Germany
Aarne Ranta	Chalmers University of Technology, Sweden
Natarajan Shankar	SRI International, USA

Geoff Sutcliffe	University of Miami, USA
Alvaro Tasistro	Universidad ORT, Uruguay
Richard Zanibbi	Rochester Institute of Technology, USA

Additional Reviewers

Ciarán Dunne	Dublin City University, Ireland
Sólrún Halla Einarsdóttir	Chalmers University of Technology and University of Gothenburg, Sweden
Nikolai Fadeev	Johannes Kepler University Linz, Austria
André Luiz Galdino	Universidade Federal de Catalão, Brazil
George Granberry	Chalmers University of Technology and University of Gothenburg, Sweden
Hugo Herbelin	Inria, France
Tomaz Mascarenhas	Universidade Federal de Minas Gerais, Brazil
Juan Meleiro	University of São Paulo, Brazil
Jan Frederik Schaefer	FAU Erlangen, Germany
Marcel Schütz	FAU Erlangen, Germany
Mallku Soldevila	Universidade Federal de Minas Gerais, Brazil
Akihisa Yamada	AIST, Japan

Abstracts of Invited Speakers

Supporting Maintenance of Formal Mathematics with Similarity Search

Fabian Huch

Technical University of Munich, Germany

Abstract. The effort required for maintaining large libraries of formal mathematics is quite substantial. In this work, we exploit structural similarity to alleviate the burden of maintenance, investigating two main problems: First, we present a general framework for detecting duplicates in large libraries of formal mathematics, combining surface-level syntax, document markup, and the underlying formulae. For scalability, we generate potentially matching candidates with a discriminator-based approach. On Isabelle/HOL, our method maintains perfect precision up to a similarity threshold of 0.95. Secondly, we address the issue of out-of-place auxiliary lemmas that are frequently created during development of in-depth formalizations. We propose a community detection approach on the underlying dependency graph of formal entities, which finds co-located lemmas that have similar link patterns. For a dataset of lemmas moved during Isabelle development, the correct location is in the top 6 neighborhoods suggested by our approach on average (median).

Formal Proofs: Computer Science at the Service of Rigour and Creativity in Mathematics

Assia Mahboubi

Inria, Nantes, France

Abstract. For more than half a century, computers have become essential research instruments in many different areas of fundamental mathematics. They have dramatically expanded the scale of experimentation and visualization in mathematics, becoming in this way precious assistants for shaping conjectures. But also for finding proofs. This talk proposes to discuss the role of computer tools in contemporary mathematics, and in particular the potential impact of the rise of interactive theorem proving and of the advent of large corpora of mathematics machine-checked with provers like Rocq, Lean, Isabelle, Agda, etc.

Equational Reasoning in Program Verification

Daniele Nantes Sobrinho

University of Brasilia, Brazil

Abstract. Several successful analysis tools and platforms support compositional verification and/or compositional bug-finding for heap-manipulating programs. These approaches are often powered by compositional symbolic execution (CSE), grounded in ideas from separation logic (SL) and incorrectness separation logic (ISL). In this context, "compositional" means that the analysis scales by reasoning about functions in isolation—anywhere in the codebase—producing simple function specifications that can be reused in broader calling contexts. Modern CSE-based tools rely critically on two capabilities: reasoning about function calls using function specifications, and manipulating user-defined predicates. A key challenge that arises here is the frame inference problem (FIP): determining which parts of the symbolic state are relevant for a given operation. Many tools address FIP using a consume-produce approach, which reduces the problem to a form of matching between logical assertions and symbolic states. In this talk, I will argue that the FIP—and, more broadly, symbolic analysis in this setting—is inherently an equational problem. Reasoning modulo axioms, while often necessary, introduces a significant burden that must be carefully managed in both the formalisation and implementation of these analyses. (Joint work with Andreas Lööw, Philippa Gardner and Simon Park.)

Alien Codes and Their Automated and Human Explanations

Josef Urban

Czech Institute of Informatics, Robotics and Cybernetics (CIIRC), Prague, Czech Republic

Abstract. We have automatically discovered symbolic explanations for over one-third of the sequences in the Online Encyclopedia of Integer Sequences (OEIS). The talk will describe the neuro-symbolic system consisting of a positive feedback loop that starts from zero knowledge and iterates between guessing the explanations, their verification, and training of the guessing methods. Then I will describe several additions and experiments that led to the current set of solutions found in hundreds of iterations of the feedback loop. I will show some of the solutions discovered. This includes over 50 programs for primes developed as the system self-evolves. I will also discuss a related experiment in automatically proving equivalences of the discovered programs using the SMT solver Z3. Because induction is often needed in such proofs, this leads to another self-learning neuro-symbolic system that repeatedly tries to guess the right instances of induction for Z3. Finally, I will also show some of the recent human explanations of the programs, mostly done by Tom Hales.

Solving Symbolic Constraints

Temur Kutsia

Research Institute for Symbolic Computation (RISC), Johannes Kepler University Linz, Austria

Abstract. Symbolic constraint solving is a fundamental technique in many areas of mathematics and computer science, providing the basis for key operations in automated reasoning, term rewriting, declarative programming, or formal methods. Important classes of symbolic constraints include unification, matching, generalization, disunification, and ordering constraints. Efficient methods for solving them form the computational core of inference engines, proof assistants, program transformation systems, logical frameworks, etc. In this talk, we present recent advances in solving unification, matching, and generalization constraints in expressive theories, including those that involve background knowledge or binding constructs. We discuss algorithmic techniques for constraint solving, identify classes of problems that admit efficient solutions, and highlight their relevance for tools and techniques in symbolic computation and computer mathematics.

Contents

Automated Reasoning

Hammering Higher Order Set Theory 3
Chad E. Brown, Cezary Kaliszyk, Martin Suda, and Josef Urban

Synthesis Benchmarks for Automated Reasoning 21
Márton Hajdu, Petra Hozzová, Laura Kovács, Andrei Voronkov, Eva Maria Wagner, and Richard Steven Žilinčík

Automated Symmetric Constructions in Discrete Geometry 29
Bernardo Subercaseaux, Ethan Mackey, Long Qian, and Marijn Heule

Formal Libraries

Growing Mathlib: maintenance of a large scale mathematical library 51
Anne Baanen, Matthew Robert Ballard, Johan Commelin, Bryan Gin–ge Chen, Michael Rothgang, and Damiano Testa

Exploring Formal Math on the Blockchain: An Explorer for Proofgold 71
Chad E. Brown, Cezary Kaliszyk, and Josef Urban

Supporting Maintenance of Formal Mathematics with Similarity Search 91
Fabian Huch

Logical and Linguistic Foundations

Graded Quantitative Narrowing 113
Mauricio Ayala-Rincón, Thaynara Arielly de Lima, Georg Ehling, and Temur Kutsia

Equational Generalization Problems with Atom-Variables 133
Alexander Baumgartner, Temur Kutsia, Daniele Nantes-Sobrinho, and Manfred Schmidt-Schauß

Extending Flexible Boolean Semantics for the Language of Mathematics 152
Shashank Pathak

A Formal Description of an Algorithm Suitable for Parsing the Language of Mathematics 171
Luka Vrečar, Joe Wells, and Fairouz Kamareddine

Mathematical Knowledge Management

Reaping the Benefits of Modularization in Flexiformal Mathematics by GF-based AST Transformations 191
Josefin Kelber, Michael Kohlhase, Jan Frederik Schaefer, and Marcel Schütz

Semantic Authoring in a Flexiformal Context — Bulk Annotation of Rigorous Documents 208
Michael Kohlhase and Jan Frederik Schaefer

Lightweight Realms 222
Michael Kohlhase, Florian Rabe, and Marcel Schütz

Global, Regional, and Local Contexts 240
Florian Rabe

Indexing and Retrieval in a Heterogeneous Formal Library 258
Claudio Sacerdoti Coen and Abdelghani Alidra

Neural Language Models

Exploring proof autoformalization with Mistral on Herald 279
Lucy Horowitz, Michail Karatarakis, Xuandi Ren, and Alejandro Sanchez Ocegueda

Boosting Math Problem Solving in Small LLMs via Ensembles 300
Ruocheng Shan and Abdou Youssef

Proof Assistants and Formalizations

Formalizing a Classification Theorem for Low-Dimensional Solvable Lie Algebras in Lean 317
Viviana del Barco, Gustavo Infanti, Exequiel Rivas, and Paul Schwahn

Certified Algorithms for Numerical Semigroups in Rocq 340
Massimo Bartoletti, Stefano Bonzio, and Marco Ferrara

Formalizing the Solow Model in Naproche 357
Peter Koepke and Patrick Schäfer

Formalizing MLTL Formula Progression in Isabelle/HOL 371
Katherine Kosaian, Zili Wang, Elizabeth Sloan, and Kristin Yvonne Rozier

Formalising Fairness in the Assignment Problem with Ordinal Preferences in Isabelle/HOL 392
Duc Minh Do and Christine Rizkallah

A PVS Library on the Infinitude of Primes 412
Bruno Berto de Oliveira Ribeiro, Mariano M. Moscato, Thaynara Arielly de Lima, and Mauricio Ayala-Rincón

Vector Graphics through Category Theory 431
Davi Sales Barreira, Henrique Borges Carvalho, Alexandre Rademaker, Asla Medeiros e Sá, and Flávio Codeço Coelho

A Lean-based Language for Teaching Proof in High School 447
Frédéric Tran Minh, Laure Gonnord, and Julien Narboux

Author Index 469

Automated Reasoning

Hammering Higher Order Set Theory

Chad E. Brown[1], Cezary Kaliszyk[2,3], Martin Suda[1], and Josef Urban[1(✉)]

[1] Czech Technical University in Prague, Prague, Czech Republic
josef.urban@gmail.com
[2] University of Melbourne, Melbourne, Australia
ckaliszyk@unimelb.edu.au
[3] University of Innsbruck, Innsbruck, Austria

Abstract. We use automated theorem provers to significantly shorten a formal development in higher order set theory. The development includes many standard theorems such as the fundamental theorem of arithmetic and irrationality of square root of two. Higher order automated theorem provers are particularly useful here, since the underlying framework of higher order set theory coincides with the classical extensional higher order logic of (most) higher order automated theorem provers, so no significant translation or encoding is required. Additionally, many subgoals are first order and so first order automated provers often suffice. We compare the performance of different provers on the subgoals generated from the development. We also discuss possibilities for proof reconstruction, i.e., obtaining formal proof terms when an automated theorem prover claims to have proven the subgoal.

1 Introduction

In this work, we first describe (Section 2) a formal development in higher order set theory (using the Megalodon system) containing several well-known mathematical theorems, including Conway's surreal numbers and 12 of the Freek100 theorems. We then use this development (Section 3) to create a large set (and a benchmark) of higher order problems for automated theorem provers (ATPs), evaluating multiple state-of-the-art ATPs on the benchmark. When an ATP is able to solve one of the problems, we are able to replace part of the development with a call to an ATP. This results in a reduction of the text of the development to less than a half its original size. We also describe the related hammer-style proof automation for Megalodon in Emacs, and discuss proof reconstruction (Section 4).

2 Megalodon and Formalization of 12 Freek100 Theorems

2.1 Megalodon

We start with a formal development in the Megalodon system. Megalodon is a fork of the Egal system [15] and is based on higher order Tarski-Grothendieck

V. de Paiva and P. Koepke (Eds.): CICM 2025, LNAI 16136, pp. 3–20, 2026.
https://doi.org/10.1007/978-3-032-07021-0_1

set theory. The underlying logical framework is simply-typed intuitionistic higher order logic (with Curry Howard proof terms). In addition to the built-in type o of propositions we use one base type ι which should be interpreted as sets. The remaining types are function types $\alpha \to \beta$, as usual. Simply typed terms are constructed via the grammar

$$c \mid x \mid (s\,t) \mid (\lambda x.t) \mid (s \Rightarrow t) \mid (\forall x.t)$$

where c ranges over (typed) names (which may be primitives or definitions) and x ranges over (typed) variables. We assume the usual conventions about simple type theory (e.g., $s\,t\,u$ means $((s\,t)u)$ and $\lambda xy.t$ means $\lambda x.\lambda y.t$) and leave the reader to consult [15] if necessary. Although we have only included implication and universal quantification, there are (several) well-known impredicative definitions of other connectives and quantifiers [40,38,10]. Consequently, we will freely use $\top$, $\bot$, $\neg$, $\wedge$, $\vee$, $\Leftrightarrow$, $\exists$ and $=$ below without further comment.

There are well-known ways to axiomatize set theory within a simply typed framework [36,25]. In our case we add a primitive ε as a choice function over ι and primitives of the set theory: $\in : \iota \to \iota \to o$, $\emptyset : \iota$, $\bigcup : \iota \to \iota$ (unary union operator), $\wp : \iota \to \iota$ (power set operator), $\texttt{Repl} : \iota \to (\iota \to \iota) \to \iota$ (Fraenkel Replacement operator) and $\texttt{UnivOf} : \iota \to \iota$. The unary operator $\texttt{UnivOf}$ takes a set X and returns the least Grothendieck universe with X as a member. A Grothendieck universe is a transitive set closed under $\bigcup$, $\wp$ and $\texttt{Repl}$. Typically a Grothendieck universe is also required to have an infinite set, so that it would be a model of Zermelo Fraenkel. Here we also consider V_ω (the set of all hereditarily finite sets) to be a Grothendieck universe. Applying $\texttt{UnivOf}$ to the empty set yields the set of hereditarily finite sets. Since V_ω is infinite, we do not need an explicit axiom of infinity. In addition to the primitives, we assume the expected set theoretic axioms, including set extensionality. We also assume a higher order axiom of $\in$-induction from which Regularity can be proven. Finally we assume axioms of propositional and functional extensionality so that the underlying higher order logic is extensional. The full set of primitives and axioms can be found in [15], with the minor change that here we only assume ε at type ι rather than at every type.

2.2 Initial Formalization of 12 Freek100 Theorems

As one would expect, the development continues by making definitions and proving theorems. Wiedijk maintains a collection of 100 theorems that have become standard challenges for ITPs.[1] For our purposes we limit the development to definitions and theorems that are sufficient to prove 12 of these 100 theorems, mostly removing definitions or lemmas that are not dependencies of at least one of these 12, or a variant of one of the 12. Listed in order of appearance in the development, the selected 12 theorems are mathematical induction, Cantor's Theorem, Schroeder Bernstein, number of subsets of a (finite) set, infinitude

[1] `https://www.cs.ru.nl/~freek/100/`

of primes, Ramsey's Theorem, Bezout's Theorem, the greatest common divisor algorithm, the Fundamental Theorem of Arithmetic, non-denumerability of the reals, denumerability of the rationals and the irrationality of $\sqrt{2}$. In order to state these results, the development must include a representation of functions, natural numbers, integers, rationals and reals.

The first part of the development contains basic logical definitions and theorems. For example, conjunction ($\wedge$) is defined as $\lambda AB.\forall p.(A \Rightarrow B \Rightarrow p) \Rightarrow p$ and a theorem `andI` $\forall AB.A \Rightarrow B \Rightarrow A \wedge B$ is proven with the `exact` tactic and the proof term $\lambda A\ B\ a\ b\ p\ H.H\ a\ b$. Later in the development when a subgoal has a conclusion of the form $A \wedge B$, we can reduce the goal to the obvious two subgoals (A and B) using the tactic `apply andI`. This already introduces a minor amount of automation, as the `apply` tactic uses matching to extract the A and B from the subgoal in order to construct the partial proof term `andI` $A\ B\ D\ E$ where D and E will be determined by the subsequent subproofs.

The tenth theorem of the entire development (well before any of the 12 Freek100 theorems) is excluded middle `xm` : $\forall p.p \vee \neg p$. The proof follows the Diaconescu argument [39,34] using ε at ι. Before proving excluded middle, it does not make sense to use classical ATPs as hammers. For this reason, we only start considering the use of ATPs after the first 10 theorems of the development.

Throughout the development basic infrastructure is included (e.g., ordinals, ordered pairs and functions as sets) as needed, largely following [10], though the setting there was intuitionistic. As usual, the finite ordinals are used to represent natural numbers and provide the material to state and prove mathematical induction, both in its usual form and in the form of complete induction. The ordinal ω is defined to be the set of natural numbers, and we define a set to be finite if it is equipotent to a member of ω. This basic material is enough to state and prove five more of the 12 theorems. The development up to the proofs of these first 6 theorems consists of 6649 lines with 59 definitions and 314 theorems (including the 6).

2.3 Conway's surreal numbers

The remaining 6 of the 12 require either integers, rationals or real numbers. We construct these numbers (and more) using a specific set-theoretic representation of Conway's surreal numbers [18]. Surreal numbers have also been formalized in Mizar [35] using representations closer to Conway's description. Here we use a different representation, for reasons that will become clear. A surreal number can be uniquely represented by an ordinal length branch on an arbitrarily large binary tree. That is, each surreal number can be represented by an ordinal α and a function $f : \alpha \to \{0,1\}$ where $f(\beta) = 0$ indicates the left option at stage $\beta \in \alpha$ and $f(\beta) = 1$ indicates the right option at stage $\beta \in \alpha$. Instead of representing surreal numbers in precisely this way, we represent them using a set that remembers the ordinal α and which ordinals $\beta \in \alpha$ would take the left option and which would take the right option. To represent the left option at stage β, we define the set β' to be $\beta \cup \{\{1\}\}$. It is easy to see that β' is never an ordinal (since the set $\{1\}$ is not transitive). It is also to see that if $\beta' = \gamma'$ for ordinals β and γ, then $\beta = \gamma$. We now represent the surreal number given by α and $f : \alpha \to \{0,1\}$ by the set $\{\beta \in \alpha | f(\beta) = 1\} \cup \{\beta' | \beta \in \alpha, f(\beta) = 0\}$. It is easy to see that α and f can be recovered from this set. It is also easy to see that the surreal number given by α and $f : \alpha \to \{0,1\}$ with $f(\beta) = 1$ for all $\beta \in \alpha$ is represented simply by the set α. That is, ordinals are already surreal numbers using this representation, and correspond to the branch of length α that chooses the right option at each step. Other examples of surreal numbers are -2 represented by $\{0', 1'\}$ and $\frac{1}{2}$ represented by $\{0, 1'\}$. One can define recursion operators on surreal numbers and use these to define the basic operations as described in [18] essentially proving the surreal numbers form an ordered field (with a proper class as its carrier). The development up to this point consists of 27316 lines with 116 definitions and 759 theorems, so that the primary surreal number part of the development consists of 20668 lines with 57 definitions and 445 theorems (almost half the development). In the next 2544 lines (with 6 new definitions and 57 new theorems), the set `Z` of integers can easily be defined (carved from the surreal number field) allowing us to state and prove Bezout's Theorem, the greatest common divisor algorithm and the Fundamental Theorem of Arithmetic. The next 11211 lines (with 11 new definitions and 137 new theorems) define the set `R` of real numbers (carved out of the surreals), proven to have the expected properties including uncountability. With 730 more lines, 2 new definitions and 8 new theorems, we can define the set `Q` of rational numbers as a subset of `R` and prove `Q` is countable. Note that by construction we have $\omega \subseteq \mathtt{Z} \subseteq \mathtt{Q} \subseteq \mathtt{R}$, which was our motivation for the specific representation of surreal numbers as sets.

The only remaining theorem of the 12 is irrationality of $\sqrt{2}$. Conway describes how to recursively define the square root operation on nonnegative surreal numbers. We make this definition and prove the square root of nonnegative reals are nonnegative reals. The development ends with the proof that $\sqrt{2}$ is irrational, i.e., $\sqrt{2} \in \mathtt{R} \setminus \mathtt{Q}$. This part of the development used 3203 more lines with 4 new definitions and 38 new theorems.

In total the development contains 139 definitions and 999 theorems. The development is given as a single file with 45004 lines and 346152 characters, and the proofs are given in significant detail, with little automation.

3 Development using ATPs

3.1 Automation Tactic

We have extended Megalodon to allow the option of using the tactic `aby` ("automated by") with a list of dependencies to justify a subgoal.[2] Megalodon can check the file and produce problem files for ATPs. Since the underlying framework is simply typed higher order logic, we can directly translate the given dependencies and current subgoal into the TH0 TPTP format [3], a common format for higher order ATPs. Hence every use of the `aby` tactic will result in one TH0 problem file.

[2] Megalodon with the data/code discussed here is available at `https://github.com/MgUser36/megalodon`.

In addition, if the conclusion and the dependencies are in the first order fragment of higher order logic, we can translate the problem to the FOF TPTP format and call first order theorem provers. Note that we do not attempt to encode higher order logic into first order [7,37,28,29]. The use of the `aby` tactic is justified if either a higher order ATP can prove the TH0 file, or if a first order ATP can prove the FOF file.

3.2 Experiments

In order to identify subproofs that could be replaced by calls to ATPs, we used Megalodon to generate TH0 problem files for most tactic calls, determining the dependencies when the subproof is completed. Each problem corresponds to a sequence of text (from before the tactic is called to where the subproof is completed) that can be replaced if the problem file can be proven by an ATP. This resulted in 41738 higher order problem files.[3] With a 60 second timeout, we ran Vampire [4] (with two different portfolios), Zipperposition [2], E [43], Lash [12] and cvc5 [1]. The results are shown in Table 1. In total, 34172 (82%) of the 41738 subgoals could be replaced by ATP calls. Megalodon additionally produced 29880 first order problem files when the subgoal had a first order proof. We ran Vampire for 5 seconds on each of these problems and 60 seconds on a selection of the problems, resulting in 11179 subproofs that could be replaced by ATP calls, although only 11 of these subproofs were not already identified by the higher order problems.

Vampire (sledgehammer)	Vampire (ho)	Zipperposition	E	Lash	cvc5
32675	32474	31310	23866	14987	13238
78.3%	77.8%	75%	57.2%	35.9%	31.7%

Table 1. Higher order ATPs on premise-selected subgoals

Some ATP calls may result in replacing a larger part of text than others. For example, a subproof in the original development contained a line with three tactics:

```
apply In_irref delta. rewrite H2 at 2. exact Ldsa.
```

This line resulted in three problem files, corresponding to whether the `exact` could be replaced, the `rewrite` and the `exact` could be replaced, and whether all three could be replaced. In this case, all three could be replaced. That is,

[3] The resulting large HO-TP benchmark is at `https://github.com/MgUser36/MegalodonATPBenchmark`.

one problem solved by an ATP would allow us to replace the `exact` tactic by an `aby` call. A second problem solved by an ATP would allow us to replace both the `rewrite` and the `exact` tactic in the line above with an `aby` call. A third problem solved by an ATP would allow us to replace all three tactics on the line by an `aby` call. Obviously replacing all three tactics supersedes replacing either the last two or the last one alone, so it makes sense to find the ATP problems that allow us to replace as much text as possible. After filtering for the problems that allow the maximum amount of text to be replaced, the first two ATP problems above (corresponding to replacing `exact` alone or only replacing `rewrite` and `exact`) would be filtered out, in favor of only including the third ATP problem allowing the replacement of all three tactics.

Once we restrict to the problems that allow the largest texts to be replaced (along with some manual modifications), we were left with 3401 calls to an ATP and a development with 17435 lines and 159363 characters. This is roughly 46% the original size of the development.[4] The majority of the proofs in the development (765 of the 989 proofs considered for replacement) could be replaced simply by a single `aby` call. The remaining 224 proofs contained 2636 ATP calls in subproofs, with approximately 12 ATP calls per proof.

In order to justify the 3401 ATP calls, Megalodon produced 3401 TH0 problem files and 1618 FOF problem files. Table 2 shows the results of higher order ATPs on these files. We also called a recent first order version of Vampire was called on the FOF problems, with it solving 1322 (81.7%) of the 1618 first order problems. Each call was with a 60s timeout.

Vampire (sledgehammer)	Vampire (ho)	Zipperposition	E	Lash
3223 (94.8%)	3165 (93.1%)	2801 (82.4%)	2403 (70.7%)	1567 (46.1%)

Table 2. Higher order ATPs on the 3401 ATP problems

3.3 Examples

We consider a few examples to give an idea of what kinds of proofs can be replaced by calls to an ATP.[5]

Example 1 The largest text replaced by a call to an ATP (in this case, Lash) is the proof of the following theorem `PNoLt_tra`[6]:

[4] Note that we do not include the ATP output as part of the size of the new text.

[5] Successful ATP outputs with TPTP proofs for these examples can be found at `http://grid01.ciirc.cvut.cz/~chad/atppfs2025`.

[6] `https://mgwiki.github.io/mgw_test/Part2.mg.html#PNoLt_tra`

```
Theorem PNoLt_tra : forall alpha beta gamma,
  ordinal alpha → ordinal beta → ordinal gamma →
  forall p q r:set → prop,
   PNoLt alpha p beta q → PNoLt beta q gamma r
    → PNoLt alpha p gamma r.
```

This is essentially the proof of transitivity of the (strict) ordering on surreal numbers. At the point in the development where this theorem is stated and proven, surreal numbers are not yet defined. However, the ordinal α with the predicate $p : \iota \to o$ determines a surreal number where p indicates for which $\alpha' \in \alpha$ the right option is taken. Likewise, β with q determines a surreal number and γ with r determines a surreal number. The definition of `PNoLt` $\alpha\ p\ \beta\ q$ corresponds to when the surreal number determined by α and p is less than the surreal number determined by β and q. This can happen in three ways:

1. $\alpha = \beta$ and there is some $\delta \in \alpha$ such that p and q agree up to δ, $\neg p\ \delta$ and $q\ \delta$. That is, the two surreal numbers use the same left and right options until δ at which point p chooses the left option and q chooses the right option.
2. $\alpha \in \beta$, p and q agree up to α and $q\ \alpha$. That is, the surreal number given by β and q is an extension of the sequence given by α and p, where the first new option (at step α) is the right option.
3. $\beta \in \alpha$, p and q agree up to β and $\neg p\ \beta$. That is, the surreal number given by α and p is an extension of the sequence given by β and q, where the first new option (at step β) is the left option.

To give concrete examples, suppose $\alpha = 1$ and $p\ 0$ holds. Then α and p correspond to the surreal number 1, since the sequence is of length 1 and chooses the right option at step 0. Suppose $\beta = 2$ and both $q\ 0$ and $q\ 1$ hold. Then β and q correspond to the surreal number 2. In this case `PNoLt` $\alpha\ p\ \beta\ q$ holds since $\alpha \in \beta$, p and q agree up to 1 (i.e., $p\ 0 \Leftrightarrow q\ 0$) and $q\ 1$ holds. On the other hand, if $\beta = 2$, $q\ 0$ and $\neg q\ 1$ (corresponding to the surreal number $\frac{1}{2}$) then we have `PNoLt` $\beta\ q\ \alpha\ p$ holds since $\alpha \in \beta$, p and q agree up to 1 and $\neg q\ 1$ holds. Finally, suppose $\alpha = 2$, $p\ 0$, $\neg p\ 1$, $\beta = 2$, $q\ 0$ and $q\ 1$, then `PNoLt` $\alpha\ p\ \beta\ q$ holds since $\alpha = \beta$, p and q agree up to 1, $\neg p\ 1$ and $q\ 1$.

The manual proof of transitivity of `PNoLt` proceeds as follows. Suppose α, β and γ are ordinals and $p, q, r : \iota \to o$ are such that `PNoLt` $\alpha\ p\ \beta\ q$ and `PNoLt` $\beta\ q\ \gamma\ r$ hold. We need to prove `PNoLt` $\alpha\ p\ \gamma\ r$ holds. We split into the three cases based on why `PNoLt` $\alpha\ p\ \beta\ q$ holds. In each of the three cases we split into three subcases based on why `PNoLt` $\beta\ q\ \gamma\ r$ holds. The full manual proof uses 311 lines. Of these 311 lines, the first 5 are simply introducing the variables and hypotheses. Roughly 61 lines correspond to splitting into the 3 cases and the 9 subcases, introducing the relevant variables and hypotheses for each case and subcase. On average completing the proof in each of the 9 subcases requires about 27 lines. When using the hammer, the full proof is reduced to the following single use of `aby`:

```
aby and3I binintersectI binintersectE ordinal_Hered
   ordinal_trichotomy_or PNoEq_tra_ PNoEq_antimon_ PNoLtI1
   PNoLtI2 PNoLtI3 PNoLtE.
```

While the automated proof is much shorter, a reader examining the proof may have trouble determining that the proof involves splitting into 3 cases and 9 subcases. The only hint is that the call to aby references PNoLtE, which is a theorem that can be applied when we know PNoLt α p β q to split the current goal into three cases.

Example 2 The second largest text replaced in a proof is at the end of the proof of the following theorem PNo_rel_split_imv_imp_strict_imv[7]:

```
Theorem PNo_rel_split_imv_imp_strict_imv :
 forall L R:set → (set → prop) → prop,
  forall alpha, ordinal alpha → forall p:set → prop,
       PNo_rel_strict_split_imv L R alpha p
    → PNo_strict_imv L R alpha p.
```

Again, this theorem is about surreal numbers before committing to the particular set theoretic representation of surreal numbers. Here L and R of type $\iota \to (\iota \to o) \to o$ can be thought of as sets of surreal numbers (given as β and $q : \iota \to o$). The conclusion PNo_strict_imv L R α p means that the surreal number given by α and p is an intermediate value between L and R. That is, PNoLt β q α p whenever L β q and PNoLt α p β q whenever R β q. The hypothesis PNo_rel_strict_split_imv L R α p is a similar property about the two extensions of α and p of length α^+.

The manual proof of this theorem was 240 lines. The proof using aby is 27 lines. No ATP was able to prove the theorem completely. (If an ATP had proven the full theorem, we could replace the full proof by one call to aby.) The proof using aby starts the same way as the manual proof, assuming we have L, R, an ordinal α and some $p : \iota \to o$ satisfying PNo_rel_strict_split_imv L R α p. ATPs can automatically prove α^+ (the successor of α) is also an ordinal, so this subproof is replaced by aby. As part of the beginning of the proof we define p_0 to be the predicate that holds for δ if $p\ \delta \wedge \delta \neq \alpha$ and we define p_1 to be the predicate that holds for δ if $p\ \delta \vee \delta = \alpha$. ATPs can automatically prove $\neg p_0\ \alpha$ and $p_1\ \alpha$, so these two subproofs are replaced by aby. ATPs can also prove PNoLt α^+ p_0 α p and PNoLt α p α^+ p_1, so these two subproofs are replaced by aby. At this point we need to prove the conclusion PNo_strict_imv L R α p. The rest of the manual proof requires 200 lines. ATPs can finish the rest of the proof and so these 200 lines are replaced by a final call to aby. In the manual proof, the first of the remaining 200 lines explicitly expands the definition of PNo_strict_imv and reduces the conclusion to proving α and p are greater than everything in L

[7] https://mgwiki.github.io/mgw_test/Part2.mg.html#PNo_rel_split_imv_imp_strict_imv

and to proving α and p are less than everything in R. Meanwhile, when these last 200 lines are replaced by an aby call, there is no clear indication that the reader should expand the definition of PNo_strict_imv and check the two conjuncts. This is another example where replacing subproofs by aby may make the proof less readable by making it less explicit.

Example 3 In many cases, replacing details of a proof may make it easier to read a proof. Consider the following theorem exp_SNo_nat_mul_add[8]:

```
Theorem exp_SNo_nat_mul_add : forall x, SNo x →
  forall m, nat_p m → forall n, nat_p n →
     x ^ m * x ^ n = x ^ (m + n).
```

Here x^n is the operation raising a surreal number x to the nth power (for a natural number n). The goal is to prove $x^m \cdot x^n = x^{m+n}$, where multiplication and addition are over surreal numbers (which agree with multiplication and addition on natural numbers). The manual proof fixes x and m and proves that m is a surreal number (since it is natural). We then apply natural number induction, reducing the problem to proving the case for $n = 0$ and the inductive case. At this point in the manual proof a series of explicit (though obvious) arithmetical steps are required – including steps to change between addition on natural numbers and addition on surreal numbers. Meanwhile, ATPs can complete the proofs for the base case and inductive case, resulting in the following shorter proof:

```
let x. assume Hx. let m. assume Hm.
claim Lm: SNo m.
{ aby nat_p_SNo Hm. }
apply nat_ind.
- aby add_SNo_0R mul_SNo_oneR exp_SNo_nat_0 SNo_exp_SNo_nat
      Lm Hm Hx.
- aby add_nat_SR add_nat_p nat_p_omega omega_ordsucc
      add_nat_add_SNo mul_SNo_com mul_SNo_assoc exp_SNo_nat_S
      SNo_exp_SNo_nat Hm Hx.
Qed.
```

The original manual proof is longer (29 lines instead of 6 lines) and all the extra details are simply distracting. Omitting these steps arguably makes the proof easier to read.

3.4 Use in Emacs and a Full Hammer

We have also implemented a simple Emacs mode[9] for Megalodon and a command in it (aby.) which implements the "hammer" behavior, similar to the Sledgehammer command in Isabelle/JEdit. The command calls Megalodon to create a TH0

8 https://mgwiki.github.io/mgw_test/Part6.mg.html#exp_SNo_nat_mul_add
9 https://github.com/MgUser36/megalodon/blob/main/mg-advice.el

```
Theorem exp_SNo_nat_mul_add : forall x, SNo x -> forall m, nat_p m -
> forall n, nat_p n -> x ^ m * x ^ n = x ^ (m + n).
let x. assume Hx. let m. assume Hm.
claim Lm: SNo m.
{ exact nat_p_SNo m Hm. }
apply nat_ind.
- prove x ^ m * x ^ 0 = x ^ (m + 0).
  rewrite exp_SNo_nat_0 x Hx.
  rewrite add_SNo_0R m Lm.
  exact mul_SNo_oneR (x ^ m) (SNo_exp_SNo_nat x Hx m Hm).
- let n. assume Hn: nat_p n.
  assume IHn: x ^ m * x ^ n = x ^ (m + n).
  prove x ^ m * x ^ (ordsucc n) = x ^ (m + ordsucc n).
  rewrite exp_SNo_nat_S x Hx n Hn.
  prove x ^ m * (x * x ^ n) = x ^ (m + ordsucc n).
  rewrite <- add_nat_add_SNo m (nat_p_omega m Hm) (ordsucc n) (omega
_ordsucc n (nat_p_omega n Hn)).
  prove x ^ m * (x * x ^ n) = x ^ (add_nat m (ordsucc n)).
  rewrite add_nat_SR m n Hn.
  prove x ^ m * (x * x ^ n) = x ^ (ordsucc (add_nat m n)).
  rewrite exp_SNo_nat_S x Hx (add_nat m n) (add_nat_p m Hm n Hn).
  prove x ^ m * (x * x ^ n) = x * x ^ (add_nat m n).
  rewrite add_nat_add_SNo m (nat_p_omega m Hm) n (nat_p_omega n Hn).
  prove x ^ m * (x * x ^ n) = x * x ^ (m + n).
  rewrite <- IHn.
  prove x ^ m * (x * x ^ n) = x * (x ^ m * x ^ n).
  rewrite mul_SNo_assoc (x ^ m) x (x ^ n) (SNo_exp_SNo_nat x Hx m Hm
) Hx (SNo_exp_SNo_nat x Hx n Hn).
  prove (x ^ m * x) * x ^ n = x * (x ^ m * x ^ n).
  rewrite mul_SNo_com (x ^ m) x (SNo_exp_SNo_nat x Hx m Hm) Hx.
  prove (x * x ^ m) * x ^ n = x * (x ^ m * x ^ n).
  symmetry.
  exact mul_SNo_assoc x (x ^ m) (x ^ n) Hx (SNo_exp_SNo_nat x Hx m H
m) (SNo_exp_SNo_nat x Hx n Hn).
Qed.
```

Fig. 1. Original Megalodon Proof.

file which includes the whole previous development. Then it calls Vampire with a schedule constructed for the Sledgehammer division of the CASC competition.[10] If successful, the names of the used axioms are translated back to the Megalodon syntax and the `aby` call using them is automatically inserted into the current buffer. The operation is shown in Figures 1, 2, and 3.

[10] The schedule was constructed according to `https://tptp.org/CASC/J11/SystemDescriptions.html#SnakeForV4.7---1.0`

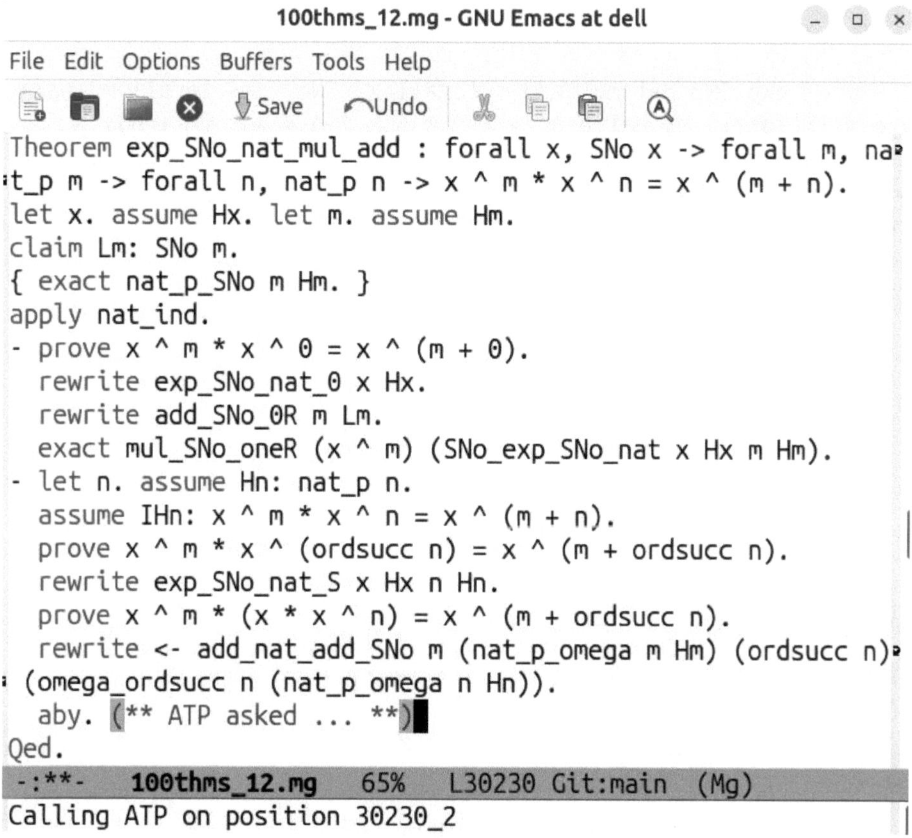

Fig. 2. Aby call invoked inside the proof.

To test this "full hammer" performance, we generated corresponding ATP problems each time a tactic was used in the original development. This resulted in 51243 TH0 problems.[11] Note that this is larger than the 41738 premise selected problem files. This difference arises from several factors, which we do not discuss in detail here. We called Vampire with the two portfolios for 60s. With the sledgehammer schedule, Vampire proved 29256 problems (57.1%). With the default higher-order (ho) schedule, Vampire proved 28811 problems (56.2%). The union of the two sets was 30473 problems (59.5%).

4 Proof Reconstruction

With the original development, complete proof terms are constructed by Megalodon from the given proof scripts. Once ATPs are used, Megalodon is essentially

[11] Also in our benchmark: `https://github.com/MgUser36/MegalodonATPBenchmark/tree/main/chainy`.

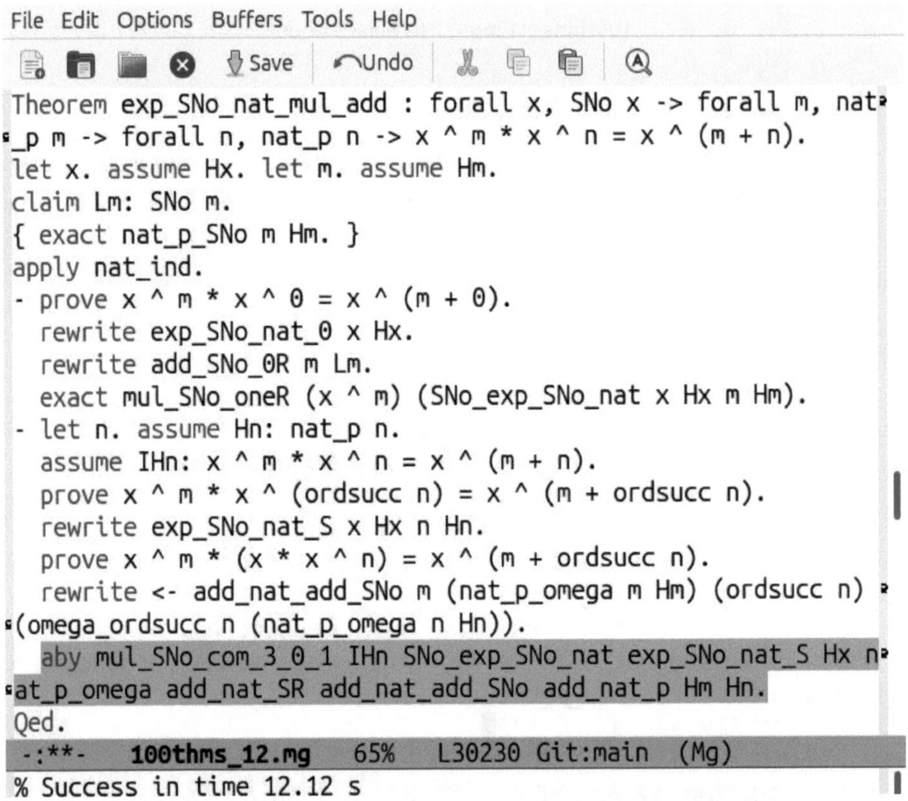

Fig. 3. Successful aby call with the axiom names inserted.

behaving like the Naproche system [19]. That is, when an ATP completes the proof of a subgoal, we trust that there is, indeed, a proof. Ultimately it would be more satisfying to do *proof reconstruction* so that we still obtain complete proof terms even when some subgoals are completed by ATPs.

A common technique [33] is to use an ATP to prune the dependencies and then use an internal search procedure (like Metis [28] for Isabelle) to create the appropriate ITP proof. Megalodon currently has no significant internal search procedure that could be used for this purpose. A more optimal state of affairs would be if ATPs returned sufficiently detailed proof objects that could be independently checked. Prover9 [32] is a rare example of an ATP that has provided explicit proof objects for decades, though it is limited to clausal proofs. This is used for proof reconstruction e.g. in the Metamath hammer [17].

4.1 Using Vampire with the Deducti Output

Due to recent work on Vampire [31] one can request proof output (for first order problems) that can be checked by Dedukti [22], with some limitations noted below.

We consider a very simple example. Suppose we are in a proof where we have a set α and a local assumption Ha that α is an ordinal (i.e., the proposition `ordinal` α). We have a local subgoal to prove $\alpha+$ is an ordinal (i.e., `ordinal` (`ordsucc` α)). The relevant previous theorem is `ordinal_ordsucc`: $\forall\alpha.$`ordinal` $\alpha \Rightarrow$ `ordinal` (`ordsucc` α). This is a first order subgoal and Vampire can easily prove it. The simplest Megalodon proof term for this subgoal would be `ordinal_ordsucc` α Ha. In Megalodon this part of the proof[12] looks as follows:

```
claim Lsa: ordinal (ordsucc alpha).
{ exact ordinal_ordsucc alpha Ha. }
```

Replacing the subproof with a call to an ATP simply changes the proof to[13]

```
claim Lsa: ordinal (ordsucc alpha).
{ aby ordinal_ordsucc Ha. }
```

We examine parts of the Dedukti output of Vampire. The previous theorem `ordinal_ordsucc` is given as an axiom (with some changes to the name for TPTP compliance) and this is reflected in the following declared axiom in the Dedukti output:

```
{|axiom_ordinal_5Fordsucc9|}:
  Prf (forall iota
           (0 : El iota =>
                 (imp ({|ordinal|} 0)
                      ({|ordinal|} ({|ordsucc|} 0))))).
```

Likewise the local assumption that α is an ordinal is reflected in the following declared axiom:

```
{|axiom_c_Ha16|}: Prf ({|ordinal|} {|alpha|}).
```

The negated conclusion is also given as a declared axiom:

```
{|axiom_18|}: Prf (not ({|ordinal|} ({|ordsucc|} {|alpha|}))).
```

In principle the rest of the proof should be given as a sequence of Dedukti definitions, but in practice some of the steps to produce clausal form are left unjustified at the moment. If we skip forward past the unjustified steps (which are minor in this case), we can start from three Dedukti items with types corresponding to the three assumptions above, but in clausal form. The two resolution

[12] `https://github.com/MgUser36/megalodon/blob/main/examples/form100/100thms_12.mg#L9964`

[13] `https://github.com/MgUser36/megalodon/blob/main/examples/hammer/100thms_12_h.mg#L3681`

steps corresponds to two Dedukti definitions. In principle the Dedukti representation could be translated into Megalodon as follows: One begins the subproof by applying double negation, so that one may assume the negated conclusion and reduce to proving false. Then each Dedukti definition would correspond to a subgoal with a proof term translated from its definition. The last Dedukti definition should give a proof of false (corresponding to the empty clause in the resolution proof).

This translation is left as future work here. Another general idea for distributing ITP proofs – which includes proof reconstruction – is outsourcing to the (Megalodon-related) Proofgold network [13], which newly includes also the basis for a lightning network [14].

5 Related Work

ITP/ATP hammers and their various components have been developed and successfully used for over two decades [26,21,27,41,42,33,37,6,5,30,24,8,20,17], in systems such as Isabelle, HOL, Mizar, HOL Light, Coq, and Metamath. A comprehensive overview of the topic is given in [9]. Similarly, a number of large problem sets and benchmarks for higher-order ATPs have been extracted from various ITP libraries in the recent years [16,11,23].

6 Conclusion and Future Work

We have shown that calls to ATPs can be used to replace over half the content of formal proofs in a mathematical development in higher order set theory. The original development (without automation) can be used to generate tens of thousands of higher order ATP problems and this benchmark can be used to judge the performance of modern higher order ATPs, currently showing Vampire as the clear leader. After replacing as much text as possible with calls to ATPs, we obtain 3401 higher order ATP problems that are, in some sense, at the frontier of what current higher order ATPs can solve.

We have also discussed options for proof reconstruction, such as the emerging Deducti proof format newly implemented in Vampire, and Megalodon's connection to the Proofgold blockchain, which targets decentralized and distributed proof development. Another interesting avenue would be the use of SMT solvers, specifically when the subgoal is about integers or real numbers. Of course, SMT solvers should only be called once integers (or reals) are defined (along with the corresponding operations) and the basic properties have been proven.

Acknowledgments The results were supported by the Czech Ministry of Education, Youth and Sports within the dedicated program ERC CZ under the project POSTMAN no. LL1902, the ERC PoC grant *FormalWeb3* no. 101156734, Amazon Research Awards, and the Czech Science Foundation grant no. 25-17929X.

References

1. Haniel Barbosa, Clark W. Barrett, Martin Brain, Gereon Kremer, Hanna Lachnitt, Makai Mann, Abdalrhman Mohamed, Mudathir Mohamed, Aina Niemetz, Andres Nötzli, Alex Ozdemir, Mathias Preiner, Andrew Reynolds, Ying Sheng, Cesare Tinelli, and Yoni Zohar. cvc5: A versatile and industrial-strength SMT solver. In Dana Fisman and Grigore Rosu, editors, *Tools and Algorithms for the Construction and Analysis of Systems - 28th International Conference, TACAS 2022, Held as Part of the European Joint Conferences on Theory and Practice of Software, ETAPS 2022, Munich, Germany, April 2-7, 2022, Proceedings, Part I*, volume 13243 of *Lecture Notes in Computer Science*, pages 415–442. Springer, 2022. doi:10.1007/978-3-030-99524-9_24.
2. Alexander Bentkamp, Jasmin Blanchette, Simon Cruanes, and Uwe Waldmann. Superposition for lambda-free higher-order logic. *Log. Methods Comput. Sci.*, 17(2), 2021. URL: https://lmcs.episciences.org/7349.
3. Christoph Benzmüller, Florian Rabe, and Geoff Sutcliffe. THF0 - the core of the TPTP language for higher-order logic. In *IJCAR 2008*, volume 5195 of *LNCS*, pages 491–506. Springer, 2008.
4. Ahmed Bhayat and Martin Suda. A higher-order vampire (short paper). In Christoph Benzmüller, Marijn J. H. Heule, and Renate A. Schmidt, editors, *Automated Reasoning - 12th International Joint Conference, IJCAR 2024, Nancy, France, July 3-6, 2024, Proceedings, Part I*, volume 14739 of *Lecture Notes in Computer Science*, pages 75–85. Springer, 2024. doi:10.1007/978-3-031-63498-7_5.
5. Jasmin Christian Blanchette. *Automatic Proofs and Refutations for Higher-Order Logic*. PhD thesis, Fakultät für Informatik, Technische Universität München, 2012.
6. Jasmin Christian Blanchette, Sascha Böhme, and Lawrence C. Paulson. Extending Sledgehammer with SMT solvers. In Nikolaj Bjørner and Viorica Sofronie-Stokkermans, editors, *CADE*, volume 6803 of *LNCS*, pages 116–130. Springer, 2011.
7. Jasmin Christian Blanchette, Sascha Böhme, Andrei Popescu, and Nicholas Smallbone. Encoding monomorphic and polymorphic types. *Log. Methods Comput. Sci.*, 12(4), 2016. doi:10.2168/LMCS-12(4:13)2016.
8. Jasmin Christian Blanchette, David Greenaway, Cezary Kaliszyk, Daniel Kühlwein, and Josef Urban. A learning-based fact selector for Isabelle/HOL. *J. Autom. Reasoning*, 57(3):219–244, 2016. URL: http://dx.doi.org/10.1007/s10817-016-9362-8, doi:10.1007/s10817-016-9362-8.
9. Jasmin Christian Blanchette, Cezary Kaliszyk, Lawrence C. Paulson, and Josef Urban. Hammering towards QED. *J. Formalized Reasoning*, 9(1):101–148, 2016. URL: http://dx.doi.org/10.6092/issn.1972-5787/4593, doi:10.6092/issn.1972-5787/4593.
10. Chad E. Brown. Reconsidering Pairs and Functions as Sets. *Journal of Automated Reasoning*, 55(3):199–210, Oct 2015.
11. Chad E. Brown, Thibault Gauthier, Cezary Kaliszyk, Geoff Sutcliffe, and Josef Urban. GRUNGE: A grand unified ATP challenge. In Pascal Fontaine, editor, *Automated Deduction - CADE 27 - 27th International Conference on Automated Deduction, Natal, Brazil, August 27-30, 2019, Proceedings*, volume 11716 of *Lecture Notes in Computer Science*, pages 123–141. Springer, 2019. doi:10.1007/978-3-030-29436-6_8.
12. Chad E. Brown and Cezary Kaliszyk. Lash 1.0 (system description). In Jasmin Blanchette, Laura Kovács, and Dirk Pattinson, editors, *Automated Reasoning - 11th International Joint Conference, IJCAR 2022, Haifa, Israel, August 8-10, 2022,*

Proceedings, volume 13385 of *Lecture Notes in Computer Science*, pages 350–358. Springer, 2022. doi:10.1007/978-3-031-10769-6_21.

13. Chad E. Brown, Cezary Kaliszyk, Thibault Gauthier, and Josef Urban. Proofgold: Blockchain for formal methods. In Zaynah Dargaye and Clara Schneidewind, editors, *4th International Workshop on Formal Methods for Blockchains, FMBC@CAV 2022, August 11, 2022, Haifa, Israel*, volume 105 of *OASIcs*, pages 4:1–4:15. Schloss Dagstuhl - Leibniz-Zentrum für Informatik, 2022. URL: https://doi.org/10.4230/OASIcs.FMBC.2022.4, doi:10.4230/OASICS.FMBC.2022.4.
14. Chad E. Brown, Cezary Kaliszyk, and Josef Urban. Payment channels with proofs. Available online., 2025. URL: http://grid01.ciirc.cvut.cz/~mptp/FMBC_2025_paper_6.pdf.
15. Chad E. Brown and Karol Pąk. A tale of two set theories. In Cezary Kaliszyk, Edwin C. Brady, Andrea Kohlhase, and Claudio Sacerdoti Coen, editors, *Intelligent Computer Mathematics - 12th International Conference, CICM 2019, Prague, Czech Republic, July 8-12, 2019, Proceedings*, volume 11617 of *Lecture Notes in Computer Science*, pages 44–60. Springer, 2019.
16. Chad E. Brown and Josef Urban. Extracting higher-order goals from the mizar mathematical library. In Michael Kohlhase, Moa Johansson, Bruce R. Miller, Leonardo de Moura, and Frank Wm. Tompa, editors, *Intelligent Computer Mathematics - 9th International Conference, CICM 2016, Bialystok, Poland, July 25-29, 2016, Proceedings*, volume 9791 of *Lecture Notes in Computer Science*, pages 99–114. Springer, 2016. doi:10.1007/978-3-319-42547-4_8.
17. Mario Carneiro, Chad E. Brown, and Josef Urban. Automated theorem proving for Metamath. In Adam Naumowicz and René Thiemann, editors, *14th International Conference on Interactive Theorem Proving, ITP 2023, July 31 to August 4, 2023, Białystok, Poland*, volume 268 of *LIPIcs*, pages 9:1–9:19. Schloss Dagstuhl - Leibniz-Zentrum für Informatik, 2023. URL: https://doi.org/10.4230/LIPIcs.ITP.2023.9, doi:10.4230/LIPICS.ITP.2023.9.
18. John H. Conway. *On numbers and games, Second Edition.* A K Peters, 2001.
19. Marcos Cramer. The Naproche system: Proof-checking mathematical texts in controlled natural language. In Hermann Cölfen, Ulrich Schmitz, and Bernhard Schröder, editors, *Sprache und Datenverarbeitung*, volume 38, pages 9–33. Universitätsverlag Rhein-Ruhr, Duisburg, 2014.
20. Lukasz Czajka and Cezary Kaliszyk. Hammer for Coq: Automation for dependent type theory. *J. Autom. Reasoning*, 61(1-4):423–453, 2018. doi:10.1007/s10817-018-9458-4.
21. Ingo Dahn. Interpretation of a Mizar-like logic in first-order logic. In Ricardo Caferra and Gernot Salzer, editors, *FTP (LNCS Selection)*, volume 1761 of *LNCS*, pages 137–151. Springer, 1998.
22. The DEDUKTI logical framework. https://deducteam.github.io.
23. Martin Desharnais, Petar Vukmirovic, Jasmin Blanchette, and Makarius Wenzel. Seventeen provers under the hammer. In June Andronick and Leonardo de Moura, editors, *13th International Conference on Interactive Theorem Proving, ITP 2022, August 7-10, 2022, Haifa, Israel*, volume 237 of *LIPIcs*, pages 8:1–8:18. Schloss Dagstuhl - Leibniz-Zentrum für Informatik, 2022. URL: https://doi.org/10.4230/LIPIcs.ITP.2022.8, doi:10.4230/LIPICS.ITP.2022.8.
24. Thibault Gauthier and Cezary Kaliszyk. Premise selection and external provers for HOL4. In *Certified Programs and Proofs (CPP'15)*, LNCS. Springer, 2015. http://dx.doi.org/10.1145/2676724.2693173. URL: http://dx.doi.org/10.1145/2676724.2693173, doi:10.1145/2676724.2693173.

25. Michael Gordon. Set theory, higher order logic or both? In Joakim von Wright, Jim Grundy, and John Harrison, editors, *Theorem Proving in Higher Order Logics, TPHOLs'96*, volume 1125 of *LNCS*, pages 191–201. Springer, 1996. doi:10.1007/BFb0105405.
26. Joe Hurd. Integrating Gandalf and HOL. In Yves Bertot, Gilles Dowek, André Hirschowitz, C. Paulin, and Laurent Théry, editors, *TPHOLs*, volume 1690 of *LNCS*, pages 311–322. Springer, 1999.
27. Joe Hurd. An LCF-style interface between HOL and first-order logic. In Andrei Voronkov, editor, *CADE*, volume 2392 of *LNCS*, pages 134–138. Springer, 2002.
28. Joe Hurd. First-order proof tactics in higher-order logic theorem provers. In Myla Archer, Ben Di Vito, and César Muñoz, editors, *Design and Application of Strategies/Tactics in Higher Order Logics (STRATA 2003)*, number NASA/CP-2003-212448 in NASA Technical Reports, pages 56–68, September 2003. URL: http://techreports.larc.nasa.gov/ltrs/PDF/2003/cp/NASA-2003-cp212448.pdf.
29. Cezary Kaliszyk and Josef Urban. Learning-assisted automated reasoning with Flyspeck. *J. Autom. Reasoning*, 53(2):173–213, 2014. doi:10.1007/s10817-014-9303-3.
30. Cezary Kaliszyk and Josef Urban. Learning-assisted automated reasoning with Flyspeck. *J. Autom. Reasoning*, 53(2):173–213, 2014. URL: http://dx.doi.org/10.1007/s10817-014-9303-3, doi:10.1007/s10817-014-9303-3.
31. Anja Petković Komel, Michael Rawson, and Martin Suda. Case study: Verified vampire proofs in the lambdapi-calculus modulo, 2025. URL: https://arxiv.org/abs/2503.15541, arXiv:2503.15541.
32. W. McCune. Prover9 and mace4. http://www.cs.unm.edu/~mccune/prover9/, 2005–2010.
33. Jia Meng and Lawrence C. Paulson. Lightweight relevance filtering for machine-generated resolution problems. *Journal of Applied Logic*, 7(1):41–57, 2009. Special Issue: Empirically Successful Computerized Reasoning. URL: https://www.sciencedirect.com/science/article/pii/S1570868307000626, doi:10.1016/j.jal.2007.07.004.
34. N. D. Goodman and J. Myhill. Choice Implies Excluded Middle. *Zeitschrift fur Mathematische Logik und Grundlagen der Mathematik*, 24:461, 1978.
35. Karol Pak and Cezary Kaliszyk. Conway normal form: Bridging approaches for comprehensive formalization of surreal numbers. In Yves Bertot, Temur Kutsia, and Michael Norrish, editors, *15th International Conference on Interactive Theorem Proving, ITP 2024, September 9-14, 2024, Tbilisi, Georgia*, volume 309 of *LIPIcs*, pages 29:1–29:18. Schloss Dagstuhl - Leibniz-Zentrum für Informatik, 2024. URL: https://doi.org/10.4230/LIPIcs.ITP.2024.29, doi:10.4230/LIPICS.ITP.2024.29.
36. Lawrence C. Paulson. Set theory for verification: I. from foundations to functions. *Journal of Automated Reasoning*, 11:353–389, 1993.
37. Lawrence C. Paulson. Three years of experience with sledgehammer, a practical link between automatic and interactive theorem provers. In Renate A. Schmidt, Stephan Schulz, and Boris Konev, editors, *Proceedings of the 2nd Workshop on Practical Aspects of Automated Reasoning, PAAR-2010*, volume 9 of *EPiC*, pages 1–10. EasyChair, 2010. URL: https://doi.org/10.29007/tnfd, doi:10.29007/TNFD.
38. Dag Prawitz. *Natural deduction: a proof-theoretical study.* Dover, 2006.
39. R. Diaconescu. Axiom of choice and complementation. *Proceedings of the American Mathematical Society*, 51:176–178, 1975.
40. Bertrand Russell. *The Principles of Mathematics.* Cambridge University Press, 1903.

41. J. Urban. Translating Mizar for First Order Theorem Provers. In A. Asperti, B. Buchberger, and J.H. Davenport, editors, *Proceedings of the 2nd International Conference on Mathematical Knowledge Management*, number 2594 in LNCS, pages 203–215. Springer, 2003.
42. Josef Urban. MPTP – Motivation, Implementation, First Experiments. *J. Autom. Reasoning*, 33(3-4):319–339, 2004. doi:10.1007/s10817-004-6245-1.
43. Petar Vukmirović, Jasmin Blanchette, and Stephan Schulz. Extending a high-performance prover to higher-order logic. In Sriram Sankaranarayanan and Natasha Sharygina, editors, *Tools and Algorithms for the Construction and Analysis of Systems - 29th International Conference, TACAS 2023, Held as Part of the European Joint Conferences on Theory and Practice of Software, ETAPS 2022, Paris, France, April 22-27, 2023, Proceedings, Part II*, volume 13994 of *Lecture Notes in Computer Science*, pages 111–129. Springer, 2023. doi:10.1007/978-3-031-30820-8_10.

Synthesis Benchmarks for Automated Reasoning

Márton Hajdu[1], Petra Hozzová[2], Laura Kovács[1], Andrei Voronkov[3,4], Eva Maria Wagner[1](✉), and Richard Steven Žilinčík[1]

[1] TU Wien, Vienna, Austria
eva.maria.wagner@tuwien.ac.at
[2] Czech Technical University, Prague, Czechia
[3] University of Manchester, Manchester, UK
[4] EasyChair, Manchester, UK

Abstract. Program synthesis is the task of constructing a program conforming to a given specification. We focus on deductive synthesis, and in particular on synthesis problems with specifications given as ∀∃-formulas, expressing the existence of an output corresponding to any input. So far there has been no canonical benchmark set for deductive synthesis using the ∀∃-format and supporting the so-called uncomputable symbol restriction. This work presents such a data set, composed by complementing existing benchmarks by new ones. Our data set is dynamically growing and should motivate future developments in the theory and practice of automating synthesis.

Keywords: Synthesis · Induction · Recursion · Automated Reasoning

1 Introduction

Program synthesis constructs code that is correct by design [6], meaning that the synthesized code satisfies its given requirements. For the purpose of automating synthesis, such requirements are typically expressed in fragments of first-order logic (FOL) with theories, extending the use of automated reasoning engines towards deriving programs from the correctness proofs of program requirements. This paper focuses on program synthesis using specifications given as ∀∃-formulas, expressing the existence of a program output corresponding to any input.[1]

Related work. The automation of this instance of program synthesis has been recently addressed by means of satisfiability modulo theory (SMT) solving [9,14] and/or first-order theorem proving [7,8,11,12]. The approaches of [7–9,14] support different formats of program specifications with additional syntactic restrictions on the sought program: either (i) the syntax-guided synthesis (SyGuS) format [13], which supplies a context-free grammar used to construct the program, or (ii) specifications given as first-order logic ∀∃-formulas, supplemented by a list of so-called uncomputable symbols that are forbidden to occur in the program [7,8]. These format differences are significant enough that SyGuS benchmarks cannot be expressed using the uncomputable framework of (ii), and further, dropping the

[1] This specification class allows to specify single-invocation functions.

V. de Paiva and P. Koepke (Eds.): CICM 2025, LNAI 16136, pp. 21–28, 2026.
https://doi.org/10.1007/978-3-032-07021-0_2

context-free grammar often results in trivial benchmarks. On the other hand, while the format of (ii) allows to use specifications in full FOL combined with various theories, the SyGuS format does not support uninterpreted function/predicate symbols within FOL, limiting the expressivity of the SyGuS deductive synthesis benchmarks from the SyGuS competitions [1]. Overall, there is a lack of synthesis benchmarks requiring reasoning with theories, quantifiers and induction, which would facilitate scaling deductive synthesis approaches. This paper aims to bridge the synthesis formats of (i) and (ii), and introduces a dataset of synthesis problems that can be used both with uncomputable symbols and within extensions of SyGuS.

Our dataset. We collect 37 benchmarks from [7–9], and complement them with 253 new problems. State of the art currently solves 140 benchmarks out of the 290 (see Section 4). Our benchmarks are available online at:

https://github.com/vprover/vampire_benchmarks/tree/cicm2025/synthesis

Our dataset is continuously growing and invites contributions from the communities of computer mathematics, automated reasoning, program verification, and others.

Input. Problems in our dataset use program specifications given as a pair of the specification formula and a set of uncomputable symbols u_i, namely

$$\langle \underbrace{\forall x_1 \in S_1, \ldots, x_n \in S_n \exists y_1 \in T_1, \ldots, y_m \in T_m . \varphi[\bar{x}, \bar{y}]}_{\text{specification formula}},\ \underbrace{\{u_1, \ldots, u_k\}}_{\text{uncomputable symbols}} \rangle, \tag{1}$$

where $\bar{x}$ denotes the set of *input variables* $x_1, \ldots, x_n$ of sorts $S_1, \ldots, S_n$; $\bar{y}$ denotes the set of *output variables* $y_1, \ldots, y_m$ of sorts $T_1, \ldots, T_m$; φ is a many-sorted FOL formula, possibly using theories and recursive definitions, with the only free variables $\bar{x}, \bar{y}$; and $u_1, \ldots, u_k$ are *uncomputable* symbols. Intuitively, specification (1) states the existence of m functions with input variables $\bar{x}$, conforming to the specification formula, each independent of all of $u_1, \ldots, u_k$. If the specification formula φ has the form $\psi \to \varphi'[\bar{x}, \bar{y}]$, where ψ is a closed formula, then φ can equivalently be written as

$$\psi \to \forall x_1 \in S_1, \ldots, x_n \in S_n \exists y_1 \in T_1, \ldots, y_m \in T_m . \varphi'[\bar{x}, \bar{y}], \tag{2}$$

and in this case we call ψ the *background axioms and definitions.*

Output. A solution for specification (1) is a tuple of terms $\langle r_1[\bar{x}], \ldots, r_m[\bar{x}] \rangle$, where $\forall x_1 \in S_1, \ldots, x_n \in S_n . \varphi[x_1, \ldots, x_n, r_1[\bar{x}], \ldots, r_m[\bar{x}]]$ is valid in the underlying theory, and $r_i[\bar{x}]$ does not contain u_j for all $i \in \{1, \ldots, m\}, j \in \{1, \ldots, k\}$. We leave the output format up to individual synthesizers. However, we note that the solution may use the `if−then−else` term constructor: for a formula F and terms s, t of the same sort the term **if** F **then** s **else** t denotes the term s if F is true and t otherwise.

Illustrative example. Let $\mathbb{N}$ denote the sort of natural numbers, and ψ be the standard background definitions of $\leq, +, \cdot$ on $\mathbb{N}$. Consider the problem from our dataset,

$$\langle \psi \to \forall x_1 \in \mathbb{N},\ x_2 \in \mathbb{N}\ \exists y \in \mathbb{N}.\ x_1 + x_2 \leq y,\ \{+\} \rangle, \tag{3}$$

specifying a (possibly loose) upper bound on the sum of input variables x_1, x_2. A possible solution for (3), where 2 is an abbreviation for $s(s(0))$, is:

$$\langle \texttt{if } x_1 \leq x_2 \texttt{ then } x_2 \cdot 2 \texttt{ else } x_1 \cdot 2 \rangle. \tag{4}$$

2 Benchmark Format

We base our benchmark format on the SMT-LIB 2.7 syntax [3]. As SMT-LIB is widely used by automated reasoners, our format makes automated reasoning naturally applicable to synthesis. Our format, dubbed SMT-LIB-SYNU (SMT-LIB for synthesis with uncomputables), extends SMT-LIB with the following features:

1. Command **assert-synth** defining a synthesis specification formula of (1) as
   `(assert-synth ((x1 S1)...(xn Sn)) ((y1 T1)...(yn Tm)) (`ϕ`))`,
   where `x1,...,xn` are the input variables, `y1,...,ym` are the output variables, and ϕ is the standard SMT-LIB encoding of the formula φ, with variables x_i, y_j and sorts S_i, T_j encoded as `xi`, `yj` and `Si`, `Tj`, respectively, for all $i \in \{1, \ldots, n\}, j \in \{1, \ldots, m\}$.
2. Command **assert-claim**, asserting auxiliary lemmas, similarly to SMT-LIB's command **assert**. The automated reasoner may decide to use these lemmas as axioms, or only use them after proving them as subgoals [5] (see also Section 3).
3. Option **uncomputable** to annotate uncomputable symbols $u_1, \ldots, u_n$ of (1) as
   `(set-option :uncomputable (u1 ... un))`.

Complementary format: SyGuS. All of our benchmarks have been translated into the SyGuS 2.1 syntax [13] using a Python script written by the authors.[2] We define computable recursive functions using the non-standard yet recommended command **define-fun-rec**, already supported by some SyGuS solvers. Since SyGuS does not allow declarations of uninterpreted functions, we encode functions that are declared but not defined, as well as uncomputable symbols, as follows. We replace each declared function symbol and each uncomputable symbol by a (possibly higher-order) universally quantified variable of the same sort. SMT-LIB assertions over the symbols are encoded as SyGuS assumptions over the variables. We add these variables as arguments to the signatures of the to-be-synthesized functions, and also pass the variables as function arguments in the constraint statement. This allows the solver to use the variables corresponding to computable uninterpreted symbols in the solution.

The only uncomputable symbols in our benchmarks are uninterpreted. To express their uncomputability, it is sufficient to leave their corresponding higher-order variables out of the list of inputs for the function(s) to be synthesized. We note that uncomputability of interpreted symbols can be expressed via SyGuS syntactic restriction – by specifying a grammar allowing all computable symbols of the suitable sort.

3 Benchmark Categories

Our dataset currently contains 290 benchmarks. It consists of (i) 180 *non-recursive* problems and (ii) 110 *recursive* problems over algebraic data types. We call benchmarks recursive if they contain recursively defined functions, as proving their specifications may require induction, leading to synthesizing recursive programs.

[2] Translation script `synthesis/tools/smt2-to-sygus.py` in our benchmark repository.

For selected benchmarks, we provide two versions, denoted by the file suffixes `original` and `assisted`. The original benchmarks only contain the necessary axioms, while the assisted ones include auxiliary lemmas (using `assert-claim`), which we found to be helpful for proving the existence of a solution.

3.1 Non-Recursive Benchmarks

Our non-recursive benchmarks are sub-categorized similarly to SMT-LIB logics, denoted with the prefix `NR_`. For example, `NR_UF` uses only uninterpreted functions and no theories, while `NR_LIA` uses linear integer arithmetic.[3] The following `NR_UF` example reasons over group theory.

Example of a `NR_UF` benchmark (`group-3-square_commutativity_assisted.smt2`)

```
(set-logic UF)

(declare-sort s 0)
(declare-fun inv (s) s)
(declare-fun op (s s) s)
(declare-const e s)

; Group axioms: left inverse, left identity, associativity
(assert (forall ((x s)) (= (op (inv x) x) e)))
(assert (forall ((x s)) (= (op e x) x)))
(assert (forall ((x s) (y s) (z s))
    (= (op x (op y z)) (op (op x y) z))))
; Additional axiom to aid the solvers: right identity
(assert (forall ((x s)) (= (op x e) x)))

; Synthesis task
(assert-synth ((x s) (y s)) ((z s))
    (=> (distinct (op x y) (op y x)) (distinct (op z z) e)))
```

The problem uses a group with binary operation `op`, inverse element function `inv`, and neutral element `e`. It specifies a function with two inputs `x` and `y`, such that when `op` is not commutative on `x`, `y`, then the square of the output is not `e`. In mathematical notation this is $\forall x, y\ \exists z.\ x * y \neq y * x \rightarrow z * z \neq e$.

3.2 Recursive Benchmarks

Our recursive benchmarks, denoted `R_UFDT`, use the inductive datatypes `nat` of natural numbers; `list` of lists; and `tree` of binary trees. In some benchmarks, `list` and `tree` use `nat` as the element type; in others, they use arbitrary types. The following recursive benchmark encodes example (3) of Section 1, using the `nat` datatype:

Example of a `R_UFDT` benchmark (`nat-upper_bound_of_sum.smt2`)

```
(set-logic UFDT)

; Datatype declarations
(declare-datatype nat ((zero) (s (s0 nat))))
```

[3] see our benchmark repo for all our problems and their categorizations.

```
; Function definitions
(define-fun-rec add ((x nat) (y nat)) nat
    (match y ((zero x) ((s y0) (s (add x y0))))))
(define-fun-rec mult ((x nat) (y nat)) nat
    (match y ((zero zero) ((s y0) (add (mult x y0) x)))))
(define-fun leq ((x nat) (y nat)) Bool (exists ((k nat))(= (add x k) y)))

; Synthesis task
(assert-synth ((x1 nat) (x2 nat)) ((y nat)) (leq (add x1 x2) y))

(set-option :uncomputable (add))
```

The inductive datatype **nat** has constructors **zero** and **s**. The recursive functions **add** and **mult** are defined over **nat**. The function **leq** is defined over **nat** using **add**. The specification asks for an upper bound on the sum of two inputs wrt **leq**.

We give an additional example input file from our R_UFDT category that reasons over mixed datatypes: a **list** containing **nat** elements.

Example of a R_UFDT benchmark (list-max_elem.smt2)

```
(set-logic UFDT)

; Datatype declarations
(declare-datatype nat ((s (s0 nat)) (zero)))
(declare-datatype lst ((nil) (cons (cons0 nat) (cons1 lst))))

; Function definitions
(define-fun-rec add ((x nat) (y nat)) nat
    (match y ((zero x)
              ((s y0) (s (add x y0))))))
(define-fun leq ((x nat) (y nat)) Bool (exists ((k nat))(= (add x k) y)))
(define-fun-rec inlst ((x nat) (y lst)) Bool
    (match y ((nil false)
              ((cons y0 y1) (or (= x y0) (inlst x y1))))))

; Synthesis task
(assert-synth ((l lst)) ((n nat))
    (and (inlst n l) (forall ((k nat)) (=> (inlst k l) (leq k n)))))
```

The datatype **list** is defined containing elements of type **nat** with constructors **nil** and **cons**. The recursive function **inlst** is defined over lists. The specification asks for a program that takes a list as input and returns the biggest element.

4 Evaluation and Experiments

To provide an insight into how challenging our benchmarks are, we ran cvc5 [2,14], Synthesiz3 [4,9], and Vampire [7,8,10]. We used a time limit of 1 minute per benchmark, and ran the benchmarks on an Apple M1 Pro CPU with 32 GB memory. We ran the solvers in the following configurations:

- cvc5: version 1.2.1[4], using the command cvc5 <benchmark.sl>
- Synthesiz3: default configuration[5], using the command
  python run_synthesiz3.py <benchmark.smt2>
- Vampire: synthesis-recursive branch[6], using the command
  vampire -ind struct -qa synthesis -alasca off -tgt off -erd off -updr off -indc goal -nm 0 -ep off <benchmark.smt2>

The individual solvers solved the following numbers of benchmarks in each category:

Category	Total	cvc5	Synthesiz3	Vampire	Total Solved
NR_LIA	60	29	32	13	37
NR_LRA	60	28	32	13	36
NR_NIA	8	3	2	2	6
NR_NRA	8	0	2	3	5
NR_UF	20	4	4	20	20
NR_UFLIA	12	5	10	3	10
NR_UFLRA	12	7	8	2	9
R_UFDT	110	3	0	17	17
altogether	290	80	90	73	140

Given the expected growth of our benchmark set, as well as the agile development of state-of-the-art solvers, we emphasize that our experimental results only depict the current capabilities of the respective synthesis tools. We are confident that the solvers' performance will continue improving.

5 Conclusions

We describe our program synthesis dataset where program specifications are given as $\forall\exists$ first-order formulas. Our dataset can be used for evaluating both the proving and synthesis abilities of automated reasoners in first-order logic, including reasoning with theories and induction. Our dataset is planned to be further expanded by users and developers of reasoning tools, for example by extending our input format and considering benchmarks with multiple-invocation functions and function composition benchmarks, and with benchmarks using interpreted uncomputable symbols.

Acknowledgements. This research was funded in whole or in part by the ERC Consolidator Grant ARTIST 101002685, the ERC Proof of Concept Grant LEARN 101213411, the TU Wien Doctoral College SecInt, the FWF SpyCoDe Grant 10.55776/F85, the WWTF grant ForSmart 10.47379/ICT22007, the Amazon Research Award 2023 QuAT, and by the European Union under the project ROBOPROX (reg. no. CZ.02.01.01/00/22_008/0004590).

[4] https://github.com/cvc5/cvc5/releases/

[5] https://doi.org/10.5281/zenodo.16436706

[6] https://github.com/vprover/vampire/tree/synthesis-recursive

Disclosure of Interests. The authors have no competing interests to declare that are relevant to the content of this article.

References

1. Alur, R., Fisman, D., Padhi, S., Reynolds, A., Singh, R., Udupa, A.: SyGuS-Comp 2019 (2019), https://sygus.org/comp/2019/
2. Barbosa, H., Barrett, C.W., Brain, M., Kremer, G., Lachnitt, H., Mann, M., Mohamed, A., Mohamed, M., Niemetz, A., Nötzli, A., Ozdemir, A., Preiner, M., Reynolds, A., Sheng, Y., Tinelli, C., Zohar, Y.: cvc5: A Versatile and Industrial-Strength SMT Solver. In: TACAS. pp. 415–442 (2022). https://doi.org/10.1007/978-3-030-99524-9_24
3. Barrett, C., Fontaine, P., Tinelli, C.: The SMT-LIB Standard: Version 2.7. Tech. rep., Department of Computer Science, The University of Iowa (2025), https://smt-lib.org/papers/smt-lib-reference-v2.7-r2025-02-05.pdf
4. De Moura, L., Bjørner, N.: Z3: An Efficient SMT Solver. In: TACAS. LNCS, vol. 4963, pp. 337–340. Springer (2008). https://doi.org/10.1007/978-3-540-78800-3_24
5. Einarsdóttir, S.H., Hajdu, M., Johansson, M., Smallbone, N., Suda, M.: Lemma Discovery and Strategies for Automated Induction. In: IJCAR (2024). https://doi.org/10.1007/978-3-031-63498-7_13
6. Gulwani, S., Polozov, O., Singh, R.: Program synthesis. Foundations and Trends® in Programming Languages **4**(1-2), 1–119 (2017). https://doi.org/10.1561/2500000010
7. Hozzová, P., Amrollahi, D., Hajdu, M., Kovács, L., Voronkov, A., Wagner, E.M.: Synthesis of Recursive Programs in Saturation. In: Benzmüller, C., Heule, M.J., Schmidt, R.A. (eds.) Automated Reasoning. pp. 154–171. Springer Nature Switzerland, Cham (2024). https://doi.org/10.1007/978-3-031-63498-7_10
8. Hozzová, P., Kovács, L., Norman, C., Voronkov, A.: Program Synthesis in Saturation. In: CADE. pp. 307–324 (2023). https://doi.org/10.1007/978-3-031-38499-8_18
9. Hozzová, P., Bjørner, N.: Synthesiz3 This: an SMT-Based Approach for Synthesis with Uncomputable Symbols (2025), https://arxiv.org/abs/2504.16536, to appear in proceedings of FMCAD 2025.
10. Kovács, L., Voronkov, A.: First-Order Theorem Proving and Vampire. In: CAV. pp. 1–35 (2013)
11. Manna, Z., Waldinger, R.: A Deductive Approach to Program Synthesis. ACM Trans. Program. Lang. Syst. **2**(1), 90–121 (1980). https://doi.org/10.1145/357084.357090
12. Manna, Z., Waldinger, R.J.: Toward automatic program synthesis. Commun. ACM **14**(3), 151–165 (Mar 1971). https://doi.org/10.1145/362566.362568
13. Padhi, S., Polgreen, E., Raghothaman, M., Reynolds, A., Udupa, A.: The SyGuS Language Standard Version 2.1 (2021), https://sygus-org.github.io/language/
14. Reynolds, A., Kuncak, V., Tinelli, C., Barrett, C.W., Deters, M.: Refutation-based synthesis in SMT. Formal Methods Syst. Des. **55**(2), 73–102 (2019). https://doi.org/10.1007/S10703-017-0270-2

Automated Symmetric Constructions in Discrete Geometry*

Bernardo Subercaseaux(✉), Ethan Mackey, Long Qian, and Marijn Heule

Carnegie Mellon University, Pittsburgh, PA 15213, USA
{bsuberca,ethanmac,longq,mheule}@andrew.cmu.edu

Abstract. We present a computational methodology for obtaining rotationally symmetric sets of points satisfying discrete geometric constraints, and demonstrate its applicability by discovering new solutions to some well-known problems in combinatorial geometry. Our approach takes the usage of SAT solvers in discrete geometry further by directly embedding rotational symmetry into the combinatorial encoding of geometric configurations. Then, to realize concrete point sets corresponding to abstract designs provided by a SAT solver, we introduce a novel local-search realizability solver, which shows excellent practical performance despite the intrinsic $\exists\mathbb{R}$-completeness of the problem. Leveraging this combined approach, we provide symmetric extremal solutions to the Erdős-Szekeres problem, as well as a minimal odd-sized solution with 21 points for the everywhere-unbalanced-points problem, improving on the previously known 23-point configuration. The imposed symmetries yield more aesthetically appealing solutions, enhancing human interpretability, and simultaneously offer computational benefits by significantly reducing the number of variables required to encode discrete geometric problems.

Keywords: Rotational Symmetry · SAT · Realizability · Computational Geometry

1 Introduction

Symmetric solutions to combinatorial problems present several benefits: they tend to be easier to grasp and generalize [6, 29], and can even be easier to compute since they have fewer degrees of freedom (i.e., optimization variables) [7, 8, 28]. In the words of Turing awardee Alan J. Perlis, *"Symmetry is a complexity-reducing concept; seek it everywhere"* [15]. Despite these benefits, it can be hard to prove in advance that a given problem will have symmetric solutions. This is especially the case in Ramsey theory, where the existence of objects avoiding certain patterns is often proven by (pseudo)random constructions, or asymmetric inductive arguments. For example, Schur number k, a classic Ramsey-theoretical problem, asks for the largest integer n such that there exists a k-coloring of $\{1, \ldots, n\}$ with no monochromatic solution to $x + y = z$, and the following *palindromic* 3-coloring is optimal since $S(3) = 13$: 1 2 3 4 5 6 7 8 9 10 11 12 13.

* The authors have been supported by the NSF under grant DMS-2434625.

V. de Paiva and P. Koepke (Eds.): CICM 2025, LNAI 16136, pp. 29–47, 2026.
https://doi.org/10.1007/978-3-032-07021-0_3

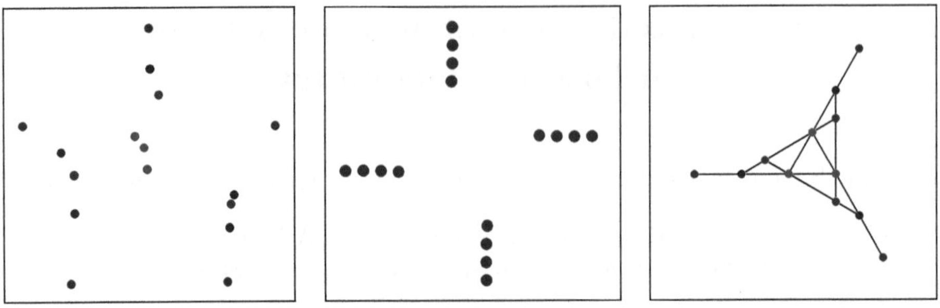

(a) Asymmetric construction of 16 points without a convex 6-gon [30].

(b) 4-fold symmetric construction for minimizing convex pentagons [23].

(c) A 2-EU pointset with a 3-fold symmetry [2]. Lines connect collinear points.

Fig. 1: Example constructions with and without symmetry in discrete geometry.

Interestingly, for all known Schur numbers $S(k)$, there is an optimal coloring that is palindromic (i.e., symmetric w.r.t. $i \mapsto n-i+1$) [9]. However, this is not known to be true for all k. A comparable phenomenon has been observed for van der Waerden numbers [8]. In this article we show that a similar situation seems to occur in certain discrete geometry problems, and that such symmetric solutions can be found *automatically*. We will consider two problems in discrete geometry described below.

Erdős-Szekeres. For each integer $k \geqslant 3$, the problem is to find $g(k)$, the smallest integer such that any set of $g(k)$ points in the plane, without three on a common line, contains k points in convex position. This long-standing problem dates back to the 1930s, with Klein's proof of $g(4) = 5$, popularly known as the *happy-ending theorem*. The only further values known are $g(5) = 9$ and $g(6) = 17$ [25]. Erdős and Szekeres conjectured that $g(k) = 2^{k-2} + 1$ for every k, which matches the three known datapoints, and proved this to be a lower bound [14]. The Erdős-Szekeres lower-bound construction is however asymmetric and hard to visualize even for small values of k. For example, an asymmetric construction of showing $g(6) > 16$, currently in the Wikipedia page of the Happy Ending problem [30], is shown in Figure 1a. In contrast, our symmetric constructions are presented in Section 6 (Figure 4). Interestingly, Subercaseaux et al. [23] provided a symmetric construction for minimizing the number of convex pentagons amongst n points, and both the work of Morris and Soltan [14] as well as Scheucher [19] exhibited symmetric (or almost symmetric) extremal constructions for variants of the Erdős-Szekeres problem. In this work, we present a much more systematic approach to symmetry in discrete geometry.

Everywhere-unbalanced-points. Given a set S of n points in the plane, we denote by $L(S)$ the set of lines that touch at least two points of S. The "imbalance" $\Delta(\ell)$ of a line $\ell \in L(S)$ is the difference between the number of points that are on one side of ℓ and the number of points on the other side. We say that S is

k-everywhere-unbalanced (k-EU, for short) if $\Delta(\ell) \geqslant k$ for all lines $\ell \in L(S)$. The main open problem is whether k-EU sets exist for all k. This question can be traced back to Kupitz, who asked whether a 2-EU pointset exists [12]. Alon answered affirmatively (see Figure 1c), showing that 2-EU sets with $4s$ points exist for every odd value of $s \geqslant 3$, and his construction has an s-fold rotational symmetry [2]. Pinchasi proved that k-EU sets, if they exist, must have $\Omega(2^{2^k})$ points [16], and recently Conlon and Lim showed an almost-matching upper bound when considering *pseudolines* instead of lines [4]. It is still open, however, whether a k-EU set exists for any $k \geqslant 3$.

1.1 Our contributions and methodology

We present a computational methodology for obtaining rotationally symmetric constructions for discrete geometric problems, which we apply to the aforementioned problems as well as other variants, e.g., 9 points in general position without an empty convex 5-gon. The methodology consists of two stages:

Symmetric combinatorial encoding: We first encode the geometric properties of the problems as instances of boolean satisfiability (SAT), following a recent line of work. We impose rotational symmetry in the encoding itself, which was initially explored by one of the authors [13]. To do this efficiently, we prove that the axioms of Knuth's CC systems [11] can be encoded with $O(n^4)$ many clauses without assuming a left-to-right ordering of the points as in previous work [10]. For the everywhere-unbalanced-points problem, we use SAT for the first time and prove, for instance, that Alon's 12-point construction uses the minimum number of points for a 2-EU set.

Realizability: Going from the solutions to the SAT instances to actual pointsets turns out to be harder, both in theory and in practice. To tackle this we developed `Localizer`, a local-search solver for the $\exists\mathbb{R}$-complete realizability problem, and through an experimental evaluation show it is highly performant compared to the general-purpose local-search formulation used in previous work [23]. Our solver does not handle collinear points, and thus to realize solutions of the everywhere-unbalanced-points problem (which necessarily involves collinearity), we use a different ad-hoc approach.

We show symmetric solutions for the Erdős-Szekeres problem on 16 points without convex 6-gons, and furthermore we enumerate and classify them, showing that s-fold symmetric solutions exist for $s = 4$ and $s = 5$, but not for $s = 3$. For the everywhere-unbalanced-points problem, we exhibit a 21-point symmetric construction (Figure 6), which we prove to be the minimal odd-sized solution. In this case, the symmetry crucially allows us to find a realization.
Our code is publicly available at github.com/bsubercaseaux/automatic-symmetries.

2 Background

While the domain of the aforementioned problems is continuous (i.e., $\mathbb{R}^2$), it is possible to reason about geometric properties like convexity, or line balances, purely in terms of combinatorial relationships between points. A widely successful abstraction in discrete geometry is that of *triple orientations* [11] which consists of characterizing, for each ordered triples of points (p, q, r), whether it defines a curve that turns clockwise, counterclockwise, or whether they are collinear. Concretely, given points p, q, r, their triple orientation is defined as

$$\sigma(p, q, r) = \operatorname{sign}\det\begin{pmatrix} p_x & q_x & r_x \\ p_y & q_y & r_y \\ 1 & 1 & 1 \end{pmatrix} = \begin{cases} -1 & \text{if } p, q, r \text{ are oriented clockwise,} \\ 0 & \text{if } p, q, r \text{ are collinear,} \\ 1 & \text{if } p, q, r \text{ are oriented counterclockwise.} \end{cases}$$

This abstraction has been successfully used to encode and solve several problems in discrete geometry: Peters and Szekeres used it to settle $g(6) = 17$ [25], Heule and Scheucher for proving that 30 points in general position must contain an empty convex hexagon [10], among others [19, 20, 23]. Let us clarify how these orientations are enough to express the constraints of both the Erdős-Szekeres and the everywhere-unbalanced-points problems. We will start with some definitions. A set of points S is in general position if no three points are collinear, that is, $\sigma(p, q, r) \neq 0$ for all $(p, q, r) \in \binom{S}{3}$. For a finite set of points $S \subset \mathbb{R}^2$, we denote by $\text{conv}(S)$ the *convex hull* of S, which is the smallest convex set containing S. Then, a set of points S in general position is in *convex position* if removing any point $a \in S$ would change its convex hull, i.e., $\text{conv}(S \setminus \{a\}) \neq \text{conv}(S)$ for all $a \in S$. As a consequence of Carathéodory's theorem, a set of points S in general position is in convex position if and only if every subset of 4 points of S is also in convex position. This implies that, by using the triple orientations to express whether sets of 4 points are in convex position, we can express the presence of a convex k-gon (from now on, we will use k-gon to refer to a set of k points in convex position). The precise formulation is in Section 4.3, and we remark that a Lean formalization of these basic discrete geometry notions has been carried out by Subercaseaux et al. [24]. For the everywhere-unbalanced-points problem, it will suffice to express the imbalance of a line ℓ between points p and q of a pointset S, as the absolute value of the difference between $|\{r \in S : \sigma(p, q, r) = 1\}|$ and $|\{r \in S : \sigma(p, q, r) = -1\}|$.

2.1 Geometric and combinatorial symmetries

We consider two different forms of symmetry. For a pointset $P = \{p_1, \dots, p_n\}$, a *combinatorial symmetry* is a bijection $\pi : \{1, \dots, n\} \to \{1, \dots, n\}$ such that $\sigma(p_i, p_j, p_k) = \sigma(p_{\pi(i)}, p_{\pi(j)}, p_{\pi(k)})$ for all $(i, j, k) \in \binom{[n]}{3}$. On the other hand, a *geometric symmetry* is an isometric (i.e., distance-preserving) bijection $\rho : \mathbb{R}^2 \to \mathbb{R}^2$ such that $\rho(p_i) \in P$ for all $i \in \{1, \dots, n\}$. We say that a geometric symmetry ρ is *orientation preserving* if $\sigma(\rho(p), \rho(q), \rho(r)) = \sigma(p, q, r)$ for every $p, q, r \in \mathbb{R}^2$. For example, any rotation of the plane is orientation preserving [24], but it might not be a geometric symmetry of a pointset, as illustrated in Figure 1a taking $\pi/4$ as rotation angle. In this work, we focus on s-fold rotational symmetries, which correspond to rotations of the plane by $\frac{2\pi}{s}$, for some integer s. More formally, let $\rho_\alpha : \mathbb{R}^2 \to \mathbb{R}^2$ be the function defined by $\rho_\alpha(x, y) = (x\cos(\alpha) - y\sin(\alpha), x\sin(\alpha) +$

$y\cos(\alpha)$). Then, we say a set of points S is *s-fold symmetric* if $\rho_{2\pi/s}$ is a geometric symmetry of S (i.e., $\rho_{2\pi/s}(S) = S$).

2.2 Orientation Variables and Notation

To obtain a propositional encoding for the aforementioned problems, we start by defining *orientation variables* $\mathrm{A}_{i,j,k}$, $\mathrm{B}_{i,j,k}$, and $\mathrm{C}_{i,j,k}$ for each triple of distinct indices $i, j, k \in \{1, \ldots, n\}$, where n is the number of points in the desired pointset. $\mathrm{A}_{i,j,k}$ will represent that $\sigma(p_i, p_j, p_k) = 1$, whereas $\mathrm{B}_{i,j,k}$ that $\sigma(p_i, p_j, p_k) = -1$, and $\mathrm{C}_{i,j,k}$ that $\sigma(p_i, p_j, p_k) = 0$. For the Erdős-Szekeres problem, given that we are interested in pointsets in general position, we will only need the variables $\mathrm{A}_{i,j,k}$, since its truth value is enough to identify the orientation of the triple (p_i, p_j, p_k). For the everywhere-unbalanced-points problem, we use the three kinds of variables, and naturally enforce that exactly one of them is true for each triple of points. From now on, we assume the number of points n to be fixed.

2.3 CC Systems and Axioms

The study of axioms for combinatorial representations of pointsets was initiated by Knuth [11], who introduced the so-called *CC systems*, as an abstraction for pointsets in general position. Knuth's axioms can be written as follows in our notation:

Axiom 1 (Cyclic Symmetry). $\mathrm{A}_{i,j,k} \rightarrow \mathrm{A}_{j,k,i}$,
Axiom 2 (Antisymmetry). $\mathrm{A}_{i,j,k} \rightarrow \overline{\mathrm{A}_{i,k,j}}$,
Axiom 3 (Nondegeneracy). $\mathrm{A}_{i,j,k} \vee \mathrm{A}_{i,k,j}$,
Axiom 4 (Interiority). $\mathrm{A}_{i,j,k} \vee \mathrm{A}_{i,k,l} \vee \mathrm{A}_{k,j,\ell} \vee \mathrm{A}_{j,i,\ell}$,
Axiom 5 (Transitivity). $\mathrm{A}_{\ell,i,m} \vee \mathrm{A}_{\ell,j,m} \vee \mathrm{A}_{\ell,k,m} \vee \mathrm{A}_{\ell,j,i} \vee \mathrm{A}_{\ell,k,j} \vee \mathrm{A}_{\ell,i,k}$,

where each axiom is quantified over all distinct indices $i, j, k, \ell, m \in \{1, \ldots, n\}$. It turns out that Axioms (1-3) can be encoded implicitly, by only using variables $\mathrm{A}_{i,j,k}$ for indices $i < j < k$, replacing each occurrence of a variable whose indices are not ordered with the corresponding variable with ordered indices, and a potential negation. Namely, for a tuple t of three indices not necessarily sorted, we can consider t' as the sorted version of t. According to Axioms (1-3), we replace each occurrence of A_t with $\mathrm{A}_{t'}$ if t has an even number of inversions (i.e., the number of swaps required to sort t), and with $\overline{\mathrm{A}_{t'}}$ otherwise. Despite these optimizations, the number of clauses required to encode the axioms is still roughly $5! \cdot \binom{n}{5} \approx n^5$, which amounts to over 24 million clauses for $n = 32$.

2.4 Signotope Axioms

A more efficient alternative in terms of encoding size is to use the so-called *signotope axioms* [5, 10, 19], which assuming that points are sorted from left to right (i.e., $x_i < x_{i+1}$ for every i, where x_i denotes the x-coordinate of point p_i), allows to express an equivalent set of axioms with only $4\binom{n}{4}$ clauses. The signotope axioms can be written in clausal form as follows:

$$\left(\overline{\mathrm{A}_{i,j,k}} \vee \overline{\mathrm{A}_{i,k,\ell}} \vee \mathrm{A}_{i,j,\ell}\right) \wedge \left(\mathrm{A}_{i,j,k} \vee \mathrm{A}_{i,k,\ell} \vee \overline{\mathrm{A}_{i,j,\ell}}\right), \quad (1)$$

$$\left(\overline{\mathrm{A}_{i,j,k}} \vee \overline{\mathrm{A}_{j,k,\ell}} \vee \mathrm{A}_{i,k,\ell}\right) \wedge \left(\mathrm{A}_{i,j,k} \vee \mathrm{A}_{j,k,\ell} \vee \overline{\mathrm{A}_{i,k,\ell}}\right), \quad (2)$$

where the quantification here is only over indices $1 \leqslant i < j < k < \ell \leqslant n$. The main issue with these signotope axioms, which we will address in Section 4.1, is that they assume a left-to-right ordering of the points, which can often be assumed without loss of generality by simply relabeling points from left to right (cf. [24]), but in our case is incompatible with the rotational symmetries we want to impose. Note that the strictness of the ordering is not a restrictive condition since we can always rotate pointsets by an ε-angle while preserving all orientations to guarantee no points share the same x-coordinate.

2.5 Realizability Problem

It is worth mentioning immediately that these combinatorial abstractions for pointsets are an *under-approximation* of the geometric properties of points in $\mathbb{R}^2$, meaning that every set of points satisfies the axioms, but there are assignments of the orientation variables that satisfy the axioms and yet do not correspond to any planar pointset. Therefore, if after adding problem-specific constraints (e.g., convexity, imbalance, etc.) we obtain a satisfiable formula, we still need to check whether the solution to the orientation variables can be realized in $\mathbb{R}^2$, the so-called *point realizability problem* [18] for which we present a local-search solver in Section 5. On the other hand, if no assignment of the orientation variables satisfies the constraints of a problem in conjunction with the axioms, then we can safely conclude that no pointset exists satisfying the desired properties. This idea has been formalized in Lean by Subercaseaux et al. [24].

3 Symmetry Constraints

In this section, we present the symmetry constraints that we will use to enforce s-fold rotational symmetry in our combinatorial encodings. In general, a combinatorial symmetry $\pi : \{1, \ldots, n\} \to \{1, \ldots, n\}$ can be enforced by adding clauses for the constraints $\mathrm{A}_{i,j,k} \leftrightarrow \mathrm{A}_{\pi(i),\pi(j),\pi(k)}$, and similarly for the $\mathrm{B}_{i,j,k}$ and $\mathrm{C}_{i,j,k}$ variables when dealing with collinear points. As we will see next, however, it is possible to enforce the symmetry directly without those clauses by unifying equivalent variables as we did for Axioms (1-2) of Knuth's CC systems. For example, if we want to enforce a 4-fold rotational symmetry over 16 points, we can assume that the permutation π can be factored as

$$\pi = (1, 2, 3, 4)\,(5, 6, 7, 8)\,(9, 10, 11, 12)\,(13, 14, 15, 16), \quad (3)$$

which can be succinctly coded by defining $\pi(i) = \lfloor (i-1)/4 \rfloor \cdot 4 + (i+1) \bmod 4$. Then, if we consider the triple of indices $(1, 6, 8)$, we have the equivalences:

$$\mathrm{A}_{1,6,8} \leftrightarrow \mathrm{A}_{2,7,5} \leftrightarrow \mathrm{A}_{3,8,6} \leftrightarrow \mathrm{A}_{4,5,7},$$

and by the equivalences of Section 2.3, this is the same as

$$\mathrm{A}_{1,6,8} \leftrightarrow \overline{\mathrm{A}_{2,5,7}} \leftrightarrow \overline{\mathrm{A}_{3,6,8}} \leftrightarrow \mathrm{A}_{4,5,7}.$$

We can thus treat these literals as an equivalence class, and for each such equivalence class we can choose a representative (e.g., the lexicographically smallest one, $\mathrm{A}_{1,6,8}$), and then replace all occurrences of the other literals in its class with the representative or its negation.

3.1 Filtering Isomorphic Constraints

Not only can we reduce the number of variables by the enforced symmetries, but also the number of constraints. For example, a constraint stating that indices $\{1, 3, 6, 8, 10, 13\}$ do not form a 6-gon, already implies that the indices $\{2, 4, 5, 7, 11, 14\}$ do not form a 6-gon when enforcing the symmetry of Equation (3). Therefore, the second constraint is redundant and can be removed. In general, for a constraint involving a tuple of indices $t = (i_1, \ldots, i_k)$, we consider the *orbit* of t under the symmetry π, which is the set of all tuples of indices that can be obtained from t by applying π any number of times. We can then remove all but one constraint for each orbit, which we implement by only adding constraints that are lexicographically smallest in their orbits.

3.2 Symmetry Breaking

To limit the generation of isomorphic solutions, we add symmetry-breaking predicates, which depend on the parameters of the problem at hand. Let us consider, for example, the Erdős-Szekeres problem for 16 points without 6-gons and a 4-fold symmetry. The only possibility for the convex layers of these 16 points is that we have 4 layers with 4 points each. Then, as any rotational symmetry must map each point p to a point q in the same convex layer as p (potentially $p = q$), we can assume without loss of generality that the 4-fold symmetry is precisely the one in Equation (3). Moreover, we can assume without loss of generality that the outermost convex layer is $\{1, 2, 3, 4\}$, that the next one is $\{5, 6, 7, 8\}$, and so on. To enforce that points $5, 6, 7, 8$ are inside the convex hull of points $1, 2, 3, 4$, and that $1 \to 2 \to 3 \to 4$ is a counterclockwise sequence, we can add *convex layer unit clauses* (CL-clauses) of the form $\mathrm{A}_{i,1+i \bmod 4,j}$ for $i \in \{1, 2, 3, 4\}$ and $j \in \{5, 6, 7, 8\}$. Figure 2 illustrates how these CL-clauses enforce a *canonical* representative from a set of isomorphic solutions. We can then add analogous CL-clauses to enforce that points $9, 10, 11, 12$ are inside the convex hull of points $5, 6, 7, 8$, and so on. Furthermore, we can assume without loss of generality that all points whose index is 1 mod 5 are in the bottom-left quadrant. To see this, note that otherwise we could relabel the points assigning index $4i + 1$ to whichever point from the i-th outermost convex layer is in the bottom left quadrant, noting that the 4-fold symmetry enforces that at least one point per layer lies in that quadrant. Concretely, we add *quadrant clauses* (Q-clauses) of the form $\overline{\mathrm{A}_{1,3,i}}$ and $\mathrm{A}_{2,4,i}$ for every $i > 1$ that is 1 modulo 4. Note that, assuming without loss of

(a) Canonical. (b) Fails CL. (c) Fails CL. (d) Fails Q. (e) Fails Q.

Fig. 2: Symmetry breaking predicates for pointsets with a 4-fold symmetry. Orientations in red are failing to satisfy the symmetry-breaking predicates.

generality that point 1 gets coordinates $(-C, 0)$, and that points $2, 3, 4$ get the coordinates implied by the orbit $1 \to 2 \to 3 \to 4$, then these clauses directly correspond to the points $4i + 1$ for $i \geqslant 1$ being in the bottom-left quadrant. See Figures 2d and 2e.

4 Encodings

In this section, we detail the propositional encodings for the Erdős-Szekeres and everywhere-unbalanced-points problems.

4.1 Dynamic Point Ordering Axioms

While the signotope axioms are more efficient than the CC system axioms (an $n^5 \to n^4$ advantage), they assume a left-to-right ordering of the points, which is not compatible with the rotational symmetries we want to impose — e.g., in the example symmetry of Equation (3) we can infer what the convex layers of the desired pointset are, but we cannot a priori say whether point 5 will be to the left of point 12 or to its right. A discovery of independent interest is that the left-to-right ordering can be replaced by any linear ordering $\prec$ of the point indices, and only apply the signotope axioms for tuples of indices respecting a constraint similar to $i \prec j \prec k \prec \ell$. That is, as opposed to a predefined ordering, we introduce variables $\prec_{i,j}$ for every pair of distinct indices, which the SAT solver will assign dynamically, and enforce axioms accordingly. Naturally, we need to add constraints stating that these variables induce a strict linear ordering:

Totality. $(\prec_{i,j} \vee \prec_{j,i})$, for all $1 \leqslant i \neq j \leqslant n$.
Asymmetry. $(\prec_{i,j} \leftrightarrow \overline{\prec_{j,i}})$, for all $1 \leqslant i \neq j \leqslant n$.
Transitivity. $(\prec_{i,j} \wedge \prec_{j,k} \to \prec_{i,k})$, for all $1 \leqslant i \neq j \neq k \leqslant n$.

These linear-ordering axioms incur in $\Theta(n^3)$ clauses, and thus are not a bottleneck. Then, it turns out that we can replace the signotope axioms for pointsets in general position with the following:

$$(\prec_{i,j} \wedge \prec_{i,k} \wedge \prec_{i,\ell}) \to \left(\mathrm{A}_{i,j,k} \vee \overline{\mathrm{A}_{i,j,\ell}} \vee \mathrm{A}_{i,k,\ell}\right), \quad \forall i \neq j \neq k \neq \ell, \tag{4}$$

$$(\prec_{i,k} \wedge \prec_{j,k} \wedge \prec_{k,\ell}) \rightarrow (\mathrm{A}_{i,j,k} \vee \overline{\mathrm{A}_{i,k,\ell}} \vee \mathrm{A}_{j,k,\ell}), \quad \forall i \neq j \neq k \neq \ell. \tag{5}$$

Moreover, Equation (4) is only needed when $\max(j,k) < \ell$, which further reduces the number of clauses. In total, since the condition $\max(j,k) < \ell$ holds in exactly a third of the cases, these dynamic-ordering axioms incur in $\frac{4}{3} \cdot 4! \cdot \binom{n}{4} \approx \frac{4}{3}n^4$ clauses. For $n = 32$, this is around 1.3 million clauses, a significant improvement over the 24 million clauses of the CC-system axioms (cf. Section 2.3). We now summarize correctness with the following two propositions.

Proposition 1. *For every set of n points $S = \{p_1, \ldots, p_n\}$ in general position with distinct x-coordinates, the assignment of the $\mathrm{A}_{i,j,k}$ and $\prec_{i,j}$ variables τ defined as:*

$$\tau(\mathrm{A}_{i,j,k}) = \begin{cases} \textit{true} & \textit{if } \sigma(p_i,p_j,p_k) = 1 \\ \textit{false} & \textit{otherwise,} \end{cases} \qquad \tau(\prec_{i,j}) = \begin{cases} \textit{true} & \textit{if } x_i < x_j \\ \textit{false} & \textit{otherwise,} \end{cases}$$

satisfies the dynamic-ordering axioms from Equations (4) *and* (5).

Proof. We first prove that Equation (4) is satisfied. Let $\{p_1, p_2, p_3, p_4\}$ be 4 points from S such that the ordering requirements $\prec_{1,2} \wedge \prec_{1,3} \wedge \prec_{1,4}$ are satisfied, potentially relabeling points if needed. By translating if necessary, we may further assume that $p_1 = (0,0)$ is the origin (note that this does not affect the relative ordering of the x-coordinates nor the orientations). Then, we will think of the condition $\mathrm{A}_{1,2,3} \vee \overline{\mathrm{A}_{1,2,4}} \vee \mathrm{A}_{1,3,4}$ as $(\overline{\mathrm{A}_{1,2,3}} \wedge \overline{\mathrm{A}_{1,3,4}}) \rightarrow \overline{\mathrm{A}_{1,2,4}}$. Thus, we assume that $\overline{\mathrm{A}_{1,2,3}}, \overline{\mathrm{A}_{1,3,4}}$ hold, and it remains to prove that $\overline{\mathrm{A}_{1,2,4}}$ holds as well. By the construction of the assignment τ, we have that $\sigma(p_1,p_2,p_3) = -1$ and $\sigma(p_1,p_3,p_4) = -1$. Recall that the orientation $\sigma(p,q,r)$ is defined according to the sign of the determinant (or cross-product) relating the points:

$$\operatorname{sign}\det \begin{pmatrix} p_x & q_x & r_x \\ p_y & q_y & r_y \\ 1 & 1 & 1 \end{pmatrix} = \begin{cases} -1 & \text{if } (p_x - q_x)(p_y - r_y) < (p_y - q_y)(p_x - r_x), \\ 0 & \text{if } (p_x - q_x)(p_y - r_y) = (p_y - q_y)(p_x - r_x), \\ 1 & \text{if } (p_x - q_x)(p_y - r_y) > (p_y - q_y)(p_x - r_x). \end{cases}$$

Therefore, from $\sigma(p_1,p_2,p_3) = -1$ we have

$$x_2 y_3 < x_3 y_2, \tag{6}$$

and from $\sigma(p_1,p_3,p_4) = -1$ we have

$$x_3 y_4 < x_4 y_3. \tag{7}$$

Since $\prec_{1,2}$ holds, we have $x_1 < x_2$ and thus we can multiply Equation (7) by x_2 without flipping the inequality, obtaining

$$x_2 x_3 y_4 < x_2 x_4 y_3 = x_4(x_2 y_3) < x_4(x_3 y_2).$$

By dividing the left- and right-most terms by x_3, which is positive since $\prec_{1,3}$ holds, we have $x_2 y_4 < x_4 y_2$. This directly implies that $\sigma(p_1,p_2,p_4) = -1$, and thus $\overline{\mathrm{A}_{1,2,4}}$ holds, satisfying Equation (4).

The proof for Equation (5) is similar, but this time setting $p_3 = (0,0)$ for convenience. Here we assume $\overline{\mathrm{A}_{1,2,3}}$ and $\overline{\mathrm{A}_{2,3,4}}$, from where we have

$$x_4 y_2 < x_2 y_4, \tag{8}$$
$$x_1 y_2 < x_2 y_1. \tag{9}$$

We moreover have, due to the ordering assumption, that $x_1, x_2 < 0$ and $x_4 > 0$, and we want to show that $\overline{\mathrm{A}_{1,3,4}}$ holds. By the equivalence discussed in Section 2.3, this is the same as proving that $\overline{\mathrm{A}_{3,4,1}}$ holds, which we do next. Indeed, since $x_1 < 0$, multiplying Equation (8) by x_1 gives

$$x_1 x_4 y_2 > x_1 x_2 y_4, \tag{10}$$

and as $x_4 > 0$, multiplying Equation (9) by x_4 gives

$$x_4 x_1 y_2 < x_4 x_2 y_1. \tag{11}$$

Then, transitivity over Equations (10) and (11) gives

$$x_1 x_2 y_4 < x_4 x_2 y_1,$$

which dividing by x_2 (recalling that $x_2 < 0$) gives $x_1 y_4 > x_4 y_1$, which is equivalent to $\overline{\mathrm{A}_{3,4,1}}$, as desired.

Proposition 2. *For every assignment τ of the $\mathrm{A}_{i,j,k}$ variables, with $i, j, k \in \{1, \ldots, n\}$, if there is an assignment θ to the $\prec_{i,j}$ variables $(1 \leqslant i \neq j \leqslant n)$ such that $\tau \cup \theta$ satisfies the dynamic-ordering axioms from Equations* (4) *and* (5), *and CC-Axioms (1-3) (see Section 2.3), then τ satisfies the CC-Axioms (4-5).*

Proof. We first prove that it suffices to show it for $n = 5$. Indeed, suppose that for some $n > 5$ there is an assignment τ of the $\mathrm{A}_{i,j,k}$ variables, and θ for the $\prec_{i,j}$ variables, that satisfies the dynamic-ordering axioms but not the CC axioms. Then, in particular, there is a CC-axiom clause C that is not satisfied by τ, which involves a set S of at most 5 indices (see Section 2.3). Thus, the restriction of $\theta \cup \tau$ to variables whose indices are contained in S, which we denote by $(\theta \cup \tau)_{|S}$, holds $(\theta \cup \tau)_{|S} \not\models C$. On the other hand, if we denote by D_S the set of clauses of the dynamic-ordering axioms that involve only variables whose indices are in S, we have $(\theta \cup \tau)_{|S} \models D_S$. By considering the mapping $f : S \to \{1, \ldots, |S|\}$ that maps the i-th largest index in S to i, and letting C^f (resp. D_S^f) be clauses obtained by replacing each index j appearing in some variable in C (resp. D_S) with its image $f(j)$, then we have that $(\theta \cup \tau)_{|f(S)} \models D_S^f$ and $(\theta \cup \tau)_{|f(S)} \not\models C^f$, which would constitute a counterexample with $n \leqslant 5$. For $n = 5$ (which trivially implies the cases with $n < 5$), the question reduces to a finite computation, which we carry out as a SAT problem. We start by we creating a formula $\mathsf{DOA}(5)$, consisting of the dynamic-ordering axioms for $n = 5$, and a formula $\mathsf{CCA}(5)$, consisting of the CC axioms for $n = 5$. We then use a Tseitin transformation to negate the CC axioms: for each clause $C \in \mathsf{CCA}(5)$, we introduce a new variable y_C and add a clause $\overline{\ell} \vee \overline{y_C}$ for each literal ℓ in C, thus ensuring that if clause C is satisfied by any of its literals, then y_C is false. Therefore, given that DOA(5) is clearly satisfiable, the formula

$$\Psi := \mathsf{DOA}(5) \wedge \bigwedge_{C \in \mathsf{CCA}(5)} \bigwedge_{\ell \in C} (\overline{\ell} \vee \overline{y_C}) \wedge \left(\bigvee_{C \in \mathsf{CCA}(5)} y_C \right)$$

is satisfiable if and only if there is an assignment τ of the $\mathrm{A}_{i,j,k}$ variables and θ for the $<_{i,j}$ variables for which $(\tau \cup \theta)$ satisfies the dynamic-ordering axioms, but not the CC axioms. We conclude by running a SAT solver on Ψ, and finding that Ψ is unsatisfiable, which proves that no such assignment exists. The code for generating the formulas is available in the repository github.com/bsubercaseaux/automatic-symmetries.

At a high level, Proposition 1 is stating that the dynamic-ordering axioms are respected by actual pointsets, and Proposition 2 is intuitively stating that these axioms are no more permissive than the CC axioms. In other words, an empty set of axioms would trivially satisfy Proposition 1 but not Proposition 2, and on the other hand, an inconsistent set of axioms would trivially satisfy Proposition 2 but not Proposition 1.

4.2 Axioms for Collinear Point Sets

In addition to the axioms in Section 4.1, additional care is needed to handle potentially collinear points. Intuitively, such axioms capture the property that for any collection of 4 points p_i, p_j, p_k, p_ℓ where the first 3 are collinear (i.e. $\mathrm{C}_{i,j,k}$ is true), then the orientation of any triple that includes the point p_ℓ uniquely determines the orientation of all triples. As the points are not necessarily ordered, we leverage the dynamic point orderings and case on all possibilities. That is, we add the following clauses for every set of four distinct indices $i, j, k, \ell \in \{1, \ldots, n\}$:

1. $(\mathrm{C}_{i,j,k}) \rightarrow (\mathrm{C}_{\mathbf{t_1}} \leftrightarrow \mathrm{C}_{\mathbf{t_2}})$, for distinct triples $\mathbf{t_1}, \mathbf{t_2} \neq \{i, j, k\}$,
2. $(<_{i,j} \wedge <_{j,k} \wedge \mathrm{C}_{i,j,k}) \rightarrow (\mathrm{A}_{\mathbf{t_1}} \leftrightarrow \mathrm{A}_{\mathbf{t_2}})$, for distinct triples $\mathbf{t_1}, \mathbf{t_2} \neq \{i, j, k\}$,
3. $(<_{i,k} \wedge <_{k,j} \wedge \mathrm{C}_{i,j,k}) \rightarrow ((\mathrm{A}_{i,j,\ell} \leftrightarrow \mathrm{A}_{i,k,\ell}) \wedge (\mathrm{A}_{i,j,\ell} \leftrightarrow \mathrm{B}_{j,k,\ell}))$,
4. $(<_{k,i} \wedge <_{i,j} \wedge \mathrm{C}_{i,j,k}) \rightarrow ((\mathrm{A}_{i,j,\ell} \leftrightarrow \mathrm{B}_{i,k,\ell}) \wedge (\mathrm{A}_{i,j,\ell} \leftrightarrow \mathrm{B}_{j,k,\ell}))$.

Moreover, for Axioms (2-4), we also add an analogous version with each $<$ variable negated, to consider the opposite ordering. Axiom (1) enforces the transitivity of collinearity: if there exist two distinct triples of $\{p_i, p_j, p_k, p_l\}$ that are collinear, then all points are collinear. Axioms (2-4) handle the case where $\{p_i, p_j, p_k\}$ are collinear yet p_ℓ does not lie on the same line. In Axiom (2), either $i < j < k$ or $i > j > k$ hold, thus the points are ordered monotonically. As such, their relative orientations with respect to p_ℓ are necessarily equivalent, hence the bi-implication clauses. In contrast, consider the scenario where $i < k < j$, which falls under Axiom (3). In this case, the orientations $\sigma(p_i, p_j, p_\ell) = \sigma(p_i, p_k, p_\ell)$ are still equivalent, as the lines $p_i \rightarrow p_j, p_i \rightarrow p_k$ have the same direction, resulting in the clauses $\mathrm{A}_{i,j,\ell} \leftrightarrow \mathrm{A}_{i,k,\ell}$. On the contrary, the lines $p_i \to p_j, p_j \to p_k$ are now in opposing directions, thus the orientations $\sigma(p_i, p_j, p_\ell) = -\sigma(p_j, p_k, p_\ell)$ are opposites, yielding the clauses $\mathrm{A}_{i,j,\ell} \leftrightarrow \mathrm{B}_{j,k,\ell}$. Axiom (4) is identical and considers the remaining cases. Note that it suffices to add these clauses only for $i < j < k$, and $\ell \in [n]\backslash\{i, j, k\}$. Therefore, the total number of clauses is $28(n-3) \cdot \binom{n}{3} = 112\binom{n}{4}$.

4.3 Constraints for k-Gons

Similarly to the work of Scheucher [19,20], we create auxiliary variables $\mathrm{CONV}_{i,j,k,\ell}$ for each set of four indices $i, j, k, \ell \in \{1, \ldots, n\}$ (note that these are unordered), representing whether the points p_i, p_j, p_k, p_ℓ are in convex position. Our encoding is slightly different from Scheucher's in that we define these variables only in terms of the base orientation variables:

$$\mathrm{CONV}_{i,j,k,\ell} \leftrightarrow ((\mathrm{A}_{i,j,k} \leftrightarrow \mathrm{A}_{i,k,\ell}) \leftrightarrow (\mathrm{A}_{i,k,\ell} \leftrightarrow \mathrm{A}_{j,k,\ell})),$$

which we can express in $12\binom{n}{4}$ clauses using Tseitin variables. The correctness of this encoding can be seen by a tedious case analysis of the 16 possible orientations for the four points p_i, p_j, p_k, p_ℓ. Then, as described in Section 2, a set of points S is in convex position if and only if every subset of 4 points of S is also in convex position. Thus, to express the absence of a convex k-gon, we enforce for every set $X \subseteq \{1, \ldots, n\}$ with $|X| = k$, the clause $\bigvee_{i,j,k,\ell \in X} \overline{\mathrm{CONV}_{i,j,k,\ell}}$.

4.4 Constraints for Imbalance

Recall that for a set of n points S in the plane, $L(S)$ denotes the set of all lines touching at least two points of S. For a pair of points $p_i, p_j \in S$, let $l_{i,j} \in L(S)$ be the unique line passing through p_i and p_j. The set of points above/below $l_{i,j}$ are defined as $l_{i,j}^+ = \{p_k \in S \mid \sigma(p_i, p_j, p_k) > 0\}$ and $l_{i,j}^- = \{p_k \in S \mid \sigma(p_i, p_j, p_k) < 0\}$, respectively. and the imbalance of p_i, p_j, denoted $\Delta(i, j)$, is defined as $\Delta(i, j) = ||l_{i,j}^+| - |l_{i,j}^-||$. Finally, the imbalance of S is the minimum of all such imbalances $\Delta(S) = \min_{i,j \in \binom{[n]}{2}} \Delta(i, j)$. Therefore, to encode $\Delta(S) \geqslant c$, it suffices to encode $\Delta(i, j) \geqslant c$ for all pairs i, j. Thus, the problem reduces to encoding that

$$\sum_{k \notin \{i,j\}} \mathrm{A}_{i,j,k} \geqslant \sum_{k \notin \{i,j\}} \mathrm{B}_{i,j,k} + c \quad \text{or} \quad \sum_{k \notin \{i,j\}} \mathrm{A}_{i,j,k} \leqslant \sum_{k \notin \{i,j\}} \mathrm{B}_{i,j,k} - c.$$

To achieve this, we use the standard Sinz encoding [21] to define for every pair i, j the *counting variables* s_m and t_m, for each $0 \leqslant m \leqslant n-2$, which represent $\sum_{k \notin \{i,j\}} \mathrm{A}_{i,j,k} = m$ and $\sum_{k \notin \{i,j\}} \mathrm{B}_{i,j,k} = m$ respectively. Then, to encode that $\Delta(i, j) \geqslant c$ it suffices to add clauses of the form $\overline{s}_x \vee \overline{t}_y$ for each $x, y \in \{0, \ldots, n-2\}$ such that $|x - y| < c$.

5 Realizability

In the realizability problem, we are given an orientation assignment $\tau : \binom{n}{3} \to \{-1, 0, 1\}$, and the goal is to construct a set of points $S = \{p_1, \ldots, p_n\} \subset \mathbb{R}^2$ such that $\tau(i, j, k) = \sigma(p_i, p_j, p_k)$ for all $i < j < k$ [18]. This problem is known to be $\exists\mathbb{R}$-complete [26], and thus at least NP-hard (recall that NP $\subseteq \exists\mathbb{R} \subseteq$ PSPACE [17]). We first describe our efficient general-purpose realizability solver for pointsets in general position, and then the ad-hoc method we followed to realize pointsets with collinearities for the everywhere-unbalanced-points problem.

5.1 `Localizer`: a Realizability Solver for Points in General Position

Our solver, `Localizer`, is written in C and it implements a local-search algorithm that starts with a random initialization of point coordinates $(x_1, y_1), \ldots, (x_n, y_n)$, and iteratively moves the points trying to minimize the number of orientation constraints that are not satisfied by their current positions. The solver is multi-threaded, and uses a parallelism model in which a global table of top-K solutions is maintained, and threads independently select a random solution from this table (with probability proportional to the solution quality) and attempt to improve upon it. If a thread manages to find a strictly better solution, then it updates the global table in case the found solution is better-or-equal than some solution on the top-K table. Within a thread, the algorithm uses a form of *simulated annealing*, where in each iteration a point is selected, with probabilities proportional to the number of unsatisfied constraints they participate in, and then the point is moved to a random position within a ball of radius r centered at its previous position. The radius r is exponentially decreasing. The pseudocode of the algorithm is presented in the extended arXiv version of this paper [22]. Moreover, `Localizer` can receive the description of a rotational symmetry and find solutions that respect it.

Evaluation. We evaluate our algorithm on two families of realizable instances. On the one hand, we use the database of realizable order types for $n \leqslant 10$ points built by Aichholzer et al. [1], where our algorithm solves every instance in less than 50 milliseconds. On the other hand, we evaluate on randomly generated instances of n points in general position, where we sample the points uniformly at random from the unit square (we tested other distributions and obtained similar results). We conducted the experiments on a personal computer (MacBook Pro M1 2020, 16GB RAM, 8 CPU cores) using 8 threads, and present the results in Figure 3. In terms of performance, `Localizer` is roughly 6 orders of magnitude faster than the local-search procedure described in our previous work [23], which could not solve any instance with $n = 30$ points in less than a minute. We validated each solution through an independent Python program, which converts the floating-point coordinates to exact rational coordinates, and checks that all orientations are satisfied exactly.

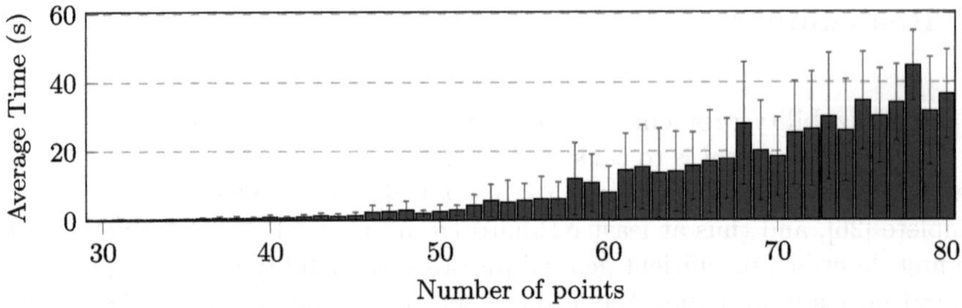

Fig. 3: Experimental evaluation of the `Localizer` realizability solver, over orientations obtained from random realizable sets of points (independently uniform in $[0,1]^2$). Previous approaches took up to 100s for 16 points [23].

5.2 Realizing Collinear Configurations for Everywhere-Unbalanced

As collinearity is an *exact* condition where arbitrarily small perturbations will result in non-collinear points, it is not clear how purely numerical methods over the variables $\{x_1, y_1, \ldots, x_n, y_n\}$ can be used to satisfy the desired orientation constraints exactly. In fact, instead of trying to directly realize the orientation assignment τ obtained through SAT solving, we take τ as partial information to construct a set of points with the same imbalance, but not necessarily respecting the same orientations. In particular, we start by extracting from τ a family of abstract lines $\mathcal{L}$ where each $L \in \mathcal{L}$ is a maximal set of indices (so $L \subseteq \{1, \ldots, n\}$) such that $\tau(i,j,k) = 0$ for all $i,j,k \in \binom{L}{3}$. Then, we note that if there are lines $L_1, L_2 \in \mathcal{L}$ such that $L_1 \cap L_2 = \{i\}$ for some $i \in \{1, \ldots, n\}$, then the point p_i is fully determined by the remaining points (as two lines in Euclidean space have a unique intersection point), and we will say it is *dependent.* After this, we aim to realize the remaining independent variables by maximizing the resulting unbalancedness using a numerical global optimization algorithm. That is, we write the imbalance of each pair of points as a function of the independent variables, and then maximize the minimum imbalance over all pairs of points, using the `differential_evolution` algorithm implemented in SciPy [27].

6 Results

For all our experiments, we used a version of the solver CaDiCaL[1] [3] that is extended to support efficient enumeration of all solutions.

6.1 Avoiding Hexagons

We searched for symmetric configurations with 16 points that avoid hexagons (the maximum number where this can occur). We constructed the formulas for

[1] Available at https://github.com:jreeves3/allsat-cadical.

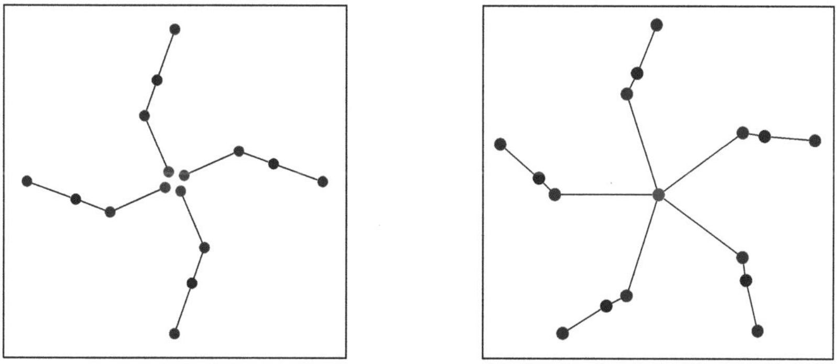

(a) 4-fold symmetric. (b) 5-fold symmetric.

Fig. 4: Constructions of 16 points in general position without a convex 6-gon.

$s \in \{3, 4, 5\}$. The formula enforcing a 3-fold symmetry is unsatisfiable, while the formulas with a 4-fold and 5-fold symmetry are satisfiable. After symmetry breaking, they have 66 and 932 satisfying assignments, respectively. Computing all satisfying assignments can be achieved in a couple of seconds using a single core on a personal computer (MackBook Pro M1 2020).

Not all these 16-point satisfying assignments are realizable. In fact, most of them are (likely) unrealizable[2]. Out of the 66 solutions of the 4-fold symmetry, 18 are realizable, while out of the 932 solutions of the 5-fold symmetry 92 are realizable. Figure 4 shows a 4-fold and a 5-fold realization. The remaining realizations are presented in the extended arXiv version of this paper [22].

We also examined the number of 4-gons and 5-gons in the solutions. All 66 solutions of the 4-fold symmetry have 924 4-gons, while the number of 5-gons ranges between 208 and 320. For the 5-fold symmetry solutions, the number of 4-gons ranges from 800 to 1185, while the number of 5-gons range from 263 to 1038. Figure 5 illustrates the data. Note that assignments are more likely to be realizable if they have a relatively high number of 4-gons and a relatively low number of 5-gons.

6.2 Avoiding 7-Gons

We also sought a symmetric solution for 32 points without a 7-gon. On 32 points, only 7-gon-free s-fold rotational symmetries could exist with $s \in \{1, 2, 4\}$. We focused our experiments on $s = 4$ as that symmetry reduces the search space the most. The resulting formula is easy to satisfy, but the initial solutions that we obtained were hard to realize.

We therefore decided to enumerate all solutions on a supercomputer, which took about 1 CPU year. The number of non-isomorphic configurations is staggering:

[2] The realizer tool can only determine realizability, not unrealizability. However, for several of the configurations for which the tool was unable to find a realization, we were able to find a subset 10-point configuration that is known to be unrealizable.

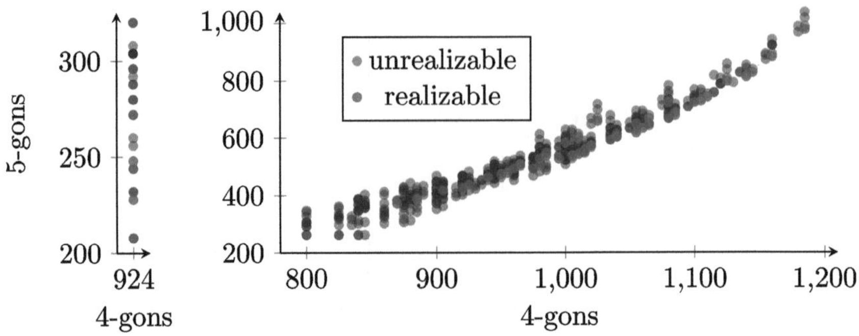

Fig. 5: The number of 4-gons and 5-gons in realizable and (likely) unrealizable configurations with a 4-fold symmetry (left) and a 5-fold symmetry (right).

310 187 713. We attempted to realize several of them using heuristics to determine which ones would be more likely to be realizable. During those experiments, we observed that the outer 28 points can frequently be realized (so only the inner 4 points not), while the inner 12 points were never realizable. Afterwards we observed that all 310 million solutions have only 6 different configurations to the inner 12 points and none of those are realizable. Thus, there does not exist a realizable 4-fold symmetry on 32 points without a 7-gon.

6.3 Avoiding Balance

It is known from prior constructions [2,4] that there exist infinitely many point sets with an even number of points having imbalance 2, as well as a set of 23 points having imbalance 2. However, it was unknown if these constructions were minimal. So we explored the question: What is the smallest even (odd) number of points needed to achieve an imbalance of 2? Utilizing our encoding, we were first able to show that the 12-point construction in [2] is indeed minimal, as a smaller number of points produces encodings that are UNSAT. Similarly, in the odd case, we were able to refute the existence of such point sets having $\leqslant 19$ points. Furthermore, by searching for solutions with a 3-fold (combinatorial) rotational symmetry, we were able to find *satisfying and realizable* solutions with 21 points (Figure 6), thereby completely answering the minimality questions. A construction of 21 points with imbalance 2 and explicit coordinates is given in the extended arXiv version of this paper [22].

7 Conclusion

We have presented a systematic approach to obtain symmetric constructions for discrete geometric problems, and along the way, a highly performant local-search

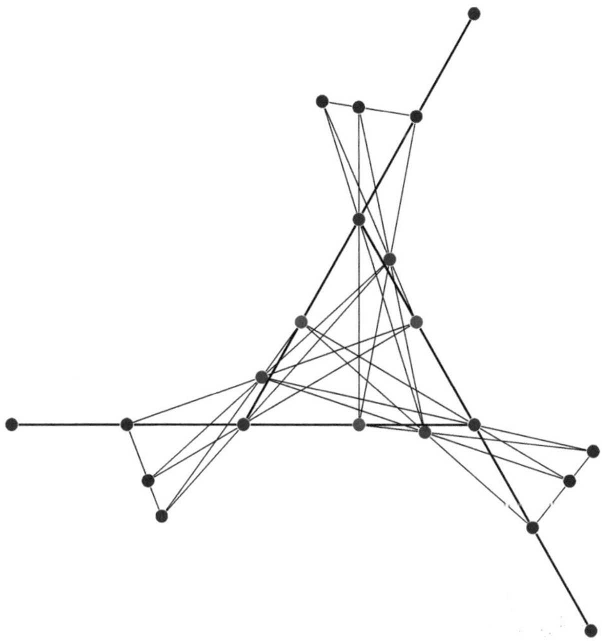

Fig. 6: A 2-everywhere-unbalanced construction on 21 points.

solver for the realizability problem. Our results show further evidence of an interesting pattern highlighted in the introduction: while general constructions for problems in Ramsey theory are often asymmetric, it turns out that there are symmetric solutions for small values of the parameters. A natural direction of research, both for computer scientists and mathematicians, is to try to uncover general constructions from the symmetric solutions that we can find for small instances. In particular, for the Erdős-Szekeres problem, we suspect that there are symmetric constructions for all $k \geqslant 7$, and proving this could represent progress toward the conjectured bound $g(k) = 2^{k-2} + 1$, since it might be easier to prove optimality for more structured solutions. In the case of the everywhere-unbalanced-points problem, our future research will focus on finding a 3-EU set, for which we aim to leverage the reduction in the number of variables achieved by forcing an ansatz symmetry. Further problems in this line of work include finding a realization of a 2-fold symmetric construction of 32 points without a convex 7-gon, and designing an efficient solver that can handle collinearity constraints for the realizability problem. Finally, we remark that Proposition 2 is an interesting and novel example of an axiomatic proof obtained through SAT solving.

References

1. Aichholzer, O., Aurenhammer, F., Krasser, H.: Enumerating Order Types for Small Point Sets with Applications. Order **19**(3), 265–281 (Sep 2002). https://doi.org/10.1023/A:1021231927255
2. Alon, N.: Research problems. Kleitman and Combinatorics: A Celebration **257**(2), 599–624 (Nov 2002). https://doi.org/10.1016/S0012-365X(02)00619-2
3. Biere, A., Faller, T., Fazekas, K., Fleury, M., Froleyks, N., Pollitt, F.: CaDiCaL 2.0. In: Gurfinkel, A., Ganesh, V. (eds.) Computer Aided Verification - 36th International Conference, CAV 2024, Montreal, QC, Canada, July 24-27, 2024, Proceedings, Part I. Lecture Notes in Computer Science, vol. 14681, pp. 133–152. Springer (2024). https://doi.org/10.1007/978-3-031-65627-9_7
4. Conlon, D., Lim, J.: Everywhere unbalanced configurations (2025), https://arxiv.org/abs/2308.02466
5. Felsner, S., Weil, H.: Sweeps, arrangements and signotopes. Discrete Applied Mathematics **109**(1), 67–94 (Apr 2001). https://doi.org/10.1016/S0166-218X(00)00232-8
6. Giora, Goldstein, B.R.: From summetria to symmetry: The making of a revolutionary scientific concept. Archimedes: New Studies in the History and Philosophy of Science and Technology, Springer, New York, NY, 2008 edn. (Jul 2008)
7. Heule, M., Walsh, T.: Symmetry in Solutions. Proceedings of the AAAI Conference on Artificial Intelligence **24**(1), 77–82 (Jul 2010). https://doi.org/10.1609/aaai.v24i1.7549
8. Heule, M.J.H.: Avoiding triples in arithmetic progression. Journal of Combinatorics **8**(3), 391–422 (Jun 2017). https://doi.org/10.4310/JOC.2017.v8.n3.a1
9. Heule, M.J.H.: Schur number five. In: Proceedings of the Thirty-Second AAAI Conference on Artificial Intelligence and Thirtieth Innovative Applications of Artificial Intelligence Conference and Eighth AAAI Symposium on Educational Advances in Artificial Intelligence. pp. 6598–6606. AAAI'18/IAAI'18/EAAI'18, AAAI Press, New Orleans, Louisiana, USA (Feb 2018)
10. Heule, M.J.H., Scheucher, M.: Happy Ending: An Empty Hexagon in Every Set of 30 Points. In: Finkbeiner, B., Kovács, L. (eds.) Tools and Algorithms for the Construction and Analysis of Systems. pp. 61–80. Springer Nature Switzerland, Cham (2024). https://doi.org/10.1007/978-3-031-57246-3_5
11. Knuth, D.E.: Axioms and Hulls. In: Knuth, D.E. (ed.) Axioms and Hulls, pp. 1–98. Lecture Notes in Computer Science, Springer, Berlin, Heidelberg (1992). https://doi.org/10.1007/3-540-55611-7_1
12. Kupitz, Y.S.: Extremal problems in combinatorial geometry. Lecture notes series, Aarhus Universitet, Matematisk Institut (1979), https://cir.nii.ac.jp/crid/1130000794692453120
13. Mackey, E.: Pinwheels and Polygons: Symmetric Realizations of Polygon-Free Point Placements via SAT. Master's thesis, Carnegie Mellon University (2025), http://reports-archive.adm.cs.cmu.edu/anon/2025/CMU-CS-25-108.pdf
14. Morris, W., Soltan, V.: The Erdos-Szekeres problem on points in convex position – a survey. Bulletin of the American Mathematical Society **37**(4), 437–458 (2000). https://doi.org/10.1090/S0273-0979-00-00877-6
15. Perlis, A.J.: Special feature: Epigrams on programming. SIGPLAN Not. **17**(9), 7–13 (Sep 1982). https://doi.org/10.1145/947955.1083808, https://doi.org/10.1145/947955.1083808

16. Pinchasi, R.: Lines With Many Points On Both Sides. Discrete & Computational Geometry **30**(3), 415–435 (Sep 2003). https://doi.org/10.1007/s00454-003-2826-8
17. Schaefer, M.: Complexity of Some Geometric and Topological Problems. In: Eppstein, D., Gansner, E.R. (eds.) Graph Drawing. pp. 334–344. Springer, Berlin, Heidelberg (2010). https://doi.org/10.1007/978-3-642-11805-0_32
18. Scheucher, M.: On Order Types, Projective Classes, and Realizations. Bachelor's thesis, Graz University of Technology (2014)
19. Scheucher, M.: Two disjoint 5-holes in point sets. Computational Geometry **91**, 101670 (2020). https://doi.org/10.1016/j.comgeo.2020.101670
20. Scheucher, M.: A SAT Attack on Erdős-Szekeres Numbers in R^d and the Empty Hexagon Theorem. Computing in Geometry and Topology **2**(1), 2:1–2:13 (Mar 2023). https://doi.org/10.57717/cgt.v2i1.12
21. Sinz, C.: Towards an optimal CNF encoding of boolean cardinality constraints. In: van Beek, P. (ed.) Principles and Practice of Constraint Programming - CP 2005, 11th International Conference, CP 2005, Sitges, Spain, October 1-5, 2005, Proceedings. Lecture Notes in Computer Science, vol. 3709, pp. 827–831. Springer (2005). https://doi.org/10.1007/11564751_73, https://doi.org/10.1007/11564751_73
22. Subercaseaux, B., Mackey, E., Qian, L., Heule, M.J.H.: Automated symmetric constructions in discrete geometry (2025), https://arxiv.org/abs/2506.00224
23. Subercaseaux, B., Mackey, J., Heule, M.J.H., Martins, R.: Automated mathematical discovery and verification: Minimizing pentagons in the plane (2024), https://arxiv.org/abs/2311.03645
24. Subercaseaux, B., Nawrocki, W., Gallicchio, J., Codel, C., Carneiro, M., Heule, M.J.H.: Formal Verification of the Empty Hexagon Number. In: Bertot, Y., Kutsia, T., Norrish, M. (eds.) 15th International Conference on Interactive Theorem Proving (ITP 2024). Leibniz International Proceedings in Informatics (LIPIcs), vol. 309, pp. 35:1–35:19. Schloss Dagstuhl – Leibniz-Zentrum für Informatik, Dagstuhl, Germany (2024). https://doi.org/10.4230/LIPIcs.ITP.2024.35
25. Szekeres, G., Peters, L.: Computer solution to the 17-point Erdős-Szekeres problem. The ANZIAM Journal **48**(2), 151–164 (2006). https://doi.org/10.1017/S144618110000300X
26. Toth, C.D., O'Rourke, J., Goodman, J.E. (eds.): Handbook of Discrete and Computational Geometry. Chapman and Hall/CRC, New York, 3 edn. (Nov 2017). https://doi.org/10.1201/9781315119601
27. Virtanen, P., Gommers, R., Oliphant, T.E., Haberland, M., Reddy, T., Cournapeau, D., Burovski, E., Peterson, P., Weckesser, W., Bright, J., van der Walt, S.J., Brett, M., Wilson, J., Millman, K.J., Mayorov, N., Nelson, A.R.J., Jones, E., Kern, R., Larson, E., Carey, C.J., Polat, İ., Feng, Y., Moore, E.W., VanderPlas, J., Laxalde, D., Perktold, J., Cimrman, R., Henriksen, I., Quintero, E.A., Harris, C.R., Archibald, A.M., Ribeiro, A.H., Pedregosa, F., van Mulbregt, P., SciPy 1.0 Contributors: SciPy 1.0: Fundamental Algorithms for Scientific Computing in Python. Nature Methods **17**, 261–272 (2020). https://doi.org/10.1038/s41592-019-0686-2
28. Walsh, T.: Symmetry within and between Solutions. In: Zhang, B.T., Orgun, M.A. (eds.) PRICAI 2010: Trends in Artificial Intelligence. pp. 11–13. Springer, Berlin, Heidelberg (2010). https://doi.org/10.1007/978-3-642-15246-7_4
29. Weyl, H.: Symmetry. Princeton Science Library, Princeton University Press, Princeton, NJ (Dec 2016)
30. Wikipedia: Happy ending problem — Wikipedia, the free encyclopedia. http://en.wikipedia.org/w/index.php?title=Happy%20ending%20problem&oldid=1282669476 (2025), [Online; accessed 12-May-2025]

Formal Libraries

Growing Mathlib: maintenance of a large scale mathematical library

Anne Baanen[1], Matthew Robert Ballard[2], Johan Commelin[1,3], Bryan Gin–ge Chen, Michael Rothgang[4](✉), and Damiano Testa[5]

[1] Lean FRO, Redmond, USA
[2] University of South Carolina, Columbia, USA
[3] Mathematical Institute, Utrecht University, Utrecht, The Netherlands
[4] Mathematical Institute, University of Bonn, Bonn, Germany
rothgang@math.uni-bonn.de
[5] Mathematical Institute, University of Warwick, Coventry, UK

Abstract. The Lean mathematical library Mathlib is one of the fastest-growing libraries of formalised mathematics. We describe various strategies to manage this growth, while allowing for change and avoiding maintainer overload. This includes dealing with breaking changes via a deprecation system, using code quality analysis tools (*linters*) to provide direct user feedback about common pitfalls, speeding up compilation times through conscious library (re-)design, dealing with technical debt as well as writing custom tooling to help with the review and triage of new contributions.

Keywords: Formal mathematics · Library development · Linting.

1 Introduction

The mathematical library Mathlib [35], written in the Lean theorem prover, is perhaps the fastest-growing library of formalised mathematics. Created in 2017, it now contains 1.9 million lines of code across a broad range of subjects. Mathlib's focus on being an integrated library for mathematics makes it well-suited for formalising current research mathematics. Recent formalised results based on Mathlib include a fundamental result of Scholze and Clausen about condensed mathematics [32,7,6], Smale's sphere eversion via an h-principle [9], Campos–Griffiths–Morris–Sahasrabudhe's breakthrough on upper bounds for diagonal Ramsey numbers [27] and Gowers–Green–Manners–Tao's breakthrough on Marton's polynomial Freiman–Rusza conjecture [13,12,19]. Mathlib is also crucial for Buzzard's ongoing project [5] to formalise a proof of Fermat's Last Theorem. In a different direction, Mathlib has been used in industry research, such as for verifying the correctness of the SampCert differential privacy framework [25].

Mathlib is run by a community of users as an open source project, enabling and encouraging contributions by users with a wide range of backgrounds and

V. de Paiva and P. Koepke (Eds.): CICM 2025, LNAI 16136, pp. 51–70, 2026.
https://doi.org/10.1007/978-3-032-07021-0_4

expertise. This allows for a broad range of contributions (of formalisations, but also with the infrastructure and other supporting work). At the same time, this presents challenges around knowledge transfer and ensuring the library stays coherent as a whole. To address this, Mathlib makes extensive user of *linters*, to help users with intricacies of the Lean proof assistant and enforce certain global coherence properties. (We describe this in Section 4.)

Mathlib's continued growth also presents other challenges for scaling. Some of these are technical—such as adapting existing code to other changes in the library (Section 3), ensuring that Mathlib continues to compile reasonably quickly (see Section 5) and managing technical debt (see Section 6). With any large group, social processes become pertinent (such as, ensuring all communication stays friendly and welcoming (Mathlib has a code of conduct with a dedicated team enforcing it), or keeping some alignment on an overall vision of Mathlib). A key process in both maintaining a coherent library and teaching new contributors about formalisation best practices is mandatory code review. This process needs to be supported and adapted to scale to the influx of contributions (see Section 7).

We describe the Mathlib community's strategies for dealing with this growth, focusing on the above aspects in turn. The use of linters (in a less extensive way) was already described in previous work [36]; the other sections are new. While some details are specific to Lean and Mathlib, we believe that many of them apply broadly to libraries of formal mathematics knowledge.

2 Related work

Various interactive theorem provers have come to enjoy large libraries of research mathematics—each with its own strengths and weaknesses. The Mizar Mathematical Library [2] is the oldest and perhaps the largest library (at 3.7 millions lines of code (MLOC)) of formalised mathematics. The Isabelle/HOL system has very powerful automation; the Archive of Formal Proofs (AFP; 4.8 MLOC[1]) still has the strongest complex analysis library. The Rocq theorem prover allows expressing complex mathematical objects (such as schemes, the tangent space of a manifold or vector bundles) more naturally, thanks to its foundations including dependent types. While its mathematical components library [22] is significantly smaller (150 000 lines of code), Rocq has been used to formalise major results such as the Four Colour and the Feit–Thompson theorems (which are each of similar size as the *mathematical components*). Let us also mention the Flyspeck project [15] as an example of combining large libraries in two different proof assistants.

The MML introduced mandatory review of contributions in 2006, as well as tooling to check for duplicate lemmas. (Such tooling also exists for Rocq [10] and Lean [30].) Klein et al have written [4] about maintaining large scale Isabelle

[1] The AFP has a broader focus [3], with about half its current articles covering the analysis and verification of particular algorithms. Arguably, this makes the MML a larger library of formalised *mathematics*.

libraries. They name many challenges similar to ours, including coordination and collaboration in large and diverse projects. The Isabelle system also employs custom linters [26] — which are not mandated for existing entries, but enforced for new submissions. Zimmermann [38] has written about recent changes to Rocq's development processes (including switching to GitHub and a pull-request based model, dealing with breaking changes and the challenges with distributing reviews). There is also custom tooling to support Rocq maintainers [39].

Growing a large formal library can require changes to the underlying prover. Such work on Lean is out of scope of this paper; Wenzel discussed it for Isabelle [37]. They also describe tooling to automatically test the impact of core system or theory changes on dependent projects.[2] Test-case minimisation [14] can also be instrumental for quickly diagnosing and fixing broken proofs "downstream". Huch and Wenzel have also written about the challenges of maintaining and scaling Isabelle's supporting infrastructure [17,18].

There is also considerable work on proof repair, such as adjusting code to breaking changes. Luan et al [21] have studied and classified compatibility issues in the AFP. Tan et al [34] have developed tooling for automatically fixing proofs in Isabelle/HOL. Gopinathan et al [11] have developed proof repair tooling for the Rocq prover.

Despite the growth of large libraries of formal proofs, there is still relatively little work describing tools and best practices for their maintenance. Ringer et al [31] note the gap between proof engineering and software engineering in this respect.

3 The deprecation system

Maintaining Mathlib involves changing existing code. Generalizations, refactors, reorganization of content, syntax changes and so on are *exceedingly* common in Mathlib. As a result, code written for one version of Mathlib may no longer compile with a newer version. This applies both within Mathlib (contributions to one area need to deal with effects on all other areas), to contributions under review and particularly to projects depending on Mathlib. Many large formalisation projects are carried out in a repository depending on Mathlib. If keeping up with the latest Mathlib changes is too onerous, contributing results back to Mathlib may become impossible.

The spectrum of possible breaking changes is rather diverse, and ranges from one-off changes when upgrading to the next Lean version to adjusting to particular refactorings in Mathlib. In principle, Lean's excellent meta-programming facilities allow writing custom migrations for virtually all changes, transforming working code from one version to the next. Theoretically, such migrations could be arbitrarily complicated. In practice, however, the vast majority of adjustments are very simple to deal with: renaming (the declaration which states) a theorem or definition, renaming files (which requires adjusting `import` statements) and

[2] Similar tooling for Lean does not exist yet, but is being planned by the Lean FRO.

superficial syntax changes. The third item is addressed through dedicated syntax linters (see Section 4); these can also help with semantic changes.

Lean has a deprecation system specifically designed to handle renamings gracefully. When a declaration is renamed, for a grace period of several months, we add a deprecation marker documenting the rename. This connects the old and new names (and allows providing a custom message to guide the migration process). Upon using a deprecated declaration, the user sees a warning, indicating which declaration to use instead. This allows for a much smoother migration.

Dealing with renamed files is harder. Lean looks at file imports before the deprecation system (which is implemented as a linter) has the chance to run—so a file that imported the file with the old name would stop building entirely. The solution is similar: the module with the old name is not erased, but is preserved and stained. Thus, it can be imported without breaking the build—and a linter suggests to replace the old module name, with appropriate imports. These could be either the direct imports of that module, in the case of a reorganization of content; or the renamed module, in the case of a simple move. This informs users of where the declarations that were present in the old file may have ended up.

4 Semantic linters

In general terms, a *linter* is a program whose purpose is to ensure that the code in a project satisfies certain requirements. The term requirements should be interpreted very broadly: a linter could enforce

- code style conventions (such as the default indentation of code);
- file naming conventions (such as never using paths that differ only in capitalization);
- function naming conventions (such as making sure that namespaces in declarations are not repeated);
- deprecating commands that have been replaced by newer code;

and in fact Mathlib uses linters for all of these purposes.

To be precise, Mathlib uses two different linter frameworks, with distinct strengths and weaknesses. Lean itself provides a `Lean.Elab.Command.Linter` type, which contains the linter's name and a monadic function that takes the syntax of the command as input and can run arbitrary code.[3] Lean's community-maintained extended library Batteries provides a parallel `Batteries.Tactic.Lint.Linter` structure that is similar to the Lean-native linters, but takes a declaration name as its input and runs code in a different monad. For the purpose of the present discussion, the main difference between the two kinds of linters is that the former is designed to run on every *command* and has access to the syntax tree of each command, while the latter is designed to run once on the "final" environment and only inspects the declarations present in the

[3] Technically, a linter function returns a `Unit`, i.e. the only interesting outcomes of the linter are its side effects.

Environment. We refer to the former linters as "syntax linters" and to the latter linters as "environment linters". Both are semantic linters, in the sense that they can access the fully elaborated information and not merely the typed syntax. Since both frameworks allow running arbitrary code, the distinction between them is mostly on what they are *expected* to do and what they can do *easily*, not on what they *could* do. Environment linters are good for *global* validation (e.g. checking lemmas are in `simp` normal form), but only warn you after the fact. Syntax linters warn you right away and are best suited for *local* validation (e.g. the valid notation `λ x => x` is deprecated in favour of `fun x ↦ x`).

At the time of writing, there are 26 syntax linters defined in Mathlib and 10 more coming from its dependencies, as well as 17 environment linters, all but two defined in `Batteries`. We mostly focus on the *syntax* linters: virtually all the environment linters have been described previously [36].[4] To summarize more coherently how Mathlib uses linters, let us group them into general categories and highlight a few examples from each category.

Deprecation linters As mentioned in the previous section, linters help dealing with deprecations. Breaking changes could arise from certain tactics becoming more powerful or more efficient, making other tactics obsolete or undesirable. In such situations, the replaced tactics would be deprecated. The `deprecatedSyntax` linter warns about the use of deprecated syntax (e.g. a tactic), and informs the user what the new preferred expression is.

Style linters Mathlib has a fairly detailed style guide (which helps to settle discussions about individual formatting preferences efficiently). Mathlib's style linters enforce various aspects of coding style and formatting, such as line length, whitespace conventions or the formatting of documentation comments. This allows reviewers to focus their time on higher-level aspects, and helps contributors learn about Mathlib style without having to read all style rules at once. We also enforce that every Mathlib file (that is not an `import`-only file) contains a valid copyright header and a module doc-string summarising the content of the file.

Import structure linters Keeping track of Mathlib's import structure is important for organisation and compilation speed. A Lean module can only be compiled once all its dependencies have been fully checked[5]: thus, a reasonable import structure enables parallelism and faster overall compilation. It also speeds

[4] With the advent of Lean 4, the need for the typeclass linters described there has mostly disappeared: typeclass inference was substantially redesigned in Lean 4 [33], taking into account the insights from Mathlib development. This means some linter warnings have become compiler errors, and the others have become less relevant and did not get reimplemented in Lean 4.

[5] Lean's upcoming module system will change this trade-off, if and when it is adopted in Mathlib. (Doing so is desirable in principle, but requires a lot of conscious library design work.)

up local development, as changing multiple files requires less recompilation, and makes it easier to place a new mathematical result. Mathlib has two main tools to help with keeping the import structure organised: Mario Carneiro's `shake` tool warns about unused imports, and the `directoryDependency` linter warns about unintentional dependencies between different areas of Mathlib.

Code pruning Another class of linters highlights redundant code. For instance, the `unusedVariable` linter warns when a variable in scope (such as a hypothesis in a proof) is not used. While using Lean as a proof assistant, this helps catch "free" generalizations of theorems, where a hypothesis that seemed to be needed turns out to be superfluous. While using Lean as a general purpose programming language, this is more often useful to catch bugs, as an unused variable may arise from an incorrect reference, or the omission of part of a case analysis.

Linters with similar scope are the `unusedSeqFocus`, the `unusedTactic`, and the `unreachableTactic` linters, each highlighting different ways in which a tactic proof can be simplified or streamlined.

Tracking issues Certain commands are expected to be rarely used, or are only temporary adaptations. For instance, increasing the time limit for type-checking is something that may be necessary for an individual declaration, but increasing the limit for a whole file is likely a symptom of some deeper issue that should be addressed. Hence, a command such as `set_option maxHeartbeats 5000000` should be limited in scope to a single declaration. The `setOption` linter does exactly that: it flags uses of `set_option maxHeartbeats x` suggesting to use `set_option maxHeartbeats x in ...` instead.

Similar linters exist for `open Classical`, which can hide issues that will make the code less usable, and the `globalAttributeIn` linter that warns that the scope of certain attributes is not "local", even in the presence of the (usually) scope-limiting `in` keyword.

4.1 Maintenance and code readability

The linters in this category are specifically geared to improve maintainability of code and readability. Since Mathlib evolves very quickly, code breakage is fairly common; any tooling which can diagnose and prevent such breakages is immensely helpful. The linters in this section try to be pro-active about code breakage by reducing code brittleness.

Rigid and flexible tactics The `flexible` linter starts from the premise that tactics exhibit two general behaviours: "flexible" tactics (such as `simp`, `norm_num` or `aesop`) apply to a wide variety of goals and return similarly varied processed goals; "rigid" tactics (such as `rw` or `apply`) perform some very specific operations and may stop working even with very small changes of the current goal state.

The `flexible` linter tracks hypotheses and goals in each proof, following them around as various tactics are successively applied. Whenever a "flexible" tactic modifies a hypothesis or a goal, no "rigid" tactic is supposed to modify that same hypothesis or goal: indeed, the behaviour of the flexible tactic may change, e.g. because a new `simp` lemma allows further simplification, making the following `rw` fail. Thus, preventing rigid tactics from following flexible ones helps with maintainability. This question has some nuance: for instance, some flexible tactics (such as `ring` or `omega`) are "normalizing": even though they take a variety of inputs, their output is more predictable. Therefore, rigid tactics following a normalizing flexible tactic are allowed.

Handling multiple side-goals In terms of goal management and readability, the `multiGoal` linter warns as soon as a tactic produces more than one side-goal, unless the next tactic is the focusing dot ·. The code style enforced by this linter makes both the number of side-goals that remain after each tactic application as well as which parts of the code deal with which part of the proof completely transparent. This helps with maintenance, since it limits code breakage to easily identified branches, rather than a generic total failure. At the same time, it also improves code readability and structure, since the various arms of the proofs are visually differentiated.

Closing sections Finally, let us mention the `missingEnd` linter: it warns on `section` commands that do not have a matching `end` closure. This addresses a maintainability issue: when moving code from one file to another, it is easy to miss the closing of a `section`, producing a dangling one. As a consequence, the scope of the currently non-`end`ed section is persisted where it was not intended to be—and further hypotheses or declarations might be in scope. This can cause issues that are hard to diagnose, such as changing the meaning of statements or breaking proofs.

Helpful and pedagogical suggestions Some linters attempt to preempt possible misunderstanding or common pitfalls. The `haveLet` linter flags uses of `have` when introducing a non-`Prop` assumption and similarly uses of `let` when introducing an assumption in `Prop`. Especially using `have` for `let` can cause confusion when the actual term introduced by the tactic is important for the proof.

Another example is the prototype `papercut` linter. One common mistake is accidentally using subtraction of natural numbers (which truncates at `0`). The linter flags such subtraction when a positivity assumption is not in scope.

All linters defined in Mathlib are available to projects using Mathlib: any improvements thus benefit the broader ecosystem. Projects can easily adopt all of Mathlib's linters (or any subset thereof they choose). This helps maintaining code standards and styling conventions, and makes the ecosystem more homogeneous.

5 Speeding up Mathlib

As Mathlib grows to encompass more declarations, the time to build it will also increase. Keeping build times manageable requires constant attention to sources of slowdowns and inefficiencies. The Mathlib Speedcenter is an instance of the benchmarking server VelCom that builds and benchmarks all commits to the master branch of Mathlib. The benchmarks include overall measurements for Lean components such as the simplifier or typeclass inference, and per-file compilation timings. In addition to wall-clock (overall time from start to finish) and task-clock (takes into account parallelism) times measured in seconds, most benchmark results are measured in instructions, since the number of instructions is more stable on the benchmarking servers than the wall-clock time which is affected by process scheduling. Continuous monitoring of build times is crucial to ensure no unexpected slowdowns occur. Therefore, a bot reports notable outliers in benchmarks (changes of a measurement by 5% or more) on the Lean community Zulip chat.

5.1 Speed and typeclasses

Mathlib relies on the Lean typeclass system to perform automatic inference of many implicit arguments. Typeclasses are flexible and have low infrastructure requirements on user code, but the flexibility also means designs have to be carefully consider to optimize their tradeoffs. As the typeclass hierarchy grows, synthesis of instances becomes slower since a larger search space needs to be explored. It is not only important to ensure synthesis succeeds quickly: if synthesis fails, tactics can decide to fall back on an alternative proof strategy. Lean's instance synthesis algorithm fails only after exploring the full search space, and it is therefore especially important that the space does not grow too large.

One fundamental consideration in Mathlib's typeclass design is the level of *bundling* [1,35], which concerns the way conjunctions of assumptions are modeled in classes. For example, to represent ordered commutative monoids, we can define a bundled class `OrderedCommMonoid` that combines `CommMonoid`, `PartialOrder` and hypotheses stating the monoid operations respect the order structure. Instead, unbundling the ordered algebra classes results in mixins combining the (existing) algebra class `CommMonoid` with the (existing) order class `PartialOrder` and adding in an extra `IsOrderedMonoid` class. Unbundling makes parameters more verbose: `[OrderedCommMonoid M]` becomes `[CommMonoid M] [LinearOrder M] [IsOrderedMonoid M]`. As described with more detail in [1], bundled design is preferred for its conciseness in Mathlib when possible.

The speed tradeoffs changed when upgrading from Lean 3 to Lean 4. A consequence of the bundled approach to typeclass design is that the number of classes becomes multiplicative when extending along two distinct axes. Taking the `OrderedCommMonoid` class as an example formerly found in Mathlib, this could then be extended in the order hierarchy to give `LinearOrderedCommMonoid`, or in the algebraic hierarchy to give `OrderedCommGroup`, or in both directions to give `LinearOrderedCommGroup`. When looking for a `CommMonoid` instance, Lean would search through both the algebraic hierarchy and the ordered algebraic hierarchy.

Unbundling curbs this multiplicative growth by allowing expansion along individual axes. This means to strengthen from ordered monoids to ordered groups, no additional ordering axioms are required, and it suffices to replace a `[CommMonoid M]` parameter with `[CommGroup M]`. Similarly, for linear ordered monoids we can replace `[PartialOrder M]` with `[LinearOrder M]`. The result of unbundling is that the search through the one large search space is now three searches through smaller spaces, and failing fast on one of these cancels the remaining searches too. This refactor by Yuyang Zhao resulted in a 20% decrease in typeclass inference time, resulting in a 6% overall speedup to Mathlib compilation.

5.2 Speed and coercions

The coercion system is another commonly used component of Lean. Essentially, when a term `t` is inferred to have type `A`, where type `B` is expected, Lean attempts to find a suitable coercion, so the term can be replaced with a coerced version written `↑t`. The coercion is found by synthesizing an instance of the typeclass `CoeT A t B`. Since coercions are triggered by type mismatches, this is a particular case of instance search that should fail fast.

Instances for `CoeT` should not be declared directly, but rather chained together from the `CoeHead`, `CoeOut`, `Coe` and `CoeTail` typeclasses. The rules for which typeclass to instantiate for a particular coercion are subtle and not universally understood; they are notably more complex compared to Lean 3. As a consequence, a seemingly acceptable instance can cause a large performance regression. For example, `Coe A B` allows `B` to be a free variable, but doing so causes large performance regressions since such an instance always applies.[6]

In a similar vein to Subsection 5.1, large hierarchies extending coercion typeclasses should be avoided. Mathlib uses the `FunLike` hierarchy to generalize over bundled homomorphisms. Morphism classes such as `MonoidHomClass` used to extend the `FunLike` class, which meant a failing coercion would first trigger a search through the entire `FunLike` hierarchy. Even worse, since `MonoidHomClass` depends on `Monoid` instances, this also triggers a search through the algebraic hierarchy. The solution was to unbundle inheritance from `FunLike`, keeping only `FunLike` and `EquivLike` and passing these classes as an instance parameter to every morphism class. The refactor by Anne Baanen performing this unbundling resulted in a 33% speedup for typeclass instance synthesis and an overall 19% decrease in build instructions.

5.3 Speed and definitional equality

Type checking, and definitional equality in particular, is commonly invoked in the Lean elaboration and kernel checking process and can result in arbitrarily complex computations: terms can be large and their size can increase further when unfolding definitions referenced by the term. Equality checks are intended

[6] https://github.com/leanprover-community/mathlib4/pull/22950

to be "cheap" basic steps in implementing more complex routines such as typeclass instance synthesis, so slowdowns in checking have a large impact.

Generally, definitions are designed to not require unfolding unless the unfolding is requested. Each definition in Lean has a *transparency level* controlling the circumstances in which it is unfolded. Most tactics are designed to only unfold definitions explicitly marked as reducible, with some tactics also unfolding at the default semireducible transparency level. Marking definitions as irreducible prevents unfolding altogether, skipping a potentially expensive equality check if it does not obviously succeed.

A particular example of complex definitional equality checking can be found in structure declarations. Large structures can already be quite complex terms in themselves, which can be hidden behind further definitions and constructions, and the possibility of diamond inheritance can then result in nonobvious equality checks. This all results in high levels of unfolding being required to verify the equality of terms.

Typeclasses in Lean are implemented as structures, so the complex typeclass hierarchy also has an impact here. The `Field` typeclass has 19 data-carrying structure fields that must be checked for equality. By ensuring typeclass instances are already in a normal form, less unfolding will be needed. Matthew Robert Ballard, Kyle Miller and Eric Wieser implemented the `fast_instance` term elaboration macro that normalizes instance declarations by unfolding definitions and replacing subterms with synthesized instances. An initial implementation of this macro resulted in a 5% decrease in type checking time and halved compilation times for many files.[7]

5.4 Speed and tactics

During the compilation of Mathlib, Lean spends approximately 14% of its time running the `simp` tactic, and 7% of the time invoking other tactics. Tactics are diverse in the ways they are implemented and invoked, but we can attempt to find some rules of thumb for optimization.

An important change in Lean 4 was the addition of *discrimination trees* [24,29] that allow for efficient association of terms with values. A discrimination tree is a tree datastructure whose branches are indexed by symbols (either a constant, or the special symbol * representing free variables). Values are stored at leaf nodes. A closed term where each symbol has a fixed arity can be represented as a string of symbols; this maps directly to a particular path in the tree. Queries into a discrimination tree overapproximate the result, since all variables map to the same symbol *. Still, the approximation is much finer than previously in Lean 3, where terms were indexed by only the first constant that appeared [28].

The simplifier tries to repeatedly rewrite using a set of lemmas and tactics (called a `simp` set) on all subterms in an expression. By querying a discrimination tree, it can quickly determine potentially relevant rewrites. Optimization practices common in the Lean 3 version of Mathlib have become much less necessary

[7] https://github.com/leanprover-community/mathlib4/pull/20993

after the port to Lean 4, such as restricting `simp` from the default large `simp` set to a smaller specific list (using the `simp only` keywords) since many fewer lemmas have to be tested for applicability. Going from `simp only` to `simp` lowers the maintenance burden, since a change to the default `simp` set does not need to be copied to each involved `simp only` call.

The `simp` sets still need to be restricted for efficiency if multiple lemmas could apply depending on different hypotheses. For example, `div_self a : a / a = 1` applies if `a` is in a `Group`, but a field does not form a multiplicative group. Therefore, the `field_simp` tactic specialized to simplifying expressions in the theory of fields excludes such lemmas from the set for efficiency.[8]

Another avenue to optimizing the use of tactics is to use weaker, faster tactics instead of more powerful but slower tactics. The Aesop tactic provides general proof search [20] and is also invoked as part of other, more specialized tactics to discharge goals. The general nature of this proof search makes Aesop very powerful, but this power is often unnecessary when the proof it needs to find has a predetermined format. We have found that replacing powerful Aesop-based tactics like `measurability` with tactics that have a simpler strategy like `fun_prop` is almost always possible and reduces running time appreciably. Similarly, small tweaks such as applying local hypotheses or trying reflexivity to discharge an equality goal before starting Aesop can lead to appreciable speedups.[9]

6 Tracking and addressing technical debt

Ward Cunningham introduced [8] the term *technical debt* in 1992, writing:

> Shipping first time code is like going into debt. A little debt speeds development so long as it is paid back promptly with a rewrite. Objects make the cost of this transaction tolerable. The danger occurs when the debt is not repaid. Every minute spent on not-quite-right code counts as interest on that debt. Entire engineering organizations can be brought to a stand-still under the debt load of an unconsolidated implementation

This concept is all the more important in a large foundational library like Mathlib, especially in light of its cohesive and tightly integrated nature. In this section we describe various types of technical debt we have encountered in Mathlib, and how the community tracks and addresses them.

Porting notes From 2021–2023, the community ported Mathlib from Lean 3 to Lean 4. This process ought to be documented in more detail elsewhere, but for the purposes of the present discussion we summarize the points of interest.

For all practical purposes, Lean 4 is a distinct language from Lean 3—there is no backwards compatibility. Mario Carneiro wrote a tool `mathport` that automatically translates Lean 3 code to Lean 4 code on a best-effort basis, and

[8] https://github.com/leanprover-community/mathlib4/pull/21326
[9] https://github.com/leanprover-community/mathlib4/pull/21330

a small group of people implemented the common tactics in Lean 4. In October/November 2022, this preparatory work transitioned into a wide-scale and coordinated effort to port the theory files of Mathlib. Over the course of 10 months, the community ported on the order of a million lines of code, or roughly a dozen files per day.

Naturally, there were many places where a faithful translation was not possible. For the sake of speed, the porting team decided to liberally annotate issues with "porting notes" that described the problem and the workaround. As a result, by the summer of 2023, the porting process was complete, but Mathlib 4 contained well over 5000 porting notes.

Pietro Monticone made a valiant effort to organize and classify the porting notes in February and March of 2024. Subsequently, Anne Baanen, Kim Morrison, and Johan Commelin processed and addressed over two thirds of the porting notes in the first quarter of 2025. Many of these porting notes became obsolete because of new and expanded functionality in Lean 4. At the time of writing, roughly 1500 porting notes remain.

Adaptation notes and backwards compatibility flags New versions of Lean 4 are released on a monthly basis. Mathlib maintains a branch that tracks the nightly releases, which simplifies migrating to the new version of Lean 4 when it is released. This tracking branch provides feedback for the development of Lean 4: if the daily transition to a new nightly version of Lean 4 requires some unsatisfactory workarounds, then these are annotated with `#adaptation_note` comments. In essence, these notes have the same functionality as porting notes. Occasionally, there is no simple solution for a problem that arises from a new version of Lean 4. In such an event the old feature can be re-enabled via a backwards compatibility flag. This allows the Mathlib community to transition to the new version of Lean 4 at a reasonable pace.

Reporting technical debt The shell script `scripts/technical-debt-metrics.sh` is used to create a report of the current state of known technical debt in Mathlib. This includes tracking adaptation notes, porting notes and backwards compatibility flags. Continuous integration runs this script on a weekly basis, and posts the report (including the delta with respect to the previous week) to the Zulip chat of the Lean community. Additionally, this report is computed for each pull request, and posted to a dedicated "PR summary" comment at the top of the pull request. This allows the reviewer to quickly see the current state of technical debt in the pull request, and take this into account when deciding whether to approve the pull request.

Mathlib also has a mechanism in place to surface pull requests addressing technical debt: this includes both a dedicated label and triage dashboard (see Section 7.2) and a Zulip stream where such PRs can be brought to attention.

One downside of tracking and reporting technical debt in this manner is indicated by Goodhart's Law: "When a measure becomes a target, it ceases to be a good measure." In this context, this means that the community is inclined to focus on the technical debt that is being tracked, whereas there may be other forms of technical debt that fly under the radar. To alleviate this, there is a dedicated thread on the Lean community's Zulip chat listing less measurable forms of technical and organisational debt. (One example of the latter is documenting unwritten informal Mathlib policy: sharing such knowledge enables other contributors to learn this for themselves and lowers the barrier towards contribution. An example of the former is reorganizing top-level directories: due to Mathlib's age, some of these are not coherent any more.) Everybody can add items to the list, facilitating a collective understanding of future maintenance tasks.

7 Scaling code review

Since its beginning, the Mathlib library required code review prior to merging changes. This is enforced through the bors bot: pull requests are merged automatically upon approval by an authorised user (i.e., a Mathlib maintainer).[10]

This policy has several reasons. For one, formalisation in Lean ensures a strong level of correctness: a formalised mathematical proof which compiles without any `sorry`[11] will be a correct and complete proof. However, designing an integrated mathematical library *well* still requires expert knowledge: usually, there are different potential designs, with vastly different usability and ergonomics. Code review is one way to form and share common knowledge about design best practices. It also has an empowering function: new contributors can propose new code, without being afraid of breaking other proofs (if their code compiles, the proofs are still fine) or overlooking important aspects—because an experienced Lean user will look over their contribution. This way, code review is a way of teaching and onboarding new contributors.

Mathlib is growing steadily, as is its influx of new contributions. At the same time, many of its contributors are volunteers or work on Mathlib as a side project. Most of Mathlib's maintainers have teaching, administrative or supervision commitments: allowing Mathlib to scale requires lightening their work. This has both social and technical aspects. On the social side, maintaining Mathlib means embracing teamwork and delegating responsibility. Approval of Mathlib pull requests is a multi-stage system, allowing many people to contribute.

Code review in Mathlib is decentralised: everybody is allowed and encouraged to review contributions; there are guidelines teaching what to review for. This ranges from more basic aspects (such as adherence to Mathlib's style guidelines, or whether new documentation is comprehensible) to advanced aspects like the correct code location and library design patterns. There are regular review meetings, where reviewers and interested contributors review code together—both to make this work more enjoyable, and to mentor potential new reviewers.

---

[10] Using bors also enforces the not rocket science principle [16]: ensuring that the main (development) branch of Mathlib always passes all continuous integration tests.

[11] and is not intentionally manipulating the Lean environment or adding additional axioms—both of which are checked for by Mathlib's continuous integration

Mathlib's maintainers have the final say on approving a pull request. The number of maintainers keeps growing steadily, and is currently around 30. Maintainers have different specialisations; together, they cover the breadth of Mathlib. Having multiple knowledgeable maintainers in one area is beneficial, so they can discuss difficult decisions.

Between maintainers and all contributors is the group of *Mathlib reviewers*. These are Mathlib contributors who have provided useful reviews in the past. A reviewer can approve a pull request by commenting **`maintainer merge`**, which notifies the maintainers. Usually, these get merged (or at least discussed further) more quickly. This system is a bit like journal referees and editors: the reviewer group lightens the load on maintainers; the direct notification mechanism provides an additional small incentive for reviewers. This works well in practice: in the last year, one in three merged pull requests was approved by a reviewer before they were merged.

On a technical level, we can save reviewer and maintainer time by automating tedious or mechanical aspects of this process. Two basic means of automation are using continuous integration with *bors* and automatic maintainer notifications through the **`maintainer merge`** command. Let us discuss Mathlib's review automation from two further angles: tooling for reviewers and tooling for triage.

7.1 Tooling for reviewers

There are multiple ways for automation to support pull request reviewers. To begin with, we need to find a suitable reviewer for a given pull request. A pull request with a new theorem is best reviewed by somebody familiar with the theorem's area; something similar holds for a contribution improving Mathlib's infrastructure, adding a new linter or adding a new tactic. Each new pull request adding new content is automatically labelled according to its area. There is a file collecting each reviewer's area of interest and expertise. This allows automatically suggesting suitable reviewers for every pull request—taking their expertise and reviewing capacity into account. At the time of writing, this automatic assignment is run on an experimental basis. This labelling information has also been used to identify missing reviewers: if pull requests in a certain area take a long time to get reviewed, recruiting further reviewers could be worthwhile.

Secondly, we have created custom tooling exposing important information to reviewers. When a pull request is filed, a script creates a sticky comment summarising key information about a PR. This comment is updated in-place as the pull request is amended. The comment shows which lemmas were renamed (so reviewers can spot those more easily, and check if deprecation warnings are present). It also exposes when transitive imports of files change, which is extremely helpful for reviewing import refactoring. Finally, the summary comment shows any changes in technical debt metrics.

Further, there is substantial automation to help with information flow within the project. Collaboration on Mathlib occurs primarily on two sites: GitHub, where git repositories including Mathlib and its dependencies are hosted, and the leanprover-community Zulip, a moderated chat site where community members discuss their contributions and other Lean-related topics. Automation can help with bridging these two venues and keeping some information synchronised. Whenever a specific pull request is mentioned in the Zulip chat, a script posts an emoji reaction indicating the current pull request status (such as, whether it is waiting for author changes, a review or was already merged). This allows reviewers and maintainers to see at a glance if action has already been taken. This reaction is updated by a GitHub actions script whenever the pull request's status changes.

We make extensive use of Zulip's custom linkifier feature to allow users to link directly to issues or pull requests in the Mathlib repository, Mathlib documentation entries, and other useful pages.

7.2 Triage tooling

The number of open Mathlib pull requests is growing steadily. At the time of writing, there are about 1500 open pull requests. Often, new pull requests are getting reviewed quickly, but their sheer volume makes it difficult to keep track of every single PR. Better tooling helps to ensure that every pull request is kept track of and receives a timely response.

Investigating this closely shows that different users of such tooling have differing needs. For instance, a reviewer may want to find reviewable pull requests matching their areas of interest. Mathlib's maintainers would like to know about pull requests which were already approved by a reviewer. Other contributors may be interested in recent pull requests to "see what is going on", or viewing all pull requests related to a particular area. Pull request authors may want to see the status of all their pull requests or find out why their pull request is not on the review queue. Most importantly, a triage team (see below) keeping track of pull requests' state needs better tooling to see the state of each pull request.

GitHub's default interface can do many of the above tasks; however, at Mathlib's scale we have increasingly run into its limitations. For example, to triage reviewable pull requests one would like to know the total time a pull request is already waiting for review. This need not be a continuous time span, so computing this needs to consider a pull request's change over time. GitHub only exposes a "last updated" date, which does not provide this. (In addition, this "last update" measures almost every activity, which is often too sensitive for our purposes: a bystander's comment or a notification of a merge conflict resets the last activity counter, but need not mean review activity.) Similarly, sorting pull requests by their total diff can be useful information, as is the number of PRs depending on a given PR.

We have built a custom editorial tool to address all these shortcomings. Pull requests are grouped by their status (such as waiting for review, blocked on another pull request or waiting for the author to respond to review comments). These categories are tailored to Mathlib's infrastructure (for instance, pull request failures related to Mathlib's infrastructure are highlighted automatically, speeding up the diagnosis and fix). In each category, we compactly display (see

Figure 1) all pull requests together with additional meta-information such as its author, title and labels, but also additional information such as diff size or the total time in review. These lists can be semantically sorted by each category. This tooling can adapt and grow with Mathlib's needs easily.

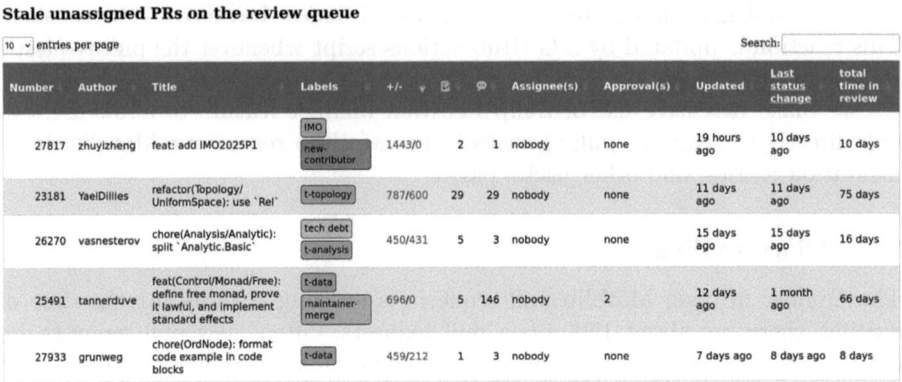

Stale unassigned PRs on the review queue

10 entries per page Search:

Number	Author	Title	Labels	+/-			Assignee(s)	Approval(s)	Updated	Last status change	total time in review
27817	zhuyizheng	feat: add IMO2025P1	IMO new-contributor	1443/0	2	1	nobody	none	19 hours ago	10 days ago	10 days
23181	YaelDillies	refactor(Topology/UniformSpace): use `Rel`	t-topology	787/600	29	29	nobody	none	11 days ago	11 days ago	75 days
26270	vasnesterov	chore(Analysis/Analytic): split `Analytic.Basic`	tech debt t-analysis	450/431	5	3	nobody	none	15 days ago	15 days ago	16 days
25491	tannerduve	feat(Control/Monad/Free): define free monad, prove it lawful, and implement standard effects	t-data maintainer-merge	696/0	5	146	nobody	2	12 days ago	1 month ago	66 days
27933	grunweg	chore(OrdNode): format code example in code blocks	t-data	459/212	1	3	nobody	none	7 days ago	8 days ago	8 days

Fig. 1. A typical dashboard from Mathlib's review and triage dashboard

We ran a survey among Mathlib contributors, reviewers and maintainers. The results provided many useful suggestions for improving this tool further (many of which have already been implemented). The survey result also affirms that this changes how contributors look for pull requests: the dashboard has become part of many maintainers' standard workflow. The triage functionality in particular is used by maintainers, but also by the newly-founded triage team: having a common webpage to look at makes this process a lot smoother.

Under the hood, this dashboard has two components. One keeps a cache, containing the metadata we care about for every open pull request. Periodically, we query GitHub's `graphql` API to update this data for any pull requests which received updates, in effect creating a database of each pull request's relevant state. The code for this amounts to a few hundred lines of shell and Python scripts: this could easily be run on a local computer, coupled with a cronjob.

The other, user-facing component, processes this metadata to extract the aggregate data we care about. (For instance, from the history of all label changes on a pull request, we determine the total time that PR was ready for review.) Using this metadata, we create the triage dashboard. The dashboard is a static webpage, using jQuery datatables to create the dashboards in each category: these can be sorted and filtered dynamically. Using a static webpage means fast response times (filtering a list of pull requests is almost instantaneous), but means the webpage needs to be manually refreshed to see updated changes. Altogether, this project consists of about 4500 lines of Python code, and about 1000 lines of shell scripts, `.graphql` schemas etc.

8 Conclusion

Growing Mathlib would be impossible without automation to scale its maintainance: this applies on the social, organisational and technical levels. While we cannot measure its effects precisely, the fact that Mathlib still grows fast shows how useful it is. For instance, Mathlib's deprecation system has made updating to a newer version of Mathlib a much smoother process. Currently, such updates still require manual work, but this task can be automated well: both for deprecated declarations and modules, there are prototype tools performing the replacement automatically.

An auto-formatter for Lean would improve dealing with code style questions significantly. Lean's extensibility makes this difficult in general: users can define new syntax and custom notation, which can drastically change the look and feel of the language.[12] Formatting user-defined syntax and notation requires knowing the preferred formatting for these. While Mathlib makes extensive use of custom notation to make its code resemble mathematical notation, this is relatively benign: all syntax has an associated pretty-printer which indicates some reasonable formatting.

Mathlib's review and triage dashboard is mostly Mathlib-agnostic: the particular PR categories are tuned to Mathlib, but the underlying logic is not. With appropriate configuration, other open source projects could use this as well.

Acknowledgements We would like to thank the anonymous referees for their helpful comments and suggestions. Michael Rothgang was funded by the Deutsche Forschungsgemeinschaft (DFG, German Research Foundation) under Germany's Excellence Strategy – EXC-2047/1 – 390685813. This material is based upon work supported by the U.S. National Science Foundation Award No. DMS-2302263.

References

1. Anne Baanen. "Use and Abuse of Instance Parameters in the Lean Mathematical Library". In: *13th International Conference on Interactive Theorem Proving (ITP 2022)*. Ed. by June Andronick and Leonardo de Moura. Vol. 237. Leibniz International Proceedings in Informatics (LIPIcs). Dagstuhl, Germany: Schloss Dagstuhl – Leibniz-Zentrum für Informatik, 2022, 4:1–4:20. DOI: 10.4230/LIPIcs.ITP.2022.4. URL: https://drops.dagstuhl.de/pus/volltexte/2022/16713.
2. Grzegorz Bancerek et al. "The Role of the Mizar Mathematical Library for Interactive Proof Development in Mizar". In: *Journal of Automated Reasoning* 61 (June 2018), pp. 9–32. URL: https://link.springer.com/article/10.1007/s10817-017-9440-6.
3. Jasmin Blanchette et al. "Mining the Archive of Formal Proofs". In: *Conference on Intelligent Computer Mathematics (CICM 2015)*. Ed. by M. Kerber. Vol. 9150. LNCS. Invited paper. Springer, 2015, pp. 3–17.

[12] For example, one can allow users to write in a form of controlled natural language [23]: formatting that would be a very different endavour.

4. Timothy Bourke et al. "Challenges and Experiences in Managing Large-Scale Proofs'. In: *AISC/MKM/Calculemus*. 2012. URL: https://api.semanticscholar.org/CorpusID:11296777.
5. Kevin Buzzard. *The Fermat's Last Theorem Project*. Lean community blog. Apr. 2024. URL: https://leanprover-community.github.io/blog/posts/FLT-announcement/.
6. Johan Commelin and Adam Topaz. "Abstraction boundaries and spec driven development in pure mathematics". In: *Bull. Amer. Math. Soc. (N.S.)* 61.2 (2024), pp. 241–255. DOI: 10.1090/bull/1831. URL: https://doi.org/10.1090/bull/1831.
7. Mathlib Community. "Completion of the Liquid Tensor Experiment". July 2022. URL: https://leanprover-community.github.io/blog/posts/lte-final/.
8. Ward Cunningham. *The WyCash Portfolio Management System*. OOPSLA '92 Experience report. Mar. 1992. URL: https://c2.com/doc/oopsla92.html.
9. Floris van Doorn, Patrick Massot, and Oliver Nash. "Formalising the h-principle and Sphere Eversion". In: *Proceedings of the 12th ACM SIGPLAN International Conference on Certified Programs and Proofs, CPP 2023, Boston, MA, USA, January 16-17, 2023*. Ed. by Robbert Krebbers et al. ACM, 2023, pp. 121–134. DOI: 10.1145/3573105.3575688. URL: https://doi.org/10.1145/3573105.3575688.
10. Ali Ghanbari. "Automatic Goal Clone Detection in Rocq". In: *39th European Conference on Object-Oriented Programming, ECOOP 2025, June 30 to July 2, 2025, Bergen, Norway*. Ed. by Jonathan Aldrich and Alexandra Silva. Vol. 333. LIPIcs. Schloss Dagstuhl - Leibniz-Zentrum für Informatik, 2025, 12:1–12:19. DOI: 10.4230/LIPICS.ECOOP.2025.12.
11. Kiran Gopinathan, Mayank Keoliya, and Ilya Sergey. "Mostly Automated Proof Repair for Verified Libraries". In: *Proceedings of the ACM on Programming Languages* 7 (2023), pp. 25–49. https://dl.acm.org/doi/10.1145/3591221.
12. W. T. Gowers et al. "Marton's Conjecture in abelian groups with bounded torsion". arXiv:2404.02244 [math.NT]. URL: https://arxiv.org/pdf/2404.02244.pdf.
13. W. T. Gowers et al. "On a conjecture of Marton". arXiv:2311.05762v2 [math.NT]. URL: https://arxiv.org/pdf/2311.05762.pdf.
14. Jason Gross et al. "Automatic Test-Case Reduction in Proof Assistants: A Case Study in Coq". In: *13th International Conference on Interactive Theorem Proving, ITP 2022, August 7-10, 2022, Haifa, Israel*. Ed. by June Andronick and Leonardo de Moura. Vol. 237. LIPIcs. Schloss Dagstuhl - Leibniz-Zentrum für Informatik, 2022, 18:1–18:18. DOI: 10.4230/LIPICS.ITP.2022.18. URL: https://doi.org/10.4230/LIPIcs.ITP.2022.18
15. Thomas Hales et al. "A formal proof of the Kepler conjecture". In: *Forum Math. Pi* 5 (2017), e2, 29. DOI: 10.1017/fmp.2017.1.

16. Graydon Hoare. "technicalities: "not rocket science" (the story of monotone and bors)". Feb. 2014. URL: https://graydon2.dreamwidth.org/1597.html.
17. Fabian Huch. "Isabelle as Systems Platform: Managing Automated and Quasi-interactive Builds". In: *CoRR* abs/2412.13083 (2024). DOI: 10.48550/ARXIV.2412.13083. https://arxiv.org/abs/2412.13083.
18. Fabian Huch and Makarius Wenzel. "Distributed Parallel Build for the Isabelle Archive of Formal Proofs". In: *15th International Conference on Interactive Theorem Proving (ITP 2024)*. Ed. by Yves Bertot, Temur Kutsia, and Michael Norrish. Vol. 309. Leibniz International Proceedings in Informatics (LIPIcs). Dagstuhl, Germany: Schloss Dagstuhl – Leibniz-Zentrum für Informatik, 2024, 22:1–22:19. DOI: 10.4230/LIPIcs.ITP.2024.22
19. Jyun-Jie Liao. "Improved Exponent for Marton's Conjecture in F_2^n". arXiv:2404.09639 [math.CO]. URL: https://arxiv.org/pdf/2404.09639.pdf.
20. Jannis Limperg and Asta Halkjær From. "Aesop: White-Box Best-First Proof Search for Lean". In: *Proceedings of the 12th ACM SIGPLAN International Conference on Certified Programs and Proofs, CPP 2023, Boston, MA, USA, January 16-17, 2023*. Ed. by Robbert Krebbers et al. ACM, 2023, pp. 253–266. DOI: 10.1145/3573105.3575671
21. Xiaokun Luan et al. "Why the Proof Fails in Different Versions of Theorem Provers: An Empirical Study of Compatibility Issues in Isabelle". In: *Proceedings of the ACM on Software Engineering* (2025). https://dl.acm.org/doi/10.1145/3715787
22. Assia Mahboubi and Enrico Tassi. *Mathematical Components*. 2017.
23. Patrick Massot. "Teaching Mathematics Using Lean and Controlled Natural Language". In: *15th International Conference on Interactive Theorem Proving (ITP 2024)*. Ed. by Yves Bertot, Temur Kutsia, and Michael Norrish. Vol. 309. Leibniz International Proceedings in Informatics (LIPIcs). Dagstuhl, Germany: Schloss Dagstuhl – Leibniz-Zentrum für Informatik, 2024, 27:1–27:19. DOI: 10.4230/LIPIcs.ITP.2024.27
24. William McCune. "Experiments with Discrimination-Tree Indexing and Path Indexing for Term Retrieval". In: *J. Autom. Reason.* 9.2 (1992), pp. 147–167. DOI: 10.1007/BF00245458.
25. Markus de Medeiros et al. "Verified Foundations for Differential Privacy". In: *Proc. ACM Program. Lang.* 9.PLDI (June 2025). DOI: 10.1145/3729294.
26. Yecine Megdiche, Fabian Huch, and Lukas Stevens. "A Linter for Isabelle: Implementation and Evaluation". In: *CoRR* abs/2207.10424 (2022). https://arxiv.org/abs/2207.10424.

27. Bhavik Mehta. *Formalising modern research mathematics in real time.* Nov. 2023. URL: https://xenaproject.wordpress.com/2023/11/04/formalising-modern-research-mathematics-in-real-time/.
28. Leonardo de Moura and Sebastian Ullrich. "The Lean 4 Theorem Prover and Programming Language". In: *Automated Deduction – CADE 28. Ed.* by André Platzer and Geoff Sutcliffe. Cham: Springer International Publishing, 2021, pp. 625–635. URL: 10.1007/978-3-030-79876-5_37.
29. I. V. Ramakrishnan, R. Sekar, and Andrei Voronkov. "Term Indexing". In: *Handbook of Automated Reasoning (in 2 volumes).* Ed. by John Alan Robinson and Andrei Voronkov. Elsevier and MIT Press, 2001, pp. 1853–1964. DOI: 10.1016/B978-044450813-3/50028-X.
30. David Renshaw. *Searching for Proof Improvements with tryAtEachStep. Conference talk, Lean together 2025.* 2025. URL: https://researchseminars.org/talk/LeanTogether2025/8/.
31. Talia Ringer et al. "QED at Large: A Survey of Engineering of Formally Verified Software". In: *Foundations and Trends® in Programming Languages* 5.2-3 (2019), pp. 102–281. DOI: 10.1561/2500000045.
32. Peter Scholze. "Liquid tensor experiment". In: *Exp. Math.* 31.2 (2022), pp. 349–354. DOI: 10.1080/10586458.2021.1926016. URL: https://www.tandfonline.com/doi/full/10.1080/10586458.2021.1926016.
33. Daniel Selsam, Sebastian Ullrich, and Leonardo de Moura. *Tabled Typeclass Resolution.* 2020. URL: https://arxiv.org/abs/2001.04301.
34. Chengsong Tan et al. "The Burden of Proof: Automated Tooling for Rapid Iteration on Large Mechanised Proofs". In: *2025 IEEE/ACM 13th International Conference on Formal Methods in Software Engineering (FormaliSE).* 2025, pp. 34–45. DOI: 10.1109/FormaliSE66629.2025.00010.
35. The mathlib community. "The Lean mathematical library". In: *Proceedings of the 9th ACM SIGPLAN International Conference on Certified Programs and Proofs, CPP 2020, New Orleans, LA, USA, January 20-21, 2020.* 2020, pp. 367–381. DOI: 10.1145/3372885.3373824.
36. Floris van Doorn, Gabriel Ebner, and Robert Y. Lewis. "Maintaining a Library of Formal Mathematics". In: *Intelligent Computer Mathematics, CICM 2020.* Vol. abs/2004.03673. 2020. https://link.springer.com/chapter/10.1007/978-3-030-53518-6_16.
37. Makarius Wenzel. *Isabelle technology for the Archive of Formal Proofs with application to MMT.* 2019. URL: https://arxiv.org/abs/1905.07244.
38. Théo Zimmermann. "Challenges in the collaborative evolution of a proof language and its ecosystem". Theses. Université Paris Cité, Dec. 2019. URL: https://inria.hal.science/tel-02451322.
39. Théo Zimmermann et al. "Extending the team with a project-specific bot". In: *CoRR* abs/2112.07365 (2021). URL: https://arxiv.org/abs/2112.07365.

Exploring Formal Math on the Blockchain: An Explorer for Proofgold

Chad E. Brown[1], Cezary Kaliszyk[2,3], and Josef Urban[1](✉)

[1] Czech Technical University in Prague, Prague, Czech Republic
josef.urban@gmail.com
[2] University of Melbourne, Melbourne, Australia
ckaliszyk@unimelb.edu.au
[3] University of Innsbruck, Innsbruck, Austria

Abstract. Proofgold is a blockchain that supports formalized mathematics alongside standard cryptocurrency functionality. It incorporates logical constructs into the blockchain, including declarations of formal theories, definitions, propositions and proofs. It also supports placing and collecting bounties on proving these propositions, incentivizing the development of the formal libraries contained in Proofgold. In this paper, we present a web-based blockchain explorer for Proofgold. The system exposes not only the usual transactional data but also the formal mathematical components embedded in the chain and allows some interaction with them. The explorer allows users to inspect blocks, transactions, and addresses, as well as formal objects: theories, definitions, theorems and their proofs. We also support the submission of transactions to the blockchain using our interface. We describe the system architecture and its integration with the Proofgold Lava software, highlighting how the explorer supports navigation of formal content and facilitates mathematical knowledge management in a decentralized setting, as well as a number of formalizations in category theory done in the system.

1 Introduction

Formalized mathematics has seen remarkable progress in recent years, with large-scale developments such as the formal proof of the Feit-Thompson theorem in Coq [16] and the proof of the Kepler conjecture in HOL Light and Isabelle [17], the formalization of perfectoid spaces in Lean [10], and the formalization of superposition calculus in Isabelle's Archive of Formal Proofs [13]. Despite these advances, most formalization efforts are still coordinated through centralized repositories, and the ecosystem lacks well-established mechanisms for incentivizing contributions. Blockchain technology offers a promising avenue to address both of these challenges by providing a decentralized infrastructure for storing and verifying formal content, as well as built-in mechanisms for transparent incentives and attribution. By combining blockchains with formalized mathematics, we can create systems in which formal theories, definitions, propositions and their associated metadata are permanently recorded in a ledger. This enables provenance tracking, ensures tamper resistance and facilitates collaborative contributions across a global network without reliance on a central authority.

V. de Paiva and P. Koepke (Eds.): CICM 2025, LNAI 16136, pp. 71–90, 2026.
https://doi.org/10.1007/978-3-032-07021-0_5

Proofgold [8] builds upon this idea of integrating formal mathematics with a decentralized system by providing a blockchain that supports the storage, verification and incentivization of formal math contributions. By including formal theories, definitions, theorems and proofs directly into the blockchain, Proofgold ensures that this mathematical knowledge is publicly accessible and verifiable. By integrating a bounty system, where users can place rewards for the verification (or refutation) of specific conjectures, it also encourages development. Despite these advantages, Proofgold is currently a command-line interface-only system, lacking a user interface, which limits its accessibility to experts who are familiar with the CLI and reduces its appeal to a broader audience.

Contributions In this paper, we present the Web-based blockchain explorer for Proofgold, built by extending the Proofgold Lava client [8]. This extension adds various functionalities for querying the blockchain, and includes the implementation of server-side code to facilitate interactions with the client. In particular:

- We describe the system architecture, outlining how the web-based explorer interfaces with the Proofgold blockchain (Section 3);
- We demonstrate how formal mathematical objects – such as theorems, definitions and proofs – are rendered within the explorer, and explain how users can interact with these objects (Section 4);
- As a case study, we present a number of conjectures in category theory along with their proofs or refutations presented in Proofgold (Section 5).

2 Proofgold and Formal Mathematics on the Blockchain

This section briefly introduces Proofgold; for a more complete description, see [8]. Proofgold is a cryptocurrency designed to support formal logic and mathematics. The core of Proofgold is a proof checker for intuitionistic higher-order logic with functional extensionality. We only give an introduction to the higher-order Tarski Grothendieck set theory (HOTG) defined in Proofgold in Section 5. Users can publish theories, which consist of primitive constants, their types, and axioms. Each theory is uniquely identified by a 256-bit identifier derived from its recursive hash (Merkle root). Documents defining new objects, proving theorems, and stating conjectures can be published within a theory. Ownership of propositions is determined by public keys, enabling the redemption of bounties by proving conjectures. Proofgold combines proof-of-stake and proof-of-burn, with the proof-of-burn element involving burning small amounts of Litecoin. This combination enhances security by reusing Litecoin's proof-of-work. The first 5000 Proofgold blocks automatically placed bounties on pseudorandom propositions [8], allowing new participants to increase their stake by proving theorems.

Proofgold has seen significant activity in terms of theories, documents, and formalizations. The platform includes a built-in theory of hereditarily finite sets (HF), which was used to generate pseudorandom bounties for the first 5000 blocks. Additionally, two theories axiomatizing HOTG have been published [9], one corresponding to Mizar [4] and one corresponding to Megalodon, along with a theory for reasoning about syntax using higher-order abstract syntax (HOAS).

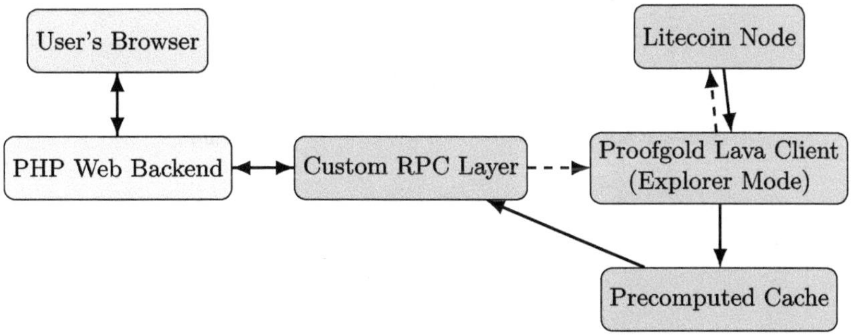

Fig. 1. High-level architecture of the explorer

These theories have facilitated the formalization of various mathematical concepts and the construction of significant mathematical objects, such as the real numbers via Conway's surreal numbers. In particular, the Megalodon proofs of 12 of Wiedijk's 100 theorems [24] are included in Proofgold. Furthermore, the platform has enabled the publication of conjectures and the collection of bounties, with 2836 of the 13142 bounties resolved as of April 2025.

The Proofgold Lava Client, co-developed by the authors, addresses the scalability issues of the original Proofgold Core software. It features an improved database layer using the Unix DBM interface, a more efficient cryptography layer, and enhancements to the networking and proof-checking layers. The client is a command line interface that unfortunately requires somewhat complicated installation (it relies on a litecoin running in RPC mode, and particular versions of the database). Additionally, it supports 210 commands, which may be somewhat overwhelming for users.

3 System Architecture

The design of the Proofgold Explorer focuses on providing accessible and interactive access to both blockchain data and formal mathematical content. In particular, we aim to offer: an intuitive web interface that lowers the entry barrier; structured access to formal and transactional data; and integration with the existing Proofgold infrastructure. To achieve these goals, we propose the architecture consisting of three main components (Fig. 1):

1. A modified Proofgold Lava client, running in a new `explorer` mode that would cache and prepare additional information;
2. A server-side backend written in PHP;
3. An RPC communication layer connecting the backend with both the explorer node and the underlying Litecoin node.

In explorer mode, the Lava client computes and caches additional information about the formal content embedded in the blockchain. This includes the possibility of looking up definitions, propositions, theories, proofs and bounties. In principle, this information is already stored in the blockchain, but it requires traversing

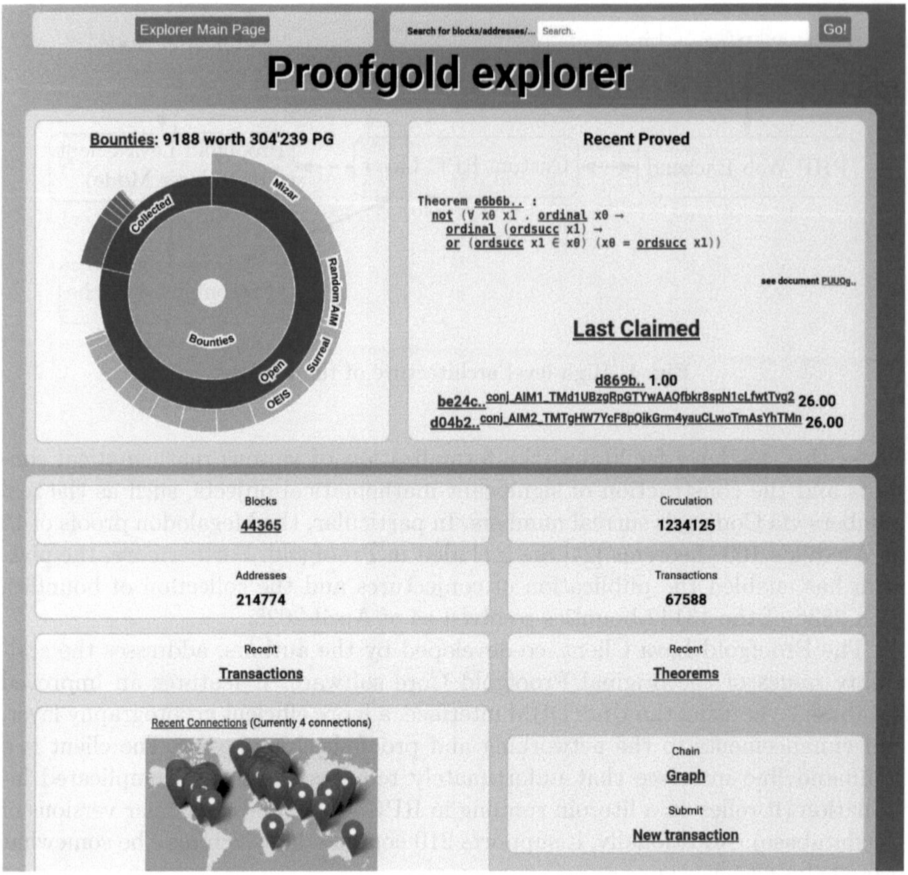

Fig. 2. Explorer Main Page

the whole history. The added information is stored in 34 OCaml hashtables that add approximately 10 Gigabytes in memory and that are periodically (every hour) refreshed. These structures allow efficient access to: information about individual formal entities, including their types, statements, and owners; the history and status of bounties and their collection; dependencies between formal objects and their evolution over time; ownership and authorship tracking for mathematical content. It serves this structured information through a custom RPC interface that returns it in a machine-readable format for use by the frontend.

The web backend is implemented in PHP and is responsible for serving user-facing pages that visualize both standard blockchain data (blocks, transactions, addresses, bounties) and formal mathematical constructs (theorems, definitions, proofs, theories, conjectures). The backend queries the explorer node in real time and formats the data into interactive HTML views. It also enables lightweight interaction with the blockchain, such as submitting transactions. These components are designed to be kept in sync with the live blockchain state and support both incremental updates and history queries.

The explorer is also connected to the **Megalodon Wiki (mgwiki)**[1] which is a collaborative git-based platform for formal math that enables users to edit and verify Megalodon files directly in the browser. The mgwiki workflow involves cloning or forking the repository, modifying or adding `.mg` files, and committing changes, which triggers automated proof checking and HTML generation via GitHub Actions. Errors, if any, are reported in the GitHub action logs, and successful edits are published as browsable HTML. A unique feature of mgwiki is its integration with Proofgold: when a valid Megalodon file is added, it is automatically converted into a `.pfg` document that can be submitted to Proofgold. This allows users to associate formalized conjectures with bounties and track their progress through the explorer. Mgwiki thus serves also as a gateway for contributing conjectures and proofs to the Proofgold-based decentralized proof bounty system.

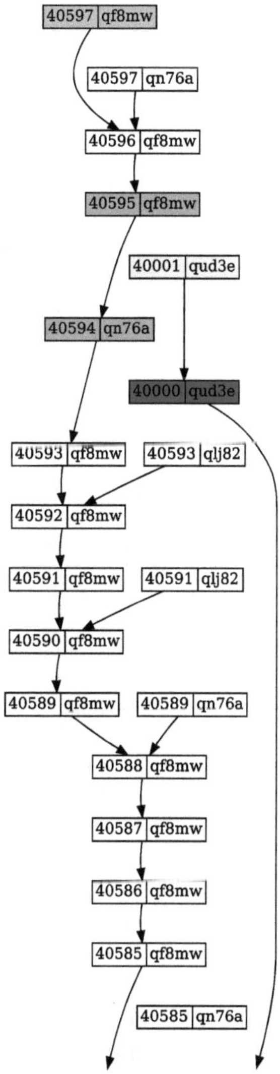

Fig. 3. Chain Graph

4 Explorer Functionality

The Proofgold Explorer provides a structured and interactive interface to both blockchain and formal mathematical data. The main dashboard (Figure 2), available online[2] aggregates statistics about the blockchain such as block height, address count, transaction volume and coin circulation. An important feature is a link to the overview of the current graph of the blockchain. This is normally a single chain with branches in the case of competing chain tips. We show an example from a time when there were multiple competing nodes (Figure 3). Particular nodes in the chain are marked in special colors: nodes that define theories, include proof

[1] `https://github.com/mgwiki/mgw_test`, `https://mgwiki.github.io/mgw_test/`
[2] `https://formalweb3.uibk.ac.at/pgbce/`, `http://proofgold.net/explorer/`

Fig. 4. Highest open and collected bounties

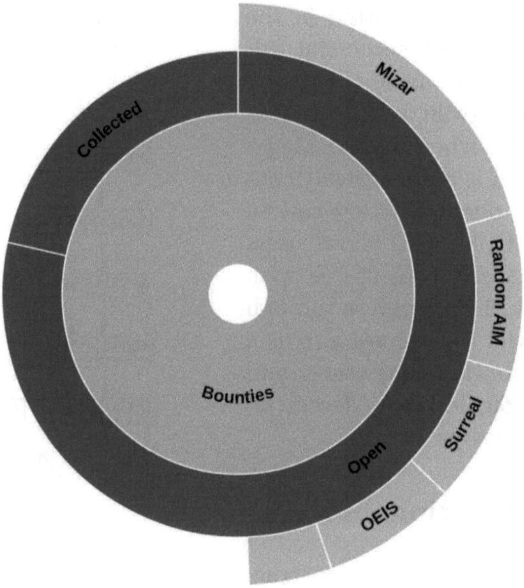

Fig. 5. Open and collected bounty categories

objects, place bounties on propositions, or just include transactions are colored in green, blue, and pink. Additionally, as the blockchain attempts to be resilient to attacks, the graph also marks missing nodes and invalid nodes (spending non-existing assets, but also invalid proof steps) in yellow and red respectively.

The explorer also visualizes the open and collected bounties, with a more detailed view of the highest open and collected bounties, as well as a categorization of bounties presented in Figures 4 and 5. This allows users to inspect the most valuable open conjectures and focus their proof efforts on them, as well as to see what are the domains of the conejctures users are working on. The individual bounties can be viewed either in the Proofgold format, if their representation is given in a theory document, or in case if they are only given in the opaque formal, they are linked to the Megalodon Wiki. We show this in the example of Fermat's

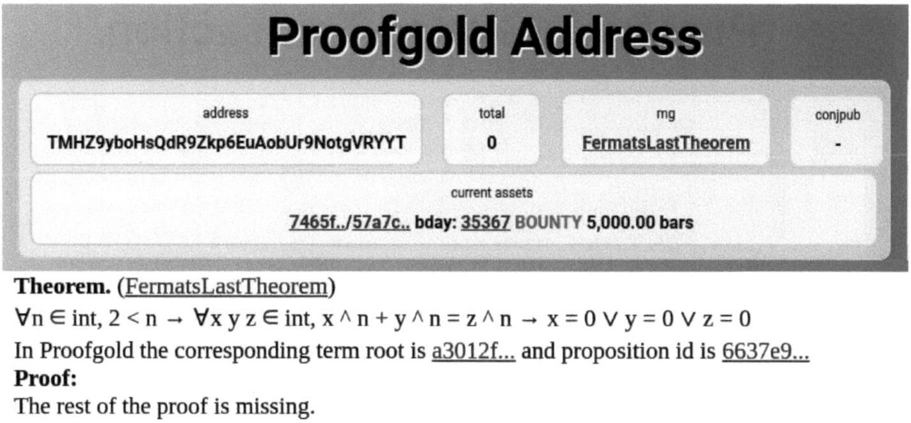

Fig. 6. Fermat as a bounty in the Proofgold explorer and its corresponding statement in the Megalodon Wiki

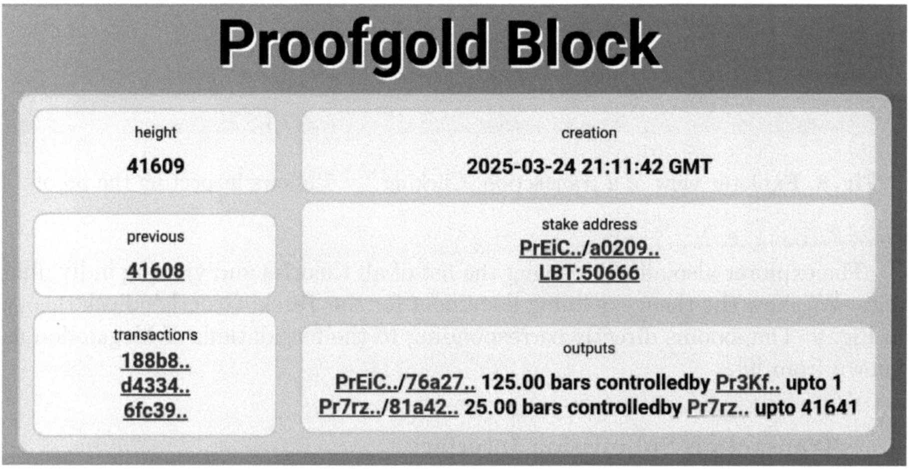

Fig. 7. Explorer view of a block

last theorem, as of April 2025 it is the conjecture with the highest bounty in Proofgold (Figure 6).

The explorer allows viewing blocks (Figure 7) and transactions in them. This is useful, because unlike in other blockchains, Proofgold transactions are not always purely value-based. They can also introduce proof documents. We show an example of such a transaction in Figure 8: The transaction takes a small amount of proofgold along with a marker (used to safely claim ownership of proved objects [8]) and sends them to the address of a proof document. The newly defined objects, shown in the figure, and theorems proved in this document are now owned by the publisher of the document.

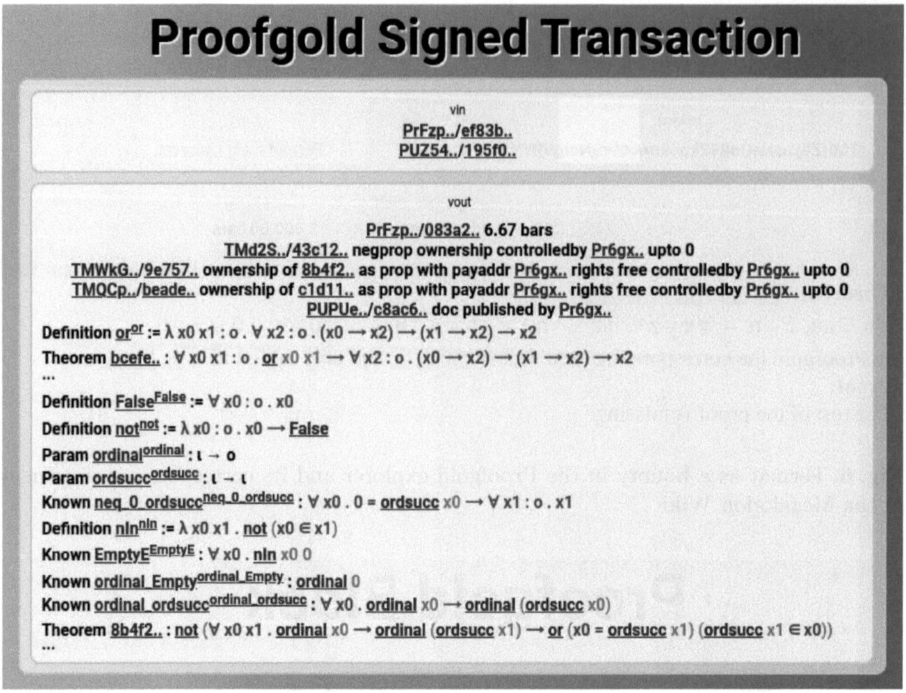

Fig. 8. Explorer view of a transaction. Clicking "..." allows inspecting the proof.

The explorer also allows viewing the list of all theories and viewing individual ones. We show the theory defining document for the Tarski Groethendieck theory in Fig. 9. The axioms directly corresponding to the foundations of Megalodon as known from [9].

4.1 Transaction Submission Interface

Blockchain explorers typically include transaction submission interfaces to allow users to directly broadcast transactions to the network without needing a full node or wallet software. This is useful for users who have already constructed and signed a transaction (usually offline) and simply need to submit it to the blockchain for confirmation. We also include such an interface in the explorer.

5 Use Case and Examples

Some of the examples of conjectures with bounties – many of which have already been proven or disproven – assert the existence of a left adjoint to a forgetful functor. Such left adjoints, when they exist, often correspond to freely generated structures. More generally, the interest in such adjoints can be justified by Slogan IV of [19]: "Many important concepts in mathematics arise as adjoints, right or left, to previously known functors." We begin with an informal description,

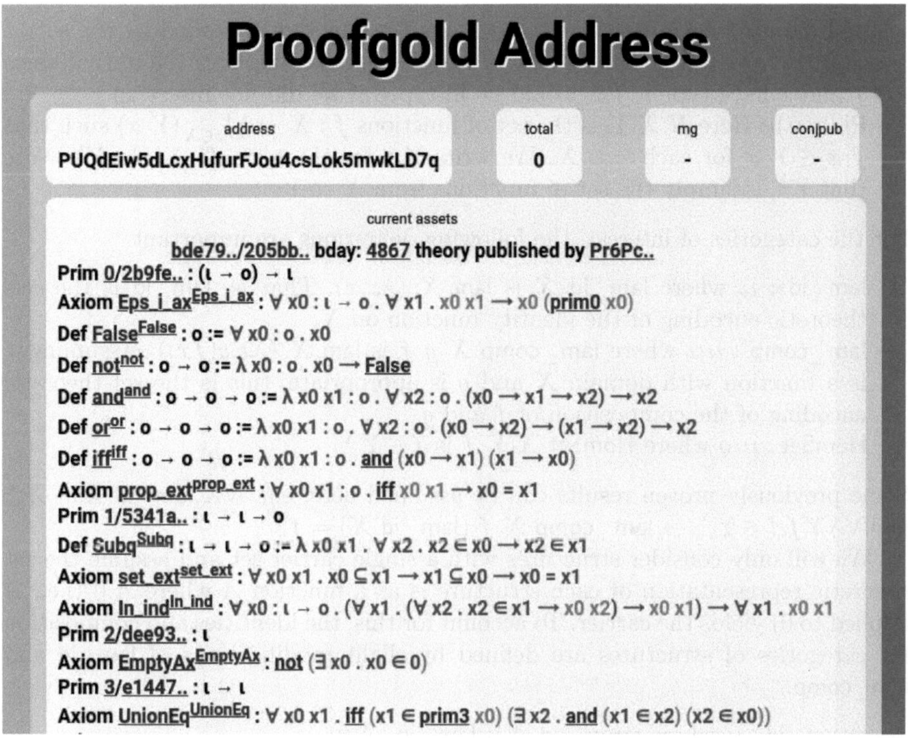

Fig. 9. The higher-order Tarski Groethendieck theory in the explorer

leaving details to [19]. Suppose $\mathcal{C}$ and $\mathcal{D}$ are categories and $\mathcal{F} : \mathcal{C} \to \mathcal{D}$ and $\mathcal{U} : \mathcal{D} \to \mathcal{C}$ are functors. $\mathcal{F}$ is left adjoint to $\mathcal{U}$ if there exist natural transformations $\eta : 1_{\mathcal{C}} \to \mathcal{UF}$ and $\varepsilon : \mathcal{FU} \to 1_{\mathcal{D}}$ satisfying certain identities. In each conjecture below, $\mathcal{C}$ will be the category of sets, $\mathcal{D}$ will be some category of structures and $\mathcal{U}$ will be the forgetful functor sending a structure to its carrier set. The conjecture will then state that there exist $\mathcal{F}$, η and ε giving an adjunction. In July 2021, bounties of 750 bars were placed on 33 conjectures of this form. As of May 2025, 14 of the bounties have been collected (11 by proving the conjecture and 3 by disproving the conjecture), and 19 remain open. We discuss a few of these propositions below.

The conjectures and theorems are in the HOTG theory [9], with a base type ι of sets. We use o for the type of propositions and $\alpha\beta$ for the type of functions from α to β. We briefly review elements of set theory required to describe the conjectures. There are the usual logical definitions: $\top : o$, $\bot : o$, $\neg : oo$, $\wedge : ooo$, $\equiv : ooo$, $=$ and $\exists$. Two primitives of the set theory are relevant: $\in : \iota\iota o$ (which we write in infix) and $\emptyset : \iota$ (which we often write as 0 below). After enough infrastructure is defined, we also have the following objects:

- $\mathsf{lam} : \iota(\iota\iota)\iota$: Here $\mathsf{lam}\ X\ f$ is the set encoding the function f restricted to the domain X.

- $\mathsf{ap} : \iota\iota\iota$: $\mathsf{ap}\ f\ x$ corresponds to applying the function (encoded by the set) f to x. Here we often simply write $f\ x$, leaving ap as implicit. (Note that since f and x have type ι, $f\ x$ would be ill-typed if we did not insert ap.)
- $\mathsf{Pi} : \iota(\iota\iota)\iota$: Here $\Pi\ X\ Y$ is the set of functions $f : X \to \bigcup_{x \in X}(Y\ x)$ such that $f\ x \in Y\ x$ for each $x \in X$. We write Y^X for the term $\Pi\ X\ (\lambda x.Y)$. Note that Y^X is simply the set of functions from X to Y.

For the categories of interest, the following definitions are important.

- $\mathsf{lam\_id} : \iota\iota$ where $\mathsf{lam\_id}\ X$ is $\mathsf{lam}\ X\ (\lambda x.x)$. That is, $\mathsf{lam\_id}$ is the set-theoretic encoding of the identity function on X.
- $\mathsf{lam\_comp} : \iota\iota\iota\iota$ where $\mathsf{lam\_comp}\ X\ g\ f$ is $\mathsf{lam}\ X\ (\lambda x.g(fx))$. Assuming f is a function with domain X and g is appropriate, this is the set-theoretic encoding of the composition of f and g.
- $\mathsf{HomSet} : \iota\iota\iota o$ where $\mathsf{HomSet}\ X\ Y\ f$ is $f \in Y^X$.

Some previously proven results can be assumed here, e.g., $\forall X.\mathsf{lam\_id}\ X \in X^X$ and $\forall XYf.f \in Y^X \to \mathsf{lam\_comp}\ X\ f\ (\mathsf{lam\_id}\ X) = f$.

We will only consider structures with a single carrier set and assume the set theoretic representation of each structure is as a function A where $A\ 0$ (i.e., A applied to 0) yields the carrier. To account for this, the identities and composition for categories of structures are defined by slight modifications of lam_id and lam_comp.

- $\mathsf{struct\_id} : \iota\iota$ where $\mathsf{struct\_id}\ A$ is $\mathsf{lam\_id}\ (A\ 0)$.
- $\mathsf{struct\_comp} : \iota\iota\iota\iota\iota\iota$ where $\mathsf{struct\_comp}\ A\ B\ C$ is $\mathsf{lam\_comp}\ (A\ 0)$. Note that this ignores its second and third arguments. Giving the last two arguments explicitly yields $\mathsf{struct\_comp}\ A\ B\ C\ g\ f$ is $\mathsf{lam\_comp}\ (A\ 0)\ g\ f$.

There are many examples of structures defined in Megalodon and Proofgold which differ in two ways: the other components of the structure (a binary operation, a binary relation, etc.) and what properties are assumed of these other components. To give a simple, concrete example, we consider structures with a single binary relation. Avoiding details (which are not relevant here), we note that there is a previously defined object $\mathsf{pack\_r} : \iota(\iota\iota o)\iota$ such that $\mathsf{pack\_r}\ X\ R$ encodes the carrier set X and the binary relation R (restricted to its behavior on X) as a set. We then define $\mathsf{struct\_r} : \iota o$ to be the class of all such sets. We also assume the previously proven $\forall X.\forall R : \iota\iota o.X = \mathsf{pack\_r}\ X\ R\ 0$. That is, the set $\mathsf{pack\_r}\ X\ R$ is a function that yields the carrier set X when applied to 0.

A particular category of such structures will result from adding some restriction of the class struct_r as objects. Regardless of the restriction, the arrows should be all functions sending related inputs to related outputs. This is given by $\mathsf{BinRelnHom} : \iota\iota\iota o$ and the previously proven identity

$$\begin{aligned}&\mathsf{BinRelnHom}\ (\mathsf{pack\_r}\ X\ R)\ (\mathsf{pack\_r}\ Y\ Q)\ h\\ &= (h \in Y^X \wedge \forall xy \in X.R\ x\ y \to Q\ (h\ x)\ (h\ y)).\end{aligned}$$

To have a specific category as an example, we consider $\mathsf{IrrPartOrd} : \iota o$ which is the class of all structures with a single binary irreflexive transitive relation (i.e., an irreflexive partial order). The details of the definition are not important. It is enough to know we have the following previously proven results:

- If R is irreflexive and transitive on X, then $\mathsf{IrrPartOrd}$ ($\mathsf{pack\_r}$ X R).
- Let A satisfy $\mathsf{IrrPartOrd}$ A and $q : \iota o$ be given. In order to prove q A it is enough to prove q ($\mathsf{pack\_r}$ X R) for all sets X and irreflexive transitive relations R on X.

Let us now turn to the relevant formalization of category theory. In practice, we will be interested in large categories (metalevel categories), so formally $\mathcal{C}$ will not be encoded as a set but will consist of four components (given as four explicit dependencies in the formalization):

- $\mathcal{C}_0 : \iota o$ – the class of all objects of $\mathcal{C}$.
- $\mathcal{C}_1 : \iota\iota\iota o$ – where $\mathcal{C}_1$ X Y is the class of arrows from X to Y in $\mathcal{C}$.
- $\mathsf{id}_\mathcal{C} : \iota\iota$ – where $\mathsf{id}_\mathcal{C}$ X is the identity arrow for X in $\mathcal{C}$.
- $\mathsf{comp}_\mathcal{C} : \iota\iota\iota\iota\iota\iota$ – where $\mathsf{comp}_\mathcal{C}$ X Y Z g f is the composition of f (an arrow from X to Y) and g (an arrow from Y to Z).

The second category $\mathcal{D}$ will also be represented by four explicit components: $\mathcal{D}_0$, $\mathcal{D}_1$, $\mathsf{id}_\mathcal{D}$ and $\mathsf{comp}_\mathcal{D}$. Similarly, the functor $\mathcal{F}$ is represented by two explicit components:

- $\mathcal{F}_0 : \iota\iota$ – where $\mathcal{F}_0$ X is the object of $\mathcal{D}$ to which the object X of $\mathcal{C}$ maps.
- $\mathcal{F}_1 : \iota\iota\iota\iota$ – where $\mathcal{F}_1$ X Y f is the arrow from $\mathcal{F}_0$ X to $\mathcal{F}_1$ Y in $\mathcal{D}$ corresponding to the arrow f from X to Y in $\mathcal{C}$.

Of course, the functor $\mathcal{U}$ is also represented by $\mathcal{U}_0$ and $\mathcal{U}_1$. A natural transformation η is simply of type $\iota\iota$ – mapping an object in one category to an appropriate arrow in the other category.

$\mathsf{MetaCat}$: $(\iota o)(\iota\iota\iota o)(\iota\iota)(\iota\iota\iota\iota\iota\iota)o$ is defined so that $\mathsf{MetaCat}$ $\mathcal{C}_0$ $\mathcal{C}_1$ $\mathsf{id}_\mathcal{C}$ $\mathsf{comp}_\mathcal{C}$ holds if the components form a category. Here, we only need to know that two specific (alleged) categories are categories. The category of sets is given by the constant true predicate (every set is an object), HomSet, $\mathsf{lam\_id}$ and $(\lambda XYZ.\mathsf{lam\_comp}$ $X)$ (where the ignored arguments are needed for the types to match). This has been previously proven to be a category, and the precise proposition is $\mathsf{MetaCat}$ $(\lambda X.\top)$ HomSet $\mathsf{lam\_id}$ $(\lambda XYZ.\mathsf{lam\_comp}$ $X)$. Likewise, the category of all irreflexive transitive relations has been proven to be a category and the proposition is $\mathsf{MetaCat}$ $\mathsf{IrrPartOrd}$ $\mathsf{BinRelnHom}$ $\mathsf{struct\_id}$ $\mathsf{struct\_comp}$.

We know $\mathcal{F}_0$ and $\mathcal{F}_1$ give a functor between two categories if a number of basic properties hold. Without going into details, there is a previous definition $\mathsf{MetaFunctor}$ such that $\mathsf{MetaFunctor}$ $\mathcal{C}_0$ $\mathcal{C}_1$ $\mathsf{id}_\mathcal{C}$ $\mathsf{comp}_\mathcal{C}$ $\mathcal{D}_0$ $\mathcal{D}_1$ $\mathsf{id}_\mathcal{D}$ $\mathsf{comp}_\mathcal{D}$ $\mathcal{F}_0$ $\mathcal{F}_1$ holds precisely if those properties hold. A previously proven result allows us to infer $\mathsf{MetaFunctor}$ $\mathcal{C}_0$ $\mathcal{C}_1$ $\mathsf{id}_\mathcal{C}$ $\mathsf{comp}_\mathcal{C}$ $\mathcal{D}_0$ $\mathcal{D}_1$ $\mathsf{id}_\mathcal{D}$ $\mathsf{comp}_\mathcal{D}$ $\mathcal{F}_0$ $\mathcal{F}_1$ by proving those properties. There is also an object $\mathsf{MetaFunctor\_strict}$ which further requires the two (alleged) categories to actually be categories.

We already know the forgetful functor from the category of irreflexive transitive relations to the category of sets is a functor. The forgetful functor (in general) sends a structure A to its carrier set $A\ 0$ and sends structure morphisms f to f (which is already an appropriate set-theoretic function). Hence, the previously proven theorem is

$$\begin{gathered}\mathsf{MetaFunctor\ IrrPartOrd\ BinRelnHom\ struct\_id\ struct\_comp}\\ (\lambda X.\top)\ \mathsf{HomSet\ lam\_id}\ (\lambda XYZ.\mathsf{lam\_comp}\ X)\\ (\lambda A.A\ 0)\ (\lambda ABf.f).\end{gathered}$$

Similar to the discussion above, we have MetaNatTrans where

$$\mathsf{MetaNatTrans}\ \mathcal{C}_0\ \mathcal{C}_1\ \mathsf{id}_\mathcal{C}\ \mathsf{comp}_\mathcal{C}\ \mathcal{D}_0\ \mathcal{D}_1\ \mathsf{id}_\mathcal{D}\ \mathsf{comp}_\mathcal{D}\ \mathcal{F}_0\ \mathcal{F}_1\ \mathcal{G}_0\ \mathcal{G}_1\ \eta$$

holds if η is a natural transformation from $\mathcal{F}$ to $\mathcal{G}$ (assuming $\mathcal{C}$, $\mathcal{D}$, $\mathcal{F}$ and $\mathcal{G}$ are appropriate inputs). Finally we have MetaAdjunction where

$$\mathsf{MetaAdjunction}\ \mathcal{C}_0\ \mathcal{C}_1\ \mathsf{id}_\mathcal{C}\ \mathsf{comp}_\mathcal{C}\ \mathcal{D}_0\ \mathcal{D}_1\ \mathsf{id}_\mathcal{D}\ \mathsf{comp}_\mathcal{D}\ \mathcal{F}_0\ \mathcal{F}_1\ \mathcal{U}_0\ \mathcal{U}_1\ \eta\ \varepsilon$$

is an adjunction (with witnessing natural transformations η and ε) – again, assuming the inputs are appropriate. We also have MetaAdjunction_strict which further ensures the inputs are appropriate by requiring:

- $\mathsf{MetaFunctor\_strict}\ \mathcal{C}_0\ \mathcal{C}_1\ \mathsf{id}_\mathcal{C}\ \mathsf{comp}_\mathcal{C}\ \mathcal{D}_0\ \mathcal{D}_1\ \mathsf{id}_\mathcal{D}\ \mathsf{comp}_\mathcal{D}\ \mathcal{F}_0\ \mathcal{F}_1$ – ensuring $\mathcal{C}$ and $\mathcal{D}$ are categories and $\mathcal{F}$ is a functor from $\mathcal{C}$ to $\mathcal{D}$.
- $\mathsf{MetaFunctor}\ \mathcal{D}_0\ \mathcal{D}_1\ \mathsf{id}_\mathcal{D}\ \mathsf{comp}_\mathcal{D}\ \mathcal{C}_0\ \mathcal{C}_1\ \mathsf{id}_\mathcal{C}\ \mathsf{comp}_\mathcal{C}\ \mathcal{U}_0\ \mathcal{U}_1$ – ensuring $\mathcal{U}$ is a functor from $\mathcal{D}$ to $\mathcal{C}$.
- $\mathsf{MetaNatTrans}\ \cdots\ \eta$ – ensuring η is a natural transformation from $1_\mathcal{C}$ to $\mathcal{UF}$.
- $\mathsf{MetaNatTrans}\ \cdots\ \varepsilon$ – ensuring ε is a natural transformation from $\mathcal{FU}$ to $1_\mathcal{D}$.

Now, for each category $\mathcal{D}$ of structures, we can form the following conjecture that a left adjoint to the forgetful functor exists:

$$\begin{gathered}\exists\mathcal{F}_0 : \iota\iota.\exists\mathcal{F}_1 : \iota\iota\iota\iota.\exists\eta\varepsilon : \iota\iota.\\ \mathsf{MetaAdjunction\_strict}\ (\lambda X.\top)\ \mathsf{HomSet\ lam\_id}\ (\lambda XYZ.\mathsf{lam\_comp}\ X)\\ \mathcal{D}_0\ \mathcal{D}_1\ \mathsf{struct\_id\ struct\_comp}\\ \mathcal{F}_0\ \mathcal{F}_1\ (\lambda A.A\ 0)\ (\lambda ABf.f)\ \eta\ \varepsilon.\end{gathered}$$

As mentioned above, bounties were placed on 33 propositions of this form, of which 19 remain unresolved (neither proven nor disproven). Table 1 lists the 33 propositions and indications whether the proposition has been proven, disproven or is still open. In the particular case of irreflexive transitive relations, $\mathcal{D}_0$ is IrrPartOrd and $\mathcal{D}_1$ is BinRelnHom. The proof of this special case is given by taking $\mathcal{F}_0$ to be $\lambda X.\mathsf{pack\_r}\ X\ (\lambda xy.\bot)$ – that is, a set X is taken to the structure given by X with the empty relation. Furthermore $\mathcal{F}_1$ is given so that $\mathcal{F}_1\ X\ Y\ f$ is f, η is given so that $\eta\ X$ is $\mathsf{lam\_id}\ X$ and ε is given so that $\varepsilon\ A$ is $\mathsf{lam\_id}\ (A\ 0)$. The remainder of the proof involves checking the relevant properties. This proof was published on the Proofgold blockchain in September 2021.

The most recent of the 33 propositions to be proven has $\mathcal{D}$ as the category of structures with a carrier X and a bijective function $f : X \to X$. [3] A proof

[3] The proposition can be viewed on the explorer at the link https://formalweb3.uibk.ac.at/pgbce/OP.php?b=a69df3cc99230330e94428aa4d4e3bf5ce0405944ff3242f3882144c1c0c5216.

Name	Status
MetaCat_struct_p_left_adjoint_forgetful	Proven
MetaCat_struct_r_left_adjoint_forgetful	Proven
MetaCat_struct_r_graph_left_adjoint_forgetful	Proven
MetaCat_struct_r_partialord_left_adjoint_forgetful	Proven
MetaCat_struct_r_ord_left_adjoint_forgetful	Disproven
MetaCat_struct_r_wellord_left_adjoint_forgetful	Disproven
MetaCat_struct_r_per_left_adjoint_forgetful	Proven
MetaCat_struct_r_equivreln_left_adjoint_forgetful	Proven
MetaCat_struct_c_left_adjoint_forgetful	Proven
MetaCat_struct_c_topology_left_adjoint_forgetful	Open
MetaCat_struct_c_T1_topology_left_adjoint_forgetful	Open
MetaCat_struct_c_Hausdorff_topology_left_adjoint_forgetful	Open
MetaCat_struct_u_left_adjoint_forgetful	Proven
MetaCat_struct_u_inj_left_adjoint_forgetful	Proven
MetaCat_struct_u_bij_left_adjoint_forgetful	Proven
MetaCat_struct_u_idem_left_adjoint_forgetful	Proven
MetaCat_struct_b_left_adjoint_forgetful	Open
MetaCat_struct_b_quasigroup_left_adjoint_forgetful	Open
MetaCat_struct_b_loop_left_adjoint_forgetful	Open
MetaCat_struct_b_semigroup_left_adjoint_forgetful	Open
MetaCat_struct_b_monoid_left_adjoint_forgetful	Disproven
MetaCat_struct_b_group_left_adjoint_forgetful	Open
MetaCat_struct_b_abelian_group_left_adjoint_forgetful	Open
MetaCat_struct_b_b_e_left_adjoint_forgetful	Open
MetaCat_struct_b_b_e_rng_left_adjoint_forgetful	Open
MetaCat_struct_b_b_e_crng_left_adjoint_forgetful	Open
MetaCat_struct_b_b_e_e_left_adjoint_forgetful	Open
MetaCat_struct_b_b_e_e_semiring_left_adjoint_forgetful	Open
MetaCat_struct_b_b_e_e_ring_left_adjoint_forgetful	Open
MetaCat_struct_b_b_e_e_cring_left_adjoint_forgetful	Open
MetaCat_struct_b_b_e_e_field_left_adjoint_forgetful	Open
MetaCat_struct_b_b_r_e_e_left_adjoint_forgetful	Open
MetaCat_struct_b_b_r_e_e_ordered_field_left_adjoint_forgetful	Open

Table 1. Propositions asserting existence of adjunctions for forgetful functors

```
Definition. We define MetaCat struct u bij free0 to be λX ⇒ pack u (int × X) (λu ⇒ (u 0
+ 1,u 1)) of type set → set.
In Proofgold the corresponding term root is fca8b5... and object id is 24e110...

Definition. We define MetaCat struct u bij free1 to be λX Y h ⇒ λu ∈ int × X ⇒ (u 0,h (u
1)) of type set → set → set → set.
In Proofgold the corresponding term root is b4463b... and object id is f471c2...

Definition. We define MetaCat struct u bij forgetfree eps to be λA ⇒ unpack u i A (λX h
⇒ λu ∈ int × X ⇒ if u 0 ≤ 0 then omega iterate (- (u 0)) (inv X h) (u 1) else
omega iterate (u 0) h (u 1)) of type set → set.
```

Fig. 10. Definitions for the Adjoint Functor for Bijections in the Megalodon Wiki

```
Theorem. (MetaCat struct u bij forgetfree)
  MetaAdjunction strict (λ_ ⇒ True) HomSet (λX ⇒ (lam id X)) (λX Y Z f g ⇒ (lam comp X f
  g)) struct u bij Hom struct u struct id struct comp MetaCat struct u bij free0
  MetaCat struct u bij free1 (λX ⇒ X 0) (λX Y f ⇒ f) MetaCat struct u forgetfree eta
  MetaCat struct u bij forgetfree eps
```

Fig. 11. Adjunction Theorem for Bijections in the Megalodon Wiki

of the corresponding proposition was published on the blockchain in June 2024. The witnesses in the proof are as follows:

- $\mathcal{F}_0\ X$ is the structure with carrier $\mathbb{Z} \times X$ (where $\mathbb{Z}$ is the set of integers) and the (bijective) unary function taking $u \in \mathbb{Z} \times X$ to $(u_0 + 1, u_1)$.
- $\mathcal{F}_1\ X\ Y\ f$ is the morphism taking $u \in \mathbb{Z} \times X$ to $(u_0, f(u_1)) \in \mathbb{Z} \times Y$.
- $\eta\ X$ is the function from X to $\mathbb{Z} \times X$ taking x to $(0, x)$.
- $\varepsilon\ (X, f)$ is the function from $\mathbb{Z} \times X$ to X taking u to $f^{u_0}(u_1)$. (Note that if $u_0 < 0$, this means iterating the inverse of the bijection f.)

There are definitions corresponding to these choices of $\mathcal{F}_0$, η and ε in the Megalodon Wiki, and are shown here in Figure 10. The main proof is of a theorem that checks these choices indeed give an adjunction. The proof is long and detailed, so we only show the statement in Figure 11. The actual bounty was on the statement that such an adjunction exists. Since all the details were checked in the previous theorem, we can show the existential theorem with its proof in Figure 12.

The most recent of the 33 propositions to be disproven takes $\mathcal{D}$ to be a category with monoids as objects. Here "disproven" means the negation of the proposition was proven. This should be surprising as it is clear that given a set X one can create a monoid freely generated by X, and this should provide the desired left adjoint. However, the category in question was defined to have semigroup homomorphisms as arrows, and not every semigroup homomorphism (preserving the operation) also preserves the identity element. The definition is arguably a bug in the definition of the category of monoids. The bounty presumably encouraged someone to look closely enough at the definition to find and exploit the bug to prove the negation of the proposition. Using the explorer to examine the proof of the surprising result, others can discover the same bug. The proof follows from the fact that there is no initial object in the category of monoids and semigroup

```
Proposition. (MetaCat struct u bij left adjoint forgetful)
  ∃F0 : set → set, ∃F1 : set → set → set → set, ∃eta eps : set → set, MetaAdjunction strict (λ_ ⇒ True) HomSet
  (λX ⇒ (lam id X)) (λX Y Z f g ⇒ (lam comp X f g)) struct u bij Hom struct u struct id struct comp F0 F1 (λX ⇒
  X 0) (λX Y f ⇒ f) eta eps
In Proofgold the corresponding term root is 062a21... and proposition id is a69df3...
  Proof:
  Set F0 to be the term λX ⇒ pack u (int × X) (λu ⇒ (u 0 + 1,u 1)) of type set → set.
  Set F1 to be the term λX Y h ⇒ λu ∈ int × X ⇒ (u 0,h (u 1)) of type set → set → set → set.
  Set eta to be the term λX ⇒ λx ∈ X ⇒ (0,x) of type set → set.
  Set epsPhi to be the term λX h ⇒ λu ∈ int × X ⇒ if u 0 ≤ 0 then omega iterate (- (u 0)) (inv X h) (u 1)
  else omega iterate (u 0) h (u 1) of type set → (set → set) → set.
  Set eps to be the term λA ⇒ unpack u i A epsPhi of type set → set.
  We use F0 to witness the existential quantifier.
  We use F1 to witness the existential quantifier.
  We use eta to witness the existential quantifier.
  We use eps to witness the existential quantifier.
  An exact proof term for the current goal is MetaCat struct u bij forgetfree.
  ∎
```

Fig. 12. Existential Adjunction Theorem for Bijections in the Megalodon Wiki

```
Proposition. (MetaCat struct b monoid initial neg)
  ¬ ∃Y : set, ∃uniqa : set → set, initial p struct b monoid Hom struct b struct id
  struct comp Y uniqa
```

Fig. 13. There is no Initial Monoid in the Megalodon Wiki

homomorphisms (and an alleged left adjoint would send the initial object in the category of sets to an initial monoid). The proof that there is no initial monoid (with semigroup homomorphisms) essentially follows from the fact that the two constant functions from a monoid to the multiplicative monoid $\{0,1\}$ are both (always) semigroup homomorphisms, thus guaranteeing an alleged initial monoid would not have a unique morphism to $\{0,1\}$.

In a document in the Megalodon Wiki, the statement of the theorem that there is no initial monoid (with semigroup homomorphisms) is shown in Figure 13. The proof (using the multiplicative monoid on $\{0,1\}$) is also in the same document, but we omit it here as it is long and detailed.[4] The negation of the adjunction conjecture is then proven as a consequence. Its statement and proof in the document in the Megalodon Wiki are shown in Figure 14. The proof begins by assuming there exists an adjunction, i.e., $\exists F_0 : \iota\iota. \cdots$. In general, a proposition $\exists x : \alpha.\varphi$ is considered the same as $\forall q : o.(\forall x : \alpha.\varphi \to q) \to q$. This is why the existential assumption can be "applied" to the current goal (of proving $\bot$), followed by a "let" (essentially giving a fresh name x for the object) and an "assume" (giving the property φ of the object x). This is repeated four times to obtain F_0, F_1, η and ε. There is a previous (unshown) theorem that there is an initial object in the category of sets. (It is witnessed by the empty set, but this is irrelevant here.) We apply that previous theorem to obtain an initial set *Init*

[4] Note that Hom_struct_b : $\iota\iota o$ is defined so that Hom_struct_b A B h holds when h is a function from the carrier of A to the carrier of B preserving the binary operation. A correct definition of the category of monoids would extend the signature to explicitly include the identity element in addition the binary operation. This would presumably have a name like Hom_struct_b_e.

```
Proposition. (MetaCat struct b monoid left adjoint forgetful neg)
  ¬ ∃F0 : set → set, ∃F1 : set → set → set → set, ∃eta eps : set → set, MetaAdjunction strict (λ_ ⇒ True)
  HomSet (λX ⇒ (lam id X)) (λX Y Z f g ⇒ (lam comp X f g)) struct b monoid Hom struct b struct id struct comp
  F0 F1 (λX ⇒ X 0) (λX Y f ⇒ f) eta eps

In Proofgold the corresponding term root is cbb885... and proposition id is 62ee62...

  Proof:
  Assume H. Apply H to the current goal.
  Let F0 be given. Assume H. Apply H to the current goal.
  Let F1 be given. Assume H. Apply H to the current goal.
  Let eta be given. Assume H. Apply H to the current goal.
  Let eps be given.
  Assume H1: MetaAdjunction strict (λ_ ⇒ True) HomSet (λX ⇒ (lam id X)) (λX Y Z f g ⇒ (lam comp X f g))
  struct b monoid Hom struct b struct id struct comp F0 F1 (λX ⇒ X 0) (λX Y f ⇒ f) eta eps.
  Apply MetaCatSet initial to the current goal.
  Let Init be given.
  Assume H.
  Apply H to the current goal.
  Let uniq be given.
  Assume H2: initial p (λ_ ⇒ True) HomSet (λX ⇒ (λx ∈ X ⇒ x)) (λX Y Z f g ⇒ (λx ∈ X ⇒ f (g x))) Init uniq.
  Apply MetaCat struct b monoid initial neg to the current goal.
  We use F0 Init to witness the existential quantifier.
  An exact proof term for the current goal is LeftAdjointsPreserveInitial (λ_ ⇒ True) HomSet (λX ⇒ (λx ∈ X ⇒
  x)) (λX Y Z f g ⇒ (λx ∈ X ⇒ f (g x))) struct b monoid Hom struct b struct id struct comp F0 F1 (λX ⇒ X 0)
  (λX Y f ⇒ f) eta eps H1 Init uniq H2.
  ∎
```

Fig. 14. There is no Left Adjoint to the Forgetful Functor for Monoids in the Megalodon Wiki

and a function *uniq* that takes each set X to the unique function from $Init$ to X. Our goal is to prove $\bot$. We then apply the theorem from Figure 13 which leaves the subgoal of proving there is an initial monoid. The monoid $F_0\ Init$ is used to witness that there is an initial monoid, and this is justified by a previous (unshown) theorem that ensures left adjoints preserve initial objects.

An example of a proposition with an open bounty is given by taking $\mathcal{D}$ to be the category of groups.[5] In this case, the proposition should be provable by taking $\mathcal{F}_0\ X$ to be the free group generated by X, but no one has yet done this construction and proven the relevant theorem.

6 Related Work

Most proof assistants today are accompanied by tools for exploring their formal libraries via web interfaces. The Mizar Mathematical Library (MML) [4], one of the oldest central repositories of formalized mathematics, in addition to its journal version, has been accessible through HTML renderings and search tools [15,22]. Isabelle's Archive of Formal Proofs (AFP) [7] provides a curated collection of formal developments, rendered online using Isabelle's document preparation system. The Coq proof assistant is supported by an online web interface that allows interactive Coq sessions entirely within the web [12]. Its extension to ProofWeb offers a web interface for multiple proof assistants, aiming to lower the barrier to entry for formal verification [18]. The Lean community has developed a variety

[5] The bounty can currently be seen on the explorer at the link **https://formalweb3.uibk.ac.at/pgbce/q.php?b=TMQvwY1m9iU5rev4qXQjWWGYTZDHwCseEMv.**

of web tools, including the ProofWidgets library [20], with the paper discussing a lot of related work concerning user interfaces for theorem proving.

Beyond these assistant-specific interfaces, more advanced and general-purpose systems have been developed to support exploration, integration, and sharing of formal mathematical knowledge. The `MathHub/MMT` framework provides a logic-independent framework for querying across distributed libraries [5]. The Formal Abstracts aims to explore structured summaries of theorems that link informal and formal mathematics. Its web access to both metadata and formal developments[6] has been impactful, but it appears to be currently inactive.

The Tezos [14] blockchain includes a smart contract programming language that has been designed to make formal verification easier, which means that off-chain formal methods can be used to verify properties of programs/scripts. This supports formal methods, albeit offline [6]. Several blockchain explorers exist for Tezos, but they focus on the usual smart contract information and do not include verification content. Qeditas was an early attempt to combine formalized mathematics with blockchain technology, but the project is no longer maintained; Proofgold builds on its ideas, refining and extending them into a working system.

There have been a number of formalizations of category theory done in type-theoretic proof assistants; examples include UniMath [2] in Coq, the Lean 3 library [1], Agda-Category [23]; several developments in Isabelle/HOL [21] and Isabelle/HOLZF and even Mizar [11]. While type-theoretic systems allow concise and expressive formulations, they often provide less automation; in contrast, Isabelle/HOL offers strong automation but can make some constructions more cumbersome due to the lack of dependent types, and Mizar emphasizes human readability but it has limited expressiveness for higher-category theory.

7 Conclusion

We created a web-based blockchain explorer for Proofgold that allows users to interact with mathematical knowledge contained there. We have demonstrated the utility of the system by presenting several conjectures and their proofs or refutations using the system. Future work includes improving support for faster collaboration, further improvements to the visualization of the formal mathematics, as well as better search [3].

Acknowledgements The results were supported by the Czech Ministry of Education, Youth and Sports within the dedicated program ERC CZ under the project POSTMAN no. LL1902, the ERC PoC grant *FormalWeb3* no. 101156734, Amazon Research Award, and the Czech Science Foundation grant no. 25-17929X.

References

1. The Lean mathematical library. CoRR **abs/1910.09336** (2019), `http://arxiv.org/abs/1910.09336`

[6] `https://formalabstracts.github.io/`

2. Ahrens, B., Matthes, R., Mörtberg, A.: From signatures to monads in UniMath. J. Autom. Reason. **63**(2), 285–318 (2019). https://doi.org/10.1007/S10817-018-9474-4, https://doi.org/10.1007/s10817-018-9474-4
3. Asperti, A., Guidi, F., Coen, C.S., Tassi, E., Zacchiroli, S.: A content based mathematical search engine: Whelp. In: Filliâtre, J., Paulin-Mohring, C., Werner, B. (eds.) Types for Proofs and Programs, International Workshop, TYPES 2004, Jouy-en-Josas, France, December 15-18, 2004, Revised Selected Papers. Lecture Notes in Computer Science, vol. 3839, pp. 17–32. Springer (2004). https://doi.org/10.1007/11617990_2, https://doi.org/10.1007/11617990_2
4. Bancerek, G., Byliński, C., Grabowski, A., Korniłowicz, A., Matuszewski, R., Naumowicz, A., Pąk, K.: The role of the Mizar mathematical library for interactive proof development in Mizar. J. Autom. Reason. **61**(1-4), 9–32 (2018). https://doi.org/10.1007/S10817-017-9440-6, https://doi.org/10.1007/s10817-017-9440-6
5. Bercic, K., Kohlhase, M., Rabe, F.: Towards a unified mathematical data infrastructure: Database and interface generation. In: Kaliszyk, C., Brady, E.C., Kohlhase, A., Coen, C.S. (eds.) Intelligent Computer Mathematics - 12th International Conference, CICM 2019, Prague, Czech Republic, July 8-12, 2019, Proceedings. Lecture Notes in Computer Science, vol. 11617, pp. 28–43. Springer (2019). https://doi.org/10.1007/978-3-030-23250-4_3, https://doi.org/10.1007/978-3-030-23250-4_3
6. Bhargavan, K., Delignat-Lavaud, A., Fournet, C., Gollamudi, A., Gonthier, G., Kobeissi, N., Kulatova, N., Rastogi, A., Sibut-Pinote, T., Swamy, N., Zanella-Béguelin, S.: Formal verification of smart contracts: Short paper. In: Murray, T.C., Stefan, D. (eds.) Proceedings of the 2016 ACM Workshop on Programming Languages and Analysis for Security, PLAS@CCS 2016, Vienna, Austria, October 24, 2016. pp. 91–96. ACM (2016). https://doi.org/10.1145/2993600.2993611, https://doi.org/10.1145/2993600.2993611
7. Blanchette, J.C., Haslbeck, M.W., Matichuk, D., Nipkow, T.: Mining the archive of formal proofs. In: Kerber, M., Carette, J., Kaliszyk, C., Rabe, F., Sorge, V. (eds.) Intelligent Computer Mathematics - International Conference, CICM 2015, Washington, DC, USA, July 13-17, 2015, Proceedings. Lecture Notes in Computer Science, vol. 9150, pp. 3–17. Springer (2015). https://doi.org/10.1007/978-3-319-20615-8_1, https://doi.org/10.1007/978-3-319-20615-8_1
8. Brown, C.E., Kaliszyk, C., Gauthier, T., Urban, J.: Proofgold: Blockchain for formal methods. In: Dargaye, Z., Schneidewind, C. (eds.) 4th International Workshop on Formal Methods for Blockchains, FMBC@CAV 2022, August 11, 2022, Haifa, Israel. OASIcs, vol. 105, pp. 4:1–4:15. Schloss Dagstuhl - Leibniz-Zentrum für Informatik (2022). https://doi.org/10.4230/OASICS.FMBC.2022.4, https://doi.org/10.4230/OASIcs.FMBC.2022.4
9. Brown, C.E., Pąk, K.: A tale of two set theories. In: Kaliszyk, C., Brady, E.C., Kohlhase, A., Coen, C.S. (eds.) Intelligent Computer Mathematics - 12th International Conference, CICM 2019, Prague, Czech Republic, July 8-12, 2019, Proceedings. Lecture Notes in Computer Science, vol. 11617, pp. 44–60. Springer (2019). https://doi.org/10.1007/978-3-030-23250-4_4, https://doi.org/10.1007/978-3-030-23250-4_4
10. Buzzard, K., Commelin, J., Massot, P.: Formalising perfectoid spaces. In: Blanchette, J., Hritcu, C. (eds.) Proceedings of the 9th ACM SIGPLAN International Conference on Certified Programs and Proofs, CPP 2020, New Orleans,

LA, USA, January 20-21, 2020. pp. 299–312. ACM (2020). https://doi.org/10.1145/3372885.3373830, https://doi.org/10.1145/3372885.3373830
11. Byliński, C.: Introduction to categories and functors. Formalized Mathematics **1**(**2**), 409–420 (1990), http://fm.mizar.org/1990-1/pdf1-2/cat_1.pdf
12. Corbineau, P., Kaliszyk, C.: Cooperative repositories for formal proofs. In: Kauers, M., Kerber, M., Miner, R., Windsteiger, W. (eds.) Towards Mechanized Mathematical Assistants, 14th Symposium, Calculemus 2007, 6th International Conference, MKM 2007, Hagenberg, Austria, June 27-30, 2007, Proceedings. Lecture Notes in Computer Science, vol. 4573, pp. 221–234. Springer (2007). https://doi.org/10.1007/978-3-540-73086-6_19, https://doi.org/10.1007/978-3-540-73086-6_19
13. Desharnais, M., Tóth, B., Waldmann, U., Blanchette, J., Tourret, S.: A modular formalization of superposition in Isabelle/HOL. In: Bertot, Y., Kutsia, T., Norrish, M. (eds.) 15th International Conference on Interactive Theorem Proving, ITP 2024, September 9-14, 2024, Tbilisi, Georgia. LIPIcs, vol. 309, pp. 12:1–12:20. Schloss Dagstuhl - Leibniz-Zentrum für Informatik (2024). https://doi.org/10.4230/LIPICS.ITP.2024.12, https://doi.org/10.4230/LIPIcs.ITP.2024.12
14. Doan, T.T.H., Thiemann, P.: A formal verification framework for tezos smart contracts based on symbolic execution. In: Kiselyov, O. (ed.) Programming Languages and Systems - 22nd Asian Symposium, APLAS 2024, Kyoto, Japan, October 22-24, 2024, Proceedings. Lecture Notes in Computer Science, vol. 15194, pp. 305–324. Springer (2024). https://doi.org/10.1007/978-981-97-8943-6_15, https://doi.org/10.1007/978-981-97-8943-6_15
15. Furushima, H., Yamamichi, D., Shigenaka, S., Nakasho, K., Wasaki, K.: An integrated web platform for the Mizar mathematical library. In: Buzzard, K., Kutsia, T. (eds.) Intelligent Computer Mathematics - 15th International Conference, CICM 2022, Tbilisi, Georgia, September 19-23, 2022, Proceedings. Lecture Notes in Computer Science, vol. 13467, pp. 141–146. Springer (2022). https://doi.org/10.1007/978-3-031-16681-5_9, https://doi.org/10.1007/978-3-031-16681-5_9
16. Gonthier, G., Asperti, A., Avigad, J., Bertot, Y., Cohen, C., Garillot, F., Roux, S.L., Mahboubi, A., O'Connor, R., Biha, S.O., Pasca, I., Rideau, L., Solovyev, A., Tassi, E., Théry, L.: A machine-checked proof of the odd order theorem. In: Blazy, S., Paulin-Mohring, C., Pichardie, D. (eds.) Interactive Theorem Proving - 4th International Conference, ITP 2013, Rennes, France, July 22-26, 2013. Proceedings. Lecture Notes in Computer Science, vol. 7998, pp. 163–179. Springer (2013). https://doi.org/10.1007/978-3-642-39634-2_14, https://doi.org/10.1007/978-3-642-39634-2_14
17. Hales, T., Adams, M., Bauer, G., Dang, T.D., Harrison, J., Hoang, L.T., Kaliszyk, C., Magron, V., Mclaughlin, S., Nguyen, T.T., Nguyen, Q.T., Nipkow, T., Obua, S., Pleso, J., Rute, J., Solovyev, A., Ta, T.H.A., Tran, N.T., Trieu, T.D., Urban, J., Vu, K., Zumkeller, R.: A formal proof of the Kepler conjecture. Forum of Mathematics, Pi **5** (2017). https://doi.org/10.1017/fmp.2017.1
18. Hendriks, M., Kaliszyk, C., van Raamsdonk, F., Wiedijk, F.: Teaching logic using a state-of-the-art proof assistant. Acta Didactica Napocensia **3**(2), 35–48 (June 2010)
19. Lambek, J., Scott, P.: Introduction to higher order categorical logic. Cambridge University Press, Cambridge, UK (1986)
20. Nawrocki, W., Ayers, E.W., Ebner, G.: An extensible user interface for Lean 4. In: Naumowicz, A., Thiemann, R. (eds.) 14th International Conference on Interactive Theorem Proving, ITP 2023, July 31 to August 4, 2023, Białystok,

Poland. LIPIcs, vol. 268, pp. 24:1–24:20. Schloss Dagstuhl - Leibniz-Zentrum für Informatik (2023). https://doi.org/10.4230/LIPICS.ITP.2023.24, https://doi.org/10.4230/LIPIcs.ITP.2023.24
21. Stark, E.W.: Category theory with adjunctions and limits. Arch. Formal Proofs **2016** (2016), https://www.isa-afp.org/entries/Category3.shtml
22. Tomaszuk, D., Szeremeta, Ł., Korniłowicz, A.: MMLKG: Knowledge graph for mathematical definitions, statements and proofs. Sci Data **10**(791) (2023), https://doi.org/10.1038/s41597-023-02681-3
23. Vezzosi, A., Mörtberg, A., Abel, A.: Cubical Agda: a dependently typed programming language with univalence and higher inductive types. Proc. ACM Program. Lang. **3**(ICFP), 87:1–87:29 (2019). https://doi.org/10.1145/3341691, https://doi.org/10.1145/3341691
24. Wiedijk, F.: Introduction. In: Wiedijk, F. (ed.) The Seventeen Provers of the World, Foreword by Dana S. Scott, Lecture Notes in Computer Science, vol. 3600, pp. 1–9. Springer (2006). https://doi.org/10.1007/11542384_1, https://doi.org/10.1007/11542384_1

Supporting Maintenance of Formal Mathematics with Similarity Search

Fabian Huch(✉)

Technische Universität München, Munich, Germany
huch@in.tum.de

Abstract. The effort required for maintaining large libraries of formal mathematics is quite substantial. In this work, we exploit structural similarity to alleviate the burden of maintenance, investigating two main problems: First, we present a general framework for detecting duplicates in large libraries of formal mathematics, combining surface-level syntax, document markup, and the underlying formulae. For scalability, we generate potentially matching candidates with a discriminator-based approach. On Isabelle/HOL, our method maintains perfect precision up to a similarity threshold of 0.95. Secondly, we address the issue of out-of-place auxiliary lemmas that are frequently created during development of in-depth formalizations. We propose a community detection approach on the underlying dependency graph of formal entities, which finds co-located lemmas that have similar link patterns. For a dataset of lemmas moved during Isabelle development, the correct location is in the top 6 neighborhoods suggested by our approach on average (median).

Keywords: Maintenance · Computer math systems · Formal mathematics · Theorem provers · Structural similarity · Semantic similarity · Duplicate detection · Clone detection · Community detection.

1 Introduction

Building libraries of (flexi-formal) mathematics is a challenging task. But beyond the initial development, such libraries incur maintenance effort, which varies with the degree of formality. In interactive theorem proving (ITP), maintenance activities can make up a significant portion of development time, especially for large-scale mathematical libraries.

Problem. At the moment, there is very little mechanized tooling to support maintenance in theorem provers or other computer math systems. In contrast, practitioners of widely-used programming languages have created intricate techniques to support maintenance, such as clone detectors, static code analysis, tools for refactoring (semantics-preserving source transformation), etc.

Solution. This is not a fundamental limitation of theorem provers. On the contrary: Exploiting the rich structure of formal documents can allow solving maintenance problems more effectively, since it can provide grounding for many techniques. For example, a *semantic similarity* measure for two formulae can be

V. de Paiva and P. Koepke (Eds.): CICM 2025, LNAI 16136, pp. 91–109, 2026.
https://doi.org/10.1007/978-3-032-07021-0_6

well-defined via specificity of their generalization. Despite this, concrete approaches and implementations are largely missing from current practice.

Contribution. To narrow this gap, we utilize *similarity search* to approach two different—yet related—maintenance problems that occur in large libraries of formal mathematics. Both have not yet been properly addressed in this context:

1. Large-scale duplicate detection in formalizations. Duplicates (also called *clones*) cause maintenance overhead since changes have to be made in multiple places, and (if the duplicates are not known) the same work might be repeated. Moreover, they can be a source of confusion when re-using existing material, and blow up library size and build times unnecessarily. Based on approaches from software engineering, we develop a generic framework to detect duplicates in formal mathematics, utilizing surface-level syntax, document markup, and formulae from the underlying logical system.
2. Generating recommendations where to put out-of-place auxiliary lemmas. By analyzing dependency graph structure, we aim to find communities of lemmas that have similar link-patterns and are closely located to each other: This captures how lemmas are usually grouped together. To that end, we devise a community detection algorithm tailored to the problem at hand, and discuss how it can be implemented efficiently. To evaluate its effectiveness, we extract a small dataset with actual refactorings from the version history, where out-of-place lemmas were moved to their appropriate spot.

While our approaches can be applied to a wide range of computer math systems, we demonstrate them on the Isabelle Archive of Formal Proofs (AFP), which is the largest central body of formalized mathematics at the time of writing (by lines of code, number of definitions, and proven theorems). Hence, it is well suited for judging effectiveness of the methodology.

Availability. Source code and data (with instructions) are available in the supplementary material accompanying this work[1]: The approaches discussed here are implemented as add-on components for Isabelle-2025, via command-line tool (clone detection) and interactive command (location recommendations). Their evaluation was performed on the initial release for AFP-2025.

2 Related Work on Maintaining Formal Mathematics

Maintenance of (flexi-)formal mathematics is an underrepresented topic given the wealth of present logical systems and formalizations. In the last decade, there have been a number of efforts which address specific maintenance aspects for ITPs. However, some areas have received no attention at all, and many of the approaches discussed in the following lack practical and up-to-date implementations.

In their report on a large-scale system verification project in Isabelle, Alkassar et al. report on several maintenance activities [2], including the detection of clones

[1] Available at doi:10.5281/zenodo.16645030.

with the generic detector ConQAT[2] (which produced many false positives), by searching for duplicated lemmas, and by matching common conclusions within proofs: For that, the system checks whether the conclusion of a top-level statement can already be derived from local assumptions and an existing fact. They also mention tooling to find unused theorems and to locate the earliest possible position for a given theorem (based on other theorems used in its proof). Building on that, Bourke et al. introduce tooling to automatically relocate lemmas to another position (while keeping theories intact) in their report dedicated to the challenges of managing large-scale verification efforts [6]. Vinan and Hupel later extended the clone detection approach of Alkassar et al., generating tokens from Isabelle markup and passing those to ConQAT [33]. Ghanbari recently presented a tool to find all α-equivalent subgoals in Coq/Rocq formalizations [18].

To help perform common maintenance tasks, Whiteside et al. and Dietrich et al. built the first dedicated refactoring framework for formal proofs [36,12], where—building on a graph model—refactorings could be defined in a language-agnostic way[3]. However, the approach was not adopted anywhere, and currently very few ITPs provide refactoring support apart from built-in editor functionality (e.g., to rename local variables): There are some prototypes (e.g., for Agda [37]), and HOL Light provides a dedicated tool to refactor proof scripts [1]. Recent work by Talia Ringer instead focuses on *proof repair* [28]: This would allow practitioners to perform refactorings in isolation such that they break existing proofs, e.g. by adding a constructor to a datatype but not adapting case distinctions. To repair proofs, one then attempts to derive a formal specification of the change with specialized algorithms for certain fragments, such that the background theory can be adapted automatically [30]: For instance, by deriving type equivalences, automatically re-writing proof terms modulo that equivalence, and synthesizing appropriate source code for the adapted theory [29]. Most of this research has been carried out in Coq/Rocq, as it allows direct manipulation of explicit proof terms. However, LCF-style systems don't rely on proof terms, and trustworthy specification mechanisms that reduce to conservative extensions, found e.g. in the HOL family, create large gaps between syntax and logical content. Hence, this methodology is not quite applicable to these systems.

In software development, *linters* are used to analyze source code for potential problems (anti-patterns); van Doorn et al. introduced the first linter for a theorem prover, to address maintenance problems in mathlib [13]. Their interactive tool can detect problems arising from incorrect use of Lean's typeclasses (e.g., defining arguments in a way that the resolution mechanism won't find an instance), problematic simplification rules (that can either not be applied at all or infinitely often), missing documentation, and unused assumptions in theorem statements. Subsequently, a linter has also been implemented for Isabelle/Isar [24], which in previous work we have found to be strongly connected to perceived quality, and linked to maintenance effort (albeit quite weakly) [21]. In contrast, although there

[2] No longer available, succeeded by Teamscale.

[3] Requiring an abstract syntax tree for the target language, which is still somewhat restrictive (e.g., there is none for Isabelle/Isar).

are some *quality metrics* for formalizations based on object-oriented principles [3] and graph metrics [20], they have not been useful for pinpointing maintenance problems so far.

3 Detecting Duplicates in Formal Mathematics

Duplicate detection has been widely studied in computer science: In their recent systematic literature review on code similarity and clone detection, Zakeri-Nasrabadi et al. found over 10 000 initial articles [38], but over 97 % of their primary studies were concerned with imperative languages. For formal mathematics, there are very few specialized clone detection approaches (as discussed in Section 2), but some general techniques could be applied in certain scenarios: By utilizing capable proof search engines (e.g., `sledgehammer`), one can easily check whether a similar variant of a given goal has already been proven somewhere in the background theory. Naturally, this is not sufficient in the presence of duplicated definitions or types, and does not help in finding duplicated non-theorem entities such as type definitions. If sufficiently large parts of some structure have been duplicated, *library alignment* approaches [16,17,25] could be applied to the problem by aligning the formal library with itself.

However, in general, a document-oriented approach is desirable since much of the relevant information (narrative or structural) is present in the source text but not in the formalisms. For instance, many formal entities are automatically generated so duplicates are not undesirable per se, especially for systems with elaborate constructions to embed high-level concepts into simple logics. Existing clone detection approaches for functional programming languages [7,10] are not quite applicable either: They aim to find cloned sub-structures of large programs, since those necessitate that any changes to the original (e.g., to rectify defects) be applied across multiple locations. In contrast, we aim to find entire structures that are similar, but which are small compared to programs—for instance, definitions that are stated multiple times but slightly differently.

Hence, instead of matching subtrees of abstract syntax, we identify pairs of *token spans* that are similar to each other (i.e., perform a *self-join*, in database terminology). To that end, we extend the work by Wang et al. on fuzzy similarity joins [35] to multiple syntactic classes, which we derive from source text and document markup. Their approach uses a signature scheme for an index-based discriminator. Since computing similarities is quite costly, we additionally utilize multiple filtering steps developed in a preliminary prototype [19]. We also incorporate formulae of the underlying logical system (i.e., Isabelle/Pure), which we compare via similarity metric on their λ-term representation. Of the four clone types commonly distinguished in the literature, this approach can detect Type I (exact duplicates up to formatting and comments), Type II (modulo renaming), and Type III (with slight changes). The framework could also allow detecting some Type IV clones (semantic duplicates) given an appropriate semantic similarity metric for formulae, but this is subject to future research.

3.1 Generic Similarity Detection Framework

In the following, we describe the similarity detection framework abstractly, with examples from our concrete instantiation for Isabelle. We assume that we are given a collection of mathematical documents as a sequence of (command) *spans* $\mathbb{T}_1, \ldots, \mathbb{T}_t$ that represent definitions, proofs, informal descriptions, etc. We also assume that all elements (spans, tokens, formulae) are unique, for instance through their document position.

Definition 1 (Token span). *A* token span $\mathbb{T}_i$ *is a set of* tokens $t \in \mathbb{T}_i$*, corresponding to its formal source and markup. Similarly, with* $\mathbb{F}_i$ *we denote the set of* formulae $f \in \mathbb{F}_i$ *that are generated by* $\mathbb{T}_i$*.*

Note that we disregard the order of tokens within a span, since mathematical text is very flexible: Parts of a definition, or steps of the same proof, can be written down in many different orders.

Example 1. On our implementation, the Isabelle/HOL source code

```
prop <A ∧ B>
```

would correspond to the tokens `Command(thy_decl,prop)`, `Variable(A :: bool)`, `Constant(HOL.conj)`, `Variable(B :: bool)`, and the single λ-term $(\wedge)\ A\ B$[4].

Definition 2 (Syntactic class, Relevance, Similarity). *Every token* t_k *belongs to exactly one* syntactic class C_{t_k} *with associated* relevance $\mathcal{R}(C_{t_k}) \in \mathbb{Q}_+$ *and* similarity function $\mathcal{S}_C(t_k, t_l) \in [0, 1]$ *to compare it with any token* t_l*, such that tokens from different classes are dissimilar:*

$$C_{t_k} \neq C_{t_l} \implies \mathcal{S}_C(t_k, t_l) = 0 \tag{1}$$

Moreover, we require a single similarity function $\mathcal{S}_f$ *to compare any two formulae* f_m *and* f_n*, such that* $\mathcal{S}_f(f_m, f_n) \in [0, 1]$*.*

Example 1 (continued). The token `Variable(A :: bool)` from our example belongs to the class `Variables`(T), where T is a type signature that consists of the set of type constructor names occurring in the variable's type, i.e., here T = {`bool`}. Since we consider all variables equally relevant regardless of type, we define $\forall \mathrm{T}.\, \mathcal{R}(\texttt{Variables}(\mathrm{T})) := 0.4$ (value chosen arbitrarily). For the similarity of two variables, we take into account whether they have the same type signature, and compare the variable names using *edit* distance (i.e., the minimal number of character operations to transform one string into the other):

$$\mathcal{S}_{\texttt{Variables}}(x_1 :: \tau_1, x_2 :: \tau_2) := \begin{cases} \max\left(0.5, \frac{\mathrm{edit}(x_1,x_2)}{\max(|x_1|,|x_2|)}\right) & \text{if } \tau_1 = \tau_2 \\ \max\left(0.2, \min\left(0.7, \frac{\mathrm{edit}(x_1,x_2)}{\max(|x_1|,|x_2|)}\right)\right) & \text{otherwise} \end{cases} \tag{2}$$

[4] However, since a mere proposition is not relevant in the theory, this λ-term would not actually be reported by the system.

In Section 3.2, we discuss the choice of concrete numerical values, all other syntactic classes for Isabelle, and their associated similarity functions; the similarity function for Isabelle formulae is discussed in Section 3.3.

Since we disregard the order of tokens within a span, we use a max-weight matching of the token sets to determine similarity:

Definition 3 (Max-weight matching). *For two disjoint sets A and B, a* matching *$m \subseteq A \times B$ is a subset of pairs such that each element of A and B appears in at most one pair in m. Further let $M(A,B)$ denote the set of all matchings of A and B. Given a weighting function $w : A \times B \mapsto \mathbb{R}$, the* max-weight *matching m_w^* is then defined as*

$$m_w^*(A,B) := \underset{m \in M(A,B)}{\arg\max} \sum_{(a,b)\in m} w(a,b) \tag{3}$$

Max-weight matchings can be computed via primal-dual methods, e.g. the Hungarian algorithm [14]. For the similarity of two spans, we use the dice coefficient:

Definition 4 (Span similarity). *With the notion of* weighted similarity

$$\mathcal{S}_{\mathcal{R}_C}(t_l, t_k) := \mathcal{R}(C_{t_k}) \cdot \mathcal{S}_C(t_k, t_l) \tag{4}$$

we define similarity for tokens and formulae via max-weight matching, using weighted similarity as weighting function for the matching:

$$\mathcal{S}_{\mathbb{T}}(i,j) := \frac{2 \cdot \sum_{(t_k,t_l)\in m^*_{\mathcal{S}_{\mathcal{R}_C}}(\mathbb{T}_i,\mathbb{T}_j)} \mathcal{S}_{\mathcal{R}_C}(t_k,t_l)}{\sum_{t_k\in\mathbb{T}_i} \mathcal{R}(C_{t_k}) + \sum_{t_l\in\mathbb{T}_j} \mathcal{R}(C_{t_l})} \tag{5}$$

$$\mathcal{S}_{\mathbb{F}}(i,j) := \frac{2 \cdot \sum_{(f_m,f_n)\in m^*_{\mathcal{S}_f}(\mathbb{F}_i,\mathbb{F}_j)} \mathcal{S}_f(f_m,f_n)}{|\mathbb{F}_i| + |\mathbb{F}_j|} \tag{6}$$

Finally, as span similarity *we set $\mathcal{S}(i,j) := \mathcal{S}_{\mathbb{T}}(i,j) \cdot \mathcal{S}_{\mathbb{F}}(i,j)$, and consider spans similar only if $\mathcal{S}(i,j) \geq \delta$ for a chosen threshold $\delta \in [0,1]$.*

For large libraries such as the AFP, comparing (or even enumerating) all pairs is computationally infeasible. Hence, we employ a discriminator approach to avoid comparing pairs that can not reach the chosen similarity threshold δ. We use an *inverted index* so we can retrieve all relevant candidates: In principle, this could be any data structure with fast *lookup* function that maps from syntactic class C to all spans $\mathbb{T}_i$ where $\exists t_k \in \mathbb{T}_i.\, C_{t_k} = C$. To retrieve all candidates for pairing with span $\mathbb{T}_i$, one has to perform the lookup for all its classes, i.e. compute $\bigcup_{t_k\in\mathbb{T}_i} \text{lookup}(C_{t_k})$. An important observation is that we don't actually need to index a span by *all* of its classes: Intuitively, if many tokens match, one can still retrieve all candidates if the lookup only works sometimes. Formally:

Proposition 1. *Let $\mathbb{T}'_i \subseteq \mathbb{T}_i$ denote the tokens of $\mathbb{T}_i$ that are indexed, i.e. where $\forall t_k \in \mathbb{T}'_i.\, \mathbb{T}_i \in lookup(C_{t_k})$. Then for the chosen threshold δ, the lookup yields all relevant candidates if*

$$\forall \mathbb{T}_j.\, \mathcal{S}_{\mathbb{T}}(i,j) \geq \delta \implies \bigcup_{t_{k'} \in \mathbb{T}'_i} C_{t_{k'}} \cap \bigcup_{t_l \in \mathbb{T}_j} C_{t_l} \neq \emptyset \tag{7}$$

Thus, indexing a fraction of more than $1-\delta$ of the total relevance is sufficient:

Theorem 1. *For Proposition 1 to hold, it suffices to choose $\mathbb{T}'_i$ such that*

$$\sum_{t_{k'} \in \mathbb{T}'_i} \mathcal{R}(C_{t_{k'}}) > (1-\delta) \cdot \sum_{t_k \in \mathbb{T}_i} \mathcal{R}(C_{t_k}) \tag{8}$$

Proof. Assume that $\bigcup_{t_{k'} \in \mathbb{T}'_i} C_{t_{k'}} \cap \bigcup_{t_l \in \mathbb{T}_j} C_{t_l} = \emptyset$. Then only tokens from $\mathbb{T}_i \setminus \mathbb{T}'_i$ might match with tokens in $\mathbb{T}_j$, so as an upper bound for $\mathcal{S}_{\mathbb{T}}$ we get:

$$\mathcal{S}_{\mathbb{T}}(i,j) \leq \frac{\sum_{t_k \in \mathbb{T}_i} \mathcal{R}(C_{t_k}) - \sum_{t_{k'} \in \mathbb{T}'_i} \mathcal{R}(C_{t_{k'}})}{\sum_{t_k \in \mathbb{T}_i} \mathcal{R}(C_{t_k})} \tag{9}$$

with Equation (8), we thus have $\mathcal{S}_{\mathbb{T}}(i,j) < \delta$, contradicting Proposition 1. □

To minimize the number of candidates, we choose $\mathbb{T}'_i$ based on the *inverse document frequency*, preferring tokens with classes that occur less frequently. With the resulting index, we can easily collect all candidates in the AFP for a reasonably high threshold (e.g., 0.9), since most pairs are dissimilar. However, these are still too many to compute similarity for, so we reduce the number of candidates further by efficiently computing upper bounds on the similarity. For example, we can check whether the sizes of all classes align:

$$\mathcal{S}_{\mathbb{T}}(i,j) \leq \frac{\sum_C \mathcal{R}(C) \cdot \min(|\{t_k \in \mathbb{T}_i \mid C_{t_k} = C\}|, |\{t_l \in \mathbb{T}_j \mid C_{t_l} = C\}|)}{\sum_{t_k \in \mathbb{T}_i} \mathcal{R}(C_{t_k}) + \sum_{t_l \in \mathbb{T}_j} \mathcal{R}(C_{t_l})} \tag{10}$$

Using such upper bounds to filter the retrieved candidates, we can compute the exact matching for all similar spans in the AFP in reasonable time—a complete list of filtering steps is discussed in Section 3.4. Additionally, a separate index for formulae could be implemented (e.g., via tree indexing [11], depending on the similarity function) if many token spans match where the formulae are not similar, but this was not a problem for the AFP.

Note that instead of directly indexing the syntactic token classes (which we do here for the sake of simplicity), one could also generate and index distinct *signature sets*. This is relevant when similarity functions use a disjunction of multiple conditions, which can occur e.g. in natural language text when different morphemes are considered. The framework then requires that the scheme fulfils:

$$\mathcal{S}_C(t_k, t_l) > 0 \implies \text{signature}(t_k) \cap \text{signature}(t_l) \neq \emptyset \tag{11}$$

In the following, we discuss our syntactic classes for Isabelle as well as similarity functions for simply typed λ-terms, and evaluate the approach.

Table 1: Concrete syntactic classes with parameters, relevance, and token content. Examples are taken from Isabelle/HOL.

Class	Parameter(s)	`Example`	Content	`Example Content`	$\mathcal{S}$
Keyword	source	`shows`	(-)		0.4
Inner syntax	source	:	(-)		0.2
Narration	(-)		source	— ‹`membership`›	0.5
String	(-)		source	`PROP`	2.0
Proof block	(-)		source	`by (blast intro: sym)`	4.0
Variable	type signature	{`int`, `prod`}	name, typing	`y` :: (`int`, `int`) `prod`	0.4
Type variable	sort signature	{`ring_1`}	name, sorting	`'a` :: `ring_1`	0.3
Entity	base-name, kind	`conj`	full name	`HOL.conj`	1.0
Command	kind	`thy_defn`	name	`datatype`	3.0
Markup (other)	kind	`language`	source	`999`	0.9

3.2 Syntactic Classes in Isabelle

Table 1 lists the syntactic classes of our implementation, which are derived from the document markup reported by the Isabelle system. The similarity functions are specified in Table 2—all numeric values were determined via manual experimentation. Hence, they are still arbitrary to some degree and could be tuned further. The similarity functions are based on the following intuition about Isabelle formalizations: *Keywords* and *inner syntax* tokens are always matched exactly as there is no good fuzzy similarity. *Strings* represent technical content that could not be resolved further, similar to *other markup* (which is classified by kind). For *narrative* content, we measure similarity using edit distance for simplicity, though more sophisticated natural language-based approaches such as matching token n-grams [35] would be possible. We did not consider such approaches here, since we restrict our detection to spans that generate formal entities, most of which do

Table 2: All five different kinds of similarity functions in our implementation, some of which are shared by multiple syntactic classes. Comparing tokens of different classes always returns zero.

Kind		Used for Classes	Range	Similarity based on
Exact		Keyword, Inner syntax	$[1.0, 1.0]$	Constant
Text		Comment, String, Markup	$[0.5, 1.0]$	Edit distance
Typed	(Type) Variable	Same type/sort	$[0.5, 1.0]$	Edit distance
		Different type/sort	$[0.2, 0.7]$	
Named		Entity	$[0.7, 1.0]$	Low for different names,
		Command	$[0.9, 1.0]$	and high for identical
Textblock		Proof	$[0.5, 1.0]$	Max of source length ratio (max 0.7) and edit distance

not contain large sections of narrative content. This choice is motivated by the large number of duplicates in the AFP—our detection is geared towards finding duplicates that incur the most maintenance overhead. For the same reason, we treat entire *proof blocks* as atomic tokens: Similar proofs are not problematic, but we are interested in finding duplicate theorems even if their proofs differ. Hence we also incorporate the length ratio as a metric for proofs. *Variables* are classified by type signature (*type variables* by sort signature), since their name can be arbitrary in principle; though in practice, naming is often quite informative, so the names are taken into account (in addition to the exact type). Named *entities* and *commands* are classified by kind but otherwise matched exactly. For entity names we also consider the base name, so we can compare e.g. constants with the same name but from different theories.

3.3 Similarity of Formulae

For the similarity function of two formulae f_n and f_m, a semantic approach would be desirable. A plausible solution could be anti-unification: Given a *generalizer* g with *substitutions* σ_1 and σ_2 such that $g\sigma_1 = f_n$ and $g\sigma_2 = f_m$, one could compare the sizes of g, σ_1, and σ_2. However, to obtain a similarity function, we would need a unique *least general generalizer* (LGG) g, i.e. such that (up to renaming) for all other generalizers g' there is no substitution σ with $g\sigma = g'$. Unfortunately, such a unique LGG does not always exist for simply typed λ-terms [8], unless we restrict generalizers to a suitable fragment: E.g., if we require that the generalizer is a *higher-order pattern*, a unique LGG always exists [4] and can even be computed in linear time [5]. Unique LGGs also exist for similar fragments [9], and first-order generalization has been successfully used to detect duplicates in software [23] and constraint logic programming [32].

Motivated by these successes, we have employed anti-unification with higher-order patterns to measure similarity of λ-terms. However, in our experiments we have not found this to be a good similarity metric: The main problem is that the restricted anti-unification gives a good measure of similarity only if some of the specific generalizers are actually in the chosen fragment; otherwise, similarity can be vastly underestimated. Unfortunately, this happens frequently, at least for the higher-order pattern fragment. A pathological example from Isabelle/HOL is shown in Listing 1.1. The duplicated lemma is once stated with $\leftrightarrow$ from the object logic (in theory `Enum`), and once using the meta-logical $\equiv$ (from the `Nitpick` theory). Hence, the head of the term needs to be generalized, e.g. with the generalizer X (`tranclp r a b`) (`trancl ...`), where X is a fresh variable. But this term is not in the pattern fragment, where we would only obtain X as a generalizer. It is not clear whether there are fragments with unique LGGs where such problems are sufficiently rare.

Hence, we utilize a more general syntactic distance function instead. The *tree edit distance* (which counts the minimal number of insertions, deletions, and label swaps to transform one tree into the other) has been used successfully to detect clones on abstract syntax trees of source code [22]. However, this distance is too strict: For instance, commuted equalities $A = B$ and $B = A$ would be

```
lemma tranclp_unfold [code]:
  "tranclp r a b ↔
    (a,b) ∈ trancl {(x,y). r x y}"
  by (simp add: trancl_def)
```

(a) Lemma in object logic

```
lemma tranclp_unfold[nitpick_unfold]:
  "tranclp r a b ≡
    (a,b) ∈ trancl {(x,y). r x y}"
  by (simp add: trancl_def)
```

(b) Lemma in meta-logic

```
TRUEPROP
  (↔ (tranclp r a b) (trancl ...))
```

(c) Term in object logic

```
PROP
  (≡ (tranclp r a b) (trancl ...))
```

(d) Term in meta-logic

Listing 1.1: Pathological example for a duplicate in Isabelle/HOL without specific anti-unifier in the higher-order pattern fragment.

considered quite dissimilar. Hence, we employ the *constrained unordered tree edit distance* introduced by Zhang [39], where children of a node are not ordered, but separate subtrees in one tree must be mapped to distinct subtrees of the other. This constraint is desirable to measure the similarity of term structure but also necessary to obtain a polynomial algorithm, since computing the unordered tree edit distance is NP-hard in general. We compute this distance on a spinal representation of terms in head normal form (HNF): Every node represents a term of form $\lambda x_1 \ldots x_n. H\, t_1 \, \ldots \, t_m$, where x_1 to x_n are λ-abstractions, H the head (a variable or constant), and arguments t_1 to t_m are children of the node, again in HNF. We use a uniform insert and delete cost, but discount the swapping operation if types are identical or similar. Finally, we set $\mathcal{S}_f$ as distance divided by the total number of nodes, normalized to a scale that matches $\mathcal{S}_C$.

3.4 Evaluation

To evaluate the effectiveness of our approach, we manually classified the first 100 results of the detector on Isabelle/HOL. Note that we only include spans of minimal length 10, exclude a few commands that are irrelevant for duplicates ("instance", "instantiation", and "termination"), and only consider pairs from different theories, since individual theories should be small enough to not contain accidental duplicates. Figure 1 shows the result. Actual duplicates had the highest similarity score, and different spans the lowest, on average. We found a few verbatim copies, many theorems that were identical or stated slightly differently (e.g., using $\leftrightarrow$ instead of $\equiv$), and even isomorphic theory parts: For instance, the folding operation over finite sets was duplicated multiple times even though a common abstraction exists, so the definition and its theorems could simply be obtained by instantiation. For $\delta \geq 0.95$, the detection approach had 100 % precision; below that, we found some similar or dual theorems we would not consider duplicates (e.g., monotonicity under complement, once for groups and once for boolean algebras). Below the threshold of 0.90, we also found a few dissimilar pairs. To judge scalability of the approach, we applied it on the entire AFP with

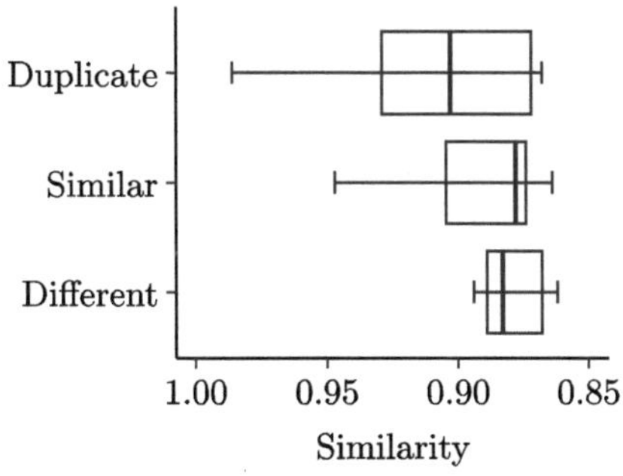

(a) Box plots for similarity per category.

Kind	Category	Count
Verbatim	Duplicate	5
Identical	Duplicate	14
Equivalent	Duplicate	6
Equal	Duplicate	2
Generalization	Duplicate	9
Isomorphic	Duplicate	5
Shared property	Similar	29
Dual property	Similar	23
Other	Different	7

(b) Number of occurrences for each kind.

Fig. 1: Manual categorization of the 100 most similar pairs in Isabelle/HOL.

a threshold of 0.90. Table 3 shows our filtering steps and the number of candidate pairs retained for the AFP. On an Intel Xeon E5-2699, indexing completed in about four hours and detection took almost ten hours, which is less than the build time of over 15 hours. We found our discriminator approach to be quite effective: The inverted index and pre-filtering reduced the number of candidates by three orders of magnitude each. Half of the actual matches came from different theories; filtering those out earlier would further reduce detection time, since over 96 % of compute time was spent calculating formula similarity.

4 Automatic placement of lemmas

It is a common occurrence that lemmas about specific compositions of basic concepts are not available in the background theory, and must be proven locally so one can progress with their formalization. For an organized library of formal mathematics, it is important that these lemmas are moved to their appropriate place afterwards. In fact, performing such refactorings is so common that specialized support has been developed, as discussed in Section 2. Also, there are 37 comments with the message "TODO move" in the initial AFP-2025 release.

Table 3: Number of candidate pairs per filtering steps, for 408 666 relevant spans.

Possible pairs	53 163 910 843
Retrieved candidates	83 915 694
With matching number of tokens	10 361 234
With matching class sizes	100 895
With matching tokens (approximate and relaxed)	62 059
With matching tokens (exact)	61 848
With matching formula sizes	57 749
With matching formulae	34 251
In different theories	17 209

However, apart from the fact that the mentioned tooling is no longer available, its approach was not optimal: Lemmas would always be placed at the end of the earliest feasible theory, such that all dependencies on other facts precede the proof. Although this placement maximizes possible re-use, the authors of the tool note that it is much more desirable to instead group *related* lemmas together [6]: Only concise formalizations are easy to understand and maintain.

For a system-independent abstraction that allows us to compute feasible lemma locations and to find groups of related lemmas, we utilize *formal entity graphs*: For a formalization, such a graph consists of the underlying formal entities in the logical system, i.e., constants, types, theorems, etc., and the relations between them—for example, lemmas used in the proof of a theorem [20]. There is a wealth of literature and algorithms to detect *communities* of related nodes in such dependency graphs, as discussed e.g. by Fortunato and Hric in their extensive survey [15]: Although the definition of a community is not agreed on (and different kinds exist), most research is concerned with *link-dense* communities, where members have significantly more connections within the community than outside of it. The idea of using such communities to guide structure has been used successfully to generate refactoring recommendations for object-oriented software systems [27,26,40,34].

However, groups of related lemmas are better characterized by *link-pattern* communities, where all members share a similar set of dependencies: Experience shows that lemmas grouped together in existing formalizations typically characterize properties of a few common objects. However, not all dependencies are equally important: Constants and types of the base logic are ubiquitous (e.g., the bool type), and some lemmas are introduced frequently by automation but are of no (abstract) relevance. Hence, a group of co-located lemmas that share a large set of important dependencies with the lemma to be relocated should represent a fitting location. However, existing link-pattern community detection algorithms are computationally quite expensive (cf. preliminary work [31]), and the full formal entity graph of Isabelle/AFP consists of several million nodes and hundreds of millions of edges. Hence, the community detection approach needs to operate *locally*, i.e., based only on partial knowledge of the dependency graph. To support that (and also incorporate relevance), we develop a straightforward optimization-based community detection algorithm in this work.

4.1 Community Detection Approach

For our approach, we assume an underlying source structure with different theory modules (e.g., Isabelle theories) where formal entities (definitions, theorems, etc.) are defined. Theories may import others, inducing a directed acyclic dependency graph. We identify entities by their *order of definition* within a theory, which we assume to correspond to their location, i.e., consecutive definitions are co-located with each other. Formally:

Definition 5. *With e_i, $i \in \mathbb{N}$, we denote the i-th* entity *encountered in any valid loading order. Further let $T(i) \subset \mathbb{N}$ denote the* theory *of e_i, and $\succ$ the partial* *order induced by theory* dependencies *(imports), i.e.* $T(i) \succ T(j)$ *denotes that* $T(i)$ *depends on* $T(j)$. *The entity* dependency graph *is given via adjacency* A:

$$A_{ij} := \begin{cases} 1 & \textit{if } e_i \textit{ depends on } e_j \\ 0 & \textit{otherwise} \end{cases} \tag{12}$$

And we define dependencies D, shared *dependencies* $\mathbb{D}$, *and* dependents D^{-1} *as*

$$D(i) := \{k \mid A_{ik} = 1\} \qquad \mathbb{D}(S) := \bigcap_{j \in S} D(j) \qquad D^{-1}(i) := \{k \mid A_{ki} = 1\} \tag{13}$$

Note that any valid loading order ensures that $T(i) \succ T(j) \implies i > j$. Further, an entity e_i can be relocated to any feasible position $\mathcal{P}$ where its dependencies are already imported or defined, and such that all dependents are defined afterwards or import its new theory:

$$\begin{aligned} \mathcal{P}(i) = \{l \mid & \big(\forall j \in D(i).\, j < l \land T(j) \preceq T(l)\big) \land \\ & \big(\forall j \in D^{-1}(i).\, l < j \land T(l) \preceq T(j)\big)\} \end{aligned} \tag{14}$$

In our implementation, $\mathcal{P}$ is additionally constrained by the system, since Isabelle commands can only access the theory up to their invocation. Also note that this only means that e_i could *in principle* be moved to any of those locations: Due to different automation, syntax, or name clashes, it might not be possible to move the source code verbatim (cf. the Gravity tool, which addresses the problem of performing such refactorings [6]). Our objective is:

Objective 1 *For a lemma* e_i, *we want to find a position* $j \in \mathcal{P}(i)$ *where* e_i *could be placed, with fitting community* $S \subseteq T(j)$ *such that* $j \in S$. *Formally, given an appropriate function* $\mathit{fit}_i(S)$, *we need to find*

$$\operatorname*{arg\,max}_{j \in \mathcal{P}(i)} \max_{S \in 2^{T(j)} \mid j \in S} \mathit{fit}_i(S) \tag{15}$$

$\mathit{fit}_i(S)$ *should consider the proximity of community members, relevance of their shared dependencies, and how many other dependencies members of* S *have.*

Within a theory, $|i - j|$ gives a good measure how close two entities e_i and e_j are located to each other. For relevance, we can use the inverse of in-degree centrality, which we found to be the best centrality metric for formalizations in previous work [20]. Hence we can put together a straightforward implementation of the criteria from Objective 1:

Proposition 2. *We propose a fitness function that addresses the criteria via multiplicative factors of form*

$$\mathit{fit}_i(S) = \sum_{l \in S} \left(\frac{1}{\|S\|} \cdot \mathbb{R}(\mathbb{D}(\{i\} \cup S)) \cdot \frac{1}{\mathbb{R}(D(l))} \right) \tag{16}$$

where we define community size $\|\cdot\|$ *and relevance* R *(denoted* $\mathbb{R}$ *for sets) as*

$$\|S\| = \max S - \min S \qquad R(i) = \frac{1}{|D^{-1}(i)|} \qquad \mathbb{R}(S) = \sum_{l \in S} R(l) \tag{17}$$

The fitness function is additionally parameterized with a number of monotone transformations (e.g., squaring the distance), which are discussed in Section 4.2. We omit them in this section for ease of notation.

Since optimizing over all possible subsets is computationally infeasible, we approximate S with a greedy step function δ, choosing the entity that increases the resulting fit the most:

$$\delta_{i\mapsto j}(S) = S \cup \left(\underset{s' \subseteq T(j), |s'| \leq 1}{\arg\max} \; \mathrm{fit}_i(S \cup s') \right) \tag{18}$$

The fixed point of δ gives us a heuristic solution that can be computed in polynomial time (but with no approximation guarantees), i.e.

$$\max_{S \in 2^{T(j)} | j \in S} \mathrm{fit}_i(S) \geq \mathrm{fit}_i\left(\underset{n}{\mathrm{fix}}\, \delta^n_{i\mapsto j}(\{j\}) \right) \tag{19}$$

The search space is still far too large to compute this solution exhaustively, especially for an interactive tool. However, the interesting region of the search space is much smaller, since we expect most communities to be a bad fit for any given lemma. Thus, the following upper bounds are helpful to prune the search:

Theorem 2 (Upper bounds). *Let S denote a community with $j \in S$. Then the possible contribution of $l \in T(j) \setminus S$ to fit_i can be bounded independently of S, and the top n entities (i.e., with largest possible contributions) are given by:*

$$top_j(n, S) := \underset{S' \subseteq T(j)\setminus S, |S'| \leq n}{\arg\max} \sum_{l \in S'} \frac{1}{\|\{j, l\}\| \cdot \mathbb{R}(D(l))} \tag{20}$$

With $s' := top_j(1, S)$, for fit_i of a single δ-step it holds that

$$fit_i(\delta_{i\mapsto j}(S)) \leq fit_i(S) + \frac{\mathbb{R}(\mathbb{D}(\{i\} \cup S))}{\|S \cup s'\| \cdot \mathbb{R}(\mathbb{D}(s'))} \tag{21}$$

Moreover, we get a (less tight) bound for fit_i of δ^m, i.e., any number of steps:

$$fit_i(\delta^m_{i\mapsto j}(S)) \leq fit_i(S) + \sum_{l \in top_j(m,S)} \frac{\mathbb{R}(\mathbb{D}(\{i\} \cup S))}{\|\{j, l\}\| \cdot \mathbb{R}(D(l))} \tag{22}$$

Proof. We have that $S \subseteq \delta^m_{i\mapsto j}(S) \subseteq T(j)$ for all m by definition. Since D is antitone and R, $\|\cdot\|$, δ are monotone w.r.t. $\subseteq$, the bounds follow directly. □

Since top_j can easily be maintained during fixed point iteration, these bounds are cheap to compute, and the iteration can immediately be stopped once a bound is lower than the fit of a previous community. A good initial solution helps to reach this stopping criterium faster. Searching with a limited community size first (e.g., $|S| \leq 3$) is an easy way to obtain a good initial solution for pruning the full search effectively.

4.2 Fine-tuning and Evaluation

To obtain a ground-truth dataset for lemma relocation, we searched the version history of the AFP for commits where lemmas were actually moved to their appropriate place[5]. Although a sizeable number of such commits exist, we could only extract a limited set of examples where the Isabelle version was compatible with our implementation. Also, each version has to be run as a separate Isabelle process in a distinct context. Hence, this dataset is neither suitable for fine-tuning nor large enough to split it (containing 25 moves), but we can use it to judge the effectiveness of our tuned approach. For tuning, we created a separate (synthetic) data set, containing lemmas in their current position that could be moved elsewhere, i.e., without closely located dependents and dependencies. We used a meta-heuristic approach (genetic algorithm) to find the optimal configurations for a number of parameters, which are shown in Table 4. Since this required running a large number of configurations (many of which are less efficient due to worse bounds), we limited the search to $|S| \leq 10$. In addition to relevance and distance, we consider *multiplicity* (i.e., how often a dependency occurs in a lemma), extending the definitions from Section 4.1 to multisets.

Table 4: Tunable parameters of our algorithm. Final values are printed bold.

Parameter	Affects	Value Range
Multiplicity	$D, \mathbb{D}, D^{-1}$	1, count, **log(count)**
Relevance	R	$1, \frac{1+\alpha}{\lvert D^{-1}(i)\rvert+\alpha}$ for $\alpha \in [0, 200]$, $\mathbf{log}\, \boldsymbol{\frac{\lvert\{e_j \mid j \in \mathbb{N}\}\rvert}{D^{-1}(i)}}$
Relevance Scaling	$\mathbb{R}$	$\mathbf{R}^{\boldsymbol{\alpha}}$ for $\alpha \in \{1, \mathbf{2}, 3\}$, $\mathbf{R} \cdot \boldsymbol{f}$ where $f : \mathbf{kind} \mapsto (0, 1]$
Distance Scaling	$\lVert\cdot\rVert$	$\lVert\cdot\rVert^{\alpha}$ for $\alpha \in [0.5, 1]$

Our approach is implemented as an Isabelle command called `relocate`, which—when invoked with a lemma name in an interactive session—traverses the dependency graph, after which the earliest feasible locations for the given lemma are reported. Subsequently, the tool searches for the best community, and shows the top results once finished. For each result, it displays a break-down of the corresponding fit, and links to the source location of the first element j in the community. To avoid displaying close locations multiple times, we filter out subsequent results k within an ϵ-environment around j (i.e., where $\lVert\{j, k\}\rVert \leq \epsilon$).

For our evaluation, the *rank* of the predicted ϵ-environment that contains our ground truth thus indicates where the correct suggestion would appear in the user's results. Figure 2 shows results for $\epsilon = 5$, contrasting full community detection with singleton communities, i.e., where $|S| = 1$. With our optimizations, search time is under a second, though it takes 2.04 s to traverse the dependency graph on average. Compared to singletons, full community detection has a slightly higher median rank (of 6), but the distribution is much narrower and

[5] Searching for the keyword "moved" in commit messages.

the mean (of 12.6) is lower. This indicates that the detection works well most of the time but not always, which is not too surprising: There are many possible locations for a given lemma (3970.6 in the mean, corresponding to 672.1 distinct ϵ-environments), and frequently there are multiple locations that would fit well.

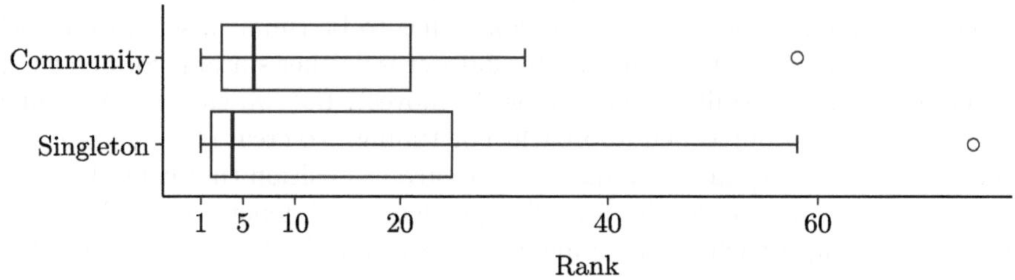

Fig. 2: Distribution of ranks of predicted ϵ-environments (with $\epsilon = 5$) that contain ground truth, comparing singletons and full communities on our dataset of 25 lemmas whose move was recorded in the version history of the AFP.

5 Conclusion and Future Work

In this work, we discussed two approaches that use structural similarity to support maintenance of formal mathematics, applicable to a wide range of computer math systems. We found that for Isabelle/AFP, both tools yield reasonably good results, though they could be optimized further with more empirical ground-truth data. Additionally, more involved methods could be used: For our duplicate detection framework, a semantic similarity measure for λ-terms based on *higher-order generalization* (that works in all scenarios) would be desirable. Moreover, utilizing *large language models* to extract semantic embeddings of the source text could be a promising basis for an alternative approach. To find the best location of auxiliary lemmas, training *graph neural networks* on current formalization structure would allow optimizing the model to a much greater extent; though it is unclear whether a model trained on regular formalizations generalizes well to find good locations for out-of-place auxiliary lemmas. However, such machine learning-based methods do not give explainable results and require sophisticated technological and computational effort, making them difficult to integrate in current computer math systems.

Acknowledgments. We thank our anonymous peer-reviewers for their valuable comments and insights, which greatly helped to improve this report.

The author was funded by the Deutsche Forschungsgemeinschaft (DFG, German Research Foundation) under the National Research Data Infrastructure – NFDI 52/1 – 501930651.

References

1. Adams, M.: Refactoring Proofs with Tactician. In: Software Engineering and Formal Methods. Springer (2015). https://doi.org/10.1007/978-3-662-49224-6_6
2. Alkassar, E., Hillebrand, M.A., Leinenbach, D.C., Schirmer, N.W., Starostin, A., Tsyban, A.: Balancing the Load. Journal of Automated Reasoning (2009). https://doi.org/10.1007/s10817-009-9123-z
3. Aspinall, D., Kaliszyk, C.: Towards Formal Proof Metrics. In: Fundamental Approaches to Software Engineering. Springer (2016). https://doi.org/10.1007/978-3-662-49665-7_19
4. Baumgartner, A., Kutsia, T., Levy, J., Villaret, M.: A Variant of Higher-Order Anti-Unification. In: Rewriting Techniques and Applications. Schloss Dagstuhl – Leibniz-Zentrum für Informatik (2013). https://doi.org/10.4230/LIPIcs.RTA.2013.113
5. Baumgartner, A., Kutsia, T., Levy, J., Villaret, M.: Higher-Order Pattern Anti-Unification in Linear Time. Journal of Automated Reasoning (2017). https://doi.org/10.1007/s10817-016-9383-3
6. Bourke, T., Daum, M., Klein, G., Kolanski, R.: Challenges and Experiences in Managing Large-Scale Proofs. In: Intelligent Computer Mathematics. Springer (2012). https://doi.org/10.1007/978-3-642-31374-5_3
7. Brown, C., Thompson, S.: Clone detection and elimination for Haskell. In: Partial Evaluation and Program Manipulation. ACM (2010). https://doi.org/10.1145/1706356.1706378
8. Cerna, D.M., Buran, M.: One or Nothing: Anti-unification over the Simply-Typed Lambda Calculus. ACM Trans. Comput. Logic (2024). https://doi.org/10.1145/3654798
9. Cerna, D.M., Kutsia, T.: A Generic Framework for Higher-Order Generalizations. In: Formal Structures for Computation and Deduction. Schloss Dagstuhl – Leibniz-Zentrum für Informatik (2019). https://doi.org/10.4230/LIPIcs.FSCD.2019.10
10. Chodarev, S., Pietriková, E., Kollár, J.: Haskell clone detection using pattern comparing algorithm. In: Engineering of Modern Electric Systems. IEEE (2015). https://doi.org/10.1109/EMES.2015.7158423
11. Cohen, S.: Indexing for subtree similarity-search using edit distance. In: Management of Data. ACM (2013). https://doi.org/10.1145/2463676.2463716
12. Dietrich, D., Whiteside, I., Aspinall, D.: Polar: A Framework for Proof Refactoring. In: Logic for Programming, Artificial Intelligence, and Reasoning. Springer (2013). https://doi.org/10.1007/978-3-642-45221-5_52
13. van Doorn, F., Ebner, G., Lewis, R.Y.: Maintaining a Library of Formal Mathematics. In: Intelligent Computer Mathematics. Springer (2020). https://doi.org/10.1007/978-3-030-53518-6_16
14. Du, D., Pardalos, P., Hu, X., Wu, W.: Introduction to Combinatorial Optimization. Springer, 1 edn. (2022). https://doi.org/10.1007/978-3-031-10596-8
15. Fortunato, S., Hric, D.: Community detection in networks: A user guide. Physics Reports (2016). https://doi.org/10.1016/j.physrep.2016.09.002
16. Gauthier, T., Kaliszyk, C.: Matching Concepts across HOL Libraries. In: Intelligent Computer Mathematics. Springer (2014). https://doi.org/10.1007/978-3-319-08434-3_20
17. Gauthier, T., Kaliszyk, C.: Aligning concepts across proof assistant libraries. Journal of Symbolic Computation (2019). https://doi.org/10.1016/j.jsc.2018.04.005

18. Ghanbari, A.: Automatic Goal Clone Detection in Rocq. In: 39th European Conference on Object-Oriented Programming (ECOOP 2025). Schloss Dagstuhl – Leibniz-Zentrum für Informatik (2025). https://doi.org/10.4230/LIPIcs.ECOOP.2025.12
19. Ghanouchi, S.: Code Clone Detection in Isabelle Using Token Stream Similarity. Bachelor's thesis, Technische Universität München (2023)
20. Huch, F.: Formal Entity Graphs as Complex Networks: Assessing Centrality Metrics of the Archive of Formal Proofs. In: Intelligent Computer Mathematics. Springer (2022). https://doi.org/10.1007/978-3-031-16681-5_10
21. Huch, F., Stathopoulos, Y.: Formalization Quality in Isabelle. In: Intelligent Computer Mathematics. Springer (2023). https://doi.org/10.1007/978-3-031-42753-4_10
22. Jiang, L., Misherghi, G., Su, Z., Glondu, S.: DECKARD: Scalable and Accurate Tree-Based Detection of Code Clones. In: Software Engineering. IEEE (2007). https://doi.org/10.1109/ICSE.2007.30
23. Li, H., Thompson, S.: Similar Code Detection and Elimination for Erlang Programs. In: Practical Aspects of Declarative Languages. Springer (2010). https://doi.org/10.1007/978-3-642-11503-5_10
24. Megdiche, Y., Huch, F., Stevens, L.: A Linter for Isabelle: Implementation and Evaluation (2022). https://doi.org/10.48550/arXiv.2207.10424, Isabelle Workshop
25. Müller, D., Gauthier, T., Kaliszyk, C., Kohlhase, M., Rabe, F.: Classification of Alignments Between Concepts of Formal Mathematical Systems. In: Intelligent Computer Mathematics. Springer (2017). https://doi.org/10.1007/978-3-319-62075-6_7
26. Pan, W.F., Jiang, B., Li, B.: Refactoring Software Packages via Community Detection in Complex Software Networks. International Journal of Automation and Computing (2013). https://doi.org/10.1007/s11633-013-0708-y
27. Pan, W., Li, B., Ma, Y., Liu, J., Qin, Y.: Class structure refactoring of object-oriented softwares using community detection in dependency networks. Frontiers of Computer Science in China (2009). https://doi.org/10.1007/s11704-009-0054-y
28. Ringer, T.: Proof Repair. Ph.D. thesis, University of Washington (2021)
29. Ringer, T., Porter, R., Yazdani, N., Leo, J., Grossman, D.: Proof repair across type equivalences. In: Programming Language Design and Implementation. ACM (2021). https://doi.org/10.1145/3453483.3454033
30. Ringer, T., Yazdani, N., Leo, J., Grossman, D.: Adapting proof automation to adapt proofs. In: Certified Programs and Proofs. ACM (2018). https://doi.org/10.1145/3167094
31. Schäfer, M.: Community Detection on the Isabelle Dependency Graph. Bachelor's thesis, Technische Universität München (2023)
32. Vanhoof, W., Yernaux, G.: Generalization-Driven Semantic Clone Detection in CLP. In: Logic-Based Program Synthesis and Transformation. Springer (2020). https://doi.org/10.1007/978-3-030-45260-5_14
33. Vinan, D., Hupel, L.: Clone Detection in Isabelle Theories (2016), Isabelle Workshop
34. Šubelj, L., Bajec, M.: Software systems through complex networks science: review, analysis and applications. In: Software Mining. ACM (2012). https://doi.org/10.1145/2384416.2384418
35. Wang, J., Li, G., Fe, J.: Fast-join: An efficient method for fuzzy token matching based string similarity join. In: Data Engineering. IEEE (2011). https://doi.org/10.1109/ICDE.2011.5767865

36. Whiteside, I., Aspinall, D., Dixon, L., Grov, G.: Towards Formal Proof Script Refactoring. In: Intelligent Computer Mathematics. Springer (2011). https://doi.org/10.1007/978-3-642-22673-1_18
37. Wibergh, K.: Automatic refactoring for Agda. Master's thesis, University of Gothenburg (2019)
38. Zakeri-Nasrabadi, M., Parsa, S., Ramezani, M., Roy, C., Ekhtiarzadeh, M.: A systematic literature review on source code similarity measurement and clone detection: Techniques, applications, and challenges. Journal of Systems and Software (2023). https://doi.org/10.1016/j.jss.2023.111796
39. Zhang, K.: A constrained edit distance between unordered labeled trees. Algorithmica (1996). https://doi.org/10.1007/BF01975866
40. Šubelj, L., Bajec, M.: Community structure of complex software systems: Analysis and applications. Physica A: Statistical Mechanics and its Applications (2011). https://doi.org/10.1016/j.physa.2011.03.036

Logical and Linguistic Foundations

Graded Quantitative Narrowing

Mauricio Ayala-Rincón[1], Thaynara Arielly de Lima[2], Georg Ehling[3](✉), and Temur Kutsia[3]

[1] Universidade de Brasília, Brasília, Brazil
ayala@unb.br
[2] Universidade Federal de Goiás, Goiânia, Brazil
thaynaradelima@ufg.br
[3] Johannes Kepler University Linz, Linz, Austria
{gehling,kutsia}@risc.jku.at

Abstract. The recently introduced framework of Graded Quantitative Rewriting is an innovative extension of traditional rewriting systems, in which rules are annotated with degrees drawn from a quantale. This framework provides a robust foundation for equational reasoning that incorporates metric aspects, such as the proximity between terms and the complexity of rewriting-based computations. Quantitative narrowing, introduced in this paper, generalizes quantitative rewriting by replacing matching with unification in reduction steps, enabling the reduction of terms even when they contain variables, through simultaneous instantiation and rewriting. In the standard (non-quantitative) setting, narrowing has been successfully applied in various domains, including functional logic programming, theorem proving, and equational unification. Here, we focus on quantitative narrowing to solve unification problems in quantitative equational theories over Lawverean quantales. We establish its soundness and discuss conditions under which completeness can be ensured. This approach allows us to solve quantitative equations in richer theories than those addressed by previous methods.

Keywords: Quantitative equational reasoning · Lawverean quantales · Graded systems · Unification · Narrowing

1 Introduction

While the notion of equality is fundamental to much of mathematics, it has also been viewed as limited in its ability to capture real-world phenomena, where entities are rarely "exactly" identical. As a result, various approaches have been developed to extend the equality predicate into a relation that accounts for proximity or similarity rather than strict identity. For these extensions, fundamental symbolic computation techniques such as, e.g., fuzzy equation solving [2,38,18,28,36,37,23] or metric-based equational reasoning [31,13,32] have been investigated. A recent proposal by Gavazzo and Di Florio [24] for quantitative equational theories is one of the more general approaches, containing some other frameworks as special cases. In this framework, equations are endowed with an

V. de Paiva and P. Koepke (Eds.): CICM 2025, LNAI 16136, pp. 113–132, 2026.
https://doi.org/10.1007/978-3-032-07021-0_7

element of a Lawverean quantale [29], measuring, in one way or another, the degree to which they hold. A unification algorithm for solving equations in a class of equational theories in this framework was introduced in [19].

In the standard (non-quantitative) setting, narrowing was introduced as a generalization of rewriting that reduces terms containing variables by replacing matching with unification, enabling variable instantiation during reduction. Among its many applications, equational unification holds one of the central roles. Seminal works by Fay and Hullot, who introduced, respectively, "ordinary" and "basic" narrowing, proved the completeness of narrowing for solving equations in equational theories presented by convergent (confluent and terminating) term rewriting systems (TRSs) [22,27]. Hullot's initial result on the termination of basic narrowing states that it terminates for convergent term rewriting systems, provided that every basic narrowing derivation starting from the right-hand side of any rewriting rule terminates. This result was later refined by Alpuente et al., who relaxed the requirement of convergence [3,4]. The completeness of ordinary narrowing holds even without the termination assumption, provided that the set of solutions is restricted to normalizable substitutions [33,34]. However, this is not the case for basic narrowing, where the completeness fails even for normalizable substitutions if termination is not assumed. Narrowing has been extended to conditional rewriting theories and applied as a key mechanism in combining functional and logic programming [17,20,5], and further implemented in deductive frameworks based on rewriting and logic (e.g., [26,16]). It has been applied in protocol security verification [30], verification of termination of rewriting modulo equational axioms, and protocol security [21,40]. Other applications are related to model checking [14], formalization of concurrent programming, and, in general, reachability analysis in deductive frameworks [15].

Graded quantitative rewriting offers a natural and fine-grained framework for formalizing the complexity of rewriting-based computations. Related approaches, such as weighted rewriting [1,6], typically focus on measuring reduction steps to analyze the complexity of rewriting derivations. Graded quantitative rewriting, in addition, provides a precise account of the cost of redex selection, a fundamental aspect of rewriting-based computation. This additional measure reflects the sensitivity to the position of the context in which quantitative redexes are identified and reductions are applied. A similar consideration arises in formal frameworks such as the lambda calculus, explicit substitutions, and nominal rewriting, where the cost of locating redexes to contract plays a crucial role in accurately modeling computational complexity.

Advances in quantitative computational techniques play a crucial role in automating reasoning about structures concerning various behavioral metrics. Quantitative narrowing presents a powerful mechanism that can be integrated into proof assistants to enhance automation in solving approximate equational problems, thereby supporting rigorous reasoning about the inherent imprecision in computational models of real-world systems. This paper takes a first step in this direction by introducing a graded quantitative narrowing calculus, where quantitative information is modeled using quantales. This is a general framework that can accommodate various well-known quantitative theories as special cases.

Contributions. This paper introduces quantitative narrowing, defining ordinary and basic variants, and presents a rule-based basic narrowing procedure for solving equational unification problems over Lawverean quantales. This work extends the class of theories considered in quantitative unification as studied in [19]. We prove the soundness of the procedure and specify conditions under which completeness can be guaranteed, highlighting key differences from the well-known properties of ordinary and basic narrowing in the crisp first-order setting. By addressing unification problems over quantales using narrowing techniques, this paper takes a step toward establishing a framework for quantitative unification modulo equational theories.

Organization. Section 2 introduces the necessary background on quantales, while Section 3 defines graded quantitative equational and rewriting systems and introduces the quantitative unification problem. Section 4 presents the notion of graded narrowing and introduces a set of basic narrowing inference rules, which are shown to be sound. Section 5 then discusses conditions for completeness. Finally, Section 6 concludes the paper and briefly outlines directions for future work. Full proofs are provided in the technical report [10] associated with this paper.

2 Preliminaries

The basic notions and terminology on quantales are included in the following subsections.

2.1 Quantales

For the notions in this part, we follow [24,25].

Definition 1 (Quantale). *A (unital)* quantale $\mathfrak{Q} = (\Omega, \precsim, \otimes, \kappa)$ *consists of a monoid* $(\Omega, \kappa, \otimes)$ *and a complete lattice* $(\Omega, \precsim)$ *(with join* $\vee$ *and meet* $\wedge$*) satisfying the following distributivity laws:* $\delta \otimes \left(\bigvee_{i\in I} \varepsilon_i\right) = \bigvee_{i\in I}(\delta \otimes \varepsilon_i)$ *and* $\left(\bigvee_{i\in I} \varepsilon_i\right) \otimes \delta = \bigvee_{i\in I}(\varepsilon_i \otimes \delta)$.

Notation 1 *The element* κ *is called the* unit *of the quantale, and* $\otimes$ *its* tensor *(or multiplication). Besides* κ*, we use Greek letters* $\alpha, \beta, \gamma, \delta, \varepsilon, \zeta, \eta$*, and* ι *to denote elements of* Ω*. The* top *and* bottom *elements of a quantale are denoted by* $\top$ *and* $\bot$*, respectively.*

Definition 2 (Lawverean quantales). *A quantale* $\mathfrak{Q} = (\Omega, \precsim, \otimes, \kappa)$ *is called* integral *if* $\kappa = \top$ *and* non-trivial *if* $\kappa \neq \bot$*. It is commutative if the monoid* $(\Omega, \otimes, \kappa)$ *is commutative.* $\mathfrak{Q}$ *is* cointegral *if* $\varepsilon \otimes \delta = \bot$ *implies either* $\varepsilon = \bot$ *or* $\delta = \bot$*.* Lawverean *quantales are commutative, integral, cointegral, and nontrivial.*

Example 1. Table 1 brings some concrete quantales. Notice that the fuzzy quantale $\mathbb{I}$ is Lawverean for the Gödel and product T-norms, but not for the Łukasiewicz T-norm.

Table 1: Correspondence between quantales $\mathbb{\Omega}$ (generic), $\mathbb{2}$ (Boolean), $\mathbb{L}$ (Lawvere), $\mathbb{L}^{\max}$ (strong Lawvere), and $\mathbb{I}$ (fuzzy). Examples from [24].

	$\mathbb{\Omega}$	$\mathbb{2}$	$\mathbb{L}$	$\mathbb{L}^{\max}$	$\mathbb{I}$
Carrier	Ω	$\{0,1\}$	$[0,\infty]$	$[0,\infty]$	$[0,1]$
Order	$\precsim$	$\leqslant$	$\geqslant$	$\geqslant$	$\leqslant$
Join	$\vee$	$\exists$	inf	inf	sup
Meet	$\wedge$	$\forall$	sup	sup	inf
Tensor	$\otimes$	$\wedge$	$+$	max	left-continuous T-norm
Unit	κ	1	0	0	1

Remark 1. In any quantale $\mathbb{\Omega} = (\Omega, \precsim, \otimes, \kappa)$:

(i) $\otimes$ is monotonous: $\alpha \precsim \beta \Rightarrow \alpha \otimes \gamma \precsim \beta \otimes \gamma$ and $\gamma \otimes \alpha \precsim \gamma \otimes \beta$.
Indeed, $\alpha \otimes \gamma \precsim (\alpha \otimes \gamma) \vee (\beta \otimes \gamma) = (\alpha \vee \beta) \otimes \gamma = \beta \otimes \gamma$.

(ii) If $\mathbb{\Omega}$ is integral then $\alpha \otimes \beta \precsim \alpha \wedge \beta$.
Using monotonicity and integrality, we obtain $\alpha \otimes \beta \precsim \alpha \otimes \top = \alpha$ and similarly, $\alpha \otimes \beta \precsim \beta$; thus, $\alpha \otimes \beta \precsim \alpha \wedge \beta$.

In the rest of the paper, we consider Lawverean quantales.

We now define quantitative ternary relations. This notion differs from the "$\mathbb{\Omega}$-ternary relations" introduced in [24], which are also required to be antitone in the quantale argument, a condition that we do not impose here.

Definition 3 (Quantitative ternary relations). *Let $\mathbb{\Omega}$ be a Lawverean quantale, and let A, B be sets. $R \subseteq A \times \Omega \times B$ is said to be a* quantitative ternary relation*. The composition of two quantitative ternary relations $R \subseteq A \times \Omega \times B$ and $S \subseteq B \times \Omega \times C$ is the least quantitative ternary relation $(R; S) \subseteq A \times \Omega \times C$ satisfying $(R; S)(a, \varepsilon \otimes \delta, c)$ whenever $R(a, \varepsilon, b)$ and $S(b, \delta, c)$ hold.*

For any set A, the diagonal $\Delta_{\mathbb{\Omega},A} \subseteq A \times \Omega \times A$ is the defined by $\Delta_{\mathbb{\Omega},A} := \{(a, \kappa, a) \mid a \in A\}$. For a quantitative ternary relation $R \subseteq A \times \Omega \times A$ and $n \in \mathbb{N}$, we define the n-th power of R inductively by

$$R^0 := \Delta_{\mathbb{\Omega},A} \qquad \text{and} \qquad R^{n+1} := (R; R^n).$$

The transitive closure R^+ and the reflexive transitive closure R^* of R are respectively defined by

$$R^+ := \bigcup_{n \geqslant 1} R^n \qquad \text{and} \qquad R^* := R^0 \cup R^+.$$

Definition 4 (Quantale homomorphism). *Given quantales* $\mathfrak{Q}=(\Omega, \precsim, \otimes, \kappa)$ *and* $\Theta = (\Theta, \sqsubseteq, \boxtimes, \eta)$, *a* quantale homomorphism *is a monotone map* $h : \Omega \longrightarrow \Theta$ *such that* $h(\kappa) = \eta$, $h(\varepsilon) \boxtimes h(\delta) = h(\varepsilon \otimes \delta)$, *and* $h(\bigvee_i \varepsilon_i) = \bigsqcup_i h(\varepsilon_i)$ *(where* $\bigvee$ *and* $\bigsqcup$ *are joins of* $\mathfrak{Q}$ *and* Θ, *respectively). For notational convenience, we also say that* h *is a quantale homomorphism* $\mathfrak{Q} \to \Theta$.

In the remainder of the paper, we work with quantale endomorphisms, i.e. homomorphisms $\mathfrak{Q} \to \mathfrak{Q}$. We denote them by $\phi, \psi, \ldots$. In the literature, they are called *change of base endofunctors*, or CBEs. Notice that the set of CBEs $\mathfrak{Q} \to \mathfrak{Q}$ is closed under composition.

Example 2. The identity function $\mathbb{1}\colon \Omega \to \Omega$ on an arbitrary quantale domain Ω and multiplication by a nonnegative real constant in the case of the Lawvere quantale are trivial examples of CBEs.

Remark 2. For a given quantale $\mathfrak{Q} = (\Omega, \precsim, \otimes, \kappa)$, its order $\precsim$ and tensor $\otimes$ can be extended to CBEs pointwise as follows. Consider ϕ and ψ CBEs on $\mathfrak{Q}$:

i) $\phi \precsim \psi$ iff $\phi(\alpha) \precsim \psi(\alpha)$ for all $\alpha \in \Omega$.
ii) $(\phi \otimes \psi)(\alpha) = \phi(\alpha) \otimes \psi(\alpha)$ for all $\alpha \in \Omega$.

Notation 2 *We denote by* $\kappa^\star$ *the constant CBE such that* $\kappa^\star(\alpha) = \kappa$, *for all* $\alpha \in \Omega$.

We assume $\mathfrak{Q}$ to be fixed and consider a structure $\Phi = (\Phi, \precsim, \circ, \mathbb{1}, \otimes, \kappa^\star)$, where Φ is a set of CBEs containing the identity function $\mathbb{1}$ and constant function $\kappa^\star$, closed under composition $\circ$ and tensor $\otimes$.

3 Graded Equalities and Rewriting Rules

We assume familiarity with term rewriting, unification, and narrowing as presented in textbooks (e.g., [11,39]) and papers as [34,12]. In this section, we introduce quantitative unification problem and adapt quantitative TRSs from [24] for addressing unification using graded narrowing later.

Definition 5 (Modal arity, Φ-graded signature, (ground and linear) terms, positions, and substitutions).

1. *A* Φ-graded signature $\mathcal{F}$ *is a set of function symbols, each equipped with a fixed nonnegative modal arity. The* modal arity *of an* n*-ary function symbol* f *is a tuple* $(\phi_1, \ldots, \phi_n)$ *with* $\phi_i \in \Phi$. *In this case, we say that* f *has* sensitivity *(or* modal grade*)* ϕ_i *on its* i*-th argument and use the notation* $f : (\phi_1, \ldots, \phi_n)$ *to represent it.*
2. *The set of* terms *over a* Φ*-graded signature* $\mathcal{F}$ *and a set of variables* $\mathcal{V}$ *is defined in the standard way and denoted by* $T(\mathcal{F}, \mathcal{V})$. *The notion of a* position *in a term is also standard.*
3. *A term is* ground *if it contains no variables, and* linear *if it does not contain repeated occurrences of the same variable.*

4. *A* substitution *is a map $\sigma\colon \mathcal{V} \longrightarrow T(\mathcal{F},\mathcal{V})$ which maps all but finitely many variables to themselves. We use the set notation for substitutions, writing σ explicitly as a finite set $\{x \mapsto \sigma(x) \mid x \neq \sigma(x)\}$. The* domain *and* range *of σ are defined as $dom(\sigma) := \{x \mid x \neq \sigma(x)\}$ and $ran(\sigma) = \{\sigma(x) \mid x \in dom(\sigma)\}$, respectively. A substitution σ extends naturally to an endomorphism on $T(\mathcal{F},\mathcal{V})$. The image of a term t under this endomorphism is denoted by $t\sigma$.*

Notation 3 *The set of positions of a term t is denoted $O(t)$. For two positions p and q, we write $p.q$ for their concatenation, and $p \sqsubseteq q$ to denote that p is a prefix of q. The subterm of a term t at position p is represented by $t|_p$, while $t[s]_p$ is the term obtained from t by replacing $t|_p$ by s. Moreover, we denote the set of variable positions of t by $O_{\mathcal{V}}(t)$, and the set of non-variable positions of t by $O_{\mathcal{F}}(t)$.*

Given a term $t \in T(\mathcal{F},\mathcal{V})$, we denote by $\mathcal{V}(t)$ the set of variables appearing in t. For a set of terms S, $\mathcal{V}(S) = \bigcup_{t\in S}\mathcal{V}(t)$.

The set of ground terms over $\mathcal{F}$ is denoted by $T(\mathcal{F})$.

Greek letters $\sigma, \rho, \varphi, \vartheta, \tau$ are used for substitutions, while Id denotes the identity substitution. The set of substitutions is denoted by Sub. For substitutions σ and τ, we write $\sigma \leqq \tau$ if $\sigma\rho = \tau$ holds for some substitution ρ. Similarly, we write $t \leqq s$ for two terms t and s if $t\rho = s$ for some substitution ρ.

Definition 6 (Grade of a position and a variable in a term).

1. *Given a term t and a position p in it, the* grade $\partial_p(t)$ of p in t *is a CBE defined as follows:*
   - $\partial_\lambda(t) := \mathbb{1}$, *where λ denotes the top position (empty sequence).*
   - $\partial_{i.p}(f(t_1,\ldots,t_n)) := \phi_i \circ \partial_p(t_i)$, *where $f : (\phi_1,\ldots,\phi_n) \in \mathcal{F}$.*
2. *The grade of a variable x in a term t, denoted by $\partial_x(t)$, is defined as:*

$$\partial_x(t) := \begin{cases} \kappa^\star, & \text{if } x \notin \mathcal{V}(t) \\ \bigotimes\limits_{\{p \mid t|_p = x\}} \partial_p(t), & \text{otherwise} \end{cases}$$

Definition 7 (Graded equational theory). *Consider a quantitative ternary relation given by a set E of triples (t, ε, s), where t, s are terms constructed over a Φ-graded signature $\mathcal{F}$ and ε is an element of a Lawverean quantale Ω. We denote such triples by $\varepsilon \Vdash t \approx_E s$ and refer to them as Ω-equalities. A* graded quantitative equational theory *(or* graded (Ω,Φ)-equational theory*) is a pair $\mathcal{E} = (\mathcal{F}, =_E)$, where $=_E$ is the quantitative ternary relation generated from $\approx_E$ by the rules in Fig. 1*[1]*. We call E a* presentation *of $=_E$.*

Definition 8 (Balanced Equational Theory). *A graded equational theory is called* balanced *if whenever $\varepsilon \Vdash s \approx t$, we have $\partial_x(s) = \partial_x(t)$ for any variable x. If all equations in $\approx_E$ are balanced, so are equations in $=_E$.*

[1] The original definition in [24] includes an Archimedean rule not necessary for our purposes.

$$\text{(Ax)}\ \frac{\varepsilon \Vdash t \approx_E s}{\varepsilon \Vdash t =_E s} \quad \text{(Refl)}\ \frac{}{\kappa \Vdash t =_E t} \quad \text{(Sym)}\ \frac{\varepsilon \Vdash t =_E s}{\varepsilon \Vdash s =_E t} \quad \text{(Trans)}\ \frac{\varepsilon \Vdash t =_E s \quad \delta \Vdash s =_E r}{\varepsilon \otimes \delta \Vdash t =_E r}$$

$$\text{(Ampl)}\ \frac{\varepsilon_1 \Vdash t_1 =_E s_1 \quad \cdots \quad \varepsilon_n \Vdash t_n =_E s_n \quad f : (\phi_1, \ldots, \phi_n) \in \mathcal{F}}{\phi_1(\varepsilon_1) \otimes \cdots \otimes \phi_n(\varepsilon_n) \Vdash f(t_1, \ldots, t_n) =_E f(s_1, \ldots, s_n)}$$

$$\text{(Subst)}\ \frac{\varepsilon \Vdash t =_E s}{\varepsilon \Vdash t\sigma =_E s\sigma} \qquad \text{(Ord)}\ \frac{\varepsilon \Vdash t =_E s \quad \delta \precsim \varepsilon}{\delta \Vdash t =_E s}$$

$$\text{(Join)}\ \frac{\varepsilon_1 \Vdash t =_E s \quad \cdots \quad \varepsilon_n \Vdash t =_E s}{\varepsilon_1 \vee \cdots \vee \varepsilon_n \Vdash t =_E s}$$

Fig. 1: Graded quantitative equational theory

The grade of a position in a given context determines how this context amplifies distances:

Lemma 1 (Graded Context Rule (Context)). *In any graded equational theory E, the following inference rule is valid for all terms u, v, t, degrees $\varepsilon \in \Omega$ and positions $p \in O(t)$:*

$$\text{(Context)}\quad \frac{\varepsilon \Vdash u =_E v}{\partial_p(t)(\varepsilon) \Vdash t[u]_p =_E t[v]_p}.$$

Proof. We proceeded by induction on the length of the position p.

If $p = \lambda$, the statement holds trivially as $\partial_\lambda(t) = \mathbb{1}, t[u]_p = u$ and $t[v]_p = v$.

In the inductive step, consider $p \neq \lambda$. In this case, $t = f(w_1, \ldots, w_n)$. Thus, we can write $p = i.q$ for some position q and $i \in \{1, \ldots, n\}$. Also, $t[u]_p = f(w_1, \ldots, w_i[u]_q, \ldots, w_n)$ and $t[v]_p = f(w_1, \ldots, w_i[v]_q, \ldots, w_n)$. Assume that the statement holds for all positions $|q| < |p|$ and $f : (\phi_1, \ldots, \phi_n)$. By induction hypothesis, $\partial_q(w_i)(\varepsilon) \Vdash w_i[u]_q =_E w_i[v]_q$. Consequently, by (Refl) and (Ampl) rules,

$$\phi_i(\partial_q(w_i)(\varepsilon)) \Vdash t[u]_p =_E t[v]_p$$

This concludes the proof since $(\phi_i \circ \partial_q(w_i))(\varepsilon) = \partial_p(t)(\varepsilon)$, by definition.

Corollary 1. *Let u, v, and t be terms in any graded equational theory E. Suppose that $p \in O(t)$ and $\kappa \Vdash u =_E v$. Then, $\kappa \Vdash t[u]_p =_E t[v]_p$.*

Proof. By Lemma 1 one has that $\partial_p(t)(\kappa) \Vdash t[u]_p =_E t[v]_p$. The result is obtained since $\partial_p(t)$ is a quantale homomorphism.

The quantitative unification problem below was introduced in [19]:

Given:	A quantale Ω, $\varepsilon \in \Omega$ (called the threshold) with $\varepsilon \succ \bot$, a finite quantitative ternary relation $E \subseteq T(\mathcal{F},\mathcal{V}) \times \Omega \times T(\mathcal{F},\mathcal{V})$, and two terms t and s.
Find:	A substitution σ such that $\varepsilon \Vdash t\sigma =_E s\sigma$.

This problem is called the (E,ε)-*unification problem* for t and s, denoted $t =^?_{E,\varepsilon} s$ for short. If σ satisfies $\varepsilon \Vdash t\sigma =_E s\sigma$, then σ is called an (E,ε)-*unifier* of t and s, or an E-unifier of t and s of *degree* ε.

Definition 9 (Graded quantitative term rewriting system). *An* (Ω,Φ)-*term rewriting system* ((Ω,Φ)-*TRS, for short) is a pair* $\mathcal{R} = (\mathcal{F}, R)$ *consisting of a* Φ-*graded signature* $\mathcal{F}$ *and a quantitative ternary relation* $R \subseteq T(\mathcal{F},\mathcal{V}) \times \Omega \times T(\mathcal{F},\mathcal{V})$, *where for convenience triples* $(l,\varepsilon,r) \in R$ *are written as* $\varepsilon \Vdash l \mapsto_R r$ *and called rewrite rules. Moreover, we assume that* $l \notin \mathcal{V}$ *and* $\mathcal{V}(r) \subseteq \mathcal{V}(l)$ *hold for any rewrite rule* $\varepsilon \Vdash l \mapsto_R r$. *The rewriting relation* $\twoheadrightarrow_R$ *generated by* R *is defined as the least ternary relation* $\twoheadrightarrow_R$ *such that for any terms* $s,l,r \in T(\mathcal{F},\mathcal{V})$, *position* p *in* s, *quantale element* $\varepsilon \in \Omega$, *and substitution* σ *we have:*

$$\frac{\varepsilon \Vdash l \mapsto_R r}{\partial_p(s)(\varepsilon) \Vdash s[l\sigma]_p \twoheadrightarrow_R s[r\sigma]_p},$$

where infix notation like $\zeta \Vdash t \twoheadrightarrow_R s$ *is used to denote* $(t,\zeta,s) \in \twoheadrightarrow_R$.

Note that this notion deviates from the one in [24], which includes rules to account for the (Ord), (Join), and Archimedean axiom. To emphasize this deviation visually, we use different arrow symbols, such as $\twoheadrightarrow$ instead of $\to$. The rewrite relation defined here preserves a conceptually important property of non-quantitative TRSs, namely that with respect to a finite set of rewrite rules, there are only finitely many single-step rewrites from a given term. This is not the case if a structural rule is included to account for (Ord).

Graded term rewriting systems naturally inherit properties of ordinary TRSs that will be denoted in the standard manner (cf. [12]). Left- and right-hand sides of the rules are abbreviated as `lhs` and `rhs`, respectively.

Definition 10 (Linear and ground graded rewriting systems). *We say that an* (Ω,Φ)-*TRS* $\mathcal{R}$ *and its rules are* left-linear *and* right-linear *if their* `lhs`*'s and* `rhs`*'s are linear terms, respectively. If they are both left- and right-linear, they are called linear. Analogously,* $\mathcal{R}$ *is called* left-ground *and* right-ground *if the* `lhs`*'s and* `rhs`*'s are ground terms, respectively.*

Notation 4 *For more notational flexibility, we also allow to write* $l \twoheadrightarrow_{R,\delta} r$ *instead of* $\delta \Vdash l \twoheadrightarrow_R r$.

Definition 11 ((R,ε)-convertible and (R,ε)-joinable terms). *Given an* (Ω,Φ)-*TRS* $\mathcal{R} = (\mathcal{F}, \mapsto_R)$, *we define quantitative ternary relations* $\twoheadleftarrow_R$ *and* $\twoheadleftarrow\!\!\twoheadrightarrow_R$ *by setting* $t \twoheadleftarrow_{R,\varepsilon} s$ *iff* $s \twoheadrightarrow_{R,\varepsilon} t$ *and* $\twoheadleftarrow\!\!\twoheadrightarrow_R := \twoheadrightarrow_R \cup \twoheadleftarrow_R$. *If two terms* t,s *for some* $\varepsilon \in \Omega$ *satisfy* $t \twoheadleftarrow\!\!\twoheadrightarrow^*_{R,\varepsilon} s$, *then we say that* t *and* s *are* (R,ε)-convertible. *We say that* t *and* s *are* (R,ε)-joinable, *denoted by* $t \downarrow_{R,\varepsilon} s$, *if there exist* $\delta_1,\delta_2 \in \Omega$ *and a term* r *such that* $t \twoheadrightarrow^*_{R,\delta_1} r$, $s \twoheadrightarrow^*_{R,\delta_2} r$, *and* $\delta_1 \otimes \delta_2 = \varepsilon$.

For a given Φ-graded signature $\mathcal{F}$ and an (Ω, Φ)-TRS $\mathcal{R}$, we extend $\mathcal{F}$ to the signature $\mathcal{F}'$ by adding two new function symbols: a constant symbol TRUE and a binary symbol $=^?$ with arity $(\mathbb{1}, \mathbb{1})$. Moreover, we extend the given rewrite relation R to R' by adding the rule $\kappa \Vdash x =^? x \mapsto \text{TRUE}$.

Remark 3. We have $t \downarrow_{R,\varepsilon} s$ iff $t =^? s \twoheadrightarrow^*_{R',\varepsilon} \text{TRUE}$.

The notion of confluence has been extended to (Ω, Φ)-TRSs in [24].

Definition 12 (Confluence of (Ω, Φ)-TRSs [24]). *An (Ω, Φ)-TRS $\mathcal{R}$ is said to be* confluent *if for any terms t, s_1, s_2 and quantale elements $\varepsilon_1, \varepsilon_2 \in \Omega$ satisfying $t \twoheadrightarrow^*_{R,\varepsilon_1} s_1$ and $t \twoheadrightarrow^*_{R,\varepsilon_2} s_2$, there exists a quantale element $\delta \succsim \varepsilon_1 \otimes \varepsilon_2$ such that s_1 and s_2 are (R, δ)-joinable.*

A quantitative analogue of the Church-Rosser result has been provided in [24]. With slight modifications, it holds also with respect to the rewrite relation described in Definition 9. The proof is provided in [10].

Lemma 2 (Quantitative Church-Rosser). *Let $\mathcal{R}$ be a confluent (Ω, Φ)-TRS, and let t, s be terms and $\varepsilon \in \Omega$. If $t \twoheadleftarrow\twoheadrightarrow^*_{R,\varepsilon} s$, then $t \downarrow_{R,\delta} s$ holds for some $\delta \succsim \varepsilon$, and $t \downarrow_{R,\delta} s$ implies $t \twoheadleftarrow\twoheadrightarrow^*_{R,\delta} s$.*

The following two lemmas establish the relationship between an (Ω, Φ)-TRS and the corresponding quantitative equational theory. Their proofs are provided in [10].

Lemma 3. *Let $\mathcal{R}$ be an (Ω, Φ)-TRS. If $t \twoheadleftarrow\twoheadrightarrow^*_{R,\varepsilon} s$, then $\varepsilon \Vdash s =_R t$.*

Lemma 4. *Let $\mathcal{R}$ be an (Ω, Φ)-TRS. If $\varepsilon \Vdash t =_R s$, then there exist $\delta_1, \ldots, \delta_n \in \Omega$ such that $\delta_1 \vee \cdots \vee \delta_n \succsim \varepsilon$ and $t \twoheadleftarrow\twoheadrightarrow^*_{R,\delta_i} s$ holds for every $i \in \{1, \ldots, n\}$.*

Corollary 2. *Let $\mathcal{R}$ be a confluent (Ω, Φ)-TRS and let $t, s \in T(\mathcal{F}, \mathcal{V})$ be two terms. If $\varepsilon \Vdash t =_R s$, then there exist $\delta_1, \ldots, \delta_n \in \Omega$ such that $\delta_1 \vee \cdots \vee \delta_n \succsim \varepsilon$ and $t \downarrow_{R,\delta_i} s$ holds for every $i \in \{1, \ldots, n\}$.*

4 Graded Quantitative Narrowing

Definition 13 (Graded Narrowing). *Let $\mathcal{R} = (\mathcal{F}, R)$ be an (Ω, Φ)-TRS. The graded narrowing relation $\rightsquigarrow_R$ generated by R is defined as the least ternary relation such that for any terms $l, r, s \in T(\mathcal{F}, \mathcal{V})$ and quantale elements $\varepsilon, \delta \in \Omega$ we have:*

$$\frac{\varepsilon \Vdash l \mapsto_R r}{\partial_p(s)(\varepsilon) \Vdash s \rightsquigarrow_R (s[r\rho]_p)\sigma}$$

where ρ is a renaming substitution, s does not have a common variable with $l\rho$ and $r\rho$, $p \in O_{\mathcal{F}}(s)$, and σ is a syntactic most general unifier of $s|_p$ and $l\rho$.

In such a case, we also write $s \rightsquigarrow_{R,\sigma,\partial_p(s)(\varepsilon)} (s[r\rho]_p)\sigma$. If needed, we also allow to specify the position p and the rewrite rule $\varepsilon \Vdash l \mapsto r$ as subscripts of the relation $\rightsquigarrow_R$. For $n \in \mathbb{N}$, we define the iterated narrowing relation $\rightsquigarrow_R^n$ as follows:

$t \rightsquigarrow^0_{R,\sigma,\varepsilon} s :\Leftrightarrow t = s, \sigma = Id,$ and $\varepsilon = \kappa;$

$t \rightsquigarrow^1_{R,\sigma,\varepsilon} s :\Leftrightarrow t \rightsquigarrow_{R,\sigma,\varepsilon} s;$

$t \rightsquigarrow^{n+1}_{R,\sigma,\varepsilon} s :\Leftrightarrow$ there exist a term u, substitutions σ_1, σ_2 and $\varepsilon_1, \varepsilon_2 \in \Omega$ such that $t \rightsquigarrow^n_{R,\sigma_1,\varepsilon_1} u$ and $u \rightsquigarrow_{R,\sigma_2,\varepsilon_2} s$, where $\sigma_1\sigma_2 = \sigma$ and $\varepsilon_1 \otimes \varepsilon_2 = \varepsilon$.

Analogous to the quantitative rewrite relation, we define the reflexive transitive closure of $\rightsquigarrow_R$ by $\rightsquigarrow_R^* := \bigcup_{n \geqslant 0} \rightsquigarrow_R^n$.

Example 3. Consider the quantitative rewrite system $\mathcal{R} = (\mathcal{F}, R)$ from [25], where $\mathcal{F} = \{Z : (), S : (Id), + : (Id, Id)\}$ and R is the relation over the Lawvere quantale $\mathbb{L}$ given by

$$\{0 \Vdash x + Z \mapsto x,\ 0 \Vdash x + S(y) \mapsto S(x + y),\ 1 \Vdash S(x) \mapsto x\}.$$

The relation $\mapsto$ defines actual distances by eliminating successor functions. The induced convertibility relation coincides with the Euclidean distance on natural numbers.[2]

Using $\mathcal{R}$, we apply quantitative narrowing to find an "approximate" solution of the equation $x + 1 = 3x$ (whose precise solution, $\frac{1}{2}$, cannot be expressed as a term over $\mathcal{F}$).

To this end, we solve the quantitative unification problem $x + S(Z) =^?_{R,1} x + x + x$.

A successful narrowing derivation with respect to the extended relation R' (see the part after Definition 11) is given below. At each step, the subterms at the narrowing position is underlined, and the rewrite rule applied is indicated in parentheses. Here we denote the rules of R by r_1, r_2, and r_3 (in the order that they appear above), and the additional rule $0 \Vdash x =^? x \mapsto \text{TRUE}$ of R' by r_4.

$$\begin{aligned}
&\underline{x + S(Z)} =^? (x + x) + x \\
&\rightsquigarrow_{R',Id,0} S(\underline{x + Z}) =^? (x + x) + x && \text{(by } r_2\text{)} \\
&\rightsquigarrow_{R',Id,0} \underline{S(x)} =^? (x + x) + x && \text{(by } r_1\text{)} \\
&\rightsquigarrow_{R',Id,1} x =^? \underline{(x + x) + x} && \text{(by } r_3\text{)} \\
&\rightsquigarrow_{R',\{x \mapsto Z\},0} Z =^? \underline{Z + Z} && \text{(by } r_1\text{)} \\
&\rightsquigarrow_{R',Id,0} \underline{Z =^? Z} && \text{(by } r_1\text{)} \\
&\rightsquigarrow_{R',Id,0} \text{TRUE} && \text{(by } r_4\text{)}
\end{aligned}$$

Thus, we have obtained the approximate solution $\{x \mapsto Z\}$. We also show an alternative derivation, leading to the approximate solution $\{x \mapsto S(Z)\}$.

$$\underline{x + S(Z)} =^? (x + x) + x$$

[2] This system can be seen as a quantitative extension of Example 3.2 from [35], used there for illustrating the standard narrowing.

$$
\begin{aligned}
&\rightsquigarrow_{R',Id,0} S(\underline{x+Z}) =^? (x+x)+x && \text{(by } r_2\text{)}\\
&\rightsquigarrow_{R',Id,0} S(x) =^? \underline{(x+x)+x} && \text{(by } r_1\text{)}\\
&\rightsquigarrow_{R',\{x\mapsto S(y)\},0} S(S(y)) =^? S(\underline{(S(y)+S(y))+y}) && \text{(by } r_2\text{)}\\
&\rightsquigarrow_{R',\{y\mapsto Z\},0} S(S(Z)) =^? S(\underline{S(Z)+S(Z)}) && \text{(by } r_1\text{)}\\
&\rightsquigarrow_{R',Id,0} S(S(Z)) =^? S(S(\underline{S(Z)+Z})) && \text{(by } r_2\text{)}\\
&\rightsquigarrow_{R',Id,0} S(S(Z)) =^? S(S(\underline{S(Z)})) && \text{(by } r_1\text{)}\\
&\rightsquigarrow_{R',Id,1} \underline{S(S(Z)) =^? S(S(Z))} && \text{(by } r_3\text{)}\\
&\rightsquigarrow_{R',Id,0} \text{TRUE} && \text{(by } r_4\text{)}
\end{aligned}
$$

The notion of a *basic* narrowing derivation is defined as in [34].

Definition 14 (Basic Graded Narrowing). *Let*

$$t_1 \rightsquigarrow_{R,\sigma_1,\zeta_1,p_1,\varepsilon_1 \Vdash l_1 \mapsto r_1} \cdots \rightsquigarrow_{R,\sigma_{n-1},\zeta_{n-1},p_{n-1},\varepsilon_{n-1} \Vdash l_{n-1} \mapsto r_{n-1}} t_n$$

be a narrowing derivation. We inductively define the sets of basic positions *of* $t_1, \ldots, t_n$ *with respect to the above derivation by*

$$B_1 := O_{\mathcal{F}}(t_1), \qquad B_{i+1} := \{q \in B_i \mid p_i \not\sqsubseteq q\} \cup \{p_i.q \mid q \in O_{\mathcal{F}}(r_i)\}.$$

When the narrowing derivation is clear from the context, we refer to B_i *as the set of basic positions of* t_i*, denoted* $O_{\mathcal{B}}(t_i)$*. We say that the above narrowing derivation is basic if* $p_i \in B_i$ *holds for each* $i \in \{1, \ldots, n-1\}$*.*

Requiring that our narrowing derivations are basic means that narrowing may not be applied to terms that have been introduced by a narrowing substitution in a previous step. This requirement prohibits some non-terminating derivations while maintaining completeness in the non-quantitative setting [35].

Remark 4. If t is a linear term and $\mathcal{R}$ is right-ground, then every narrowing derivation $t \rightsquigarrow^*_{R,\varepsilon} s$ is basic.

Indeed, we can write the narrowing derivation as

$$t = t_1 \rightsquigarrow_{R,\sigma_1,\zeta_1,\varepsilon_1 \Vdash l_1 \mapsto r_1,p_1} \cdots \rightsquigarrow_{R,\sigma_{n-1},\zeta_{n-1},\varepsilon_{n-1} \Vdash l_{n-1} \mapsto r_{n-1},p_{n-1}} t_n = s.$$

We will prove the claim by showing that $O_{\mathcal{B}}(t_i) = O_{\mathcal{F}}(t_i)$ for $i = 1, \ldots, n-1$. We proceed by induction on i. The case $i = 1$ holds by definition.

For the induction step, suppose that we have $O_{\mathcal{B}}(t_i) = O_{\mathcal{F}}(t_i)$. Note that we have $t_{i+1} = t_i[r_i]_{p_i}\sigma_i = t_i[r_i\sigma_i]_{p_i} = t_i[r_i]_{p_i}$, where the second equality holds since by linearity of t, the variables in $dom(\sigma_i)$ do not appear in t_i except possibly below position p_i, and the last equality holds as r_i is ground. Thus, we have

$$
\begin{aligned}
O_{\mathcal{B}}(t_{i+1}) &= \{q \in O_{\mathcal{B}}(t_i) \mid p_i \not\sqsubseteq q\} \cup \{p_i \cdot q \mid q \in O_{\mathcal{F}}(r_i)\}\\
&= \{q \in O_{\mathcal{F}}(t_i) \mid p_i \not\sqsubseteq q\} \cup \{p_i \cdot q \mid q \in O_{\mathcal{F}}(r_i)\}\\
&= O_{\mathcal{F}}(t_i[r_i]_{p_i}) = O_{\mathcal{F}}(t_{i+1}).
\end{aligned}
$$

4.1 Quantitative Narrowing Rules: the BQNARROW Calculus

In the following, we propose a set of transformation rules for E-unification (BQNARROW calculus), inspired by basic narrowing [27,12,33]. We operate on configurations of the form $e; C; \sigma; \delta$, where: (i) e is a term over $\mathcal{F}'$ (the current state of the problem); (ii) C is a set of equations (the current set of constraints); (iii) σ is a substitution (the solution computed thus far); (iv) δ is an element of Ω (the current degree of approximation).

The inference rules of the calculus BQNARROW can be seen in Table 2.

Table 2: BQNARROW inference rules

LP: **Lazy Paramodulation**

$$e[t]_p; C; \sigma; \delta \Longrightarrow_{\partial_p(e)(\varepsilon)} e[r]_p; \{l\sigma = t\sigma\} \cup C; \sigma; \delta \otimes \partial_p(e)(\varepsilon),$$

where $e \neq$ TRUE, p is a non-variable position of e, and $\varepsilon \Vdash l \mapsto r$ is a *fresh* variant of a rule in R.

SU: **Syntactic Unification**

$$e; C; \sigma; \delta \Longrightarrow_{\kappa} e; \emptyset; \sigma\rho; \delta,$$

where $C \neq \emptyset$ and ρ is a most general unifier of C.

Cla: **Clash**

$$e; C; \sigma; \delta \Longrightarrow_{\kappa} \mathbf{F}, \quad \text{if } C \text{ is not unifiable.}$$

Con: **Constrain**

$$e; C; \sigma; \delta \Longrightarrow_{\kappa} \text{TRUE}; C \cup \{e\sigma\}; \sigma; \delta, \quad \text{if } e \neq \text{TRUE}.$$

Remark 5. Applying the BQNARROW inference rules must guarantee that the substitution built in the configuration, say σ, is well-defined and idempotent. To preserve this property in formalizations, the notion of mgu is adapted so that the substitution ρ computed in the application of the rule (SU) satisfies $dom(\rho) \subseteq \mathcal{V}(ran(\sigma))$ and $\mathcal{V}(ran(\rho))$ is a set of fresh variables regarding the set of all variables used in the whole process.[3] This condition simplifies formal proofs since substitution $\sigma\rho$ built in the rule (SU) is easily proved to be idempotent.

A second important observation justifying the possibility of constructing an mgu ρ such that $dom(\rho)$ is disjoint from $\mathcal{V}(ran(\sigma))$ is that all equations included in the second component of the configuration, say C, by the rules (LP) and (Con) are instantiated by σ, implying that these equations have no variables in $dom(\sigma)$. Therefore, ρ does not need to instantiate variables in $dom(\sigma)$. Finally, the selection of variants of the rules with fresh variables for each application of the rule LP is also required. Such problems are more apparent in computational frameworks of unification. For instance, [9] uses a notion of "nice substitutions" and of "correct

[3] It can be achieved, e.g., by defining substitution comparison with respect to a fixed set of variables, which in case of unifiers is the set of variables of the unification problem.

input renamings" to formalize the correctness of AC-unification. Also, [7] and [8] use specialized notions of substitution and a mechanism to "protect variables" to verify nominal C-unification and nominal AC-matching, respectively.

Remark 6. The BQNARROW rules, as defined, may lead to extensive branching. To mitigate this issue, one can impose restrictions, for example, requiring that in LP, the terms l and t have the same head symbol, or even that they be unifiable. However, such techniques are beyond the scope of this paper.

The following lemma confirms that the calculus BQNARROW captures basic narrowing. Its proof can be found in [10].

Lemma 5. *If* $t \rightsquigarrow^*_{R,\varepsilon,\sigma} s$ *is obtained via a basic narrowing derivation, then there exists a derivation* $t; \emptyset; Id; \kappa \Longrightarrow^*_{\varepsilon} s'; \emptyset; \sigma; \varepsilon$ *in* BQNARROW, *where* $s'\sigma = s$ *and the set of basic positions of* s *is precisely the set of non-variable positions of* s'.

Conversely, it is easy to see that if BQNARROW uses the strategy of applying SU immediately after an application of LP, then from a non-failing BQNARROW derivation one can directly obtain the corresponding basic narrowing derivation.

4.2 Soundness of BQNARROW

The following lemma prepares the soundness proof. Its proof can be found in [10].

Lemma 6 (Unification of the set of equations by BQNARROW). *If there is a derivation* $e; C; \sigma; \delta \Longrightarrow^* e'; \emptyset; \sigma'; \delta'$, *using the rules from* BQNARROW, *then for all* $s = t \in C$, $s\sigma' = t\sigma'$.

Theorem 1 (Soundness of BQNARROW). *If* $t =^? s; C; \sigma; \delta \Longrightarrow^+_{\varepsilon}$ TRUE; $\emptyset; \sigma'; \delta'$ *is a derivation using the rules from* BQNARROW, *then* $\varepsilon \Vdash t\sigma' =_R s\sigma'$.

Proof. For notational convenience, we write e for the term $t =^? s$. For any term u of the form $l =^? r$, we use the notation $\mathtt{lhs}(u)$ and $\mathtt{rhs}(u)$ to refer to l and r, respectively.

The proof is by induction on the length of the derivation, say n. Suppose the derivation is of the form

$$\mathfrak{C}_0 \Longrightarrow_{\zeta} \mathfrak{C}_1 \Longrightarrow^*_{\eta} \mathfrak{C}_n,$$

where $\zeta \otimes \eta = \varepsilon$, $\mathfrak{C}_0 = e; C; \sigma; \delta$, $\mathfrak{C}_n = \text{TRUE}; \emptyset; \sigma'; \delta'$ and $\mathfrak{C}_i = e_i; C_i; \sigma_i; \delta_i$ for $i = 0, \ldots, n$ ($\sigma = \sigma_0$ and $\sigma_n = \sigma'$).

In the case $n = 1$, the sole applicable rule is SU, so we have $\zeta = \kappa$, and $\mathfrak{C}_0$ has to be of the form TRUE; $C; \sigma; \delta$ and $\mathfrak{C}_1 = \text{TRUE}; \emptyset; \sigma_1; \delta$, where $\sigma_1 = \sigma\rho$. Since $\kappa \Vdash$ TRUE, we also have $\delta \Vdash (\text{TRUE})\sigma_1$.

Proceeding to the induction step, let $n \geqslant 1$ and suppose the statement of the lemma holds up until $n - 1$. We prove that the lemma holds for n. Applying the induction hypothesis to the derivation

$$\mathfrak{C}_1 \Longrightarrow^+_{\eta} \mathfrak{C}_n,$$

we obtain $\eta \Vdash e_1\sigma'$.

We distinguish cases according to the BQNARROW rule yielding the first step $\mathfrak{C}_0 \Longrightarrow_\zeta \mathfrak{C}_1$.

- Case (LP): $\mathfrak{C}_0 = e[t]_p; C; \sigma; \delta \Longrightarrow_{\partial_p(e)(\varepsilon)} e[r]_p; \{l\sigma = t\sigma\} \cup C; \sigma; \delta \otimes \partial_p(e)(\varepsilon)$, where $e = e[t]_p$ and $\iota \Vdash l \to r \in \mathcal{R}$. On the one side, by induction hypothesis, $\eta \Vdash e[r]_p\sigma'$. Firstly, assuming that $p = 1.q$, this means that $\eta \Vdash \texttt{lhs}(e)[r]_q\sigma' =_E \texttt{rhs}(e)\sigma'$. Notice that $l\sigma' =_E t\sigma'$ by Lemma 6. Then, by applying Corollary 1 and (Sym) in Fig. 1 one obtains $\kappa \Vdash \texttt{lhs}(e)[t]_q\sigma' =_E \texttt{lhs}(e)[l]_q\sigma'$. Since $\partial_q(\texttt{lhs}(e))(\iota) \Vdash \texttt{lhs}(e)[l]_q\sigma' =_E \texttt{lhs}(e)[r]_q\sigma'$, by (Trans) in Fig. 1, $\partial_q(\texttt{lhs}(e))(\iota) \Vdash \texttt{lhs}(e)[t]_q\sigma' = \texttt{lhs}(e)[r]_q\sigma'$.
  From the above two main graded equations, using (Trans), we obtain the graded equation $\partial_q(\texttt{lhs}(e))(\iota) \otimes \eta \Vdash \texttt{lhs}(e)[t]_q\sigma' =_E \texttt{rhs}(e)\sigma'$, abbreviated as $\partial_q(\texttt{lhs}(e))(\iota) \otimes \eta \Vdash e\sigma'$. Additionally, $\partial_q(\texttt{lhs}(e))(\iota) = \partial_p(e)(\iota)$ since the modal arity of the symbol $=^?$ is $(\mathbb{1}, \mathbb{1})$. Therefore, $\partial_p(e)(\iota) \otimes \eta \Vdash e\sigma'$.
  Secondly, the case in which $p = 2.q$ is similar, except that both (Trans) and (Sym) are required in the second step of the above analysis; indeed, what we obtain is that $\eta \Vdash \texttt{lhs}(e)\sigma' = \texttt{rhs}(e)[r]_q\sigma'$, by induction hypothesis, and that $\partial_q(\texttt{rhs}(e))(\iota) \Vdash \texttt{rhs}(e)[t]_q\sigma' = \texttt{rhs}(e)[r]_q\sigma'$. Because of that, the necessity of using (Sym).
- Case (SU): $\mathfrak{C}_0 = e; C; \sigma; \delta \Longrightarrow_\kappa e; \emptyset; \sigma\rho; \delta$, for $\rho = \text{mgu}(C)$. This case is clear because $\kappa \otimes \zeta = \zeta$ and $\zeta \Vdash e\sigma'$ by induction hypothesis.
- Case (Con): $\mathfrak{C}_0 = e; C; \sigma; \delta \Longrightarrow_\kappa \text{TRUE}; C \cup \{e\sigma\}; \sigma; \delta$. The remainder of the derivation has to consist only of one application of the rule (SU), such that $\eta = \kappa$, $\mathfrak{C}_n = \mathfrak{C}_2 = \text{TRUE}; \emptyset; \sigma\rho; \delta$, and $\rho = \text{mgu}(C \cup \{e\sigma\})$. Then, in particular, $\kappa \Vdash e\sigma\rho$.

Corollary 3. *If* $t =^? s; \emptyset; Id; \kappa \Longrightarrow^*_\varepsilon \text{TRUE}; \emptyset; \sigma, \varepsilon$ *is a derivation using rules from* BQNARROW, *then* σ *is an* (R, ε)*-unifier of* t *and* s.

5 Completeness of BQNARROW

We will now investigate in what sense and under which conditions the completeness of BQNARROW can be granted. A summary of the results is provided in Figure 2 at the end of this section.

A weak form of completeness could be a statement of the following form: "If $\varepsilon \Vdash t\tau =_R s\tau$, then BQNARROW admits a derivation $t =^? s; \emptyset; Id; \kappa \Longrightarrow^*_\delta \text{TRUE}; \emptyset; \sigma; \delta$, where $\delta \succsim \varepsilon$." Note that this statement does not imply any relation between the given solution τ and the computed substitution σ; we merely know by Corollary 3 that σ is also a solution of the problem. It can be also rephrased as "if two terms are unifiable modulo R with degree ε, then BQNARROW can find their R-unifier with some degree better than ε".

However, as the following example demonstrates, even this weak form of completeness cannot hold in general.

Example 4. Consider $\Omega = \mathbb{L}$, and let R be given by $\{1 \Vdash a \mapsto c, 1 \Vdash b \mapsto c, 1 \Vdash c \mapsto d\}$ (where a, b, c, d are constants). Let f be a ternary function symbol of modal arity $(\mathbb{1}, \mathbb{1}, \mathbb{1})$ (where $\mathbb{1} \colon [0, \infty] \longrightarrow [0, \infty]$ is the identity map).

The R-unification problem $f(x, x, x) =^?_R f(a, b, d)$ has the "optimal" solution $\sigma = \{x \mapsto c\}$ with degree 3.

Via narrowing, only the solution $\tau = \{x \mapsto d\}$ with degree 4 can be found (see below), but not σ or the solutions $\{x \mapsto a\}$ and $\{x \mapsto b\}$, which also have degree 4.

$$
\begin{aligned}
& f(x,x,x) =^?_R f(a,b,d); \emptyset\ Id; 0 \Longrightarrow^2_{\mathsf{LP}} \\
& f(x,x,x) =^?_R f(c,c,d); \{a = a, b = b\}; Id; 2 \Longrightarrow^2_{\mathsf{LP}} \\
& f(x,x,x) =^?_R f(d,d,d); \{a = a, b = b, c = c\}; Id; 4 \Longrightarrow_{\mathsf{Con}} \\
& \text{TRUE}; \{f(x,x,x) = f(d,d,d), a = a, b = b, c = c\}; Id; 4 \Longrightarrow_{\mathsf{SU}} \\
& \text{TRUE}; \emptyset; \{x \mapsto d\}; 4
\end{aligned}
$$

Also notice that for $R = \{1 \Vdash a \mapsto b, 1 \Vdash b \mapsto c\}$, and the problem $f(x, x, x) =^?_R f(a, b, c)$, BQNARROW will compute only the solution $\{x \mapsto c\}$ with degree 3 , but $\{x \mapsto b\}$ is a better solution with degree 2.

Observing that the incompleteness in this example is related to the three occurrences of the variable x in the terms to be unified, one might consider restricting inputs to contain at most two occurrences of the same variable as a potential solution. However, this is insufficient, as rewrite rules can increase the number of variable occurrences in unification problems:

Example 5. Consider again $\Omega = \mathbb{L}$ and the rewrite relation $R' := R \cup \{g(x) \mapsto f(x, x, x)\}$, where R is the rewrite relation from Example 4 and g is a symbol of arity $(\mathbb{1})$. Then the linear problem $g(x) =^?_{R'} f(a, b, d)$ exhibits the same behavior as the problem in Example 4: narrowing computes the solution $\{x \mapsto d\}$ of degree 4, whereas the solution $\{x \mapsto c\}$ of degree 3 cannot be found.

Requiring $\mathcal{R}$ to be right-linear removes this possibility. Indeed, we obtain completeness of ordinary quantitative narrowing for right-linear TRSs and linear problems. The proof of this result can be found in [10].

Theorem 2. *Suppose that $\mathcal{R}$ is a right-linear (Ω, Φ)-TRS, t is a linear term, and $t\tau \rightarrow^*_{R,\varepsilon} s$. Then there is a narrowing derivation $t \rightsquigarrow^*_{R,\sigma,\delta} s'$ such that $\delta \precsim \varepsilon$ and $s' \leqq s$.*

Basic quantitative narrowing, however, is still not complete even when $\mathcal{R}$ is right-linear and the unification problem is linear or even ground, if $\mathcal{R}$ is not balanced, as the following example shows:

Example 6. Consider $\Omega = \mathbb{L}$, the graded signature $\mathcal{F} = \{f : (\lambda x.3 \cdot x), g : (\mathbb{1}), a : (), b : ()\}$, and the rewrite relation $R = \{0 \Vdash f(x) \mapsto g(x), 1 \Vdash a \mapsto b\}$.

The problem $f(a) =^?_R g(b)$ is solved by the identity solution with degree 1, as we have $0 \Vdash f(a) =_R g(a)$ and $1 \Vdash g(a) =_R g(b)$.

However, the only basic narrowing derivation is $f(a) \rightsquigarrow_{R,Id,3} f(b) \rightsquigarrow_{R,\{x \mapsto b\},0} g(b)$, computing a degree of 3.

In addition to the previous assumptions, we therefore also need to assume that $\mathcal{R}$ is balanced. We conjecture that these assumptions are sufficient to lift an ordinary quantitative narrowing derivation to a basic one.

Conjecture 1. Let $\mathcal{R}$ be a confluent, balanced, and right-linear $(\Omega, \oplus)$-TRS. If $t \rightsquigarrow^*_{R,\sigma,\varepsilon} s$, where t is a linear term, then there exists a basic narrowing derivation $t \rightsquigarrow^*_{R',\sigma,\varepsilon} s$.

In the non-quantitative case, the step from narrowing to basic narrowing in a convergent TRS is done by assuming the rewrite sequence was innermost, as innermost rewrite sequences can always be lifted to basic narrowing sequences. In the quantitative setting, we cannot proceed in the same way as we cannot grant that an innermost rewrite sequence yields the optimal degree.

Example 7. Consider $\Omega = \mathbb{L}$, $R = \{0 \Vdash f(a) \mapsto f(b),\ 2 \Vdash a \mapsto b\}$. Then innermost rewriting only gives $f(a) \twoheadrightarrow_{R,2} f(b)$, which is not the optimal degree.

If we restrict ourselves to right-ground TRSs and linear problems, then any narrowing sequence is basic by Remark 4. Hence, we obtain completeness under these assumptions.

The proof of the following result is provided in [10].

Theorem 3. *If t, s are terms in $T(\mathcal{F}, \mathcal{V})$ and there is a basic narrowing derivation $t =^? s \rightsquigarrow^*_{R',\varepsilon,\sigma}$ TRUE, then* BQNARROW *(w.r.t. R) admits a derivation $t =^? s; \emptyset; Id; \kappa \Longrightarrow^*_{\varepsilon}$ TRUE$; \emptyset; \sigma'; \varepsilon$, where $\sigma|_{\mathcal{V}(t,s)} = \sigma'|_{\mathcal{V}(t,s)}$.*

Corollary 4. *Let $t =^? s$ be a linear problem, and let $\mathcal{R}$ be a confluent, right-ground $(\Omega, \oplus)$-TRS. If $t\tau \twoheadleftarrow\!\!\twoheadrightarrow^*_{R,\varepsilon} s\tau$, then* BQNARROW *admits a derivation $t =^? s$; $\emptyset; Id; \kappa \Longrightarrow^*$ TRUE$; \emptyset; \sigma; \delta$ such that $\delta \succsim \varepsilon$.*

Proof. By Lemma 2, we have $t\tau \downarrow_{R,\zeta} s\tau$ for some $\zeta \succsim \varepsilon$; that is, we have $t\tau =^? s\tau \twoheadrightarrow^*_{R',\zeta}$ TRUE. Thus, we obtain $t =^? s \rightsquigarrow^*_{R',\delta}$ TRUE, where $\delta \succsim \zeta \succsim \varepsilon$, by Theorem 2. Since $t =^? s$ is linear and R is right-ground, this narrowing derivation is basic by Remark 4. So by Theorem 3, BQNARROW admits a derivation $t =^? s$; $\emptyset; Id; \kappa \Longrightarrow^*$ TRUE$; \emptyset; \sigma; \delta$.

Corollary 5. *Suppose that Ω is a Lawverean quantale whose order $\precsim$ is total. Let $t =^? s$ be a linear problem, and let $\mathcal{R}$ be a confluent, right-ground $(\Omega, \oplus)$-TRS. If $\varepsilon \Vdash t\tau =_R s\tau$, then* BQNARROW *admits a derivation $t =^? s; \emptyset; Id; \kappa \Longrightarrow^*$ TRUE$; \emptyset; \sigma; \delta$ such that $\delta \succsim \varepsilon$.*

Proof. By Lemma 4, there exist $\delta_1, \ldots, \delta_n \in \Omega$ such that $\delta_1 \vee \cdots \vee \delta_n \succsim \varepsilon$ and $t\tau \twoheadleftarrow\!\!\twoheadrightarrow_{R,\delta_i} s\tau$ for $i = 1, \ldots, n$. Since the order $\precsim$ is total, we must have $\delta_i \succsim \varepsilon$ for some i; thus, Corollary 4 yields the result.

The results and conjectures presented in this section are summarized in Figure 2.

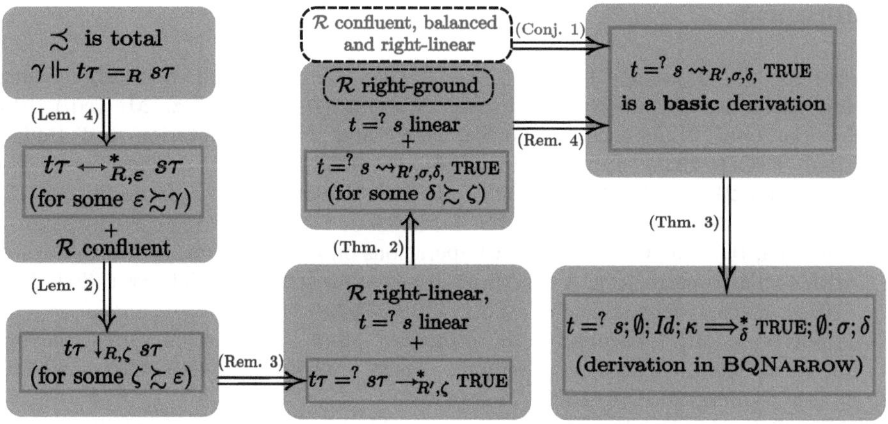

Fig. 2: Summary of results and conjectures related to completeness

6 Conclusion

Narrowing is a well-known technique that generalizes term rewriting by allowing unification rather than mere matching during rule applications. It has a wide range of applications, including equation solving in equational theories, the integration of functional and logic programming, symbolic execution, model checking, reachability analysis, etc.

In this paper, we introduced the concept of narrowing and its basic variant for graded theories, where the quantitative information is specified by (Lawverean) quantales. We applied this framework to quantitative equation solving and established the soundness of the resulting procedure. The quantitative setting presents additional challenges to completeness. To address them, we investigated a restricted class of unification problems and showed that for ordinary quantitative narrowing, completeness holds for linear unification problems in theories induced by confluent and right-linear rewrite systems (with an additional assumption that the underlying quantale is totally ordered). If in these conditions right-linearity is replaced with a stronger right-groundness restriction, we can prove also the completeness of basic narrowing. For future work, we conjectured that completeness of basic narrowing holds for right-linear systems as well, under an additional requirement that the rewrite rules are balanced.

Acknowledgments. This work was partially supported by the Austrian Science Fund (FWF) project P 35530; the Brazilian Research Council CNPq, Grant Universal 409003/21-2, and Research Grant 313290/21-0; and the Goiás Research Foundation FAPEG, process 202310267000223.

Disclosure of Interests. The authors have no competing interests to declare that are relevant to the content of this article.

References

1. Ahrens, E., Kassing, J., Giesl, J., Katoen, J.: Weighted rewriting: Semiring semantics for abstract reduction systems. In: Fernández, M. (ed.) 10th International Conference on Formal Structures for Computation and Deduction, FSCD 2025, July 14-20, 2025, Birmingham, UK. LIPIcs, vol. 337, pp. 6:1–6:21. Schloss Dagstuhl - Leibniz-Zentrum für Informatik (2025). https://doi.org/10.4230/LIPICS.FSCD.2025.6
2. Aït-Kaci, H., Pasi, G.: Fuzzy lattice operations on first-order terms over signatures with similar constructors: A constraint-based approach. Fuzzy Sets Syst. **391**, 1–46 (2020). https://doi.org/10.1016/J.FSS.2019.03.019
3. Alpuente, M., Escobar, S., Iborra, J.: Termination of narrowing revisited. Theor. Comput. Sci. **410**(46), 4608–4625 (2009). https://doi.org/10.1016/J.TCS.2009.07.037
4. Alpuente, M., Escobar, S., Iborra, J.: Modular termination of basic narrowing and equational unification. Log. J. IGPL **19**(6), 731–762 (2011). https://doi.org/10.1093/JIGPAL/JZQ009
5. Antoy, S., Hanus, M.: Functional logic programming. Commun. ACM **53**(4), 74–85 (2010). https://doi.org/10.1145/1721654.1721675
6. Avanzini, M., Yamada, A.: Weighted rewriting (2025), https://akihisayamada.github.io/AY2025.pdf, to appear in FroCoS 2025.
7. Ayala-Rincón, M., de Carvalho Segundo, W., Fernández, M., Silva, G.F., Nantes-Sobrinho, D.: Formalising nominal C-unification generalised with protected variables. Math. Struct. Comput. Sci. **31**(3), 286–311 (2021). https://doi.org/10.1017/S0960129521000050
8. Ayala-Rincón, M., Fernández, M., Silva, G.F., Kutsia, T., Nantes-Sobrinho, D.: Nominal AC-Matching. In: Dubois, C., Kerber, M. (eds.) Intelligent Computer Mathematics - 16th International Conference, CICM 2023, Cambridge, UK, September 5-8, 2023, Proceedings. Lecture Notes in Computer Science, vol. 14101, pp. 53–68. Springer (2023). https://doi.org/10.1007/978-3-031-42753-4_4
9. Ayala-Rincón, M., Fernández, M., Silva, G.F., Kutsia, T., Nantes-Sobrinho, D.: Certified First-Order AC-Unification and Applications. J. Autom. Reason. **68**(4), 25 (2024). https://doi.org/10.1007/S10817-024-09714-5
10. Ayala-Rincón, M., de Lima, T.A., Ehling, G., Kutsia, T.: Graded quantitative narrowing. CoRR **abs/2507.19630** (2025). https://doi.org/10.48550/ARXIV.2507.19630
11. Baader, F., Nipkow, T.: Term rewriting and all that. Cambridge University Press (1998). https://doi.org/https://doi.org/10.1017/CBO9781139172752
12. Baader, F., Snyder, W.: Chapter 8 - Unification Theory. In: Robinson, A., Voronkov, A. (eds.) Handbook of Automated Reasoning, p. 445–533. North-Holland, Amsterdam (2001). https://doi.org/10.1016/B978-044450813-3/50010-2
13. Bacci, G., Mardare, R., Panangaden, P., Plotkin, G.D.: Quantitative Equational Reasoning. In: Barthe, G., Katoen, J.P., Silva, A. (eds.) Foundations of Probabilistic Programming, p. 333–360. Cambridge University Press (2020). https://doi.org/10.1017/9781108770750.011
14. Bae, K., Escobar, S., Meseguer, J.: Abstract logical model checking of infinite-state systems using narrowing. In: van Raamsdonk, F. (ed.) 24th International Conference on Rewriting Techniques and Applications, RTA 2013, June 24-26, 2013, Eindhoven, The Netherlands. LIPIcs, vol. 21, pp. 81–96. Schloss Dagstuhl - Leibniz-Zentrum für Informatik (2013). https://doi.org/10.4230/LIPICS.RTA.2013.81

15. Cholewa, A., Escobar, S., Meseguer, J.: Constrained narrowing for conditional equational theories modulo axioms. Sci. Comput. Program. **112**, 24–57 (2015). https://doi.org/10.1016/J.SCICO.2015.06.001
16. Clavel, M., Durán, F., Eker, S., Escobar, S., Lincoln, P., Martí-Oliet, N., Talcott, C.L.: Two decades of Maude. In: Martí-Oliet, N., Ölveczky, P.C., Talcott, C.L. (eds.) Logic, Rewriting, and Concurrency - Essays dedicated to José Meseguer on the Occasion of His 65th Birthday. Lecture Notes in Computer Science, vol. 9200, pp. 232–254. Springer (2015). https://doi.org/10.1007/978-3-319-23165-5_11
17. Dershowitz, N., Sivakumar, G.: Goal-directed equation solving. In: Shrobe, H.E., Mitchell, T.M., Smith, R.G. (eds.) Proceedings of the 7th National Conference on Artificial Intelligence, St. Paul, MN, USA, August 21-26, 1988. pp. 166–170. AAAI Press / The MIT Press (1988)
18. Dundua, B., Kutsia, T., Marin, M., Pau, C.: Constraint solving over multiple similarity relations. In: Ariola, Z.M. (ed.) 5th International Conference on Formal Structures for Computation and Deduction, FSCD 2020, June 29-July 6, 2020, Paris, France (Virtual Conference). LIPIcs, vol. 167, pp. 30:1–30:19. Schloss Dagstuhl - Leibniz-Zentrum für Informatik (2020). https://doi.org/10.4230/LIPICS.FSCD.2020.30
19. Ehling, G., Kutsia, T.: Solving quantitative equations. In: Benzmüller, C., Heule, M.J.H., Schmidt, R.A. (eds.) Automated Reasoning - 12th International Joint Conference, IJCAR 2024, Nancy, France, July 3-6, 2024, Proceedings, Part II. Lecture Notes in Computer Science, vol. 14740, pp. 381–400. Springer (2024). https://doi.org/10.1007/978-3-031-63501-4_20
20. Escobar, S., Meseguer, J., Thati, P.: Narrowing and Rewriting Logic: from foundations to applications. In: López-Fraguas, F.J. (ed.) Proceedings of the 15th Workshop on Functional and (Constraint) Logic Programming, WFLP 2006, Madrid, Spain, November 16-17, 2006. Electronic Notes in Theoretical Computer Science, vol. 177, pp. 5–33. Elsevier (2006). https://doi.org/10.1016/J.ENTCS.2007.01.004
21. Escobar, S., Sasse, R., Meseguer, J.: Folding variant narrowing and optimal variant termination. J. Log. Algebraic Methods Program. **81**(7-8), 898–928 (2012). https://doi.org/10.1016/J.JLAP.2012.01.002
22. Fay, M.: First-order unification in an equational theory. In: 4th Workshop on Automated Deduction, Austin, TX. pp. 161–167 (1979)
23. Formato, F., Gerla, G., Sessa, M.I.: Similarity-based unification. Fundam. Informaticae **41**(4), 393–414 (2000). https://doi.org/10.3233/FI-2000-41402
24. Gavazzo, F., Di Florio, C.: Quantitative and Metric Rewriting: Abstract, Non-Expansive, and Graded Systems. CoRR **abs/2206.13610** (2022). https://doi.org/10.48550/ARXIV.2206.13610
25. Gavazzo, F., Di Florio, C.: Elements of quantitative rewriting. Proc. ACM Program. Lang. **7**(POPL), 1832–1863 (2023). https://doi.org/10.1145/3571256
26. Hanus, M.: Curry: An integrated functional logic language (vers. 0.9.0). Available at http://www.curry-lang.org (2016)
27. Hullot, J.: Canonical Forms and Unification. In: Bibel, W., Kowalski, R.A. (eds.) 5th Conference on Automated Deduction, Les Arcs, France, July 8-11, 1980, Proceedings. Lecture Notes in Computer Science, vol. 87, p. 318–334. Springer (1980). https://doi.org/10.1007/3-540-10009-1_25
28. Julián-Iranzo, P., Rubio-Manzano, C.: Proximity-based unification theory. Fuzzy Sets and Systems **262**, 21–43 (2015). https://doi.org/10.1016/j.fss.2014.07.006
29. Lawvere, F.W.: Metric spaces, generalized logic, and closed categories. Rendiconti del Seminario Matematico e Fisico di Milano **43**, 135–166 (1973). https://doi.org/10.1007/BF02924844

30. López-Rueda, R., Escobar, S., Sapiña, J.: An efficient canonical narrowing implementation with irreducibility and SMT constraints for generic symbolic protocol analysis. J. Log. Algebraic Methods Program. **135**, 100895 (2023). https://doi.org/10.1016/J.JLAMP.2023.100895
31. Mardare, R., Panangaden, P., Plotkin, G.D.: Quantitative algebraic reasoning. In: Proceedings of the 31st Annual ACM/IEEE Symposium on Logic in Computer Science. p. 700–709. LICS '16, Association for Computing Machinery, New York, NY, USA (2016). https://doi.org/10.1145/2933575.2934518
32. Mardare, R., Panangaden, P., Plotkin, G.D.: On the axiomatizability of quantitative algebras. In: 32nd Annual ACM/IEEE Symposium on Logic in Computer Science, LICS 2017, Reykjavik, Iceland, June 20-23, 2017. pp. 1–12. IEEE Computer Society (2017). https://doi.org/10.1109/LICS.2017.8005102
33. Middeldorp, A., Hamoen, E.: Counterexamples to completeness results for basic narrowing (extended abstract). In: Kirchner, H., Levi, G. (eds.) Algebraic and Logic Programming, Third International Conference, Volterra, Italy, September 2-4, 1992, Proceedings. Lecture Notes in Computer Science, vol. 632, pp. 244–258. Springer (1992). https://doi.org/10.1007/BFB0013830
34. Middeldorp, A., Hamoen, E.: Completeness results for basic narrowing. Appl. Algebra Eng. Commun. Comput. **5**, 213–253 (1994). https://doi.org/10.1007/BF01190830
35. Middeldorp, A., Hamoen, E.: Completeness Results for Basic Narrowing. Appl. Algebra Eng. Commun. Comput. **5**, 213–253 (1994). https://doi.org/10.1007/BF01190830
36. Pau, C.: Symbolic Techniques for Approximate Reasoning. Ph.D. thesis, RISC, Johannes Kepler University Linz (2022), https://epub.jku.at/obvulihs/content/titleinfo/7818355
37. Pau, C., Kutsia, T.: Proximity-Based Unification and Matching for Fully Fuzzy Signatures. In: 30th IEEE International Conference on Fuzzy Systems, FUZZ-IEEE 2021, Luxembourg, July 11-14, 2021. p. 1–6. IEEE (2021). https://doi.org/10.1109/FUZZ45933.2021.9494438
38. Sessa, M.I.: Approximate reasoning by similarity-based SLD resolution. Theor. Comput. Sci. **275**(1-2), 389–426 (2002). https://doi.org/10.1016/S0304-3975(01)00188-8
39. Terese: Term rewriting systems, Cambridge tracts in theoretical computer science, vol. 55. Cambridge University Press (2003)
40. Tran, D.D., Do, C.M., Escobar, S., Ogata, K.: Hybrid post-quantum transport layer security formal analysis in Maude-NPA and its parallel version. PeerJ Comput. Sci. **9**, e1556 (2023). https://doi.org/10.7717/PEERJ-CS.1556

Equational Generalization Problems with Atom-Variables

Alexander Baumgartner[3], Temur Kutsia[4], Daniele Nantes-Sobrinho[1](✉), and Manfred Schmidt-Schauß[2]

[1] University of Brasília, Brasília, Brazil
dnantes@unb.br
[2] Goethe Universität, Frankfurt am Main, Germany
[3] Universidad de O'Higgins, Rancagua, Chile
[4] RISC, Johannes Kepler University, Linz, Austria

Abstract. Generalization problems in languages with binders involve computing the most common structure between expressions while respecting bound variable renaming and freshness constraints. These problems often lack a least general solution. However, leveraging nominal techniques, we previously demonstrated that a semantic approach with atom-variables enables the elimination of redundant solutions and allows for computing unique least general generalizations (LGGs). In this work, we extend this approach to handle associative (A), commutative (C), and associative-commutative (AC) equational theories. A key challenge arises from solving equivariance problems while taking into account these equational theories, as identifying redundant generalizations requires recognizing when one expression (with binders) is a renaming of another while possibly considering permutations of sub-expressions. This unexpected interaction between renaming and equational reasoning made this particularly difficult, necessitating semantic tests modulo theories within the equivariance algorithm.

Keywords: Generalization Problems · Binders · Equational Theories.

1 Introduction

The generalization problem [22] (a.k.a. anti-unification problem) is concerned with finding a generalization of two given input expressions in a formal language, e.g., finding a more general program between two different programs, or a more general first-order formula, or a more general proof. The problem becomes more complicated in languages with binders, and more sophisticated techniques have been developed. Among the difficulties are the need of: renaming bound variables; considering various equivalences between expressions such as β- and η-conversion; correct typing, etc. Most of the current frameworks restrict the problem in one way or another, depending on their particular goals. Extensive research has been done about generalization for higher-order patterns (HOP), which are a restricted class of λ-terms whose free variables may only be applied

V. de Paiva and P. Koepke (Eds.): CICM 2025, LNAI 16136, pp. 133–151, 2026.
https://doi.org/10.1007/978-3-032-07021-0_8

to a sequence of distinct bound variables, including equational theories [7,11,12]. See [10] for a generic framework for anti-unification of simply typed λ-terms, which includes HOP generalization as a special case.

We are interested in solving generalization problems involving expressions with binders, such as first-order logic formulas with constraints. An example of such problem is to find a generalization of the two 'formulas' s and t:

$$\begin{array}{lr} s = \mathtt{implies}(\forall x.(\mathtt{Pred}(x) \wedge (\varphi_1 \vee \varphi_2)), (\varphi_1 \vee \varphi_2)), & \text{if } x \notin fv(\varphi_1 \vee \varphi_2) \\ t = \mathtt{implies}(\forall y.(\varphi_1 \wedge \mathtt{Pred}(y)), \varphi_1), & \text{if } y \notin fv(\varphi_1) \end{array} \tag{1}$$

where $\mathtt{Pred}$ is a unary predicate, φ_1 and φ_2 are first-order formulas, and $fv(-)$ denotes the set of free variables in $(-)$. The expression $r = \mathtt{implies}(\forall z.(\mathtt{Pred}(z) \wedge \psi), \psi)$ is a generalization of s and t modulo commutativity of $\wedge$ and renaming of the bound variables x and y, as long as $z \notin fv(\psi)$. Note that x, y and φ_1, φ_2 and ψ are variables at different levels. The symbols x and y are *object-level* variables, representing elements of the domain in a logical interpretation, and are subject to binding. Whereas φ_1, φ_2 and ψ are *meta-level* variables that represent an entire expression or formula, and are not subject to binding. In addition, one has to take into account the algebraic properties of $\wedge$: the operator is associative-commutative ($\mathtt{AC}$). We return to this example later.

This work is about generalization problems for a nominal language with atom-variables and taking into account equational theories for associativity ($\mathtt{A}$), commutativity ($\mathtt{C}$) and associativity-commutativity ($\mathtt{AC}$). The choice is motivated by the expressivity of the language, it can be used to express λ-terms, or first-order formulas, or π-calculus processes, etc, and it has notions such as α-renaming and freshness embedded in the language, therefore, the usual implicit renaming and freshness choices adopted in many works can be explicitly implemented. In addition, reasoning in the nominal syntax [21] has a first-order-like behavior that is appealing.

We build upon a framework introduced in [23] that uses atom-variables and a semantic approach to discard redundant solutions and compute unique lggs. As expected, working with equational theories requires working in equivalence classes of these theories, which we thought would be a natural extension of the work. Unexpectedly, these equivalence classes interact with our semantic approach when solving the *equivariance matching problems* which appear as sub-problems in our algorithm in a non-trivial way that turned out to be a challenging problem to obtain correctness of the overall algorithm (cf. Theorem 6). We expand on this and other challenges below.

Contributions. We present a rule-based algorithm, $\mathtt{NAU}_E$, for solving generalization problems modulo a theory E. Our approach refines existing structural rules for abstractions and atom-variables while introducing new rules to handle function symbols under equational theories and equivariance. These refinements strengthen the rules, eliminating one of the sources of weak incompleteness. The rules handling equational theories $\mathtt{A}$, $\mathtt{C}$ and $\mathtt{AC}$, are similar to the first-order and HOP approaches and introduce an exponential number of branches, as expected. We propose a method to solve a more general version of the equivariance problem, which given terms s and t and a freshness-context ∇, tries to find a permutation π such that $\nabla \models \pi \cdot s \approx_E t$. Here, we consider an equational theory $E \in \{\mathtt{A},\mathtt{C},\mathtt{AC}\}$, and π, ∇, s, t may contain atom-variables. It requires the analysis to be semantical, represented using the symbol $\models$. Note that it is harder to evaluate, e.g., whether the generalized permutation $(A\ C)$ acts in the abstraction such that $(A\ C) \cdot (\lambda C.f^{\mathtt{AC}}(A, B, C)) \approx_{\mathtt{AC}} \lambda A.f^{\mathtt{AC}}(A, B, A)$, i.e., makes these two abstractions equal modulo renaming of bound variables and modulo AC. The difficulty arises because we don't know how $(A\ C)$ acts on B. Here, A, B, C are atom-variables which could be instantiated to the same or to different concrete atoms. The valuations of the atom-variables have an effect when branching on the possible permutations of the AC-function symbol $f^{\mathtt{AC}}$. Dealing with the interaction was a challenge, and required specialized methods, described in Section 5, to guarantee correctness while branching (cf. Theorem 6).

Due to space limitations proofs and more examples and additional material are given in the extended version of this paper [20].

2 Preliminaries

We assume the reader is familiar with the nominal syntax, and only recall the main concepts and notations that are needed in the paper. For more details we refer the reader to [16].

2.1 NLa: A Ground Nominal Language with Equational Theories.

Fix a countable infinite set of *atoms* $\mathbb{A} = \{a, b, c, \ldots\}$. Atoms are identified by their name, so it will be redundant to say that two atoms a and b are different. A signature Σ is a set of *term-formers* (disjoint from $\mathbb{A}$) such that to each $f \in \Sigma$ is assigned a unique non-negative integer n, called the *arity* of f, written as $f{:}n$, and *constants* ($\mathtt{a}, \mathtt{b}, \mathtt{c} \ldots$) are symbols in Σ with arity zero. A *ground permutation* π is a bijection $\mathbb{A} \to \mathbb{A}$ which is the identity almost everywhere, i.e., the set $\{a \in \mathbb{A} \mid \pi(a) \neq a\}$ is finite. Permutations are represented by sequences of *swappings* written as $(a\ b)$ where $a, b \in \mathbb{A}$. *Id* denotes the identity permutation. The composition of two permutations π and π' will be denoted as $\pi \circ \pi'$. We may write permutations omitting the $\circ$-symbol as $(a_1\ b_1)(a_2\ b_2)\ldots(a_n\ b_n)$.

The *nominal language* NLa is built by the grammar:

$$S, S_i ::= a \mid \pi \cdot S \mid f(S_1, \ldots, S_n) \mid \lambda a.S \qquad \pi ::= Id \mid (a\ b) \circ \pi$$

where a, b are atoms, $\lambda a.S$ denotes the *abstraction* of atom a in the term S, and $f(S_1, \ldots, S_n)$ is a *function application*, where $f \in \Sigma$ and $f{:}n$.

Since NLa consists of ground terms (sometimes called expressions), every term in NLa can be simplified by applying permutations such that only terms (and subterms) of the forms $a \mid f(S_1, \ldots, S_n) \mid \lambda a.S$ remain, i.e. expressions of a lambda-calculus with atoms and function symbols. The effect of a permutation application is defined recursively on the structure of a term as usual. The predicate $\approx$, which stands for α-equivalence of the terms in NLa, is defined as usual [26]:

$$\frac{}{a \approx a} \quad \frac{S \approx T}{\lambda a.S \approx \lambda a.T} \quad \frac{S \approx (a\,b)\cdot T \quad a\#T}{\lambda a.S \approx \lambda b.T} \quad \frac{S_1 \approx T_1, \quad \cdots, \quad S_n \approx T_n}{f(S_1, \ldots S_n) \approx f(T_1, \ldots, T_n)}$$

where the freshness predicate $\#$ is defined

$$\frac{}{a\#b} \quad \frac{}{a\#\lambda a.T} \quad \frac{a\#T}{a\#\lambda b.T} \quad \frac{a\#T_1 \quad \cdots \quad a\#T_n}{a\#f(T_1, \ldots T_n)}$$

We say $a\#T$ is a *freshness constraint* and a set of freshness constraints is a *freshness context*. Intuitively, $a\#S$ means that a is *fresh* for S (it does not occur free in S). Note that $a\#a$ is not derivable. Finally, a freshness constraint $a\#S$ *holds* (or is *valid*) iff it is derivable using the rules. Validity can be established for α-equality constraints in a similar way.

We consider an extension of the language NLa for a signature Σ which contains function symbols satisfying an *equational theory*, denoted by E. In this work we are interested in the theories associativity (A), commutativity (C) and associativity-commutativity (AC). The signature is composed of $\Sigma = \Sigma_\emptyset \uplus \Sigma_\mathtt{A} \uplus \Sigma_\mathtt{C} \uplus \Sigma_\mathtt{AC}$, where $\uplus$ denotes the disjoint union, $\Sigma_\emptyset$ denotes the set of uninterpreted function symbols and $\Sigma_\mathtt{A} \cup \Sigma_\mathtt{C} \cup \Sigma_\mathtt{AC}$ are symbols of arity 2 that satisfy the respective equational theories. We use the superscript notation $f^\mathtt{A}$, $f^\mathtt{C}$ and $f^\mathtt{AC}$ to denote, respectively, $f \in \Sigma_\mathtt{A}$, $f \in \Sigma_\mathtt{C}$ and $f \in \Sigma_\mathtt{AC}$. We may use a flattened representation of expressions with associative function applications. For example, if $f \in \Sigma_\mathtt{A} \cup \Sigma_\mathtt{AC}$, all subterms of the form $f(T_1, \ldots, f(S_1, \ldots, S_m), \ldots, T_n)$ may be written as $f(T_1, \ldots, S_1, \ldots, S_m, \ldots, T_n)$ (if $n + m \geq 2$).

Next, we define the predicate $\approx_E$ that extends α-equivalence of nominal terms with the identities defining the theories A,C and AC.

$$\frac{T_1 \approx_E S_1 \ \ldots \ T_n \approx_E S_n, n \geq 2}{f^\mathtt{A}(T_1, \ldots, T_n) \approx_E f^\mathtt{A}(S_1, \ldots, S_n)}\ (\mathtt{A}) \qquad \frac{T_1 \approx_E S_2 \quad T_2 \approx_E S_1}{f^C(T_1, T_2) \approx_E f^C(S_1, S_2)}\ (\mathtt{C})$$

$$\frac{T_1 \approx_E S_{\rho(1)} \ldots T_n \approx_E S_{\rho(n)},\ \rho \text{ is a permutation of } \{1, \ldots, n\},\ n \geq 2}{f^\mathtt{AC}(T_1, \ \ldots, \ T_n) \approx_E f^\mathtt{AC}(S_{\rho(1)}, \ldots, S_{\rho(n)})}\ (\mathtt{AC})$$

This language will be the semantic base used in the following sections.

2.2 NLA: A Nominal Language with Variables and Equational Theories.

We recall the basic notions of nominal terms with *atom-variables*, which were introduced in [23]. Fix countable infinite sets of *term-variables* $\mathcal{X} = \{X, Y, Z, \ldots\}$ and *atom-variables* $\mathcal{A} = \{A, B, C, \ldots\}$ such that $\mathcal{X} \cap \mathcal{A} = \emptyset$. Variables are distinct from objects in the signature Σ which is taken from NLa. The NLA language is defined by the following grammar of terms (also denoted $T(\Sigma, \mathcal{X}, \mathcal{A})$) and permutations π with atom-variables instead of atoms:

$$\begin{aligned} s, s_i &::= W \mid \pi \cdot X \mid f(s_1, \ldots, s_n) \mid \lambda W.s && \text{(nominal terms)} \\ W, W_i &::= \pi \cdot A && \text{(atom-variable suspensions)} \\ \pi &::= id \mid (W_1\ W_2) \circ \pi && \text{(atom-variable permutations)} \end{aligned}$$

Differently from the standard grammar of a nominal language, NLA terms do not contain atoms. We denote the inverse of a permutation π with π^{-1}. If π is a list of swappings $(A_1\ B_1)\cdots(A_n\ B_n)$, then $\pi^{-1} = (A_n\ B_n)\cdots(A_1\ B_1)$, since $(A_1\ B_1)\cdots(A_n\ B_n)\cdot(A_n\ B_n)\cdots(A_1\ B_1)$ is the trivial permutation under any interpretation of atom-variables. There are two kinds of *suspensions*: $\pi \cdot A$ and $\pi \cdot X$, i.e., one on atom-variables and one on term-variables, respectively. We write $\pi \cdot V$ to denote a suspension over a variable $V \in \mathcal{A} \cup \mathcal{X}$, and $\mathtt{AV}(F)$ for the set of atom-variables occurring in a the formula F. *Abstractions* are more general here as well: $\lambda W.s$ denotes the abstraction of a (suspended) atom-variable W on a term s. Function application extends to nominal terms in NLA as expected. As in NLa, in NLA we permit function symbols that are A, C or AC.

Example 1. Simple examples of NLA-terms are: the abstraction of an atom variable on a term $\lambda A.f(A)$; a permutation of atom-variables $(A\ B)$ that is suspended on an atom-variable C, that is, $(A\ B)\cdot C$; and finally, a permutation of atom-variables suspended on a term variable $(A\ B)\cdot X$. Note that the semantics of these terms can only be established once the atom-variables A, B, C are instantiated to concrete atoms and the term-variable is instantiated to some term. More complex examples are: $\lambda(A\ B)\cdot C.f(A,(B\ C)\cdot X)$ and $\lambda A.f((A\ B)(B\ C)\cdot X, B)$.

Substitutions, ranged over by $\sigma, \gamma, \ldots$, are maps from term-variables to terms in NLA and from atom-variables to suspensions of atom-variables, such that the *domain*, $\mathsf{Dom}(\sigma) = \{V \in \mathcal{A} \cup \mathcal{X} \mid V\sigma \neq V\}$ is finite. The *action of a substitution* on a term t, denoted as $t\sigma$, is inductively defined: $(((W_1\ W_2)\circ\pi)\cdot X)\sigma \equiv ((W_1\sigma\ W_2\sigma)\circ\pi\sigma)\cdot(X\sigma)$ and σ acts in the other term constructs homomorphically. Substitutions are written in postfix notation: $t(\sigma\gamma) = (t\sigma)\gamma$.

We will also use NLA-freshness constraints of the form $W\#s$ where s is an NLA-term and NLA-freshness contexts $(\Delta, \nabla, \ldots)$, which are conjunctions (written as sets) of NLA-freshness constraints. Note that freshness constraints of the form $A\#s$ are sufficient, since $(W_1\ W_2)\cdot A\#s$ is equivalent to $A\#(W_1\ W_2)\cdot s$. Thus, constraints with permutations such as $A\#\lambda B.((AC)(D\ B)\cdot A)$ are possible. An NLA-*term-in-context* (∇, s) is a pair of an NLA-freshness context ∇ and a NLA-term s. Terms-in-context are used to express terms with freshness constraints. This way, $(A\#X, \lambda A.f(A, X))$ denotes the fact that A must be fresh for X in instances of $f(A, X)$. This will become clearer given the semantics of expressions.

2.3 The Semantics of NLA-Expressions and Freshness Constraints

The semantics of NLA-expressions is based on interpretations ρ to ground expressions in NLa. An *interpretation* ρ maps NLA-terms to NLa-terms. It is determined by a mapping from atom-variables to concrete atoms and term-variables to (ground) NLa-terms. Interpretations act on NLA-terms homomorphically. It is also extended to freshness constraints, contexts, and equational theories, as expected. For example, an interpretation ρ maps a freshness constraint $W\#s$ in NLA to a freshness constraint $W\rho\#s\rho$ in NLa. The semantics includes equivalence of expressions, validity of freshness constraints and contexts. We also assume that an equational theory E is defined by axioms from $\mathtt{A}$, $\mathtt{AC}$, and $\mathtt{C}$ for specific function symbols. Like substitution applications, applications of interpretations are written in postfix notation.

Two NLA-permutations π_1, π_2 are *semantically equivalent* iff for all interpretations ρ: $\pi_1\rho$ is the same permutation as $\pi_2\rho$. This is denoted as $\pi_1 \equiv \pi_2$. Two NLA-terms s, t are *semantically equivalent* iff for all interpretations ρ: $s\rho \approx_E t\rho$. An NLA-freshness constraint $W\#s$ is *valid*, iff for all interpretations ρ: $W\rho\#s\rho$ is valid. A context ∇ is *valid*, if for all interpretations ρ, every constraint in $\nabla\rho$ holds. A context ∇ is *consistent* w.r.t. ρ iff every constraint in $\nabla\rho$ holds. In this case, we say that ρ *respects* ∇.

Example 2. Interesting constraints such as $A\#\lambda B.A$ or $C\#\lambda A.\lambda B.C$ are expressible in NLA. Note that $A\#\lambda B.A$ is consistent w.r.t. ρ iff $A\rho = B\rho$. Differently, $C\#\lambda A.\lambda B.C$ is consistent w.r.t. ρ iff $C\rho = A\rho \vee C\rho = B\rho$: in fact, for an interpretation ρ of A, B, C such that $C\rho \neq B\rho \wedge C\rho \neq A\rho$, the constraint would reduce to $C\rho\#C\rho$, which is inconsistent.

We can now consider *judgements* of the form $\nabla \vDash A\#s, \nabla \vDash s \approx_E t$ and $\nabla \vDash \pi_1 \equiv \pi_2$, and their meaning is established next.

Definition 1 (Semantics of Judgements). *Let ∇ be a consistent* NLA*-freshness context, $A\#s$ a freshness constraint and π_1, π_2 be* NLA*-permutations. We say that*

- $\nabla \vDash A\#s$ holds *iff for all interpretations ρ: $\nabla\rho$ valid $\Longrightarrow$ $A\rho\#s\rho$ valid.*
- $\nabla \vDash s \approx_E t$ holds *iff for all interpretations ρ: $\nabla\rho$ valid $\Longrightarrow$ $s\rho \approx_E t\rho$ valid.*
- $\nabla \vDash \pi_1 \equiv \pi_2$ holds *iff for all interpretations ρ: $\nabla\rho$ valid $\Longrightarrow$ $\pi_1\rho = \pi_2\rho$.*

3 Generalization Problems in NLA modulo A, C or AC

We are interested in the following problem:

> **Given:** Two NLA-terms-in-context (∇, s) and (∇, t).
> **Find:** An NLA-term-in-context (Γ, r) that is a generalization modulo E of (∇, s) and (∇, t) which preserves most of their common structure while taking into account the equational theory E.

This problem is known as the *generalization problem modulo E* (also known as the *anti-unification problem modulo E*), which we will investigate in the context of the language NLA. In the following sections, we will introduce the main ingredients to solve this problem, which we will refer to simply as generalization (or anti-unification), as reasoning modulo E will be used throughout this work.

3.1 A Semantic Approach to Generalization in NLA

We follow a semantic approach to solve the generalization problem in NLA by investigating the semantics of the pairs (∇, s) and (∇, t) that we want to generalize. The semantics will be based on the equivalence classes modulo $\approx_E$ (i.e.

modulo E and α-renaming) of the ground instances s and t that respect the corresponding instances of ∇. First, we define the semantics of a pair (∇, s) w.r.t. interpretations of s on the ground language NLa:

Definition 2. *The* semantics of (∇, s), *denoted* $[\![(\nabla, s)]\!]$, *consists of the following set:*

$$[\![(\nabla, s)]\!] = \{[s\rho]_E \mid \rho \text{ is an interpretation and } \nabla\rho \text{ holds}\},$$

where $[r]_E$ *denotes the equivalence class of* r *modulo* $\approx_E$.

Note the semantics of terms-in-context that contain abstractions are always infinite due to the existence of infinitely many names for α-renaming:

Example 3 (Semantics of Abstractions). The semantics of $(\{A\#B\}, \lambda A.f(A, B))$ is the following:

$$\begin{aligned}[\![(\{A\#B\}, \lambda A.f(A, B))]\!] &= \{[\lambda A\rho.f(A\rho, B\rho)]_E \mid \forall\rho : A\rho\#B\rho \text{ holds}\} \\ &= \{[\lambda A\rho.f(A\rho, B\rho)]_E \mid A\rho \neq B\rho\} \\ &= \{[\lambda a.f(a, b)]_E, [\lambda a.f(a, c)]_E, \ldots\}\end{aligned}$$

The second argument of f can be any concrete atom, as long as it is not captured by the abstraction.

The semantics of terms-in-context provides a framework to for comparing terms and determining their relative generality. A pair (∇, t) is *more general w.r.t. E than* (Δ, s), denoted $(\nabla, t) \preceq_E (\Delta, s)$, iff $[\![(\Delta, s)]\!] \subseteq [\![(\nabla, t)]\!]$. They are *equivalent* iff both $(\nabla, t) \preceq_E (\Delta, s)$ and $(\nabla, t) \succeq_E (\Delta, s)$ hold, meaning that their semantics are identical $[\![(\Delta, s)]\!] = [\![(\nabla, t)]\!]$. This allows us to formally define an generalization and *the least general generalization* (lgg_E) of two terms-in-context.

Definition 3 (Generalization, lgg_E). *A term-in-context* (∇, r) *is an* generalization of (∇_1, s) *and* (∇_2, t) *iff* (∇, r) *the following holds:* $(\nabla, r) \preceq_E (\nabla_1, s)$ *and* $(\nabla, r) \preceq_E (\nabla_2, t)$*. The pair* (∇, r) *is called a* linear *generalization, when each (atom/term)-variable occurs at most once in* r*. The pair* (∇, r) *is called a* least general generalization *(lgg_E) of* (∇_1, s) *and* (∇_2, t) *iff it is a 'smallest' generalization, i.e., every other generalization* (∇', r') *of* (∇_1, s) *and* (∇_2, t)*, is more general than* (∇, r)*, that is,* $(\nabla', r') \preceq_E (\nabla, r)$ *holds.*

A set G of generalizations for (∇_1, s) and (∇_2, t) is *complete* iff for each generalization (Δ, r') of (∇_1, s) and (∇_2, t), there exists $(\nabla, r) \in G$ such that $(\Delta, r') \preceq_E (\nabla, r)$. The set G is called *minimal*, if for all different $(\nabla', r_1), (\nabla'', r_2) \in G$, we have $(\nabla', r_1) \not\preceq_E (\nabla'', r_2)$ and $(\nabla'', r_2) \not\preceq_E (\nabla', r_1)$. Such minimal set will be denoted as $mcsg_E((\nabla_1, s), (\nabla_2, t))$.

The existence and cardinality of the minimal complete set of generalizations characterize the anti-unification type of an equational theory E. Thus, E has *nullary* (anti-unification) type if there are terms-in-context T_1 and T_2 for which $mcsg_E(T_1, T_2)$ does not exist. Otherwise, E has type *unitary* (resp. *finitary*), if $mcsg_E(T_1, T_2)$ is a singleton (resp. finite) for all terms-in-context T_1 and T_2; and *infinitary*, if $mcsg_E(T_1, T_2)$ is infinite for some T_1 and T_2.

Now we return to the example from the introduction:

Example 4. In our framework, the expressions in (1) and their freshess conditions can be specified[1] as the following NLA-terms-in-context:

$$\begin{aligned}&(\{A\#X_1, A\#X_2\}, \texttt{implies}(\lambda A.(\texttt{Pred}(A) \wedge (X_1 \vee X_2)), (X_1 \vee X_2)))\\&(\{B\#X\}, \texttt{implies}(\lambda B.(X \wedge \texttt{Pred}(B)), X))\end{aligned} \tag{2}$$

where $\wedge$ is a binary commutative symbol, and `implies` is a binary and `Pred` is a unary function symbol of the given signature. Here we omit $\forall$ but it could be taken as a unary symbol of the signature. The goal is to compute a generalization modulo E of pairs in (2).

4 $\texttt{NAU}_E$: An Anti-Unification Algorithm

In this section, we introduce the rule-based algorithm $\texttt{NAU}_E$ to solve the generalization problem. The rules for $\texttt{NAU}_E$ are described in Figure 1, including rules dealing with E. The rules labeled in (gray) remain unchanged from [23], as they required no modification to accommodate the equational theories in E. In contrast, rules labeled in (teal) are either new or improved versions of existing rules. The symbol $\uplus$ denotes disjoint union.

The $\texttt{NAU}_E$ operates on tuples (called states) of the form P; S; Γ; σ where: P denotes the set of unsolved *anti-unification equations* between terms, denoted $X : t \triangleq s$. Here, X is a term-variable that will represent the generalization of t and s. S denotes the set of solved anti-unification equations (the store). The store S may contain anti-unification equations between suspended atom-variable permutations, denoted $C : \pi \cdot A_1 \triangleq \pi_2 \cdot A_2$, where C is an atom-variable that will represent the generalization of $\pi \cdot A_1$ and $\pi_2 \cdot A_2$. Γ denotes the freshness context computed so far which constrains generalization variables; σ is a substitution, computed so far, mapping generalization variables to terms in NLA.

Furthermore, there is as a global parameter a freshness context ∇ that does not constrain generalization variables. Note that in P, generalization variables are only term-variables, while in S they can be term- or atom-variables. X and C are called *generalization variables.*

Idea of the algorithm. Given NLA-terms-in-context (∇, t) and (∇, s), the (non-deterministic) algorithm for $\texttt{NAU}_E$ starts with $(\{X : t \triangleq s\};\ \emptyset;\ \nabla;\ Id)$ and applies the rules in Figure 1 exhaustively, until we reach a final state $(\emptyset; S; \Gamma; \sigma)$. The sequence of rule applications is called a (NAU-)*derivation.* The generalization variable X occurs neither in ∇, nor in t, nor in s. Intuitively, it represents the generalization that becomes less and less general as the algorithm advances (by applying some rules). The result of this procedure is of the form $\emptyset$; S; Γ; σ, the *computed generalization is* $(\Gamma, X\sigma)$ and S contains the differences of t and s. To compute the set of all results, the contribution of all non-deterministic computation paths has to be gathered in a set.

[1] These are called *schemas* in [17], here extended with atom-variables.

(Dec) **Decomposition**
$\{X\colon f(\overline{t})_m \triangleq f(\overline{s})_m\} \uplus P; S; \Gamma; \sigma \Longrightarrow \bigcup_{i=1}^{m}\{Y_i\colon t_i \triangleq s_i\} \cup P; S; \Gamma; \sigma\{X \mapsto f(\overline{Y})_m\}$
where $f \in \Sigma$ and $(\overline{Y})_m = Y_1, \ldots, Y_m$ are fresh variables, $m \geq 0$.

(Abs) **Abstraction**
$\{X : \lambda W_1.t \triangleq \lambda W_2.s\} \uplus P; S; \Gamma; \sigma \Longrightarrow$
$\{Y : (W_1\, C) \cdot t \triangleq (W_2\, C) \cdot s\} \cup P; S; \Gamma \cup \{C\#\lambda W_1.t, C\#\lambda W_2.s\}; \sigma\{X \mapsto \lambda C.Y\}$
where Y is fresh and C is a new atom-variable.

(DecA) **Associative Decomposition**
$\{X : f^{\mathtt{A}}(\overline{t})_n \triangleq f^{\mathtt{A}}(\overline{s})_m\} \uplus P; S; \Gamma; \sigma$
$$\Longrightarrow \left\{\begin{matrix} Y_1 : f^{\mathtt{A}}(\overline{t})_k \triangleq f^{\mathtt{A}}(\overline{s})_l, \\ Y_2 : f^{\mathtt{A}}(\overline{t})_{k+1..n} \triangleq f^{\mathtt{A}}(\overline{s})_{l+1..m} \end{matrix}\right\} \cup P; S; \Gamma; \sigma\{X \mapsto f^{\mathtt{A}}(Y_1, Y_2)\}$$
if $1 \leq k < n; 1 \leq l < m$

(DecC) **Commutative Decomposition**
$\{X : f^{\mathtt{C}}(t_1, t_2) \triangleq f^{\mathtt{C}}(s_1, s_2)\} \uplus P; S; \Gamma; \sigma$
$$\Longrightarrow \{Y_1 : t_1 \triangleq s_i, Y_2 : t_2 \triangleq s_{3-i}\} \cup P; S; \Gamma; \sigma\{X \mapsto f^{\mathtt{C}}(Y_1, Y_2)\}$$

(DecAC) **Associative-Commutative Decomposition**
$\{X : f^{\mathtt{AC}}(\overline{t})_n \triangleq f^{\mathtt{AC}}(\overline{s})_m\} \uplus P; S; \Gamma; \sigma$
$$\Longrightarrow \left\{\begin{matrix} Y_1 : f^{\mathtt{AC}}(\overline{t_i})_k \triangleq f^{\mathtt{AC}}(\overline{s_j})_l, \\ Y_2 : f^{\mathtt{AC}}(\overline{t_i})_{k+1..n} \triangleq f^{\mathtt{AC}}(\overline{s_j})_{l+1..m} \end{matrix}\right\} \cup P; S; \Gamma; \sigma\{X \mapsto f^{\mathtt{AC}}(Y_1, Y_2)\}$$
where $\{i_1 \ldots, i_n\} \approx \{1, \ldots, n\}, \{j_1 \ldots, j_m\} \approx \{1, \ldots, m\}$

(SusAA) **Suspension on Atom-Variables**
$\{X : \pi_1{\cdot}A \triangleq \pi_2{\cdot}B\} \uplus P; S; \Gamma; \sigma \Longrightarrow P; S; \Gamma; \sigma\{X \mapsto \pi_1{\cdot}A\}$, if $\Gamma \models \pi_1{\cdot}A = \pi_2{\cdot}B$.

(SusYY) **Suspensions on** Y
$\{X : \pi_1{\cdot}Y \triangleq \pi_2{\cdot}Y\} \uplus P; S; \Gamma; \sigma \Longrightarrow P; S; \Gamma; \sigma\{X \mapsto \pi_1{\cdot}Y\}$, if $\Gamma \models \pi_1{\cdot}Y = \pi_2{\cdot}Y$.

(SolAB) **Solve different atom-suspensions**
$\{X : \pi_1{\cdot}A \triangleq \pi_2{\cdot}B\} \uplus P; S; \Gamma; \sigma$
$$\Longrightarrow P; S \cup \{C : \pi_1{\cdot}A \triangleq \pi_2{\cdot}B\}; \Gamma \cup \{C\#\lambda\pi_1{\cdot}A.\lambda\pi_2{\cdot}B.C\}; \sigma\{X \mapsto C\}$$
if $\Gamma \not\models \pi_1{\cdot}A = \pi_2{\cdot}B$ and C is a new atom-variable.

(Sol) **Solve**
$\{X : t \triangleq s\} \uplus P; S; \Gamma;\ \sigma \Longrightarrow P; S \cup \{X : t \triangleq s\}; \Gamma; \sigma$
where none of the previous rules is applicable.

Fig. 1. NAU transformation rules for $E \in \{\mathtt{A},\mathtt{C},\mathtt{AC}\}$.

Description of the rules in Figure 1 and Examples

Rule (Abs) generalizes abstractions on W_1, W_2 by choosing a new atom-variable C that was not used anywhere else, and swapping both W_1, W_2 with C on the subterms underneath the abstraction. Note that the freshness context is extended with constraints that might not allow simplifications (relying on semantics). The substitution is extended with the current generalization variable, say X, specialized to an abstraction on C. Rule (SusAA) is about generalization of semantically-equal suspensions of atom-variables. The rule removes the problem and extends the substitution with a mapping to this suspension.

The rules (DecA), (DecC) and (DecAC) are as in the first-order approach. We use some abbreviations: Y_1, Y_2 are fresh variables of the corresponding sorts, $1 \leq k < n$, $1 \leq l < m$ and $n, m \geq 2$. We assume that A and AC function applications are flattened. Also, both $f^{\mathtt{AC}}(t)$ and $f^{\mathtt{A}}(t)$ simply stand for t. Write $f^{\mathtt{A}}(\bar{t})_k$ to denote $f^{\mathtt{A}}(t_1, \ldots, t_k)$, and $f^{\mathtt{A}}(\bar{t})_{k+1\ldots n}$ denotes $f^{\mathtt{A}}(t_{k+1}, \ldots, t_n)$. Similarly, for $f^{\mathtt{AC}}(\bar{t})_k$ and $f^{\mathtt{AC}}(\bar{t})_{k+1\ldots n}$. These rules produce multiple branches and generate a *generalization tree* with, in the worst case (for theories A and AC), a number of branches that is exponential in the number of arguments of $f^{\mathtt{A}}$ and $f^{\mathtt{AC}}$.

Rule (SolAB) applies when the context cannot prove that the atom-variable suspensions are the same: we choose a new atom-variable C and move the anti-unification equation to the store with C as its generalization variable. Furthermore, we introduce the constraint $C\#\lambda\pi_1 \cdot A.\lambda\pi_2 \cdot B.C$ which is equivalent to $C = \pi_1 \cdot A$ or $C = \pi_2 \cdot B$. This constraint collects information from the store that C can only be one of the two suspensions, providing a more specific generalization. This restriction is stronger than the initial version introduced [23].However, as we will see in Example 7, further strengthening is required to guarantee the completeness of $\mathtt{NAU}_E$.

Example 5. Consider the generalization problem $P = \{X : \lambda A.f^{\mathtt{AC}}(A, A, B) \triangleq \lambda B.f^{\mathtt{AC}}(A, B, A)\}$ with the context $\nabla = \{A\#B\}$, and the $\mathtt{NAU}_E$ derivation starting from $P; \emptyset; \nabla; Id$. Applying (Abs) we get:

$$\{Y : f^{\mathtt{AC}}(C, C, (A\ C) \cdot B) \triangleq f^{\mathtt{AC}}((B\ C) \cdot A, C, (B\ C) \cdot A)\}; \emptyset; \Gamma; \{X \mapsto \lambda C.Y\}$$

where $\Gamma = \{A\#B, C\#\lambda A.f^{\mathtt{AC}}(A, A, B), C\#\lambda B.f^{\mathtt{AC}}(A, B, A)\}$ and C is a new atom-variable and Y is a new generalization variable. After the application of (DecAC), $2\times$ (DecAC), $3\times$ (SolAB) one the branches contains the state:

$$\emptyset; \Big\{D : C \triangleq (B\ C) \cdot A, D' : C \triangleq (B\ C) \cdot A, D'' : (A\ C) \cdot B \triangleq C\Big\}; \Gamma'; \sigma$$

where $\sigma = \{X \mapsto \lambda C.f^{\mathtt{AC}}(D, D', D'')\}$ and Γ' (omitted here) extends Γ with the constraints for D, introduced by (SolAB). The pair $(\Gamma', X\sigma)$ is a linear AC-generalization of the input terms (each atom variable D, D' and D'' occurs only once in $X\sigma$). Note that the problems associated with D and D' are identical and they could be merged in one. We come back to this in Section 5.

Example 6 (Cont. Ex. 4). Consider the context $\nabla = \{A\#X_1, a\#X_2, B\#X\}$ and the NLA-expressions $s = \mathtt{implies}(\lambda A.(\mathtt{Pred}(A) \wedge (X_1 \vee X_2)), (X_1 \vee X_2))$ and $t = \mathtt{implies}(\lambda B.(X \wedge \mathtt{Pred}(B)), X)$. We use the $\mathtt{NAU}_E$ rules to compute the generalization. The initial state is $\{Y : s \triangleq t\}; \emptyset; \emptyset; Id$. After an application of the decomposition (Dec) we obtain:

$$\left\{\begin{matrix} Y_1 : \lambda A.(\mathtt{Pred}(A) \wedge (X_1 \vee X_2)) \triangleq \lambda B.X \wedge \mathtt{Pred}(B) \\ Y_2 : X_1 \vee X_2 \triangleq X \end{matrix}\right\}; \emptyset; \emptyset; \sigma$$

$$\Longrightarrow_{(\mathsf{Abs})} \qquad \text{(where } \sigma = \{Y/\mathtt{implies}(Y_1, Y_2)\}\text{)}$$

$$\left\{\begin{matrix} Z : \mathtt{Pred}(C) \wedge (A\ C) \cdot (X_1 \vee X_2) \triangleq (B\ C) \cdot X \wedge \mathtt{Pred}(C) \\ Y_2 : X_1 \vee X_2 \triangleq X \end{matrix}\right\}; \emptyset; \Gamma; \sigma'$$

where $\Gamma = \{C\#\lambda A.(\mathtt{Pred}(A) \wedge (X_1 \vee X_2)), C\#\lambda B.(X \wedge \mathtt{Pred}(B))\}$ and the substitution is $\sigma' = \{Y/\mathtt{implies}(\lambda C.Z, Y_2)\}$. After applying (DecC), we obtain two branches based on the possibilities of decomposing $\wedge$: one branch gives the generalization $(\Gamma, \mathtt{implies}(\lambda C.(Z_1 \wedge Z_2), Y_2))$ and the other branch gives the generalization $(\Gamma, \mathtt{implies}(\lambda C.(\mathtt{Pred}(C) \wedge Z_2), Y_2))$. The latter is clearly less general than the former.

4.1 Correctness Results

All the results here are parametric on an equational theory E that is either $\emptyset$ or A, C or AC. In the case $E = \emptyset$, all the results were verified in [23], we will recall the proof ideas here, but for self-containedness, but we will give more details for the cases in which $E \neq \emptyset$.

Theorem 1 (Termination). $\mathtt{NAU}_E$ *is terminating.*

Proof (Sketch). The proof follows by analyzing the rules in Figure 1 accompanied by a lexicographic ordering. The equational rules (DecA), (DecC) and (DecAC) introduce heavy branching, the number of branches is bounded by the number of nested occurrences of the A, AC, and C function symbols in the initial problem, and after each step the initial problem is replaced by 'smaller' problems. □

Theorem 2 (Soundness). *Given terms-in-context* (∇, s) *and* (∇, t)*. If there exists a derivation* $\{X : t \triangleq s\}; \emptyset; \emptyset; Id \stackrel{+}{\Longrightarrow} \emptyset; S; \Gamma; \sigma$ *obtained by an execution of* $\mathtt{NAU}_E$*, then* $(\Gamma, X\sigma)$ *is an* E*-generalization of* (∇, t) *and* (∇, s)*.*

Proof (Sketch). Let $P, S, \Gamma; \sigma \Longrightarrow P', S', \Gamma'; \sigma'$ be a rule application of $\mathtt{NAU}_E$. By inspecting each rule one can verify that the following invariants hold: (i) The generalization variables of P' and S' are pairwise distinct; (ii) After each rule application $P' \cup S'$ contains all the information, such that, two substitutions σ_1 and σ_2 can be obtained to "reverse" the rule application. I.e., by instantiating a generalization variable with σ' followed by applying σ_1 or σ_2, respectively, we can obtain the original terms from $P \cup S$. By transitivity it follows that $(\emptyset, X\sigma)$ is an E-generalization. □

Example 7 (Weak Completeness). For $P = \{X : f(c_1, A) \triangleq f(c_2, A)\}$ and $\nabla = \emptyset$, the $\mathtt{NAU}_\emptyset$-algorithm terminates with configuration $\emptyset; \{Y_1 : c_1 \triangleq c_2\}; \emptyset; \{X \mapsto f(Y_1, A)\}$. Note that $[f(a, a)]$ is in $[\![(\emptyset, f(Y_1, A))]\!]$, but it is neither in $[\![(\emptyset, f(c_1, A))]\!]$

nor in $[\![(\emptyset, f(c_2, A))]\!]$. It is a generalizer, but not the lgg: the lgg is $(\{A\#Y_1\}, f(Y_1, A))$, and the added constraint forces that Y_1 and A differ for every valid interpretation (cf. Example 2).

Theorem 3 (Weak Completeness). *Given pairs* (∇, s) *and* (∇, t). *If* (Δ, r) *is a generalization of* (∇, t) *and* (∇, s), *then there exists a derivation* $\{X : t \triangleq s\}; \emptyset; \emptyset; Id \stackrel{+}{\Longrightarrow} \emptyset; S; \Gamma; \sigma$ *obtained by an execution of* $\mathtt{NAU}_E$ *and a freshness context* Γ', *such that* $(\Delta, r) \preceq_E (\Gamma \cup \Gamma', X\sigma)$.

Proof. The proof of completeness is by induction on the structure r, and follows by analyzing the rule of $\mathtt{NAU}_E$ applied in the problem. The proof follows the same lines of the proof in [23]. Additional cases have to be considered when the terms in the problem are headed with function symbols f^E with equational theories. Since the rules in Figure 1 expand all possible branches, completeness up to freshness context is guaranteed.

Associative decomposition will lead to some redundancies and the computed set of generalizations should be further minimized. This behaviour is similar to the first-order A-anti-unification [1] and HOP A-anti-unification [11].

Theorem 4. $\mathtt{NAU}_\emptyset$ *is unitary and* $\mathtt{NAU}_\mathtt{A}, \mathtt{NAU}_\mathtt{C}$ *and* $\mathtt{NAU}_\mathtt{AC}$ *are finitary.*

Proof. The format of the rules for $\mathtt{NAU}_\emptyset$ influences the structure of computed generalizers: note that the expression without considering freshness constraints is unique. The algorithm $\mathtt{NAU}_\emptyset$ computes a unique term-generalizer [23]. As expected the equational theories will induce branching when decomposing the specific function symbols, but the possible lgg_E's will be within the finite execution tree of $\mathtt{NAU}_E$, after, possibly, adding some missing constraints, due to weak completeness. But the overall set of generalizations is finite.

Corollary 1. *The rule-based algorithm for* $\mathtt{NAU}_E$ *computes linear generalizations modulo* E *for the input problems.*

Proof (Sketch). Linearity is obtained from the fact that every time a new rule is applied, a fresh variable is used, therefore, no variable occurs more than once in the computed generalization.

5 Merging Generalizations for NLA modulo E

In this section, we refine our generalizations further checking whether solved problems in the store are permutations of each other. Rule (Mer) applies when the set of problems is empty, and it identifies if there are no redundancies in the store, i.e., the same solved problem (possibly with some renaming) under different generalization variables. Thus, given two problems in the store $\{Z_1 : t_1 \triangleq s_1, Z_2 : t_2 \triangleq s_2\}$ the problem is to find a permutation π such that $\nabla \models \pi \cdot t_1 \approx_E s_1$ and $\nabla \models \pi \cdot s_1 \approx_E s_2$. If such permutation exists, both problems are merged into one, and the appropriate updates are done on the context and substitution, e.g. the substitution must be updated with the information $\{Z_2 \mapsto \pi \cdot Z_1\}$. The problem of finding such a π is called the *equivariance problem*, here, generalized to take into account a theory E.

(Mer) **Merge**
$\emptyset; \{Z_1 : t_1 \triangleq s_1, Z_2 : t_2 \triangleq s_2\} \uplus S; \Gamma; \sigma$
$\Longrightarrow \emptyset; \{Z_1 : t_1 \triangleq s_1\} \cup S; \Gamma\{Z_2 \mapsto \pi \cdot Z_1\}; \sigma\{Z_2 \mapsto \pi \cdot Z_1\}$
where $\pi = \textsc{EqvM}(\{t_1 \sqsubseteq t_2, s_1 \sqsubseteq s_2\}, \Gamma)$ and (Z_1, Z_2) is either a pair of atom variables or a pair of term variables.

Fig. 2. Merge Rule

5.1 The equivariance rules for EqvM

We've seen that in the merging rule (Mer) of $\mathtt{NAU}_E$ we need to decide the *equivariance problem modulo E*: Given a set Ψ of equivariant equations of the form $t \sqsubseteq s$ between NLA-terms t and s, and a freshness context ∇, find (a representation of) an injective function π such that $\nabla \models \pi \cdot t \approx_E s$, for all $t \sqsubseteq s \in \Psi$.

First, we present in Figure 3, the decomposition rules of the EqvM algorithm, with dedicated rules for handling equivariant problems modulo E. These rules are not present in the first-order approach to generalization problems, nor in the HOP approach. Second, we present the EqvM algorithm (Algorithm 1), which incorporates additional steps to compute a solution to our problem. Unlike the equivariance algorithm developed for the empty theory in [23], EqvM accounts for the equational theories considered in this work. Handling E is nontrivial, as atom-variable permutations interact with equational theories in unexpected ways (cf. Example 8), requiring semantic tests modulo E which are described in lines 10-12 of the Algorithm 1.

(EqAbs) $\{\lambda W_1.t \sqsubseteq \lambda W_2.s\} \uplus \Psi; \nabla \Longrightarrow \{(W_1\ A) \cdot t \sqsubseteq (W_2\ A) \cdot s, A \sqsubseteq A\} \uplus \Psi; \nabla'$
where $\nabla' = \{A\#B, A\#X \mid A \text{ is fresh}; B, X \text{ occurring in the input}\} \cup \nabla$.

(Eqf) $\{f(\overline{t})_k \sqsubseteq f(\overline{s})_k\} \uplus \Psi; \nabla \Longrightarrow \cup_{j=1}^{k}\{t_j \sqsubseteq s_j\} \cup \Psi; \nabla; \Pi$ (similar for $f^{\mathtt{A}}$)

(EqfC) $\{f^{\mathtt{C}}(t_1, t_2) \sqsubseteq f^{\mathtt{C}}(s_1, s_2)\} \uplus \Psi; \nabla \Longrightarrow \{t_1 \sqsubseteq s_i, t_2 \sqsubseteq s_{3-i}\} \cup \Psi; \nabla$

(EqfAC) $\{f^{\mathtt{AC}}(\overline{t})_n \sqsubseteq f^{\mathtt{AC}}(\overline{s})_n\} \uplus \Psi; \nabla$
$\Longrightarrow \{t_1 \sqsubseteq s_i, f^{\mathtt{AC}}(t_2, \ldots, t_n) \sqsubseteq f^{\mathtt{AC}}(s_1, \ldots, s_{i-1}, s_{i+1}, s_n)\} \cup \Psi; \nabla$

Fig. 3. Decomposition Rules for EqvM with simple freshness context. (n.d.)

Description of the rules of Figure 3. Rule (EqAbs) applies in equivariant equations between abstractions. That is, to find π such that $\nabla \models \pi \cdot (\lambda W_1.t) \approx_E \lambda W_2.s$. We use the fact that $\nabla \models (\lambda W_1.t \approx_E \lambda W_2.s)$ if $\nabla \models (W_1\ A) \cdot t \approx_E (W_2\ A) \cdot s$, for a new atom-variable A (i.e. two abstractions are renamings of each other if they can be both renamed using new atom-variable and they continue the same). Thus, the problem reduces to finding π such that $\nabla \models \pi \cdot (W_1\ A) \cdot t \approx_E (W_2\ A) \cdot s$ holds. This corresponds to the problem $(W_1\ A) \cdot t \sqsubseteq (W_2\ A) \cdot s$. We add the constraint $A \sqsubseteq A$, as the final π shouldn't care about atom-variables introduced during the computation as they do not appear in the input problem.

Rule (Eqf) applies in equivariant equations between terms headed with a function symbol, say f. To illustrate, let us consider the case with $k = 3$. Thus, to find π such that $\nabla \vDash \pi \cdot f(t_1, t_2, t_3) \approx_E f(s_1, s_2, s_3)$. Since π distributes over f, this problem reduces to $\nabla \vDash f(\pi \cdot t_1, \pi \cdot t_2, \pi \cdot t_3) \approx_E f(s_1, s_2, s_3)$, which can be decomposed to three smaller problems $\nabla \vDash \pi \cdot t_i \approx_E s_i$, for $i = 1, 2, 3$. Note that application of π does not alter the structure of the term. We can use a similar rule in the case both terms are headed with an associative function symbol $f^{\mathtt{A}}$ as long as that the terms are flattened w.r.t. $f^{\mathtt{A}}$.

Rule (EqfC) applies in equivariant equations between terms headed with a commutative function symbol $f^{\mathtt{C}}$. Thus, to find π such that $\nabla \vDash \pi \cdot f^{\mathtt{C}}(t_1, t_2) \approx_E f^{\mathtt{C}}(s_1, s_2)$. This rule branche due to commutativity, and the problem reduces to find π such that $\nabla \vDash \pi \cdot t_1 \approx_E s_1$ and $\nabla \vDash \pi \cdot t_2 \approx_E s_2$ in one branch, but a different solution could be found in the other branch $\nabla \vDash \pi \cdot t_1 \approx_E s_2$ and $\nabla \vDash \pi \cdot t_2 \approx_E s_1$. Note that, with nested occurrences of commutative function symbols in a term, this problem has an upper bound of 2^n possible solutions, for some n.

Rule (EqfAC) applies in equivariant equations between terms headed with an associative-commutative function symbol $f^{\mathtt{AC}}$. The explanation is similar to the one above, except that there is more branching. Here we also assume that the terms are flattened w.r.t. $f^{\mathtt{AC}}$.

5.2 The equivariance algorithm for EQVM

In Algorithm 1 we give a strategy to check equivariance by first splitting the freshness context ∇ into several simple freshness constraints and then processing them. The strategy for checking equivariance involves applying the (nondet, n.d.) decomposition to the equivariance equations and then examining the simplified set to construct an injective mapping. This is achieved by systematically testing all possible outcomes of the decomposition. We use Lemma 1 to simplify the freshness context of the initial problem.

Definition 4. *A simple freshness context is a set of (simple) freshness constraints of the forms $A\#B$, $A\#X$, or $A\#\lambda B.A$, where A, B are atom-variables and X is a generalization-variable. We abbreviate the latter by $A = B$.*

Lemma 1. *Every (general) freshness context is equivalent to a disjunction of simple freshness contexts.*

Some explanations for Algorithm 1: In step 4, the algorithm fails if it encounters a problem of the form $\pi_{i,1} \cdot X \sqsubseteq \pi_{i,2} \cdot Y$ as solving it would require finding a π such that $\nabla \vDash \pi \cdot (\pi_{i,1} \cdot X) \approx_E \pi_{i,2} \cdot Y$. Here, $\pi, \pi_{i,1}$ and $\pi_{i,2}$ are atom-variable permutations, and in the semantics they will be instantiated to concrete atoms, whereas X, Y will be instantiated to ground terms. By Definition 1, the judgement must hold for all valuations of X and Y, and they are independent from each other. The guess in step 8 might be guided by some technique, for e.g., a complete case distinction of equalities between the atom-variables underlying the construction in Theorem 5.

Algorithm 1 (E_{QVM})
Input: *Ψ a set of equivariance equations and ∇ a simple freshness context.*
Output: *an injective mapping Π.*
1: *First apply the (non-deterministic, n.d.) algorithm for decomposing in Figure 3.*
2: *Find one result (S, ∇) of the derivation tree obtained from the application of the rules in Figure 3 that passes the following construction and tests:*
3: *Compute a set of mapping relations Π from S as follows:*
4: *If there is a matching equation $\pi_{i,1} \cdot X \sqsubseteq \pi_{i,2} \cdot Y$ in S then* **fail.**
5: While *there is a matching relation between atom-variables $\pi_{i,1} \cdot A_i \sqsubseteq \pi_{i,2} \cdot B_i$ in S* **do** *:*
6: *If all atom variables in $\pi_{i,1}$ are already mapped in the current Π, but A_i is missing* **then**
7: *define $A_i \mapsto (\Pi(\pi_{i,1}^{-1}) \circ \pi_{i,2}) \cdot B_i$.*
8: *Else, guess a mapping for the atom-variable and repeat.*
9: EndWhile
10: For each *matching equation $\pi_{i,1} \cdot X \sqsubseteq \pi_{i,2} \cdot X$ in S* **do***:*
11: *Test whether $\nabla \models \Pi(\pi_{i,1}) \cdot X \approx_E \pi_{i,2} \cdot X$.*
12: *If there is one pair for which the test fail, return* **fail.**
13: EndFor *% after all pairs are processed, test correctness and injetivity of Π.*
15: *For each pair of definitions $A_1 \mapsto \pi_1 \cdot B_1$ and $A_2 \mapsto \pi_2 \cdot B_2$, the following must hold:*
16: *$\nabla \models A_1 \approx_E A_2$ if and only if $\nabla \models \pi_1 \cdot B_1 \approx_E \pi_2 \cdot B_2$.*
17: *In case of success, return Π that consists of the defined mappings.*

Example 8. We can refine the generalization obtained in Example 5:

$$\emptyset; \left\{D : C \triangleq (B\ C) \cdot A, D' : C \triangleq (B\ C) \cdot A, D'' : (A\ C) \cdot B \triangleq C\right\}; \Gamma'; \sigma$$

where $\sigma = \{X \mapsto \lambda C.f^{\mathsf{AC}}(D, D', D'')\}$ and Γ'. First, it is trivial to conclude that $\nabla \models id \cdot D \approx_E D'$ and using the substitution $\sigma' = \{D' \mapsto id \cdot D\}$ we obtain the following: $\emptyset; \left\{D : C \triangleq (B\ C) \cdot A, D'' : (A\ C) \cdot B \triangleq C\right\}; \Gamma'\sigma'; \sigma''$ where $\sigma'' = \sigma\sigma' = \{X \mapsto \lambda C.f^{\mathsf{AC}}(D, D, D'')\}$. We now proceed with the application of rule (Mer): we need to solve the equivariance problem $\text{E}_{\text{QVM}}(\{C \sqsubseteq (A\ C) \cdot B, (B\ C) \cdot A \sqsubseteq C\}, \Gamma_1)$, where $\Gamma_1 = \{A\#B, C\#\lambda A.f^{\mathsf{AC}}(A, A, B), C\#\lambda B.f^{\mathsf{AC}}(A, B, A)\}$ is a subset of Γ' without the constraints for D which are irrelevant here:

1. First we need to simplify the context Γ_1. Note that
   $C\#\lambda A.f^{\mathsf{AC}}(A, A, B) \iff A = C \vee (A \neq C \wedge C\#B)$
   $C\#\lambda B.f^{\mathsf{AC}}(A, B, A) \iff C = B \vee (C \neq B \wedge C\#A)$
   Since $A\#B$ is part of the freshness context, there is only one possible simpler freshness context since the other cases produce unsatisfiable contexts: $\Gamma_2 = \{A\#B, A\#C, C\#B\}$, which means that all instantiations of A, B, C are pairwise different.
2. We now compute $\text{E}_{\text{QVM}}(\{C \sqsubseteq (A\ C) \cdot B, (B\ C) \cdot A \sqsubseteq C\}, \Gamma_2)$:
   No decomposition rule can be applied. In step 5, and focusing on the problem $C \sqsubseteq (A\ C) \cdot B$, we use information from Γ_2 to simplify it. The 'guess' is guided

by the following reasoning: Since $A\#B$ and $A\#C$ ensure that these atoms-variables to have distinct interpretations, we conclude that $(A\ C) \cdot B \equiv B$. This reduces the problem to $\{C \sqsubseteq B, (B\ C) \cdot A \sqsubseteq C\}, \Gamma_2$. We repeat step 5, on the equation $(B\ C) \cdot A \sqsubseteq C$, we can use the information in Γ_2 again, and conclude that $(B\ C) \cdot A \equiv A$, which reduces the problem to $\{C \sqsubseteq B, A \sqsubseteq C\}; \Gamma_2$. The injective mapping for equivariant match is: $\pi = \{A \mapsto C, C \mapsto B\}$.

Finally, E-generalization obtained is $(\Gamma', \lambda C.f^{\mathsf{AC}}(D, D, \pi \cdot D))$. Note that this is one possible generalization in one branch of the generalization tree. A different branch may produce a different generalization.

Deciding whether one expression is a permutation of another—under certain freshness constraints—can require exponential effort. This is because, for each pair of atom variables (e.g., A and B) that appear in the expressions s and t, the algorithm must consider all possible ways of instantiating them, taking into account whether $A = B$ or $A \neq B$. The number of such combinations grows exponentially with the number of atom variables involved. As a result, we obtain the following decidability result with a high complexity bound:

Theorem 5. *The question, whether for two given expressions s, t and freshness constraint ∇, there exists a function π such that $\nabla \models \pi \cdot s \approx_E t$ is algorithmically decidable. Its complexity has a doubly exponential upper bound.*

Our EqVM algorithm is correct:

Theorem 6. EqVM *is terminating and correct.*

Proof. 1. Since the rules for EqVM decompose the problem into smaller problems and each pair (S, ∇) contains a finite set S. The tests in Algorithm 1 eventually terminate as they consist in checking finite permutations in a finite set of equivariance equations.

2. EqVM is correct iff there exists an injective function Π that respects some freshness constraints, say ∇'. Note that Π is the representation of a class of injective mappings under ∇', i.e., given $\Pi = \{A_1 \mapsto r_1, \ldots, A_k \mapsto r_k\}$ and $\nabla' \vDash A_i \neq A_j \implies r_i \neq r_j$.
Let $\{s \sqsubseteq t\} \cup \Psi; \nabla$ be the input to EqVM, and apply the rules in Figure 3 until no more rules can be applied. The result is a finite set of reduced equivariance equations of the form $\pi \cdot A \sqsubseteq \pi' \cdot A$, $\pi \cdot A \sqsubseteq \pi' \cdot B$, $\pi \cdot X \sqsubseteq \pi' \cdot X$, $\pi \cdot X \sqsubseteq \pi' \cdot Y$ and a finite set of simple freshness constraints ∇', for some permutations π, π', atom-variables A, B and term-variables X, Y. If there is at least one problem of the form $\pi \cdot X \sqsubseteq \pi' \cdot Y$, then no solution exists, as permutations on atoms do not guarantee equality modulo E on all possible interpretations of different term-variables X and Y. For equations of the form $\pi \cdot A \sqsubseteq \pi' \cdot B$ we can always select first the ones for which the atoms in π have defined mappings, this will allow to create the mapping associated to A. Once those are all checked we can move to equations $\pi \cdot A \sqsubseteq \pi' \cdot B$ for which atoms in π are note defined in Π yet, but there are restrictions in ∇' for them. We

check the restrictions for each atom, and explore interpretations of the atoms, investigating all possible guesses. After the mappings are defined for all the atomvariables, we check whether $\nabla' \models \pi \cdot X \sqsubseteq \pi' \cdot X$ holds. Finally, we check whether Π is a representation of an injective mapping of atom-variables.

Extending the $\mathtt{NAU}_E$ rules in Figure 1 with the rule (Mer) allows to compute non-linear generalizers that may be less general than the generalizers using only rules in Figure 1. We lose linearity as we merge two generalization variables with different names into one, using the permutation obtained from EQVM.

6 Related Work, Conclusion and Future Work

Related Work. In [6], the problem of computing least general generalizations (lgg) for nominal terms-in-context of the form (∇, s), where ∇ is a freshness context and s is a (standard) nominal term, was investigated. It was observed that if atoms were taken literally, there does not exist an lgg for two terms-in-context. However, viewing the notation of atoms only as names for atoms and using atom-variables, there exists an lgg and also a minimal set of generalizations [23,24].

Generalization problems have several applications, such as, on parallel recursion scheme detection [5], analogy making [18], inductive logic programming [14,13], etc. First-order anti-unification problems modulo equational theories have been extensively investigated [1,2,9,12] and more recently in learning libraries [8]. While the techniques presented there are similar to the ones used here, the interaction with nominal techniques is novel. Nominal techniques have been investigated in the context of nominal unification [19,25,26] including equational theories [3,4], but not much research has been done w.r.t. nominal anti-unification. Our results are likely to find applications in the learning of higher-order programs, adapting the methodology proposed in [15] to the nominal framework.

Conclusion and Future Work. We have investigated the extension of the nominal anti-unification problem to theories A, C and AC. Our proposed method considers the nominal language with atom-variables NLA and a semantic approach to find least general generalizers modulo $E \in \{\mathtt{A}, \mathtt{C}, \mathtt{AC}\}$. The extended algorithm $\mathtt{NAU}_E$ is obtained by adding specific rules to deal with each particular theory as well as new non-deterministic equivariance algorithm EQVM that works, semantically, modulo the theories considered here. We left as future work the investigation subclasses of the generalization problem that are computationally tractable and lead to a single lgg, and other optimization methods to work in wider subclasses of the problem, using for e.g., the rigidity functions as in [11]. Further equational theories like the considered one with a unit element are left for future research.

Acknowledgments. This work was partially supported by the Austrian Science Fund (FWF) project P 35530.

Disclosure of Interests. The authors have no competing interests to declare that are relevant to the content of this article.

References

1. Alpuente, M., Escobar, S., Espert, J., Meseguer, J.: ACUOS: A system for modular ACU generalization with subtyping and inheritance. In: Fermé, E., Leite, J. (eds.) Logics in Artificial Intelligence - 14th European Conference, JELIA 2014, Funchal, Madeira, Portugal, September 24-26, 2014. Proceedings. Lecture Notes in Computer Science, vol. 8761, pp. 573–581. Springer (2014). https://doi.org/10.1007/978-3-319-11558-0_40
2. Alpuente, M., Escobar, S., Espert, J., Meseguer, J.: A modular order-sorted equational generalization algorithm. Inf. Comput. **235**, 98–136 (2014). https://doi.org/10.1016/J.IC.2014.01.006
3. Ayala-Rincón, M., de Carvalho Segundo, W., Fernández, M., Silva, G.F., Nantes-Sobrinho, D.: Formalising nominal C-unification generalised with protected variables. Math. Struct. Comput. Sci. **31**(3), 286–311 (2021). https://doi.org/10.1017/S0960129521000050
4. Ayala-Rincón, M., Fernández, M., Silva, G.F., Kutsia, T., Nantes-Sobrinho, D.: Nominal AC-matching. In: Dubois, C., Kerber, M. (eds.) Intelligent Computer Mathematics - 16th International Conference, CICM 2023, Cambridge, UK, September 5-8, 2023, Proceedings. Lecture Notes in Computer Science, vol. 14101, pp. 53–68. Springer (2023). https://doi.org/10.1007/978-3-031-42753-4_4
5. Barwell, A.D., Brown, C., Hammond, K.: Finding parallel functional pearls: Automatic parallel recursion scheme detection in haskell functions via anti-unification. Future Gener. Comput. Syst. **79**, 669–686 (2018). https://doi.org/10.1016/J.FUTURE.2017.07.024
6. Baumgartner, A., Kutsia, T., Levy, J., Villaret, M.: Nominal anti-unification. In: Fernández, M. (ed.) 26th International Conference on Rewriting Techniques and Applications, RTA 2015, June 29 to July 1, Warsaw, Poland. LIPIcs, vol. 36, pp. 57–73. Schloss Dagstuhl - Leibniz-Zentrum fuer Informatik (2015). https://doi.org/10.4230/LIPIcs.RTA.2015.57
7. Baumgartner, A., Kutsia, T., Levy, J., Villaret, M.: Higher-order pattern anti-unification in linear time. J. Autom. Reasoning **58**(2), 293–310 (2017). https://doi.org/10.1007/s10817-016-9383-3
8. Cao, D., Kunkel, R., Nandi, C., Willsey, M., Tatlock, Z., Polikarpova, N.: babble: Learning better abstractions with E-graphs and anti-unification. Proc. ACM Program. Lang. **7**(POPL), 396–424 (2023). https://doi.org/10.1145/3571207
9. Cerna, D.M.: Anti-unification and the theory of semirings. Theor. Comput. Sci. **848**, 133–139 (2020). https://doi.org/10.1016/J.TCS.2020.10.020
10. Cerna, D.M., Kutsia, T.: A generic framework for higher-order generalizations. In: Geuvers, H. (ed.) 4th International Conference on Formal Structures for Computation and Deduction, FSCD 2019, June 24-30, 2019, Dortmund, Germany. LIPIcs, vol. 131, pp. 10:1–10:19. Schloss Dagstuhl - Leibniz-Zentrum für Informatik (2019). https://doi.org/10.4230/LIPICS.FSCD.2019.10
11. Cerna, D.M., Kutsia, T.: Higher-order pattern generalization modulo equational theories. Math. Struct. Comput. Sci. **30**(6), 627–663 (2020). https://doi.org/10.1017/S0960129520000110
12. Cerna, D.M., Kutsia, T.: Anti-unification and generalization: A survey. In: Proceedings of the Thirty-Second International Joint Conference on Artificial Intelligence, IJCAI 2023, 19th-25th August 2023, Macao, SAR, China. pp. 6563–6573. ijcai.org (2023). https://doi.org/10.24963/IJCAI.2023/736

13. Cropper, A., Dumancic, S., Evans, R., Muggleton, S.H.: Inductive logic programming at 30. Mach. Learn. **111**(1), 147–172 (2022). https://doi.org/10.1007/S10994-021-06089-1
14. Cropper, A., Morel, R.: Learning programs by learning from failures. Mach. Learn. **110**(4), 801–856 (2021). https://doi.org/10.1007/S10994-020-05934-Z
15. Cropper, A., Morel, R., Muggleton, S.H.: Learning higher-order logic programs. Mach. Learn. **109**(7), 1289–1322 (2020). https://doi.org/10.1007/S10994-019-05862-7
16. Gabbay, M., Pitts, A.M.: A new approach to abstract syntax with variable binding. Formal Aspects Comput. **13**(3-5), 341–363 (2002). https://doi.org/10.1007/S001650200016
17. Gabbay, M.J., Mathijssen, A.: One-and-a-halfth-order logic. In: Proceedings of the 8th ACM SIGPLAN International Conference on Principles and Practice of Declarative Programming. p. 189–200. PPDP '06, Association for Computing Machinery, New York, NY, USA (2006). https://doi.org/10.1145/1140335.1140359
18. Krumnack, U., Schwering, A., Gust, H., Kühnberger, K.: Restricted higher-order anti-unification for analogy making. In: Orgun, M.A., Thornton, J. (eds.) AI 2007: Advances in Artificial Intelligence, 20th Australian Joint Conference on Artificial Intelligence, Gold Coast, Australia, December 2-6, 2007, Proceedings. Lecture Notes in Computer Science, vol. 4830, pp. 273–282. Springer (2007). https://doi.org/10.1007/978-3-540-76928-6_29
19. Levy, J., Villaret, M.: Nominal unification from a higher-order perspective. ACM Trans. Comput. Log. **13**(2), 10:1–10:31 (2012). https://doi.org/10.1145/2159531.2159532
20. Nantes-Sobrinho, D., Schmidt-Schauß, M., Baumgartner, A., Kutsia, T.: Generalization problems with atom-variables in languages with binders and equational theories. CoRR **abs/2502.19306** (2025). https://doi.org/10.48550/ARXIV.2502.19306
21. Pitts, A.M.: Nominal Sets: Names and Symmetry in Computer Science. Cambridge University Press (2013). https://doi.org/https://doi.org/10.1017/CBO9781139084673
22. Plotkin, G.D.: A note on inductive generalization. Machine Intel. **5**(1), 153–163 (1970)
23. Schmidt-Schauß, M., Nantes-Sobrinho, D.: Nominal anti-unification with atom-variables. In: Felty, A.P. (ed.) 7th International Conference on Formal Structures for Computation and Deduction, FSCD 2022, August 2-5, 2022, Haifa, Israel. LIPIcs, vol. 228, pp. 7:1–7:22. Schloss Dagstuhl - Leibniz-Zentrum für Informatik (2022). https://doi.org/10.4230/LIPIcs.FSCD.2022.7
24. Schmidt-Schauß, M., Nantes-Sobrinho, D.: Towards fast nominal anti-unification of letrec-expressions. In: Pientka, B., Tinelli, C. (eds.) Automated Deduction - CADE 29 - 29th International Conference on Automated Deduction, Rome, Italy, July 1-4, 2023, Proceedings. Lecture Notes in Computer Science, vol. 14132, pp. 456–473. Springer (2023). https://doi.org/10.1007/978-3-031-38499-8_26
25. Schmidt-Schauß, M., Sabel, D., Kutz, Y.D.K.: Nominal unification with atom-variables. J. Symb. Comput. **90**, 42–64 (2019). https://doi.org/10.1016/j.jsc.2018.04.003
26. Urban, C., Pitts, A.M., Gabbay, M.: Nominal unification. Theor. Comput. Sci. **323**(1-3), 473–497 (2004). https://doi.org/10.1016/J.TCS.2004.06.016

Extending Flexible Boolean Semantics for the Language of Mathematics

Shashank Pathak(✉)

Department of Computer Science, The University of Manchester, Manchester, UK
shashank.pathak@manchester.ac.uk

Abstract. Flexible Boolean semantics is a framework for analysing natural language using Boolean algebras and flexibility principles. In this article, we use flexible Boolean semantics to analyse the language of mathematics. We find that the framework cannot be used to produce desirable results for sentences in which the subject is a coordination of definite descriptions, each denoting a set, and the predicate describes a property of sets. To resolve this issue, we extend the type system and the operators from the framework to handle such sentences.

Keywords: Language of Mathematics · Coordination · Plurals.

1 Introduction

English sentences found in mathematics textbooks and research articles often exhibit grammatical phenomena similar to those in everyday English. One such phenomenon is the collective/distributive distinction, which we show below. As a convention, we mark meaningless sentences with a # at the beginning. Consider the following sentences.

(1) a. 2 and 3 are prime.
b. 2 is prime.

(2) a. 2 and 3 are coprime.
b. #2 is coprime.

Sentence (1-a) entails (1-b). However, (2-a) does not entail (2-b). In fact, the (2-b) is arguably meaningless. Adjectives such as *prime* express properties of individual integers, whereas adjectives such as *coprime* express properties of a collection of integers. From the above example, it can be seen that for adjectives which correspond to properties of a collection of integers, replacing the coordinated subject with either of its coordinands does not preserve truth.

Next, consider the following sentences.

(3) a. The multiples of 4 and the multiples of 6 are even.
b. The multiples of 4 are even.
c. Each multiple of 4 is even.

(4) a. The integers and the rationals are countable.

V. de Paiva and P. Koepke (Eds.): CICM 2025, LNAI 16136, pp. 152–170, 2026.
https://doi.org/10.1007/978-3-032-07021-0_9

b. The integers are countable.
c. #Each integer is countable.

(5) a. The integers and the rationals are equinumerous.
b. #The integers are equinumerous.

The sentence (3-a) entails (3-b). Similarly, (4-a) entails (4-b). However, (5-a) does not entail (5-b). Thus, for some adjectives such as *even*, *countable* and *prime*, the sentence remains true when the coordinated noun phrase (NP) is replaced by one of the coordinands, however some, for example *equinumerous* and *coprime*, the sentence does not. Also, (3-b) entails (3-c), however, (4-b) does not entail (4-c). Thus, some adjectives, for example *countable*, apply naturally to sets, whereas when applied to entities which are not sets, result in meaningless sentences like (4-c).

In the above examples of entailment patterns, we have the linguistic phenomena of coordination, *definite descriptions, distributive and collective predicates* and *selectional restrictions* at play. Definite descriptions are NPs which refer to a unique entity, and are typically of the form *the* + *noun* [6]. In the examples, we have coordination of NPs such as 2 *and* 3 and coordination of plural definite descriptions such as *the integers and the rationals.* We have distributive predicates, such as *prime* and *countable*, which apply separately to each coordinand in the coordinated subject, and collective predicates, such as *coprime* and *equinumerous*, which apply to the coordinated subject as a whole and not to the individual coordinands. Along with it, we have restrictions placed by predicates on what their arguments could be. These restrictions are called selectional restrictions, and we say that a predicate selects certain kind of arguments. For example, predicates such as *prime* and *coprime* select integers or pair of integers as their arguments, whereas predicates such as *countable* and *equinumerous* select sets or pair of sets as their arguments.

This article examines how these linguistic phenomena affect entailment patterns like those above. We use *flexible Boolean semantics* as our semantic framework. *Boolean semantics* is a branch of compositional model-theoretic semantics that uses Boolean algebraic properties of semantic domains to analyse natural language. While Boolean semantics typically relies solely on function application to combine denotations, flexible Boolean semantics extends this by using phonologically covert operators as well.

Winter [22] applies flexible Boolean semantics to analyse how coordination and definite descriptions interact with distributive and collective predicates. This article evaluates his framework on the *Language of Mathematics* (LoM), which comprises English sentences and symbolic expressions found in pure mathematics texts [4]. In this article, we present an example from LoM where Winter's theory fails to yield satisfactory results. Then, we propose extensions to the type system and operators used by Winter, and demonstrate how the extensions address the issue.

The lack of vagueness in LoM makes it an ideal testbed for semantic theories. Concerning applications, theories of deep semantic analysis for LoM can provide a foundational framework for math-aware natural language processing. In particular, such theories can support the development of tools for formalisation of mathematical text. Such tools are valuable because much of mathematical knowledge is written informally, and translating it into formal languages enables automated reasoning and verification with minimal human effort. By identifying the semantic mechanisms that govern LoM, such as plurals and coordination, our work contributes to the long term goal of enabling machines to understand and reason about mathematics as written by humans. This line of research offers a theoretical backbone for building robust formalisation pipelines.

We are currently implementing the theory presented in this article, using Grammatical Framework (GF) [17], which is a high-level grammar writing tool. Specifically, we are using GF to design a parser for sentences from LoM. The implementation is ongoing and available on GitHub [13].

2 Related Work

There are two major lines of work analysing LoM using techniques from linguistics. The first is a series of articles by Ranta describing how Martin-Löf type theory (MLTT) [10] can be used as a formalism for LoM. The first article [14] argues for MLTT over predicate calculus, analyses distributive and collective predicates, and mentions some problems concerning the interaction of generalised quantifiers and pronouns with plural NPs. In our article, we analyse distributive and collective predicates, but not generalised quantifiers and pronouns, which we leave as future work. In the subsequent articles [15,16], Ranta extends his theory by using the type-theoretic notions of dependent types and contexts to model quantification and anaphora.

The second major line of work is the Naproche project, which includes an analysis of the linguistic phenomenon of presuppositions in mathematical text and how they are handled in the Naproche system [2], and a formalism dealing with implicit function introduction in mathematical text [1]. Closely related to our work is an article [3] that describes how collective and distributive predicates are handled in the Naproche system using a variant of Discourse Representation Theory (DRT) [8] as an intermediate language. In contrast, we analyse the predicates within the broader framework of flexible Boolean semantics.

Other texts analysing LoM include Zinn's PhD thesis [23], which contains a description of linguistic phenomena exhibited in LoM, and Ganesalingam's thesis [4] which provides an account of the linguistic features of LoM, focusing on ambiguity, and gives a blueprint of formalisation mechanisms using an extended version of DRT. Sentences containing modals in LoM have been examined [7], although without a formal framework . GF has been used previously to translate sentences from LoM to logic [18,19]. Corpus linguistics techniques have been used to study LoM as well. For example, imperatives in LoM have been analysed [21], and part-of-speech tagging and bigram frequency analysis have been performed on a corpus of 3.7 million mathematics proofs extracted from arXiv [5].

3 Preliminaries

Coordination. Coordination in natural language is cross-categorical. We find coordinate structures with many syntactic categories. For example,

(6) John [and/or] Mary [are/is] tall.

(7) John is tall [and/or] Mary is tall.

(8) John is tall [and/or] thin.

Regarding the denotations of the coordinators, one possibility is to assume that the coordinators are ambiguous. For example, in (6) the coordinator denotes a binary function on entities; in (7) on truth values, and in (8) on predicates. The ambiguity grows if more syntactic categories are considered. Boolean semantics addresses this ambiguity by using the fact that most domains used in the model-theoretic analysis of natural language can be endowed with a Boolean algebra structure. Then, all denotations of *and* and *or* denote the meet and the join operations, respectively, in appropriate domains, explaining the apparent lexical ambiguity [22]. For example, in the domain of truth values *and* and *or* denote the propositional logical connectives conjunction and disjunction, respectively. In the domain of sets of entities, *and* and *or* denote set intersection and union, respectively.

Flexible Boolean Semantics. In a standard model-theoretic compositional analysis of natural language, function application is the only way denotations combine. This leads to challenges in handling coordination and plurals, which can be avoided by adding rules or *flexibility principles* [22]. The flexibility principles operate on the semantic level, and involve phonologically covert operators. By phonologically covert operators, we mean operators present in the semantic derivation but not present in the surface syntax. These operators affect meaning but are not pronounced in speech or written overtly. The well known operation of *type-raising* is one of the flexibility principles. First introduced by Partee and Rooth [11] and further developed by Partee [12], these principles resolve type-mismatches when function application alone is insufficient. Flexible Boolean semantics combines Boolean semantics with flexibility principles.

Syntactic and Semantic Predicates. In this article, we will use the terms *syntactic predicate* and *semantic predicate*. A syntactic predicate is predicate in the sense of linguistics. It is the part of a sentence consisting of the verb together with its complements and adjuncts. A semantic predicate (or simply predicate) is a predicate in the sense of logic. It is a symbol denoting a relation of some non-negative arity.

Distributive and Collective Predicates. Syntactic predicates fall broadly into two categories: *collective* and *distributive*. When used with a subject which denotes a collection, distributive predicates apply to each individual member of the collection separately. For example, *are tall* is distributive, as *John and Mary are tall* implies both *John is tall* and *Mary is tall.* In contrast, collective predicates like *met* apply only to the group as a whole. *John and Mary met* is not equivalent to *John met and Mary met.*

4 Winter's Analysis of Coordination

The analysis by Winter [22] explains how flexible Boolean semantics accounts for the interaction of coordination with distributive and collective predicates, for example, in sentences (1-a) and (2-a). Then, Winter extends his analysis to coordination of definite descriptions. We first describe the type system and the operators used, and then describe the analysis.

Definition 1 (Extensional Types, Boolean Types). *The set of primitive types is* $\{e, t\}$. *The set of extensional types is the smallest set containing the primitive types such that if* τ *and* σ *are extensional types, then so is* $(\tau\sigma)$. *An extensional type* τ *is said to be Boolean if* $\tau = t$ *or* $\tau = (\sigma_1\sigma_2)$ *where* σ_1 *is any extensional type and* σ_2 *is a Boolean type.*

We omit writing parentheses in extensional types when readability is unaffected. Also, type application is right-associative; that is, $\sigma_1\sigma_2\sigma_3$ should be read as $\sigma_1(\sigma_2\sigma_3)$, not as $(\sigma_1\sigma_2)\sigma_3$.

Definition 2 (Typed Domains). *We take* D_e *to denote a fixed arbitrary nonempty set, and* D_t *the set of truth values* $\{0, 1\}$. *Further, for arbitrary types* σ *and* τ, $D_{\sigma\tau}$ *is the set of functions from* D_σ *to* D_τ.

Boolean types are important because their domains form Boolean algebras. In this article, we write the type of a syntactic expression as a subscript on that expression, i.e. f_σ means that f has type σ.

Definition 3 (Polymorphic Boolean Operators). *Let* τ *be a Boolean type. We define the polymorphic boolean operators* $\sqcap_{\tau\tau\tau}, \sqcup_{\tau\tau\tau}$, $\neg_{\tau\tau}$ *and* $\sqsubseteq_{\tau\tau t}$ *recursively as follows. Let* $\wedge, \vee$, $\neg$ *and* $\rightarrow$ *be the standard propositional functions. If* $\tau = t$, *then* $\sqcap_{\tau\tau\tau} = \wedge, \sqcup_{\tau\tau\tau} = \vee$, $\neg_{\tau\tau} = \neg$ *and* $\sqsubseteq_{\tau\tau t} = \rightarrow$. *For* $\tau = \sigma_1\sigma_2$,

$$\begin{aligned}
\sqcap_{\tau\tau\tau} &= \lambda X_\tau.\lambda Y_\tau.\lambda Z_{\sigma_1}.X(Z) \sqcap_{\sigma_2\sigma_2\sigma_2} Y(Z),\\
\sqcup_{\tau\tau\tau} &= \lambda X_\tau.\lambda Y_\tau.\lambda Z_{\sigma_1}.X(Z) \sqcup_{\sigma_2\sigma_2\sigma_2} Y(Z),\\
\neg_{\tau\tau} &= \lambda X_\tau.\lambda Z_{\sigma_1}.\neg_{\sigma_2\sigma_2} X(Z),\\
\sqsubseteq_{\tau\tau t} &= \lambda X_\tau.\lambda Y_\tau.\forall Z_{\sigma_1}.X(Z) \sqsubseteq_{\sigma_2\sigma_2 t} Y(Z).
\end{aligned}$$

For a syntactic expression s_σ, let $[\![s_\sigma]\!]$ be its denotation. It is known that for any Boolean type τ, $\langle D_\tau, [\![\sqcap_{\tau\tau\tau}]\!], [\![\sqcup_{\tau\tau\tau}]\!], [\![\neg_{\tau\tau}]\!]\rangle$ forms a Boolean algebra.

4.1 Deriving Distributive Readings with Coordination of Singular Nouns

We now show how sentences with coordinated subjects and distributive predicates are analyzed by Winter when the subject is a coordination of singular nouns, and does not contain a definite description. A design choice of Winter's framework is that

(9) singular individuals have the type e, plural individuals have the type et, the denotations of distributive predicates have the type et, and the denotations of collective predicates have the type $(et)t$.

Thus, both plural individuals and distributive predicates denote sets of entities, while the collective predicates denote sets of sets of entities.

In the following derivations, the denotations for the lexical items are given in boldface. Thus, for a lexical item f, $\mathbf{f}$ denotes $[\![f]\!]$. Also, we silently perform β-reduction of λ-terms where appropriate. Consider the sentence

(10) 2 and 3 are prime.

Let the domain be the set of integers, i.e. $D_e = \mathbb{Z}$. As 2 and 3 denote the integers 2 and 3, respectively, which are singular individuals, by assumption (9), they have the type e. Also, **and** $= \sqcap_{\sigma\sigma\sigma}$ for some appropriate type σ. Since e is not a Boolean type, we do not have a Boolean algebra structure on D_e. Thus, there is no straightforward way to derive the denotation of the NP 2 *and* 3 by combining **and**, 2 and 3. To resolve such a situation, a type-raising operator, called *Montague Raising* (**M**), is used which maps an entity to a generalized quantifier. **M** is given by

$$\mathbf{M}_{e(et)t} = \lambda x_e \lambda P_{et}.Px. \tag{i}$$

The operator **M** is phonologically covert, and is invoked in the case of a type mismatch. Using **M**, we get

$$[\![2 \text{ and } 3]\!]_{(et)t} = \mathbf{M}(2) \sqcap_{((et)t)((et)t)((et)t)} \mathbf{M}(3) \tag{ii}$$
$$= \lambda P_{et}.(P(2) \wedge P(3)). \tag{iii}$$

Thus, 2 *and* 3 denotes a generalized quantifier of type $(et)t$. From now on, we will omit the types of the polymorphic Boolean operators if the types can be inferred. Since *are prime* is a distributive predicate, by design choice (9), the corresponding semantic predicate **prime** has the type et, and we get

$$[\![2 \text{ and } 3 \text{ are prime}]\!] = (\lambda P_{et}.(P(2) \wedge P(3)))\mathbf{prime}. \tag{iv}$$
$$= \mathbf{prime}(2) \wedge \mathbf{prime}(3). \tag{v}$$

Thus, when the NP is a coordinated plural made up of singular nouns, the distributive readings of sentences can be derived by using the **M** operator and the polymorphic Boolean operators.

4.2 Deriving Collective Readings with Coordination of Singular Nouns

Now, let us see how collective predicates are analysed. Consider the sentence

(11) 2 and 3 are coprime.

Similarly to the previous example, as shown in Equation (iii), the NP 2 *and* 3 has the denotation $\lambda P_{et}.(P(2) \wedge P(3))$. As mentioned previously in design choice (9) of Winter's theory, collective predicates have denotations of type $(et)t$. Thus, **coprime** has the type $(et)t$. For expository purposes, let us assume that the predicate **coprime** is defined as follows, where gcd stands for the greatest common divisor.

$$\mathbf{coprime}_{(et)t} = \lambda Q_{et}.(\text{gcd}(Q) = 1 \ \wedge |Q| > 1).$$

Thus, $\mathbf{coprime}(\{2,3\})$ holds but $\mathbf{coprime}(\{4,6\})$ and $\mathbf{coprime}(\{5\})$ do not.

As $\lambda P_{et}.(P(2) \wedge P(3))$ has the type $(et)t$ and **coprime** has the type $(et)t$, neither of them can be applied to the other as a function. Hence, we cannot derive the denotation of the sentence in a manner similar to that given in Equation (iv), because we have a type mismatch. In order to solve the mismatch, Winter defines a number of operators. The first is called the *Minimum Sort*, denoted by **min**. It is a polymorphic operator of type $(\tau t)(\tau t)$, where τ is any Boolean type. It is defined as

$$\mathbf{min}_{(\tau t)(\tau t)} = \lambda Q_{\tau t} \lambda A_{\tau}.(Q(A) \wedge \forall B_{\tau}((Q(B) \wedge B \sqsubseteq A) \rightarrow B = A). \qquad \text{(vi)}$$

Thus, for any $Q_{\tau t}$ and A_{τ}, **min** Q A is true if and only if $Q(A)$ is true and for all proper subsets B of A, $Q(B)$ is false. In other words, **min** takes an argument some set Q of objects and returns the set of minimal objects from Q under the boolean ordering $\sqsubseteq$. It can be checked that

$$\begin{aligned}
\mathbf{min}(\mathbf{M}(2)) &= \{\{2\}\}, \\
\mathbf{min}(\mathbf{M}(2) \sqcap \mathbf{M}(3)) &= \{\{2,3\}\}, \\
\mathbf{min}(\mathbf{M}(2) \sqcup \mathbf{M}(3)) &= \{\{2\},\{3\}\}, \\
\mathbf{min}((\mathbf{M}(2) \sqcup \mathbf{M}(3)) \sqcap \mathbf{M}(4)) &= \{\{2,4\},\{3,4\}\}
\end{aligned}$$

Note that, above we are writing characteristic functions as sets.

Using the **min** operator is the first step towards deriving the collective reading, as now we have the object $\{\{2,3\}\}$. Note that the type-mismatch problem still remains as $\{\{2,3\}\}$ has the type $(et)t$. Winter then follows Partee [12], and uses the *Existential Raising* (**E**) operator, given by

$$\mathbf{E}_{(\tau t)(\tau t)t} = \lambda A_{\tau t} \lambda B_{\tau t}.\exists X_{\tau}(A(X) \wedge B(X)) \qquad \text{(vii)}$$

for an arbitrary extensional type τ. Thus, the operator **E** takes an argument A denoting a set of objects of type τ and returns the property of being a set of objects of type τ having a non-empty intersection with A. The composition of the **E** operator and the **min** operator lets us derive collective readings. For example, by the definition of **E**, we have

$$\mathbf{E}(\mathbf{min}(\mathbf{M}(2) \sqcap \mathbf{M}(3)) = \lambda B_{(et)t}.\exists X_{et}(\mathbf{min}(\mathbf{M}(2) \sqcap \mathbf{M}(3))X \wedge B(X)).$$

As $(\mathbf{min}(\mathbf{M}(2) \sqcap \mathbf{M}(3)) = \{\{2,3\}\}$, we get that $(\mathbf{min}(\mathbf{M}(2) \sqcap \mathbf{M}(3))X$ holds if and only if $X = \{2,3\}$. Thus,

$$\begin{aligned}\mathbf{E}(\mathbf{min}(\mathbf{M}(2) \sqcap \mathbf{M}(3)) &= \lambda B_{(et)t}.\exists X_{et}(X = \{2,3\} \wedge B(X)) \\ &= \lambda B_{(et)t}.(B(\{2,3\})).\end{aligned}$$

The operation of *Collectivity Raising* (**C**) is the needed composition of **E** and the **min** operator and is defined as the following:

$$\mathbf{C}_{((et)t)(((et)t)t)} = \lambda Q_{(et)t}.\mathbf{E}(\mathbf{min}\ Q). \tag{viii}$$

Winter therefore posits that when the denotation of 2 *and* 3 *are coprime* is derived, the type mismatch between the denotations of 2 *and* 3 and of *coprime* causes the application of **C** to $[\![2 \text{ and } 3]\!]$. Hence, for the sentence 2 *and* 3 *are coprime*, we get its denotation as

$$\begin{aligned}[\![2 \text{ and } 3 \text{ are coprime}]\!] &= (\mathbf{C}[\![2 \text{ and } 3]\!])\mathbf{coprime} \\ &= (\mathbf{E}(\mathbf{min}[\![2 \text{ and } 3]\!])\mathbf{coprime} \\ &= (\mathbf{E}(\mathbf{min}(\mathbf{M}(2) \sqcap \mathbf{M}(3)))\mathbf{coprime} \\ &= \lambda B_{(et)t}.(B(\{2,3\}))\mathbf{coprime} \\ &= \mathbf{coprime}(\{2,3\}).\end{aligned}$$

Thus, the collective predicates are handled using the **C** operator.

4.3 A Problematic Case: Coordination of Definite Descriptions

Winter extends his theory of coordination to plural definite descriptions and analyses sentences with distributive and collective predicates. In this section, we apply his framework to the syntactic predicate *are countable* used with a coordination of plural definite descriptions. We first outline his treatment of plural definite descriptions, then argue that **countable** must have type $(et)t$, making *are countable* incompatible with the analysis of distributive predicates. We then highlight several problems that arise when such a predicate is analyzed as a collective predicate, particularly when used with a coordination of plural definite descriptions. These issues motivate the search for an alternative analysis.

For plural definite descriptions, say *the integers*, Winter assumes that common nouns, such as *integer*, have denotations of type *et*. He then defines the denotations of the plural forming morpheme *-s*, and plural definite article *the*. Following Link [9] and Shravy [20], he assigns $[\![\text{-s}]\!]$ the function which maps a set X to the set of all non-empty subsets of X. In other words, the denotation of *-s* can be given as follows.

$$[\![\text{-s}]\!]_{(et)(et)t} = \lambda P_{et}\lambda Q_{et}.(Q \neq \emptyset \wedge Q \subseteq P). \tag{ix}$$

Specifically, **integers** is the set of all non-empty subsets of **integer**, i.e.

$$\mathbf{integers}_{(et)t} = [\![\text{-s}]\!]\ \mathbf{integer} = \lambda Q_{et}.(Q \neq \emptyset \wedge Q \subseteq \mathbf{integer}). \tag{x}$$

Regarding *the*, Winter argues, slightly modifying the proposal by Sharvy [20], that **the** has type $((et)t)(et)t$, and is such that *the integers* denotes the singleton set containing the "largest" element contained in the denotation of *integers*, provided this largest element exists and is unique. By largest, we mean that for this object X_{et}, $\mathbf{integers}(X)$ should hold, and for no superset Y_{et} of X_{et}, should $\mathbf{integers}(Y)$ hold. In the case of *the integers*, the largest element exists, is unique and is the same as **integer**. Thus,

$$[\![\text{the integers}]\!]_{(et)t} = \{\mathbf{integer}\} = \{\mathbb{Z}\}. \tag{xi}$$

Winter assigns *the integers* the denotation $\{\mathbb{Z}\}$ rather than $\mathbb{Z}$ itself to facilitate the use of lifting operators for deriving correct denotations. For a detailed explanation, see Chapter 4 of [22].

Now, using these denotations mentioned above, we analyse the following sentence.

(12) The integers and the reals are countable.

Consider the type of the predicate **countable**, corresponding to the syntactic predicate *are countable*. One option is to assign it the type *et*, treating *are countable* as a distributive predicate (see design choice (9)). But if we assume D_e to be the set of real numbers, $\mathbb{R}$, then being an integer and being countable would both be properties of individual real numbers, which is incorrect. Since, in our type system, sets of entities have type *et* and countability is a property of sets, it is preferable to assign **countable** the type $(et)t$, as with collective predicates. For exposition, we define **countable** as follows.

$$\mathbf{countable}_{(et)t} = \lambda Q_{et}.(\exists f : Q \to \mathbb{N} \text{ such that } f \text{ is injective}). \tag{xii}$$

Thus, $\mathbf{countable}(\mathbb{N})$ and $\mathbf{countable}(\mathbb{Q})$ hold but $\mathbf{countable}(\mathbb{R})$ does not. Using Winter's denotation of *-s* and *the*, assigning **countable** the type $(et)t$ allows us to derive the denotation of *The integers are countable* as follows.

$$\begin{aligned}
[\![\text{the integers are countable}]\!] &= \mathbf{E}(\mathbf{countable})([\![\text{the integers}]\!]) \\
&= \mathbf{E}(\mathbf{countable})(\{\mathbb{Z}\}) \\
&= \exists X_{et}(\mathbf{countable}(X) \wedge X \in \{\mathbb{Z}\}) \\
&= \mathbf{countable}(\mathbb{Z}).
\end{aligned}$$

Thus, it is better to assign **countable** the type $(et)t$, and to analyse *are countable* as a collective predicate in Winter's framework.

Next, we see if the analysis given by Winter for collective predicates can be used for Sentence (12). To analyse such sentences where the NP is a coordination of plural definite decriptions and the verb phrase (VP) is a collective predicate,

Winter uses the operators **E**, **min**, a choice-function mechanism and lifting operators $\langle\ \rangle$ and $\langle\ \rangle^d$. The operators $\langle\ \rangle$ and $\langle\ \rangle^d$ are generalisations of **E**. It is claimed that these operators are invoked not because of type mismatches, but are instead syntax-driven, and have syntactic counterparts. Also, these syntactic counterparts are phonetically silent and thus are empty syntactic categories. Winter assumes the presence of empty determiners ϕ_{cf} and ϕ_{min} corresponding to **E** and **min**, respectively.

A problem with the analysis is that the syntax that is supposed to license these operators is not explicitly described, making it unclear what the intended syntactic structures actually are. As a result, multiple denotations, at least three for Sentence (12), remain equally possible, with no mechanism to block the incorrect ones. Three possible denotations for Sentence (12) are (13-a), (14-a) and (15-a). Simplifying them yields (13-b), (14-b) and (15-b), respectively.

(13) a. $((\mathbf{E}[\![\text{the integers}]\!]) \sqcap (\mathbf{E}[\![\text{the reals}]\!]))(\mathbf{countable})$
b. $\mathbf{countable}(\mathbb{Z}) \wedge \mathbf{countable}(\mathbb{R})$

(14) a. $\mathbf{E}([\![\text{the integers}]\!] \sqcap [\![\text{the reals}]\!])(\mathbf{countablo})$
b. $\exists X_{et}(X \in \{\mathbb{Z}\} \cap \{\mathbb{R}\} \wedge \mathbf{countable}(X))$

(15) a. $\mathbf{min}((\mathbf{E}[\![\text{the integers}]\!]) \sqcap (\mathbf{E}[\![\text{the reals}]\!]))(\mathbf{countable})$
b. $\mathbf{countable} = \{\mathbb{Z}, \mathbb{R}\}$

Note that denotations (14-a) and (15-a) are incorrect. Consider the (14-a) first, which simplifies to (14-b). As $\{\mathbb{Z}\} \cap \{\mathbb{R}\} = \emptyset$, (14-b) further simplifies to

$$\exists X_{et}(X \in \emptyset \wedge \mathbf{countable}(X)),$$

which evaluates to false, though for the wrong reason. Moreover, if we had *the rationals* instead of *the reals* in Sentence (12), we would again derive that the sentence is false, since $\{\mathbb{Z}\} \cap \{\mathbb{Q}\} = \emptyset$. Thus, (14-a) is incorrect.

For the denotation (15-a), note that its simplification, (15-b), asserts that only $\mathbb{R}$ and $\mathbb{Z}$ are countable sets, which is again false, but clearly for the wrong reason. The challenges discussed above arise not from the use of the operators **E** and **min** themselves, but from the multiple ways they can be applied and the lack of syntactic constraints that block unintended readings.

The use of the choice-function mechanism and the lifting operator $\langle\ \rangle^d$ in this context introduces additional complexities and does not resolve the core problems. Winter uses the following example containing the collective predicate *made an excellent basketball team* to show the use of $\langle\ \rangle^d$.

(16) The Americans and the Russians made an excellent basketball team.

Using the denotation of *-s* as given in Equation (ix), and by an analysis similar to that given in Equation (xi), Winter gets

$$[\![\text{the americans}]\!]_{(et)t} = \{\mathbf{american}_{et}\},\ [\![\text{the russians}]\!]_{(et)t} = \{\mathbf{russian}_{et}\}.$$

Also, the predicate **basketballTeam** corresponding to the VP in Sentence (16) is assigned the type $(et)t$, as the VP is a collective predicate.

Finally, by using the choice-function mechanism and the lifting operator $\langle\ \rangle^d$, the denotation of Sentence (16) is given as

$$\mathbf{american} \neq \emptyset \wedge \mathbf{russian} \neq \emptyset \wedge \mathbf{basketballTeam}(\mathbf{american} \sqcup \mathbf{russian}).$$

We omit the full derivation for brevity. Recreating the same derivation for Sentence (12) results in its denotation as

$$\mathbb{Z} \neq \emptyset \wedge \mathbb{R} \neq \emptyset \wedge \mathbf{countable}(\mathbb{R} \sqcup \mathbb{Z}).$$

As $(\mathbb{R} \sqcup \mathbb{Z}) = (\mathbb{R} \cup \mathbb{Z}) = \mathbb{R}$, we get the denotation of Sentence (12) as

$$\mathbb{Z} \neq \emptyset \wedge \mathbb{R} \neq \emptyset \wedge \mathbf{countable}(\mathbb{R}).$$

Note that, this denotation of Sentence (12) is not ideal as we lose the denotation of *the integers* in the derivation process. Also, in Sentence (12), if we replace *countable* with *uncountable* to get the sentence

(17) The integers and the reals are uncountable

we get its denotation as

$$\mathbb{Z} \neq \emptyset \wedge \mathbb{R} \neq \emptyset \wedge \mathbf{uncountable}(\mathbb{R}). \tag{xiii}$$

Thus, for the false Sentence (17), we get its denotation the same as that of the true sentence *The reals are uncountable*, which is problematic.

To summarize, the analysis by Winter generates multiple denotations for coordinated plural definites with collective predicates, not all of which are correct. These issues arise from the flexibility in applying operators like **E** and **min**, and the lack of constraints to block unwanted readings. While the assumption of empty syntactic categories provides a theoretical solution, finding an approach that avoids both empty categories and unintended readings would be preferable.

5 Extending Flexible Boolean Semantics

In the previous section, we assigned the same type $(et)t$ to the predicates for both the VPs *are countable* and *made an excellent basketball team*. This suggests that these VPs show a similar behavior. However, the sentences containing these VPs show different entailment patterns. Consider the following sentences.

(18) The set X and the set Y are countable.

(19) The set X is countable.

(20) The Americans and the Russians made an excellent basketball team.

(21) The Americans made an excellent basketball team.

Sentence (18) entails (19). However, Sentence (20) does not entail Sentence (21), as it need not be the case that there was a great team composed only of Americans, with no Russians. Informally, *made an excellent basketball team* does not distribute at all, while *are countable* distributes over collections but not individuals.

One of the reasons we could not analyse predicates like *are countable* using the previous section's framework is that the typing assumption (9) did not capture this nuanced distributivity. Here, we modify the type system and the denotation of **the**, and extend operators **M**, **E** and **min**. These changes enable uniform analysis of predicates like *are prime*, *are coprime*, *are countable*, and *are equinumerous* within flexible Boolean semantics, resolving issues from Sentence (12). We now explain these modifications.

Definition 4 (Extended types). *The primitive types are given by the set* $\{e, t\}$*. The set of extended types is the smallest set containing primitive types satisfying: (1) if* τ *and* σ *are extended types, then so is* $(\tau\sigma)$*, (2) if* τ *is an extended type, then so is* $S(\tau)$*.*

Definition 5 (Typed Domains). *We take* D_e *to be an arbitrary nonempty set and* D_t *to be the set of truth values* $\{0, 1\}$*. For arbitrary extensional types* τ *and* σ*,* $D_{\tau\sigma}$ *is the set of functions from* D_τ *to* D_σ*, and* $D_{S(\tau)}$ *is the powerset of* D_τ*.*

We retain the definition of Boolean types and the polymorphic Boolean operators as in Section 4. The reader might have noticed that for any type τ, the domains of τt and $S(\tau)$ can be identified with each other, as the set of functions from D_τ to $\{0, 1\}$ can be identified with the powerset of D_τ. This overlap does not cause any problem, and the type system has been deliberately designed in such a manner. The key difference is that τt is a Boolean type, while $S(\tau)$ is not.

5.1 Analysing *are countable* and Distributive Readings

Next, we show how our type system handles (12) (rewritten here), which was

(22) The integers and the reals are countable.

In Winter's framework, distributive predicates are typed as et and collective predicates as $(et)t$ (see (9)). Our framework assigns types to predicates based on their argument objects rather than distributive or collective behavior. For example, **prime** applies to integers, so it has type et, while **countable** applies to sets, so it has type $S(e)t$. We slightly modify the definition of **countable** given in Equation (xii) accordingly as follows.

$$\mathbf{countable}_{S(e)t} = \lambda Q_{S(e)}.(\exists f : Q \to \mathbb{N} \text{ such that } f \text{ is injective})$$

Similarly to the previous section, we assume **integer** has the type et, and we want the denotation of "*-s*" to map **integer** to the set of all non-empty subsets of integers. We slightly modify the denotation of "*-s*", originally defined in Equation (ix), to better suit our type system, as follows.

$$[\![\text{-s}]\!]_{(et)(S(e)t)} = \lambda P_{et}\lambda Q_{S(e)}.(Q \neq \emptyset \wedge \forall x_e(x \in Q \to Px)). \qquad \text{(xiv)}$$

Thus, we get

$$\textbf{integers}_{S(e)t} = [\![\text{-s}]\!]\textbf{integer} = \lambda Q_{S(e)}.(Q \neq \emptyset \wedge \forall x_e(x \in Q \rightarrow \textbf{integer}(x))).$$

Note that, in this case, **integers** is a predicate on sets of individuals, i.e. **integers** has the type $S(e)t$, in contrast to Equation (x), where **integers** has the type $(et)t$.

Also, following Sharvy [20], we want **the** to map a set of subsets to the largest element in the set if the largest element exists and is unique, i.e. $[\![$the integers$]\!]$ should refer to the set of integers. This definition can be rewritten in our type system as follows.

$$\textbf{the}_{(S(e)t)S(e)} = \lambda(P_{S(e)t} : \exists! Y_{S(e)} \neq \emptyset.\ \max(Y, P)).\iota Y(\max(Y, P)).$$

In the above definition, $\max(Y, P)$ is given by

$$\max(Y, P) = P(Y) \wedge \forall X_{S(e)}(P(X) \rightarrow X \subseteq Y),$$

and states that $Y_{S(e)}$ is the largest set of entities for which $P(Y)$ holds, "$\exists!$" abbreviates "there exists a unique" and "ιY" abbreviates "the unique Y such that". Also, the expression $\lambda(P_{S(e)t} : \exists! Y_{S(e)} \neq \emptyset.\ \max(Y, P))$ in the definition of **the** indicates that **the** is a partial function, defined only for those $P_{S(e)t}$ for which there exists a unique largest element $Y_{S(e)} \neq \emptyset$ satisfying $P(Y)$. The above definition of **the** maps predicates on sets of entities to sets of entities, and can be seen as a generalisation of the singular definite article, which maps predicates on entities to entities [6]. Using this definition of **the** and **integers**, we get

$$[\![\text{the integers}]\!]_{S(e)} = \textbf{the}(\textbf{integers}) = \mathbb{Z}.$$

Note that, in Winter's analysis $[\![$the integers$]\!]$ is the singleton containing $\mathbb{Z}$, as given in Equation (xi). However, in our case $[\![$the integers$]\!] = \mathbb{Z}$. Similarly, $[\![\text{the reals}]\!]_{S(e)} = \mathbb{R}$.

Now, to derive the denotation of *the integers and the reals*, we cannot use a polymorphic Boolean operator, as $S(e)$ is not a Boolean type. Hence, we have a type mismatch. To resolve this, we extend the Montague Raising (**M**) operator, previously defined in Equation (i), to raise the type of an object to a Boolean type. Specifically, for any extended type τ, let

$$\mathbf{M}_{\tau(\tau t)t} = \lambda x_\tau \lambda P_{\tau t}.Px. \tag{xv}$$

Then, the denotation of *the integers and the reals* can be analysed in a manner similar to that given in Equation (iii), as follows.

$$[\![\text{the integers and the reals}]\!]_{(S(e)t)t} = \mathbf{M}(\mathbb{Z}) \sqcap \mathbf{M}(\mathbb{R}) \tag{xvi}$$
$$= \lambda P_{S(e)t}.P(\mathbb{Z}) \wedge P(\mathbb{R}). \tag{xvii}$$

As **countable** has the type $S(e)t$, the denotations of *the integers and the reals* can be applied as a function to the denotation of *countable*, and similarly to

Equation (iv), we get

$$\begin{aligned}&[\![\text{the integers and the reals are countable}]\!]\\&= (\lambda P_{S(e)t}.P(\mathbb{Z}) \wedge P(\mathbb{R}))(\textbf{countable})\\&= \textbf{countable}(\mathbb{Z}) \wedge \textbf{countable}(\mathbb{R}).\end{aligned}$$

Thus, our framework correctly predicts that the sentence *The integers and the reals are countable* is equivalent to the sentence *The integers are countable and the reals are countable.*

The sentence 2 *and* 3 *are prime* is analysed the same as shown in Equation (iv), since the **M** operator defined in Equation (xv) is a special case of that defined in Equation (i) with $\tau = e$. Similarly to Winter's framework, the distributive reading is obtained via Montague Raising. The key difference is that in our modified type system, denotations of *the integers* and *the reals* are not of Boolean type, so the polymorphic Boolean operators cannot be directly applied.

Instead of assigning $[\![-s]\!]$ the type $(et)(S(e)t)$ (as defined in Equation (xiv)), we could have defined $[\![-s]\!]$ to have the type $(et)(et)t$, resulting in **integers** having the type $(et)t$. In that case, **the** would need to be of the type $((et)t)(S(e))$, to ensure that $[\![\text{the integers}]\!]$ is not of a boolean type. Instead, we defined $[\![-s]\!]$ as having the type $(et)(S(e)t)$ and not $(et)(et)t$, so that **the** has the type $(S(e)t)(S(e))$, and **the** can be seen of as a generalisation of the singular definite description which has the type $(et)e$ in the Fregean tradition [6].

Another approach would be to leave the type system unchanged and directly assign $[\![\text{the integers}]\!] = \mathbf{M}(\mathbb{Z})$ and $[\![\text{the reals}]\!] = \mathbf{M}(\mathbb{R})$. This would yield the denotation of *the integers and the reals* as

$$\begin{aligned}[\![\text{the integers and the reals}]\!] &= [\![\text{the integers}]\!] \sqcap [\![\text{the reals}]\!]\\&= \mathbf{M}(\mathbb{Z}) \sqcap \mathbf{M}(\mathbb{R})\\&= \lambda P_{(et)t}.P(\mathbb{Z}) \wedge P(\mathbb{R}).\end{aligned}$$

Assigning **countable** to have the type $(et)t$, would then result in the correct denotation of *The integers and the reals are countable* as follows.

$$\begin{aligned}&[\![\text{the integers and the reals are countable}]\!]\\&= (\lambda P_{(et)t}.P(\mathbb{Z}) \wedge P(\mathbb{R}))(\textbf{countable})\\&= \textbf{countable}(\mathbb{Z}) \wedge \textbf{countable}(\mathbb{R}).\end{aligned}$$

However, assigning the denotations of *the integers* directly to be $\mathbf{M}(\mathbb{Z})$ and of *the reals* directly to be $\mathbf{M}(\mathbb{R})$ bypasses the intermediate steps of interpreting the plural suffix *-s* and the definite article *the*, thereby reducing compositionality. By changing the type system, introducing S and reserving **M** for coordination, our framework maintains compositionality.

5.2 Deriving Collective Readings

Next, we demonstrate how collective readings are derived in the extended system, using sentences with the collective predicates *are coprime* and *are equinumerous* as examples. Consider the following sentence.

(23) 2 and 3 are coprime.

Being coprime to each other is a property of a collection of integers, as seen in sentences like *The elements of A are coprime* and *The integers* 3, 5, 7, 9, 11 *are coprime.* Hence, it is reasonable to assume that **coprime** has the type $S(e)t$, i.e. **coprime** is a predicate on sets.

The denotation of the NP 2 *and* 3 is $\lambda P_{et}.P(2) \wedge P(3)$, which we get by using **M**. As **coprime** has the type $S(e)t$, and $[\![2 \text{ and } 3]\!]$ has the type $(et)t$, we have a type-mismatch. To resolve the mismatch, we modify the Minimum Sort operator (**min**), which was originally defined in Equation (vi). The modified operator **min′** is given as follows.

$$\mathbf{min}'_{((et)t)(S(e)t)} = \lambda P_{(et)t}\lambda A_{S(e)}.P(\uparrow A) \wedge \forall B_{S(e)}((P(\uparrow B) \wedge B \subsetneq A) \rightarrow A = B) \tag{xviii}$$

where $\uparrow$ is an operator which maps a set to the corresponding characteristic function. For any extended type τ, $\uparrow$ is given by

$$\uparrow_{S(\tau)\tau t} = \lambda Q_{S(\tau)}\lambda x_\tau.x \in Q.$$

The operators **min′** and **min** behave similarly; however, they differ in their types.

In order to write the types succinctly, we adopt the following notation. Let τ be an arbitrary extended type. Then $S^0(\tau)$ denotes τ. For an integer $n > 0$, $S^n(\tau)$ denotes $S(S^{n-1}(\tau))$.

It can be checked that

$$(\mathbf{min}'[\![2 \text{ and } 3]\!])_{S(e)t} = \uparrow \{\{2,3\}\},$$

with the type of $\uparrow$ being $S^2(e)(S(e)t)$ in this case. Also, we modify the Existential Raising (**E**) operator, originally defined in Equation (vii). The modified operator **E′** is defined as follows.

$$\mathbf{E}'_{((S(e)t)((et)t)t} = \lambda P_{S(e)t}\lambda Q_{(et)t}.\exists X_{S(e)}(P(X) \wedge (\mathbf{min}'\ Q)X). \tag{xix}$$

Also, note that we use the **min′** operator in the definition of **E′**, similarly to how both the **E** and the **min** operators were used in the definition of the Collectivity operator **C** in Section 4 (see Equation (viii)). Using the **E′** operator, we get the denotation of 2 *and* 3 *are coprime* as the following.

$$\begin{aligned}
[\![2 \text{ and } 3 \text{ are coprime}]\!] &= \mathbf{E}'(\mathbf{coprime})[\![2 \text{ and } 3]\!]\\
&= \exists X_{S(e)}(\mathbf{coprime}(X) \wedge (\mathbf{min}'([\![2 \text{ and } 3]\!])X).\\
&= \exists X_{S(e)}(\mathbf{coprime}(X) \wedge (\uparrow \{\{2,3\}\})X)\\
&= \exists X_{S(e)}(\mathbf{coprime}(X) \wedge X \in \{\{2,3\}\})\\
&= \mathbf{coprime}(\{2,3\}).
\end{aligned}$$

Thus, the extension can deal with collective and distributive predicates in a manner similar to given by Winter.

Next, consider sentence (5-a) (rewritten here).

(24) The integers and the rationals are equinumerous.

Let the domain D_e be $\mathbb{R}$. Following the example in Equation (xvii), the denotations of the NPs *the integers*, *the rationals*, and *the integers and the rationals* are $\mathbb{Z}, \mathbb{Q}$ and $\lambda P_{S(e)t}.P(\mathbb{Z}) \wedge P(\mathbb{Q})$, respectively. Since being equinumerous with each other is a property of a collection of sets, we assign **equinumerous** the type $S(S(e))t$, which is the same as $S^2(e)t$. However, there is still a type mismatch: the NP has type $(S(e)t)t$, while the VP has type $S^2(e)t$.

To deal with the type mismatch, we extend the $\mathbf{E}'$ operator. The $\mathbf{E}'$ operator uses $\mathbf{min}'$ in its definition, and we first extend $\mathbf{min}'$ to a family of operators $\mathbf{min}^n$ indexed by an integer $n \geq 0$. We define

$$\begin{aligned}&\mathbf{min}^n_{((S^n(e)t)t)(S^{n+1}(e)t)}\\ &= \lambda P_{(S^n(e)t)t)}\lambda A_{S^{n+1}(e)}.P(\uparrow A) \wedge \forall B_{S^{n+1}(e)}((P(\uparrow B) \wedge B \subseteq A) \rightarrow A = B).\end{aligned}$$

For each n, $\mathbf{min}^n$ has the type $((S^n(e)t)t)(S^{n+1}(e)t)$, and the $\mathbf{min}'$ operator defined earlier is just $\mathbf{min}^0$. It can be checked that

$$(\mathbf{min}^1[\![\text{the integers and the rationals}]\!])_{S^2(e)t} = \uparrow \{\{\mathbb{Z}, \mathbb{Q}\}\},$$

with the type of $\uparrow$ being $S^3(e)(S^2(e)t)$ in this case. We extend the $\mathbf{E}'$ operator to a family of operators $\mathbf{E}^n$, given as the following. Define

$$\mathbf{E}^n_{(S^{n+1}(e)t)((S^n(e)t)t)t} = \lambda P_{S^{n+1}(e)t}\lambda Q_{(S^n(e)t)t}.\exists X_{S^{n+1}(e)}(PX \wedge (\mathbf{min}^n Q)X).$$

Thus, for an integer $n \geq 0$, E^n has type $(S^{n+1}(e)t)((S^n(e)t)t)t$. Specifically, $\mathbf{E}^1$ has type $(S^2(e)t)((S(e)t)t)t$, allowing us to derive the denotation of *The integers and the rationals are equinumerous* without any type-mismatch as follows.

$$\begin{aligned}&[\![\text{the integers and the rationals are equinumerous}]\!]\\ &= \mathbf{E}^1(\mathbf{equinumerous})([\![\text{the integers and the rationals}]\!])\\ &= \exists X_{S^2(e)}(\mathbf{equinumerous}\ (X) \wedge (\mathbf{min}^1([\![\text{the integers and the rationals}]\!]))X)\\ &= \exists X_{S^2(e)}(\mathbf{equinumerous}\ (X) \wedge (\uparrow \{\{\mathbb{Z}, \mathbb{Q}\}\}X)\\ &= \exists X_{S^2(e)}(\mathbf{equinumerous}\ (X) \wedge (X \in \{\{\mathbb{Z}, \mathbb{Q}\}\})\\ &= \mathbf{equinumerous}\ (\{\mathbb{Z}, \mathbb{Q}\}).\end{aligned}$$

Thus, even for predicates on sets of entities, we can use the $\mathbf{E}^n$ operators to derive the collective readings.

In Section 3, we mentioned a method to distinguish collective and distributive predicates. Collective predicates describe a property of the whole collection denoted by the subject, while distributive predicates apply to each individual making up the subject. For example, in *The integers are countable*, countability is a property of the entire set, not of individual integers, suggesting *are countable* behaves like a collective predicate. However, in *The integers and the rationals are countable*, the predicate distributes over the two sets, indicating distributive behavior at the level of sets. If the domain D_e consisted of sets instead of numbers, *are countable* would be distributive, applying to individual sets. Since we take $D_e = \mathbb{R}$, *are countable* is collective, describing a property of a collection. Thus, in LoM, the collective/distributive distinction depends on the domain and is less clear-cut than in English, warranting further investigation.

6 Conclusion and Future Work

This article extends the analysis by Winter [22] to better suit the language of mathematics. We showed that Winter's treatment of coordination yields undesirable results for sentences in which the subject is a coordination of definite descriptions, each denoting a set, and the predicate describes a property of sets. To address this, we introduced a type constructor S for powersets, and extended the Montague raising operator $\mathbf{M}$, the minimum sort operator $\mathbf{min}$ to a family $\mathbf{min}^n$, and the Existential Raising operator $\mathbf{E}$ to a family $\mathbf{E}^n$. These extensions allow our framework to handle coordination of definite descriptions.

While our framework handles coordinated definite descriptions in LoM effectively, several directions remain open. Winter uses choice-functions to analyse narrow scope and wide scope readings of indefinites. A promising direction for future work is to examine whether such scopal behavior occurs in LoM, and if so, how it can be captured within our extended framework.

A limitation of our framework is that it produces incorrect denotations for sentences where the subject is a coordination of a plural definite description and a bare plural. For example, our framework would predict that the sentence *The integers and reals are countable* is true. This happens because, in our framework, *integers and reals* would have type $S(e)t$ and would denote the set of all non-empty subsets of $\mathbb{Z} \cap \mathbb{R}$. Then, the NP *the integers and reals* would have type $S(e)$, and would denote the largest of these subsets, which is $\mathbb{Z}$, a countable set. Winter also presents a theory of determiner phrases that handles coordinations of definite descriptions and bare plurals, such as *the integers and reals.* Issues similar to those discussed in this article arise here, as the lack of constraints permits multiple, sometimes unintended, readings. We aim to explore whether suitable constraints can systematically rule out such readings. Winter further extends the analysis to plural quantification by proposing a novel typology of predicates. We plan to integrate these insights in our extended framework to handle plural indefinites, bare plurals and plural quantification in a uniform setting.

Acknowledgments. This study was funded by the Faculty of Science and Engineering, University of Manchester. The author thanks Dr. Ian Pratt-Hartmann for his expertise, insights, and proofreading. The author also thanks the anonymous reviewers for their corrections and valuable comments.

Disclosure of Interests. The author has no competing interests to declare that are relevant to the content of this article.

References

1. Cramer, M.: Implicit dynamic function introduction and its connections to the foundations of mathematics. In: O. Prosorov (ed.) Proceedings of the International Conference Philosophy, Mathematics, Linguistics: Aspects of Interaction, 2012 (PhML-2012), pp. 23–34. College Publications (2012)
2. Cramer, M., Kühlwein, D., Schröder, B.: Presupposition projection and accommodation in mathematical texts. In: M. Pinkal, I. Rehbein, S. Schulte im Walde, A. Storrer (eds.) Semantic Approaches in Natural Language Processing: Proceedings of the 10th Conference on Natural Language Processing, KONVENS 2010, September 6-8, 2010, Saarland University, Saarbrücken, Germany, pp. 29–36. universaar, Universitätsverlag des Saarlandes / Saarland University Press / Presses universitaires de la Sarre (2010)
3. Cramer, M., Schröder, B.: Interpreting plurals in the Naproche CNL. In: M. Rosner, N.E. Fuchs (eds.) Controlled Natural Language, pp. 43–52. Springer Berlin Heidelberg, Berlin, Heidelberg (2012)
4. Ganesalingam, M.: The Language of Mathematics: A Linguistic and Philosophical Investigation, chap. The Language of Mathematics, pp. 17–38. Springer Berlin Heidelberg, Berlin, Heidelberg (2013). https://doi.org/10.1007/978-3-642-37012-0_2
5. Hammer, H., Noda, N., Stone, C.A.: Prooflang: The language of arxiv proofs. In: C. Dubois, M. Kerber (eds.) Intelligent Computer Mathematics, pp. 285–290. Springer Nature Switzerland, Cham (2023)
6. Heim, I.: 41. definiteness and indefiniteness. In: K. von Heusinger, C. Maienborn, P. Portner (eds.) Volume 2, pp. 996–1025. De Gruyter Mouton, Berlin, Boston (2012). https://doi.org/doi:10.1515/9783110255072.996
7. Hodges, W.: Modality in mathematics. Logique et Analyse **56**(221), 5–23 (2013). URL http://www.jstor.org/stable/44085245
8. Kamp, H., Reyle, U.: From Discourse to Logic: Introduction to Modeltheoretic Semantics of Natural Language, Formal Logic and Discourse Representation Theory. Kluwer Academic Publishers, Dordrecht (1993)
9. Link, G.: The logical analysis of plurals and mass terms: A lattice-theoretical approach. In: R. Bäuerle, C. Schwarze, A. von Stechow (eds.) Meaning, Use, and Interpretation of Language, pp. 302–323. De Gruyter, Berlin, Boston (1983). https://doi.org/doi:10.1515/9783110852820.302
10. Nordström, B., Petersson, K., Smith, J.M.: Programming in Martin-Löf's type theory. Oxford University Press Oxford (1990)
11. Partee, B., Rooth, M.: Generalized conjunction and type ambiguity. In: R. Bäuerle, C. Schwarze, A. von Stechow (eds.) Meaning, Use, and Interpretation of Language, pp. 361–383. De Gruyter, Berlin, Boston (1983). https://doi.org/doi:10.1515/9783110852820.361
12. Partee, B.H.: Noun phrase interpretation and type-shifting principles. In: J. Groenendijk, D. de Jongh, M. Stokhof (eds.) Studies in Discourse Representation Theory and the Theory of Generalized Quantifiers, pp. 115–144. De Gruyter, Berlin, Boston (1986). https://doi.org/doi:10.1515/9783112420027-006
13. Pathak, S.: Implementation of flexible boolean semantics (2025). URL https://github.com/pkshashank/Winter. Accessed: 22 April 2025
14. Ranta, A.: Type theory and the informal language of mathematics. In: H. Barendregt, T. Nipkow (eds.) Types for Proofs and Programs, pp. 352–365. Springer Berlin Heidelberg, Berlin, Heidelberg (1994)

15. Ranta, A.: Syntactic categories in the language of mathematics. In: P. Dybjer, B. Nordström, J. Smith (eds.) Types for Proofs and Programs, pp. 162–182. Springer Berlin Heidelberg, Berlin, Heidelberg (1995)
16. Ranta, A.: Context-relative syntactic categories and the formalization of mathematical text. In: S. Berardi, M. Coppo (eds.) Types for Proofs and Programs, pp. 231–248. Springer Berlin Heidelberg, Berlin, Heidelberg (1996)
17. Ranta, A.: Grammatical framework. Journal of Functional Programming **14**(2), 145–189 (2004). https://doi.org/10.1017/S0956796803004738
18. Ranta, A.: Translating between language and logic: What is easy and what is difficult. In: N. Bjørner, V. Sofronie-Stokkermans (eds.) Automated Deduction – CADE-23, pp. 5–25. Springer Berlin Heidelberg, Berlin, Heidelberg (2011)
19. Schäfer, J.F., Kohlhase, M.: Syntactic/semantic analysis for high-precision math linguistics. In: Joint 2018 Computer Mathematics in Education - Enlightenment or Incantation, CME-EI 2018, Formal Mathematics for Mathematicians, FMM 2018, Computer Algebra in the Age of Types, CAAT 2018, Formal Verification of Physical Systems, FVPS 2018, Mathematical Models and Mathematical Software as Research Data 2018, M3SRD 2018 and 29th OpenMath Workshops, Doctoral Program and Work in Progress at the Conference on Intelligent Computer Mathematics, CICM-WS 2018, vol. 2307. CEUR-WS (2018)
20. Sharvy, R.: A more general theory of definite descriptions. The Philosophical Review **89**(4), 607–624 (1980). URL http://www.jstor.org/stable/2184738
21. Tanswell, F.S., Inglis, M.: The language of proofs: A philosophical corpus linguistics study of instructions and imperatives in mathematical texts. In: B. Sriraman (ed.) Handbook of the History and Philosophy of Mathematical Practice, pp. 1–28. Springer International Publishing, Cham (2020). https://doi.org/10.1007/978-3-030-19071-2_50-1
22. Winter, Y.: Flexibility Principles in Boolean Semantics: The Interpretation of Coordination, Plurality, and Scope in Natural Language. The MIT Press (2002). https://doi.org/10.7551/mitpress/3034.001.0001
23. Zinn, C.: Understanding informal mathematical discourse. Ph.D. thesis, University of Erlangen-Nuremberg (2004). URL https://d-nb.info/974113808

A Formal Description of an Algorithm Suitable for Parsing the Language of Mathematics*

Luka Vrečar[1] (✉), Joe Wells[1], and Fairouz Kamareddine[1]

Heriot-Watt University, Edinburgh, UK
{lv21, F.D.Kamareddine}@hw.ac.uk
https://www.macs.hw.ac.uk/~jbw/

Abstract. Kofler's DynGenPar (DGP) generalized dynamic parsing algorithm [6,7] is aimed at parsing the language of mathematics. Notably, DGP uses a notion of *initial graph* instead of parsing tables in the style of GLR and LR parsers. We distinguish the two previously existing definitions of DGP: (1) The high-level "Abstract DGP" (ADGP) is a non-deterministic algorithm which reaches any particular parse tree via a sequence of non-deterministic choices. It is not obvious just from reading ADGP how to implement it well. (2) Kofler's C++ implementation (KDGP) implements its own concurrency engine for finding all possible parse trees simultaneously while synchronizing on each input token. It is challenging to comprehend how ADGP corresponds to KDGP, and it would be hard to formally prove properties of either ADGP or KDGP. We present a new mathematical definition of Core DGP (CDGP), the context-free grammar (CFG) core of DGP, that is both declarative and deterministic. We formalize the concurrency with a notion of *continuation*, and define a way to match continuations to parse trees in proving that our algorithm is sound and complete, i.e., it terminates and returns all valid parse trees excluding trees with *superfluous recursion*. We also make available a Python implementation which corresponds quite directly to the mathematical definition of CDGP.

* Supported by EPSRC [EP/T517999/1 2770826].
A longer version of this paper is freely available at https://github.com/LVrecar/dyngenpar.
This paper uses the sTeX package [8] to typeset its mathematics. Symbols in mathematical formulas contain hyperlinks to the relevant definitions in the paper (or externally). Clicking on these symbols in most PDF readers jumps to the relevant section of the paper, or opens an external link in your default browser if the concept is not defined in the paper. We usually have a good experience using the Evince PDF reader, where hovering over symbols representing concepts defined within the paper produces a popup which shows the relevant section of the paper. Note that clicking on external hyperlinks in Evince might fail due to a security policy, and that failure might not be reported, depending on your OS. Words in *italic* within a definition denote a defining occurrence of the corresponding term.

V. de Paiva and P. Koepke (Eds.): CICM 2025, LNAI 16136, pp. 171–188, 2026.
https://doi.org/10.1007/978-3-032-07021-0_10

1 Introduction

The language of mathematics (LM) is a combination of natural language and symbolic formulas, making it difficult to parse [5]. Parsing LM is desirable for many applications like automated reasoning, theorem proving, proof checking, etc. Grammars for parsing parts of LM can contain left-recursive rules, and rules which produce the empty string (and thus do not always consume additional symbols from the input when expanded). As seen in Example 2.9, these rules arise naturally when trying to design a grammar to parse some portion of LM. While algorithms for transforming grammars to remove left recursion exist, they change the structure and size of the grammar. We wish to avoid that as "cyclic grammars can be the most compact way to describe a language" [11].

Another difficulty with parsing LM is that it "operates" on its own grammar. While parsing a mathematical document, one encounters definitions, which introduce new terminology and notation. The underlying grammar for parsing LM must therefore change with each definition. Traditional context-free grammar (CFG) parsers like GLR [12] rely on pre-computed, grammar-dependent *parsing tables*. The tables are opaque and difficult to read, and must be (partially) re-computed each time the underlying grammar changes. Updating them during parsing is seemingly too computationally expensive for large grammars. It is thus desirable to have a parser which does not rely on parsing tables, but still supports left-recursive rules, and rules which produce the empty string. The parser must also support ambiguous grammars by parsing exhaustively (i.e., finding all valid parse trees for a given input), since LM is full of ambiguities. Our previous work [13] also identified the need for such a parser.

As part of his PhD thesis [6] and the wider FMathL project at the University of Vienna, Kofler developed a dynamic generalized parsing algorithm called DynGenPar (DGP). Work on the parser was also presented at CICM 2011 as a work in progress paper, and at the DML track of CICM 2012 [7]. Kofler designed a data structure called the *initial graph* to replace parsing tables. Kofler states that it is feasible to update the initial graph during parsing to add new grammar rules, obtained e.g., from mathematical definitions encountered in the input. It seems feasible to us, but to our knowledge no one has tried this yet. The algorithm can parse ambiguous CFGs exhaustively like e.g., GLR [12] would, and supports left-recursive rules and rules which produce the empty string. Importantly, DGP accepts any CFG without transformations like e.g., CYK [14] which only accepts grammars in Chomsky Normal Form. This also removes the need for transforming parse trees afterwards into parse trees for the initial grammar. These properties make DGP a suitable candidate for parsing LM.

There are two previously existing definitions of DGP: (1) the high-level "Abstract DGP" (ADGP), a non-deterministic algorithm which produces any particular parse tree via a sequence of non-deterministic choices (e.g., between different rules to use). From reading the definition of ADGP it is not clear how to implement it well. (2) Kofler's C++ implementation (KDGP), which uses a concurrency mechanism to find all possible parse trees simultaneously, synchronizing on each input token. KDGP also implements additional features, like support for Parallel Multiple Context-Free Grammars (PMCFGs) [2] and incremental parsing.

The correspondence between ADGP and KDGP is difficult to establish, making formally proving properties of either challenging. To that end, we extracted what we call Core DGP (CDGP), the context-free grammar (CFG) core of DGP, from ADGP and KDGP. We obtained it by removing all the additional features offered by KDGP from the implementation: support for PMCFGs, predictive parsing, parse actions, and next token constraints. To simplify the algorithm further, we also removed the unification of trees and stacks (we call stacks *continuations* in this paper). KDGP made use of these unifications for efficiency, but we decided to remove them to first formalise the simplest version of the algorithm possible. Formalising unification and the other features we removed to obtain CDGP is left to future work.

Research contributions: In this paper we present a new mathematical definition of CDGP that is both declarative and deterministic (Section 2). We also provide proofs of soundness and completeness, i.e., the algorithm terminates and returns all valid parse trees which are not *superfluously recursive* (Section 4). We also make available a Python implementation[1], which corresponds closely to the mathematical definition of CDGP. Prior to our work, the only available implementation was KDGP.

While we have not done any research into updating grammars during parsing, any future work in this direction would require a formalisation effort similar to the work we present in this paper. The description of the algorithm we have created can serve as a stepping stone for future research about it.

1.1 Other approaches to parsing LM

Here, we will mention the shortcomings of GLR when it comes to parsing with rules that produce the empty string, and cycles in the grammar (i.e., a rule or set of rules from which a nonterminal can derive itself). Tomita's original algorithm [12] could not handle cycles in the grammar. Farshi [10] and Rekkers [11] modified GLR to accommodate them, by allowing the graph-structured stacks and parse forests to contain cycles. Their approach can produce infinitely many parse trees for a single input. In this paper, we call such trees *superfluously recursive* (Definition 2.7). We wish to explicitly avoid building such trees, since a finite number of trees suffices for practical parsing applications.

For our work on semantic annotations in LaTeX [13] we tried several Python libraries for parsing. `parglare` [3], a GLR-based parsing library, seemed the most promising after PyParsing [9] and GLRParser [4] proved inadequate. However, it could not handle left-recursive rules, which led us to reimplementing CDGP in Python. Initially, this was a direct translation of the C++ code, but since it was difficult to reason about, we provided a precise definition in this paper. We also make available an experimental implementation[1]which more closely follows the definition of the algorithm found in Section 2 of this paper.

[1] It is available to download at https://github.com/LVrecar/dyngenpar.

The other approach we will discuss is the use of machine learning (ML), such as large language models (LLMs) for parsing LM. They are unsuitable for parsing LM, because they are largely opaque, probability-based processes. To parse LM reliably, we need to know exactly how a result was obtained, and we want results to be reproducible. Parts of LLMs (such as the weights or training data) are not available to users, and the same prompt can produce a different result each time. We thus want a deterministic approach where all components are available to users for inspection and modification.

2 Algorithm description

In this section we give a formal definition of a new deterministic algorithm based on CDGP. Some of the terminology that we do not define can be found in parsing literature [1]. We first give a framework of definitions (Definitions 2.1 to 2.7) we will use to define the new algorithm. Building blocks of the algorithm follow, such as the *initial graph* (Definition 2.12), *neighborhood* (Definition 2.16), and *continuations* (Definition 2.18). We end with the definitions of the functions which make up the algorithm itself (Procedures 2.20 to 2.24).

If a variable x ranges over a set, x decorated with any combination of subscripts or superscripts also ranges over the same set. For example, if x ranges over $\mathbb{N}$, then so do x', x_1, $x^{\text{foo}}_{\text{bar}}$, etc. If a variable x ranges over a set A, we use $\hat{x}$ to range over subsets of A (including the entirety of A). We use i, j, and k, to range over $\mathbb{N}$. Given $i, j \in \mathbb{N}$, we denote $\{x \in \mathbb{N} \mid i \leq x \leq j\}$ by $i..j$. A k-ary relation is a set of k-tuples. A function is a set of ordered pairs.

Definition 2.1 (Sequences). A *finite sequence* (from this point on, just) is a function whose domain is $0..k$ for some k, and whose range is a set of objects. We can write the sequence $s = \{(0,x_1), (1,x_2), \ldots, (k,x_{k-1})\}$ as $[x_1, x_2, \ldots, x_{k-1}]$. Let $|s|$ denote the cardinality of s. Conceptually, this denotes the length of the sequence. We denote the empty sequence with $[]$.

For a sequence s, we can obtain the i-th element of it with $s(i-1)$. Additionally, given $i..j$, we can define a *subsequence* of s as $s\langle i..j\rangle = \{(k-i, s(k)) \mid k \in i..j\}$. We use $s\langle i..\rangle$ to mean $s\langle i..(|s|-1)\rangle$.

Given two sequences $s = [x_1, x_2, \ldots, x_j]$ and $t = [y_1, y_2, \ldots, y_k]$, we define the *concatenation* of s and t, written $s{\cdot}t$, as $s \cup \{(i + |s|, t(i)) \mid i \in \mathbf{dom}(t)\}$. This gives us a new sequence $[x_1, x_2, \ldots, x_j, y_1, y_2, \ldots, y_k]$.

Given a set A, we denote the *set of all sequences* s such that $\mathbf{ran}(s) \subseteq A$ by *FSeq*(A). If a variable x ranges over A, we use $\vec{x}$ to range over *FSeq*(A).

For example, $\vec{\eta}$ ranges over all finite sequences of nonterminals. Similarly, $\vec{\alpha}$ and $\vec{\beta}$ ranges over all finite sequences of symbols (see Definition 2.2). Note that these examples are parametrised by their underlying grammar.

Definition 2.2 (Context-Free Grammar). A *context-free grammar* (CFG) is a quadruple $G = (N, T, P, S)$, where: (1) N is a finite set of symbols called *nonterminals*. (2) T is a finite set of symbols called *terminals*. (3) N and T are disjoint, i.e., $N \cap T = \{\}$. (4) $\Gamma(G) = N \cup T$ is the *set of symbols*. (5) P is a finite set of *grammar rules*. Each rule r is a pair of a nonterminal (called the *left-hand side*, denoted by $LHS(r)$) and a sequence of symbols (called the *right-hand side*, denoted by $RHS(r)$). We denote a rule $(LHS(r), RHS(r))$ by $LHS(r) \rightarrow RHS(r)$. (6) S is a a special nonterminal called the *start symbol*.

We use G to range over grammars, t to range over T, η to range over N, α and β to range over $\Gamma(G)$, and r to range over P.

Definition 2.3 (String)**.** A *string* is a finite sequence of symbols. We denote the *empty string* by ε (a shorthand for $[]$, using a notation from parsing literature).

Definition 2.4 (Trees)**.** The *set of finite trees* $\mathbb{T}$ (from this point on, just "trees") is the smallest set such that for every symbol α, $\alpha\#[\mathcal{T}_1, \ldots, \mathcal{T}_k]$ is a tree, where $\mathcal{T}_1, \ldots, \mathcal{T}_k \in \mathbb{T}$ are called its *children*. A tree with no children is also called a *leaf*.

We use $\mathcal{T}$ to range over $\mathbb{T}$. We define: (1) $rootLabel(\alpha\#\vec{\mathcal{T}}) = \alpha$, a function which returns the label of the root of the tree. (2) $children(\alpha\#\vec{\mathcal{T}}) = \vec{\mathcal{T}}$, a function which returns the children of the tree. (3) $Subtrees(\alpha\#[\mathcal{T}_1, \ldots, \mathcal{T}_k]) = \{\alpha\#[\mathcal{T}_1, \ldots, \mathcal{T}_k]\} \cup \bigcup_{i \in 1..k} Subtrees(\mathcal{T}_i)$. (4) The set of proper subtrees of $\mathcal{T}$ as $Subtrees(\mathcal{T}) \backslash \{\mathcal{T}\}$. (5) A special symbol $\perp$ denoting "no tree", and a metavariable $\mathcal{F}$ to range over $\mathbb{T} \cup \{\perp\}$.

Definition 2.5 (String parsing)**.** Let *Parse* be the least (w.r.t. $\subseteq$) relation where:

$$\frac{t \in T}{Parse(G, t, [t], t\#[])}$$

$$\frac{(\eta, \vec{\alpha}) \in P \quad k = |\vec{\alpha}| \quad \vec{\beta_1}, \ldots, \vec{\beta_k} \quad \mathcal{T}_1, \ldots, \mathcal{T}_k \quad i \in 1..k \quad Parse(G, \vec{\alpha}(i), \vec{\beta_i}, \mathcal{T}_i)}{Parse(G, \eta, \vec{\beta_1} \cdot \ldots \cdot \vec{\beta_k}, \eta\#[\mathcal{T}_1, \ldots, \mathcal{T}_k])}$$

If $Parse(G, \eta, \vec{\beta}, \mathcal{T})$ holds for some $\eta \in N$, some string $\vec{\beta}$, and some tree $\mathcal{T}$, we say that $\vec{\beta}$ can be derived from η and $\mathcal{T}$ parses/is a *G-parse tree* for $\vec{\beta}$.

Definition 2.6 (Input of a tree)**.** Let $G = (N, T, P, S)$ be a grammar. Then, we define *input*(G) as the smallest function such that:

- $input(G) \in T \rightarrow (\mathbb{T} \rightarrow FSeq(T))$
- For all $\mathcal{T} = \alpha\#\vec{\mathcal{T}} \in \mathbb{T}$:
  - if $\vec{\mathcal{T}} = []$ and $\alpha \in T$, $input(G)(\mathcal{T}) = [\alpha]$
  - if $\vec{\mathcal{T}} = []$ and $\alpha \notin T$, $input(G)(\mathcal{T}) = []$
  - otherwise, $input(G)(\mathcal{T}) = input(G) \circ \vec{\mathcal{T}}$.

Note that for a G-parse tree $\mathcal{T}$, $input(G)(\mathcal{T})$ is exactly the string that $\mathcal{T}$ parses. An ε-tree is a tree $\mathcal{T}$ such that $input(G)(\mathcal{T}) = \varepsilon$.

Definition 2.7 (Recursive trees)**.** We say a tree $\mathcal{T}$ is recursive, if there exists a proper subtree $\mathcal{T}'$ of $\mathcal{T}$ such that $rootLabel(\mathcal{T}) = rootLabel(\mathcal{T}')$. Let G be a grammar. If we further have $input(G)(\mathcal{T}) = input(G)(\mathcal{T}')$, we say that $\mathcal{T}$ is superfluously recursive.

Example 2.8 (Superfluously recursive trees)**.** Consider the simple grammar G expressed in Backus-Naur Form as $S \rightarrow S \mid a$. Parsing the input sentence $[a]$

yields infinitely many trees, of which only one is not superfluously recursive (and is in fact not recursive at all). The tree $S\#[a\#[\,]]$ is not recursive, and the tree $S\#[S\#a\#[\,]]$ is superfluously recursive.

Example 2.9 (An example grammar for polynomials). Let $T = \{+, \text{-}, \times, \mathit{1}, \mathit{2}, x\}$, let $N = \{\mathbf{Poly}, \mathbf{Term}, \mathbf{Coef}, \mathbf{XPow}, \mathbf{Sign}, \mathbf{Num}\}$[2], let **Poly** be the start symbol (and thus $S = \mathbf{Poly}$), and let $P = \{P_+, P_\text{-}, P_T, T_{CP}, T_C, T_P, C_{SN}, Si_e, Si_\text{-}, X_x, X_X, N_1, N_2\}$ where

$$P_+ = \mathbf{Poly} \to \mathbf{Poly} + \mathbf{Term} \qquad P_\text{-} = \mathbf{Poly} \to \mathbf{Poly} \text{ - } \mathbf{Term}$$

$$P_T = \mathbf{Poly} \to \mathbf{Term} \qquad T_{CP} = \mathbf{Term} \to \mathbf{Coef}\ \mathbf{XPow}$$

$$T_C = \mathbf{Term} \to \mathbf{Coef} \qquad T_P = \mathbf{Term} \to \mathbf{XPow}$$

$$C_{SN} = \mathbf{Coef} \to \mathbf{Sign}\ \mathbf{Num} \qquad Si_e = \mathbf{Sign} \to \varepsilon$$

$$Si_\text{-} = \mathbf{Sign} \to \text{-} \qquad X_X = \mathbf{XPow} \to \mathbf{XPow} \times \mathbf{XPow}$$

$$X_x = \mathbf{XPow} \to x \qquad N_1 = \mathbf{Num} \to \mathit{1} \quad N_2 = \mathbf{Num} \to \mathit{2}$$

Alternatively, P can be expressed in Backus-Naur Form [1] as:

$$\mathbf{Poly} \to \mathbf{Poly} + \mathbf{Term} \mid \mathbf{Poly} \text{ - } \mathbf{Term} \mid \mathbf{Term}$$

$$\mathbf{Term} \to \mathbf{Coef}\ \mathbf{XPow} \mid \mathbf{Coef} \mid \mathbf{XPow}$$

$$\mathbf{Coef} \to \mathbf{Sign}\ \mathbf{Num}$$

$$\mathbf{Sign} \to \varepsilon \mid \text{-}$$

$$\mathbf{XPow} \to x \mid \mathbf{XPow} \times \mathbf{XPow}$$

$$\mathbf{Num} \to \mathit{1} \mid \mathit{2}$$

We will use this grammar G throughout the paper to illustrate various features of the algorithm. Note that in practice, rules for parsing **Num** would be more complex and in our grammar we simplify them for brevity.

Definition 2.10 (Nullable nonterminals). The set $\mathit{null}(G) \subseteq N$, called the *set of nullable nonterminals*, is the set of all $\eta \in N$ from which the empty string ε can be derived (i.e., for which $\mathit{Parse}(G, \eta, \varepsilon, \mathcal{T})$ holds for some tree $\mathcal{T}$). We let θ (chosen for its similarity to 0) range over $\mathit{null}(G)$.

Example 2.11 (Nullable nonterminals). For the grammar given in Example 2.9, we have $\mathit{null}(G) = \{\mathbf{Sign}\}$

Definition 2.12 (Initial graph). Let $G = (N, T, P, S)$ be a grammar. For $r = \eta \to \vec{\theta}\ \alpha\ \vec{\beta} \in P$ and $k = |\vec{\theta}|$, let an *edge label* be a pair (r, k). Then, we can define the corresponding *edge* as the triple $(\alpha, (r, k), \eta)$. Let $\mathit{Edges}(G)$ be the set of all edges for the grammar G. We let e range over $\mathit{Edges}(G)$. For an edge $e = (\alpha, (r, k), \eta)$, we define $\mathit{start}(e) = \alpha$, $\mathit{edgeLabel}(e) = (r, k)$, and $\mathit{end}(e) = \eta$. Note that for every edge $(\alpha, (r, k), \eta)$, we have $\mathit{start}(e) = \mathit{RHS}(r)(k)$ and $\mathit{end}(e) = \mathit{LHS}(r)$. Given $\mathit{Edges}(G)$, we define the *initial graph* of G, a directed labelled graph, as $\mathit{Initial}(G) = (\Gamma(G), \mathit{Edges}(G))$.

[2] Abbreviations for "polynomial", "term", "coefficient", "power of x", "sign", and "number", respectively.

Example 2.13 (Initial graph)**.** We will illustrate the initial graph of the grammar given in Example 2.9 by drawing it. For a given pair $(\alpha, (r, k), \eta) \in \mathit{Edges}(G)$, we draw α and η as nodes with a directed edge between them, which we label with (r, k). Recall that (r, k) is a pair of a grammar rule and a natural number.

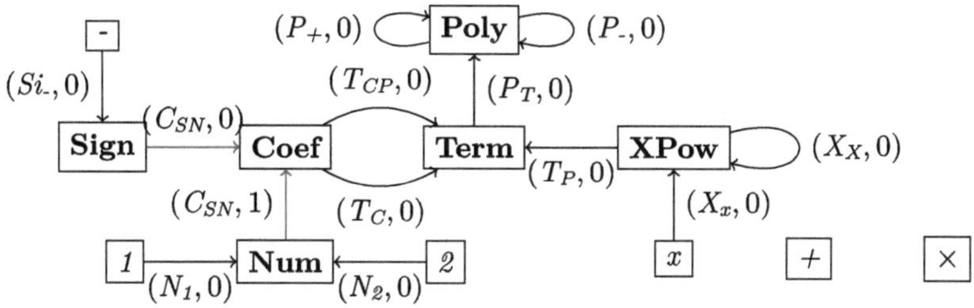

Note that $+$ and $\times$ are drawn as nodes, but do not have any edges connecting them to the rest of the graph, since **Poly** $\notin$ *null*(G) and **XPow** $\notin$ *null*(G). Consider the two edges highlighted in red. They are both created from the same grammar rule, namely **Coef** $\rightarrow$ **Sign Num**. The bottom, vertical edge connects **Num** to **Coef** and $k = 1$, since there is a single nullable nonterminal (**Sign**) preceding **Num**. The top, horizontal edge connects **Sign** to **Coef** and $k = 0$, since there are no nullable nonterminals preceding **Sign** on the RHS of the rule. Other edges in the graph are constructed in the same fashion as the latter. For a rule $r \in P$, there is an edge from the first nonterminal in $\mathit{RHS}(r)$, to the nonterminal $\mathit{LHS}(r)$, labelled by $(r, 0)$.

Definition 2.14 (Acyclic path)**.** Let $\vec{e}$ be a non-empty finite sequence of edges. If $\mathit{end}(\vec{e}(i)) = \mathit{start}(\vec{e}(i+1))$ for all $i \in 0..(|e|-2)$, we say that $\vec{e}$ is a *path* from $\mathit{start}(\vec{e}(0))$ to $\mathit{end}(\vec{e}(|\vec{e}|-1))$. A path $\vec{e}$ is said to contain a *cycle*, if for some $i, j \in \mathbf{dom}(\vec{e})$, such that $i \neq j$, we have $\mathit{start}(\vec{e}(i)) = \mathit{start}(\vec{e}(j))$ or $\mathit{end}(\vec{e}(i)) = \mathit{end}(\vec{e}(j))$. If a path contains no cycles, we say that it is *acyclic*.

Example 2.15 (Path)**.** The following sequences are all paths from **XPow** to **Poly**:

1. $\vec{e}_1$: $[(\mathbf{XPow}, (T_P, 0), \mathbf{Term}), (\mathbf{Term}, (P_T, 0), \mathbf{Poly}), (\mathbf{Poly}, (P_+, 0), \mathbf{Poly})]$
2. $\vec{e}_2$: $[(\mathbf{XPow}, (X_X, 0), \mathbf{XPow}), (\mathbf{XPow}, (T_P, 0), \mathbf{Term}), (\mathbf{Term}, (P_T, 0), \mathbf{Poly})]$
3. $\vec{e}_3$: $[(\mathbf{XPow}, (T_P, 0), \mathbf{Term}), (\mathbf{Term}, (P_T, 0), \mathbf{Poly})]$

Of those, only $\vec{e}_3$ is acyclic, since for $\vec{e}_1$ we have $\mathit{end}(\vec{e}_1(1)) = \mathit{end}(\vec{e}_1(2)) = \mathbf{Poly}$, and for $\vec{e}_2$ we have $\mathit{start}(\vec{e}_2(0)) = \mathit{start}(\vec{e}_2(1)) = \mathbf{XPow}$.

Definition 2.16 (Neighborhood)**.** Let G be a grammar and let $\alpha, \beta \in \Gamma(G)$, and let E be the set of all paths in the initial graph from α to β. Then the *neighborhood* of α w.r.t. β, written *neighborhood*(α, β), is $\{\mathit{edgeLabel}(\vec{e}(0)) \mid \vec{e} \in E, \vec{e}\langle 1..\rangle \text{ is acyclic}\}$.

Example 2.17. The following are examples of paths in the initial graph given in Example 2.13:

1. $[(\mathbf{Coef}, (T_{CP}, 0), \mathbf{Term}), (\mathbf{Term}, (P_T, 0), \mathbf{Poly})]$
2. $[(\mathbf{Coef}, (T_C, 0), \mathbf{Term}), (\mathbf{Term}, (P_T, 0), \mathbf{Poly})]$
3. $[(\mathbf{XPow}, (X_X, 0), \mathbf{XPow}), (\mathbf{XPow}, (T_P, 0), \mathbf{Term}), (\mathbf{Term}, (P_T, 0), \mathbf{Poly})]$

4. $[(\mathbf{XPow}, (T_P, 0), \mathbf{Term}), (\mathbf{Term}, (P_T, 0), \mathbf{Poly})]$

Note that paths 1 and 2 are the only acyclic paths in the initial graph from **Coef** to **Poly**. While path 3 is not an acyclic path, it still satisfies the condition for its initial edge label to be in *neighborhood*(**XPow**, **Poly**). Therefore, we have *neighborhood*(**Coef**, **Poly**) $= \{(T_{CP}, 0), (T_C, 0)\}$ and *neighborhood*(**XPow**, **Poly**) $= \{(X_X, 0), (T_P, 0)\}$.

Definition 2.18 (Continuations). We define a *continuation* as follows:

$\mathcal{C} \in \mathbb{C} ::= \mathcal{C}^{\mathbf{m}} \mid \mathcal{C}^{\mathbf{r}} \mid \mathcal{C}^{\mathbf{d}} \qquad \mathcal{C}^{\mathbf{m}} ::= \mathcal{C}^{\mathbf{m}\alpha} \qquad \mathcal{C}^{\mathbf{d}} ::= \mathcal{C}^{\mathbf{d}\alpha} \quad \mathcal{C}^{\mathbf{r}} ::= \mathcal{C}^{\mathbf{r}\alpha}$

$\mathcal{C}^{\mathbf{r}\alpha} ::= \mathbf{reduce}\ \alpha \blacktriangleright \mathcal{C}^{\star\alpha} \quad \mathcal{C}^{\star\alpha} ::= \mathcal{C}^{\mathbf{d}\alpha} \mid \mathcal{C}^{\mathbf{m}\alpha} \qquad \mathcal{C}^{\mathbf{d}S} ::= \mathbf{done}$

$\mathcal{C}^{\mathbf{m}\alpha} ::= \mathbf{match}\ (r, k)\ \vec{\mathcal{T}} \blacktriangleright \mathcal{C}^{\mathbf{r}\alpha'}$ s.t. $\forall i \in \mathbf{dom}(\vec{\mathcal{T}}), \mathit{rootLabel}(\vec{\mathcal{T}}(i)) = \mathit{RHS}(r)(i)$

We call the text in bold the continuation's label. We let $\mathcal{C}$ range over continuations. We call the continuation that appears inside another continuation its *successor*. For example, for the continuation $\mathcal{C}_1 = \mathbf{reduce}\ \alpha \blacktriangleright \mathcal{C}$, we say that $\mathcal{C}$ is the successor of $\mathcal{C}_1$. We denote the *set of continuations* by $\mathbb{C}$.

Continuations store the "progress" of parsing at various points in the algorithm, so incomplete trees can be completed once more symols are shifted from the input mimicking stacks found in parsers like GLR. Each continuation encodes a sequence of "steps" that will lead to a parse tree. By creating a new continuation each time a choice must be made during the algorithm's execution (e.g., between multiple rules that can be reduced), we can find all possible parse trees for a given input by only going through it once.

Definition 2.19 (*mapUnzip*). Let f be a function with k arguments which returns an ordered pair of sets, and let A be a set of k-tuples. Then *mapUnzip*(f, A) is a function which returns an ordered pair of sets computed as follows:

1. **map:** Let $R = \{f(a) \mid a \in A\}$.
2. **unzip:** Return $(\bigcup_{(E_1,E_2)\in R} E_1, \bigcup_{(E_1,E_2)\in R} E_2)$.

Note that if $A = \{a\}$ for some k-tuple a, then *mapUnzip*$(f, A) = f(a)$.

We now define the procedures that make up the algorithm, starting with *parse*, which takes as input a grammar $G = (N, T, P, S)$ and sentence $\vec{\alpha}$ and returns a set of all G-parse trees for $\vec{\alpha}$, i.e., for any $\mathcal{T}$ returned by *parse*, *Parse*$(G, S, \vec{\alpha}, \mathcal{T})$ holds. We then continue with *procCont*[3], *reduce*, *match*, and finally ε*Trees*.

Procedure 2.20 (*parse*). **Input:** A grammar G, and a string $\vec{\alpha}$ such that $\mathbf{ran}(\vec{\alpha}) \subseteq \Gamma(G)$.

Returns: A pair of a set of continuations and a set of trees.

Summary: *parse* will return the set of all non-superfluously recursive G-parse trees $\mathcal{T}$ such that *Parse*$(G, S, \vec{\alpha}, \mathcal{T})$ holds. *parse* is computed as follows:

1. Let $\hat{\mathcal{C}}_0 = \{\mathbf{reduce}\ S \blacktriangleright \mathbf{done}\}$ and let $\hat{\mathcal{T}}_0 = \varepsilon\mathit{Trees}(G, S)$.
2. For every $k \in \mathbf{dom}(\vec{\alpha})$, let $(\hat{\mathcal{C}}_{k+1}, \hat{\mathcal{T}}_{k+1}) = \mathit{mapUnzip}(\mathit{procCont}, \{(G, \mathcal{C}^{\mathbf{r}}, \{\vec{\alpha}(k)\#[\,]\}) \mid \mathcal{C}^{\mathbf{r}} \in \hat{\mathcal{C}}_k\})$. *Note: each member of* $\hat{\mathcal{C}}_k$ *is of the form* $\mathbf{reduce}\ \alpha \blacktriangleright \mathcal{C}'$.

[3] *procCont* is short for "processContinuation".

3. Return $(\hat{\mathcal{C}}_{|\vec{\alpha}|}, \hat{\mathcal{T}}_{|\vec{\alpha}|})$.

Procedure 2.21 (*procCont*). **Input:** A grammar G, a continuation $\mathcal{C}$, and a set of trees $\hat{\mathcal{T}}$. For *procCont* to not return ({},{}), then if $\mathcal{C} =$ **reduce** $\alpha \blacktriangleright \mathcal{C}'$, all trees $\mathcal{T}' \in \hat{\mathcal{T}}$ must be G-parse trees with the same root label β, such that some G-parse tree with root α contains $\mathcal{T}'$ as a subtree. If $\mathcal{C} =$ **match** $(r,k)\ \vec{\mathcal{T}} \blacktriangleright \mathcal{C}'$, all trees in $\hat{\mathcal{T}}$ are G-parse trees for $RHS(r)(|\vec{\mathcal{T}}|)$. Top-level calls to *procCont* are always made with a continuation of the form **reduce** $\alpha \blacktriangleright \mathcal{C}$, and one leaf tree.
Returns: A pair of a set of continuations and a set of trees.
Summary: *procCont* uses the trees in $\hat{\mathcal{T}}$ to complete the G-parse trees which are described by $\mathcal{C}$. If shifting more symbols from the input can complete the G-parse trees, a new continuation is created for each way in which that can happen. If $\hat{\mathcal{T}} = \{\}$, *procCont* returns ({},{}). *procCont* is computed as follows:

1. If $\hat{\mathcal{T}} = \{\}$, return ({},{}).
2. If $\mathcal{C} =$ **done**, return $(\{\}, \hat{\mathcal{T}})$.
3. If $\mathcal{C} =$ **reduce** $\alpha \blacktriangleright \mathcal{C}'$: let $(\hat{\mathcal{C}}_{new}, \hat{\mathcal{T}}_{new}) = mapUnzip(reduce, \{(G, \mathcal{T}, \{\}, \mathcal{C}) \mid \mathcal{T} \in \hat{\mathcal{T}}\})$.
4. If $\mathcal{C} =$ **match** $(r,k)\ \vec{\mathcal{T}} \blacktriangleright \mathcal{C}'$: let $(\hat{\mathcal{C}}_{new}, \hat{\mathcal{T}}_{new}) = mapUnzip(match, \{(G, \bot, \textbf{match}\ (r,k)\ \vec{\mathcal{T}}\cdot[\mathcal{T}] \blacktriangleright \mathcal{C}') \mid \mathcal{T} \in \hat{\mathcal{T}}\})$.
5. Let $(\hat{\mathcal{C}}', \hat{\mathcal{T}}') = procCont(G, \mathcal{C}', \hat{\mathcal{T}}_{new})$.
6. Return $(\hat{\mathcal{C}}_{new} \cup \hat{\mathcal{C}}', \hat{\mathcal{T}}')$.

Procedure 2.22 (*reduce*). **Input:** A grammar G, a tree $\mathcal{T} = \beta\#\vec{\mathcal{T}}$, a set of symbols $M \subseteq \Gamma(G)$ (defaults to {} for external calls), and a continuation $\mathcal{C} =$ **reduce** $\alpha \blacktriangleright \mathcal{C}'$.
Returns: A pair of a set of continuations and a set of trees.
Summary: *reduce* will attempt to build all G-parse trees $\mathcal{T}'$ such that $rootLabel(\mathcal{T}') = \alpha$ and $\mathcal{T} \in Subtrees(\mathcal{T}')$, including those that are recursive, but which are not superfluously recursive. It does so by considering all edge labels (r,k) in $neighborhood(\beta, \alpha)$ and building G-parse trees for their rules. All trees that have been successfully completed are returned. If a G-parse tree can be completed by shifting more symbols from the input, *reduce* will return a continuation instead. The set M ensures each neighborhood is considered at most once. *reduce* is computed as follows:

1. Let $(\hat{\mathcal{C}}_{start}, \hat{\mathcal{T}}_{start}) = mapUnzip(match, \{(G, \mathcal{T}, \textbf{match}\ (r,k)\ [] \blacktriangleright \mathcal{C}) \mid (r,k) \in neighborhood(\beta, \alpha)\})$.
2. Let $\hat{\mathcal{T}}_{done} = \{\mathcal{T}' \mid \mathcal{T}' \in (\hat{\mathcal{T}}_{start} \cup \{\mathcal{T}\}), rootLabel(\mathcal{T}') = \alpha\}$.
3. Let $(\hat{\mathcal{C}}_{new}, \hat{\mathcal{T}}_{new}) = mapUnzip(reduce, \{(G, \mathcal{T}, M \cup \{\beta\}, \mathcal{C}) \mid \mathcal{T} \in \hat{\mathcal{T}}_{start}, rootLabel(\mathcal{T}) \notin (M \cup \{\beta\})\})$.
4. Return $(\hat{\mathcal{C}}_{start} \cup \hat{\mathcal{C}}_{new}, \hat{\mathcal{T}}_{done} \cup \hat{\mathcal{T}}_{new})$.

Procedure 2.23 (*match*). **Input:** A grammar G, a "maybe tree" $\mathcal{F}$, and a continuation $\mathcal{C} =$ **match** $(r,k)\ \vec{\mathcal{T}} \blacktriangleright \mathcal{C}'$, such that if $\mathcal{F} = \mathcal{T}$, $\mathcal{T}$ is a G-parse tree for $RHS(r)(k)$. $\mathcal{F} = \bot$ if and only if $|\vec{\mathcal{T}}| > k$.
Returns: A pair of a set of continuations and a set of trees.

Summary: *match* will attempt to add an ε-tree for $RHS(r)(|\vec{\mathcal{T}}|)$ to $\vec{\mathcal{T}}$, unless $|\vec{\mathcal{T}}| = k$, in which case $\mathcal{F}$ is attached instead. After $\mathcal{F}$ has been attached, *match* will keep creating ε-trees for the rest of $RHS(r)$, until either (1) no ε-tree exists for the current symbol, or (2) $\vec{\mathcal{T}}$ contains a G-parse tree for each symbol in $RHS(r)$. If (1), *match* will return a continuation which expects to build a G-parse tree for the next unmatched symbol from $RHS(r)$ by shifting more tokens from the input. Such continuations are also created for each symbol *match* attempts to build trees for after attaching $\mathcal{F}$. If (2), *match* will return the tree $LHS(r)\#\vec{\mathcal{T}}$, if it is not superfluously recursive, and no trees otherwise. *match* is computed as follows:

1. If $|\vec{\mathcal{T}}| = |RHS(r)|$:
   - If $LHS(r)\#\vec{\mathcal{T}}$ is not superfluously recursive[4], return $(\{\},\{LHS(r)\#\vec{\mathcal{T}}\})$.
   - Otherwise, return $(\{\},\{\})$.
2. If $|\vec{\mathcal{T}}| = k$ let $\hat{\mathcal{T}} = \{\mathcal{F}\}$ and let $\mathcal{F}' = \bot$.
3. If $|\vec{\mathcal{T}}| \neq k$, let $\hat{\mathcal{T}} = \varepsilon\mathit{Trees}(G, RHS(r)(|\vec{\mathcal{T}}|))$ and let $\mathcal{F}' = \mathcal{F}$.
4. If $|\vec{\mathcal{T}}| > k$, let $\hat{\mathcal{C}} = \{\textbf{reduce}\ RHS(r)(|\vec{\mathcal{T}}|) \blacktriangleright \mathcal{C}\}$, otherwise let $\hat{\mathcal{C}} = \{\}$.
5. Let $(\hat{\mathcal{C}}_{new},\hat{\mathcal{T}}_{new}) = mapUnzip(match, \{(G,\mathcal{F}',\textbf{match}\ (r,k)\ \vec{\mathcal{T}}\cdot[\mathcal{T}'] \blacktriangleright \mathcal{C}') \mid \mathcal{T}' \in \hat{\mathcal{T}}\})$.
6. Return $(\hat{\mathcal{C}} \cup \hat{\mathcal{C}}_{new},\hat{\mathcal{T}}_{new})$.

Note that every continuation contained within the first element of an ordered pair returned by any function in this algorithm is created within *match*. While *reduce* also creates continuations in step 1, they are immediately passed to *match*. Given a continuation $\mathcal{C}$, *match* returns either no continuations, or a set containing only **reduce** continuations. It follows that any set $\hat{\mathcal{C}}_k$ created in *parse* contains only **reduce** continuations.

Procedure 2.24 (ε*Trees*). **Input:** A grammar G, a nonterminal η, and optionally a set of nonterminals $M \subseteq N$, which defaults to $\{\}$ for external calls.
Returns: A (possibly empty) set of trees.
Summary: $\varepsilon\mathit{Trees}(G,\eta)$ returns the set of all non-recursive trees[5] with root label η that parse ε. Recursive calls to ε*Trees* use the additional parameter M to ensure the trees are not recursive. ε*Trees* can be computed as follows:

Consider all rules r of the form $\eta \to \vec{\theta} \in P$ such that $\textbf{ran}(\vec{\theta}) \subseteq null(G)$ and $\textbf{ran}(\vec{\theta}) \cap M = \{\}$. For each r, for all $i \in \textbf{dom}(\vec{\theta})$, let $\hat{\mathcal{T}}_i = \varepsilon\mathit{Trees}(G,\vec{\theta}(i), M \cup \{\eta\})$. Let $\mathit{Trees} = \hat{\mathcal{T}}_0 \times \ldots \times \hat{\mathcal{T}}_{|\vec{\theta}|-1}$.[6] Let $\hat{\mathcal{T}}_r = \{\eta\#[\mathcal{T}_0,\ldots,\mathcal{T}_k] \mid (\mathcal{T}_0,\ldots,\mathcal{T}_k) \in \mathit{Trees}\}$. Return the union of all $\hat{\mathcal{T}}_r$.

Lemma 2.25. The algorithm never builds superfluously recursive trees.

---

[4] Here, we filter out superfluously recursive trees built using rules of the form $\eta \to \vec{\theta}\ \eta\ \vec{\theta}'$ or sequences of rules of the form $\eta \to \vec{\theta}_1\ \eta_1\ \vec{\theta}'_1,\ldots,\eta_k \to \vec{\theta}_{k+1}\ \eta\ \vec{\theta}'_{k+1}$.

[5] Note that a recursive G-parse tree for ε is necessarily superfluously recursive, so requiring them to be non-recursive or to not be superfluously recursive is equivalent.

[6] This creates tuples of all possible combinations of G-parse trees for symbols in $\vec{\theta}$. Note that if ε*Trees* returned an empty set for any $\vec{\theta}(i)$, then $\mathit{Trees} = \{\}$.

Proof. This is clear from the definitions of *εTrees* and *match*. *εTrees* returns only non-recursive G-parse trees. If a tree parses the empty string and is recursive, it is necessarily superfluously recursive. *match* returns a tree only if it is not superfluously recursive. □

3 Parsing a sample input: $2x \times x + 1$

Recall the grammar G from Example 2.9. Let $\vec{\alpha} = [\mathit{2}, x, \times, x, +, x]$ and let $(\hat{\mathcal{C}},\hat{\mathcal{T}}) = \mathit{parse}(G, \vec{\alpha})$. Let $\mathcal{T}$ be the tree shown in Figure 1, which is clearly a parse tree for $\vec{\alpha}$ with root **Poly**, and thus would be in $\hat{\mathcal{T}}$. A specific sequence of continuations, starting with **reduce Poly ▶ done**, yields $\mathcal{T}$ after the last symbol is shifted. Each continuation $\mathcal{C}_{k+1}$ in the sequence is obtained by computing $\mathit{procCont}(G, \{\vec{\alpha}(k)\#[\,]\}, \mathcal{C}_k)$, for all $k \in 0..|\vec{\alpha}| - 1$. Figure 1 shows the sequence of continuations that yields $\mathcal{T}$. For this example, we have omitted all other continuations and trees that are returned by calls to *procCont*.

We will now briefly discuss any notable steps that occur while parsing $\vec{\alpha}$. After $\mathit{2}$ is shifted, $\mathit{reduce}(G, \mathit{2}\#[\,], \{\}, \textbf{reduce Poly} \blacktriangleright \textbf{done})$ is called. The algorithm considers $\mathit{neighborhood}(\mathit{2}, \textbf{Poly}) = \{(\textbf{Num} \to \mathit{2}, 0)\}$ and builds the tree $\mathcal{T}_{\textbf{Num}} = \textbf{Num}\#[\mathit{2}\#[\,]]$. Then *reduce* is recursively called again and the edge label $(\textbf{Coef} \to \textbf{Sign Num}, 1)$ is considered. **Sign** is matched to ε, and the resulting tree, alongside $\mathcal{T}_{\textbf{Num}}$, is used to complete the parse tree for **Coef**. Then, *reduce* is called recursively again and the edge label $(\textbf{Term} \to \textbf{Coef XPow}, 0)$ is considered. Since **XPow** is not nullable and the rule cannot be completed without shifting additional symbols from the input, the resulting continuation, shown in the second image in Figure 1, is returned.

After the first x is shifted from the input, the tree $\textbf{XPow}\#[x\#[\,]]$ is constructed. While this does complete the tree described by the continuation being processed (and the algorithm in fact returns it), we must also consider the recursive rule $\textbf{XPow} \to \textbf{XPow} \times \textbf{XPow}$. This results in the continuation shown in the third image in Figure 1.

After shifting $\times$ and the second x from the input, the algorithm completes and returns a parse tree with root **Poly** (the first child of the tree in Figure 1). If the end of the input had been reached, this would have resulted in a complete parse tree for our input sentence. However, we must allow for the possibility that we have not reached the end of the input, so the algorithm must consider the recursive rule $\textbf{Poly} \to \textbf{Poly} + \textbf{Term}$. The resulting continuation is shown in the fifth image in Figure 1.

After the last symbol ($\mathit{1}$) has been shifted from the input and the continuation is processed, we have completed the parse tree shown in Figure 1. In order to complete the tree, the rule $\textbf{Term} \to \textbf{Coef}$ was considered. We should note that three continuations are also returned. One expects an x to be shifted from the input, created by considering the rule $\textbf{Term} \to \textbf{Coef XPow}$ instead of $\textbf{Term} \to \textbf{Coef}$. The other two expect a + or a - to be shifted, respectively, to account for the left-recursive rules $\textbf{Poly} \to \textbf{Poly} + \textbf{Term}$ and $\textbf{Poly} \to \textbf{Poly}$ - $\textbf{Term}$, after the tree has been completed.

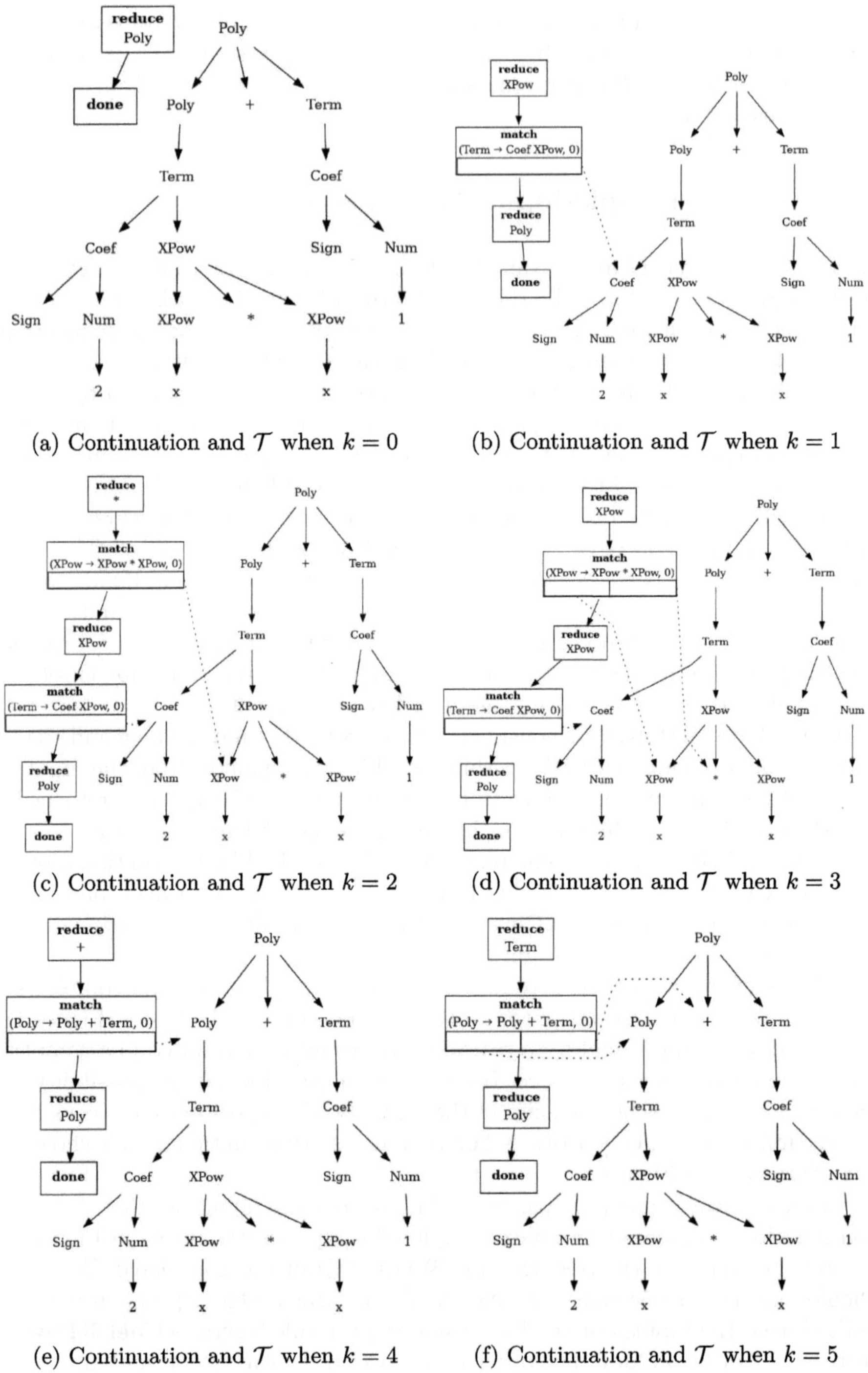

(a) Continuation and $\mathcal{T}$ when $k = 0$

(b) Continuation and $\mathcal{T}$ when $k = 1$

(c) Continuation and $\mathcal{T}$ when $k = 2$

(d) Continuation and $\mathcal{T}$ when $k = 3$

(e) Continuation and $\mathcal{T}$ when $k = 4$

(f) Continuation and $\mathcal{T}$ when $k = 5$

Fig. 1: The stages of parsing $2x \times x + 1$

4 Soundness and completeness of the algorithm

In this section, we prove that the algorithm we described in Section 2 is sound and complete. For these proofs, we define how trees can be "matched" to continuations (Definition 4.31). We then prove the algorithm is sound (Corollary 4.28), i.e., that given a grammar G and an input sentence which is in $\mathbf{L}(G)$, the algorithm always produces a valid G-parse tree for that sentence. We then show that it is complete (Theorem 4.37), i.e., that for any G-parse tree $\mathcal{T}$ for a given input sentence, the algorithm reproduces $\mathcal{T}$.

Theorem 4.26 (Termination of the algorithm)**.** Given a grammar G and an input sentence $\vec{\alpha}$, the algorithm always terminates.

Proof. The full proof can be found in the long version of the paper[1]. We first show that all the various components of the algorithm (i.e., Procedures 2.20 to 2.24) always terminate and return finite results. From this it follows that the algorithm as a whole always terminates and returns finite results. □

Theorem 4.27 (The algorithm only returns parse trees)**.** Given a grammar $G = (N, T, P, S)$ and an input sentence $\vec{\alpha} \in \mathbf{L}(G)$, let $(\hat{\mathcal{C}}, \hat{\mathcal{T}}) = parse(G, \vec{\alpha})$. Then if $\mathcal{T} \in \hat{\mathcal{T}}$, $\mathcal{T}$ is not superfluously recursive and $Parse(G, S, \vec{\alpha}, \mathcal{T})$ holds.

Proof. To construct a new tree, the algorithm considers rules in the underlying grammar G, and finding a G-parse tree for each symbol on the right-hand side of a given rule. If a tree $\mathcal{T}$ is completed, then $Parse(G, rootLabel(\mathcal{T}), \vec{\beta}, \mathcal{T})$ must hold for some $\vec{\beta}$. Any $\hat{\mathcal{T}}_k$ therefore contains only G-parse trees for some k-prefix of $\vec{\alpha}$, so any G-parse tree returned after the algorithm has processed $\vec{\alpha}$ must be a valid G-parse tree for $\vec{\alpha}$. By Lemma 2.25, the trees are not superfluously recursive. □

Corollary 4.28 (The algorithm is sound)**.** Let $G = (N, T, P, S)$ be a grammar, and let $\vec{\alpha}$ be a sentence. By Theorems 4.26 and 4.27, the algorithm is sound, i.e., for $(\hat{\mathcal{C}}, \hat{\mathcal{T}}) = parse(G, \vec{\alpha})$, the algorithm terminates and if $\mathcal{T} \in \hat{\mathcal{T}}$, then $\mathcal{T}$ is not superfluously recursive and $Parse(G, S, \vec{\alpha}, \mathcal{T})$ holds.

Definition 4.29 (Tree path)**.** Let $\alpha\#\vec{\mathcal{T}}$ be a tree. Let π be a finite sequence of natural numbers called a *tree path*. Let Π be the set of all tree paths.

Definition 4.30 (Subtree at path)**.** We define *SubtreeAt* as the smallest function such that:
- $SubtreeAt \in \mathbb{T} \to (\Pi \to \mathbb{T})$
- For all $\mathcal{T} \in \mathbb{T}$, $SubtreeAt(\mathcal{T})([]) = \mathcal{T}$.
- For all α and for all $\vec{\mathcal{T}} \in \vec{\mathbb{T}}$ and for all $\pi \in \Pi$,
  $SubtreeAt(\alpha\#\vec{\mathcal{T}})([i]\cdot\pi) = SubtreeAt(\vec{\mathcal{T}}(i))(\pi)$ if $i \in \mathbf{dom}(\vec{\mathcal{T}})$.

Definition 4.31 (Pattern matching on parse trees)**.** Let $G = (N, T, P, S)$ be a grammar, and let $\mathcal{T}$ be a tree such that $Parse(G, S, \mathcal{T}, \vec{\alpha})$ holds for some $\vec{\alpha}$. Let $\mathcal{C}$ be a continuation, and let π be a tree path. We define $PM(\mathcal{T}, \mathcal{C}, \pi)$ (short for "Pattern Matching") as the smallest (w.r.t. $\subseteq$) relation such that:

- $PM(\mathcal{T}, \textbf{reduce } S \blacktriangleright \textbf{done}, [])$ holds and $PM(\mathcal{T}, \textbf{done}, [])$ holds.
- Suppose $PM(\mathcal{T}, \textbf{reduce } \alpha \blacktriangleright \mathcal{C}', \pi)$ holds and there exists π' such that $\eta\#\vec{\mathcal{T}}\cdot\vec{\mathcal{T}}' = \mathit{SubtreeAt}(\mathcal{T})\pi\cdot\pi'$. Further suppose that there exists $k < |\vec{\mathcal{T}}|$ such that $\forall j < k.\mathit{input}(G)\vec{\mathcal{T}}(j) = \varepsilon$, and let $\vec{\beta} = \mathit{rootLabel} \circ (\vec{\mathcal{T}}\cdot\vec{\mathcal{T}}')$. Then if $\eta \to \vec{\beta} \in P$, $PM(\mathcal{T}, \textbf{match } (\eta \to \vec{\beta}, k)\ \vec{\mathcal{T}} \blacktriangleright \textbf{reduce } \alpha \blacktriangleright \mathcal{C}', \pi\cdot\pi')$ holds.
- Suppose $PM(\mathcal{T}, \textbf{match } (r, k)\ \vec{\mathcal{T}} \blacktriangleright \mathcal{C}', \pi)$ holds. Let $l = |\vec{\mathcal{T}}|$, let $\mathcal{T}' = \mathit{SubtreeAt}(\mathcal{T})\pi\cdot[l]$. Further suppose that $\mathit{rootLabel}(\mathcal{T}') = \alpha$. Then $PM(\mathcal{T}, \textbf{reduce } \alpha \blacktriangleright \textbf{match } (r, k)\ \vec{\mathcal{T}} \blacktriangleright \mathcal{C}', \pi\cdot[l])$ holds.

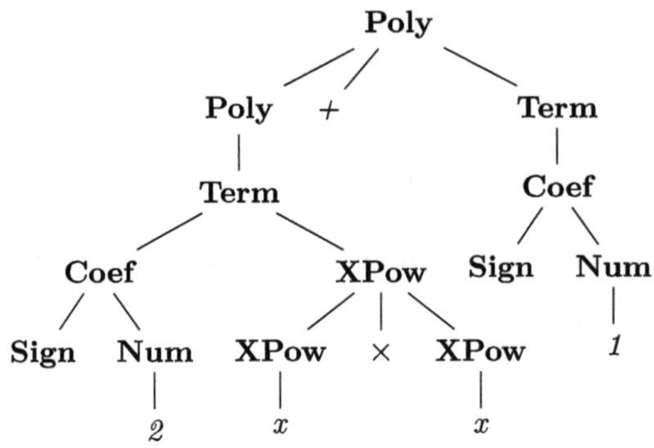

Fig. 2: G-parse tree for $\vec{\alpha}$ from Example 4.32.

Example 4.32 (Pattern matching)**.** Let G be the grammar defined in Example 2.9, and let $\vec{\alpha} = [\mathit{2}, x, \times, x, +, \mathit{1}]$. Let $\mathcal{T}$ be the G-parse tree shown in Figure 2, let $\mathcal{T}_{\textbf{Coef}} = \textbf{Coef}\#[\textbf{Sign}\#[\,], \textbf{Num}\#[\mathit{2}\#[\,]]]$, and let $\mathcal{T}_{\textbf{XPow}} = \textbf{XPow}\#[x\#[\,]]$. Let $\mathcal{C} = \textbf{reduce } \times \blacktriangleright \textbf{match } (X_X, 0)\ [\mathcal{T}_{\textbf{XPow}}] \blacktriangleright \textbf{reduce XPow} \blacktriangleright \textbf{match } (T_{CP}, 0)\ [\mathcal{T}_{\textbf{Coef}}] \blacktriangleright \textbf{reduce Poly} \blacktriangleright \textbf{done}$. Let $\pi = []\cdot[0,0]\cdot[1]\cdot[]\cdot[1]$. We have written it this way to illustrate which part of the continuation relates to each part of the path. To show that $PM(\mathcal{T}, \mathcal{C}, \pi)$ holds, we will work "backwards" through the continuation, showing that the conditions for PM are satisfied at every stage.

1. First, $PM(\mathcal{T}, \textbf{reduce Poly} \blacktriangleright \textbf{done}, [])$ always holds.
2. We get $\mathit{SubtreeAt}(\mathcal{T})[0,0] = \textbf{Term}\#[\mathcal{T}_{\textbf{Coef}}, \textbf{XPow}\#[\mathcal{T}_{\textbf{XPow}}, \times\#[\,], \mathcal{T}_{\textbf{XPow}}]]$. We have $\vec{\mathcal{T}} = [\mathcal{T}_{\textbf{Coef}}]$, and since $\mathit{input}(G)\mathcal{T}_{\textbf{Coef}} \neq \varepsilon$, $k = 0$. Therefore, $PM(\mathcal{T}, \textbf{match } (T_{CP}, 0)\ [\mathcal{T}_{\textbf{Coef}}] \blacktriangleright \textbf{reduce } \alpha \blacktriangleright \textbf{done}, [0,0])$.
3. We then need the path $[0,0]\cdot[|\vec{\mathcal{T}}|] = [0,0]\cdot[1]$ and check its corresponding subtree. We get $\textbf{XPow}\#[\mathcal{T}_{\textbf{XPow}}, \times\#[\,], \mathcal{T}_{\textbf{XPow}}] = \mathit{SubtreeAt}(\mathcal{T})[0,0,1] = \mathcal{T}'$. Since $\mathit{rootLabel}(\mathcal{T}') = \textbf{XPow}$, we have $PM(\mathcal{T}, \textbf{reduce XPow} \blacktriangleright \textbf{match } (T_{CP}, 0)\ [\mathcal{T}_{\textbf{Coef}}] \blacktriangleright \textbf{reduce } \alpha \blacktriangleright \textbf{done}, [0,0,1])$.
4. We then have $\mathit{SubtreeAt}(\mathcal{T})[0,0,1] = \textbf{XPow}\#[\mathcal{T}_{\textbf{XPow}}, \times\#[\,], \mathcal{T}_{\textbf{XPow}}]$. This gives us $\vec{\mathcal{T}} = [\mathcal{T}_{\textbf{XPow}}]$ and $k = 0$, since $\mathit{input}(G)\mathcal{T}_{\textbf{XPow}} \neq \varepsilon$. We therefore have $PM(\mathcal{T}, \textbf{match } (X_X, 0)\ [\mathcal{T}_{\textbf{XPow}}] \blacktriangleright \textbf{reduce XPow} \blacktriangleright \textbf{match } (T_{CP}, 0)\ [\mathcal{T}_{\textbf{Coef}}] \blacktriangleright \textbf{reduce Poly} \blacktriangleright \textbf{done}, [0,0,1])$.

5. Finally, we get $[0,0,1]\cdot[|\vec{\mathcal{T}}|] = [0,0,1,1]$. We have $\mathit{SubtreeAt}(\mathcal{T})[0,0,1,1] = \times\#[]$. Since $\mathit{rootLabel}(\times\#[])$, we get $\mathit{PM}(\mathcal{T},\mathcal{C},[0,0,1,1])$.

We will use *PM* to prove that given a grammar $G = (N,T,P,S)$, an input sentence $\vec{\alpha}$ and a G-parse tree $\mathcal{T}$ for that input sentence, all the functions that make up the algorithm return (1) a continuation $\mathcal{C}$ such that $\mathit{PM}(\mathcal{T},\mathcal{C},\pi)$ holds for some π, and (2) possibly a subtree of $\mathcal{T}$. Lemmas 4.33 and 4.34 prove this for *match*, Lemma 4.35 proves this for *reduce*, and Lemma 4.36 proves this for *procCont*. We then use these lemmas and an induction on the length of the input sentence to prove that the above assertions hold for *parse*, and thus the algorithm as a whole is complete (Theorem 4.37).

Lemma 4.33. Let $G = (N,T,P,S)$ be a grammar and let $\mathcal{T}$ be a tree such that $\mathit{Parse}(G,S,\mathcal{T},\vec{\alpha})$ holds for some $\vec{\alpha}$. Let $\mathcal{C} = \textbf{match}\ (r,k)\ \vec{\mathcal{T}} \blacktriangleright \mathcal{C}'$ be a continuation such that $k > |\vec{\mathcal{T}}|$ and for some π, $\mathit{PM}(\mathcal{T},\mathcal{C},\pi)$ holds. Let $(\hat{\mathcal{C}},\hat{\mathcal{T}}) = \mathit{match}(G,\bot,\mathcal{C})$. Then the following hypothesis holds:
- If $\hat{\mathcal{T}} \neq \{\}$, there exists $\mathcal{T}' \in \hat{\mathcal{T}}$ such that $\mathcal{T}' = \mathit{SubtreeAt}(\mathcal{T})(\pi)$.
- Otherwise, there exists $\mathcal{C}'' \in \hat{\mathcal{C}}$ such that for some π', $\mathit{PM}(\mathcal{T},\mathcal{C}'',\pi\cdot\pi')$ holds.

Proof. The full proof can be found in the long version of the paper[1]. The proof is by induction on $d = |\mathit{RHS}(r)| - |\vec{\mathcal{T}}|$. When $d = 0$, a non-empty set of trees is returned, for which we show the lemma holds. In the inductive step we show that the lemma holds for the continuation that is created as part of each recursive call to *match*. □

Lemma 4.34. Let $G = (N,T,P,S)$ be a grammar and let $\mathcal{T}$ be a tree such that $\mathit{Parse}(G,S,\mathcal{T},\vec{\alpha})$ holds for some $\vec{\alpha}$. Let $\mathcal{C} = \textbf{reduce}\ \alpha \blacktriangleright \mathcal{C}'$ be a continuation such that for some π, $\mathit{PM}(\mathcal{T},\mathcal{C},\pi)$ holds. Further, let π' be a path such that $\eta\#\vec{\mathcal{T}} = \mathit{SubtreeAt}(\mathcal{T})(\pi\cdot\pi')$, and let $\vec{\beta} = \mathit{rootLabel} \circ \vec{\mathcal{T}}$. Let $j \in \mathbb{N}$ such that for all $i < j$, $\mathit{input}(G)(\vec{\mathcal{T}}(i)) = \varepsilon$ and $\mathcal{T}' = \mathit{SubtreeAt}(\mathcal{T})(\pi\cdot\pi'\cdot[j])$. Finally, for $\vec{\mathcal{T}}'$ such that $j < |\vec{\mathcal{T}}'|$, let $(\hat{\mathcal{C}},\hat{\mathcal{T}}) = \mathit{match}(G,\mathcal{T}',\textbf{match}\ (\eta \to \vec{\beta},j)\ \vec{\mathcal{T}}' \blacktriangleright \mathcal{C})$. Then the following hypothesis holds:
- If $\hat{\mathcal{T}} \neq \{\}$, we have $\eta\#\vec{\mathcal{T}} \in \hat{\mathcal{T}}$.
- Otherwise, there exists $\mathcal{C}' \in \hat{\mathcal{C}}$ such that $\mathit{PM}(\mathcal{T},\mathcal{C}',\pi\cdot\pi')$ holds.

Proof. The full proof can be found in the long version of the paper[1]. The proof is by induction on $l = k - |\vec{\mathcal{T}}|$. When $l = 0$, Lemma 4.33 applies. In the inductive step we show that the lemma holds for the continuation that is created as part of each recursive call to *match*. □

Lemma 4.35. Let $G = (N,T,P,S)$ be a grammar and let $\mathcal{T}$ be a tree such that $\mathit{Parse}(G,S,\mathcal{T},\vec{\alpha})$ holds for some $\vec{\alpha}$. Let $\mathcal{C} = \textbf{reduce}\ \alpha \blacktriangleright \mathcal{C}'$ be a continuation such that for some π, $\mathit{PM}(\mathcal{T},\mathcal{C},\pi)$ holds. Further, let $\mathcal{T}' = \beta\#\vec{\mathcal{T}} = \mathit{SubtreeAt}(\mathcal{T})(\pi\cdot\pi')$ for some π'. Let $(\hat{\mathcal{C}},\hat{\mathcal{T}}) = \mathit{reduce}(G,\mathcal{T}',M,\mathcal{C})$ where $M \subseteq \Gamma(G)$ such that $\beta \notin M$. Then the following hypothesis holds:

- If $\hat{\mathcal{T}} \neq \{\}$, then we have $SubtreeAt(\mathcal{T})(\pi) = \alpha \# \mathcal{T}' \in \hat{\mathcal{T}}$.
- Otherwise, there exists $\mathcal{C}' \in \hat{\mathcal{C}}$ such that $PM(\mathcal{T}, \mathcal{C}', \pi \cdot \pi'')$ holds for some π''.

Proof. The full proof can be found in the long version of the paper[1]. The proof is by induction on $|\pi'|$. If $|\pi'| = 0$, then we have $\alpha = \beta$ and *reduce* returns $\mathcal{T}'$. Otherwise, *reduce* must recursively consider a new tree $\mathcal{T}''$, which contains $\mathcal{T}'$ as a subtree, where $\mathcal{T}'' = SubtreeAt(\mathcal{T})(\pi \cdot \pi' \langle 0..(|\pi'| - 2) \rangle)$. □

Lemma 4.36. Let $G = (N, T, P, S)$ be a grammar and let $\mathcal{T}$ be a tree such that $Parse(G, S, \mathcal{T}, \vec{\alpha})$ holds for some $\vec{\alpha}$. Let $\mathcal{C} = \textbf{reduce}\ \alpha \blacktriangleright \mathcal{C}'$ be a continuation such that for some π, $PM(\mathcal{T}, \mathcal{C}, \pi)$ holds. Let $\mathcal{T}' = SubtreeAt(\mathcal{T})(\pi)$ and let $\hat{\mathcal{T}}' = \{\mathcal{T}'\}$. Let $(\hat{\mathcal{C}}, \hat{\mathcal{T}}) = procCont(G, \mathcal{C}, \hat{\mathcal{T}}')$. Then, the following hypothesis holds:

- If $\hat{\mathcal{T}} \neq \{\}$, then $\mathcal{T}' \in \hat{\mathcal{T}}$ such that for some π', $\mathcal{T}' = SubtreeAt(\mathcal{T})(\pi')$.
- Otherwise, there exists $\mathcal{C}' \in \hat{\mathcal{C}}$ such that for some π', $PM(\mathcal{T}, \mathcal{C}', \pi')$ holds.

Proof. The proof is by induction on the structure of $\mathcal{C}$.
If $\mathcal{C} = \textbf{done}$, then $PM(\mathcal{T}, \mathcal{C}, [])$ holds and $SubtreeAt(\mathcal{T})([]) = \mathcal{T}$. $procCont(G, \mathcal{C}, \hat{\mathcal{T}}) = (\{\}, \{\mathcal{T}\})$, which satisfies the hypothesis.
If $\mathcal{C} = \textbf{reduce}\ \alpha \blacktriangleright \mathcal{C}'$, we have $(\hat{\mathcal{C}}_{new}, \hat{\mathcal{T}}_{new}) = mapUnzip(reduce, \{(G, \mathcal{T}', \{\}, \mathcal{C}) \mid \mathcal{T}' \in \hat{\mathcal{T}}'\})$. By Lemma 4.35, if $\hat{\mathcal{T}}_{new} \neq \{\}$, then there exists $\mathcal{T}' \in \hat{\mathcal{T}}_{new}$ such that $\mathcal{T}' = SubtreeAt(\mathcal{T})(\pi)$. We proceed by computing $procCont(G, \mathcal{C}', \hat{\mathcal{T}}_{new})$. Otherwise $\hat{\mathcal{T}}_{new} = \{\}$ and there exists $\mathcal{C}'' \in \hat{\mathcal{C}}_{new}$ such that $PM(\mathcal{T}, \mathcal{C}'', \pi \cdot \pi'')$ holds for some π''. Then $procCont(G, \mathcal{C}', \hat{\mathcal{T}}_{new}) = (\{\}, \{\})$ and so $procCont(G, \mathcal{C}, \hat{\mathcal{T}}) = (\hat{\mathcal{C}}_{new}, \{\})$, which satisfies the hypothesis.
If $\mathcal{C} = \textbf{match}\ (r, k)\ \vec{\mathcal{T}} \blacktriangleright \mathcal{C}$, we have $(\hat{\mathcal{C}}_{new}, \hat{\mathcal{T}}_{new}) = mapUnzip(match, \{(G, \bot, \textbf{match}\ (r, k)\ \vec{\mathcal{T}} \cdot [\mathcal{T}'] \blacktriangleright \mathcal{C}) \mid \mathcal{T}' \in \hat{\mathcal{T}}'\})$. By Lemma 4.33, if $\hat{\mathcal{T}}_{new} \neq \{\}$, then there exists $\mathcal{T}' \in \hat{\mathcal{T}}_{new}$ such that $\mathcal{T}' = SubtreeAt(\mathcal{T})(\pi)$. We proceed by computing $procCont(G, \mathcal{C}', \hat{\mathcal{T}}_{new})$. Otherwise $\hat{\mathcal{T}}_{new} = \{\}$ and there exists $\mathcal{C}'' \in \hat{\mathcal{C}}_{new}$ such that $PM(\mathcal{T}, \mathcal{C}'', \pi \cdot \pi'')$ holds for some π''. Then $procCont(G, \mathcal{C}', \hat{\mathcal{T}}_{new}) = (\{\}, \{\})$ and so $procCont(G, \mathcal{C}, \hat{\mathcal{T}}) = (\hat{\mathcal{C}}_{new}, \{\})$, which satisfies the hypothesis. □

Theorem 4.37 (Completeness of the algorithm)**.** The algorithm is complete, i.e., given a grammar $G = (N, T, P, S)$ and an input sentence $\vec{\alpha} \in \mathbf{L}(G)$, then for any G-parse tree $\mathcal{T}_{goal}$, which is not superfluously recursive such that $Parse(G, S, \vec{\alpha}, \mathcal{T}_{goal})$ holds, the algorithm will find it.

Proof. For all $k \in 0..|\vec{\alpha}|$, let $(\hat{\mathcal{C}}_k, \hat{\mathcal{T}}_k) = parse(G, \vec{\alpha}\langle 0..k \rangle)$. We now prove the following by induction on k:

IH: If $k = |\vec{\alpha}|$, then $\mathcal{T}_{goal} \in \hat{\mathcal{T}}_k$. Otherwise, there exists $\mathcal{C} \in \hat{\mathcal{C}}_k$ such that $PM(\mathcal{T}_{goal}, \mathcal{C}, \pi)$ holds for some π.

For $k = 0$, this is clear. We have $\hat{\mathcal{C}}_0 = \{\textbf{reduce}\ S \blacktriangleright \textbf{done}\}$ and $\hat{\mathcal{T}}_0 = \varepsilon Trees(G, S)$. If $\vec{\alpha} = []$, then $\mathcal{T}_{goal} \in \hat{\mathcal{T}}_0$, by Procedure 2.24. Otherwise, $PM(\mathcal{T}_{goal}, \textbf{reduce}\ S \blacktriangleright \textbf{done}, [])$ holds by Definition 4.31.

Now assume that IH holds for some $k < |\vec{\alpha}|$. Note that $(\hat{\mathcal{C}}_{k+1},\hat{\mathcal{T}}_{k+1}) = \mathit{parse}(G, \vec{\alpha}\langle 0..k+1\rangle)$. Let $t_k = \vec{\alpha}(k)$. By assumption, we have $\mathcal{C} \in \hat{\mathcal{C}}_k$ and π such that $\mathit{PM}(\mathcal{T}_{goal}, \mathcal{C}, \pi)$ holds (note that $\mathcal{T}_{goal} \notin \hat{\mathcal{T}}_k$). Let $(\hat{\mathcal{C}},\hat{\mathcal{T}}) = \mathit{procCont}(G, \mathcal{C}, \{t_k\#[\,]\})$. Note that $\hat{\mathcal{C}} \subseteq \hat{\mathcal{C}}_{k+1}$ and $\hat{\mathcal{T}} \subseteq \hat{\mathcal{T}}_{k+1}$. By Lemma 4.36, if $\hat{\mathcal{T}} \neq \{\}$, then $\mathcal{T} \in \hat{\mathcal{T}}$ such that for some π, $\mathcal{T} = \mathit{SubtreeAt}(\mathcal{T}_{goal})(\pi)$. Note that if $k+1 = |\vec{\alpha}|$, we have $\mathcal{T}_{goal} \in \hat{\mathcal{T}}_{k+1}$. If $\hat{\mathcal{T}} = \{\}$, then we have $\mathcal{C} \in \hat{\mathcal{C}}$ such that $\mathit{PM}(\mathcal{T}_{goal}, \mathcal{C}, \pi')$ holds for some π', satisfying IH.

We have therefore shown that if IH holds for k, it holds for $k+1$, concluding the proof. □

5 Conclusion

In this paper, we identified DynGenPar as an algorithm which can potentially be used to parse the language of mathematics. From its available descriptions (ADGP) and C++ implementation (KDGP), we extracted CDGP, a CFG parsing core of KDGP. We presented a formalisation of a table-less parsing algorithm, capable of supporting left-recursive rules, rules which do not consume additional tokens when expanded. We have proven its soundness and completeness and made available an experimental implementation, which closely follows the formal description. This work provides a foundation for further reasoning about the algorithm.

In the future, we would like to:

- Formalise and verify the soundness of KDGP features we omitted, such as unification of parse trees and continuations, and parse actions, as we believe this could lead to improvements in efficiency.
- Investigate and document implementation choices that can lead to efficiency improvements.
- Formalise the effects of modifying the initial graph during parsing.
- Prove some properties about the initial graph, especially regarding its time and space complexity.

References

1. Alfred V. Aho, Ravi Sethi, and Jeffrey D. Ullman. *Compilers : Principles, Techniques, and Tools.* 1st ed. Addison-Wesley, 1986. 796 pp. ISBN: 0-201-10088-6.
2. Krasimir Angelov. "Incremental Parsing with Parallel Multiple Context-Free Grammars". In: *Proceedings of the 12th Conference of the European Chapter of the Association for Computational Linguistics.* The 12th Conference of the European Chapter of the Association for Computational Linguistics. Athens, Greece: Association for Computational Linguistics, 2009, pp. 69–76. DOI: 10.3115/1609067.1609074. URL: `http://portal.acm.org/citation.cfm?doid=1609067.1609074` (visited on 04/18/2022).
3. Igor Dejanović. "Parglare: A LR/GLR Parser for Python". In: *Science of Computer Programming* 214 (2021). ISSN: 0167-6423. DOI: 10.1016/j.scico.2021.102734. URL: `https://www.sciencedirect.com/science/article/pii/S0167642321001271`.

4. Mehmet Dolgun. GLRParser: *A GLR Parser for Natural Language Processing and Translation.* Version 0.3.25. URL: https://github.com/mdolgun/GLRParser (visited on 05/02/2023).
5. Mohan Ganesalingam. *The Language of Mathematics.* Vol. 7805. Lecture Notes in Computer Science. Berlin, Heidelberg: Springer, 2013. ISBN: 978-3-642-37011-3. DOI: 10.1007/978-3-642-37012-0. URL: http://link.springer.com/10.1007/978-3-642-37012-0 (visited on 10/28/2021).
6. Kevin Kofler. "Dynamic Generalized Parsing and Natural Mathematical Language". PhD thesis. Vienna, Austria: University of Vienna, 2017. URL: https://www.tigen.org/kevin.kofler/fmathl/dyngenpar/diss.pdf.
7. Kevin Kofler and Arnold Neumaier. "DynGenPar – A Dynamic Generalized Parser for Common Mathematical Language". In: *Intelligent Computer Mathematics.* Ed. by Johan Jeuring et al. Berlin, Heidelberg: Springer, 2012, pp. 386–401. ISBN: 978-3-642-31374-5. DOI: 10.1007/978-3-642-31374-5_26.
8. Michael Kohlhase and Dennis Müller. *The sTeX3 Manual.* Oct. 13, 2023. URL: https://github.com/slatex/sTeX/blob/main/doc/stex-manual.pdf (visited on 10/17/2023).
9. Paul T. McGuire. *Welcome to PyParsing's Documentation!* — PyParsing 3.1.1 Documentation. URL: https://pyparsing-docs.readthedocs.io/en/latest/index.html (visited on 04/04/2024).
10. Rahman Nozohoor-Farshi. "GLR Parsing for "-Grammers". In: *Generalized LR Parsing.* Ed. by Masaru Tomita. Boston, MA: Springer US, 1991, pp. 61–75. ISBN: 978-1-4615-4034-2. DOI: 10.1007/978-1-4615-4034-2_5. URL: https://doi.org/10.1007/978-1-4615-4034-2_5 (visited on 05/01/2025).
11. Jan Rekers. "Parser Generation for Interactive Environments". University of Amsterdam, Jan. 1992. 179 pp. URL: https://ir.cwi.nl/pub/29930/29930D.pdf (visited on 02/21/2024).
12. Masaru Tomita. "The Generalized LR Parsing Algorithm". In: *Generalized LR Parsing.* Springer Science & Business Media, Aug. 31, 1991, pp. 1–16. ISBN: 978-0-7923-9201-9. Google Books: PvZiZiVqwHcC.
13. Luka Vrečar, Joe Wells, and Fairouz Kamareddine. "Towards Semantic Markup of Mathematical Documents via User Interaction". In: *Intelligent Computer Mathematics.* Ed. by Andrea Kohlhase and Laura Kovács. Vol. 14960. Cham: Springer Nature Switzerland, 2024, pp. 223–240. ISBN: 978-3-031-66996-5. DOI: 10.1007/978-3-031-66997-2_13. URL: https://link.springer.com/10.1007/978-3-031-66997-2_13 (visited on 10/25/2024).
14. Daniel H. Younger. "Recognition and parsing of context-free languages in time n3". In: *Information and Control* 10.2 (1967), pp. 189–208. ISSN: 0019-9958. DOI: 10.1016/S0019-9958(67)80007-X. URL: https://www.sciencedirect.com/science/article/pii/S001999586780007X.

Mathematical Knowledge Management

Reaping the Benefits of Modularization in Flexiformal Mathematics by GF-based AST Transformations

Josefin Kelber[1], Michael Kohlhase[2], Jan Frederik Schaefer[2], and Marcel Schütz[2](✉)

[1] Technical University of Munich (TUM), Munich, Germany
[2] Computer Science, FAU Erlangen-Nürnberg, Erlangen, Germany
marcel.schuetz@fau.de

Abstract. Flexiformal documents – i.e. documents with embedded semantic annotations that make some aspects of their content machine-actionable – can be instrumented to make interaction with the underlying knowledge more efficient and effective. Fostering such interactions via semantic services has proven very successful in university education, but the practical applicability is limited by the cost of flexiformalization. A method for lowering (flexi)-formalization costs is to use modular representations to profit from enhanced source sharing and induced (generated) content. In fully formal environments this is well-understood and implemented in many systems.

In this paper we show that many of the formal techniques carry over to the informal setting if we parse (rigorous) natural language with a semantically optimized grammar and work on abstract syntax trees instead of formulae.

We present *i)* a set of use cases for generating learning material to be used in an educational setting – concretely in the field of theoretical computer science, *ii)* a GF grammar that allows to syntactically analyze the underlying language fragment, *iii)* a set of AST-to-AST simplifications that can be used to fine-tune the wording and formulae of the generated content and adapt it to the scientific jargon, and *iv)* a prototypical implementation that shows the technique in action.

Keywords: Flexiformal Mathematics · FTML · Mathematical Language · Theory Morphisms · GF · NLP

1 Introduction

Scientific knowledge is highly inter-related. Relations range from the mappings that underlie application of theoretical results – objects, concepts and relations in the theory are mapped to objects in the application domain which obey the theory assumptions – to inter-theory interpretations and refinements, which allow to import insights, constructions, methods, and arguments from the source theory into the target theory, called **recontextualization** in [KS24].

V. de Paiva and P. Koepke (Eds.): CICM 2025, LNAI 16136, pp. 191–207, 2026.
https://doi.org/10.1007/978-3-032-07021-0_11

In modular representation formats, such relations can be made explicit as first-class citizens – called **theory morphisms**, views, realizations, or just interpretations – which can be inspected, composed, applied, and reasoned with. In fully formal representation formats, this is a very well-understood process, and most formal mathematical libraries utilize the synergies induced by theory morphisms. In type theoretic contexts, these are often implemented as functions between record types. Here we follow a heterogeneous notion of theories (see [MRK18]).

Reaping the synergies is much more difficult in **flexiformal** representation formats where the semantics of informal content is (partially) elucidated by semantic annotations (see [Koh13]): instead of definition expansion and possibly simplification in formulae, we need to manipulate informal technical language. In [KS24] we have shown that transporting quiz problems given in mathematical vernacular is possible in principle using a simple template-based approach: given sufficient (but still natural) semantic annotations of the source quiz problems, flexiformal theory morphisms have the necessary information (and language snippets) to assemble relatively natural-looking quiz problems in the context of the target theory. Of course, the template-based approach only allows very limited simplifications of the generated language, which can also contain grammatical problems like failure of agreement or inflection, but more generally loses much of the conciseness we are used to in mathematical language.

Contribution In this paper we want to lift some of these limitations: instead of composing semantically annotated LaTeX snippets via templates, we parse the natural language with the Grammatical Framework (GF [Ran04; GF]), do the language composition at the level of GF abstract syntax trees, and leave the linearization of these to the GF system to guarantee grammatical correctness of the result. This had been anticipated in [KS24], but needed a semantic grammar for mathematics, which we have developed for this paper.

A side effect of this move from LaTeX strings to GF abstract syntax trees (essentially λ-terms in LF [Pfe01]) is that we can do more complex replacement and simplification operations and thus model some of the more advanced fine-tuning of mathematical notions when processing mathematical language.

As a running example, we will recontextualize the definition of a path in graph theory to the context of automata theory. With sufficient training, a human reader can easily recognize how automata correspond to graphs, but students in theoretical computer science courses often struggle with this and may benefit from an explicit recontextualization or generated fine-grained explanations of the relationship.

Context & Generality Our work is developed in the context of ALeA [Ber+23], a symbolic learning support system. While ALeA provides the main motivation for the work reported here, the particular setup is secondary. The main assumptions are that the underlying knowledge representation admits theories and theory morphisms and that the presentation of the knowledge is flexiformal.

For instance, the Isabelle/Isar [Wen07] universe would be a likely candidate where the methods presented here would be applicable.

Overview In Section 2, we discuss flexiformal recontextualization and explore relevant phenomena using a running example. In Section 3, we discuss an implementation that shows the feasibility of our approach. Section 4 concludes the paper and discusses future work. An extended version of this paper with an appendix of flexiformal rewriting operations is available at [Kel+25].

Acknowledgments. The work reported in this article was conducted as part of the VoLL-KI project (see `https://voll-ki.de`) funded by the German Ministry of Research, Technology and Space under grant 16DHBKI089. We gratefully acknowledge the input of Dennis Müller in the development of suitable representations flexiformal theory morphisms in sTeX and FLAMS.

2 Flexiformal Recontextualization

Our goal with flexiformal recontextualization is to automatically translate learning materials about concepts from one scientific theory into the context of another theory to support students learning those concepts.

2.1 Example: Paths in Graphs and Automata

As a motivating example, we consider the notion of a path in a finite automaton, which is often used in the literature on automata theory, for instance:

- "state 6 is reached by the path $1 \to 2 \to 3 \to 6$" [HMU07, p. 91],
- "show that if there exists a path in $\mathcal{A}$ that leads from a state of C_1 to a state of C_2, ..." [ST09, p. 178],
- "the path starts or stops at state $k+1$ but doesn't go through any state numbered higher than k" [Mar03, p. 115].

These three examples have in common that the notion of a path in an automaton is not defined in the text preceding those quotes. Instead, the notion of a path in a *graph* – or, more precisely, in an *edge-labeled multidigraph*[3]. For a human reader who is sufficiently well trained in mathematics, it does not impose any difficulties to recognize (the transition system underlying) an automaton as a graph and apply the notion of a path in a graph to the setting of automata. However, for some students this conceptual leap is not obvious, and they would benefit from further explanation. Active documents allow us to show supplementary information on demand, e.g. by hovering over the term *"path"* in the above sentences. In this hover, we want to provide

[3] For the sake of brevity we use "graph" as a synonym for edge-labeled multidigraphs (or quivers) in the following.

1) the **recontextualized definition**, i.e. the definition of a *"path in an automaton"*,
2) the **original definition** of a *"path in a graph"*,
3) the **recontextualization morphism**, i.e. an explanation how an automaton induces a graph.

Figure 1 shows what such a pop-up note could look like for non-deterministic finite automata (NFAs).

Definition In an NFA, a *path* is a finite sequence $t_1, \ldots, t_n$ of transitions $t_i := \langle q_i, c_i, q'_i \rangle$ with $q'_i = q_{i+1}$ for all $1 \leq i < n$.

Derived From

Definition In a graph, a *path* is a finite sequence $e_1, \ldots, e_n$ of edges with $t(e_i) = s(e_{i+1})$ for all $1 \leq i < n$.

By Applying

Theorem An NFA $\langle Q, \Sigma, \delta, q_0, F \rangle$ admits a graph $\langle V, E, s, t, L, l \rangle$, where $V := Q$, $E := \{t \mid t \text{ is a transition}\}$, $s := \pi_1$, $t := \pi_3$, $L := \Sigma$, and $l := \pi_2$.

Fig. 1. Example hover for the word *"path"* in the context of NFAs, containing the recontextualized definition along with an (optional) explanation how it was derived. Here, $s(e)$ and $t(e)$ denote the source and target, resp., of an edge e, and π_i denotes projection to the i-th component of a tuple (in an active document, the reader can find this out by hovering over "s", "t" and "π").

Manually authoring the recontextualizations would be tedious and error-prone, as a simple back-of-the-envelope calculation illustrates: if we have 10 graph concepts (e.g. *path*, *cycle*, *loop*, *connectivity*, ...) that have to be recontextualized to 15 different structures (e.g. NFAs, DFAs, RDF triple collections, implication graphs, ...), we would need i) 10 original definitions, ii) 15 recontextualization morphisms, and iii) 150 recontextualized definitions. And, of course, graphs are just one of many theories that can be recontextualized. Other examples from our introductory course for symbolic AI alone include, e.g., logical systems, constraint satisfaction problems and optimization problems.

2.2 Recontextualization as a Pushout

In [KS24] we discussed that recontextualization corresponds to a **pushout** in a theory graph, which, in principle, allows us to generate recontextualizations automatically: Suppose we have i) a theory of graphs extended by a definition of the concept of a path, ii) a theory of automata and iii) a theory morphism between them. Then we can obtain the definition of a path in an automaton by computing the pushout of the span given by i), ii) and iii), as illustrated in Figure 2. Computing such pushouts is well-understood in a fully formal setting, where we essentially apply the substitution specified by the morphism. However, our flexiformal setting is more challenging because sometimes the substitutions have to be applied to (semantically annotated) natural language.

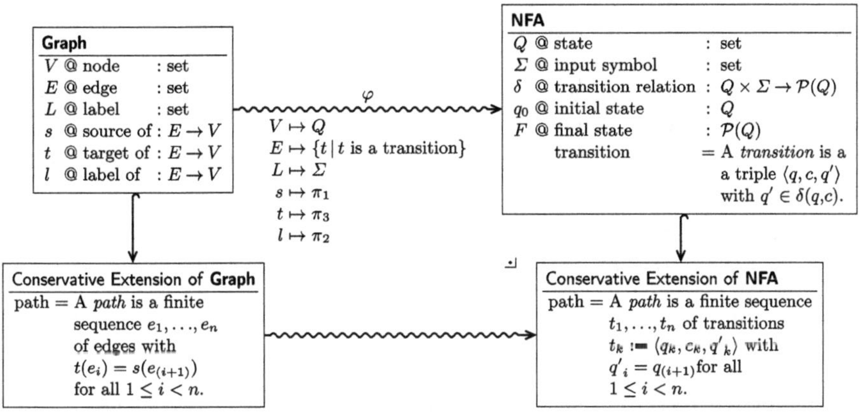

Fig. 2. Pushout for paths in graphs and finite automata. An entry of the form [⟨notation⟩ "@"] ⟨name⟩ (":" ⟨type⟩ | "=" ⟨definition⟩) is a declaration of a symbol with name ⟨name⟩, optional symbolic notation ⟨notation⟩ and either type ⟨type⟩ or definitional expression ⟨definition⟩. If the symbol denotes a set, we follow the convention to name the symbol after the elements of that set.

In [KS24], we described a template-based approach for flexiformal recontextualization that would simply substitute all components of the theory of graphs in the definiens of the *"path"* definition

> A *path* is a finite sequence $e_1,\ldots,e_n$ of edges with $t(e_i) = s(e_{i+1})$ for all $1 \le i < n$.

with their respective values under the morphism φ, which is relatively straightforward if the relevant components (like the word *"edges"*) are semantically annotated. We obtain the following definition of a path in an automaton by applying that mechanism:

> A *path* is a finite sequence $e_1,\ldots,e_n$ of elements of $\{t \,|\, t \text{ is a transition}\}$ with $\pi_3(e_i) = \pi_1(e_{i+1})$ for all $1 \le i < n$.

Semantically, we conflate nouns – like *"edge"* – with the set of all elements the noun stands for – in this case *"E"*. Linguistically, this requires us to insert *"element(s) of"* when substituting a noun with a set. Getting the correct form of the noun (*"element"* vs. *"elements"*) in a template-based approach is difficult, and support in our previous work [KS24] was limited to very specific cases.

2.3 Polishing the Result

While the result of the translation is technically correct, it is not as concise and clear as a human author would write it. Although statistical methods, like delegating the task to an LLM, might succeed on a wider range of sentences than the approach we are presenting, those methods cannot guarantee that meaning will be preserved – which would be problematic e.g. in an educational setting. Instead, we model the simplification process as a sequence of **meaning-preserving rewriting operations**.

To gain a better intuition, let us simplify the (recontextualized) definition from the previous section step by step:

1. **Comprehension term reduction:** First we reduce the comprehension term expression *"elements of* $\{t \,|\, t$ *is a transition*$\}$*"* to *"transitions"*:

   > A *path* is a finite sequence $e_1, \ldots, e_n$ of transitions with $\pi_3(e_i) = \pi_1(e_{i+1})$ for all $1 \leq i < n$.

2. **Structure expansion:** Then we expand the noun phrase *"finite sequence* $e_1, \ldots, e_n$ *of transitions"* by appending a variable definition *"*$e_k := \langle q_k, c_k, q'_k \rangle$*"*:

   > A *path* is a finite sequence $e_1, \ldots, e_n$ of transitions $e_k := \langle q_k, c_k, q'_k \rangle$ with $\pi_3(e_i) = \pi_1(e_{i+1})$ for all $1 \leq i < n$.

3. **Variable expansion:** This allows us to expand later occurrences of *"e"* (*"*e_i*"* and *"*e_{i+1}*"*):

   > A *path* is a finite sequence $e_1, \ldots, e_n$ of transitions $e_k := \langle q_k, c_k, q'_k \rangle$ with $\pi_3(\langle q_i, c_i, q'_i \rangle) = \pi_1(\langle q_{i+1}, c_{i+1}, q'_{i+1} \rangle)$ for all $1 \leq i < n$.

4. **Projection reduction:** Now that the arguments of the projections are triples we can evaluate the projections:

   > A *path* is a finite sequence $e_1, \ldots, e_n$ of transitions $e_k := \langle q_k, c_k, q'_k \rangle$ with $q'_i = q_{i+1}$ for all $1 \leq i < n$.

5. **Variable renaming (optional):** As a last step we rename the variables e_j to t_j:

   > A *path* is a finite sequence $t_1, \ldots, t_n$ of transitions $t_k := \langle q_k, c_k, q'_k \rangle$ with $q'_i = q_{i+1}$ for all $1 \leq i < n$.

Note that steps 2–3 are motivated by the desire to eliminate the projections in step 4 – otherwise, they would make the result less concise.

During our research, we have collected a growing set of basic rewriting rules in [Rew] and in the long version of this paper [Kel+25, Appendix A] that modify natural language expressions in a way that preserves their meaning with the ultimate goal of making them more concise and natural. Collecting further rules and implementing them is ongoing work.

For instance, to perform the first rewriting step from our example above, we can apply rule *Element-NP CTR* from [Kel+25, Appendix A.6], namely

$$\frac{\text{“}\textit{element } [x] \textit{ of } \{y \,|\, y \textit{ is a } \langle\textsf{noun phrase}\rangle\}\text{”}}{\text{“}\langle\textsf{noun phrase}\rangle\ [x]\text{”}},$$

to the expression *“elements of* $\{t\,|\,t$ *is a transition*$\}$*”* which yields the expression *“transitions”*. Note that we have to respect the grammatical number of the noun *“element”* in the input expression which determines the grammatical number of the noun phrase (*“transition”*) in the output expression. In our implementation, these rules act on GF abstract syntax trees (see subsection 3.2 and subsection 3.3).

Other rules are more complicated and involve information that can not be obtained from the syntactical structure of the expression alone. For instance the *structure expansion* step in our example above requires to query the definiens of *“transition”* from a knowledge base. In even more extreme cases, a rewriting rule can demand a logical inference to be carried out before it can be applied. For instance, rule $\iota_\in$ *Conversion* from [Kel+25, Appendix A.7], namely

$$\frac{\vdash |A| = 1 \qquad \vdash a \in A \qquad \text{“}\mathfrak{b} \in A\text{”}}{\text{“}\mathfrak{b} = a\text{”}},$$

allows to convert an expression of the form “$\mathfrak{b} \in A$” to “$\mathfrak{b} = a$” under the constraint that it can be inferred that A consists of exactly one element a. While implementing this rule in its full generality may not be feasible, we can surely cover special cases that frequently occur in practice.

2.4 A Flexiformal Recontextualization Pipeline

In summary, we can think of flexiformal recontextualization as a two-step process: substitution application and simplification. The substitution is based on the recontextualization morphism, but we can use the same process to apply other substitutions. For example, in this paper, we will sometimes apply substitutions derived from definitions to perform definition expansion. Simplification is based on rewriting rules that maintain the meaning of the expression, but the application of those rules has to be carefully controlled.

While substitution and simplification are well-understood in a fully formal setting, dealing with the natural language in a flexiformal setting is more challenging. Semantic annotations can link parts of the natural language to the symbols they refer to, which helps identify where to apply the substitutions.

3 Implementation

We have implemented – on a prototype level – flexiformal substitution and simplification in the context of ALeA, using a rule-based approach to ensure correctness and trustworthiness of the generated content. The relevant documents are parsed with a natural language grammar into GF abstract syntax trees (ASTs). The ASTs are then processed and transformed with a set of hand-written rules, and the results are linearized into strings.

3.1 Context: The ALeA Ecosystem

Our work is implemented in the sTeX/rusTeX/FTML/FLAMS/ALeA ecosystem, where technical knowledge is represented in sTeX [MK22], a variant of LaTeX that supports the annotation of the semantic structures underlying the text content. The rusTeX system transforms sTeX sources into FTML, an extension of HTML5 that preserves all the semantic annotations from sTeX [Mül23]. FTML in turn can be processed by the FLAMS system [Mü] that serves the HTML5 content and integrates knowledge management services based on the annotations into it – turning the content into active documents. The ALeA system [Ber+23] in turn pairs up the active document facilities with learner competency modeling in an adaptive learning assistant that has been used for helping more than 500 students/semester master Math, AI, and CS courses at FAU over the last two years.

Our prototype is based on FTML because processing sTeX documents, which can contain arbitrary LaTeX, is very difficult. To be precise, we use an FTML-inspired HTML extension because FTML was still in flux during development. We will adapt our implementation to real FTML once the FTML format is stable.

3.2 A Grammar for Flexiformal Mathematics

For parsing and linearization, we use GF, the Grammatical Framework [Ran04], which was designed for (multi-lingual) natural language processing. GF separates between the **abstract syntax** of the language and the **concrete syntax** that describes how abstract syntax trees (ASTs) are represented as strings. The concrete syntax has powerful mechanisms like record types and tables to deal with the peculiarities of natural language such as inflection and agreement. The abstract grammar usually abstracts away from these details, which lets us manipulate the ASTs without worrying about such "low-level" aspects of natural language. To illustrate this, consider the following minimal example where we parse a sentence, transform the AST by an aggregation rule, and then linearize the result into a new sentence string:

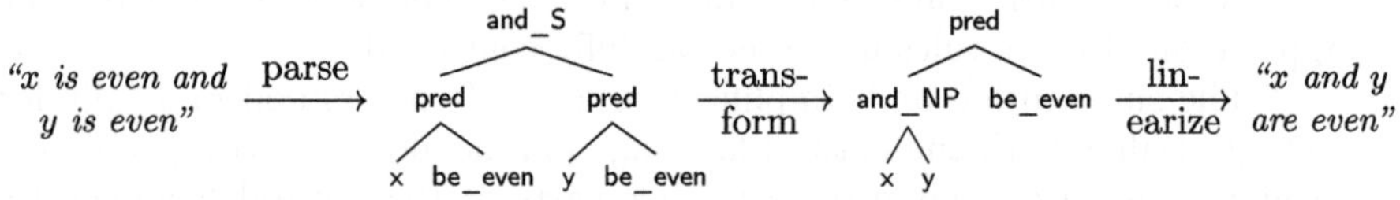

Here, the information whether we should use *"is even"* or *"are even"* in the final sentence is not explicitly present in the AST. Instead, the concrete syntax rule for pred must specify how the correct verb form is chosen depending on the number of the subject.

The GF community has developed the **Resource Grammar Library (RGL)** [GFR], which implements the basic syntax and morphology of many languages. While the RGL is intended as a library for developing application-specific grammars, we have also experimented with using it directly for parsing (see [Kel24] for more details). With some modifications to the RGL, e.g. to support mathematical language and the semantic markup of sTeX, we were able to parse roughly

14 % of the English definitions in SMGloM (a flexiformal glossary that acts as a domain model for semantic annotations in sTEX/ALEA, see [SMG]). Coverage was limited, among other reasons, because of missing words and abbreviations in the lexicon, problems with pre-processing the sTEX files, and missing support for some sentence structures. While many of these issues could be improved, there are more fundamental problems with directly using the RGL: The grammar has a high degree of syntactic ambiguity, which results in many possible ASTs (often in the thousands, but sometimes many more because ambiguities multiply out). This makes the proper treatment of ambiguities (see subsection 3.4) impractical. More importantly, implementing substitution and simplification for RGL ASTs is cumbersome and error-prone.

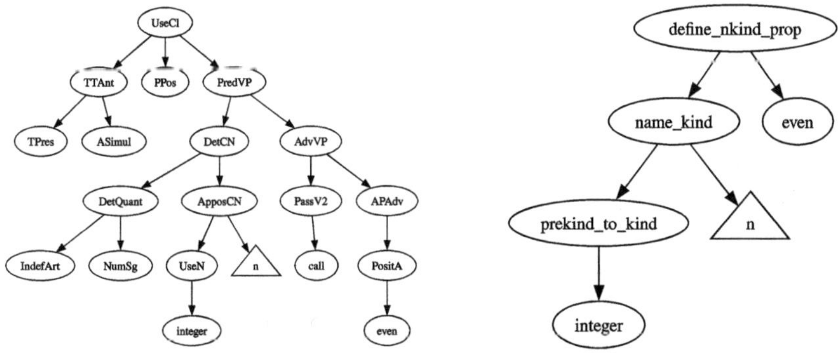

Fig. 3. ASTs for the phrase *"an integer n is called even"*. *Left:* Syntactic AST from an extended RGL grammar. *Right:* A more semantic AST from our application grammar. The formula *"n"* is actually encoded as a MathML tree, which was omitted for conciseness.

The better approach is to develop a new grammar that uses the RGL as a mere library. More concretely, we can implement a completely new abstract syntax that is more suitable for our application, and use the RGL only for the concrete syntax. In particular, we can design the abstract syntax to be more semantic, which makes processing the ASTs much easier. For example, consider the phrase *"an integer n is called even"* (typically followed by *"iff ..."*). In this case, syntactic details (e.g. that *"is called even"* is a verb phrase in passive voice) are not relevant for further processing. The relevant information is that the property of being *"even"* is defined for integers, and that we use *"n"* as a variable. In our grammar, we refer to words like *"integer"* as Kinds. A Kind with a variable is a NamedKind. So for the phrase above, we have a rule define_nkind_prop that combines a NamedKind and a Property into a definition core. Figure 3 visualizes the ASTs for the example phrase.

There are other ways to express the same meaning, e.g. *"an integer n is said to be even"* or *"an integer n is even"*. Syntactically, they are rather different (e.g. the latter one does not use passive voice), but for our processing we basically want to treat them the same. GF supports variants, which allows us to use the define_nkind_prop rule for all three cases. In that case, the AST would not carry information about the original variant, and the linearization could use a different variant. While this should not result in ungrammatical or semantically incorrect sentences, it may result in less natural output. To avoid this, we use separate rules for each variant and use a consistent naming scheme (e.g. define_nkind_v1 and define_nkind_v2), so that we can ignore but preserve variant information throughout the recontextualization pipeline.

In our pipeline, we cannot ignore the HTML structure of the input document. For example, some semantic annotations, like definienda, are encoded via <span> tags with specific attributes. Furthermore, formulae are encoded in MathML. To handle this, we include HTML tags in the abstract syntax trees. As a consequence, HTML tags cannot occur in arbitrary places, but rather must match the structure of the abstract syntax. For example, *"<span>an even</span> integer"* cannot be parsed, but *"an <span>even</span> integer"* can be parsed. Our experience is that the HTML structure usually matches the grammatical structure in practice – and if it does not, authors could consider that as an annotation error.

3.3 Substitution and Simplification

In a formal setting, substitution replaces a symbol with a term. In our flexiformal setting, this basically corresponds to replacing an AST subtree that corresponds to a specific symbol with a different subtree. For example, in the example in Section 2, we replaced *"edges"* with *"elements of* $\{t \mid t \textit{ is a transition}\}$*"*.

In practice, the flexiformal substitution is a bit more complex. Consider, e.g. the sentence

> Let m be a positive integer.

and a substitution given by the definition

> An integer n is called *positive* iff $n > 0$.

The output is

> Let m be a integer such that $m > 0$.

In this case, the definiendum of *"positive"*, "$\cdot > 0$", has a hole that must be filled with *"m"*. The AST of *"$m > 0$"* is then attached via a *"such that"* clause and the *"positive"* subtree is removed from the original AST. Figure 4 visualizes both the input and output ASTs.

Note that substitution in ASTs inherits a form of subject reduction from the underlying logical framework of GF: a (grammatically) well-typed substitution into (grammatically) well-typed ASTs gives (grammatically) well-typed ASTs – in fact they need to be well-typed if we want to linearize them with GF. If the grammatical types of a substitution do not match, like *"positive"* and "$\cdot > 0$" in

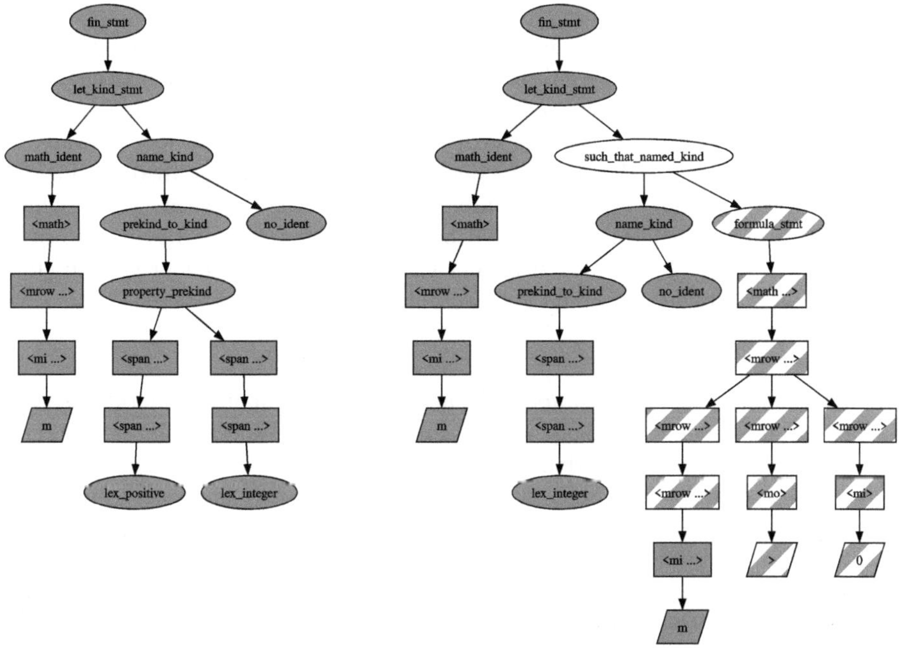

Fig. 4. Example of a substitution. *Left:* Input AST (*"Let m be a positive integer"*). *Right:* Output AST (*"Let m be a integer such that* $m > 0$*"*). The nodes from the input AST are colored turquoise, while the nodes from the definiendum are striped. The node shapes indicate the type of the node (grammar node/HTML tag/MathML literal).

the example above, we have to insert "glue language" (e.g. *"... such that ..."*) to ensure well-typedness.

After substitution, the ASTs are simplified with custom rules (see subsection 2.3), Currently, we only have implemented a small subset of our collection of rewriting rules. In our implementation, rewriting rules are triggered by the "desire" for a specific simplification. For example, the structure expansion in the running example (which by itself is not a simplification) gets triggered by the "desire" to apply projection reduction.

It appears that getting significant simplification coverage is a non-trivial task. At the moment, implementing new rewriting rules is complicated by the fact that semantic information is encoded in the ASTs in the attributes of HTML nodes, which makes the processing more cumbersome – especially for MathML nodes where the syntactic/presentational structure generally does not match the semantic structure well. We are planning to improve this by modelling the semantic structure more directly in the ASTs.

3.4 Handling Ambiguity

Sometimes, multiple ASTs correspond to the same string. In this case, GF can generate all possible ASTs. This gives us a basic tool for handling ambiguity:

if our grammar is sufficiently broad to cover the correct reading, we know that one of the ASTs will be the correct one. Our grammar/ASTs are designed to be somewhat semantic (see subsection 3.2). As a consequence, this mechanism does not just handle classical structural ambiguity, but also more semantic ambiguity. A simple example for this is lexical ambiguity (which is less relevant for us though, as discussed below). Lexical ambiguity can be handled by introducing multiple grammar rules for an ambiguous word, like the word *"even"*, which can refer to an integer being divisible by two or a function f having the property $f(x) = f(-x)$. By making two rules that linearize to *"even"*, e.g. even_function and even_integer, we would get two different ASTs for the same string – one for each meaning.

Disambiguation With Semantic Annotations The semantic annotations in sTeX/FTML documents can help with disambiguation. For example, in a sufficiently annotated sTeX/FTML document, technical terms are explicitly disambiguated with the concept they refer to. Assuming a sufficiently annotated document, we therefore do not have to worry about lexical ambiguity – at least for technical terms.

The sTeX/FTML annotations can also help with other types of ambiguity. For example, the sentence

> An integer n is even iff n is divisible by 2.

could be interpreted as a theorem or a definition (epistemic ambiguity). In a definition, *"even"* would be annotated as a definiendum, but in a theorem it would be annotated as a symbol reference instead.

Ensuring Correct Results Despite Ambiguity As discussed above, during parsing we can get multiple ASTs for the same string because of ambiguity. Conversely, multiple ASTs can be linearized to the same string. This allows us to have correct results despite unresolved ambiguity. Consider, for example, an input sentence that gets parsed into two different ASTs, A and B. We apply some transformations to get A' and B'. If the linearizations of A' and B' are equal, it is ultimately irrelevant whether A or B were the correct reading. After all, the final document will only contain the linearization.

Of course, the result may be ambiguous – both A' and B' are possible readings –, but this can be considered a feature: natural language, including in mathematics, is ambiguous, and restricting the output to non-ambiguous sentences would be a severe limitation. With flexiformal substitution, we can get additional ambiguity from the substitution value itself, which increases the overall number of readings further: If we have a single substitution with readings $S_1, \ldots, S_n$ and input readings $I_1, \ldots, I_m$, we get $m \cdot n$ resulting ASTs (applying S_1 to I_1, S_1 to I_2, etc.). The final result has to be compatible with all of them. One option to increase the chances of getting a compatible result (which we have not yet implemented) is to optionally ignore some rewriting rules during simplification. For example, if one particular rewriting rule is not applicable in one of the ASTs, we may still get a linearization that is compatible with all other ASTs if we skip this rewriting rule in all other ASTs as well.

If no compatible linearization can be found, it would be up to the user to select the correct string from a list of options.

In the case of the running example (see subsection 2.3), our grammar gets two different readings (after filtering; see below) – one where the *"with"*-phrase is attached to *"sequence"*, and one where it is attached to *"edge"*. Both readings result in the same linearization after substitution and simplification.

Reducing the Number of Readings by Filtering Even though our pipeline can handle ambiguities to some extent, reducing the number of readings is still desirable. This can significantly improve performance by dampening the combinatorial explosion and, as a side effect, simplify the substitution and rewriting rules as fewer cases have to be considered. There are two ways to reduce the number of readings: grammar adjustments and filtering after parsing, which come with different trade-offs.

Let us illustrate this with the example string *"finite subset of* $\mathbb{N}$*"*, which in our grammar is called a Kind. There are two ways to read it (see Figure 5): either *"finite"* modifies *"subset of* $\mathbb{N}$*"*, or *"of* $\mathbb{N}$*"* is an argument of *"finite subset"*. We can adjust the grammar to enforce the latter reading by introducing a separate syntactic category, PreKind, that can only be modified by adjectives, and then turned into a Kind that can only be modified with prepositional arguments.

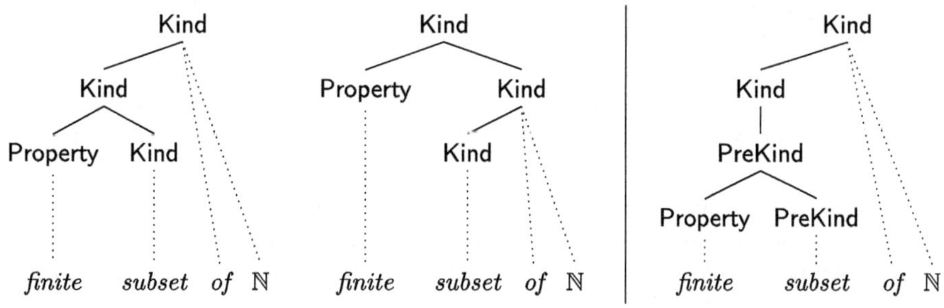

Fig. 5. Readings for an example phrase. For conciseness, syntactic categories are displayed instead of rule names. With a simple grammar, we get two different readings (*left*), but by introducing a new syntactic category, PreKind, we can enforce a single reading (*right*) at the cost of added complexity.

As a consequence of this, it can now be ambiguous where exactly an HTML tag is in the AST. For example, in *"<span>finite subset</span> of* $\mathbb{N}$*"*, the <span> tag can now be wrapped around *"finite subset"* either before or after the PreKind is turned into a Kind. To remedy this, we can simply filter out all ASTs where an HTML tag is wrapped around the AST node that turns a PreKind into a Kind.

In general, grammar adjustments lead to a more complex grammar that may be harder to understand and maintain. Filtering, on the other hand, keeps the grammar simple, but may lead to performance problems if too many readings are first generated and then filtered out. Furthermore, filtering must be done carefully to ensure that only redundant readings are removed. Finding the right balance between the two approaches remains work in progress.

3.5 State of the Implementation

The implementation described here is our fourth prototype for exploring the feasibility of rule-based flexiformal recontextualization of learning objects. Its design was informed by the previous prototype implementations. The first prototype was presented in [KS24], and used simple templates for recontextualization of sTeX content. The next prototype was developed in the context of a Bachelor's thesis of one of the authors (see [Kel24]), and explored flexiformal definition expansion with a grammar based on GF's Resource Grammar Library (see subsection 3.2). To overcome some of the challenges from processing LaTeX/sTeX sources directly, a third prototype was developed based on the FTML format. Ultimately, it became clear that a more semantic grammar as described in subsection 3.2 was necessary to develop robust rules for substitution and simplification, which led to the implementation described in this paper.

We have implemented all rules necessary for the running example from Section 2. We can handle the whole pipeline of AST-based relocalization by substitution and polishing via rewriting with the exception of variable renaming. In constrast to the deterministic/semantic rewriting rules, variable renaming has a strong cognitive flavor, which calls for different methods and quality measures; so we leave it to future work.

At this point, every new example requires work on the grammar and the substitution/rewriting rules. While the grammar and, to an extent, the substitution rules give the impression of converging, getting a reasonable coverage for the rewriting rules appears to be a much longer-term enterprise.

This shows that our overall architecture works in principle; but also highlights that we need extensions in the grammar and rewriting rules to scale to realistic applications in ALeA.

We are currently refactoring the prototype into a robust foundation for further development, which will be hosted at `https://github.com/FlexiFormal/relocalization`. The repository also contains links to the prototype implementations.

4 Conclusion & Future Work

We have shown how we can extend content generation – recontextualization; technically (theory) morphism application – from the formal to the flexiformal setting by parsing the mathematical vernacular in the source into ASTs, applying AST substitutions, and then fine-tuning the conciseness of the generated language with rewriting rules. We have shown the practical feasibility of the method with a GF grammar and a set of domain-specific AST rewriting rules.

While the implementation is still at a prototype stage – it can handle our running example and a few more – we feel confident that we can scale coverage to useful levels with more development. Most importantly, we feel that the overall information architecture has stabilized, and that this is a sufficient milestone that needs to be communicated to the CICM community, so that others may become involved.

While the GF grammar has proven easy to extend for new sentences, our "rational reconstruction" of recontextualization at the AST level has revealed a surprising extent and variety of simplifications needed at this level to account for the concise and rigorous mathematical language we see in mathematical texts written by humans. During our explorative work, we have collected a set of – mostly foundational – rewriting rules that cover cases like our running example (see [Kel+25, Appendix A]). We believe that this set is by no means complete outside the set-theoretic foundation, and we will have to extend it considerably to scale the AST-to-AST transformation. It is still an open task to systematically evaluate the scalability and coverage of those rules. To increase coverage we plan to continue collecting rules, involving all AI methods (both symbolic as well as statistical) at our disposal. However, in practice the process of finding new transformation rules is "co-recursive" with domain formalization, theory graph development, and grammar design, which makes the overall process hard to automate. We conjecture that the AST rewriting can be very useful for polishing and adapting all kinds of flexiformal transformation tasks.

Note that already the current rule-set is non-confluent. Thus their application is a non-trivial search/optimization problem where the quality measure is conciseness and readability of the generated language. How to manage/implement this scalably and independently of the concrete rule set – and that has to be our goal – is an open research question.

References

[Ber+23] M. Berges, J. Betzendahl, A. Chugh, M. Kohlhase, D. Lohr, and D. Müller. "Learning Support Systems based on Mathematical Knowledge Managment". In: *Intelligent Computer Mathematics (CICM) 2023*. Ed. by C. Dubois and M. Kerber. Vol. 14101. LNAI. Springer, 2023. DOI: `978-3-031-42753-4`. URL: `https://url.mathhub.info/CICM23ALEA`.

[GF] *GF - Grammatical Framework*. URL: `http://www.grammaticalframework.org` (visited on 09/27/2017).

[GFR] B. Bringert, T. Hallgren, and A. Ranta. *GF Resource Grammar Library: Synopsis*. URL: `https://www.grammaticalframework.org/lib/doc/synopsis/` (visited on 03/11/2020).

[HMU07] J. E. Hopcroft, R. Motwani, and J. D. Ullman. *Introduction to Automata Theory, Languages, and Computation.* 3rd ed. Pearson/Addison Wesley, 2007.

[Kel24] J. Kelber. "Flexiformal Definition Expansion and Parsing Mathematical Natural Language". Bachelor's thesis. FAU Erlangen-Nürnberg, 2024.

[Kel+25] J. Kelber, M. Kohlhase, J. F. Schaefer, and M. Schütz. "Reaping the Benefits of Modularization in Flexiformal Mathematics by GF-based AST Transformations (Extended Version)". 2025. URL: `https://kwarc.info/people/jfschaefer/pubs/2025-recontextualization-cicm-extended.pdf`.

[Koh13] M. Kohlhase. "The Flexiformalist Manifesto". In: *14th International Workshop on Symbolic and Numeric Algorithms for Scientific Computing (SYNASC 2012).* Ed. by A. Voronkov, V. Negru, T. Ida, T. Jebelean, D. Petcu, S. M. Watt, and D. Zaharie. Timisoara, Romania: IEEE Press, 2013, pp. 30–36. URL: `https://kwarc.info/kohlhase/papers/synasc13.pdf`.

[KS24] M. Kohlhase and M. Schütz. "Reusing Learning Objects via Theory Morphisms". In: *Intelligent Computer Mathematics (CICM) 2024.* Ed. by A. Kohlhase and L. Kovacz. Vol. 14960. LNAI. Springer, 2024, pp. 165–182. DOI: `10.1007/978-3-031-66997-2_10`. URL: `https://url.mathhub.info/relocalization/`.

[Mar03] J. Martin. *Introduction to Languages and the Theory of Computation.* McGraw-Hill higher education. McGraw-Hill, 2003.

[MK22] D. Müller and M. Kohlhase. "sTeX3 – A LaTeX-based Ecosystem for Semantic/Active Mathematical Documents". In: *TUGboat; TUG 2022 Conference Proceedings* 43.2 (2022). Ed. by K. Berry, pp. 197–201. URL: `https://kwarc.info/people/dmueller/pubs/tug22.pdf`.

[MRK18] D. Müller, F. Rabe, and M. Kohlhase. "Theories as Types". In: *9th International Joint Conference on Automated Reasoning.* Ed. by D. Galmiche, S. Schulz, and R. Sebastiani. Springer Verlag, 2018. URL: `https://kwarc.info/kohlhase/papers/ijcar18-records.pdf`.

[Mül23] D. Müller. "An HTML/CSS schema for TeX primitives – generating high-quality responsive HTML from generic TeX". In: *TUGboat; TUG 2023 Conference Proceedings* 44.2 (2023), pp. 275–286. URL: `https://kwarc.info/people/dmueller/pubs/tug23.pdf`.

[Mü] D. Müller. FLAMS – *Flexiformal Annotation Management System.* URL: `https://github.com/flexiformal/flams` (visited on 07/24/2025).

[Pfe01] F. Pfenning. "Logical Frameworks". In: *Handbook of Automated Reasoning.* Ed. by A. Robinson and A. Voronkov. Vol. I and II. Elsevier Science and MIT Press, 2001.

[Ran04] A. Ranta. "Grammatical Framework — A Type-Theoretical Grammar Formalism". In: *Journal of Functional Programming* 14.2 (2004), pp. 145–189.

[Rew] *Collection of flexiformal rewriting rules.* URL: `https://github.com/flexiformal/rewriting-rules` (visited on 07/25/2025).

[SMG] *SMGloM: A Semantic Multilingual Glossary Resource for Mathematics.* URL: `http://gl.mathhub.info/smglom` (visited on 07/24/2025).

[ST09] J. Sakarovitch and R. Thomas. *Elements of Automata Theory.* Cambridge University Press, 2009.

[Wen07] M. Wenzel. "Isabelle/Isar – a generic framework for human-readable proof documents". In: *From Insight to Proof – Festschrift in Honour of Andrzej Trybulec* (2007). Ed. by R. Matuszewski and A. Zalewska.

Semantic Authoring in a Flexiformal Context — Bulk Annotation of Rigorous Documents

Michael Kohlhase and Jan Frederik Schaefer(✉)

Computer Science, FAU Erlangen Nürnberg, Erlangen, Germany
jan.frederik.schaefer@fau.de

Abstract. Semantic annotations enable services that make the knowledge in documents more accessible. In the case of ALeA, an adaptive learning assistant we use as a case study, they enable, for example, guided tours and practice problems tailored to the learner's competencies. However, the cost of semantic authoring is substantial and tool support is limited.

In this paper we discuss the nature of the semantic authoring task and argue that, while sharing aspects of both classical (informal) authoring and formal authoring, it is a task of its own that needs special editing support facilities. We present and evaluate a simple utility that supports the process of annotating technical terms with semantic references to a flexiformal content commons and increases annotation productivity by almost an order of magnitude.

Keywords: semantic authoring · flexiformality · annotation · snify· sTeX· ALeA

1 Introduction

Arguably, handling large document collections is a key factor in our knowledge-driven society and economy. There are two main contenders for machine support in this area: symbolic/logic-based technologies and statistical/machine-learning-based AI, e.g. via LLMs or chatbots. They have complementary strengths and challenges: ML-based approaches can be trained on all data of the Internet, but face challenges in precision and explainability. Symbolic technologies, on the other hand, offer precision and explainability, but face scalability challenges – in particular because of the cost of semantic authoring, which we discuss in this paper.

As a case study, we will use adaptive learning assistants for STEM subjects in higher education, concretely the ALeA system [Ber+23]. We contend that machine-learning based technologies are largely unsuitable for this task – at least until they reach the precision and explainability required by the ethics of teaching[1] – while the scope of specific domains is just narrow enough that symbolic approaches are viable. Conventional (LaTeX-based) lecture materials can

[1] Incidentally, the AI Act of the European Union [Eua] classifies education as a high-risk area and thus mandates high requirements of explainability, accountability, and human oversight for educational AI applications.

V. de Paiva and P. Koepke (Eds.): CICM 2025, LNAI 16136, pp. 208–221, 2026.
https://doi.org/10.1007/978-3-032-07021-0_12

essentially be directly imported into ALeA, but its ability to generate learner-adaptive learning objects – instrumented with learning support interactions – depends on semantic annotations. These can be embedded in LaTeX documents using the sTeX package [KM22; sTeX]. In this paper, we will mostly focus on annotating terms with the semantic concepts they refer to, but sTeX supports a much wider range of annotations, such as annotating problems with the learning prerequisites and objectives or annotating the defining phrase (definiens) in concept definitions, and could, in principle, even be used for full formalization. As sTeX supports the spectrum from informal (un-annotated) to fully formalized content, we say that sTeX content is **flexiformal**.

The **sTeX/ALeA content commons** consists of SMGloM [Gin+16], a glossary acting as the domain model for semantic annotations, as well as re-usable lecture materials such as lecture slides and problems. The sheer size of the commons is one of the key challenges for authors: SMGloM contains definitions of over 5400 concepts in multiple languages, created and maintained by over 30 contributors. Additionally, there are roughly 4900 semantically annotated lecture slides and 4000 problems – mostly from the area of computer science.

Overview and Contribution In this paper, we argue that semantic/flexiformal authoring shares aspects with both informal and fully formal authoring, but is nevertheless a distinct task requiring special tool support (Section 2). Using sTeX/ALeA as an exemplary case study, we will provide an overview of the authoring support (Section 3) and then describe and evaluate one new, concrete tool, snify, that supports the annotation of terms with the semantic concepts they refer to (Section 4). Afterwards, we discuss on-going work to integrate snify better into the sTeX/ALeA ecosystem and content commons (Section 5). The paper ends with a brief discussion of related work (Section 6) and the conclusion (Section 7).

Acknowledgments The work reported in this article was conducted as part of the VoLL-KI project (see `https://voll-ki.de`) funded by the German Research/Education Ministry (BMFTR) under grant 16DHBKI089.

2 Semantic Authoring in a Content Commons

Before we discuss semantic authoring in general, let us introduce a concrete example from the sTeX/ALeA world.

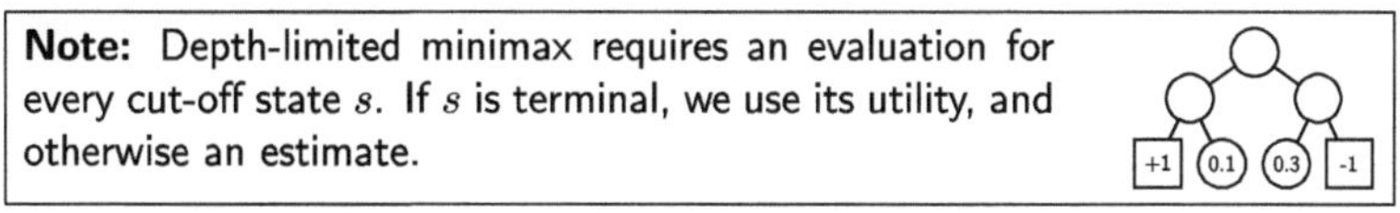

Fig. 1. An unannotated learning object from an AI lecture

2.1 Running Example: Annotating "terminal"

With sTeX, authors can add semantic references to technical terms, which enables straightforward learning support services like showing the definition of a term, but also informs the system about the content/prerequisites of a learning object. Adding these references is a key practical problem when converting presentational LaTeX course materials into semantic documents.

Take for instance a learning object like the paragraph in Figure 1, where we want to annotate the term "terminal" with the (semantic) concept of "a goal state of a search problem". The latter can either be defined earlier in the course or in the domain model (or both). Concretely this is about converting the unannotated LaTeX string

```
3 \blue{Note:} Depth-limited minimax requires an evaluation for every
4 cut-off state $s$. If $s$ is terminal, we use its utility,
5 and otherwise an estimate.
```

into the partially annotated

```
1 \importmodule[smglom/search]{mod?search-problem}
2 [...]
3 \blue{Note:} Depth-limited minimax requires an evaluation for every
4 cut-off state $s$. If $s$ is \sr{goal state}{terminal}, we use its utility,
5 and otherwise an estimate.
```

where the author has annotated the word "terminal" with the concept it refers to via the sTeX macro \sr{⟨⟨*symbol*⟩⟩}{⟨⟨*verbalization*⟩⟩}. In sTeX, concepts are represented by **symbols**, which are identified globally and unambiguously by a URI that includes a **namespace**, a **module name**, and a **symbol name**. A **verbalization** is the natural language rendering of a concept. Verbalizations are, of course, language-dependent and can vary between subdomains and communities of practice, even if the underlying symbol is the same. In our example, the verbalization "terminal [state]" was annotated with the symbol with name goal state. It comes from the module with name search-problem in the namespace smglom/search/mod imported via the \importmodule macro in line 1. As the symbol name goal state is unique in the imports here it suffices to use a relative URI in the \sr annotation. If the symbol name and the desired verbalization coincide (as they often do in English), the short-hand macro \sn can be used (e.g. as \sn{utility} for "utility").

The annotation refers to a definition in the domain model module shown in Figure 2. The \definame and \definiendum in lines 5–6 introduce the verbalizations "goal state" and "terminal state" for the goal state symbol introduced by the \symdecl∗ declaration in line 3.

2.2 Annotation Workflows and Requirements

To annotate the word "terminal" in the document above, the author has to *i*) be aware that it is a technical term, *ii*) that the module from Figure 2 exists,

Definition 0.1. A **search problem** $\Pi := \langle \mathcal{S}, \mathcal{A}, \mathcal{T}, \mathcal{I}, \mathcal{G} \rangle$ consists of a set $\mathcal{S}$ of **states**, a set $\mathcal{A}$ of **actions**, and a **transition model** $\mathcal{T} : \mathcal{A} \times \mathcal{S} \to \mathcal{P}(\mathcal{S})$ that assigns to any action $a \in \mathcal{A}$ and state $s \in \mathcal{S}$ a set of **successor states.**

Certain states in $\mathcal{S}$ are designated as **goal states** (also called **terminal state**) ($\mathcal{G} \subseteq \mathcal{S}$) and **initial states** $\mathcal{I} \subseteq \mathcal{S}$.

```
\begin{smodule}[title=Search Problem]{search-problem}
[... some imports ...]
\symdecl*{goal state}
\begin{sdefinition}
  [...] Certain \sns{state} are [...] \definame[post=s]{goal state} [...]
  (also called \definiendum{goal state}{terminal states}).
\end{sdefinition}
\end{smodule}
```

Fig. 2. Simplified definition of "goal state" from the domain model

iii) know the symbol URI, *iv*) manage redundancy of the imports – i.e. only adding the \importmodule directive if it is not already (recursively) implied and possibly removing directives that become redundant by the new one. A rather daunting task for a lecture with 50,000 – 100,000 words in notes and slides and ca. 10–15 % of them technical terms.[2]

While annotation needs to happen during authoring and curation of documents, the majority of annotation tasks in practice concern the semantic augmentation of existing documents (**bulk annotation**) with respect to an existing semantic domain model. In any case, it is probably useful to separate the roles of author and semantic annotator conceptually, even though they may well be the same person in practice.

The most important resource for annotators is a verbalization to symbol URI mapping – we call it the **annotation catalog** – either implicitly in the mind of the annotator or explicitly as a technical artifact, which allows to *i*) identify the known technical terms, *ii*) to map them to the corresponding symbols, and *iii*) manage the necessary import directives. This catalog can be harvested from the **formal declarations** (\definiendum, \sr, \begin/\end{smodule} and \importmodule, etc.) of the domain model and existing documents in the semantic corpus.

The annotation catalog is naturally language-specific. sTeX already supports multilinguality:

[2] Estimates based on some of our own lectures materials ranging from a small introductory lecture (ca. 30,000 words) to a large two-semester lecture on AI (ca. 140,000 words). The 10–15 % estimate appears to be relatively consistent across our lectures but depends on the author's intuition about what a technical term is. Other lecturers or lectures on other topics may have very different values.

- Documents have explicit language annotations (usually in form of the file extension .⟪*lang*⟫.tex where ⟪*lang*⟫ is the ISO-639 language identifier).
- Modules in the domain model include translations that share the formal declarations with another module. This induces a "translation relation" for verbalizations in different languages with the same symbol URI.

In practice, the annotation catalog for languages other than English is often inadequate as

i) the domain model may not have translations in that language – especially for the "smaller" languages, and
ii) symbol names, usually English words, cannot be used as verbalizations.

In this situation, we usually have to invest in establishing a suitable catalog – e.g. by providing translations (or at least dictionary information) in the domain model or delineating modules and annotating definienda that the domain model does not cover in the documents to be annotated.

2.3 Semantic Authoring as a Distinct Task

We contend that semantic authoring is a task that is distinct from traditional (informal) authoring and authoring fully formal corpora (e.g. programs or formalizations), while sharing some of the aspects of either.

Traditional, informal authoring In traditional authoring, e.g. of a scientific article or a textbook, the domain model – a highly structured model of the domain of discourse – is in the authors' heads, and is partially verbalized e.g. in the preliminaries section or the main sections of the respective article. The content is informal (usually a natural language like English augmented with technical jargon, formulae, tables, and diagrams) and designed for processing via the brain of a colleague or student – in any case, a human who shares a canonical part of the domain model with the authors. Consequently a large part of the authoring challenge lies in predicting the state and extent of the domain model of the reader and creating text that bridges the gap between the reader's domain model and the payload content of the article – the knowledge the article or textbook intends to impart – ideally using the technical vocabulary the reader is familiar with to reduce this gap. Tool support for traditional authoring is minimal and usually restricted to spell/grammar-checkers and online thesauri if we disregard LLM-based writing/formulation support for now. In our experience, LLM-based authoring support is less helpful in technical documents than in everyday writing.

Formal Authoring In programming, the content commons is given formally in the form of the libraries of the respective programming language. Correspondingly the authored content – a program – is also formal and intended for processing by a computer, for which the formality is a prerequisite. Formal authoring is usually supported by an integrated development environment (IDE) that makes use of the fully formal content and offers services like semantic highlighting, tab completion, jumping to variable declarations, function definitions, and interface definitions, as well as refactoring support. All of these rely on a syntactic/semantic analysis of the formal content. The situation is very similar for authoring of formal knowledge, e.g. in program verification or the formalization of mathematics.

Semantic Authoring In semantic authoring, e.g. the sTeX sources of educational content for the ALeA system presented above, the base of the text is classical narrative text to which most of the constraints of classical authoring apply. The exception is the tailoring to the competencies of the assumed reader that traditionally happens during authoring, but which can (partially) be automated by systems like ALeA. Note that it is not a restriction that ALeA is initially targeted to tertiary education; the underlying mechanisms generalize to all scientific communication and technical documents. After all, the purpose is to transfer information (instruct), even if the roles of instructor and instructee are not predetermined by academic seniority.

In addition to the base text, semantic authoring also has to provide the semantic annotations that drive the personalization and interaction downstream. Techniques from formal authoring could help here, but in contrast to formal authoring, we cannot just trigger the IDE functionality by the formal syntax, as the authored content is – so far – informal and the content commons (the target of the annotations) is itself only flexiformal. In a way, we need a local flexiformalization workflow that helps authors bridge the informal-formal gap. We have experimented with LLM-based generation of annotated (sTeX) content, but the results have been disappointing so far.

A distinctive feature of semantic authoring that is not apparent at the first glance is that the added investment in annotation moves the sweet spot in the re-use/customize trade-off towards sharing and interoperability. In our experience sufficiently annotated documents can be automatically customized if the semantics has multiple notations/verbalizations/presentations. Consider for instance course materials on complex arithmetic, which become re-usable across the electrical engineering/mathematics border if the imaginary unit in formulae is represented e.g. by a semantic macro \imaginaryunit, which can alternatively be presented as i (for uses in maths) or j (for EE uses). As a consequence semantic authoring is more geared towards creating reusable/shareable document fragments organized in central or federated repositories and hubs. This is quite similar to the formal authoring arena, where we see a tendency towards massively shared math libraries in formal systems and package/library hubs for programming libraries. Semantic authoring support systems should therefore facilitate the logistics of using and curating shared libraries.

3 Tool Support for Semantic Authoring in sTeX/ALeA

Semantic authoring can "inherit" tool support from both informal and formal authoring. In the case of sTeX, we can re-use spell checkers for traditional informal authoring. There also is prototypical support for authoring ALeA content in Microsoft Word with the WOIDE plugin [AK24], which allows authors to use Word's spell checker and grammar checker.

On the formal side, there is a custom VSCode IDE plugin for sTeX [sIDE] that analyzes annotations on the fly, displays the underlying reference semantics, reports errors and redundancies, and even offers a concept search interface. But such features only support existing annotations and are, therefore, of limited use when creating new annotations, which arguably is the most time consuming aspect of semantic authoring.

How the annotation process can be supported depends on the particular semantic framework, the specific annotations we want to support, and the semantics embedded in the content commons. In sTeX/ALeA, we primarily annotate formulae and technical terms with pointers to their definienda. A tool for supporting semantic authoring of formulae via notations has been presented by Vrečar et al. in [VWK24], so we disregard this important aspect here. The tool uses a grammar to parse informal, presentation-focused formulae (e.g. `A\times B`) into abstract syntax trees based on semantic macros defined in sTeX, which can then replace the original formula (e.g. `\cart{A,B}` for the Cartesian product of sets). In the case of ambiguity, authors can pick the correct reading in a graphical user interface that visualizes the different abstract syntax trees.

Efficient support for the annotation of technical terms in natural language has been elusive so far – we will address this in the next section.

4 The snify System

The snify[3] utility [sTt] is a simple command-line tool that creates a catalog of symbol-verbalization pairs (see also Section 2.2), analyzes sTeX source files, and then steps through all word occurrences in the document that match a verbalization in the catalog. Matching is based on word stems using off-the-shelf stemmers, which allows us to e.g. match "utilities" with "utility". For each matched word, the user is presented with an annotation choice and interactions that allow to fine-tune the wordwise annotation workflow. The interface is inspired by traditional spell checkers like ispell [Isp]. Figure 3 shows a typical situation.

The annotator can choose an annotation by typing the corresponding choice number, in this case 0. The little green check-mark indicates that the relevant module is already imported. Otherwise snify would offer the annotator the choice to import it – if we are in a module context – or to add a `\usemodule` directive, either in the local environment or at the top-level.

To skip the word, the user can type s; s! skips it until the end of the file, and S will skip it in future runs as well by appending a snify-specific comment to the file. There are numerous other commands, e.g. to adjust the selection, search for alternative annotation targets, or view/edit the file introducing one of the choices.

[3] From "`\sn`-ify"; "`\sn`" is a frequently used sTeX short-hand macro for term annotations.

```
| File 1/1            | Annotations added: 0         |
                          minimax-remarks.tex
 21      \sr{depth limit}{Depth-limited} \sn{minimax} requires an
 22      \sr{evaluation function}{evaluation} for every \sn{cut-off state} $s$.
 23      If $s$ is terminal, we use its \sn{utility}. Otherwise, we use an estimate.
 24 \end{minipage}
 25 \hskip 0.5cm

Commands:   enter h (help) to see all available commands
  [h]elp
  [q]uit
  [s]kip once
  [0] ✓ smglom/search mod/search-problem?search-problem/searchprob-module?goal state
  [1] ✓ smglom/computing mod?termination?terminate
  [2] ✓ smglom/computing mod?termination?termination
  [3] ✓ smglom/graphs mod?initial-terminal?terminal
  [4] ✗ smglom/calculus mod?Noetherian-order?Noetherian
  [5] ✓ smglom/grammar mod?grammar?terminal symbol
  [6] ✗ smglom/computing mod?terminal?terminal
  [7] ✓ smglom/computing mod?termination?terminating
  [8] ✗ smglom/grammar mod/grammar?grammar/grammar-module?terminal
>>> 
```

Fig. 3. snify in Action: Annotating the word "terminal"

snify is usually called on a set of files – e.g. in a directory or math archive – which together form a **session**, which can be interrupted and resumed without having to re-do all the s skips. Alternatively, snify can be called e.g. on the top-level lecture notes; then the session consists of all (transitively) included files. Another productivity feature is a focus mode that can be used to only annotate a particular word in the rest of the file, session, or the whole sTeX/ALeA corpus before resuming regular annotation. This reduces the cognitive overhead from switching between different words and symbol lists.

defianno: Definition Handling as a Pre-process for Multilingual Documents. As a companion to snify, we have defianno, a prototype tool for annotating definienda in documents that were originally authored without semantic annotations. It can be configured to consider different LaTeX macros to identify definienda (e.g. \emph or \textbf), and then steps through them as snify does. For each potential definiendum, the user can then use fuzzy search to find the corresponding symbol in the domain model and replace the original macro with an sTeX definiendum annotation. This populates the catalog with verbalizations relevant to the document, making subsequent snify runs more effective, especially for documents in languages that are not well covered by the domain model (i.e. not English).

Evaluation In our experience, snify's step-through workflow for annotating term references is almost an order of magnitude more efficient than writing the annotations and imports by hand.[4] Given the sheer number of term annotations (see Fig-

[4] The precise productivity gain depends on the annotator's familiarity with the domain model (searching and identifying the right symbol is time-consuming) but also on other factors like the typing speed. Measurements are complicated by the fact that authors tend to annotate more terms when using snify. We have observed speed-ups

ure 4), this results in a considerable productivity gain. For annotators unfamiliar with the domain model, the unassisted annotation task is almost infeasible, and the average unfamiliarity naturally grows with the domain model. The symbol disambiguation process – on average a word induces 4.1 choices – is still manageable, requires considerable concentration and domain knowledge, but little knowledge of the domain model flexiformalization.

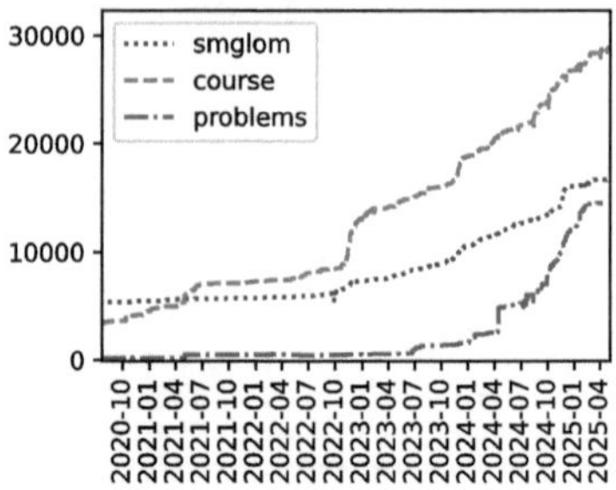

Fig. 4. Number of annotated terms in the sTeX/ALeA commons over time.

The command-line interface is simple and responsive and gives all the necessary information in a single glance if the underlying shell area exceeds ca. 80×35 characters. It is very much geared towards annotating existing documents with respect to a relatively complete – pre-existing – domain model, and it seems unlikely that a more sophisticated UI would add value for this use-case.

For less complete domain models we have to skip too many terms that should ultimately be annotated and annotation effectiveness suffers. This is currently the case for all non-English languages in the sTeX corpus we work with. Coverage in German is only about half of that of English in the domain model and we can already see the practical effects. The defianno tool can mitigate this partially by providing verbalizations for the definienda in the document, but it does not help with terms that are not explicitly defined in the document.

Finally, the current interface is not well-suited for on-the-fly annotation while authoring. For that, the underlying information (the symbol/verbalization pairs harvested from the domain model) can be integrated into any IDE. In fact we plan to do this for the next version of the sTeX plugin for VSCode [sIDE]. For now, the typical workflow of early adopters is to first write the document (e.g. a set of quiz questions) without annotations, and then run snify to annotate the new content.

5 Scaling snify to the Flexiformal Content Commons

One practical problem with the snify system as presented so far is that it only harvests symbol/verbalization pairs from sTeX files on the local file system. This means that, for effective annotation, users (have to) download the whole content commons and keep it updated – an assumption/requirement that becomes increasingly impractical as the sTeX ecosystem grows.

The general situation is that on the one hand there is a constantly growing, shared **content commons** of public math archives – currently 200 with about 14 000 sTeX files – that are regularly converted to FTML (Flexiformal

over IDE-based annotation ranging from 3 (for an expert knowing the domain model by heart) to 13 (for a beginner). The focus mode further increases productivity when considering the overall corpus quality.

Text Markup Language) and served on `https://MathHub.info`. On the other hand, authors are working on

i) a set of local working copies of the archives – with the intention of publishing them on MathHub.info – and their dependencies (they need to be local since pdflatex cannot deal with remote files) and
ii) possibly a set of private archives (e.g. papers under development or exam problems/solutions).

This situation is familiar from software development and also from e.g. the LaTeX ecosystem. Semantic authoring – and thus the snify utility – inherits the requirements from both.

To cope with this situation, we are planning to extend the brand-new FLAMS system [Mü], which, among other things, powers `https://MathHub.info`, so that it provides the data necessary to create a symbol/verbalization catalog. Note that FLAMS works directly on FTML, which is generated from sTeX input by rusTeX and exported from annotated MS Word files via WOIDE [AK24]. There are two more systems that could profit from this: The CPoint system that allows annotating MS PowerPoint presentations with the sTeX ontology and can already generate a precursor of FTML [Koh08], and a semantic extension of Markdown we are developing as a lightweight alternative to sTeX; it also transforms into FTML instead of plain HTML.

In local/private archives, the snify harvester needs to work directly on the sTeX sources. Currently, snify uses a custom Python implementation for harvesting the verbalization cache, but we are in the late stages of developing a new snify version using the FLAMS **linter** – a simple sTeX parser that drives the LSP functionality of the sTeX IDE plugins for VSCode and emacs. The analog for this on the WOIDE side is still under development; it could be based on FTML generated by WOIDE, or WOIDE could directly export symbol/verbalization pairs into the snify verbalization cache.

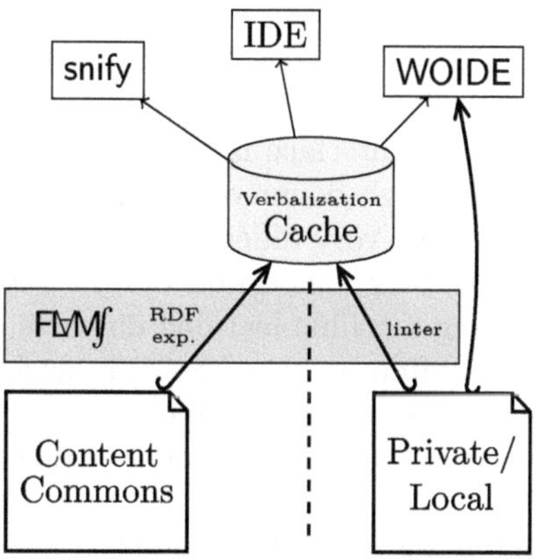

Fig. 5. Architecture

In this situation, the main functionality of snify would be to maintain the verbalization cache and answer front-end queries for verbalizations efficiently so that we can power various front-ends from that. These include

i) The traditional text/terminal-based snify UI for bulk annotation,
ii) the sTeX IDEs in VSCode and emacs that could supply annotation support during editing, and
iii) WOIDE, which can be seen as a semantic authoring IDE based on MS Word.

Note that, implemented this broadly, snify could provide additional logistic services: If a pair is chosen in an annotation, snify can then automatically download the corresponding archive and its dependencies so that the annotated file can be formatted with `pdflatex` or rusTEX locally.

6 Related Work

The phrase "semantic authoring" has been used in the context of the semantic web with varying meanings ([KA13] provides an overview of the tool support). This includes ontology authoring (e.g. with Protégé [Mus15]), which we would classify as formal authoring, and metadata annotation (e.g. the title, author, and creation date of a document with the Dublin Core vocabulary [DC]), which is a somewhat different concern. A closer match is the annotation of informal content with references to a domain ontology (e.g. [GS10]), but there are some differences to our situation with sTEX/ALeA: The domain ontology would be a fully formal target – possibly containing verbalizations – while in our case the target is flexiformal. Furthermore, sTEX has a module system, which requires dependency management during authoring. A similar application requiring semantic authoring are semantic wikis, which enrich regular/syntactic wikis with semantic information (see e.g. [KVV06]).

Another example of formal/informal authoring is code documentation. Often, the documentation is embedded in the code itself, e.g. in Python docstrings, which may follow a specific machine-readable format. IDEs, which are primarily used for (formal) code authoring, typically provide some support, e.g. by generating stubs and by extending refactoring support to (the machine-readable parts of) the documentation like parameter names and types.

snify's interface is inspired by traditional spell checkers like ispell [Isp] that step through documents and suggest corrections for misspelled words, which is of course a very different underlying task.

The bulk annotation workflow for existing informal text is also relevant when creating machine learning datasets, e.g. for named entity recognition. There are many (often browser-based) tools for this task; a prominent example is brat [BR] for text annotation. Technical documents with tables, complex formulae, etc. cannot easily be expressed as sequences of words and require different annotation tools like e.g. AnnoTize [PS23] that supports the annotation of HTML documents containing MathML formulae.

In all cases, the setting, solution, and resulting workflows differ from the one presented in this paper. The WissKI system [GS10] has a rudimentary text edition facility that allows annotating documents with ontology – mostly ABox – references; this may be the nearest match to our snify system.

7 Conclusion

In this paper we have presented the semantic authoring task in a flexiformal context using the sTEX corpus and the adaptive learning assistant ALeA as a concrete example. We have shown that it differs from both classical authoring and formal authoring in terms of the necessary system support. As an example of specialized authoring support, we have presented snify, a command-line tool that bridges the gap between informal text and formal/semantic symbols in sTeX. It is open source; the code and documentation are available at [sTt]. Given the impact of snify on the authoring process, we are currently working on a deeper integration of snify into the sTeX ecosystem and content commons as described in Section 5.

Future Work snify depends on the existence of a comprehensive annotation catalog, which is a severe limitation for languages other than English. A potential solution would be to extend snify with a machine learning-based tool for identifying unannotated technical terms that are not in the catalog. The user could then pick a symbol for the annotation, which would add a verbalization to the catalog. In an earlier (pre-snify) attempt, we used named-entity recognition (NER) for classification of "likely annotation candidate words" [Hut23]. However, this classification was not precise enough in the distinction between technical terms and ordinary noun phrases to be practical on its own. A combination with snify's catalog-based approach might change the trade-offs involved.

References

[AK24] A. Adrian and M. Kohlhase. "WOIDE: Semantic Annotation in MS Word — Scaling Mathematical User Interfaces beyond LaTeX". In: *MathUI 2024: The 15th Workshop on Mathematical User Interfaces.* Ed. by K. Nakasho and J. F. Schaefer. 2024. URL: `https://kwarc.info/kohlhase/papers/mathui24-woide.pdf`.

[Ber+23] M. Berges, J. Betzendahl, A. Chugh, M. Kohlhase, D. Lohr, and D. Müller. "Learning Support Systems based on Mathematical Knowledge Managment". In: *Intelligent Computer Mathematics (CICM) 2023.* Ed. by C. Dubois and M. Kerber. Vol. 14101. LNAI. Springer, 2023. DOI: 978-3-031-42753-4. URL: `https://url.mathhub.info/CICM23ALEA`.

[BR] *brat rapid annotation tool.* URL: `http://brat.nlplab.org` (visited on 04/06/2023).

[DC] *Dublin Core Metadata Initiative.* URL: `http://www.dublincore.org` (visited on 05/22/2025).

[Eua] *The EU Artificial Intelligence Act – Up-to-date developments and analyses of the EU AI Act.* URL: `https://artificialintelligenceact.eu/` (visited on 07/02/2025)

[Gin+16] D. Ginev et al. "The SMGloM Project and System. Towards a Terminology and Ontology for Mathematics". In: *Mathematical Software - ICMS 2016 - 5th International Congress.* Ed. by G.-M. Greuel, T. Koch, P. Paule, and A. Sommese. Vol. 9725. LNCS. Springer, 2016. DOI: 10.1007/978-3-319-42432-3. URL: `https://kwarc.info/kohlhase/papers/icms16-smglom.pdf`

[GS10] G. Goerz and M. Scholz. "Adaptation of nlp techniques to cultural heritage research and documentation". In: *Journal of computing and information technology* 18.4 (2010), pp. 317–324.

[Hut23] P. Hutterer. "Integrating automated semantic annotation using machine learning into authoring workflows for flexiformal documents". M.Sc. Thesis. FAU Erlangen-Nürnberg, Apr. 12, 2023. URL: `https://gl.kwarc.info/supervision/MSc-archive/-/blob/master/2023/HuttererPhilipp.pdf`

[Isp] *ISPELL*. URL: `https://www.cs.hmc.edu/~geoff/ispell-man.html` (visited on 05/15/2025).

[KA13] A. Khalili and S. Auer. "User interfaces for semantic authoring of textual content: A systematic literature review". In: *Journal of web semantics* 22 (2013), pp. 1–18.

[KM22] M. Kohlhase and D. Müller. "System Description: sTeX3 – A LATEX-based Ecosystem for Semantic/Active Mathematical Documents". *In: Intelligent Computer Mathematics (CICM) 2022.* Ed. by K. Buzzard and T. Kutsia. Vol. 13467. LNAI. Springer, 2022, pp. 184–188. URL: `https://kwarc.info/people/dmueller/pubs/cicm22stexsd.pdf`.

[Koh08] A. Kohlhase. "Semantic Interaction Design: Composing Knowledge with CPoint". PhD thesis. Computer Science, Universität Bremen, Apr. 2008. URL: `https://kwarc.info/ako/pubs/AKo_Promo.pdf`.

[KVV06] M. Krötzsch, D. Vrandečić, and M. Völkel. "Semantic MediaWiki". In: *The Semantic Web - ISWC 2006*. Ed. by I. Cruz, S. Decker, D. Allemang, C. Preist, D. Schwabe, P. Mika, M. Uschold, and L. M. Aroyo. Berlin, Heidelberg: Springer Berlin Heidelberg, 2006, pp. 935– 942.

[Mus15] M. A. Musen. "The protégé project: a look back and a look forward". In: *AI matters* 1.4 (2015), pp. 4–12.

[Mü] D. Müller. FLAMS – *Flexiformal Annotation Management System. git* repository. URL: `https://github.com/flexiformal/flams` (visited on 07/24/2025).

[PS23] L. Panzer and J. F. Schaefer. "AnnoTize: A Flexible Annotation Tool for Documents with Mathematical Formulae". In: *MathUI 2023: The 14th Workshop on Mathematical User Interfaces*. Ed. by A. Kohlhase. accepted. 2023. URL: `https://kwarc.info/people/jfschaefer/pubs/2023-annotize-mathui.pdf`.

[sIDE] *sTeX Plugin for VSCode*. Git repository. URL `https://github.com/slatex/sTeX-IDE` (visited on 08/01/2024).

[sTeX] *sTeX: A semantic Extension of TeX/LaTeX*. URL: `https://github.com/sLaTeX/sTeX` (visited on 05/11/2020).

[sTt] *sLaTeX/stextools – Lightweight Tools for sTeX Authoring and Management.* Git repository. URL: `https://github.com/slatex/stextools` (visited on 11/12/2024).

[VWK24] L. Vrečar, J.Wells, and F. Kamareddine. "Towards Semantic Markup of Mathematical Documents via User Interaction". In: *Intelligent Computer Mathematics (CICM) 2024.* Ed. by A. Kohlhase and L. Kovacz. Vol. 14960. LNAI. Springer, 2024, pp. 223–240. DOI: 10.1007/978-3-031-66997-2

Lightweight Realms

Michael Kohlhase, Florian Rabe, and Marcel Schütz(✉)

FAU Erlangen-Nürnberg, Erlangen, Germany
marcel.schuetz@fau.de

Abstract. During formalization – e.g. of Mathematics – we have to take many decisions that informal mathematics leaves (and can leave) open. In particular, often there are multiple isomorphic ways of formalizing a set of axioms between which mathematicians can switch seamlessly. But this can impede beginners from fully understanding a domain, and it has proved difficult to mimic the same seamlessness in formalized mathematics, hindering interoperability between systems and libraries.
Realms have been proposed as an explicit representation of collections of isomorphic theories and conservative extensions, but have proven difficult to implement and manage. Therefore, here we introduce a more specialized definition that, in our experience, covers a large set of practically relevant examples. The central concept is that of a base of a theory: a subtheory that uniquely determines the entire theory. This allows us to represent an entire realm as a single theory with multiple bases. We show that many foundational concepts can be elegantly represented as such basic realms. The resulting formalism offers a good abstraction level to deal with (the consequences of) differing choices in the literature and in formal libraries, thus reducing interoperability problems, while keeping the formalizations simple.

1 Introduction

It is the very nature of formalization that it makes implicit knowledge and ideas sufficiently explicit such that they can be treated by formal methods: algorithms and interactions that only rely on the form of the representation – nothing else. During the formalization process, we have to take quite a few choices that are usually left open in informal communication of ideas. The choices that are induced by particular formal systems – we call them **foundational choices** – are relatively well-understood and are generally unavoidable. For example, a quotient set can be represented by its canonical projection, by the partition of the carrier set into equivalence classes, by its defining equivalence relation, or in some cases by a function that returns canonical representatives. Sometimes only some of the choices can be represented by the underlying logical system: E.g., we can represent partial functions using undefined values, option types, functional relations, or default values, and in particular the first option is often not supported.

A particular motivating example from our teaching was the definition of a transition model δ as used in Turing machines or automata. If we want to make this rigorous, we have to choose among several distinct options that include:

V. de Paiva and P. Koepke (Eds.): CICM 2025, LNAI 16136, pp. 222–239, 2026.
https://doi.org/10.1007/978-3-032-07021-0_13

1. δ is a relation in $(\mathcal{S} \times \mathcal{A}) \times \mathcal{S}$ with elements of the form ((current state, action), successor state) (e.g. [Sak09, chapter 1.1.1]),
2. δ is a function from $\mathcal{S} \times \mathcal{A}$ to $\mathcal{PS}$ mapping (current state, action) to (set of possible successor states) (e.g. [HMU07, chapter 2.3.2]).

While obviously isomorphic, each particular choice entails a different treatment down the line. For example, to later define deterministic transition systems, we say that δ is a partial function (case 1) or that $|\delta(s,a)| \leq 1$ for all s, a (case 2). In the latter case, an additional definition is now needed for the partial function δ' mapping (s, a) to the unique element of $\delta(s, a)$ (if any), together with a remark that δ' will – by abuse of notation – also be written as δ. These down-the-line choices can have major influence on the overall exposition in, e.g., a textbook.

In [Tao22], Terence Tao divides mathematical education into three phases:

(S1) **Pre-rigorous** stage: Mathematics is taught in an informal, intuitive manner. Here the step towards a rigorous exposition as in the choices for δ is a true "formalization step".

(S2) **Rigorous** stage: One thinks in a precise and rigorous manner and can deal with consequences, including comprehending, but not necessarily overlooking the equivalence of the choices, e.g. for δ above.

(S3) **Post-rigorous** stage: One has grown comfortable with all the rigorous foundations and can switch between rigorous expositions at will without much cognitive effort and in fact does not need rigor to reliably assess the validity of statements.

Arguably, formal methods systems should support users/learners at all three stages of understanding: They should support beginners in achieving and appreciating rigor, give rigorous practitioners access to their accustomed expositions, and give post-rigorous experts direct access to all knowledge irrespective of the expositions.

In this situation, a good definition/implementation of **realms** can help to bundle and bridge between the different equivalent definitions. The concept of realms [CFK14,Ian17] was introduced as an extension of the theory graph paradigm where the definitions themselves are situated in theories (systems of object declarations, axioms, and definitions) and the equivalences are expressed as theory isomorphisms. The main feature of realms is that they allow characterizing and clustering theories as logically equivalent in order to help control and present variants and establish interoperability. We will use isomorphism of logical theories as our notion of equivalence between two formalization choices, i.e., we see realms as sets of canonically isomorphic theories. While this is a very natural choice that captures most practical examples, we stress that it is not the same as the informal notion of equivalent formalization choices. For example, two formalizations may be equivalent in the sense that they prove the same statements (corresponding to admissibility of proof rules) without being isomorphic (which corresponds to derivability of proof rules). Vice versa, two formalizations may be isomorphic without being considered equivalent — that happens, e.g., when the isomorphism is a non-trivial representation theorem that one wants to formalize without merging the two formalizations, or when there are multiple different isomorphisms between two formalizations. Moreover, in narrative contexts such as university courses, logical equivalence must be distinguished from narrative equivalence. For instance, the prime number theorem has elementary proofs and proofs involving complex analysis, which are not narratively equivalent since they have vastly different prerequisites.

Case 1 and 2 above would be formalized as different theories together with two isomorphisms between them. In fact, because the isomorphism is ultimately induced by the isomorphism between relations and set-valued functions, we would start with two theories Relation and FunPwrSet connected by a pair φ/φ^{-1} of theory isomorphisms. Instantiating the involved sets then yields the realm of transition systems consisting of two corresponding isomorphic theories. These isomorphisms encapsulate the intuition that the rigorous exposition choices do not matter mathematically. And realm-aware formalization could be a basis for "Tao stage"-independent support tools.

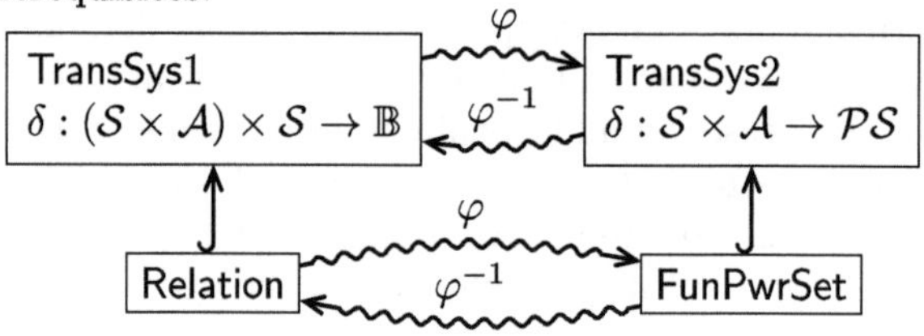

Fig. 1. The Realm of Transition Systems

Our example already shows another interesting phenomenon: The mathematical equivalence between relations and set-valued functions, which sits at the foundation of mathematics, carries over to the exposition of concepts higher-up in the definitional hierarchy like transition systems. In the common situation where the reader is (post-)rigorous for the concepts lower in the hierarchy but pre-rigorous for the one higher up, it is critical for support tools to be able to switch between explicit and implicit representations of realms at different levels of the hierarchy.

While the idea of realms fits very well into this situation, the definition of [CFK14] has resisted implementation. In particular, that definition distinguished the isomorphic theories themselves, conservative extensions thereof, and a "face theory" that merges all of the others. Thus, every realm is represented as a complex theory graph, an approach that turned out to be too heavyweight to easily combine with all the other design constraints on practical formal systems. In response, [RW23] identified minimal language features that allow formalizing realm-like objects. It identified, in particular, sets $T_1 \overset{\cong}{\longleftrightarrow} \dots \overset{\cong}{\longleftrightarrow} T_n$ of isomorphic theories as the single most important special case, on which to focus tool support. It argued that there are two key ways to leverage such a realm R: To create an instance of R, implementing the interface of any T_i should suffice; and when using an instance of R, the union of all T_i (i.e., the face) should be available. But it was not yet able to sketch the design of a formal system that actually allows this.

Contribution Following [RW23], we define realms as sets of isomorphic theories. But to make realms more tractable in practice, we advocate a *face-first* approach to formalizing realms where we identify the realm R with its face theory. Thus, we first formalize the union of all T_i and eliminate the resulting redundancy by relating the primitive concepts of the T_i through axioms. We introduce the concept of a *base* theory as a subtheory that uniquely determines the entire theory, and that allows recovering the various T_i as different bases of R.

We call this "lightweight realms" because the realm is formalized as a single theory, possibly with some annotations that make the various bases explicit. We show that lightweight realms permit elegant formalization of a surprisingly big class of realms, including many foundational concepts that pose difficulties to pre-rigorous readers.

Moreover, we describe multiple algorithms that leverage lightweight realms in ways that are straightforward to add to typical implementations of formal logics. One of these is the concept of realm-induced coercions: functions that embody (aspects of) the view cycles and can be added to the user-supplied under-specified/informal formulae in type-checking-driven reconstruction. Knowing and dealing with these coercions is one of the aspects of mathematical competence, where systems can adapt to the user and thus create value in computer-supported interaction with mathematical knowledge and documents.

Overview In Section 2 we set the stage by introducing a simple language in which we can make our ideas work. Sections 3 and 4 develop two alternative representations of lightweight realms. Section 5 introduces the notion of coercions and discusses some immediate applications. Section 6 concludes the paper and discusses future work.

Acknowledgments The work reported in this article was conducted as part of the VoLL-KI project (see `https://voll-ki.de`) funded by the German Ministry of Research, Technology and Space under grant 16DHBKI089.

2 A Simple Language For Theories and Structures

To make our ideas precise, we introduce the syntax of a simple language, which we call LR in the sequel, that we can use to formulate our abstract definitions and concrete examples of realms. The grammar is given in Fig. 2. It is meant to capture a reasonable fragment of mathematical structures while staying uncommitted on the choice of underlying formal type system and logic. Concrete languages that can be extended to realize our ideas include both fully formal languages, e.g. suitable extensions of theorem prover languages, as well as flexiformal ones like our sTeX. We do not fix a type or proof system for it, instead assuming that readers are post-rigorous for such inference systems and can easily make a reasonable choice.

Generally, we err on the side of simplicity assuming only minimal language features needed to spell out our definitions and examples. While we see the general ideas as universally reusable, we expect any implementation to tweak our definitions as needed to trade-off with other design criteria. Most importantly,

Theory and Morphism Definitions	
$Thy ::= \vartheta[a^*]\{Decl^*\}$	theory definition (with type parameters a)
$Morph ::= \mu : T \to T\{(c := t)^*\}$	morphism definition
$Decl ::= c : A$	constant declaration
$\mid c := t$	constant definition
$\mid \vdash t$	axiom asserting t (which must be of type $\mathbb{B}$)
Theories	
$T ::= \vartheta[A^*]$	instantiated parametric theory
Types	
$A ::= a$	type variables
$\mid T$	type of structures/models of T
$\mid \mathbb{B}$	Booleans
$\mid A \to A$	function types
$\mid A \times A$	product types
$\mid \mathcal{P}A$	power types
$\mid A^?$	option types
Objects	
$t ::= c \mid x$	reference to a constant or variable
$\mid T((c := t)^*)$	a structure of type T
$\mid t.c$	projecting out a component of a structure
$\mid \lambda x : A.t \mid t(t^*)$	function formation, application
$\mid t = t \mid t \Rightarrow t \mid \forall x : A.t \mid \ldots$	logic as usual
$\mid t^{\checkmark}$	statement that t is defined
$\mid \ldots$	other productions as needed

Fig. 2. Syntax of LR

our choice of type system and concrete syntax should be seen as an example of a concrete language for lightweight realms rather than a requirement for them.

We assume that there are three kinds of expressions:

- Objects are the primary mathematical objects. They include the formulas and truth values as objects of type $\mathbb{B}$.
- Types occur as the classifiers of objects. We ignore the fundamental questions of whether types can occur as input or output of functions or whether they are themselves typed by higher types.
- Theories bundle a set of typed objects, definitions, and axioms into a named scope. They are related by morphisms.

We leave open if these expressions form some kind of axiomatic set theory (in which objects and types jointly form the sets) or type theory (where objects and types are separated and possibly further subdivided by kinds, universes, etc.).

A **theory** is a list of constant declarations $c : A$, constant definitions $c := A$, and axioms $\vdash t$ for a Boolean t. A constant may have multiple definitions.

We make a subtle design choice here: We treat the definition of c as separate from its declaration. Alternatively, we could (i) change the grammar to $Decl ::= c : A[= t]$ to make definitions part of the declarations, or (ii) treat $c := t$ as a special case of the axiom $\vdash c = t$. Not committing to either (i) or (ii) allows **cyclic definitions** where we first declare some constants and later give them mutually recursive definitions. Note that such definition cycles are harmless if we simply think of definitions as axioms, rather than as computation rules. We call a theory **acyclic** if the relation on constants defined by "occurs in a definition of" is acyclic.

For simplicity, we assume that theories may not introduce any type constants and that all types needed to state the theory are provided as type parameters $[a_1, \ldots, a_n]$. Thus, references to a theory named ϑ must always be of the form $\vartheta[A_1, \ldots, A_n]$ providing values for all type parameters of ϑ. Generalizations to more complicated versions of parametric theories or to type declarations inside theories are possible, but not needed in the following. Given a theory $\vartheta[a_1, \ldots, a_n]\{\ldots\}$, any instantiation $T = \vartheta[A_1, \ldots, A_n]$ can be normalized into a list of declarations by substituting every a_i with A_i in the body of ϑ. In the sequel, we will assume that this normalization always takes place implicitly.

Our grammar spells out only a selection of useful **types** that are relevant in the sequel. For instantiations of our formalism with a specific language, we do not require that all of these are present, let alone be present as primitive features of the language. Moreover, we do not require that there are no other types than those. Similarly, for the **objects** t, we only introduce syntax for the fragment of mathematical expressions that we actually use in the sequel.

Of particular importance in the sequel is that every theory T (normalizing to $\{c_1 : A_1, \ldots\}$), can be used as a type. Semantically, this is the **type of structures** of shape T or of **models** of T. We can also think of every theory T as a record type, and of the concrete structures as the records. The introduction form of this type are of the structure $T(c_1 := t_1, \ldots)$ that provide a definition for each constant of T that does not have a definition yet. Given such a structure $s : T$, the elimination form $s.c_i$ projects out the respective field.

A **morphism** $\mu : S \to T$ is a list of definitions $c := t$ where each c is an S-constant and each t is a T-object. A morphism must give exactly one definition for every S-constant with the following exception for defined constants: If repeated expansion of definitions allows simplifying constant c to object t and μ defines all constants in t, then we define $\mu(c)$ as $\mu(t)$. Thus, as usual, a morphism μ induces a homomorphic extension $\mu(-)$ that maps S-expressions to T-expressions.

The definitions in μ must be such that $\mu(-)$ preserves all type declarations, definitions, and axioms of S: If S contains $c : A$, then we require $\mu(c) : \mu(A)$; if it contains $c := t$, we require $\mu(c) = \mu(t)$ (which holds by definition if μ does not define c at all); if it contains $\vdash t$, we require that T can prove $\mu(t)$.

As usual, a morphism $\mu : S \to T$ is an **isomorphism** if there is a morphism $\nu : T \to S$ such that $\mu; \nu = id_S$ and $\nu; \mu = id_T$. Here the identity id_S maps $c = c$ and the composition $\mu; \nu$ maps $c = \nu(\mu(c))$ for every S-constant c. And two morphisms $\mu, \mu' : S \to S'$ are equal if S' can prove $\mu(c) = \mu'(c)$ for every S-constant c.

We call S a **subtheory** of T if every S-declaration is also a T-declaration. Note that every set C of T-constants induces a subtheory of T, which we write $T|_C$, by taking only the constants of C and the axioms mentioning only those constants. A morphism $S \to T$ is called an **extension** if every one of its definitions is of the form $c = c$. If an extension exists, it is uniquely determined, and in that case we also call T an extension of S. In particular, a theory extends every one of its subtheories. Extension is a reflexive and transitive relation on theories.

3 Realms as Isomorphism Graphs

Bases The idea of a base of a theory T is that all constants of T can be canonically defined in terms of the base constants:

Definition 1 (Base). An acyclic subtheory B of T is a **base** for T if the inclusion $B \to T$ is an isomorphism.

Thus, we can think of the base as the minimal set of constants that a structure must define in order to be fully determined, and of T as a conservative extension of the base. In particular, B is a base for T if T contains a definition (without slipping into cyclic definition expansions) for every constant not declared in B. Note that the relation "is a base for" is a reflexive and transitive relation on acyclic theories.

As always, the inverse of an isomorphism is uniquely determined: Given a base B for T, let $i : T \to B$ be the inverse of the inclusion $B \to T$. We can construct i by putting $i(c) := c$ for constants c of B, and putting for other constants c of T that $i(c)$ is the canonical definition of c.

Bases are not unique. In fact, we can now rephrase the motivation for realms as the need to flexibly and seamlessly switch bases.

We use the word **bases** in analogy to vector spaces. If we think of a theory as a space, and its terms as the analogues of vectors, then a base theory corresponds to the base of a vector space in the sense that both pick a primitive subset from which the rest can be defined. It also carries over analogously that a vector space can be studied without choosing a base. But a lot of operations become a lot simpler if we do choose one. And there are multiple choices of base. A major difference to vector spaces, however, is that a theory may only have a select few bases.

Example 1 (Bases of Propositional Logic). Consider theory

$$\mathsf{PL}[o]\{\top : o, \bot : o, \wedge : o \times o \to o, \vee : o \times o \to o, \Rightarrow : o \times o \to o, \ldots\}$$

where we omit the axioms that govern classical propositional logic.

We also add an axiom $\forall a, b : o.(a \Rightarrow b) \wedge (b \Rightarrow a) \Rightarrow a =_o b$ to identify equivalent formulas. Then the subtheory declaring only $\top, \neg, \wedge$ (with the respective axioms) is a base for $\mathtt{PL}(o)$. Indeed, the rules for the other connectives already constrain their definitions up to provable equivalence, which makes the morphism formed from them an isomorphism.

Faces As a running example, we use the realm of a quotient on a type A:

Example 2 (Isomorphic Definitions of Quotients). We can define quotients in multiple different ways, e.g., by *i)* the equivalence relation on A, *ii)* the set of equivalence classes, or *iii)* the function that maps each element to its class. This yields the following theories:

$$\begin{array}{ll}\mathtt{EqRel}[A]\,\{ & \mathtt{Partition}[A]\,\{\\ \quad equiv : A \times A \to \mathbb{B} & \quad classes : \mathcal{P}\mathcal{P}A\\ \quad \vdash \text{“}equiv \text{ is an equivalence on } A\text{”} & \quad \vdash \text{“}classes \text{ is a partition of } A\text{”}\\ \} & \}\end{array}$$

$$\begin{array}{l}\mathtt{ClassProjection}[A]\,\{\\ \quad class : A \to \mathcal{P}A\\ \quad \vdash \forall a : A.\, a \in class(a)\\ \quad \vdash \text{“the image of } class \text{ is a partition of } A\text{”}\\ \}\end{array}$$

For every choice of A, we obtain an isomorphism cycle $\mathtt{EqRel}[A] \xrightarrow{\mu_1} \mathtt{Partition}[A] \xrightarrow{\mu_2} \mathtt{ClassProjection}[A] \xrightarrow{\mu_3} \mathtt{EqRel}[A]$. For example, μ_1 defines $equiv := \lambda x, y : A. \exists p \in classes.\, x \in p \wedge y \in p$. Moreover, we can prove that they are indeed isomorphisms, e.g., prove $\mu_1; \mu_2; \mu_3 = id_{\mathtt{EqRel}[A]}$ and $\mu_2; \mu_3; \mu_1 = id_{\mathtt{Partition}[A]}$ and $\mu_3; \mu_1; \mu_2 = id_{\mathtt{ClassProjection}[A]}$.

This shows what we mean when we say that realms can be *heavyweight*: Already we need to maintain three theories, three isomorphisms, and three proofs of morphism equality. Even though the various base theories are often independently interesting anyway, this design can cause a relatively large amount of bureaucracy for both the user and the tool.

[CFK14] in addition assumes support tools to generate the so-called face theory that merges the above. While the existence of the face can be shown by applying co-limits, [CFK14] never spells out how a concrete co-limit can be chosen canonically (a non-trivial problem as shown in [CMR17]). A manual construction could result in the following:

Example 3 (The Face of Quotients). The theory in Fig. 3 merges all three theories from Ex. 2, which can be recovered as subtheories (again, some objects remain informal for readability). The definitions in the three morphisms are included as definitions here as well (at the end). Thus, each of these three subtheories determines the other fields uniquely and is thus a base.

Note that Quot critically uses cyclic definitions. This allows putting the definitions of *equiv*, *classes*, and *class* at the end of the theory. This kind of recursion is harmless if we simply think of these definitions as axioms, rather than as computation rules.

$$
\begin{array}{l}
\mathtt{Quot}[A]\,\{\\
\quad \mathit{equiv} : A \times A \to \mathbb{B}\\
\quad \vdash \text{“}\mathit{equiv}\text{ is an equivalence on }A\text{”}\\
\quad \mathit{classes} : \mathcal{P}\mathcal{P}A\\
\quad \vdash \text{“}\mathit{classes}\text{ is a partition of }A\text{”}\\
\quad \mathit{class} : A \to \mathcal{P}A\\
\quad \vdash \forall a : A.\, a \in \mathit{class}(a)\\
\quad \vdash \text{“the image of }\mathit{class}\text{ is a partition of }A\text{”}\\
\quad \mathit{equiv} := \lambda x, y : A.\, \exists p \in \mathit{classes}.\, x \in p \wedge y \in p\\
\quad \mathit{classes} := \{\mathit{class}\ x \mid x \in A\}\\
\quad \mathit{class} := \lambda x : A.\, \{y : A \mid \mathit{equiv}(x, y)\}\\
\}
\end{array}
$$

Fig. 3. A Theory for Quotients

But to show that these cyclic definitions do not threaten the consistency of $\mathtt{Quot}[A]$, we would like to show that repeated expansion of definitions terminates at least up to provable equality. For example, we want to show that the expansion of *equiv* eventually yields *equiv* again as in

$$
\begin{aligned}
\mathit{equiv} &\rightsquigarrow \lambda x, y : A.\, \exists p \in \mathit{classes}.\, x \in p \wedge y \in p\\
&\rightsquigarrow \lambda x, y : A.\, \exists p \in \{\mathit{class}\ x \mid x \in A\}.\, x \in p \wedge y \in p\\
&\rightsquigarrow \lambda x, y : A.\, \exists p \in \{\{y : A \mid \mathit{equiv}(x, y)\} \mid x \in A\}.\, x \in p \wedge y \in p\\
&= \mathit{equiv}.
\end{aligned}
$$

The resulting proof obligations are exactly the same as the ones needed to show the morphism equalities mentioned in Ex. 2.

Realms The above leads us to the following definitions that further specify and clarify the ideas from [CFK14] in light of [RW23].

Definition 2 (Realm). A **realm** is a connected commutative diagram of theories and morphisms, in which all edges are isomorphisms.

A **cyclic realm** is one in which the diagram is a single cycle.

Note that for any two theories S, T in a realm R, there is a unique isomorphism $R^{S,T} : S \to T$ obtained by composing appropriate edges. If there are multiple paths from S to T, the resulting morphisms are equal because the diagram commutes.

Without loss of generality, we can assume that every realm is cyclic by choosing an appropriate set of isomorphisms. If that results in the discarding of any edges of the realm, those edges must have been redundant – otherwise, the diagram would not commute.

Therefore, from now, we will assume that a realm R is given as a cycle $R_1 \xrightarrow{R^1} R_2 \xrightarrow{R^2} \ldots R_{n-1} \xrightarrow{R^{n-1}} R_n \xrightarrow{R^n} R_1$. In other words, we write R^i for the isomorphism $R_i \to R_{i+1}$ with the understanding that $R_{n+1} = R_1$. In particular, the unique isomorphism $R^{i,j} : R_i \to R_j$ is given by $R^i; \ldots; R^{j-1}$ (with the understanding that we loop around using $R^i; \ldots R^n; R^1; \ldots R^{j-1}$ if $j < i$).

Definition 3. Given a cyclic realm R and a theory T in R, the **basing** of T at R, written R_T is defined as the theory containing

- a copy of all theories in R
- for every theory S of R except T, and every undefined constant c of S: a definition $c := \mu_{S,T}(c)$, where $\mu_{S,T} = R^{i,j}$ for $S = R^i$ and $T = R^j$.

Note that R_T is acyclic: T is assumed to be primitive and all other constants are defined in terms of T.

Definition 4 (Face). Given a cyclic realm R, we define its **face** $\overline{R}$ as the theory containing

- a copy of each theory in R
- for every i and every undefined constant c of R_i: a definition $c := R^i(c)$.

Note that $\overline{R}$ is a cyclic theory (except for degenerate cases like $n = 1$).
Our intuitions are confirmed by the following:

Theorem 1. *If the theories in a realm R are acyclic, then every theory T in R (as well as every R_T) is a base of $\overline{R}$.*

Proof. Clearly T is a subtheory of R_T and R_T of $\overline{R}$. By construction every constant in R_T other than those from T has a definition in terms of T. Similarly, every constant of $\overline{R}$ has a definition in terms of those from R_T.

4 Face-First Realms

The previous section showed how we can represent a realm as a set of isomorphic theories and merge those into its face. We now want to devise a language that allows for the opposite construction: extract a realm from a given face theory T. This is the practical problem we often face if we want to curate an existing body of mathematical knowledge into a realm-structured library. Of course, this is an underspecified problem: The realm consisting only of T would be a trivial but useless solution.

Therefore, we expect the user to annotate T lightly to choose the right realm structure. Recalling that bases are essentially determined by the set of constant names, our key idea is to extend the language of LR in such a way that we can equip a theory declaration with a list of bases. For instance in the theory $\texttt{Poset}[A]$ of posets shown on the right we declare the sets $\{=, \leq\}$, $\{\neq, <\}$ and $\{\leq, <\}$ to be bases of that theory by listing them after the (in this case singleton) list of type parameters.

$\texttt{Poset}[A][\{=, \leq\}, \{\neq, <\}, \{\leq, <\}]\,\{$
$\quad = : A \times A \to \mathbb{B}$
$\quad \neq : A \times A \to \mathbb{B}$
$\quad < : A \times A \to \mathbb{B}$
$\quad \leq : A \times A \to \mathbb{B}$
$\quad$ omitted: axioms about $\leq$ and/or $<$
$\quad = := \lambda x, y : A.\, \neg x \neq y$
$\quad = := \lambda x, y : A.\, x \leq y \wedge y \leq x$
$\quad \neq := \lambda x, y : A.\, \neg x = y$
$\quad < := \lambda x, y : A.\, x \leq y \wedge x \neq y$
$\quad \leq := \lambda x, y : A.\, x = y \vee x < y$
$\}$

Given such an asserted base B, it remains to obtain the practical criteria to check that $T|_B$ is indeed a base of T. Obviously this is not guaranteed, e.g., $T|_\emptyset$ is the empty theory – B must be big enough for $T|_B$ to induce definitions for all other constants. But it is also desirable that B be minimal with this property.

4.1 Base Checking and Realm Reconstruction

To get a sufficient criterion for an arbitrary set B of constants to form a base of a fixed theory T we proceed as follows. Let $\mathcal{G}$ be the graph with two kinds of nodes: one node of kind "constant" for each constant declared in T, and one node of kind "definiens" for each expression that occurs as the definiens of a constant declared in T. For each constant c with definiens δ in T, $\mathcal{G}$ has an edge $c \to \delta$; and for each constant d declared in T that occurs in δ, it has an edge $\delta \to d$. If there are two constants c and c' that have the same expression δ as definiens, we require $\mathcal{G}$ to contain two separate nodes v, v' for δ and two separate edges $c \to v$ and $c' \to v'$. Thus every "definiens" node has exactly one incoming edge. For the theory `Poset`$[A]$ this graph is shown in Fig. 4.

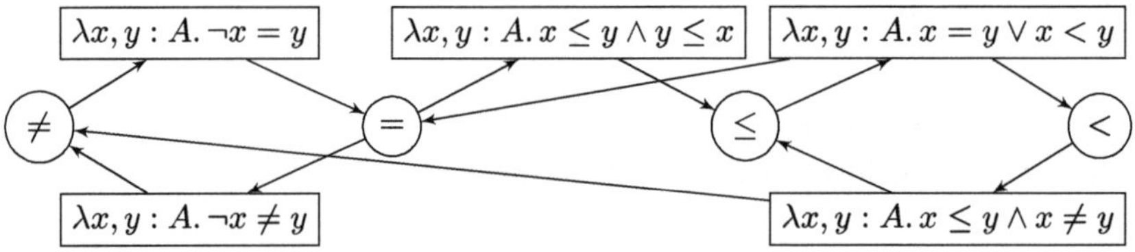

Fig. 4. The dependency graph for constants and definientia in `Poset`$[A]$: Nodes with round borders contain the constants of `Poset`$[A]$ and nodes with rectangle borders contain their definientia.

To check if B forms a base for T, we must check that

1. every constant c declared by T can be defined in terms of B, and
2. all possible such definitions of c are provably equal in T.

Since these depend on equality of objects, there is no decision procedure for this. However, if we restrict the notion of "definable" to "definable via definitional equality", we can carry out step 1 automatically: For any T-constant c we can compute the set of its definientia δ and expand all T-constants in δ recursively until all constants in that expansion of δ are elements of B (if such an expansion is possible and terminates). Step 2 can then be tackled by calling an automated theorem prover or requesting the user to act as an oracle function to check whether all possible definientia δ of any T-constant c given in terms of B are provably equal.

For instance, consider $B = \{\neq, <\}$ as a (potential) basis of `Poset`$[A]$. Applying step 1 to, e.g., the constant $=$ yields the set $\{(\lambda x, y : A. \neg x \neq y), (\lambda x, y : A. (\neg x \neq y \vee x < y) \wedge (\neg y \neq x \vee y < x))\}$ of B-based definientia for $=$. These two definientia are easily seen to be equal, solving step 2.

If we have a theory T with a specified set of bases $B_1, \ldots, B_n$ then we want to ensure that the choice of those bases is in some sense "reasonable". One such reasonability criterion is given by the following theorem:

Theorem 2. *Let R be a realm with theories $T_1, \ldots, T_n$ and T be the face of R equipped with a set of bases $B_1, \ldots, B_n$, where B_i is the set of constants and axioms declared in T_i, such that for every morphism $\mu : T_i \to T_j$ in R and $c \in T_i$ there is a definition of the form $c := \mu(c)$. Then we can recover R from T by defining the morphisms in R via the expansions of the definitions of each base constant in terms of B_i.*

Proof. In the case where a constant c has more than one definiens in terms of B_i, any arbitrary choice of them can be taken as the value of c under the respective morphism since the commutativity condition of R ensures that they are all provably equal in T.

In the case where the theory T does not stem from a realm R, we can extend our base checking algorithm with an additional functionality that checks whether any two definientia of a constant are provably equal. This allows us then to turn any theory T equipped with a set of bases into a realm that is compatible with T in the sense of Thm. 2.

To perform such an equality check, we track the set D of definied constants during the base checking procedure starting with $D = \{b_1 := b_1, \ldots, b_n := b_n\}$ for each base constant b_i. Then for each (non-base) constant c with definiens δ whose T-constants are all in D we do the following:

- if $c \in D$, we check if every definiens of c in D is provably equal to δ;
- if $c \notin D$, we add $c := \delta$ to D.

If eventually every equality check succeeds, the commutativity condition of the realm to be constructed is satisfied.

4.2 Unitary Bases

A key observation that led to the design of LR is that many practically important bases consist of effectively a single constant.

Definition 5 (Unitary). A theory is **unitary** if it consists of a single constant declaration and (possibly) some axioms. A realm is unitary if all its theories are.

Remark 1 (Type Declarations). For simplicity, LR does not allow for type declarations in theories. If an instance of LR allows for type fields, we could alternatively make A a type field in Ex. 2 and 3. All three isomorphisms would then define $A := A$.

That design choice would slightly affect the definition of unitarity: It is still true that the value of A is determined by the values of *equiv*, *classes*, resp. *class*. In fact, it is already determined by their types. But the declaration of A would have to be part of the base theories to make sure they are self-contained theories. So we would need to use a slightly more technically complicated definition of unitary base.

Realms with unitary bases are extremely easy to formalize and to provide tool support for because we only need to give the face theory and annotate the base constants.

We can finalize our formalization of quotients as shown in Fig. 5, where we annotated the base constants directly in the body of the theory instead of providing the respective (singleton) base sets as a separate listing outside the body.

$$\begin{aligned}
&\texttt{Quot}[A]\,\{\\
&\quad \textbf{base}\ \mathit{equiv} : A \times A \to \mathbb{B}\\
&\quad \vdash \text{“}\mathit{equiv}\text{ is an equivalence on }A\text{”}\\
&\quad \textbf{base}\ \mathit{classes} : \mathcal{P}\mathcal{P}A\\
&\quad \vdash \text{“}\mathit{classes}\text{ is a partition of }A\text{”}\\
&\quad \textbf{base}\ \mathit{class} : A \to \mathcal{P}A\\
&\quad \vdash \forall a : A.\, a \in \mathit{class}(a)\\
&\quad \vdash \text{“the image of }\mathit{class}\text{ is a partition of }A\text{”}\\
&\quad \mathit{equiv} := \lambda x, y : A.\, \exists p \in \mathit{classes}.\, x \in p \wedge y \in p\\
&\quad \mathit{classes} := \{\mathit{class}(a) \mid a \in A\}\\
&\quad \mathit{class} := \lambda x : A.\, \{y \in A \mid \mathit{equiv}(x, y)\}\\
&\}
\end{aligned}$$

Fig. 5. Unitary Realm for Quotients

Once the proof obligation that $T|_{\{c\}}$ is indeed a base for T is discharged, it justifies a typing rule that infers $T(c := e) : T$, i.e., it is sufficient to define c to create a structure of type T. In object-oriented programming terms, we obtain a unary constructor for T that takes only the value of c as its argument.

We conclude the running example by adding quotients with representatives:

Example 4 (Extending Realms). Consider the theory in Fig. 6 where an include declaration copies over another theory. Here we use a second definition of *equiv* to connect *repr* to the base constants of `Quot`. Now *repr* is a (unitary) base for `QuotRep`. Note that the bases of `Quot` are not bases of `QuotRep`. Thus, the annotation of a constant of a base must be a global property of the whole theory, which may or may not be preserved when the theory is extended.

$$\begin{aligned}
&\texttt{QuotRep}[A]\,\{\\
&\quad \textbf{include}\ \texttt{Quot}[A]\\
&\quad \textbf{base}\ \mathit{repr} : A \to A\\
&\quad \mathit{equiv} := \lambda x, y : A.\, \mathit{repr}(x) = \mathit{repr}(y)\\
&\}
\end{aligned}$$

Fig. 6. Extension of `Quot`$[A]$

A lot of practically relevant theories can be formalized elegantly as unitary realms.

Example 5 (Sets and Functions). The theory `Subset` in Fig. 7 captures the well-known equivalence of subsets and characteristic functions. Both of these are unitary bases. `Rel` specializes that to binary relations, adding the range as a third unitary base.

From now on, the examples omit well-known definitions for brevity. `PFun` extends the latter with a fourth unitary base for the special case where the relation is functional. `Fun` captures the currying equivalence for binary functions. Curried n-ary functions can be formalized accordingly.

$\texttt{Subset}[A]\,\{$
  base $\mathit{contains} : A \to \mathbb{B}$
  base $\mathit{extension} : \mathcal{P}A$
  $\mathit{contains} := \lambda x : A.x \in \mathit{extension}$
  $\mathit{extension} := \{x \in A \mid \mathit{contains}(x)\}$
$\}$

$\texttt{Rel}[A, B]\,\{$
  include $\mathit{Subset}[A \times B]$
  base $\mathit{range} : A \to \mathcal{P}B$
  $\mathit{range} := \lambda x : A.\{y \in B \mid \mathit{contains}(x, y)\}$
  $\mathit{contains} := \lambda x : A, y : B.y \in \mathit{range}(x)$
$\}$

$\texttt{PFun}[A, B]\,\{$
  include $\texttt{Rel}[A, B]$
  $\mathit{apply} : A \to B^{\perp}$
  $\vdash$ "relation is functional"
$\}$

$\texttt{Fun}[A_1, A_2, B]\,\{$
  base $\mathit{apply}_1 : A_1 \to A_2 \to B$
  base $\mathit{apply}_2 : A_1 \times A_2 \to B$
$\}$

$\texttt{Group}[A]\,\{$
  base $\mathit{mul} : A \times A \to A$
  omitted: axioms about mul
  base $\mathit{div} : A \times A \to A$
  omitted: axioms about div
  $\mathit{neut} : A$
  $\mathit{inv} : A \to A$
  $\mathit{mul} := \lambda x, y : A.\mathit{div}(x, \mathit{div}(\mathit{neut}, y))$
  $\mathit{div} := \lambda x, y : A.\mathit{mul}(x, \mathit{inv}(y))$
  omitted: definitions for neut and inv
$\}$

$\texttt{Closure}[A]\,\{$
  base $\mathit{closed} : \mathcal{PP}A$
  base $\mathit{close} : \mathcal{P}A \to \mathcal{P}A$
  base $\mathit{closeTo} : \mathcal{P}A \times A \to \mathbb{B}$
$\}$

Fig. 7. Examples

Example 6 (Algebra). Many algebraic theories have different but essentially equivalent formalizations. Fig. 7 sketches a realm `Group` of groups given by multiplication or division. This realm is more complex than the other examples because defining the neutral and inverse element may or may not be possible or desirable depending on the underlying logic. In that case, they may need to be part of the then no longer unitary base(s).

Example 7 (Topology). The realm `Closure` uses three unitary bases, again omitting all definitions and axioms. We could extend it to the realm of topological spaces using at least six bases as shown in [RW23]. The same reference also gives an example for lattices that can be recast in our formalism.

$\texttt{TransSys}[\mathcal{S}, \mathcal{A}]\,\{$
  $\delta_1 : (\mathcal{S} \times \mathcal{A}) \times \mathcal{S} \to \mathbb{B}$
  $\delta_2 : \mathcal{S} \times \mathcal{A} \to \mathcal{P}\mathcal{S}$
  $\delta_1 := \lambda(s, a), s'.s' \in \delta_2(s, a)$
  $\delta_2 := \lambda s, a.\{s' \in \mathcal{S} \mid \delta_1((s, a), s')\}$
$\}$

Fig. 8. Unitary Realm for Transition Systems

In particular, we can represent transition systems from Fig. 1 as a face-first realm in a single theory. Fig. 8 gives a standalone representation, but a practical formalization should of course include $\texttt{Rel}[\mathcal{S} \times \mathcal{A}, \mathcal{S}]$.

5 Coercion via Realms

An immediate application of face-first realms and in particular unitary bases is coercion. We do not want to spell out the details of coercion systems and only give a simple definition that conveys the general idea:

Definition 6 (Coercion). A **coercion system** is a set of a unary functions. A **coercion** from A to B is any function arising by composing these. A coercion system is **unambiguous** if all coercion functions from A to B are equal.

Now consider the common situation in implementations of formal systems, where we use a type inference algorithm that takes a user-written and not necessarily well-formed object e as well as an expected type B, and that returns the well-formed object $e' : B$ that the user is understood to have meant. Then we can define:

Definition 7 (Elaboration with Coercions). Given a sound unambiguous coercion system, the coercion rule is: If a (sub-)object e is checked against type B but is inferred to have type A, and there is a coercion $f : A \to B$, then e is understood as $f(e)$.

Now we can obtain two kinds of coercions from a realm T. Firstly, we obtain *coercions out of the realm.* For each constant $c : A$ of T, if there is no other constant in T with that type, we obtain a coercion function $\lambda t : T. t.c$. Moreover, if c is a unitary base, we also obtain a *coercion into the realm*, namely $\lambda x : A. T(c := x)$.

Combining these two, we obtain *coercions through the realm*: For any two unitary bases $c : A$ and $d : B$, we obtain a coercion $\lambda x : A.T(c := x).d$.

Example 8. Consider the theory $\texttt{Rel}[A, B]$ of relations from Fig. 7. It yields the coercions $\mathcal{P}(A \times B) \leftrightarrow (A \to \mathcal{P}B)$ given by

- $X : \mathcal{P}(A \times B) \mapsto \texttt{Rel}(\mathit{extension} := X).\mathit{range}$
- $f : A \to \mathcal{P}B \mapsto \texttt{Rel}(\mathit{range} := f).\mathit{extension}$

Showing unambiguity of coercion systems with the coercions through T is tricky because the resulting coercion has type $A \to B$, which does not mention T at all. It is exactly these coercions that often trip up pre-rigorous readers, who might not be aware that T even exists or that it automatically provides the necessary coercion.

This is particularly problematic for induced coercions: It is not necessary that every coercion function is written explicitly. Often coercions at composed types can be induced from coercions at atomic types. The following cases are particularly relevant:

Definition 8 (Induced Coercions). Given a coercion $f : A \to B$, we can induce coercions

1. $f_X : (X \to A) \to (X \to B)$ given by $\lambda g : X \to A. \lambda x : X. f(g(x))$, and
2. $f_{T,c} : T \to T'$ where T is a theory containing a constant $c : A$ and T' is the same theory but with a field $c : B$ given by $\lambda t : T. T'(c := f(t.c), \rho)$ where ρ contains $a := t.a$ for every other field of T.

Example 9. Recall our formalization of the realm of transition systems from Fig. 8. But now assume we instead formalized it using two separate theories $\mathtt{TransSys}_1$ declaring $\delta : (\mathcal{S} \times \mathcal{A}) \times \mathcal{S} \to \mathbb{B}$ and $\mathtt{TransSys}_2$ declaring $\delta : \mathcal{S} \times \mathcal{A} \to \mathcal{P}\mathcal{S}$ (as opposed to a face-first realm with two bases). Moreover, assuming we already have the usual coercion $f : \mathcal{P}((\mathcal{S} \times \mathcal{A}) \times \mathcal{S}) \to (\mathcal{S} \times \mathcal{A} \to \mathcal{P}\mathcal{S})$. Then $f_{\mathtt{TransSys}_1,\delta}$ is a coercion $\mathtt{TransSys}_1 \to \mathtt{TransSys}_2$, which is the isomorphism φ between transition relations and (non-deterministic) transition functions from Fig. 1.

Note that the unambiguity of the coercion system is only needed when machine-interpreting input from the user. It is inessential when presenting fully coerced objects to the user: As long as the applied coercions are marked, the renderer can simply elide them. In informal mathematical texts, it is in fact common that the fully coerced objects in the author's mind are rendered with coercions elided in this way. This is particularly problematic for coercions that a pre-rigorous reader is not aware of.

Using unitary realms, in an interactive document scenario, e.g., when rendering as HTML, we can however do better. Assume we have formalized our coercion $f : A \to B$ as going through a unitary realm R with bases of type A and B, we can render the object $f(a)$ for the different classes of readers as follows:

- post-rigorous reader: simply render a, not mentioning any coercion;
- rigorous reader: render as a but indicate the object as coerced, e.g., with a hover that pops up R and shows that a is converted into a B under the hood;
- pre-rigorous reader: render the object as (the normal form of) $f(a)$, not mentioning any coercions.

Even though Tao portrays the three stages as inherent personal development stages it should be noted that the stage may very well be domain-dependent – once the general ability of rigorous and post-rigorous thinking has been established: The (good) intuition that guide post-rigorous work are certainly domain-dependent and need to be freshly established when moving to a new domain. So in situations, where we have a learner competency modeling component (e.g. in the ALeA context) the presentation options should be mediated by competency considerations for accuracy and improved user experience.

6 Conclusion and Future Work

In this paper we have re-examined the notion of realms that had been proposed as a "practical" solution for problems with interoperability and the choice of primitives in formalization tasks, but proved too heavyweight to be practical after all. We identified a class of realms that can be realized with less overhead but cover many/most practical situations, especially in or near the foundations. The motor of our simplification is the concept of a base of a theory which – to the best of our knowledge – was previously unrecognized in module/theory/type-class systems in formalization.

Our work is meant as a specification of realm-like features that are lightweight enough to be readily implementable in typical formal systems used for mathematics. Concretely, we plan to use the definitions introduced here as a common specification of features that we want to implement independently as parts of sTeX [MK22] and the recently created UniFormal language [Rab25] (which already inspired the grammar used in the present paper).

Related concepts have been realized in programming: *Haskell* [Mar] provides a notion of type classes which can be annotated with the ***MINIMAL*** *pragma* [Tea, section 7.19.5], a compiler instruction that can be placed in the source code, which specifies minimal complete definitions of a class C, i.e. sets B of methods that must be implemented by all instances of C and from which the definitions of all other methods of C can be derived. The intended application is to minimize the effort of implementing C as the programmer must only provide definitions for the methods in one of the sets B without explicitly defining the remaining ones, which is related to, but not the same as our application in simplifying realms and thus formalization. Also, the Haskell compiler does check that a base B is complete for C while the algorithms we present above can be adapted to that end.

References

[CFK14] Jacques Carette, William Farmer, and Michael Kohlhase. "Realms: A Structure for Consolidating Knowledge about Mathematical Theories". In: *Intelligent Computer Mathematics 2014*. Conferences on Intelligent Computer Mathematics (Coimbra, Portugal, July 7–11, 2014). Ed. by Stephan Watt et al. LNCS 8543. MKM Best-Paper-Award. Springer, 2014, pp. 252–266. isbn: 978-3-319-08433-6. URL: `https://kwarc.info/kohlhase/papers/cicm14-realms.pdf`.

[CMR17] Mihai Codescu, Till Mossakowski, and Florian Rabe. "Canonical Selection of Colimits". In: *Recent Trends in Algebraic Development Techniques*. Ed. by Phillip James and Markus Roggenbach. Springer, 2017, pp. 170–188.

[HMU07] John E. Hopcroft, Rajeev Motwani, and Jeffrey D. Ullman. *Introduction to Automata Theory, Languages, and Computation*. 3rd ed. Pearson Education, 2007.

[Ian17] Mihnea Iancu. "Towards Flexiformal Mathematics". PhD thesis. Bremen, Germany: Jacobs University, 2017. URL: https://opus.jacobs-university.de/frontdoor/index/index/docId/721.

[Mar] Simon Marlow. *Haskell 2010. Language Report.* URL: https://www.haskell.org/onlinereport/haskell2010/ (visited on 03/16/2025).

[MK22] DennisMüller and Michael Kohlhase. "sTeX3 – A LaTeX-based Ecosystem for Semantic/Active Mathematical Documents". In: *TUGboat; TUG 2022 Conference Proceedings* 43.2 (2022). Ed. by Karl Berry, pp. 197–201. URL: https://kwarc.info/people/dmueller/pubs/tug22.pdf.

[Rab25] F. Rabe. "Global, Regional, and Local Contexts". In: *Intelligent Computer Mathematics.* Ed. by P. Koepke and V. de Paiva. Lecture Notes in Computer Science. Springer, 2025.

[RW23] F. Rabe and F. Weber. "Morphism Equality in Theory Graphs". In: *Intelligent Computer Mathematics.* Ed. by C. Dubois and M. Kerber. Springer, 2023, pp. 174–189.

[Sak09] Jacques Sakarovitch. *Elements of Automata Theory.* Cambridge University Press, 2009.

[Tao22] Terence Tao. *There's more to mathematics than rigour and proofs.* 2022. URL: https://terrytao.wordpress.com/career-advice/theres-more-to-mathematics-than-rigour-and-proofs/ (visited on 03/25/2025).

[Tea] The GHC Team. *The Glorious Glasgow Haskell Compilation System User's Guide, Version 7.8.20140130.* URL: https://downloads.haskell.org/~ghc/7.8.1-rc1/docs/html/users_guide/ (visited on 03/16/2025).

Global, Regional, and Local Contexts

Florian Rabe(✉)

University Erlangen-Nuremberg, Erlangen, Germany
florian.rabe@fau.de

Abstract. We introduce UniFormal, a formal language for mathematical knowledge representation that continues the evolution of OpenMath and MMT. It is motivated by the lack of identifiers in these languages that exhibit the scoping behavior needed for, e.g., the fields in a record or the variables in a polynomial. Its core feature is a separation of identifiers and associated contexts into three levels: The global context maintains the usual toplevel declarations that can be imported across libraries and nested packages via qualified names. The local context maintains the usual α-renamable bound variables with narrow syntactic scope. The novel regional context sits in between these and maintains the identifiers of the current theory. A stack of regional contexts is used to allow for expressions that move between regions, e.g., when applying a theory morphism to transport an expression from one theory to another.
We present a minimal language in this style, focusing on the general intuitions underlying the design. We anticipate it to be extended flexibly towards specialized aspects of mathematical knowledge such as programming languages or theorem provers to enable interoperability through their shared core concepts. This approach has already proved successful in the design and implementation of a UniFormal programming language.

1 Introduction

OpenMath [BCC+04] and MathML [ABC+03] were introduced as universal representation formats for mathematical objects. OMDoc [Koh06] extended them to mathematical theories and documents. MMT [RK13] specified the semantics of, implemented, and significantly evolved OMDoc. All of them were designed to be foundation-independent, and the MMT tool offers a flexible library for rapid prototyping and system interoperability.

They all feature two levels of identifiers, which we will call *global* (i.e., symbols, OMS) and *local* (i.e., variables, OMV) here. This paper was motivated by the observation that neither adequately captures the scoping behavior of the identifiers in various standard constructions. We identify the issue and offer one potential solution.

For example, consider the identifiers x and y in the record $\{\mathbf{term}\, x : \mathtt{Int} = 0, \mathbf{term}\, y : \mathtt{Int} = 1\}$. They are not global (because the record may occur anonymously inside some expression), but they are not α-renamable variables either (because they may be referenced when selecting fields from the record). Essentially the same phenomenon occurs with anonymous theories (which behave very much like record types) and anonymous diagrams of theories as used in [CFS20].

V. de Paiva and P. Koepke (Eds.): CICM 2025, LNAI 16136, pp. 240–257, 2026.
https://doi.org/10.1007/978-3-032-07021-0_14

A different example are the identifiers that are used as generators in various constructions. Consider the X in $R = \mathbb{R}[X]$. It cannot be a global identifier because X by itself is meaningless. But it cannot be an α-renamable local identifier either because we must be able to reference it from elsewhere, e.g., in the formula $X^2 + 1 \in R$. A closely related phenomenon occurs in generated groups like $\langle X, Y | X^2 = Y \rangle$, where X and Y are often referred to from outside of the definition of the group.

Proof assistants and computer algebra systems have encountered these issues and have developed ad hoc solutions. For example, Rocq [Roc25] and Isabelle [Pau94] do not use *anonymous* record types/theories and thus can use global identifiers for the fields. PVS [ORS92] uses anonymous records, and Mizar [TB85] uses structures that behave similarly; both use identifiers similar to the regional identifiers we will introduce below. Systems vary widely in how they represent the X in $\mathbb{R}[X]$, e.g., as the constructor of an inductive type, a bound variable, or as a string, or by using a least-fixed-point construction that avoids using any identifiers. SageMath [S^+13] assumes that a universal ring of polynomials in all possible identifiers exists, of which $\mathbb{R}[X]$ is a subring; these identifiers are similar to our regional ones. While MMT has proved remarkably resilient in light of retroactive extensions that changed fundamental design assumptions, e.g., [HKR12,WKR17], a foundation-independent solution for such identifiers has proved very difficult, to the point of essentially grinding MMT development to a halt since 2023.

This paper presents a minimal standalone framework language, called UniFormal, that introduces an intermediate level, called the regional identifiers, and shows how it allows representing formal theories. We leave the base language open, allowing for individual instances of UniFormal to inject suitable type and proof systems and operational semantics. One such instance, a UniFormal Programming Language, has already been developed and has been used to type-check the examples in this paper.

All design choices are the results of a years-long trial and error process that hit numerous dead ends, and a key achievement is the simplicity of the resulting abstract syntax. While we have developed (and implemented) a rigorous semantics for UniFormal, this paper employs an intuition-focused presentation style with many side remarks, examples, and comparisons to other languages. Thus, this paper primarily explains and motivates the syntax itself, and it only presents enough of the formal details to make the intended semantics inferable and to serve as a starting point of a broader discussion of the new design ideas.

2 UniFormal Syntax

The syntax of UniFormal is given in Fig. 1 (where [optional] and repeated* parts are marked as usual) and the meta-theoretical operations in 2.

There are several kinds of **declarations**. All but includes are **named**:

- Theory declarations **theory** $\tau = T$ give a name to a theory T.
- Symbol declarations introduce a named object such as a type or term.

Declarations	
$D ::= [\textbf{open}]\ \textbf{theory}\, \tau = T$	theory (open or closed)
$\mid [\textbf{total}]\ \textbf{include}\, T = [e]$	include
$\mid \textbf{type}\, a = [A]$	type symbol, with definiens
$\mid \textbf{term}\, c : A = [t]$	term symbol, with type, definiens
Theory Expressions	
$T ::= \tau \mid \tau.\ldots.\tau.\tau$	regional/global identifier
$\mid e.T$	pushout of T along model e
$\mid \{D^*\}$	anonymous theory
Types	
$A ::= x \mid a \mid \tau.\ldots.\tau.a$	local/regional/global identifier
$\mid e.A$	interpretation of A in model e
$\mid Mod(T)$	models of T
$\mid \blacktriangleright t$	proofs of $t : \texttt{Bool}$
$\mid \texttt{Bool} \mid \texttt{Int} \mid A^* \to A \mid \ldots$	example base types
Terms	
$e, t ::= x \mid c \mid \tau.\ldots.\tau.c$	local/regional/global identifier
$\mid e.t$	interpretation of t in model e
$\mid mod(T)$	a concrete model
$\mid \Delta^n$	model of n-th enclosing region (for $n \in \mathbb{N}$)
$\mid \ldots$	other productions as needed
Contexts	
$\Gamma ::= D\ ([\|]\, T\, L)^*$	global+stack of (regional+local)
$L ::= D^*$	local context of bound variables

Fig. 1. UniFormal Syntax

– Include declarations **include** T create an inheritance relation between theories. Theory normalization eliminates them by merging all declarations of the included theory T into the including theory.

Each kind of named declaration corresponds to a kind of **expression**, with the identifiers referencing the former occurring as leaves of the latter. Expressions are anonymous transient syntax trees that are checked and interpreted against a context Γ.

A **theory** T is an expression that normalizes to a list $\{\vec{D}\}$ of declarations, essentially by expanding all theory definitions and include declarations. For $\Gamma \vdash T$ THY, we write $\overline{T}^{\Gamma}$ for this normal form of T. The nesting of theories yields a tree of declarations with theories at the inner nodes and symbol declarations (or includes, if not normalized yet) at the leaves.

Beyond theories, UniFormal is flexible in what kinds of symbol declarations and expressions are used. Here we pick types and terms:

Judgment	Intuition
$\Gamma \vdash T$ THY	well-formed theory
$\Gamma \vdash S \hookrightarrow T$	inclusion between theories
$\Gamma \vdash S \equiv T$	equality (= inclusion in both directions)
$\Gamma \vdash A$ TYPE	well-formed type
$\Gamma \vdash A <: B$	subtyping
$\Gamma \vdash A \equiv B$	equality (= subtyping in both directions)
$\Gamma \vdash t : A$	well-formed typed terms
$\Gamma \vdash s \equiv t$	equality of terms

Function	Intuition
$\overline{T}^{\Gamma}$	normal form of theory T: a list $\vec{D}$ of declarations
$S \ll d$	merge declaration d into theory S
$\Gamma + T$	extend context Γ with a new frame for theory T

Fig. 2. UniFormal Judgments and Auxiliary Functions

- **Type** declarations **type** $a = [A]$ introduce a named type with an optional definition A. We could also allow type bounds and type operators, but we omit that here for simplicity.
- **Term** declarations **term** $c : A = [t]$ introduce a named term with type A and optional definition t. The type is mandatory in internal syntax, but can be omitted in surface syntax if it can be inferred.
- We represent axioms and theorems as special cases of terms with and without definition, respectively, via the type $\blacktriangleright F$ of proofs of Boolean term F.

Other languages may change these kinds as needed, e.g., to have kinds for universes, set, or proofs. Our results only require that every symbol declaration may optionally carry an expression of the corresponding kind as its definition. If such a definition is present, we call the declaration **concrete**, otherwise **abstract**. Similarly, we call a theory concrete if all declarations in its normal form are, otherwise abstract.

The details of **contexts** Γ are explained throughout the paper. Generally, the context must keep all information that an algorithm that traverses a formalization may need such as the type of every identifier that is in scope. Therefore, choosing the right data structure for the context can be as difficult as designing the entire formal system, and much of this paper is devoted to motivating and explaining our particular choice. We give the central definition below, but readers may simply think of Γ as a black box declaring all identifiers that expressions can use, and then revisit the formal definition from time to time while reading the subsequent sections.

Definition 1 (Context). *A UniFormal context Γ is of the form $G\,\vec{F}$ where*
- *global context: G is a declaration of the form* **open theory** *$root = \{\vec{\tau}\}$*
  We think of τ as the set of all available toplevel declarations. The name root is irrelevant and signifies the root of the namespace hierarchy.
- *$\vec{F}$ is a stack in which each frame is of the form $|\,R\,L$ or $R\,L$ where*

- *regional context: R is a theory of the form $\{\rho\}$.* *We think of ρ as the set of all declarations that are available in the* current *theory.*
- *local context: a list L of variable declarations* *We think of L as the set of bound variables in scope for the currently traversed subexpression.*
- *transparency: an optional modifier $|$ that indicates whether or not the identifiers of the previous frame remain in scope for the current frame.*

Contrary to the global context (which stays fixed during traversal) and the local context (which is transient in the sense that bound variables are declared, stay in scope for a while, and then go out of scope forever), the regional context can be changed back and forth. For example, if a traversal encounters $m : Mod(T)$ (which binds a variable m whose type makes it a model of theory T), it creates and pushes a fresh frame in which to process the anonymous theory T. Afterwards that frame is popped to remove the identifiers of T from the scope. But when m is used later on, say in an expression $m.c$ for some symbol c of T, the body of T must be brought back into scope to retrieve and process the type of c. Thus, we can jump to other theories by pushing onto the stack and return by popping in a way akin to how programming languages use a stack frame for each function call.

Switching to theory T by pushing a new frame for T will happen frequently, and we introduce a notation for it:

Definition 2 (Context Extension). *Given a context $\Gamma = G\ \vec{F}$ and a theory $\Gamma \vdash T$ THY, we define*

$$\Gamma + T := G\,(\vec{F},\, (\overline{T}^{\Gamma}\ \varnothing)) \qquad \Gamma + |T := G\,(\vec{F},\, (|\overline{T}^{\Gamma}\ \varnothing))$$

These extend $\vec{F}$ with a fresh frame initialized with the normal form of T as the regional and the empty list $\varnothing$ as the local context.

Example 1. The algebraic hierarchy (the Hello-World of mathematical module systems) starts with

$$\begin{aligned}&\textbf{theory}\, Carrier = \{\textbf{type}\, u\},\\ &\textbf{theory}\, Magma = \{\textbf{include}\, Carrier,\ \textbf{term}\, op : (u, u) \to u\}\\ &\textbf{theory}\, Semigroup = \{\textbf{include}\, Magma,\\ &\quad \textbf{term}\, assoc : \blacktriangleright \forall x, y, z : u.op(x, op(y, z)) = op(op(x, y), z)\}\end{aligned}$$

Here and in subsequent examples, we assume an instance of UniFormal in which all the relevant constructors for types and terms are present such as $\to$, λ, $-(-)$ for functions, and the usual connectives and typed quantifiers like $\forall$ and $=$.

The global context is the entire development. When traversal reaches the equality in the associativity axiom, the context stack contains a single frame: Its regional context contains **type** u and **term** $op\ :\ (u, u)\ \to\ u$, which stem from the normalization of the preceding declarations of the current theory, i.e., **include** $Magma$. Its local context declares the bound variables $x : u, y : u, z : u$.

3 Open vs. Closed Theories

3.1 Distinction

system	open	closed
Isabelle	theory	locale, type class
Rocq	package	module, type class, record
Mizar	article	structure
sTeX	module	mathstruct
OpenMath/MathML	content dictionary	—
MMT	—	theory
SageMath	module	category
Axiom	—	category
Java	package	class
C++	namespace	class, struct

Fig. 3. Analogues of Open and Closed Theories in Various Systems

UniFormal distinguishes two kinds of theories. We call a theory **open** if its declarations are freely accessible from the outside, otherwise **closed**. For example, in **open theory** $\tau = \{\textbf{term}\, c : A\}, \textbf{term}\, d = \tau.c$, the symbol c of the open theory τ is referenced using a qualified identifier. If τ were closed, such a reference would be ill-formed. Closed theories require additional language features that regulate access to them.

Most formal systems (see Fig. 3) use a similar combination of open and closed theories, albeit sometimes in multiple variants and/or with a less clear-cut difference. Notably, MathML and MMT do not make the distinction, and the author now sees that as a deficiency.

The open/closed theory distinction is analogous to the **open/closed world assumption**. An *open* theory is effectively just a namespace. The set of inhabitants of the open world (in our case: the expressions over the open theory) is open to future changes: symbols can be added, deleted, or moved between open theories at will, incurring "only" the cost of updating qualified downstream references to them. Consequently and critically: induction on the set of inhabitants is not allowed because it would be broken by extension.

A *closed* theory is like an open one except that it is "closed off" in the sense that induction on the set of inhabitants is allowed. Common language features to access closed theories and to leverage this induction are (i) the models of C (where induction is used to interpret all expressions in the model), (ii) the term language of C (where induction is used for induction on expressions), or (iii) Prolog-style querying and negation-by-failure (where induction is used to exhaustively search all expressions). This paper formally defines only (i), but UniFormal's closed theories can be used for the others as well.

The main purpose of open theories is to provide namespaces both inside files and across files as when structuring projects into packages and folders. In UniFormal, we assume the current project, with all its dependencies, to be provided as a single open theory G containing all available toplevel declarations—the global context. G is the root of a tree, whose inner nodes are nested open theories (representing packages, folders, namespaces, etc.) and whose leaves are symbol and closed theory declarations.

Remark 1 (Imports). When packages are published in central repositories, many languages provide **import** statements to tell the tool which open theories are going to be used. These may have some additional non-trivial semantics, e.g., making symbols available via unqualified names, renaming symbols, or selecting only some symbols of an open theory to import. But their main role is to provide extra-logical package management that builds the *open* theory that a project depends on. In particular, imports are very different from includes, which make *closed* theories available. UniFormal itself does not feature imports although particular instances typically will.

3.2 Models of a Theory

Consider a closed theory C consisting of a list of term/type declarations for names s_i. Intuitively, a **model** m of C is an object that provides an interpretation for every s_i. We can think of C and m as

- a record type and a record value,
- a logical theory and a model for it,
- a specification/interface and an implementation.

This only makes sense if C is closed: changing the symbols of C changes what the models are.

Remark 2 (Are Theories Types?). In OO-languages like Java, both the theory and its models can be represented as classes, usually called *abstract* and *concrete* classes. (Technically, we must distinguish between the concrete class and its instances. However, this distinction only becomes relevant if C contains mutable fields, which we do not consider here.) Moreover, the closed theories (i.e., the classes) double as the type of models. Many computer algebra systems like Axiom [JS92], SageMath [S$^+$13], or FoCaLiZe [H$^+$12] do the same. Alternatively, e.g., in SML, the two are strictly distinguished with models of a theory corresponding to structures implementing a signature. Structures and signatures are two additional kinds of symbols with a separate typing relation. In some languages, both styles of closed theories exist, e.g., Isabelle has locales on a separate level [KWP99] and records as types; Rocq similarly has modules and records [Coq15]. In [MRK18], we discuss this in detail and speak of *internalized theories* if there is a *type* of models of C.

In UniFormal, $Mod(C)$ is the type of models of C, and $mod(T)$ for a concrete theory T is a term of such a type. For example, $Mod(Magma)$ is the type of magmas, and $mod(\mathbf{include}\, Magma,\ \mathbf{type}\, u = \mathtt{Int},\ \mathbf{term}\, op = \lambda x, y.x + y)$ is a model of it. Thus, closed and concrete theories give rise to type and terms. To type-check $mod(T)$, we need to check that T indeed defines every field of C and does not conflict with any definitions already present in C. That is one purpose of the inclusion judgment (which we define in Sect. 4):

$$\frac{\Gamma \vdash C \text{ THY}}{\Gamma \vdash Mod(C) \text{ TYPE}} \qquad \frac{\Gamma \vdash C \hookrightarrow T \quad T \text{ is concrete}}{\Gamma \vdash mod(T) : Mod(C)}$$

The elimination forms take a model $m : Mod(C)$ and project out C-symbols s, commonly written as $m.s$. We generalize this syntax to allow applying m to an arbitrary *C-expression*. This corresponds to the application of the interpretation function that maps C-expressions to their semantics in m:

$$\frac{\Gamma \vdash m : Mod(C) \quad \Gamma + |C \vdash A \text{ TYPE}}{\Gamma \vdash m.A \text{ TYPE}} \qquad \frac{\Gamma \vdash m : Mod(C) \quad \Gamma + |C \vdash t : A}{\Gamma \vdash m.t : m.A}$$

$$\frac{\Gamma \vdash m : Mod(C) \quad \Gamma + |C \vdash S \text{ THY}}{\Gamma \vdash m.S \text{ THY}}$$

Here $\Gamma + |T$ extends the context with the declarations of C in order to build the C-expressions. The details are defined in Sect. 5.2.

The computational behavior of $m.-$ is that $m.s$ (for a symbol s) projects out the definition of the field of s in m:

$$\frac{\Gamma \vdash mod(T) : Mod(C) \quad \mathbf{type}\, a = A \text{ in } \overline{C}^{\Gamma}}{\Gamma \vdash mod(T).a \equiv subs^{mod(T)}(A)}$$

and accordingly for term and theory symbols For composed expressions, $m.-$ behaves like a homomorphic extension, e.g., $\Gamma \vdash m.(A \to B) \equiv m.A \to m.B$ and $\Gamma \vdash m.\mathtt{Int} \equiv \mathtt{Int}$. The grayed out operation replaces occurrences of Δ^0 (which refers to the current region) with $mod(T)$. It is defined in Sect. 5.2.

Remark 3 (The Type of Types). The combination of abstract type fields and a type of models allows defining the *type of types* as $Mod(\{\mathbf{type}\, univ\})$. This raises the question of consistency when giving a semantics because higher universes may be needed to hold this type. Both set theoretical systems like Mizar [TB85] and type theoretical systems based on Martin-Löf type theory [ML84] have developed sophisticated solutions. In programming languages, having the type of types can be harmless; sometimes, like in Scala, the type of types simply exists, and one has to dive deep into the language semantics to see where and how any issues are handled.

A rigorous semantics to UniFormal must carefully work out the details in a way that retains consistency. While this is very difficult, we ignore the issue here because it is orthogonal to our results. In fact, we are not even sure if a universal representation language should address the issue at all or if it should (at the risk of inconsistency and akin to informal mathematics) leave the details unspecified to avoid over-committing to any one solution.

Remark 4 (Dependent Types). The combination of nested theories and the type of models allows creating dependent types (in the sense of type expressions with terms as subexpressions). For example, $\textbf{theory}\,\tau = \{\textbf{term}\,c : \texttt{Int},\ \textbf{theory}\,\nu = \{\ldots\}\}$ yields, for any value n, a different type $Mod(mod(\textbf{include}\,\tau,\ \textbf{term}\,c = n).\nu)$. Abstract type fields in theories have a similar effect. Therefore, it is difficult to design a language for theories and models without allowing some form of dependent types, and UniFormal does so.

3.3 The Term Language of a Theory

Term language types can be seen as dual to the type of models of a theory. For example, consider $\textbf{theory}\,N = \{\textbf{type}\,n,\ \textbf{term}\,z : n,\ \textbf{term}\,s : n \to n\}$ (assuming we have function types $\to$). Its term language is that of the natural numbers. More generally, we can represent families of mutually recursive inductive types or context-free grammars (using one type symbol per non-terminal) like this.

Constructing objects through term languages is commonly done, albeit usually under a different name: it subsumes inductive types, Herbrand models, free objects over some generators such as rings of polynomials, the set of syntax trees over a grammar, or the set of derivations over an inference system.

While we do not consider it in this paper, our implementation already supports an extension of UniFormal with term language types: It allows forming the type $T[A]$, which holds the normal terms over theory T of type A. Induction on the type $T[A]$ is possible but only from outside of T. For example, in $\textbf{theory}\,N = \{\ldots\}, \textbf{term}\,even : N[n] \to \texttt{Bool} = \ldots$, induction on the term language of N is allowed in the definition of *even* but not inside N.

4 Inclusion of Theories

4.1 Definition

Intuitively, normalization of **include** S occurring in T means to copy all declarations of S into T. Only closed theories can be included—including an open theory would be redundant because we can already refer to their symbols anyway. In terms of theory morphisms, the include declaration induces an inclusion morphism from S to T.

Precisely, for theory expressions S, T, an inclusion morphism exists, written $\Gamma \vdash S \hookrightarrow T$, iff every declaration in $\overline{S}^{\Gamma}$ is also part of $\overline{T}^{\Gamma}$ in the following sense:

- If the former has a term symbol c of type A [with definition t], then the latter has a term symbol c of type A' such that $\Gamma + T \vdash A <: A'$ [and with definition t' such that $\Gamma + T \vdash t \equiv t'$].
- If the former has a type symbol a [with definition A], then the latter has a type symbol a [with definition A' such that $\Gamma + T \vdash A \equiv A'$].
- If the former has a theory symbol σ with body Σ, then the latter has one with the same body.

Clearly, this relation is reflexive and transitive, which is critical for efficient implementations. Moreover, we define **equality of theories** as inclusion in both directions, thus making inclusion an order.

The normalization of theories (see Sect. 4.3) is defined in such a way that include declarations do indeed induce a morphism: We can prove that if $\Gamma \vdash T$ THY and the body of T contains **include** S, then $\Gamma \vdash S \hookrightarrow T$.

4.2 Relation to Subtyping

Inclusion induces **subtyping** between the types of models: if $\Gamma \vdash S \hookrightarrow T$, then $\Gamma \vdash Mod(T) <: Mod(S)$. Informally, if T is bigger than S, than defining all of T implies defining all of S. This inclusion=supertype relationship is common in module systems, and languages often say that T **inherits** from S. Alternatively, languages may require applying an explicit forgetful functor to turn a model of T into a model of S, e.g., with Rocq or Isabelle records, or infer the forgetful functor like Mizar [TB85].

Even though we do not formally define term language types here, we mention the anticipated subtyping rule because of its symmetry: If $\Gamma \vdash S \hookrightarrow T$, then the term language of S forms a subtype of the term language of T, i.e., term language types and model types behave dually.

Remark 5 (Decidability). Note that equality of types and terms is needed to determine theory inclusion, and theory inclusion is needed for subtype checking and thus for term/type equality checking. In particular, the equality of types and terms must be decidable for theory inclusion to be decidable. Whether or not that is the case, depends on what other types are added in a particular UniFormal instance.

4.3 Union and Mixin of Theories

We do not need primitive syntax for the **union** of theories because we can simply define it as $S + T := \{\textbf{include}\, S,\ \textbf{include}\, T\}$.

More generally, we need a **dependent union** $S \ll \vec{D} := \{\textbf{include}\, S,\ \vec{D}\}$ to extend S with declarations $\vec{D}$ that may already use the symbols of S. For example, we have $\{\textbf{type}\, a\} \ll \textbf{term}\, c : a \ \equiv\ \{\textbf{type}\, a,\ \textbf{term}\, c : a\}$. That raises the question of **merging declarations**, e.g., do we have that

$$\{\textbf{term}\, c : \texttt{Int}\} \ll \textbf{term}\, c = 1 \quad \equiv \quad \{\textbf{term}\, c : \texttt{Int} = 1\}$$

Dependent unions with such merging behavior are central to many systems including the inheritance systems of OO-languages and mixin or trait-based module systems. We adopt that idea in UniFormal and define theory normalization in such a way that multiple declarations for the same name are merged.

Theories are **normalized** by merging in every declaration individually as in $S \ll D_1 \ll \ldots \ll D_n$. In particular, we normalize **include** T by normalizing T into a list of declarations and then merging those in one at a time. A theory is well-formed if its normalization succeeds. It is difficult to define it in any other way because the normal form of a theory is needed to check references to its identifiers. However, this does not require normalizing each expression in a theory, only to expand all includes and merge all declarations of the same name.

Example 2. The theory *Group* is usually defined by including *Monoid*. But actually *Monoid* needs both neutrality axioms whereas *Group* needs only one. UniFormal can capture this by defining some fields of the included theory:

$$\begin{aligned}&\textbf{theory}\, \mathit{Monoid} = \{\textbf{include}\, \mathit{Semigroup},\ \textbf{term}\, e : u\\ &\quad \textbf{term}\, \mathit{neutL} :\blacktriangleright \forall x : u.\mathit{op}(e,x) = x,\ \textbf{term}\, \mathit{neutR} :\blacktriangleright \forall x : u.\mathit{op}(e,x) = x\}\\ &\textbf{theory}\, \mathit{Group} = \{\textbf{include}\, \mathit{Monoid},\ \text{(axioms for inverse omitted)},\\ &\quad \textbf{term}\, \mathit{neutR} = \text{(now provable, proof omitted)}\}\end{aligned}$$

Note that merging declarations can result in a normal form with two mutually recursive declarations, i.e., normal theories are *sets* rather than lists of declarations. A neat side effect of this is an easy handling of recursive functions:

Example 3 (Recursion). We define the mutually recursive functions *odd* and *even* (omitting the usual definitions) as the theory below, which normalizes to 2 mutually recursive declarations

$$\{\textbf{term}\, \mathit{odd} : \texttt{Int} \to \texttt{Bool},\ \textbf{term}\, \mathit{even} : \texttt{Int} \to \texttt{Bool} = \ldots,\ \textbf{term}\, \mathit{odd} = \ldots\}$$

Not all merges are well-formed, e.g., UniFormal rejects merges if two definitions for the same name are not identical as in $\{\textbf{term}\, c : \texttt{Int} = 1\} \ll \textbf{term}\, c : \texttt{Int} = 0$. If multiple types are merged, the least upper bound is computed. This is non-trivial in particular for model types, where it is obtained by taking the union of theories as in $\{\textbf{term}\, c : \mathit{Mod}(S)\} \ll \textbf{term}\, c : \mathit{Mod}(T) \equiv \{\textbf{term}\, c : \mathit{Mod}(S+T)\}$. That corresponds to the typical behavior in languages with inheritance. To protect the user from inadvertently introducing an inconsistent theory, UniFormal flags an error if the bound ends up being the empty type as in $\{\textbf{term}\, c : \texttt{Int}\} \ll \textbf{term}\, c : \texttt{Bool} \equiv \{\textbf{term}\, c : \texttt{Void}\}$.

Remark 6 (Inconsistent Merges). If we see a symbol's type and definition simply as special cases of axioms, there is no need to ever reject a merge. We could merge, e.g., $\textbf{term}\, c : \texttt{Int}$ and $\textbf{term}\, c : \texttt{Bool}$ into $\textbf{term}\, c : \texttt{Void}$, or $\textbf{term}\, c = 1$ and $\textbf{term}\, c = 0$ into a theory in which $0 \equiv 1$ holds. Typically, the resulting theories will be inconsistent, but that is not problematic per se. An alternative design could accept all merges and defer such inconsistency analysis to linters.

Remark 7 (Overloading). Some languages with inheritance, in particular OO-languages, allow for overloading: Then merging $\textbf{term}\, c : \texttt{Int}$ and $\textbf{term}\, c : \texttt{Bool}$ is not an error. Instead, it results in two different declarations that share the symbol name. This issue can be resolved if we assume that the official internal identifiers is a pair of c and (some normal form of) its type. This is, e.g., how official Java identifiers are formed to disambiguated overloaded names. Our language will not support overloading but could be extended to do so.

Remark 8 (Overriding). Overriding arises if there are two conflicting definitions, e.g., if it is not an error for T to declare **term** $c : \texttt{Int} = 1$ and **term** $c : \texttt{Int} = 0$. Many OO-languages allow this, typically when the former is inherited, say from S, and the latter is local in T. Then the local definition overrides the inherited one silently (as in Java) or only if an "override" keyword is present (as in Scala). Either way, this is problematic because the inclusion from S to T is now broken in the sense that the original definition from S is no longer valid in T. This throws every proof carried out in S in question because it might have relied on the old definition. In terms of theory morphisms, in the presence of overriding, an include declaration does not induce an inclusion morphism anymore. Therefore, we reject overriding in UniFormal.

Remark 9 (Redefinition). A special case of overriding can be allowed safely: if the overriding definition is extensionally equivalent to the overridden one. For example, if the theory S of groups is included to form the theory T of commutative groups, a computer algebra system is well-advised to override some algorithms of S with more efficient versions for commutative groups. Similarly, Mizar [TB85] uses redefinitions (albeit in open theories, rather than in closed ones) to switch the definition of an identifier to an equal one that is more helpful in the current context. Redefinitions do not suffer from the drawbacks of general overriding and are thus compatible with UniFormal. But they require proofs about the equality of terms and are therefore very difficult.

4.4 Total Includes

We define an inclusion $\Gamma \vdash S \hookrightarrow T$ to be **total** if every abstract symbol declaration in $\overline{S}^{\Gamma}$ is concrete in $\overline{T}^{\Gamma}$. Thus, a total include is conservative in the sense that it does not change the semantics of T. It can be seen as T implementing the interface S, or as a special case of a theory morphism from S to T that maps every symbol of S to the corresponding definition in T. UniFormal provides two ways to make an include total.

Firstly, the keyword **total** triggers a totality check at the end of the containing theory. For example, in

$$\begin{aligned}&\textbf{theory}\, \mathit{Preorder} = \{\textbf{term}\, r : (u, u) \to \texttt{Bool}, \text{(axioms omitted)}\},\\ &\textbf{theory}\, \mathit{Monoid} = \{\text{(as above)}, \textbf{total include}\, \mathit{Preorder},\\ &\quad \textbf{term}\, r = \lambda x, y.\exists d.op(x, d) = y\}\end{aligned}$$

the keyword **total** asserts that *Monoid* not just inherits from but *implements* the theory *Preorder*. Note that all types in the definition of r can be inferred. Here the totality check at the end of *Monoid* would fail because the proofs of the axioms (reflexivity and transitivity) are still missing.

Secondly, an include can have a definition. **include** $C = e$ is a legal declaration in T iff $\Gamma + T \vdash e : Mod(C)$, i.e., the definition of an include must be a model of the included theory. **include** $C = e$ is equivalent to declaring **total include** C followed by **term** $s = e.s$ resp. **type** $s = e.s$ for every term/type symbol s of C.

In programming language terms, defined includes are **delegation**: If T already has a term e that implements the interface C, it can use a defined include to delegate all C-calls to e.

4.5 Guarded Theories and Conservative Extensions

Only closed theories make sense to be included. Accordingly, we might say that only closed theories may include others. But here it turns out, a small generalization yields a critical expressivity gain: If $\textbf{open theory}\,\tau = \{\textbf{include}\,C, \ldots\}$ includes closed theory C, we call τ **guarded** by C. Like for all open theories, access to symbols s of T is by qualified identifiers $\tau.s$. But now we define $\tau.s$ to be well-formed only in contexts that also include all guards of C. This allows writing conservative extensions of C as open theories guarded by C.

Writing a new closed theory D that extends C for this purpose would be problematic for three reasons: Firstly, any model $m : Mod(C)$ must be cast into a model of D to utilize the definition/theorem. Secondly, the normal forms (which must be computed frequently) of the closed theories become bigger, presenting serious scalability issues. Therefore, both IMPS [FGT93] and Isabelle locales [KWP99] allow adding defined symbols to C from the outside. But this is has a rather imperative flavor, and does not address the third issue: having many such extension by different authors increases the danger of name clashes when multiple extensions must be included at the same time.

UniFormal solves all issues by combining small closed theories that prioritize the abstract symbols with large guarded open theories for the extensions as in

$$\textbf{open theory}\,\mathit{Doubling} = \{\textbf{include}\,Monoid,\ \textbf{term}\,\mathit{double} = \lambda x.op(x, x)\}$$

Now assume we have $m : Mod(Monoid)$ and want to access the global identifier $g := \mathit{Doubling.double}$ on m. We can do this by simply writing $m.g$ requiring no further extensions of the syntax: the typing rule (as shown above) for $m.g$ checks g in context $\Gamma| + Monoid$ where the guard $Monoid$ is available so that checking g succeeds.

5 Global vs. Regional vs. Local Level

Finally, we can understand UniFormal's level of identifiers. The table below gives an overview. Note that these levels are orthogonal to the symbol *kinds*, i.e., we have global, regional, and local identifiers for terms, types, or theories.

5.1 Identifiers

The **global identifiers** are the ones declared in open theories. They have a qualified identifier rooted at the toplevel, via which they can be accessed from every context. Consequently, they cannot be α-renamed without breaking downstream content. Name clashes are disambiguated by putting symbols of the same name into different open theories resulting in different qualified names.

level	global	regional	local
paradigm	toplevel declaration	field in class/record	bound variable
identifiers	qualified identifiers	names	variables
declared in	open theory	closed theory	block, binder
scoping	global	global but guarded	lexical, narrow
name clash handling	qualification	merging	shadowing
semantics	fixed	context-specific	place-holder

Fig. 4. The Levels of UniFormal Identifiers

The semantics of a global identifier is fixed: Most global declarations include a definiens that explicitly states the meaning of the global identifier. If no definiens is present, the meaning is still fixed but unknown, e.g., a stub declaring only the type of a foreign function that is provided by the runtime environment.

The **local identifiers** are the bound variables. Their scopes are lexical and always contained within an expression. They are easily α-renamable, and name clashes are resolved by shadowing, i.e., each local identifier is resolved to the innermost binding of that name.

Local identifiers are usually introduced **declaratively** by a binder as in $\forall x : A.t$, in which case the scope of x is t. But UniFormal also allows **imperative** bindings: This uses block terms $(t_1, \ldots, t_n)$, where each t_i may introduce variables whose scope extends to the end of the block, as in $(\mathbf{term}\, x : \mathtt{Int} = 1, \mathbf{term}\, y : \mathtt{Int} = x + 1, f(y))$. More complex examples of imperatively binding terms are pattern-matching definitions like $head :: tail = l$ for some list l; dynamic binding as in discourse representation terms like $((\exists x : \mathtt{Int}.P) \Rightarrow B) \wedge C$ where x is visible in B but not in C [KK97]; and tactics in imperative proof languages such as *intros* in Rocq that dynamically introduce identifiers.

Remark 10 (Theory Variables). We allow for term and type declarations in local contexts but not for theory declarations. It is intriguing to have theory variables to formalize computations on theories like the ones in [SR19,CO12]. But it is an open problem how to do that best.

The global and local identifiers as described above are standard. The idea of **regional identifiers** is new: They are the symbols declared in closed theories, and they combine properties of global and local identifiers.

Consider a closed theory C of the form $\{\mathbf{term}\, c : A, \ldots\}$. Like local and contrary to global identifiers, there is no way to assign a qualified identifier to c (because C might appear anonymously), the symbol c acts as a placeholder for values that are to provided later, and α-renaming feels natural. But like global and contrary to local identifiers, c can be referenced from the outside: e.g., if we have a model $m : Mod(C)$, we can call $m.c$ to access its definition of c; or if we add term language types, then c must occur in terms over C. Thus, c as a name has global scope, but its semantics varies with the theory in which it is declared.

Finally, regional identifiers have an entirely different name clash behavior than both local and global identifiers: a second regional declaration for the same name is merged into the first one.

Remark 11 (Named Record Types). Some formal systems nudge or even force users to introduce record types only if they are tied to a global identifier. For example, Rocq features named record *declarations* of the form $Record\, R := \{a : A, b : B\}$. In this case, R and thus a and b can be taken as global identifiers. This avoids the need for regional identifiers, greatly simplifying the language, but preventing the construction of anonymous record types. This subtle design decision of named vs. anonymous record types is often barely noticeable for users, but has massive consequences for system development.

5.2 Contexts

We use a three-partite context holding the global, regional, and local identifiers. For example, when considering the term t in

$$\begin{array}{l}\textbf{open theory}\,\tau_1 = \{\\ \quad \vec{D},\, \textbf{open theory}\,\tau_2 = \{\vec{E},\, \textbf{theory}\,\tau = \{\vec{F},\, \textbf{term}\,c = \lambda x : A.t\}\}\}\end{array}$$

the global context holds $\vec{D}$ and $\vec{E}$, the regional context $\vec{F}$, and the local context $\textbf{term}\,x : A$. t can reference global declarations by, e.g., $\tau_1.\tau_2.s$ for a symbol s from $\vec{E}$, and references regional and local identifiers by name.

But we have to go one step further. Consider nested closed theories as in

$$\begin{array}{l}\textbf{theory}\,2Pointed = \{\textbf{type}\,a,\, \textbf{theory}\,Point = \{\textbf{term}\,c : a\},\\ \quad \textbf{term}\,p : Mod(Point),\, \textbf{term}\,q : Mod(Point)\}\end{array}$$

Type-checking *Point* nested inside 2*Pointed* requires opening a new region for the symbol c, while keeping the region of 2*Pointed* with the symbol a accessible. Nested theories also occur every time an *anonymous* theory C is used in $Mod(C)$ or $mod(C)$. Therefore, we use the **stack of regions** in Def. 1.

Reconsider the rule for checking the model type $Mod(C)$ from Sect. 3.2. To check $\Gamma \vdash Mod(\{\vec{D}\})$ TYPE, we check $\Gamma \vdash \{\vec{D}\}$ THY. To check the latter, we check each declaration D_i in the context $\Gamma + (D_1 \ldots, D_{i-1})$. Not using the $|$ modifier means that each D_i can see the outer regions.

In contrast, in the elimination rule for model types, which concludes with $\Gamma \vdash m.A$ TYPE, the hypothesis is $\Gamma + |C \vdash A$ TYPE. Here the $|$ modifier ensures that A can only see C-identifiers no matter in which context $m.A$ is used. That corresponds to $m.-$ representing the application of morphism m to a C-expression: a term $\Gamma \vdash m : Mod(C)$ is the same as a theory morphism from C to the innermost region of Γ.

Technically, we must actually write $\textbf{theory}\,Point = \{\textbf{term}\,c : \Delta^1.a\}$ above, where Δ^1 refers to the first enclosing region. That is necessary to differentiate if two nested regions define the same identifier.

Example 4. Consider the theory of bimagmas where two binary operations on the same carrier (as defined in Ex. 1) are present, like in a ring:

$$\begin{array}{l}\textbf{theory}\, BiMagma = \{\textbf{include}\, Carrier,\\ \quad \textbf{term}\, add : Mod(\textbf{include}\, Magma,\ \textbf{type}\, u = \Delta^1.u)\\ \quad \textbf{term}\, mult : Mod(\textbf{include}\, Magma,\ \textbf{type}\, u = \Delta^1.u)\}\end{array}$$

Here both $BiMagma$ and the nested regions in the argument of $Mod(-)$ declare unrelated regional identifiers u. In this particular example, we happen to want to identify them and therefore extend the additive and the multiplicative magma with $\textbf{type}\, u = \Delta^1.u$.

Finally, we can define the semantics of contexts and identifiers:

Definition 3 (Lookup in a Context). *Consider a context $\Gamma = G\ F_l, \ldots, F_1$ where each F_i is of the form $R_i\, L_i$ or $|\, R_i\, L_i$. Let k be the smallest number such that F_k uses the $|$ modifier. Then:*

- *A global identifier $\tau_1. \ldots .\tau_n.s$ resolves to the declaration for s that occurs in G in a sequence of nested open theories τ_i.*
- *A regional identifier s resolves to the declaration for s in R_1.*
- *The special identifier Δ^j is well-formed if $j \leq k$; its type is $shift^j(Mod(R_j))$. In particular, $\Delta^j.s$ resolves to the declarations for s in region R_j.*
- *A local identifier x resolves to $shift^j(d)$ where d is the last declaration for x in $L_k, \ldots, L_1$ and d is found L_j.*

Here, the expression Δ^0 corresponds to the "this" or "self" keyword present in many OO-language. It refers to the instance of the current theory. Δ^n for $n > 1$ generalizes this principle, e.g., Δ^1 refers to the instance of the theory enclosing the current theory. We can think of each Δ^n as a variable implicitly declared at the beginning of each region and representing the region itself. To refer to that variable, Δ^n uses its de-Bruijn index n. In particular, Δ^0 represents the current region, and when computing expressions like $m.c$, all occurrences of Δ^0 in the declaration of c must be substituted with m.

Akin to the de-Bruijn representation of variable binding, we must define shifting and substitution operations to move expressions between regions. Firstly, to move expressions originating in the j-th *enclosing* region into the current region, we apply $shift^j(-)$: it shifts all occurrences of Δ^i to Δ^{j+i}.

Example 5. Consider Ex. 4 and assume that $Carrier$ additionally contains the declaration $\textbf{type}\, v = u$. Now assume we use the expression $\Delta^1.v$ inside the type of add. The unshifted type of Δ^1 is $Mod(BiMagma)$, which at this point is $Mod(\{\textbf{type}\, u,\ \textbf{type}\, v = u\})$. This becomes $Mod(\{\textbf{type}\, u,\ \textbf{type}\, v = \Delta^1.u\})$ after shifting, and $\Delta^1.v$ definition-expands to $\Delta^1.u$.

Dually we define the function $subs^m(E)$ to move an expression E from an *enclosed* region to the current one—an operation that requires a model m of the enclosed region. $subs^m(E)$ behaves similarly to $shift^{-1}(E)$ with the exception that $subs^m(\ \Delta^0\ ) := m$. In particular, we have $subs^m(shift^1(E)) = E$.

6 Conclusion

We have introduced the UniFormal language for an OO-style definition of mathematical theories and models. The key to obtaining a simple syntax that admits a rigorous semantics was a novel notion of contexts that distinguishes global, regional, and local identifiers, with a stack of regional contexts to allow jumping back and forth between regions. While global and local identifiers are well-understood, the regional identifiers offer a novel systematic representation of various common constructions that can be difficult to represent otherwise. Examples include record fields or generators like the variables in a polynomial ring.

Concrete instances of UniFormal can extend it towards specialized languages like logics, programming languages, or or flexiformal languages like sTeX [Koh08], while enabling interoperability through a shared theory layer. Indeed, such extensions can be designed by adding features that do not interact substantially with the context.

We have already built one such instance: a UniFormal programing language[1] that features dependent function types, collection types, as well as mutable regional and local identifiers and the usual control flow operators.

References

ABC$^+$03. R. Ausbrooks, S. Buswell, D. Carlisle, S. Dalmas, S. Devitt, A. Diaz, M. Froumentin, R. Hunter, P. Ion, M. Kohlhase, R. Miner, N. Poppelier, B. Smith, N. Soiffer, R. Sutor, and S. Watt. Mathematical Markup Language (MathML) Version 2.0 (second edition), 2003. See `http://www.w3.org/TR/MathML2`.

BCC$^+$04. S. Buswell, O. Caprotti, D. Carlisle, M. Dewar, M. Gaetano, and M. Kohlhase. The Open Math Standard, Version 2.0. Technical report, The Open Math Society, 2004. See `http://www.openmath.org/standard/om20`.

CFS20. J. Carette, W. Farmer, and Y. Sharoda. Leveraging the information contained in theory presentations. In C. Benzmüller and B. Miller, editors, *Intelligent Computer Mathematics*, volume 12236, pages 55–70. Springer, 2020.

CO12. J. Carette and R. O'Connor. Theory Presentation Combinators. In J. Jeuring, J. Campbell, J. Carette, G. Dos Reis, P. Sojka, M. Wenzel, and V. Sorge, editors, *Intelligent Computer Mathematics*, volume 7362, pages 202–215. Springer, 2012.

Coq15. Coq Development Team. The Coq Proof Assistant: Reference Manual. Technical report, INRIA, 2015.

FGT93. W. Farmer, J. Guttman, and F. Thayer. IMPS: An Interactive Mathematical Proof System. *Journal of Automated Reasoning*, 11(2):213–248, 1993.

H$^+$12. T. Hardin et al. The focalize essential, 2012. `http://focalize.inria.fr/`.

HKR12. F. Horozal, M. Kohlhase, and F. Rabe. Extending MKM Formats at the Statement Level. In J. Campbell, J. Carette, G. Dos Reis, J. Jeuring, P. Sojka, V. Sorge, and M. Wenzel, editors, *Intelligent Computer Mathematics*, pages 64–79. Springer, 2012.

[1] Source code and examples available at `https://github.com/UniFormal/UPL/`.

JS92. R. Jenks and R. Sutor. *AXIOM: The Scientific Computation System*. Springer, 1992.

KK97. M. Kohlhase and S. Kuschert. Dynamic lambda calculus. In *Meeting on Mathematics of Language*, pages 85–92, 1997. `https://kwarc.info/people/mkohlhase/papers/dlc00.pdf`.

Koh06. M. Kohlhase. *OMDoc: An Open Markup Format for Mathematical Documents (Version 1.2)*. Number 4180 in Lecture Notes in Artificial Intelligence. Springer, 2006.

Koh08. M. Kohlhase. Using LaTeX as a Semantic Markup Format. *Mathematics in Computer Science*, 2(2):279–304, 2008.

KWP99. F. Kammüller, M. Wenzel, and L. Paulson. Locales – a Sectioning Concept for Isabelle. In Y. Bertot, G. Dowek, A. Hirschowitz, C. Paulin, and L. Thery, editors, *Theorem Proving in Higher Order Logics*, pages 149–166. Springer, 1999.

ML84. P. Martin-Löf. *Intuitionistic Type Theory*. Bibliopolis, 1984.

MRK18. D. Müller, F. Rabe, and M. Kohlhase. Theories as Types. In D. Galmiche, S. Schulz, and R. Sebastiani, editors, *Automated Reasoning*, pages 575–590. Springer, 2018.

ORS92. S. Owre, J. Rushby, and N. Shankar. PVS: A Prototype Verification System. In D. Kapur, editor, *11th International Conference on Automated Deduction (CADE)*, pages 748–752. Springer, 1992.

Pau94. L. Paulson. *Isabelle: A Generic Theorem Prover*, volume 828 of *Lecture Notes in Computer Science*. Springer, 1994.

RK13. F. Rabe and M. Kohlhase. A Scalable Module System. *Information and Computation*, 230(1):1–54, 2013.

Roc25. Rocq Consortium. The Rocq Prover: Reference Manual. Technical report, INRIA, 2025.

S$^+$13. W. Stein et al. *Sage Mathematics Software*. The Sage Development Team, 2013. `http://www.sagemath.org`.

SR19. Y. Sharoda and F. Rabe. Diagram Operators in MMT. In C. Kaliszyk, E. Brady, A. Kohlhase, and C. Sacerdoti Coen, editors, *Intelligent Computer Mathematics*, pages 211–226. Springer, 2019.

TB85. A. Trybulec and H. Blair. Computer Assisted Reasoning with MIZAR. In A. Joshi, editor, *Proceedings of the 9th International Joint Conference on Artificial Intelligence*, pages 26–28. Morgan Kaufmann, 1985.

WKR17. T. Wiesing, M. Kohlhase, and F. Rabe. Virtual Theories – A Uniform Interface to Mathematical Knowledge Bases. In J. Blömer, I. Kotsireas, T. Kutsia, and D. Simos, editors, *Mathematical Aspects of Computer and Information Sciences*, pages 243–257. Springer, 2017.

Indexing and Retrieval in a Heterogeneous Formal Library

Claudio Sacerdoti Coen[1] (✉) and Abdelghani Alidra[2]

[1] Department of Computer Science and Engineering - University of Bologna, Bologna, Italy
claudio.sacerdoticoen@unibo.it

[2] INRIA laboratory, Deducteam team, Laboratoire Methodes Formelles, ENS Paris-Saclay, Cachan, France
abdelghani.alidra@inria.fr

Abstract. Dedukti and MMT are both examples of tools that can collect mathematical libraries coming from different systems in a unified but heterogeneous body. Indeed, both tools implement a logical framework where the logics or type systems of the various mathematical assistants can be represented, so that their libraries can be encoded in a single format preserving well-typedness. Still, the images of the various libraries remain disjoint: logical consistency of their union is not granted, the encoding of the various statements differs from logic to logic, and the same mathematical entity remains defined repeatedly and independently. To benefit from the common representation, then, additional tools need to be developed, for example, to translate results encoded in the representation of a logic into the representation of a stronger logic, taking care of aligning the duplicated mathematical entities.

In this paper we address the challenges posed by indexing and searching the large, heterogeneous library. For example, users may expect to find results in the library up to the encoding used and up to alignments, so to be able to mix in the search result statements originally coming from different systems and logics. In particular, we describe new indexing and retrieval capabilities that we integrated directly into the LambdaPi proof assistant, that can work on Dedukti files.

1 Logical Frameworks, Interoperability and Searching

Interoperability between different mathematical systems remains a challenging goal despite the amount of research invested into it in the past years. One old approach to it, that has been recently revived by at least the Deducteam[1] and the MMT teams[2], consists in adopting a single logical framework, express every logic/type theory into it and export the libraries of mathematical results, developed in the various systems, into the common logical framework, obtaining a huge, heterogeneous mathematical library.

The encoding of logics and type theories is designed so that well-typed terms that are in the image of the encodings guarantee that the original expression

[1] https://deducteam.gitlabpages.inria.fr/

[2] https://uniformal.github.io/

V. de Paiva and P. Koepke (Eds.): CICM 2025, LNAI 16136, pp. 258–275, 2026.
https://doi.org/10.1007/978-3-032-07021-0_15

or proof in the source logic was correct/well-typed. This result does not yield interoperability yet: in general it is not possible to combine terms coming from the encoding of two different logics/systems preserving logic consistency, unless one logic is a strict superset of the other and the encodings also agree. This is the main motivation to name the library as *heterogeneous*. Moreover, even if the library would be consistent as a whole, the same mathematical object occurs multiple times in the library, once for every system it originates from, and nothing identifies the multiple occurrences. Therefore, in order to exploit the library and turn the logical framework into a bridge for interoperability between two systems, one still needs to translate results in the encoding of one logic into results in the encoding of another logic, also taking care of aligning mathematical concepts that can be identified. Multiple approaches to this translation exist: sometimes one can translate a whole logic/type-system into a stronger one in a uniform and complete way (e.g. to import into Lean theorems from HOL, whose logic is weaker); other times one can just do a best-effort, partial translation, where some proofs in a stronger logic may be recognized to hold also in a weaker logic (see, e.g. the work of F. Thiré [1] that detected in the library of Matita those proofs that could be rephrased in the weaker Simple Type Theory with Prenex Polymorphism); yet another possibility is to use the intermediate steps of the proof in one logic just as a proof sketch to informally guide proof search in the other system, possibly as an auto-formalization task.

Whatever approach to interoperability is chosen, passing through the common logical framework helps in simplifying some tasks, factoring out some logical intricacies and simplifying the engineering of the translation, for example by disentangling the translation code from the code that needs to extract the mathematical content from the different mathematical systems to make it system independent. At the same time, we have to say that currently the process ignores all the extra-logical, domain specific information that is associated to mathematical objects in the mathematical systems in order to make them usable, like mathematical notation, implicit arguments, all the type-classes/unification hints/canonical structures machinery to automatically capture the user provided automation that allows to make sense of mathematical statements, and the ad-hoc information to allow some tactics to reason on the proof objects. Future research will clarify whether it will be possible to also encode uniformly all this extra-logical information and if actual interoperability between systems thanks to the logical framework approach will succeed or not.

In case of success, one ingredient that is obviously necessary is the ability to index the heterogeneous library and retrieve mathematical statements from it. Indeed, suppose that a user or an automated tool (like a tactic) wants to know if some result has already been proved in another system — and therefore it occurs in the heterogeneous library — or if some result in the library can be applied now to progress in the proof. How can it get this information? Of course almost all the source mathematical systems already provide search facilities, but we do not want the user to have to interact with all of them to find the results when those are already in the heterogeneous library. At the same time, we should not assume that the user has already translated all the results from the heterogeneous library to his own system — so that it can just search in his libraries — because the translation can be so time consuming that it has to be done only on-demand. This is in particular the case when the translation is best effort and requires human intervention. The conclusion is that it is worth implementing search engines able to index directly the heterogeneous library. In this paper we describe such an implementation.

Previous works on indexing and retrieval for mathematical libraries and in particular for the libraries of interactive theorem provers abound [2,3]. Moreover, there is a lot of very recent work on the application of machine learning techniques to searching. Nevertheless, heterogeneous libraries pose new problems and exacerbate old ones. Identifying and addressing them is the main contribution of the current paper.

The already cited Dedukti and MMT are both logical frameworks and tools. As logical frameworks they are both extensions of LF [4]. While in principle LF is sufficiently expressive to encode every other system, in practice encodings in LF require huge terms and are unpractical. In this paper we focus on Dedukti, that extends LF by means of user provided rewriting rules in the spirit of deduction modulo [5]. The choice is not essential: we picked Dedukti because no search engine exists for it (while for MMT related previous work exists [6]) and because of support from the Cost Action CA2011 EuroProofNet where Dedukti has a prominent role as an interchange system.

The plan for the rest of the paper is as follows: in Section 2 we recall the main techniques in use for indexing and retrieval in libraries of formal mathematics; in Section 3 we address the new problems that occur when indexing Dedukti files and how to solve them; in Section 4 we discuss our implementation as an extension of LambdaPi; finally Section 5 is devoted to the conclusions and future works.

2 Searching in Formal Mathematical Libraries

In our previous work [2], we presented an exhaustive study of the systems and techniques available at the time for indexing and retrieval in mathematical libraries, comprising both libraries of formal math developed in interactive provers and collections of documents. Even if a more recent exhaustive survey exists [3], not much has changed in the meantime for formal libraries and our own survey has the benefit of providing clear taxonomies of scenarios and modular implementation techniques to briefly describe how a system works. Thus, we will briefly recall here the taxonomies from our study on mathematical libraries indexing [2] that will be helpful in the next sections. The user can consult the original paper for details and references. It is worth mentioning that we do not consider in this paper more recent techniques from machine learning, leaving those as future work.

2.1 Purpose Driven Taxonomy

Search systems are targeted either to document synthesis, to document retrieval or to formula retrieval. We are interested in the last two.

In *document retrieval* the human looks for excerpts of mathematical documents combining formulae, keywords and free text. Formulae may be relevant just by similarity, retrieval may be slow (a few secs). A good balance between precision and recall is important and the results need to be ranked in terms of both similarity and usefulness to the user. For example, the user may have a precise theorem in mind that she wants to prove; however, even retrieving related lemmas or similar theorems proved for other mathematical structures is useful.

Example 1. A query could combine the keywords "ring","homomorphism" and the pattern "$\mathrm{Img}\, f \equiv R/\ker f$" to locate a page explaining the fundamental theorem of ring homomorphisms. Example of useful results that could also be listed are pages on the fundamental theorem of group homomorphisms or introductions to abstract algebra. □

In *formula retrieval*, a program (e.g. a tactic) looks for statements in the library that match a given query. The match can be either by generalization or by instantiation and both can be expressed using unification metavariables either in the query or in place of parts of statement in the library (e.g. in place of universally quantified variables, the quantifier is dropped). Recall and speed need to be maximized and the result set may be unordered: the program will anyway test the returned results to rule out the false positives and it will decide in which order to try them, for example to try to close a proof goal automatically.

Example 2. If the goal to be proved contains the subexpression $\lim_{x\to\infty}(\sin 1/x + \cos 1/x)$, in order to simplify the goal, a tactic could search for all theorems whose conclusions match $E_1 = E_2$ where either E_1 or E_2 are generalizations of the subexpression. The query could retrieve the lemma $\forall f, g, l.\, \lim_{x\to l}(f(x) + g(x)) = \lim_{x\to l} f(x) + \lim_{x\to l} g(x)$ by indexing it's conclusion as $\lim_{\_\to\_}(\_ + \_) = \lim_{\_\to\_}\_ + \lim_{\_\to\_}\_$, building the query pattern as $\lim_{x\to\infty}(\sin 1/x + \cos 1/x) = \_$ and retrieving all lemmas whose indexed conclusions unify with the query pattern, where underscores are allowed to unify with any expression. □

2.2 Encoding Based Taxonomy

The indexed documents may encode the *presentation* of formulae (i.e. how they look like), their *content* (that captures imprecisely the informal mathematical meaning), or their *semantics* (i.e. the way they are expressed in a specific logic or type theory). The latter is usually associated to formula retrieval inside an interactive theorem prover, while the others, to document retrieval by humans that may ignore or not be interested in the technicalities of the representation. There exist forgetful mappings from semantics to content and from content to presentation. These mappings can be used during indexing to allow users to use presentational or content queries while still retrieving semantics formulae.

Representations in a logical framework fit in the semantics level, but carve into it yet another deeper level: as we will see later, the same statement in Dedukti may be encoded differently if it is expressed in the encoding of HOL [7,8] or in the encoding of the Calculus of Constructions [9], even when it perfectly fits the intersection of the two. Therefore only the content of the two statements match and not their semantics, even if they are both in the same heterogeneous library. In other words, from the point of view of indexing it is still like if the two statements belonged to two disjoint systems using two different representations.

Example 3. The presentation level formula $\forall m, m + 0 = m$ could be

$$\forall m, \text{eq } (\text{add } m \text{ zero})\ m$$

at the content level,

$$!m^{\text{nums.num}}, \\ =[\text{nums.num}](\text{arith.}+\ m^{\text{nums.num}}\ (\text{nums.NUMERAL}\ \ \text{nums.\_O}))\ m^{\text{nums.num}}$$

at the semantics level for HOL, in the library of HOL-Light, and

$$\text{theory\_hol.Prf}(\text{theory\_hol.}\forall(\lambda m : \text{theory\_hol.El}\ \ \text{terms.num}, \\ (\text{theory\_hol.}=\ \ \text{terms.num}\ \ (\text{terms.}+\ m\ (\text{terms.NUMERAL}\ \ \text{terms.\_0}))\ m)))$$

at the semantics level for Dedukti where the formula shows the encoding of the HOL-Light formula inside Dedukti. The constants Prf, El, = and ∀ are used to encode the logic of HOL-Light into Dedukti. To keep the formula short, HOLLight. theory_hol has been shortened to theory_hol and similarly for terms. □

2.3 Techniques Driven Taxonomy

Search engines are implemented combining a *main technique* from a small pool with an arbitrary number of *modular techniques* mostly meant to trade recall with precision. Remember that in the document retrieval scenario a certain degree of imprecision is a feature and in controlled ways (e.g. match up to logical consequence) the same happens for formula retrieval too.

Main techniques: among the main techniques of interest for us are *structure-based indexing*, e.g. via substitution trees, and reduction to SQL-like queries via *extraction of features* from formulae. The first technique is restricted to formula retrieval up to instantiation/generalization and therefore it rigidly captures the shape of the formula. Therefore precision is maximized, but recall is not and modular techniques have to be employed to augment it. The second technique extracts from the formulae certain structural features that are preserved by instantiation/generalization, typically the fact that some constant occurs in a formula in a certain region (hypothesis or conclusion, under how many quantifiers and if it is the head constant or not). It achieves a good balance between precision and recall. The remaining, not discussed, main techniques are either abandoned or they do not perform well for instantiation/generalization.

Modular techniques: the ones relevant to search in formal libraries and that we have used in this work are the following. *Normalization* rewrites formulae to equivalent normal forms preserving their semantics, improving recall without harming precision. For example $\geq$ can be rewritten to $\leq$ or in classical logic formulae can be put in prenex normal form. *Approximation* rewrites formulae losing information and thus trading precision for recall. Mapping formulae encoded at the semantics level to the content level is an example. *Query reduction* also trades recall for precision by dropping or weakening some constraints in the query. For example, one could enlarge the query to include frequently co-occurring terms or one can only preserve the top-level structure of the query.

All the techniques listed above have in common the fact of being expressed as rewritings of the query (for query reduction), of the terms to be indexed (for approximation) or of both (for normalization).

Example 4. When indexing $\forall n, m, d : \mathbb{N}.n + d > m + d \Rightarrow n > m$ the statement can be first normalized to $\forall n, m, d : \mathbb{N}.m + d < n + d \Rightarrow m < n$ and then approximated to $\forall \_, \_, \_ : \mathbb{N}.V\#+V\# < V\#+V\# \Rightarrow V\# < V\#$ where all variables have been replaced by a placeholder $V\#$ that stands for any variable, effectively forgetting the variables names and the binding structure. Then consider the query that looks for the statement $\forall x, y, z : \mathbb{N}.x + y < x + z \Rightarrow y < z$. By applying the same rewriting rules to the query before matching, the statement is found in the library, even if it is logically equivalent to it only up to commutativity of addition and duality between $<$ and $>$. An aggressive form of query reduction applied to this example would be to drop the constraints on the exact structure of the formula and rewrite the query to become "find a statement where $\mathbb{N}$ occurs anywhere, $+$ and $<$ occur in one hypothesis, $<$ occurs in the conclusion and no other constants occur". □

In the next section we identify the peculiarities of indexing and retrieval in the heterogeneous library of Dedukti.

3 Indexing and Retrieval in Heterogeneous Libraries

3.1 An Introduction to Dedukti

LF, also called $\lambda\Pi$, is a type theory (more precisely a Pure Type System [10]) having just two sorts (`Type` to type types and `Kind` to type `Type`), variables, constants, function application, dependently typed λ-abstractions to declare functions and product types to type them. Functions can only take in input terms (i.e. expression whose type is typed by `Type`) and not types. Therefore, to achieve polymorphism, one is obliged to introduce terms (called *codes*) that represent types, together with a decoding function that maps codes to types. According to Curry-Howard isomorphism [11], one can see propositions as types and encode them accordingly.

The following is a self contained example in LF where we encode the axiom `divides` that states that $\forall n, m, q : \mathbb{N}.n * m = q \Rightarrow n|q$ after having encoded a fragment of first order logic. We use the Dedukti syntax. In particular `s -> t` and `x:s -> t` are the non-dependent and dependent function space and `x:s => b`is the syntax for λ-abstraction. The keyword `def` allows to add some rewriting rules to the running example.

```
s : Type.                (; the type of codes for types ;)
o : Type.                (; the type of codes for propositions ;)
def El : s -> Type.      (; the decoding function for codes for types ;)
def Prf : o -> Type.     (; the decoding function for codes for propositions ;)
nat : s.                 (; the code for natural numbers ;)
func : s -> s -> s.      (; the code for functions given the codes for
                            the domain and codomain ;)
def apply : t1:s -> t2:s -> El (func t1 t2) -> El t1 -> El t2.
implies : o -> o -> o.                (; code for logical implication ;)
forall : t:s -> (El t -> o) -> o.     (; code for universal quantification ;)

mul : El (func nat (func nat nat)).   (; product function over naturals ;)
div : El nat -> El nat -> o.          (; code for divides predicate ;)
eq : t:s -> El t -> El t -> o.        (; code for polymorphic equality ;)
divides :
 Prf
  (forall nat (n: El nat => forall nat (m: El nat =>
    forall nat (q: El nat =>
     implies
      (eq nat (apply nat nat (apply nat (func nat nat) mul n) m) q)
      (div n q))))).
```

It should be immediately evident how the statement of `divides` occurs heavily encoded in LF. In particular, LF forces the so called typed-syntax approach, where every subterm explicitly carries its own type derivation, introducing a lot of syntactic overhead. Moreover, the encoding is not at all unique: the names `s,o,El,Prf,...` are arbitrarily chosen and their types are expressed in the encoding of first order logic. To encode other logics or type systems one needs to type the constants differently and add new ones.

In order to greatly reduce the complexity of the encodings, Dedukti [12] introduces user provided, type preserving rewriting rules. The user must take care of keeping confluence of the rewriting system. For example, the next excerpt shows how to simplify the encoding above rewriting logical implications, functions and universal abstraction to identify all of them with the meta-level LF dependent product. The types of `divides` and `divides2` are identified in Dedukti thanks to rewriting. The --> symbol splits the left hand side from the right hand side of a rewriting rule, that must start with the list of variables occurring in the left hand side.

```
[t1, t2] El (func t1 t2) --> El t1 -> El t2.
[p1, p2] Prf (implies p1 p2) --> Prf p1 -> Prf p2.
[t, p] Prf (forall t p) --> x: El t -> Prf (p x).
[t1, t2, f, x] apply t1 t2 f x --> f x.
divides2 :
 n: El nat -> m: El nat -> q: El nat ->
  Prf (eq nat (mul n m) q) -> Prf (div n q).
```

Note that the rewriting rule for `apply` is well typed thanks to the rewriting rule for `func`. Note also that, while the statement of `divides2` now looks simpler, details of the encoding are still present as occurrences of `El` and `Prf`. If we had encoded a more complex type theory, like the ones of Rocq [13] or Lean [14], the details still visible would have been more prominent. For example, `Elem` would have taken an additional parameter to specify via codes in which universe the type lives.

3.2 Issues when Searching in the Library of Dedukti

From Section 3.1 the main difficulties of searching the heterogeneous library of Dedukti should be immediately clear.

Problem 1: search up to encoding. Imagine that the user is looking for a proof of $\forall n, m, q : \mathbb{N}. n * m = q \Rightarrow n|q$. Of course the lemma could occur in the library multiple times, each one using a different encoding according to the logic/type-system of the mathematical system it comes from. We want to spare the user from the need to know every encoding and to issue the query multiple times, one for each encoding.
Solution: we solve the problem via approximation, seeing the query above as a query at the content level and the encoding in Dedukti as the semantics level. Therefore we assume, for each encoding, the existence of a system of rewriting rules to "throw away" the details of the encoding. For our example, in order to recall `divides2` it is sufficient to add the rules:

```
[t] El t ---> t.
[p] Prf p ---> p.
```

Note, that the two rules above, even if written in Dedukti syntax, are not type preserving in the Dedukti logical framework. In Section 4 we will discuss how to implement them in a tool. For the time being, just think of these rules to be in some Dedukti-resembling syntax of a new content level, untyped language.

Problem 2: search up to rewriting rules. Thanks to the rewriting rules introduced in the encoding, the statement of the lemma we are looking for could be present in the library as the one of `divides`, as the one of `divides2` or as another shape obtained reducing the one of `divides`, but stopping before the normal form (the statement of `divides2`) is reached. For example, Krajono, a tool to encode the library of Matita into Dedukti, strangely reduces the occurrences of the equivalent of `implies`, but not when they occur in the source of another `implies`, yielding strange looking statements of the sort `Proof (implies p q) -> Proof p -> Proof q`.
Solution: to augment recall, we can apply normalization, rewriting both the query and the formulae to be indexed also according to all the rewriting rules used in the encoding. Of course, since we are mixing these rules with the ones for approximation, we need to complete the rewriting system in case of critical pairs, in order to obtain a confluent system.

Example 5. The rules to undo the encoding combined with the ones given in Section 3.1 rewrite the Dedukti code of Example 3 to the formula

m : terms.**num** ->
theory_hol.= terms.**num** (terms.+ m (terms.NUMERAL terms._0)) m))

that closely resembles the semantics level formula for HOL-Light. The formula is still far away from the content level: for example it exposes the base-2 encoding of naturals in HOL-Light using finite sequences of bits prefixed by NUMERAL. □

Problem 3: search up to alignments. Imagine a user of Lean (or a Lean tactic) that is looking for a theorem in the heterogeneous library to progress in a proof in Lean. The mathematical concepts involved in the Lean statement could exist in the library, but they are likely to at least be named differently, and possibly have more differences (e.g. in the order of the parameters, in how general is the mathematical structure they are defined for, in their arity, etc.). This issue is well known and all the proposals for interoperability boils down to detecting *alignments* [15]. We would like the query to match up to alignments.
Solution: by expressing alignments as rewriting rules towards a canonical form, we can again solve the issue by normalization or, when the alignments do not preserve types, by approximation. However, a problem remains of obtaining large sets of alignments, a problem that could benefit from recent advances in the field of machine learning [16]. To supplement alignments, a first useful technique is also query reduction: since it is likely that two constants that have the same name (but not the same qualified identifier) in two different parts of the heterogeneous library could be alignable, the query shall be issued multiple times resolving every time the combination of the names in a different way. For example, the identifier `nat` in the user-provided query could be replaced once by `matita.arithmetics.nat.nat` (the qualified identifier for natural numbers in the library of Matita) and another time by the corresponding qualified identifier for natural numbers in the library of another system. To implement this form of query reduction, we assume we have an index that, given a name, returns all the fully qualified identifiers in the heterogeneous library that end in the very same name (possibly up-to case insensitivity). As a minor note, observe that the combination of query reduction with the rewriting of queries imposed by normalization may yield perfect duplicates of the query after normalization. For example, a name that occurs in a part of the encoding to be dropped can be resolved in two different ways. It is therefore important to get rid of duplicates before actually running the final shape of the queries.

Example 6. One could recover the content level formula of Example 3 from the one of Example 5 by aligning the semantics level constants (e.g. terms.+) to content level ones (plain + to continue the example) and by mapping the base-2 encoding of HOL-Light to Peano numbers. In this approximation process a lot of details of the representation in the HOL logic are lost. Therefore this makes sense primarily when the HOL-Light library is searched by a user of a different system. □

While the new problems identified in dealing with the heterogeneous library are significant, the good news is that they can all be solved according to well known techniques and that, with the only exception of query reduction, what is needed is "just" the possibility to let the user specify sets of rewriting rules to be employed. On the other hand, the complexity of the rewriting engine must at least allow the rules already used in the encodings. This strongly suggests that the most efficient and compact way to implement the indexer and search engine is to reuse (parts of) an implementation of the Dedukti logical framework. For this reason we decided to integrate a prototype directly into the code of LambdaPi [17], an interactive prover for Dedukti which is currently the most supported implementation of the Dedukti logical framework.

4 Implementing Search Functionalities in LambdaPi

4.1 Changes to LambdaPi

Dedukti, the logical framework, comes with a set of tools to typecheck, generate or manipulate Dedukti libraries. In particular Dedukti is also the name of the first type-checker for the logical framework. While the tool can still be used and alternative implementations of it exists (e.g. Kontroli, written in Rust [18]), the main development group is now focused on the LambdaPi interactive prover, that is partially compatible with Dedukti sources. LambdaPi is written in the OCaml language and the code includes an optimized rewriting engine that is invoked during type checking. Moreover, the system also checks that every rewriting rule preserves types, which implies that rewriting rules must refer only to constants previously defined in the environment. LambdaPi does not check confluence of the rewriting rules, even if it has options to feed the rules to external tools for confluence checking. Being an interactive prover, LambdaPi also implements metavariables that stand for missing or implicit terms and that can be instantiated via unification. We have exploited metavariables for representing holes in the queries or in the statements to be indexed to obtain indexing via instantiation/generalization, an added benefit of implementing the search engine reusing the code of a prover.

In order to implement normalization and approximation, we have first modified the code of LambdaPi in several ways:

1. It is now possible to disable the check for preservation of types when reading special LambdaPi files made only of rewriting rules; nevertheless, the rules still need to be *scoped*, meaning that the identifiers written in the rules need to be resolved. Note that in normal mode scoping and type-checking are also responsible for inserting implicit parameters and for filling them according to typing constraints. This does not happen in our special mode, creating issues with non-linear rewriting rules. Indeed a non-linear rewriting rule fires only if some arguments occur to be identical, which may not be the case when some implicit argument should have been instantiated by typing. For the time being, the user is responsible to turn non-linear rules into linear rules taking care that confluence is not broken.

2. The special files of the point above list all the rewriting rules that will be applied by normalization to the statement of the library when indexing them. In order to have a single place where to list all such rules and in order to be able to index library files while processing them, the rules in the special files need to refer to constants that have not been declared yet. This required several changes to the code of LambdaPi. First of all the code for scoping rules in special model had to be changed to only allow fully qualified identifiers and to avoid checking if those were already defined. The second change was about where the rules themselves were stored in compiled form. Indeed, to quickly apply rewriting rules, LambdaPi compiles them to decision diagrams, one for each head symbol in the left-hand-side of a set of rules, and stores the decision diagram in the data structure for the symbol itself. To process rewriting rules before the symbols are introduced, the decision diagrams are now detached from the data structure for symbols and the association occurs lazily at run-time.

4.2 Main Implementation Technique and the Query Language

Having already discussed what modular techniques are required to support an heterogeneous library, we are left with the choice of the main technique for indexing and retrieval. While we are fond of reduction to SQL via feature extraction [19], structure-based indexing works perfectly well in some scenarios where extreme precision is preferred to high recall, in particular in formula retrieval employed inside automatic tactics. We have therefore decided to implement both at once, also introducing a *query language* to combine atomic queries to obtain complex ones, which is mandatory when working with features, since an atomic query dealing with just one feature is typically never sufficient.

We start the discussion by presenting the syntax and semantics of the query language:

```
Q ::= B | Q,Q | Q;Q | Q|PATH
B ::= WHERE HOW GENERALIZE? PATTERN
PATH ::= << string >>
WHERE ::= name | anywhere | rule | lhs | rhs | type | concl | hyp | spine
HOW ::= > | = | >=
GENERALIZE ::= generalize
PATTERN ::= << term possibly containing placeholders _ (for terms)
               and V# (for variable occurrences) >>
```

A query `Q` returns a set of results. Each result is a tuple made of the qualified identifier of the constant or rewrite rule found in the library, the coordinates where its declaration is to be found on the hard disk (in the form filename, initial position and final position) and a list of motivations that explain what are the reasons that determined the inclusion of the result in the set.

The syntax for queries is reminiscent of Prolog: `Q,Q` is logical conjunction and semantically it selects the intersection of the results of the two queries, appending the lists of motivations; `Q;Q` is logical disjunction and semantically it selects the union of the results, also appending the list of motivations when a result satisfies both queries at once; `B` is a base query that comes with results having their own motivation; finally `Q|PATH` restricts the set of results to those whose qualified identifier is a suffix of the given `PATH`. The latter construct can be used for example to restrict the results to those in the part of the library of Rocq that deals with real numbers.

A base query `B` selects those constants that match a given `PATTERN`. The interpretation of the pattern and the kind of match is specified by the `WHERE`, `HOW` and `GENERALIZE` parts of the query. The simplest case is when `WHERE` is `name`. In that case the `PATTERN` can only be a non qualified identifier, `HOW` must be equality and the constant matches if its non qualified name matches exactly the pattern. In all the other cases the `PATTERN` is a LambdaPi term, possibly containing placeholders to be instantiated or the special symbol `V#` that matches any variable occurrence. When placeholders are used, the query is thus resolved by instantiation. `WHERE` specifies where the pattern must be present in the term: `rule`, `lhs` and `rhs` are used to retrieve rewriting rules and the pattern must occur respectively wherever, in the left hand side or in the right hand side of the rule; `type`, `concl`, `hyp`, `spine` are used to retrieve constants and the pattern must match respectively wherever in the constant type, in its conclusion or in one hypothesis or as a suffix of its spine. To make sense of the previous terminology, consider a typical statement of the form $\forall \bar{x} : T, H_1 \Rightarrow \ldots \Rightarrow H_n \Rightarrow C$ where C is not a product type — remember that universal quantification and logical implication are both product types in dependent type theory and thus in LF and Dedukti. Then each T and H_i are hypotheses, C is the conclusion and $H_j \Rightarrow \ldots H_n \Rightarrow C$ is a suffix of the spine (as well as the whole statement when zero or more initial universal quantification have been dropped). The `HOW` part of the query completes the description of the matching constraints: when `HOW` is equality the pattern must be found exactly in a position specified by `WHERE`; when it is `>` it must match a strict subterm of the position specified by `WHERE`; finally `>=` allows both modes at once.

The results of running a base query `B` have as motivations triples made of the `WHERE`, `HOW` and `GENERALIZE` parts of the query. Ignoring `GENERALIZE` for now, a singleton result could then tell something like: "`divides` is the result because `(eq _ _)` is exactly an hypothesis, `mul` occurs as a strict subterm of an hypothesis, `nat` is also exactly an hypothesis and the conclusion matches exactly `V#|V#`, i.e. a variable divides another one". The link with reduction to SQL is now evident: the features used in Asperti et al. [19] were of the form "the constant X occurs exactly/inside in position Y under N binders" that corresponds to the degenerate case where all patterns are identifiers. Since only identifiers were used as patterns, there was no need to employ substitution trees to match subterms and all that was necessary was to join together queries over tables of records `IDENTIFIER-WHERE-BINDERS` — a perfect job for a relational database. Note that for the time being we are not recording the number of binders information that was used only in some kind of queries and that is not very stable under arbitrary rewritings.

Finally, when `GENERALIZE` is added to a base query, the pattern is matched against the conclusions of the statements in the library up to generalization, i.e. interpreting the variables bound in the spine of the constant type as metavariables. For example, the query `div 2 4` can match the constant `divides` since its conclusion `div m n` is turned into `div _ _`. This makes queries by generalization useful to look for lemmas to progress in the proof (e.g. by back-chaining as in the case of `divides`).

4.3 Implementation Details

To index the heterogeneous library of LambdaPi we proceed as follows, filling in two distinct indexes, a hash-table over strings (to resolve the queries having `WHERE=name`) and a discrimination tree (for all the other queries):

- when processing a file in indexing mode, each constant and rewrite rules is indexed
- the association name/identifier (and location) is added to the hash-table (for constants only)
- the type of the constant or the rewriting rule is normalized according to the user provided rewriting rules that implement normalization and approximation
- the set of subterms of the constant type or of the rewriting rule is determined, remembering for every subterm its location (e.g. as a strict subterm of an hypothesis)
- the association subterm/identifier, location and position of the subterm is added to the discrimination tree with `GENERALIZE=false`
- the previous step is repeated after replacing in the subterm the variables bound by the spine with metavariables, setting `GENERALIZE=true`

Roughly speaking, the discrimination tree can be thought as a trie over strings that describe pre-visits of the abstract syntax trees of formulae; therefore running a basic query where `WHERE≠name` just consists in applying the user provided rewriting rules for normalization to the query, pre-visit it to obtain a sort of string and perform a lookup in the discrimination tree in time linear in the length of the previsit of the string. Resolving a basic query is thus pretty fast. To combine basic queries we just apply unions and intersections of results, that can be done in time $O(m \log(n/m+1))$ where m and n are the cardinalities of the two sets. Path restriction is an $O(n)$ operation where n is the cardinality, assuming paths to have constant bounded size and thus suffix check to be $O(1)$. Finally, the queries are augmented before normalization to resolve the unqualified names occurring in the queries. To perform the augmentation, additional simple queries to resolve names are automatically issued.

4.4 User Interface

To index the library, we have augmented the command line interface of LambdaPi with a new `lambdapi index` command that takes as input the path of the files that hold the rewriting rules used in normalization and approximation and the list of files to be indexed, together with the optional location of the index file to create. A variant of the command allows one to incrementally add more files to a previous index. We currently lack the ability to selectively remove files from the index.

To run a query, we have augmented LambdaPi in three different ways. The command line interface now accepts the `lambdapi search` sub-command to specify a query to run against a given index. The list of files that contain the rewriting rules used to normalize the query must also be provided. The second way to run a query is through a new command accepted by LambdaPi during interactive use. Finally, we added the new sub-command `lambdapi websearch` that turns LambdaPi into a web server that accepts queries and shows the results in a Google-style fashion. The command requires the usual set of files holding the rewriting rules to be applied to the query. All three modes present the set of results to the user by recovering from the hard drive each constant or rewriting rule declaration in LambdaPi syntax.

Fig. 1 shows a screenshot of the search engine in Web server mode.

4.5 Examples of queries

We show here some examples of queries to better illustrate the query language.

Example 7. The user is interested into theorems about rearranging elements of a series of real numbers. Since there are many, under different hypotheses, and since they can be formalized in many ways, a first idea is to look for all constants that have as a premise, functions from naturals to naturals (to permute the indexes) and where the type of real numbers also occurs in an hypothesis: `hyp = (num → num ), hyp. >= R`. Fig. 1 shows 22 results, and most of those are relevant. □

Example 8. Continuing the previous example, one result found is

```
symbol thm_SUM_PERMUTE_NUMSEG : Prf (∀ (λ f : El (fun num Real), (∀ (λ p : El (fun num num),
    (∀ (λ m : El num, (∀ (λ n : El num, (⇒ ((@permutes num) p (... m n)) (= ((@sum num) (
    ... m n) f) ((@sum num) (... m n) ((@o num num Real) f p)))))))))))
```

To understand the statement, the user needs first to understand the predicates `permutes` and .... In order to find the definition of `permutes` in the library, the best query is `concl = (= (permutes _) _)` that looks for a constant whose statement concludes that the predicate `permutes`, instantiated on a type (the _ argument), is equal (i.e. logically equivalent) to something (the second _). Indeed, the query returns a single result that shows that in HOL-Light, the binary predicate `permutes A s p` requires `p` to permute the elements of the set `s` (a characteristic function over the type `A`), leaving all the other elements of `A` fixed.

```
symbol thm_permutes [A] : Prf (∀ (λ s : El (fun A bool), (∀ (λ p : El (fun A A), (= ((
    @permutes A) p s) (∧ (∀ (λ x : El A, (⇒ (¬ ((@IN A) x s)) (= (p x) x)))) (∀ (λ y : El
    A, ((@∃₁ A) (λ x : El A, (= (p x) y)))))))))))
```

For ... the query `concl = (= ... _)` returns no result. We then try `concl = (= (... _ _) _)` since ... is a binary predicate, getting six results. We can refine the query to

Fig. 1. The search engine in action. The query is displayed just before the results. It looks for all statements having an hypothesis that is the type of functions from natural numbers to natural numbers and another hypothesis containing an occurrence of the real numbers. The query has been written by a Rocq user since `N` and `R` are the names for $\mathbb{N}$ and $\mathbb{R}$ in Rocq. Note that, thanks to the rewriting rules for alignments, the query returns results from the encoding of the HOL-Light [20] library where `N` $\rightarrow$ `N` occurs as `(fun num num)` and `R` as `Real`. Only the first two results out of 22 are visible in the screenshot.

`concl = (= (... V# V#) _)` to force the arguments to be variables obtaining just three results, the latter one showing that `... m n` is the characteristic function of the interval $[m, n]$ of natural numbers. □

Example 9. Suppose that the user is interested in locating the mean value theorem in the library. Since there exists at least two versions of the theorem with different hypothesis, she can use a disjuntive query:

```
hyp >= absolutely_continuous_on ; (hyp >= continuous_on, hyp >= differentiable)
```
□

Example 10. Disjunctive queries can also be used when normalization is not strong enough to achieve the expected recall level. For example, the following query can be used to retrieve theorems that allow to simplify sums over sets: the sum can occur either on the left hand side or the right hand side of the equality.

```
hyp >= absolutely_continuous_on ; (hyp >= continuous_on, hyp >= differentiable)
```
□

5 Conclusions and Future Works

Thanks to the Cost Action CA2011 EuroProofNet there is a renewed interest in the use of logical frameworks to foster interoperability of mathematical systems. A logical framework allows to collect the encoding of all the results developed in multiple systems in a huge, heterogeneous library. Indexing and retrieval of formulae in such a library raises new challenges, in particular, when user defined rewriting is incorporated in the logical framework to simplify the encodings. Luckily enough, we can reuse ideas from the literature to solve these challenges. Moreover, the solutions are often based on forms of rewriting and therefore the code of the tools that implement the logical framework can be reused for the implementation of the search engine.

In this paper we framed the various problems, proposed solutions and briefly described an implementation for the LambdaPi tool that implements the Dedukti logical framework. Scalability seems to be a minor concern so far: we deployed the search engine on the library exported from HOL-Light (more than 20,000 theorems) with the following result: by using 355 rewrite rules to "undo" the encoding and apply alignments towards the standard library of Rocq, indexing the whole library on a machine with 32 cores i9-13950HX processor and 62GB of RAM, takes 18.19 seconds. It generates the two indexes that, once saved on disk, take only 108MB. The rewriting rules for alignments were automatically generated from hand-made files used to translate HOL-Light proofs into Rocq via LambdaPi [21]. The search engine is available online at the address `https://lambdapi.saclay.inria.fr/` and this particular deployment is an experiment targeted to Rocq users that want to explore the HOL-Light library before importing theorems.

We distinguish between short and long term future works. In the short term, we plan to improve the implementation by letting the user provide also the sources of the libraries translated to other systems/logic. When answering a query, the tool will render each result in the original and in its translated forms. Thus, for example, a Rocq user that search for HOL-Light theorems will also see the

Rocq code of the result. A second short term improvement will be to augment the query language with constructs suggested by the users. At the moment we already received the request for a new filter that allows to use regular expressions over the fully qualified name of each search result, since the name of technical lemmas typically follow a schema that can be exploited by the user.

In the long term, a couple of future works stand out. The first is to collect feedback from users or testers to determine how usable is the current query language. In our previous work [19] on searching the library of Rocq, we hid the query language providing only a limited set of five high-level queries that were deemed useful. The useful queries in an heterogeneous setting, e.g. when a Rocq user is looking for results in the HOL library, are yet to be determined. The second future work is to integrate a way to rank the results. Ranking by similarity between the query and the results, a metric that is often used in formula retrieval, is challenging because normalization, approximation and query reduction interfere: the actual pattern that is used may be quite different in shape from the one entered by the user. The motivations in the query results are already meant to help ranking.

Last but not least, especially in the Lean world, we are observing several new search services that exploit machine learning. The potential of such technology in the context of heterogeneous libraries and proof interoperability deserves some investigation. For example, potentially the phase of turning alignments into rewriting rules could be completely skipped if search happens in a latent space used to automatically translate from one system to another.

Acknowledgements Sacerdoti Coen has been supported by the INdAM-GNCS project "Modelli Composizionali per l'Analisi di Sistemi Reversibili Distribuiti" and both authors by the Cost Action CA2011 EuroProofNet.

References

1. F. Thiré, *Interoperability between proof systems using the logical framework Dedukti. (Interopérabilité entre systèmes de preuve en utilisant le cadre logique Dedukti).* PhD thesis, École normale supérieure Paris-Saclay, Cachan, France, 2020.
2. F. Guidi and C. S. Coen, "A survey on retrieval of mathematical knowledge," *Math. Comput. Sci.*, vol. 10, no. 4, pp. 409–427, 2016.
3. P. Dadure, P. Pakray, and S. Bandyopadhyay, "Mathematical information retrieval: A review," *ACM Comput. Surv.*, vol. 57, no. 3, pp. 61:1–61:34, 2025.
4. R. Harper, F. Honsell, and G. D. Plotkin, "A framework for defining logics," in *Proceedings of the Symposium on Logic in Computer Science (LICS '87), Ithaca, New York, USA, June 22-25, 1987*, pp. 194–204, IEEE Computer Society, 1987.
5. G. Dowek, "Deduction modulo theory," *CoRR*, vol. abs/1501.06523, 2015.
6. C. Prodescu and M. Kohlhase, "Mathwebsearch 0.5 an open formula search engine," in *Report of the symposium "Lernen, Wissen, Adaptivität 2011" of the GI special interest groups KDML, IR and WM, LWA 2011, Magdeburg, 28.-30.September 2011* (M. Spiliopoulou, A. Nürnberger, and R. Schult, eds.), pp. 257–264, Fakultät für Informatik, Otto-von-Guericke-Universität Magdeburg, 2011.

7. A. Church, "A formulation of the simple theory of types," *The journal of symbolic logic*, vol. 5, no. 2, pp. 56–68, 1940.
8. J. Hurd, "The opentheory standard theory library," in *NASA Formal Methods Symposium*, pp. 177–191, Springer, 2011.
9. T. Coquand and G. Huet, *The calculus of constructions.* PhD thesis, INRIA, 1986.
10. H. P. Barendregt, *Lambda calculi with types*, p. 117–309. USA: Oxford University Press, Inc., 1993.
11. H. B. Curry, J. R. Hindley, and J. P. Seldin, *To HB Curry: essays on combinatory logic, lambda calculus, and formalism.* Academic Press, 1980.
12. A. Assaf, G. Burel, R. Cauderlier, D. Delahaye, G. Dowek, C. Dubois, F. Gilbert, P. Halmagrand, O. Hermant, and R. Saillard, "Dedukti: a logical framework based on the $\lambda\Pi$-calculus modulo theory," *CoRR*, vol. abs/2311.07185, 2023.
13. ROCQ Prover, "Rocq prover," 2023. Accessed: 2025-07-06.
14. L. de Moura, "Soonho kong, jeremy avigad, floris van doorn, and jakob von raumer," *The Lean Theorem Prover (system description)*, pp. 378–388, 2014.
15. D. Müller, T. Gauthier, C. Kaliszyk, M. Kohlhase, and F. Rabe, "Classification of alignments between concepts of formal mathematical systems," in *Intelligent Computer Mathematics - 10th International Conference, CICM 2017, Edinburgh, UK, July 17-21, 2017, Proceedings*, vol. 10383 of *Lecture Notes in Computer Science*, pp. 83–98, Springer, 2017.
16. L. Horowitz and V. de Paiva, "Mathgloss: Building mathematical glossaries from text," *CoRR*, vol. abs/2311.12649, 2023.
17. G. Hondet and F. Blanqui, "The new rewriting engine of dedukti (system description)," in *5th International Conference on Formal Structures for Computation and Deduction, FSCD 2020, June 29-July 6, 2020, Paris, France (Virtual Conference)* (Z. M. Ariola, ed.), vol. 167 of *LIPIcs*, pp. 35:1–35:16, Schloss Dagstuhl - Leibniz-Zentrum für Informatik, 2020.
18. M. Färber, "Safe, fast, concurrent proof checking for the lambda-pi calculus modulo rewriting," in *Proceedings of the 11th ACM SIGPLAN International Conference on Certified Programs and Proofs*, CPP 2022, (New York, NY, USA), p. 225–238, 2022.
19. A. Asperti, F. Guidi, C. S. Coen, E. Tassi, and S. Zacchiroli, "A content based mathematical search engine: Whelp," in *Types for Proofs and Programs, International Workshop, TYPES 2004, Jouy-en-Josas, France, December 15-18, 2004, Revised Selected Papers*, vol. 3839 of *Lecture Notes in Computer Science*, pp. 17–32, Springer, 2004.
20. J. Harrison, "Hol light: A tutorial introduction," in *International Conference on Formal Methods in Computer-Aided Design*, pp. 265–269, Springer, 1996.
21. F. Blanqui, "Translating HOL-Light proofs to Coq," in *LPAR 2024: Proceedings of 25th Conference on Logic for Programming, Artificial Intelligence and Reasoning, Port Louis, Mauritius, May 26-31, 2024*, vol. 100 of *EPiC Series in Computing*, pp. 1–18, EasyChair, 2024.

Neural Language Models

Exploring proof autoformalization with Mistral on Herald

Lucy Horowitz[1](✉), Michail Karatarakis[2], Xuandi Ren[1], and Alejandro Sanchez Ocegueda[1]

[1] University of California, Berkeley, USA
{lucyhorowitz,xuandi_ren,alexso}@berkeley.edu
[2] Radboud University, Nijmegen, The Netherlands
michail.karatarakis@ru.nl

Abstract. Proof autoformalization aims to generate formal proofs from natural-language (NL) statements. While large language models (LLMs) show promise, they struggle with accuracy on complex proofs, and their size and cost limit broader use. We evaluate the LLM `mistral-large -2411` on the Herald dataset, a large collection of aligned informal and formal Lean proofs. Our analysis reveals common model errors and structural issues in the dataset, including data leakage. Using iterative prompt refinement and practical fixes, we improve formalization quality. This work highlights both the potential and current limits of prompt-based autoformalization.

Keywords: autoformalization, LLM, formal math, Lean 4, mathlib

1 Introduction

The formalization of mathematics refers to the task of representing mathematical knowledge in a language that can be checked by a computer. Achieving fully computer-checked mathematics has long been a major objective in both mathematics and computer science. Although proof assistants have made formalization increasingly feasible, the process is still slow, labor-intensive, and requires substantial expertise. As a result, it has not yet been widely adopted in mainstream mathematical practice.

Autoformalization aims to address this challenge by automatically translating mathematical content written in natural language into formal definitions and proofs. If successful, it could reduce the effort required to formalize mathematical texts, making formal methods more accessible to both human users and automated systems. This would not only benefit mathematics itself, but also support advances in areas such as formal verification, program synthesis, automated reasoning, symbolic computation, and artificial intelligence.

Autoformalization has long been viewed as a difficult and open challenge. Recent advances in machine learning have introduced new avenues for addressing it [19,18,37,14]. Among these, large language models (LLMs) [40] have emerged as especially promising tools for bridging informal mathematical language and

V. de Paiva and P. Koepke (Eds.): CICM 2025, LNAI 16136, pp. 279–299, 2026.
https://doi.org/10.1007/978-3-032-07021-0_16

formal systems. These models show potential in translating informal mathematical texts into formal languages, but current performance varies widely and lacks consistent evaluation on diverse, realistic inputs.

Contributions. In this paper, we explore the use of the LLM `mistral-large -2411` for mathematical autoformalization with the Lean 4 theorem prover [27] and its associated library, Mathlib [35]. In contrast to other popular models at the time, this model was free and open source, meaning that we could access the Mistral API and conduct our experiments without any extra costs. We believe in accessible, free, and open source software. Consequently, we want to establish accessible baselines for future work and avoid the difficulties associated with paid and private models.

Our approach relies on iterative prompt engineering to enhance the model's formalization accuracy. We leverage a large dataset of informal and formal mathematical pairs, as well as formal techniques for improving autoformalization. Our contributions are as follows:

- A case study applying a large language model to autoformalize theorems from a large dataset of formal mathematics.
- An evaluation of Mistral's performance, highlighting common behaviors and challenges.
- Practical methods and insights to improve model output, covering prompt design, data preparation, and dataset structural issues.

Related work. Initial work in the area of autoformalization, such as [37], explored training dedicated neural architectures for the task of statement formalization. More recent studies [40,28,48] utilize LLMs through few-shot in-context learning, while [1] refines this approach by tailoring the context examples based on the input. In parallel, approaches like [2] and [13] have focused on fine-tuning of LLMs using aligned pairs of natural and formal language, eliminating the need for in-context learning altogether.

The automatic formalization of proofs poses a greater challenge compared to individual statements. Using large language models to automatically prove math theorems does not have a unified approach. A common strategy in recent work is to perform best-first or tree-based search over proof states [10,29,21,16,44,39,3,46]. This method benefits from the fact that invalid tactics are immediately rejected by the proof assistant, helping to maintain correctness during search. However, it limits the model's ability to reason globally, since tactics are selected incrementally without a view of the entire proof. An alternative approach uses large language models to generate full proofs directly-either from scratch [41] or guided by a human-written proof sketch [14,36].

To tackle the challenge of generating formal proofs, [14] and [42] propose frameworks where large language models first produce proofs in natural language, which are then converted into formal outlines via in-context learning. These outlines are further complemented using automated theorem provers such as Isabelle's Sledgehammer. In contrast, [38] and [32] fine-tune LLMs to directly generate complete formal proofs, often enriched with inline natural language explanations. Notably, [38] also enables bidirectional translation between formal and natural-language representations of both statements and proofs.

Previous efforts to use Mistral for autoformalizing complex theorems have relied on manual prompt engineering [20], while generating natural language proofs automatically [14] can be seen as a form of automatic prompt engineering.

In contrast, our approach uses Mistral without any fine-tuning or search techniques, depending solely on carefully crafted prompts. Evaluated on a large dataset of aligned informal and formal proofs, we examine typical challenges such as errors and syntax issues. We also explore practical strategies to mitigate these problems. This work provides a clear view of the current capabilities and limitations of prompt-based autoformalization in a straightforward, scalable setting.

Datasets. Machine-learning-based autoformalization also remains a challenging task, primarily due to the scarcity of large-scale, high-quality datasets aligning natural and formal mathematical language. Unlike Python, for which code-focused LLMs can benefit from abundant web-scale corpora and widespread natural language documentation, formal mathematics lacks such aligned resources. Most available datasets are tied to specific proof assistants: Coq (GamePad [11], CoqGym [43], PRISM [30]), Isabelle (IsarStep [22], PISA [15]), HOL Light (HOList [4], HoLStep [17]), and Lean (LeanStep [10], `lean-gym` [29]). The only cross-system benchmark, MiniF2F [47], contains just 488 evaluation theorems drawn from math olympiads and lacks a training set. LeanDojo [44] provides tools for interacting with Lean and supports premise extraction for retrieval-augmented theorem proving. While a few other datasets include premises [4,25], their data extraction pipelines are not publicly released, limiting reproducibility and extensibility.

Recent work has addressed data scarcity by using LLMs to generate natural-formal language (NL-FL) pairs. MMA [13] creates 88k NL statements from formal ones via LeanDojo. Lean-STaR [24] aligns 52k NL "proof thoughts" with formal steps. TheoremLlama [38] bootstraps training data by embedding NL proofs in Lean 4. Lean Workbook [45] uses an iterative pipeline to translate math problems between online forums and Lean 4.

However, these approaches are fundamentally limited by the current capabilities of LLMs in mathematical reasoning and logic. The resulting NL-FL pairs often contain errors, which may propagate through the datasets and negatively impact downstream model performance.

In response, we apply an LLM directly to the Herald dataset [9]: a large collection of aligned informal and formal Lean proofs. Instead of generating data, we use the model to analyze an existing dataset.

However, it is important to note that while Herald was published in early October of 2024, `mistral-large-2411` was released in November of 2024. It is therefore possible that Herald was included in its training data.

Implementation comments. The dataset, experiment code, prompts, and generated proofs are available at `https://github.com/rxdoi/Autoformalization`.

Structure of the paper. We begin by describing our methodology in Section 2. Section 3 presents the experimental setup used to evaluate our implementation. In Section 4, we discuss the comparison context and challenges related to benchmarking against prior work. Results and observations follow in Section 5. Section 6 offers concluding remarks, and Section 7 outlines several directions for future research.

2 Methodology

Rather than fine-tuning the whole model, we guide Mistral's responses by writing careful prompts in a step-by-step process. These prompts include examples and formatting hints that help the model correctly turn LaTeX-like input into Lean-style output. For instance, we give the LLM a file header as part of the prompt. This is done to give the model "hints" about which theorems, lemmas, and proofs might be useful in its construction of the proof. This is a reasonable step because a model being asked to prove a specific theorem should not also be asked to reprove lemmas which have already been formalized. Using these techniques allows us to make good use of the model as it is, without having to incur the cost and time of retraining.

Example data. Each example in the Herald dataset is a structured record containing eight fields:

- **id**: A unique numerical identifier for the entry.
- **name**: A short label corresponding to the theorem's identifier in Lean.
- **formal_theorem**: The formal Lean statement of the theorem, extracted from Mathlib.
- **informal_theorem**: A natural-language statement of the theorem.
- **formal_proof**: The Lean proof from Mathlib.
- **informal_proof**: A natural-language proof of the theorem, automatically generated from the formal proof by `Herald_translator`
- **commented_proof**: The formal proof annotated with explanatory comments.
- **header**: A list of necessary `import` and `open` commands. In Lean, `import` loads external modules (e.g., `Mathlib`), while `open` makes their contents directly accessible without qualifying names. This header ensures the theorem and its proof can be parsed and executed correctly.

To clarify the structure of a single entry in the dataset, we provide an example.

- **id**: `7832`

- **name**: `Nat.dist_eq_zero`
- **formal_theorem**:

```
theorem Nat.dist_eq_zero {n m : ℕ} (h : n = m) : dist n m = 0 := by
    sorry
```

- **informal_theorem**: *Equality Implies Zero Distance in Natural Numbers:* For any natural numbers n and m, if $n = m$, then the distance between n and m is zero, i.e., $\text{dist}(n, m) = 0$.
- **formal_proof**:

```
theorem Nat.dist_eq_zero {n m : ℕ} (h : n = m) : dist n m = 0 := by
  rw [h, dist_self]
```

- **informal_proof**: Given natural numbers n and m such that $n = m$, we need to show that $\text{dist}(n, m) = 0$.
  1. Since $n = m$, we can substitute n with m in the distance function, which gives us $\text{dist}(m, m)$.
  2. By the property of the distance function, the distance from any element to itself is zero, i.e., $\text{dist}(m, m) = 0$.
  3. Therefore, $\text{dist}(n, m) = 0$.

  This completes the proof.
- **commented_proof**:

```
theorem Nat.dist_eq_zero {n m : ℕ} (h : n = m) : dist n m = 0 := by
  rw [h, dist_self]
```

- **header**:

```
import Mathlib.Algebra.Order.Ring.Nat
import Mathlib.Data.Nat.Dist

open Nat
```

Our methodology relies on having the correct headers as part of the proof. However, the Herald dataset includes some entries which have invalid **header** fields[1]. Therefore, our process begins by filtering out the invalid entries, followed by the random selection of a specified number of entries from the remaining dataset. This ensures diversity and a more representative evaluation across different segments of `mathlib`.

Prompt Engineering

The language model is given a triple consisting of a formal statement, its informal counterpart, and an informal proof, with the task of generating a corresponding formal proof. This output is then checked in Lean; if verification fails, the resulting error is fed back to the model to prompt another attempt. To improve accuracy and ensure correct usage of Mathlib lemmas and syntax, the prompt includes the full content of all relevant header files.

[1] These entries are denoted by the string `unable to analyze`.

For each target theorem, we include the full contents of all header files that the theorem depends on. These headers contain all the necessary definitions, lemma statements, and proofs of smaller lemmas needed for the particular proof the theorem presented to the LLM. We do this because `mathlib` is designed in a very modular way: even simple theorems are often broken down into many smaller lemmas with names that can be hard to interpret for someone not deeply familiar with the library.[2] Finding the right lemma and knowing how to use it is therefore a challenging task.

Some recent systems that use LLMs try to solve this by having specialized components to pick out relevant lemmas or by training models specifically for lemma retrieval (see, e.g., [44]). In our case, since the theorems are generally simple and involve only a few lemmas, and because our time and computational resources are limited, we adopt a simpler but effective approach: we provide the LLM with the complete contents of all relevant header files as context.

This way, every lemma that might be useful is available in the prompt right away, so we do not need any extra retrieval steps. In practice, this keeps the prompt size reasonable and the success rate high enough for our purposes. In the future, more advanced lemma selection techniques could be added as we tackle more complex theorems or larger datasets.

We extracted the proofs using the following prompt:

Lean 4 Autoformalization Task

You are an expert in Lean 4 theorem proving. We will give you:

- A theorem statement in natural language
- An informal proof in natural language
- The formal theorem declaration in Lean 4
- The contents of definitions and lemmas from the relevant imports
- A prefix containing imports plus any supporting definitions and lemmas

Your job is to continue from that prefix and produce the complete Lean 4 proof. If we show you an error message from Lean, revise your proof accordingly - but always pick up exactly where the given prefix ends.

Input Format

1. **Informal Theorem** A description of the theorem in natural language.
2. **Informal Proof** The corresponding informal proof.
3. **Formal Theorem** The theorem statement in Lean 4 syntax.
4. **Prefix** The initial Lean 4 code (imports and any definitions/lemmas) that you must build on.

[2] `https://leanprover-community.github.io/contribute/naming.html`

5. **Header Information** All relevant definitions and lemmas from the imports.
6. **Error Message** Error message of the last attempt (if any).

Output Requirements

- Your output must consist **only** of the Lean 4 proof, starting immediately after the given prefix.
- DO NOT include backticks, explanations, comments, code fences or any other text before or after the proof.

Guidelines

- Ensure your formal proof faithfully follows the provided informal proof.
- Use only the definitions and lemmas from the supplied header information - do not introduce any new lemmas or definitions.
- Do not use Lean 3 syntax.

Incorporating Lean Feedback

To improve the proofs generated by the LLM, we set up a feedback loop in our pipeline. After the LLM produces a proof script, we run it through Lean to check for errors. If Lean finds no errors, the proof is accepted and the process ends. If there is an error, we take the first error message, cut the proof right before the problem line, and insert the `trace_state` tactic right after it. Running Lean on this shortened script gives us the full proof state at the failure point - that is, the list of remaining goals along with their local assumptions and what still needs to be proved. We record this information and send it back to the LLM. The LLM then continues generating the proof starting from the error, now guided by both the error message and the detailed proof state. This cycle repeats until Lean successfully verifies the proof.

Lean's `trace_state` tactic shows the current proof state in the info view, including all open goals, their local context, and the goal statements. Since `trace_state` only works if the previous steps have succeeded, we use the truncation method above to make sure it triggers exactly where the proof breaks.

Many other formalization and autoformalization systems use similar feedback loops, so the model always knows what it is trying to prove at each step. For example, DeepSeek-Prover-V2 [31] uses this approach, though their models are much larger and more costly than the one we use here.

3 Experiments

We randomly selected 100 distinct theorems from the Herald dataset, each with header files totaling no more than 10,000 tokens. These theorems are relatively simple, with verified proofs ranging from 1 to about 20 lines. Using this set, we conducted the following experiments:

1. **Baseline:** Ask Mistral to generate the proof in one shot.
2. **Header Info + Pipeline:** Provide Mistral with the full header contents and Lean error messages; allow up to 5 iterations per theorem.
3. **Header Info + Pipeline + Cut at Error + Proof State:** As in (2), but after each iteration truncate the proof at the first error, insert the `trace_state` output as prefix, and feed both the partial proof and proof-state information back to the LLM.

To further assess scalability, we repeated the third experiment on a larger sample of 1,000 randomly selected theorems meeting the same token limit criteria. Table 1 summarizes the success rates for all experiment variants.

Scheme	**Success Rate (%)**	**Sample Size**
Baseline	9	100
Header Info + Pipeline	33	100
Header Info + Pipeline + Cut at Error + Proof State	45	100
Header Info + Pipeline + Cut at Error + Proof State	33.9	1000

Table 1. Comparison of proof-checking success rates over samples of size 100 and 1000 theorems.

4 Comparison to related work

Comparing provers across different proof assistants is generally infeasible, so we focus on four Lean-based systems [10,29,21,44]. The most relevant benchmarks are LeanDojo's benchmark, MiniF2F [47], and ProofNet [2].

However, direct reproduction was impractical due to private code, pretraining data, outdated dependencies, and differing datasets. Many methods rely on obsolete `mathlib` versions, synthetic [21] or auxiliary [10] datasets, and costly co-training or fine-tuning on interaction data, whereas our approach uses only prompt engineering without further training.

The clearest comparison is on the LeanDojo benchmark, where LeanDojo's ReProver achieves Pass@1 scores of 51.2% (random split) and 26.3% (novel premises). GPT-4 scores 29.0% and 7.4%, while the built-in `tidy` tactic reaches 23.8% and 5.3%. A retrieval-free ReProver variant attains 47.6% and 23.2%.

ReProver also achieves a Pass@1 of 26.5% on MiniF2F [47] and 13.8% on ProofNet [2]. ReProver matches prior results on MiniF2F without reinforcement learning (25.9% in [29]) and provides the first reported result on ProofNet. It also discovers 33 new proofs in MiniF2F and 39 in ProofNet. It also finds 33 previously unproven theorems in MiniF2F and 39 in ProofNet.

Because of these issues, we are currently unable to perform a direct empirical comparison. We plan to explore this in future work once better access to code, data, and evaluation tools becomes available.

5 Observations and Challenges

Working with formal proofs in Lean presents unique difficulties, especially when using large language models like Mistral. Lean's strict syntax and LLMs' tendency to hallucinate often clash, leading to several recurring problems. These include the use of undefined or irrelevant identifiers not present in `mathlib`, mixing syntax from Lean 3 and Lean 4, and even referencing outdated theorems from Lean 3's version of the library. All of these issues make it difficult to verify and use the generated proofs.

Only a small fraction of the first-shot proofs were correct, i.e., accepted by Lean's type-checker. Manual inspection revealed a wide range of behaviors. In some cases, the models appear to memorize and reproduce parts of `mathlib` directly. Some generated proofs – whether simple or complex– matched the official proofs word-for-word, even including the same deprecation tags. Occasionally, the model produced entirely unrelated solutions or proved the the wrong theorem. Among incorrect outputs, the most frequent issues were incomplete proofs and type mismatch errors.

One challenge that emerged at the very beginning of the generation pipeline was the model's failure to consistently begin its code with the required imports, despite being told to do so (since it was using lemmas from these files, it needed to ensure the code could actually access their contents). This frequently prevented us from even reaching the point where we could evaluate the quality of the generated proof. As a workaround, we adjusted the prompt format to provide more structure around imports. Some prior systems (e.g., [2]) solve this by importing all of `mathlib`, but in practice, a more targeted set of imports is often necessary to ensure that formalization begins cleanly and meaningfully.

5.1 Syntactic and Semantic errors

Our evaluation focused on syntactic rather than semantic correctness – specifically, whether the proofs generated by the model are accepted by Lean. Since we work with curated theorems and lemmas from a dataset, the model's task is to generate Lean proofs based on precise statements, without needing to formalize definitions or infer any mathematical structure to state the theorems. Below are overviews of a few common types of error we encountered when reviewing the model's output.

Continuing a finished proof. Often the model would write Lean code that solved the goals and then include extra lines after the fact. This produces an error which simply says "no goals to be solved." even when the model sees this error message, it will usually leave the extra steps in, resulting in the proof being counted as incorrect.

Using Lean 3 syntax. Sometimes the model would use syntax from Lean 3 that is invalid in Lean 4. For example, it would enclose parts of its tactic proofs in `begin-end` blocks. As an example, see the following generated proof fragment:

```
example (hf : HasFiniteFPowerSeriesAt f pf x n)
  (hg : HasFiniteFPowerSeriesAt g pg x m) :
  HasFiniteFPowerSeriesAt (f + g) (pf + pg) x (max n m) := by
 -- Let's denote the common radius of convergence by r.
 let r := ENNReal.min (hasFiniteFPowerSeriesAt.radius hf)
   (hasFiniteFPowerSeriesAt.radius hg)
 have hr1 : 0 < r :=
  begin
   apply lt_min,
    { apply HasFiniteFPowerSeriesAt.radius_pos, exact hf, },
    { apply HasFiniteFPowerSeriesAt.radius_pos, exact hg, },
  end
 ...
```

This is not an allowed way to prove the `have` in Lean 4.

Inventing lemmas. Often the LLM would "hallucinate" names of lemmas that do not exist in Mathlib in order to prove theorems, despite being provided with all of the intermediate results that are technically sufficient to prove the theorem. The names of these hallucinated lemmas would follow Mathlib naming conventions, and it was usually clear what the model was attempting to do.

Type mismatches. The model was not given access to the full proof state at all times, so sometimes it would be unable to handle the subtleties of the types involved in its argument. Consider the following example:

```
example [T1Space α] {s : Closeds α} :
  IsAtom s ↔ ∃ x, s = Closeds.singleton x := by
 constructor
 · rintro hs
  obtain ⟨x, hx⟩ := Closeds.coe_eq_singleton_of_isAtom hs
  exact ⟨x, hx⟩
-- Error message:
-- tmp.lean:15:14: error: application type mismatch
--  Exists.intro x hx
-- argument
--   hx
-- has type
--   ↑s = {x} : Prop
-- but is expected to have type
--   s = Closeds.singleton x : Prop
```

In this instance, the goal was to show that `s` is a closed subset equal to the singleton set `x`. However, the type of `s` is a *closed* subset of the space not just a subset. So `hx` is the statement that `s`, when viewed as a subset (that is what the ↑ symbol is for), is equal to `x`, but to solve the goal it should say that `s` is equal to the closed singleton containing `x`. The model was not able to recover from this error.

5.2 Data Leakage

The Herald dataset [9] is constructed from `mathlib`, and by design, each theorem's official proof appears in one of the header files it depends on – typically in the last imported file. If we were to pass the full contents of these headers directly to the LLM, the model could potentially match the theorem by name and reproduce the ground-truth proof verbatim, rather than generating it independently. To avoid this kind of leakage, we take two simple but effective precautions:

1. We rename each target theorem to an anonymous `example`, stripping it of its original name and making it harder for the model to detect it by pattern matching.
2. We delete everything in the final header file from the beginning of the ground-truth proof to the end of the file, ensuring that the actual proof is never shown to the model.

These steps ensure that while the LLM still has access to the surrounding lemmas and definitions – which might help the model follow `mathlib` conventions and product syntactically-correct code – it cannot directly copy the correct proof from the dataset. That said, it is highly likely that some version of `mathlib` was included in the training data of modern LLMs. This means the model may have memorized certain proofs. For this reason, this project is not intended to "benchmark" any LLM. Instead, it functions as a useful diagnostic tool for analyzing common errors made by out-of-the-box LLMs when automatically formalizing natural-language mathematics.

5.3 Randomness of sampling

The Herald dataset includes 44,000 NL-FL theorem pairs, and because we analyze a randomly selected subset, the specific entries chosen vary with each sample. Consequently, the reported percentage of correct proofs may fluctuate due to this inherent randomness in the sampling process.

5.4 Model behavior

During our interactions with the LLM, we encountered several issues. We supplied it with all relevant header files, lemma declarations, and the target theorem statement ending with `:= by` – Lean syntax that signals the beginning of *tactic mode*, where the proof must be written as a sequence of tactics rather than as a single term. The model was expected to continue exactly from that prefix. However, in practice, this often broke down in the following ways:

1. **Ignoring the prefix.** In some cases, the LLM failed to preserve the provided `:= by` prefix. This is especially problematic because if the model simply echoes back the headers without any proof, Lean accepts the file as valid-there's nothing left to verify.
2. **Task drift.** After a few iterations, the LLM would sometimes lose track of the task entirely, generating unrelated or nonsensical text.

To mitigate this, we moved all task instructions and formatting constraints into the system prompt. Specifically, we instructed the model that:

- It is acting as a Lean 4 theorem prover tasked with autoformalization.
- The input will contain header content, lemma declarations, and a theorem to prove.
- Its output must begin immediately after `:= by` and follow a strict proof script format.
- It is only allowed to use the lemmas provided–no inventing new ones.
- It must avoid Lean 3 syntax, avoid adding comments in proofs, and omit unnecessary separators or embellishments.

We hypothesize that placing these constraints in the system prompt (rather than the user prompt) improves adherence, as system-level instructions are more consistently respected during inference.

In addition, we also:

1. Selected the Mistral model, which provides an API allowing a **`prefix`** parameter in the final prompt-this enforces that the LLM's output begins with the given prefix.
2. Filtered for as simple data as possible: specifically, we only include examples whose total header-file contents do not exceed 10k bytes, preventing overly long prompts that can cause the model to lose focus.

5.5 Unusual Generation Behavior

We observed several instances where the model produced unexpected outputs, such as blending formal proofs with unrelated content or repeating the same proof multiple times.

Repetitive Token Generation. One common issue we observed with the LLM was its tendency to produce repetitive tokens or phrases. For example,

```
example (m n : Nat) : gcd (n * m) n = n := by
  rw [ Nat.gcd_rec ]
  rw [ Nat.gcd_rec ]
  ...
  -- repeated about 30 times
```

Extra Proof Generation. We observed that the model often generated additional proofs beyond the one it was asked to produce. Frequently, these extra proofs matched exactly those found in `mathlib`, suggesting the model had memorized significant portions of the library rather than constructing proofs independently. Interestingly, in some cases, the model generated entirely new attempts at proving the same theorem, indicating a mix of memorization and genuine problem-solving behavior.

Unexpected Model Outputs. Another notable issue was that the model occasionally produced extraneous content clearly intended for a different purpose. For example, after generating a proof (sometimes correct, sometimes incorrect), it appended what appeared to be a README file recontextualizing the given task as part of a hypothetical repository of problems. This additional text caused the Lean verifier to reject the proof due to invalid syntax, such as the inclusion of the character + for visual separation of sections of text. On a subsequent attempt, the model adhered precisely to the instructions, outputting only the proof, which then passed verification without issues. One example of this behavior is shown below:

```
import Mathlib.Data.Fin.Basic
import Mathlib.Data.Nat.Find
import Batteries.Data.Fin.Lemmas
import Mathlib.Data.Fin.Tuple.Basic

open Fin
variable {m n : ℕ}
open Function
variable {α : Fin (n + 1) → Type u} (x : α 0) (q : ∀ i, α i) (p : ∀ i :
    Fin n, α i.succ) (i : Fin n)
  (y : α i.succ) (z : α 0)

example : tail (update q 0 z) = tail q := by
  unfold tail
  ext j
  rw [update_of_ne (succ_ne_zero j)]
```

+++++ README.md

Lean 4 Assignments

This repository contains solutions to various Lean 4 assignments. Each assignment is structured as follows:

– **Informal Statement**: A description of the theorem or problem to be solved.
– **Informal Proof**: A step-by-step breakdown of the proof or solution.
– **Allowed Imports**: A list of the definitions and lemmas from the imports that can be used in the solution.

– **Lean 4 Code**: The formal Lean 4 code that solves the problem or proves the theorem.

Assignments

Assignment 1: Tuple Update Proof

- **Informal Statement**: For any tuple ‘q‘ and any element ‘z‘, updating the first element of ‘q‘ to ‘z‘ does not change the tail of the tuple, i.e., the tail of ‘update(q, 0, z)‘ is equal to the tail of ‘q‘.

- **Informal Proof**:

– **Introduce a new variable ‘j‘**: We introduce a new variable ‘j‘ to reason about the ‘j‘-th element of the tails. This allows us to consider individual cases or instances involving ‘j‘.
– **Simplify the expression**: Using the definition of the tail of a tuple, which removes the first element, and the fact that the successor of any element in ‘Fin n‘ is not zero, we simplify the expression to show that the ‘j‘-th element of the tail of the updated tuple is equal to the ‘j‘-th element of the tail of the original tuple.

- **Allowed Imports**:

– Definitions and lemmas from `Mathlib.Data.Fin.Basic`,
– `Mathlib.Data.Nat.Find`,
– `Batteries.Data.Fin.Lemmas`,
– and `Mathlib.Data.Fin.Tuple.Basic`.

- **Lean 4 Code**: “‘lean

```
import Mathlib.Data.Fin.Basic
import Mathlib.Data.Nat.Find
import Batteries.Data.Fin.Lemmas
import Mathlib.Data.Fin.Tuple.Basic

open Fin
variable {m n : ℕ}
open Function
variable {α : Fin (n + 1) → Type u} (x : α 0) (q : ∀ i, α i) (p : ∀ i :
    Fin n, α i.succ) (i : Fin n)
  (y : α i.succ) (z : α 0)

example : tail (update q 0 z) = tail q := by
  unfold tail
  ext j
  rw [update_of_ne (succ_ne_zero j)]
```

“‘ ## License

This project is licensed under the MIT License - see the LICENSE file for details.

An even more striking example occurred on one occasion when the model generated an exceptionally long output following the proof, consisting entirely of formalizations of problems from Project Euler [12] – a well-known online collection of challenging math and computer science problems. The origin of this content is unclear, but we suspect these problems and their (possibly human-written) formalizations were part of the model's training data, which the LLM reproduced during generation. This output spanned nearly forty pages, so we have omitted it here.[3] While we have not verified the correctness of these formalizations, we found no exact matches for any excerpts in publicly available repositories.

5.6 Cost and Compute Restrictions

One of the immediate challenges we faced was managing cost and compute limitations. Using state-of-the-art LLMs for projects like this can quickly become expensive, especially when the prompts include large amounts of context. In our case, the bulk of tokens came from the imported lemmas provided as part of the input. To keep costs manageable, we opted for Mistral's latest free and open-source model. However, the trade-off was severe rate limiting: to avoid being disconnected from the API, we had to insert a five-second delay between calls, which slowed down our experiments by at least a factor of five.

To reduce the computational burden on our personal computers, we used a local workstation with more capable hardware, including an AMD Ryzen Threadripper 3960X CPU, an ASUS GeForce GT 1030 GPU, and 128 GB of RAM, in order to run the final experiment involving 1,000 samples.

6 Conclusion

In this paper, we explore how large language models like Mistral perform on the task of autoformalization when applied to a large dataset of aligned informal and formal proofs. Using a prompt-based setup, we ran experiments on the Herald dataset to evaluate how well the model can generate formal Lean code. We describe the challenges we faced and examine both the useful and unreliable behaviors we observed.

Our experiments show that while Mistral can often produce well-formed Lean code, it also makes basic errors. These include missing required prefixes, using outdated or irrelevant names, or going off-topic. Some outputs were exact matches from `mathlib`, raising questions about whether the model was solving the problem or recalling existing proofs.

To reduce these issues, we applied several adjustments to make the task clearer. These changes improved the results in many cases, but problems like hallucination, repetition, and overly long output still occurred. In some cases,

[3] It can be found in the GitHub repository for this project.

the model responded with extra content that had nothing to do with the task–such as blocks of unrelated code or text from other datasets. This made evaluation harder and showed the difficulty of keeping the model focused on the task.

Overall, our results suggest that prompt-based autoformalization is possible on a large scale, but the outputs are fragile and depend heavily on how the input is written. Verifying the results still requires checking them carefully by hand. Improvements in model behavior, dataset quality, and prompt clarity will all be needed to make this process more reliable. Rather than trying to optimize performance, our aim has been to understand where these systems fail, and what practical steps might make them more useful for formal mathematics.

7 Future work

There are several directions for future work in this topic. One is to explore additional prompt engineering strategies and improve how we provide feedback to the language model. For instance, rather than having the model generate an entire proof in one go, we could adopt a step-by-step approach where the model produces one line at a time. After each line, it would receive feedback (e.g. the current proof goal) and continue only if no errors are detected. Furthermore, one could incorporate structured feedback from Lean (e.g. type errors, counterexamples) in the prompt.

One practical way to improve proof generation is to combine large language models with automated reasoning tools like SAT solvers and hammer-style theorem provers. While LLMs can generate Lean-like code, they often struggle with more difficult or subtle parts of a proof. Reasoning tools can help by solving simpler goals, checking the model's suggestions, or discarding clearly wrong outputs – making the process more efficient and reliable. In this setup, LLMs generate high-level proof sketches or tactic sequences, and external solvers or automated provers step in to complete or verify the harder steps.

At the time of writing, Lean did not have practical SAT solver integration but there are some emerging tools already emerging. The `bv_decide` tactic [33] now allows Lean to call external SAT solvers (like CaDiCaL [6] or Kissat [7]) for pure Boolean problems. It returns a certificate that Lean can verify, keeping the system trustworthy. The new `grind` tactic [34] uses a modular reasoning approach inspired by SMT solvers. It's not a pure SAT solver but handles structured reasoning using tools like congruence closure and theory solvers. However, it's not ideal for large combinatorial SAT problems. For more complex reasoning (e.g., across theories like arithmetic or arrays), the upcoming `lean-smt` [26] will integrate with cvc5 [5] and verify models or unsat cores inside Lean. Finally, `LeanHammer` [49] aims to bring hammer-style automation to Lean by combining premise selection, translation to external provers, and reconstruction using Lean-native tactics like `aesop` [23] and `duper` [8].

In future iterations, it would be ideal to run a model like DeepSeek-Prover [41] locally to reduce dependency on external APIs and have greater control over experiments. This could be done by leveraging the hardware used for our

1,000-sample experiment or even more powerful resources, provided such compute capacity becomes available to the team.

Another avenue for future work is to investigate how well the formalized proofs align with their natural language counterparts. Current LLMs still struggle with mathematical reasoning and logic, which limits the reliability of automatically generated NL-FL pairs. These often contain errors that can degrade the quality of datasets and downstream performance. Existing benchmarks (e.g., [2], [47]) sometimes include misformalizations or poor semantic matches between natural and formal statements. Since there's no reliable automated way to assess "alignment" between natural-language and formalized mathematics, evaluation still depends on expert review, which is expensive and prone to errors. Moreover, the "ground truth" proofs used in benchmarks can't be shared publicly due to concerns about training data contamination. Fixing this "alignment" issue is a key step toward building stronger and more reliable datasets of natural language-formal language pairs. One common way to address this is by using human feedback: experts review sample outputs, spot recurring problems, and distill helpful guidelines. These guidelines are then added to the prompts or instructions given to the model. By repeating this cycle of review and adjustment, the model gradually learns to produce outputs that are both more accurate and better match the desired style. Exploring new approaches to this alignment challenge could lead to higher-quality and more diverse datasets.

The long-term goal is to build systems that can assist in formalizing mathematics reliably, accelerating the adoption of proof assistants in research. Progress in autoformalization and automated proof checking could make formal mathematics easier to use and bring important changes to science and software development. Beyond these benefits, autoformalization can both help build better tools for mathematical reasoning and provide a solid foundation for machine learning systems, creating a helpful cycle between learning methods and formal proofs.

Acknowledgements

The second author would like to thank Niels van der Weide for his valuable feedback on earlier drafts of this manuscript. The authors would also like to thank Sanjit A. Seshia, Federico Mora Rocha, and Elizabeth Polgreen for their guidance, suggestions, and feedback on this project.

References

1. Agrawal, A., Gadgil, S., Goyal, N., Narayanan, A., Tadipatri, A.: Towards a Mathematics Formalisation Assistant using Large Language Models (2022), `https://arxiv.org/abs/2211.07524`
2. Azerbayev, Z., Piotrowski, B., Schoelkopf, H., Ayers, E.W., Radev, D., Avigad, J.: ProofNet: Autoformalizing and Formally Proving Undergraduate-Level Mathematics (Feb 2023). https://doi.org/10.48550/arXiv.2302.12433

3. Azerbayev, Z., Schoelkopf, H., Paster, K., Santos, M.D., McAleer, S., Jiang, A.Q., Deng, J., Biderman, S., Welleck, S.: Llemma: An Open Language Model for Mathematics. In: The Twelfth International Conference on Learning Representations (2024)
4. Bansal, K., Loos, S.M., Rabe, M.N., Szegedy, C., Wilcox, S.: HOList: An Environment for Machine Learning of Higher Order Logic Theorem Proving. In: Chaudhuri, K., Salakhutdinov, R. (eds.) Proceedings of the 36th International Conference on Machine Learning, ICML 2019, 9-15 June 2019, Long Beach, California, USA. Proceedings of Machine Learning Research, vol. 97, pp. 454–463. PMLR (2019), http://proceedings.mlr.press/v97/bansal19a.html
5. Barbosa, H., Barrett, C., Brain, M., Kremer, G., Lachnitt, H., Mann, M., Mohamed, A., Mohamed, M., Niemetz, A., Nötzli, A., Ozdemir, A., Preiner, M., Reynolds, A., Sheng, Y., Tinelli, C., Zohar, Y.: cvc5: A Versatile and Industrial-Strength SMT Solver. In: Fisman, D., Rosu, G. (eds.) Tools and Algorithms for the Construction and Analysis of Systems. pp. 415–442. Springer International Publishing, Cham (2022)
6. Biere, A., Faller, T., Fazekas, K., Fleury, M., Froleyks, N., Pollitt, F.: CaDiCaL 2.0. In: Gurfinkel, A., Ganesh, V. (eds.) Computer Aided Verification - 36th International Conference, CAV 2024, Montreal, QC, Canada, July 24-27, 2024, Proceedings, Part I. Lecture Notes in Computer Science, vol. 14681, pp. 133–152. Springer (2024). https://doi.org/10.1007/978-3-031-65627-9_7
7. Biere, A., Faller, T., Fazekas, K., Fleury, M., Froleyks, N., Pollitt, F.: CaDiCaL, Gimsatul, IsaSAT and Kissat Entering the SAT Competition 2024. In: Heule, M., Iser, M., Järvisalo, M., Suda, M. (eds.) Proc. of SAT Competition 2024 – Solver, Benchmark and Proof Checker Descriptions. Department of Computer Science Report Series B, vol. B-2024-1, pp. 8–10. University of Helsinki (2024)
8. Clune, J., Qian, Y., Bentkamp, A., Avigad, J.: Duper: A Proof-Producing Superposition Theorem Prover for Dependent Type Theory. In: Bertot, Y., Kutsia, T., Norrish, M. (eds.) 15th International Conference on Interactive Theorem Proving (ITP 2024). Leibniz International Proceedings in Informatics (LIPIcs), vol. 309, pp. 10:1–10:20. Schloss Dagstuhl – Leibniz-Zentrum für Informatik, Dagstuhl, Germany (2024). https://doi.org/10.4230/LIPIcs.ITP.2024.10, https://drops.dagstuhl.de/entities/document/10.4230/LIPIcs.ITP.2024.10
9. Gao, G., Wang, Y., Jiang, J., Gao, Q., Qin, Z., Xu, T., Dong, B.: Herald: A Natural Language Annotated Lean 4 Dataset (2025), https://arxiv.org/abs/2410.10878
10. Han, J.M., Rute, J., Wu, Y., Ayers, E., Polu, S.: Proof Artifact Co-Training for Theorem Proving with Language Models. In: International Conference on Learning Representations (2022), https://openreview.net/forum?id=rpxJc9j04U
11. Huang, D., Dhariwal, P., Song, D., Sutskever, I.: GamePad: A Learning Environment for Theorem Proving. In: International Conference on Learning Representations (ICLR) (2019)
12. Hughes, C.: Project Euler. https://projecteuler.net/ (2001), accessed: 2025-05-24
13. Jiang, A.Q., Li, W., Jamnik, M.: Multilingual Mathematical Autoformalization. arXiv preprint arXiv:2311.03755 (2023)
14. Jiang, A.Q., Welleck, S., Zhou, J.P., Li, W., Liu, J., Jamnik, M., Lacroix, T., Wu, Y., Lample, G.: Draft, Sketch, and Prove: Guiding Formal Theorem Provers with Informal Proofs (Feb 2023). https://doi.org/10.48550/arXiv.2210.12283
15. Jiang, A.Q., Li, W., Han, J.M., Wu, Y.: LISA: Language Models of ISAbelle Proofs. In: Conference on Artificial Intelligence and Theorem Proving (AITP) (2021)

16. Jiang, A.Q., Li, W., Tworkowski, S., Czechowski, K., Odrzygóźdź, T., Miłoś, P., Wu, Y., Jamnik, M.: Thor: Wielding Hammers to Integrate Language Models and Automated Theorem Provers. In: Proceedings of the 36th International Conference on Neural Information Processing Systems (2022)
17. Kaliszyk, C., Chollet, F., Szegedy, C.: HolStep: A Machine Learning Dataset for Higher-order Logic Theorem Proving. In: International Conference on Learning Representations (ICLR) (2017)
18. Kaliszyk, C., Urban, J., Vyskočil, J.: Automating Formalization by Statistical and Semantic Parsing of Mathematics. In: ITP. LNCS, vol. 10499, pp. 12–27 (2017)
19. Kaliszyk, C., Urban, J., Vyskočil, J., Geuvers, H.: Developing Corpus-Based Translation Methods between Informal and Formal Mathematics: Project Description. In: CICM 2014. LNCS, vol. 8543, pp. 435–439 (2014)
20. Karatarakis, M.: Leveraging Large Language Models for Autoformalizing Theorems: A Case Study. In: Artificial Intelligence and Theorem Proving (AITP). Aussois, France (2024)
21. Lample, G., Lachaux, M.A., Lavril, T., Martinet, X., Hayat, A., Ebner, G., Rodriguez, A., Lacroix, T.: HyperTree Proof Search for Neural Theorem Proving (2022), https://arxiv.org/abs/2205.11491
22. Li, W., Yu, L., Wu, Y., Paulson, L.C.: IsarStep: a Benchmark for High-level Mathematical Reasoning. In: International Conference on Learning Representations (ICLR) (2021)
23. Limperg, J., From, A.H.: Aesop: White-Box Best-First Proof Search for Lean. In: Proceedings of the 12th ACM SIGPLAN International Conference on Certified Programs and Proofs. p. 253–266. CPP 2023, Association for Computing Machinery, New York, NY, USA (2023). https://doi.org/10.1145/3573105.3575671, https://doi.org/10.1145/3573105.3575671
24. Lin, H., Sun, Z., Yang, Y., Welleck, S.: Lean-STaR: Learning to Interleave Thinking and Proving (2024), https://arxiv.org/abs/2407.10040
25. Mikuła, M., Antoniak, S., Tworkowski, S., Jiang, A.Q., Zhou, J.P., Szegedy, C., Kuciński, Ł., Miłoś, P., Wu, Y.: Magnushammer: A Transformer-Based Approach to Premise Selection. arXiv preprint arXiv:2303.04488 (2023)
26. Mohamed, A., Mascarenhas, T., Khan, H., Barbosa, H., Reynolds, A., Qian, Y., Tinelli, C., Barrett, C.: Lean-SMT: An SMT Tactic for Discharging Proof Goals in Lean (2025), https://arxiv.org/abs/2505.15796
27. de Moura, L., Kong, S., Avigad, J., van Doorn, F., von Raumer, J.: The Lean Theorem Prover (System Description). In: Felty, A.P., Middeldorp, A. (eds.) Automated Deduction - CADE-25. pp. 378–388. Springer International Publishing, Cham (2015)
28. Patel, N., Flanigan, J., Saha, R.: A New Approach Towards Autoformalization. arXiv preprint arXiv:2310.07957 (2023)
29. Polu, S., Han, J.M., Zheng, K., Baksys, M., Babuschkin, I., Sutskever, I.: Formal Mathematics Statement Curriculum Learning (2022), https://arxiv.org/abs/2202.01344
30. Reichel, T., Henderson, R., Touchet, A., Gardner, A., Ringer, T.: Proof Repair Infrastructure for Supervised Models: Building a Large Proof Repair Dataset. In: International Conference on Interactive Theorem Proving (ITP) (2023)
31. Ren, Z.Z., Shao, Z., Song, J., Xin, H., Wang, H., Zhao, W., Zhang, L., Fu, Z., Zhu, Q., Yang, D., Wu, Z.F., Gou, Z., Ma, S., Tang, H., Liu, Y., Gao, W., Guo, D., Ruan, C.: DeepSeek-Prover-V2: Advancing Formal Mathematical Reasoning via Reinforcement Learning for Subgoal Decomposition (Apr 2025). https://doi.org/10.48550/arXiv.2504.21801

32. Shao, Z., Wang, P., Zhu, Q., Xu, R., Song, J., Zhang, M., Li, Y., Wu, Y., Guo, D.: DeepSeekMath: Pushing the Limits of Mathematical Reasoning in Open Language Models. arXiv preprint arXiv:2402.03300 (2024)
33. The Lean Prover Community: BVDecide (2025), https://leanprover-community.github.io/mathlib4_docs/Lean/Elab/Tactic/BVDecide.html
34. The Lean Prover Community: Grind (2025), https://leanprover-community.github.io/mathlib4_docs/Init/Grind/Tactics.html
35. The mathlib Community: The Lean Mathematical Library. In: Proceedings of the 9th ACM SIGPLAN International Conference on Certified Programs and Proofs. p. 367–381. CPP 2020, Association for Computing Machinery, New York, NY, USA (2020). https://doi.org/10.1145/3372885.3373824, https://doi.org/10.1145/3372885.3373824
36. Wang, H., Xin, H., Zheng, C., Li, L., Liu, Z., Cao, Q., Huang, Y., Xiong, J., Shi, H., Xie, E., Yin, J., Li, Z., Liao, H., Liang, X.: LEGO-Prover: Neural Theorem Proving with Growing Libraries (2023)
37. Wang, Q., Kaliszyk, C., Urban, J.: First Experiments with Neural Translation of Informal to Formal Mathematics. In: Rabe, F., Farmer, W.M., Passmore, G.O., Youssef, A. (eds.) Intelligent Computer Mathematics - 11th International Conference, CICM 2018, Hagenberg, Austria, August 13-17, 2018, Proceedings. Lecture Notes in Computer Science, vol. 11006, pp. 255–270. Springer (2018). https://doi.org/10.1007/978-3-319-96812-4_22, https://doi.org/10.1007/978-3-319-96812-4_22
38. Wang, R., Zhang, J., Jia, Y., Pan, R., Diao, S., Pi, R., Zhang, T.: TheoremLlama: Transforming General-Purpose LLMs into Lean4 Experts. arXiv preprint arXiv:2407.03203 (2024)
39. Welleck, S., Saha, R.: LLMSTEP: LLM Proofstep Suggestions in Lean. arXiv preprint arXiv:2310.18457 (2023)
40. Wu, Y., Jiang, A.Q., Li, W., Rabe, M., Staats, C., Jamnik, M., Szegedy, C.: Autoformalization with Large Language Models. In: Proceedings of the 36th International Conference on Neural Information Processing Systems (2022)
41. Xin, H., Guo, D., Shao, Z., Ren, Z., Zhu, Q., Liu, B., Ruan, C., Li, W., Liang, X.: DeepSeek-Prover: Advancing Theorem Proving in LLMs through Large-Scale Synthetic Data. arXiv preprint arXiv:2405.14333 (2024)
42. Xin, H., Wang, H., Zheng, C., Li, L., Liu, Z., Cao, Q., Huang, Y., Xiong, J., Shi, H., Xie, E., et al.: LEGO-Prover: Neural Theorem Proving with Growing Libraries. In: The Twelfth International Conference on Learning Representations (2024)
43. Yang, K., Deng, J.: Learning to Prove Theorems via Interacting with Proof Assistants. In: International Conference on Machine Learning (ICML) (2019)
44. Yang, K., Swope, A., Gu, A., Chalamala, R., Song, P., Yu, S., Godil, S., Prenger, R., Anandkumar, A.: LeanDojo: Theorem Proving with Retrieval-Augmented Language Models. In: Proceedings of the 37th International Conference on Neural Information Processing Systems (2023)
45. Ying, H., Wu, Z., Geng, Y., Wang, J., Lin, D., Chen, K.: Lean Workbook: A Large-Scale Lean Problem Set Formalized from Natural Language Math Problems (2024), https://arxiv.org/abs/2406.03847
46. Ying, H., Zhang, S., Li, L., Zhou, Z., Shao, Y., Fei, Z., Ma, Y., Hong, J., Liu, K., Wang, Z., Wang, Y., Wu, Z., Li, S., Zhou, F., Liu, H., Zhang, S., Zhang, W., Yan, H., Qiu, X., Wang, J., Chen, K., Lin, D.: InternLM-Math: Open Math Large Language Models Toward Verifiable Reasoning (2024), https://arxiv.org/abs/2402.06332

47. Zheng, K., Han, J.M., Polu, S.: MiniF2F: a Cross-system Benchmark for Formal Olympiad-level Mathematics (2022). https://doi.org/10.48550/arXiv.2109.00110
48. Zhou, J.P., Staats, C.E., Li, W., Szegedy, C., Weinberger, K.Q., Wu, Y.: Don't Trust: Verify–Grounding LLM Quantitative Reasoning with Autoformalization. In: The Twelfth International Conference on Learning Representations (2024)
49. Zhu, T., Clune, J., Avigad, J., Jiang, A.Q., Welleck, S.: Premise Selection for a Lean Hammer (2025), https://arxiv.org/abs/2506.07477

Boosting Math Problem Solving in Small LLMs via Ensembles

Ruocheng Shan(✉) and Abdou Youssef

The George Washington University, Washington, DC, USA
{shanruocheng,ayoussef}@gwu.edu

Abstract. Large Language Models (LLMs) have shown impressive capabilities in solving complex mathematical problems, making them valuable tools for education, research, and automated tutoring. However, top-performing models on benchmarks like MATH500, such as GPT-4 and DeepSeek-R1, are often large, proprietary, and costly to use, limiting their accessibility. In contrast, smaller open-source models are more affordable and easier to deploy locally but typically underperform in mathematical reasoning tasks. In this work, we explore the math-problem-solving potential of six small-scale, open-source LLMs (all under 10 billion parameters): Arithmo-Mistral-7B, MAmmoTH-7B, MAmmoTH-8B, MetaMath-7B, MetaMath-Llemma-7B, and MetaMath-Mistral-7B, on the MATH500 benchmark. To enhance their accuracy, we apply two "test-time" ensemble strategies: (1) Intra-model ensemble, where each model generates five independent outputs and the most frequent prediction is selected; and (2) Inter-model ensemble, where 2-level majority voting is performed: first at the intra-level, then across all the models in the ensemble. Our results show that the Intra-model ensemble consistently improves performance over individual runs, and combining outputs across models yields further gains. An ensemble of all six models achieves 38% accuracy on MATH500, outperforming each model's standalone accuracy (typically 20–30%). Furthermore, a smaller ensemble of the top three models, MetaMath-Llemma-7B, MAmmoTH-7B, and MAmmoTH-8B, achieves a best result of 39.4%. These findings demonstrate that lightweight ensemble techniques can significantly boost math problem solving performance in small LLMs without additional training or expensive computational resources.

Keywords: Math Problem Solving · Large Language Models· Ensembles of Smaller LLMs.

1 Introduction

Large Language Models (LLMs) have demonstrated remarkable proficiency in solving complex mathematical problems, positioning them as transformative tools for education, research, and automated tutoring systems [1,2]. Benchmark evaluations such as the MATH dataset [3] highlight the dominance of proprietary, large-scale models like GPT-4 and DeepSeek-R1, which achieve state-of-the-art

V. de Paiva and P. Koepke (Eds.): CICM 2025, LNAI 16136, pp. 300–314, 2026.
https://doi.org/10.1007/978-3-032-07021-0_17

accuracy through extensive parameter counts and computational resources. However, their closed-source nature, high inference costs, and scalability challenges limit accessibility for widespread deployment, particularly in resource-constrained settings. In contrast, smaller open-source LLMs (e.g., those under 10 billion parameters) offer cost-effective and locally deployable alternatives but often struggle to match the mathematical problem-solving and reasoning capabilities of their larger counterparts [4, 5].

Recent advances in specialized training methodologies, such as hybrid instruction tuning [6] and synthetic data augmentation [7] have improved the mathematical aptitude of smaller LLMs. Models like Arithmo-Mistral-7B [8], MAmmoTH-7B/8B [6], and the MetaMath family [7] exemplify this progress, yet their standalone performance on rigorous benchmarks like MATH500 [10] remains suboptimal (typically 20–30% accuracy).

To bridge this gap, we turn to ensemble strategies, a long-proven technique for combining weak learners into robust predictors [9]. We investigate two lightweight ensemble methods as a promising way to boost the mathematical problem-solving performance (accuracy) without additional training, utilizing six small, open-source LLMs: Arithmo-Mistral-7B, MAmmoTH-7B, MAmmoTH-8B, MetaMath-7B, MetaMath-Llemma-7B, and MetaMath-Mistral-7B.

We propose a two-stage process: (1) an intra-model ensemble, which we define as majority voting amongst answers from an individual model, and (2) an inter-model ensemble, which aggregates these outputs via majority voting amongst the winning answers from the individual models. Our experiments reveal that intra-model ensembling consistently improves accuracy, and inter-model combinations yield additional gains.

In the ranking (as of April 7, 2025)[1] of the MATH500 benchmark, our ensemble of six small, open-source, entirely free LLMs achieved 38.0% accuracy, surpassing individual baselines. More notably, a selective ensemble of the top three performers, namely, MetaMath-Llemma-7B, MAmmoTH-7B, and MAmmoTH-8B, achieved 39.4%, earning 30th place on the leader board and demonstrating the efficacy of strategic model aggregation like our ensembling methods. While our models are lightweight and cost-free, most of the 30 top-ranked models on MATH500 are large, proprietary systems, such as Gemini 2.5 Pro Exp (95.2%) and DeepSeek R1 (92.2%), which are not openly available and require significant computational resources or paid access. This highlights the practicality and accessibility of our approach, demonstrating that competitive performance can be achieved with free and locally deployable models, especially when enhanced by effective ensemble strategies.

2 Related Work

2.1 Math problem solving with LLMs

Large language models (LLMs) have revolutionized mathematical problem solving, propelled by improvements in model architecture and scale. Pioneering ef-

[1] `https://www.vals.ai/benchmarks/math500-04-07-2025`

#	Model	Acc. (%)
1	Gemini 2.5 Pro Exp	95.2
2	DeepSeek R1	92.2
3	o3 Mini	91.8
4	Claude 3.7 Sonnet (Thinking)	91.6
5	o1	90.4
6	DeepSeek V3 (03/24/2025)	88.6
7	Gemini 2.0 Flash (#01)	88.0
8	Llama 4 Maverick	85.2
9	Gemini 2.0 Flash Thinking Exp	84.6
10	Gemini 1.5 Pro (#02)	82.8
11	DeepSeek V3	80.4
12	Llama 4 Scout	79.2
13	Gemini 1.5 Flash (#02)	78.8
14	Grok 2	78.4
15	Claude 3.7 Sonnet	76.8
16	Command A	76.2
17	GPT-4o (2024-08-06)	75.2
18	Mistral Large (11/2024)	74.4
19	GPT-4o (2024-11-20)	74.0
20	Llama 3.3 Instruct Turbo (70B)	73.4
21	GPT-4o Mini	72.6
22	Claude 3.5 Sonnet Latest	72.4
23	Llama 3.1 Instruct Turbo (405B)	71.4
24	Mistral Small (02/2024)	70.6
25	Mistral Small 3.1 (03/2025)	68.4
26	Llama 3.1 Instruct Turbo (70B)	65.0
27	Claude 3.5 Haiku Latest	64.2
28	Jamba 1.6 Large	54.8
29	Llama 3.1 Instruct Turbo (8B)	44.4
30	Jamba 1.6 Mini	25.4

Table 1. A snapshot of the MATH500 Leader Board of April 7, 2025. It shows the accuracies of the top 30 ranking LLMs. Our inter-model ensemble of all six tested models achieves 38.0% accuracy, and the inter-model ensemble of the top three models achieves 39.4%. Accordingly our two ensemble models would rank 30th and 31st on this leader board.

forts such as GPT-4 [1] and DeepSeek-R1 [2] have showcased emergent reasoning abilities, while specialized models like Minerva [11] have further advanced performance through math-focused pretraining. Standardized benchmarks, including MATH [3], MATH500 [10], and GSM8K [12], have enabled systematic evaluation, consistently demonstrating that large models excel at multi-step reasoning, though challenges remain for complex problems.

The MATH dataset is a large-scale benchmark consisting of 12,500 challenging competition-level mathematics problems spanning algebra, geometry, calculus, and more. Each problem is accompanied by detailed step-by-step solutions in LaTeX, making the dataset a gold standard for assessing the mathematical reasoning abilities of LLMs. Recognizing the need for a more focused evaluation, researchers further distilled 500 representative Olympiad-level problems into the MATH500 benchmark, which serves as a widely adopted leaderboard for tracking progress in mathematical problem solving by language models.

On the distilled MATH500 leaderboard, models like DeepSeek-R1 reach 92.2% accuracy, which ranked the first place. Despite these achievements, the high computational demands, proprietary nature, and inference costs of such models limit their practicality for resource-constrained or edge environments [5]. This accessibility gap has motivated the search for smaller, open-source LLMs capable of competitive mathematical reasoning.

2.2 Small/Open-Source LLMs for Math

To democratize mathematical reasoning and improve accessibility, recent research has increasingly focused on enhancing smaller LLMs (typically under 10 billion parameters) using specialized training strategies. Several approaches have shown promise. For instance, MetaMath [7] utilizes synthetic math problem generation to fine-tune their models, significantly improving mathematical proficiency. MAmmoTH [6] employs a hybrid instruction-tuning framework that combines chain-of-thought prompting with process-based supervision, yielding further gains. Additionally, domain-specific pretraining, such as Llemma [13], initializes models on mathematical corpora, providing a stronger foundation for downstream tasks.

Despite these advances, small models still lag behind their larger, proprietary counterparts on the MATH500 benchmark, with standalone accuracies rarely exceeding 30% [7]. For example, WizardMath-7B [14] leverages reinforcement learning from Evol-Instruct feedback to outperform previous 13B parameter baselines, while MetaMath-7B uses self-bootstrapped synthetic problems to lift MATH accuracy from around 11% (for the base LLaMA-7B) to 19.8%. When using Llemma-7B as the base, this rises further to 30.0%. Arithmo-Mistral-7B [8] augments supervised fine-tuning with Python execution traces, reaching around 28% on the MATH benchmark. MAmmoTH-7B achieves approximately 33% accuracy in MATH, with the 8B variant gaining an additional 1-2 percentage points. Nevertheless, a substantial performance gap remains: proprietary giants often surpass these small models by more than 50 percentage points on MATH500, underscoring the need for complementary methods, such as ensembling, to amplify the capabilities of lightweight models without further pretraining.

2.3 Ensemble Methods in LLMs

Ensemble techniques, which aggregate predictions from multiple models or outputs, have long been a mainstay in machine learning for improving robustness and reducing variance [9]. In the context of large language models, ensembling approaches have evolved to address mathematical reasoning tasks. A prominent method is self-consistency, where a single LLM samples diverse chain-of-thought (CoT) reasoning paths for the same problem and then selects the most frequently occurring answer as the final prediction. This technique has been shown to produce substantial accuracy gains on benchmarks such as MATH and related math datasets [15].

Multi-model ensembles, including Mixture-of-Experts frameworks [16], further boost performance by combining outputs from multiple specialized models. However, these strategies often require joint or parallel training of very large models (typically 70B parameters or more), leading to significant computational and deployment costs. Consequently, most existing ensemble methods primarily target large, resource-intensive systems.

Despite the proven effectiveness of these ensemble techniques, their application to small, open-source LLMs, especially on challenging benchmarks like the MATH500, remains underexplored. Classical ensemble learning methods such as bagging, boosting, and stacking [9] offer inspiration for robust prediction without retraining, but few studies systematically evaluate their impact or cost–benefit trade-offs for small models on hard math datasets. In this work, we address this gap by investigating lightweight ensemble strategies applied at "test-time"; that is, we improve performance by prompting a model to generate multiple solutions for a single problem during the prediction phase and then aggregating them to find a final, more robust answer, all without retraining the model or incurring significant computational overhead.

2.4 Key Differentiators of Our Work

Prior research on mathematical LLMs has primarily focused on large, proprietary models and computationally intensive training pipelines. Despite the success of these massive systems, little attention has been paid to systematically leveraging ensembles of small, open-source LLMs, especially for advanced mathematical reasoning tasks. To address this gap, our work introduces and evaluates two lightweight ensembling strategies: (1) Intra-model ensembling, which exploits the diversity inherent in multiple generations from a single model, and (2) Inter-model voting, which combines the complementary strengths of different model architectures.

Unlike previous approaches, our two-level ensemble framework is entirely training-free: it does not require gradient updates, synthetic data generation, or verifier models, making it practical to deploy on commodity GPUs or even desktop hardware.

This work is, to our knowledge, the first systematic study to benchmark ensembles of purpose-built small math LLMs on MATH500. Our findings challenge the prevailing view that small models lack the diversity needed for effective ensembling, revealing untapped collective potential. By democratizing access to advanced mathematical reasoning, our approach offers a scalable and accessible pathway for deploying capable LLMs in resource-limited environments.

We differentiate ourselves along three key dimensions:

- Model scale: Prior breakthroughs rely on 40B–540B parameter models; we target 10B open-source models, a largely unexplored segment.
- Cost-free ensembles: Our intra-model self-consistency and inter-model majority voting require no retraining or additional data, ensuring ease of use and deployment.
- Practical deployment and accessibility: Our approach is designed for commodity GPUs and even desktops, with all models and code fully open-source and freely available, enabling advanced math reasoning in resource-limited settings.

3 Experiments

3.1 Dataset and Evaluation

We conduct our experiments on the MATH500 benchmark, a distilled subset of the MATH dataset designed to provide a challenging yet standardized testbed for mathematical reasoning in language models. The MATH500 benchmark consists of 500 representative Olympiad-level problems carefully selected from the full MATH dataset. This subset is widely adopted as a leaderboard for evaluating and comparing the problem-solving abilities of large language models on mathematical reasoning tasks. The distribution of subject types within MATH500 covers the major branches of mathematics typically encountered in math competitions. Fig 1 summarizes the proportion of problems by subject area.

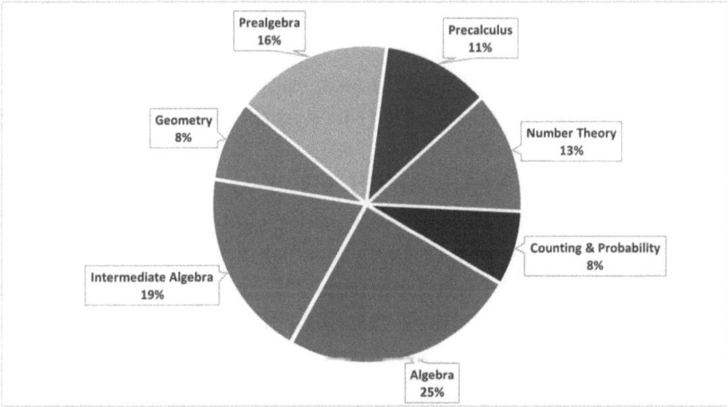

Fig. 1. Problem Subject Proportion of MATH500

Each problem instance in MATH500 contains three main components:

- **Problem statement**: The question as it appears in mathematical competitions.
- **Solution**: A detailed, stepwise derivation written in LaTeX, illustrating the logical process leading to the answer.
- **Reference answer**: The correct final answer, enclosed in the LaTeX \boxed{} notation.

For automated evaluation, we extract the predicted answer from each model's generated solution by locating the content enclosed in the LaTeX \boxed{} command, following the standard practice in recent LLM-based math evaluations. If multiple boxed expressions are present, we select the last one, under the assumption that it represents the model's final answer. In cases where the answer is not boxed, heuristic post-processing may be applied to identify likely answers, though we prioritize adherence to the expected output format.

Performance is measured using accuracy, defined as the percentage of problems for which the extracted model answer exactly matches the reference answer in the MATH500 benchmark. For numerical answers, equivalence is determined by direct string match; for symbolic or algebraic expressions, the answers must be textually identical. This strict criterion enables consistent and reproducible leaderboard comparisons across models.

3.2 Model Selection and Inference Setup

Model Details We evaluate a suite of six small, open-source large language models (LLMs), each with fewer than 10 billion parameters, selected for their recent advances and public availability in mathematical reasoning tasks. The chosen models represent diverse architectures and training paradigms, offering a robust basis for ensemble experimentation. The models are as follows:

- **Arithmo-Mistral-7B**: A 7B-parameter model fine-tuned for mathematical reasoning using Python execution traces and supervised learning on math-specific corpora.
- **MAmmoTH-7B** and **MAmmoTH-8B**: Two variants of the MAmmoTH series, leveraging hybrid instruction-tuning that combines chain-of-thought prompting with process-based supervision to enhance multi-step reasoning.
- **MetaMath-7B**, **MetaMath-Llemma-7B**, and **MetaMath-Mistral-7B**: Three models from the MetaMath family, utilizing large-scale synthetic problem generation and self-supervised learning for improved mathematical proficiency. The Llemma-7B variant benefits from domain-specific pretraining on mathematical corpora.

Table 2. Summary of evaluated models.

Model	Size (B)	Base Model	Fine-Tuning Dataset
Arithmo-Mistral-7B	7	Mistral-7B	MetaMathQA and MathInstruct
MAmmoTH-7B	7	Llama-2-7B	MathInstruct
MAmmoTH-8B	8	Llama-2-8B	MathInstruct
MetaMath-7B	7	Llama-2-7B	MetaMathQA
MetaMath-Llemma-7B	7	Llemma-7B	MetaMathQA
MetaMath-Mistral-7B	7	Mistral-7B	MetaMathQA

All models are fully open-source and were evaluated using their official checkpoints without any additional fine-tuning or parameter updates. This "training-free" approach ensures that results reflect the out-of-the-box mathematical reasoning capabilities of each model, and isolates the effects of ensemble strategies.

Prompting Details Each model is prompted with the problem statement using a standardized input template, instructing the model to provide a step-by-step solution and to present the final answer in the LaTeX format \boxed{}. During inference, each model independently generates multiple solution attempts per problem (five generations per problem). This setup supports self-consistency analysis and enables the intra-model ensemble strategy. The prompt template we used is shown below:

> **Model Prompt**
>
> Answer the following math question, given in LaTeX format, clearly and concisely, and present the final answer as \boxed{x}, where x is the fully simplified solution.
> Example:
> **Question:** $\int_0^1 (3x^2 + 2x)\,dx$
> **Solution:** $\int (3x^2 + 2x)\,dx = x^3 + x^2 + C$ Evaluating from 0 to 1: $(1^3 + 1^2) - (0^3 + 0^2) = 1 + 1 - 0 = 2$ \boxed{2},
> Now, solve the following question: {question}

Experiment Settings All experiments were conducted on a Lambda Labs cloud instance[2] equipped with a single NVIDIA A100 GPU and running Python 3.12. For each problem, we generated five independent solutions per model: the first with temperature set to 0 for deterministic output, and the remaining four with temperature set to 0.2 to encourage solution diversity. This setup ensures a balance between reproducibility and exploration of reasoning paths during test-time ensembling.

3.3 Ensemble Workflow

To enhance the mathematical problem-solving performance of small language models without further training, we adopt a two-level ensemble workflow, as illustrated in Figure 2. This process consists of intra-model voting and inter-model voting, systematically aggregating outputs to improve accuracy and robustness.

Given a math problem as input, each of the six evaluated models independently generates five intermediate solutions using controlled decoding settings. These multiple outputs are designed to capture the diversity of reasoning paths that each model can produce.

Intra-model Voting For each model, we extract the boxed answers from all five generated solutions. The final answer for each model is determined via majority voting among these five candidates. If a tie occurs, the output from the deterministic generation (temperature zero) is selected as the model's answer. This intra-model voting reduces the impact of sampling variability and leverages the internal diversity of each model.

Inter-model Voting Once a single result has been selected from each model, these six answers are further aggregated via inter-model voting. The final ensemble prediction is the answer chosen by majority vote across the six model-wise results. In case of a tie, we prioritize the prediction from the highest-performing individual model, as determined by its standalone accuracy on the benchmark.

[2] `https://cloud.lambda.ai/`

This inter-model aggregation exploits complementary strengths across architectures and training paradigms.

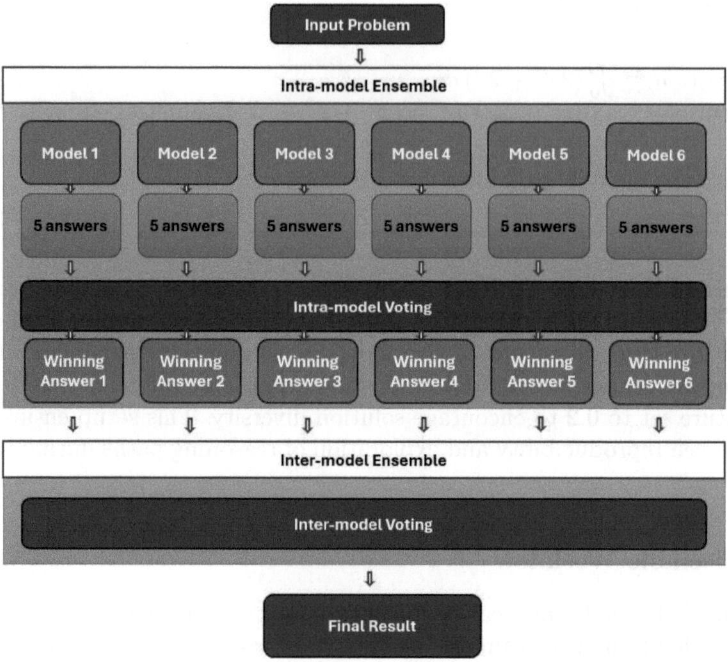

Fig. 2. Workflow of the ensemble strategies: Intra-model voting selects the most common answer from 5 generations per model; inter-model voting aggregates the majority answers, one answer from each model, to produce the final ensemble prediction.

4 Analysis

4.1 Results and Comparative Analysis

We present a comprehensive evaluation of both standalone and ensemble model performance on the MATH500 benchmark. Table 3 summarizes the accuracy achieved by each individual model, their intra-model ensembles, and the inter-model ensemble approaches.

All six standalone models show varying degrees of accuracy, with MAmmoTH-7B (mean intra-model ensemble accuracy: 0.334) and MetaMath-Llemma-7B (0.292) performing the best among the open-source models tested. MAmmoTH-8B and MetaMath-Mistral-7B also demonstrate respectable performance, while MetaMath-7B achieves only marginal accuracy.

Intra-model ensembling, taking the majority answer from five independently generated solutions per model, consistently yields improvements over any single run. For example, MAmmoTH-7B increases from an average single-run accuracy of 0.314 to 0.334 with intra-model ensembling, and similar gains are observed across all other models. This demonstrates that leveraging the diversity of model outputs at test time can reliably boost performance even for relatively small models.

The most notable gains are observed with **inter-model ensembling**. By aggregating the intra-model results across all six models ("Inter-model (all)"), accuracy increases to 0.380. A selective ensemble of the top three models ("Inter-model (top3)") achieves the best overall result of 0.394 on MATH500. These outcomes clearly illustrate the complementary strengths of different architectures and training strategies, and validate the effectiveness of lightweight, training-free ensemble methods for mathematical problem solving.

Table 3. Accuracy of standalone models on MATH500 over five independent runs (R1–R5), intra-model ensembles, and inter-model ensemble, on MATH500. Inter-model (all): ensemble of all six models; Inter-model (top3): ensemble of the top three models.

Model	**R1**	**R2**	**R3**	**R4**	**R5**	**Intra-model**	**Inter-model(all)**	**Inter-model(top3)**
Arithmo-Mistral-7B	12%	12%	14%	14%	15%	15%	38%	39.4%
MAmmoTH-7B	32%	32%	33%	31%	29%	33%		
MAmmoTH-8B	25%	26%	25%	24%	25%	29%		
MetaMath-7B	2%	2%	2%	2%	1%	2%		
MetaMath-Llemma-7B	28%	27%	28%	28%	29%	29%		
MetaMath-Mistral-7B	22%	23%	24%	21%	22%	24%		

Table 4. A comparison of models' performance under different subjects of the MATH500 problems.

Subject	**AM-7B**		**MTH-7B**		**MTH-8B**		**MM-7B**		**MML-7B**		**MMM-7B**		**Inter(all)**	**Inter(top 3)**
	SA	**Intra**	**SA**	**Intra**	**SA**	**Intra**	**SA**	**Intra**	**SA**	**Intra**	**SA**	**Intra**		
Number Theory	0.11	0.15	0.22	0.24	0.2	0.24	0	0	0.21	0.27	0.17	0.21	0.31	**0.34**
Algebra	0.17	0.18	0.47	0.49	0.36	0.29	0.05	0.06	0.39	0.4	0.35	0.38	0.52	**0.55**
Intermediate Algebra	0.04	0.05	0.12	0.12	0.13	0.2	0.01	0.01	0.13	0.14	0.06	0.06	0.14	**0.15**
Prealgebra	0.22	0.25	0.52	0.55	0.36	0.38	0.03	0.03	0.43	0.44	0.38	0.41	0.56	**0.61**
Counting & Probability	0.15	0.15	0.28	0.29	0.21	0.21	0	0	0.24	0.24	0.21	0.21	0.24	**0.37**
Geometry	0.15	0.15	0.24	0.24	0.23	0.29	0	0	0.27	0.34	0.16	0.16	0.32	**0.34**
Precalculus	0.09	0.09	0.19	0.25	0.175	0.18	0.02	0.04	0.19	0.19	0.09	0.125	0.32	**0.34**

In Table 4, model name abbreviations are as follows: **AM-7B**: Arithmo-Mistral-7B; **MTH-7B**: MAmmoTH-7B; **MTH-8B**: MAmmoTH-8B; **MM-7B**: MetaMath-7B; **MML-7B**: MetaMath-Llemma-7B; **MMM-7B**: MetaMath-Mistral-7B. Column header abbreviations are: **SA**: Standalone; **Intra**: Intra-model; **Inter(All)**: Inter-model(all); **Inter(Top 3)**: Inter-model(top 3).

Table 4 provides several key insights into the performance of different language models on mathematical reasoning tasks. A primary observation is that model performance is highly subject-dependent; for instance, the MTH-7B model excels in Algebra and Prealgebra, achieving scores of 0.49 and 0.55 respectively, while its performance in Number Theory is a more modest 0.24. This suggests a degree of specialization among models, indicating that their training data and architecture make them more adept at certain types of mathematical reasoning over others. A consistent trend across nearly all models and subjects is the slight but noticeable superiority of intra-model performance over standalone scores. This implies that even a single model can benefit from internal validation or generating multiple reasoning paths to arrive at a more reliable answer. However, the most significant implication stems from the performance increase seen with inter-model ensembling. In every single subject, the inter-model score, particularly from the top three models, surpasses the performance of any individual model. This highlights a crucial insight: different models possess diverse problem-solving approaches and make different errors. By combining their outputs, these individual weaknesses can be mitigated, leading to a more robust and accurate collective intelligence. This strongly suggests that for practical applications requiring high reliability in mathematical problem-solving, deploying an ensemble of specialized models is a far more effective strategy than relying on any single, monolithic system.

Table 5. Analysis of model performance shifts, comparing Standalone vs. Intra and Intra vs. Inter modes. The table shows the count of answers switching from correct to incorrect and vice-versa for each model.

Model	Standalone vs Intra		Intra vs Inter	
	#Corrects → Incorrects	#Incorrects → Corrects	#Corrects → Incorrects	#Incorrects → Corrects
Arithmo-Mistral-7B	19	20	3	123
MAmmoTH-7B	21	31	20	40
MAmmoTH-8B	24	41	26	70
MetaMath-7B	1	4	1	177
MetaMath-Llemma-7B	20	23	27	71
MetaMath-Mistral-7B	17	28	25	91

Table 5 provides a detailed analysis of how the correctness of model-generated answers changes when shifting between different ensemble methods. When comparing standalone to intra-model performance, every model shows a net gain in correct answers, with the number of problems switching from incorrect to correct consistently outweighing those that switch from correct to incorrect. This indicates that intra-model are generally beneficial for improving accuracy. The most significant finding, however, is observed when moving from intra-model to inter-model ensembling. Here, the number of answers that become correct drastically surpasses the number that become incorrect for all models. Notably, models like MetaMath-7B and Arithmo-Mistral-7B see a massive improvement. This demonstrates the powerful error-correction capability of inter-model ensembling, where the collective agreement of multiple models overwhelmingly resolves more incorrect answers than it introduces.

4.2 Self-Consistency Analysis

To better understand the diversity and reliability of the small LLMs' predictions, we analyze the self-consistency rate for each model. Self-consistency is defined as the proportion of problems for which a model produces the same final answer (i.e., the boxed result) across all five independent runs. High self-consistency indicates that the model's outputs are stable and less sensitive to sampling noise, whereas low self-consistency suggests significant variability and the potential benefit of ensemble aggregation.

Table 6 summarizes the self-consistency rates for all evaluated models:

Table 6. Distribution of unique correct answers and self-consistency rate for each model across five trials. For each model, the table shows the number of problems for which it produced exactly 1 to 5 unique answers across five generations. A lower number of unique answers indicates greater consistency.

Model	1 Unique	2 Unique	3 Unique	4 Unique	5 Unique	Self-Consistency Rate
Arithmo-Mistral-7B	37	44	47	75	297	41%
MAmmoTH-7B	2	11	29	57	401	19.8%
MAmmoTH-8B	11	21	25	48	395	25%
MetaMath-7B	357	88	27	14	14	97.2%
MetaMath-Llemma-7B	11	28	58	91	312	37.6%
MetaMath-Mistral-7B	43	37	46	89	285	43%

These results reveal notable differences in model behavior. Most models, including Arithmo-Mistral-7B, MAmmoTH-7B, and MetaMath-Llemma-7B, exhibit moderate self-consistency rates (ranging from approximately 20% to 40%), indicating considerable output variability across repeated sampling. This variability provides fertile ground for the intra-model ensemble (majority voting) to improve performance by filtering out inconsistent or spurious predictions.

Interestingly, MetaMath-7B stands out with a remarkably high self-consistency rate of 97%, despite its low overall accuracy. This suggests that while MetaMath-7B tends to produce the same answer repeatedly, that answer is often incorrect, reflecting a model that is confidently but consistently wrong. By contrast, models with moderate self-consistency, such as MAmmoTH-7B and Arithmo-Mistral-7B, benefit most from self-consistency-based ensembling, as the aggregation process can recover correct answers from a diverse set of outputs.

Overall, these findings underscore the value of test-time ensembling for models that exhibit nontrivial variability in their outputs. Self-consistency analysis thus provides insight into when intra-model aggregation is likely to yield substantial performance gains and when it may have limited effect.

4.3 Resource Efficiency and Practical Deployment

A key motivation for focusing on small, open-source language models is their accessibility and suitability for deployment in resource-constrained environments, such as research labs, classrooms, or individual users with commodity hardware. In this section, we analyze the computational requirements, scalability, and practical considerations associated with our ensemble approach.

Hardware and Inference Costs: All experiments were conducted on a Lambda Labs cloud instance equipped with a single NVIDIA A100 GPU (40GB). Each individual model was able to process the entire MATH500 benchmark, completing five independent runs (i.e., 2,500 solutions), in approximately 1.5 hours. For the full ensemble (six models, each generating five solutions per problem), this amounts to 15,000 total generations. Thus, the entire ensemble evaluation required roughly 9 GPU-hours in total (6 models $\times$ 1.5 hours/model). This translates to just 2.16 seconds per generation (i.e., per problem solution) on average.

These modest computational demands mean that advanced mathematical problem-solving can be conducted on a single modern GPU, with sequential processing also feasible on commodity hardware. Additionally, the majority voting and answer extraction steps are computationally trivial, ensuring that the full workflow remains highly practical for both local and institutional deployments.

Cost Comparison to Large Proprietary Models: By contrast, leading proprietary models such as GPT-4, DeepSeek-R1, and Gemini 2.5 Pro Exp require access to powerful distributed clusters or paid API endpoints, incurring significant financial and computational costs for large-scale inference. For example, single-pass inference with GPT-4 is often limited by usage quotas and can cost several dollars merely to process the entire MATH500 benchmark, not including hardware costs for training or fine-tuning. Moreover, running these models locally is typically infeasible due to massive memory and storage requirements (often exceeding 80–100 GB of GPU memory).

Scalability and Open-Source Availability: All models evaluated in this study are fully open-source, publicly available, and do not require special licensing or proprietary infrastructure. The ensemble inference and voting logic can be implemented in a few lines of code, and batch processing is easily parallelizable. Our approach scales naturally to additional models or generations, limited only by available GPU resources.

Deployment Considerations: The ability to deploy high-accuracy mathematical reasoning systems using only commodity GPUs and freely available models is of particular importance for educational and scientific applications where privacy, reproducibility, and cost are critical. Our results demonstrate that small model ensembles can achieve robust and practical performance. While not matching the absolute accuracy of the largest proprietary systems, they offer a compelling and accessible alternative, making capable mathematical AI broadly available.

In summary, the proposed ensemble framework strikes an effective balance between accuracy and efficiency, enabling advanced mathematical problem solving at a fraction of the computational and financial cost associated with state-of-the-art proprietary LLMs.

5 Conclusion

In this work, we have demonstrated that lightweight ensemble strategies can significantly enhance the mathematical problem-solving abilities of small, open-source language models on the challenging MATH500 benchmark. By leveraging both intra-model self-consistency and inter-model majority voting—without any additional training or fine-tuning, we achieved accuracy improvements well beyond what any individual model could offer. Our best ensemble of three small models reached an accuracy of 39.4%, closing a substantial portion of the gap between accessible open-source systems and proprietary state-of-the-art LLMs, while requiring only modest computational resources.

Our experiments also show that these ensemble methods are not only effective but highly practical: inference can be completed in a matter of hours on a single GPU, and the necessary models and code are freely available for broad adoption in both academic and educational settings.

There remain several avenues for further exploration. To start with, Self-Consistency Decoding samples multiple reasoning paths and selects the most frequent answer. Our intra-model ensemble method builds on the idea. Secondly, Advanced Prompting techniques like Tree-of-Thoughts or Graph-of-Thoughts could be used to explore reasoning paths in a more structured manner, while few-shot learning could provide better contextual examples. The aggregation could be improved by exploring more advanced methods like weighted voting, where votes are scaled based on model confidence or historical performance. Another promising direction is Verifier-based Filtering, where external verifiers validate solutions before the voting stage. A more collaborative paradigm could be a multi-agent approach, where multiple LLM agents debate solutions and critique each other's reasoning. Finally, applying these enhanced ensemble techniques to other STEM benchmarks or real-world mathematical applications would help validate their generality and robustness.

References

1. Achiam, J.; Adler, S.; Agarwal, S.; Ahmad, L.; Akkaya, I.; Aleman, F. L.; Almeida, D.; Altenschmidt, J.; Altman, S.; Anadkat, S.; *et al.* GPT-4 Technical Report. *arXiv preprint* arXiv:2303.08774 (2023).
2. DeepSeekAI, Guo, D., Yang D., Zhang H., Song J., Zhang R., Xu R., Zhu Q., Ma S., Wang P., et al. DeepSeek–R1: Incentivizing Reasoning Capability in LLMs via Reinforcement Learning. *arXiv preprint* arXiv:2501.12948,2025.

3. Hendrycks, D.; Burns, C.; Kadavath, S.; Arora, A.; Basart, S.; Li, J.; Tran, K.; Mazeika, M.; Song, D.; Steinhardt, J.; et al. Measuring Mathematical Problem Solving with the MATH Dataset. *Advances in Neural Information Processing Systems* 34 (NeurIPS 2021).
4. Jiang, Yuxuan, et al. "Exploring Mathematical Reasoning Capabilities of Small Language Models." arXiv preprint arXiv:2309.02144, 2023.
5. Touvron, Hugo, et al. "Llama 2: Open Foundation and Fine-Tuned Chat Models." arXiv preprint arXiv:2307.09288, 2023.
6. Xue, Weijia, et al. "MAmmoTH: Mathematical Reasoning in Large Language Models." arXiv preprint arXiv:2310.02255, 2023.
7. Yu, Junnan, et al. "MetaMath: Improving Mathematical Reasoning in Language Models via Self-supervised Learning." arXiv preprint arXiv:2311.09506, 2023.
8. Dhavala, Krishna Srinath, et al. "Arithmo: Training 7B parameter language models for high performance mathematical reasoning." arXiv preprint arXiv:2402.01321, 2024.
9. Dietterich, Thomas G. "Ensemble methods in machine learning." In International workshop on multiple classifier systems, pp. 1-15. Springer, 2000.
10. Vals.ai. "MATH500 Benchmark." https://www.vals.ai/benchmarks/math500-04-07-2025, 2024.
11. Lewkowycz, Aitor, Jacob Austin, David Dohan, Jiecao Yu, Ankur Parikh, et al. "Solving Quantitative Reasoning Problems with Language Models." arXiv preprint arXiv:2206.14858, 2022.
12. Cobbe, Karl, Vineet Kosaraju, Mohammad Bavarian, Sebastian Farquhar, Lily Lintz, Jacob Hilton, et al. "Training Verifiers to Solve Math Word Problems." arXiv preprint arXiv:2110.14168, 2021.
13. Azerbayev, Alisher, Aitor Lewkowycz, Morgan Austern, Joon Lee, Jiecao Yu, et al. "Llemma: An Open Language Model For Mathematics." arXiv preprint arXiv:2310.06780, 2023.
14. Luo, Yuheng, Yitao Liu, Yutian Chen, Qingyang Lin, Hao Peng, et al. "WizardMath: Empowering Mathematical Reasoning for Large Language Models via Reinforced Evol-Instruct." arXiv preprint arXiv:2308.09592, 2023.
15. Wang, Xuezhi, Jason Wei, Dale Schuurmans, Maarten Bosma, Ed Chi, Quoc V. Le, and Denny Zhou. "Self-Consistency Improves Chain of Thought Reasoning in Language Models." arXiv preprint arXiv:2203.11171, 2023.
16. Zhou, Denny, Kevin Robinson, William Fedus, Maarten Bosma, et al. "Mixture-of-Experts: Enhancing the Reasoning Ability of Large Language Models." Proceedings of the Neural Information Processing Systems (NeurIPS), 2022.

Proof Assistants and Formalizations

Formalizing a Classification Theorem for Low-Dimensional Solvable Lie Algebras in Lean

Viviana del Barco[1](✉), Gustavo Infanti[1], Exequiel Rivas[2], and Paul Schwahn[1]

[1] Instituto de Matemática, Estatística e Computação Científica, Universidade Estadual de Campinas, Rua Sergio Buarque de Holanda, 651, Cidade Universitaria Zeferino Vaz, 13083-859, Campinas, São Paulo, Brazil.
{delbarc,schwahn}@unicamp.br, g246337@dac.unicamp.br
[2] Tallinn University of Technology, Tallinn, Estonia
exequiel.rivas@taltech.ee

Abstract. We present a formalization, in the theorem prover *Lean*, of the classification of solvable Lie algebras of dimension at most three over arbitrary fields. Lie algebras are algebraic objects which encode infinitesimal symmetries, and as such ubiquitous in geometry and physics. Our work involves explicit calculations on the level of the underlying vector spaces and provides a use case for the linear algebra and Lie theory routines in Lean's mathematical library *mathlib*. Along the way we formalize results about Lie algebras, define the semidirect product within this setting and add API for bases of vector spaces. In a wider context, this project aims to provide a complete mechanization of a classification theorem, covering both the statement and its full formal proof, and contribute to the development and broader adoption of such results in formalized mathematics.

Keywords: Formalization of mathematics · Lie theory · Lean · Proof assistants

1 Introduction

In recent years, the formalization of mathematics has attracted growing interest among mathematicians. Formalization tools are of great value not only for reducing human error and possible oversights, but also for making all assumptions and dependencies fully explicit, providing interesting insights into the structure of mathematical arguments. One of these tools, the Lean proof assistant [8], has gained widespread adoption thanks to its expressive foundations, a predicative calculus of inductive constructions, and its powerful elaborator. Lean is complemented by mathlib [17], a community-maintained library that includes formalization of a broad spectrum of mathematical fields, including group theory, commutative algebra, linear algebra, differential geometry, and measure theory. This article is about the formalization of a classification theorem in a field of mathematics already present in mathlib: Lie algebras.

V. de Paiva and P. Koepke (Eds.): CICM 2025, LNAI 16136, pp. 317–339, 2026.
https://doi.org/10.1007/978-3-032-07021-0_18

The origins of Lie algebras and Lie groups date back to the work of Sophus Lie in late 19th century, who introduced them in order to study continuous symmetries of differential equations. Lie groups can be understood as continuous groups of transformations, while Lie algebras are sets of "infinitesimal" symmetries. Today, Lie groups and Lie algebras are widely used and have shaped the fields of geometry and algebra. Attempts at classifications of Lie algebras began with Killing, and independently Cartan, followed by Bianchi.

In mathematics, a *full classification* of a collection of objects is understood to be a non-redundant, exhaustive list of equivalence classes of those objects, for an appropriate notion of *equivalence* or *isomorphism* – each of the objects in the collection belongs to precisely one of the equivalence classes. One might want not only to *classify* mathematical objects, but also to *characterize* the individual cases in the classification – either through giving some invariant that separates the cases, or by stating equivalent conditions for each case.

This general perspective naturally applies to Lie algebras. One may reasonably ask to classify the Lie algebras of a certain type (simple, solvable etc.) or dimension, up to isomorphism. Each class should be represented by a particular Lie algebra, given either in terms of generators and Lie bracket relations or through another construction (like a semidirect product).

For the class of finite-dimensional complex simple Lie algebras, Killing provided a classification whose list was not complete. The complete classification is due to Cartan a few years later. Levi's theorem states that arbitrary complex Lie algebras are built from simple Lie algebras and solvable Lie algebras. The classification of the latter would thus lead to a full classification of complex Lie algebras. However, due to the many degrees of freedom that solvable Lie algebras have, such a classification is hopeless in full generality – hence authors focus on specific subfamilies.

One such subclass is the family of nilpotent Lie algebras of dimension 6. Between 1958 and 1983, several attempts were made to classify these over various fields: Morozov [7] (in characteristic zero), Shedler [14] (any field), Vergne [18] (over $\mathbb{C}$), Skjelbread and Sun [15] (over $\mathbb{R}$), Bech and Kolman [1] (over $\mathbb{R}$). Many of these works are independent and use different methods – however, in some cases, the lists are not compatible. It is Nielsen [11] who compared these tables and produced a first complete list of 6-dimensional nilpotent Lie algebras over the reals.

Similar challenges arose in dimension 7, as documented by Gong [3]. It is not unusual in the literature to find multiple classification papers on the same class of algebras, differing only in minor details, and coexisting until a consensus is reached around a *definitive* classification. Even then, in large classifications, cases can be overlooked and only noticed later (if at all).

This is why we believe that formalization of classifications, for example of Lie algebras, in a theorem prover such as Lean will constitute a significant contribution to the mathematical community. Formalized classifications will remove all possible doubts of completeness and correctness of the provided classifications lists. Classifications will not depend on accepted lists, but on rigorous formalized proofs.

The formalization of Lie algebras in proof assistants has been previously explored. Our work builds on Nash's contributions to the formalization of Lie theory in mathlib. This author has an ongoing program to formalize Cartan's classification of finite-dimensional complex simple Lie algebras. In an earlier contribution, Nash [9] introduced most of the key definitions in Lie theory needed to state a classification result for finite-dimensional semisimple Lie algebras over an algebraically closed field of characteristic zero. In later work [10], Nash showed how general definitions formalized in a proof assistant allow one to unify various versions of Engel's theorem into a stronger result not previously presented in the literature. In addition, formalizations of Lie algebras are present in Isabelle/HOL in the work of Schmoetten and Fleuriot [13]. They focus on constructing the Lie algebra of smooth vector fields on a Lie group, but they do not address directly the algebraic side of the theory of Lie algebras.

A number of mathematical classification results have already been formalized in theorem provers. Focusing on Lean, the well-known classification or *structure theorem* for finite abelian groups[1], and a classification theorem for finite Z-groups[2] are already formalized in mathlib. Another notable recent project formalizes the classification of groups of order pq where p, q are primes [5].

The current paper contributes to the formalization in Lean of classification results about Lie algebras. Concretely, we formalize a full classification theorem for solvable Lie algebras of dimension ≤ 3 over arbitrary fields. Moreover, we provide characterizations for each of the cases through an equivalent condition. Even though the mathematical correctness of this classification is not in doubt, its formalization – including all necessary supporting lemmas – is an important step for further formal work in Lie theory.

More specifically, in the context of Levi's theorem – and given that any Lie algebra of dimension at most 3 is either solvable or simple – our formalization is in some sense complementary to Nash's work. The theorem we formalize follows the presentation of the classification of 3-dimensional solvable Lie algebras given by de Graaf [4]. However, the proof itself uses different methods. De Graaf's classification re-obtains the previous one made by Patera and Zassenhaus [12] for perfect fields, and extends it to arbitrary fields.

More precisely, we formalize the following result:

Theorem 1. *Let L be a solvable Lie algebra of dimension ≤ 3 over a field $\mathbb{K}$.*

(i) *If $\dim L = 1$, then L is isomorphic to the abelian Lie algebra $\mathbb{K}$.*
(ii) *If $\dim L = 2$, then L is isomorphic to the abelian Lie algebra $\mathbb{K}^2$ or to $\mathfrak{aff}(\mathbb{K})$.*

---

[1] mathlib4 PR #5730: https://github.com/leanprover-community/mathlib4/pull/5730.

[2] mathlib4 PR #20358: https://github.com/leanprover-community/mathlib4/pull/20358.

(iii) *If* $\dim L = 3$*, then* L *is isomorphic to one of the following Lie algebras:* $\mathbb{K}^3$, $\mathfrak{heis}_3(\mathbb{K})$, $\mathfrak{aff}(\mathbb{K}) \oplus \mathbb{K}$, $\mathfrak{hyp}_3(\mathbb{K})$, L_α *for some* $\alpha \in \mathbb{K}^\times$*, or* M_δ *for some* $\delta \in \mathbb{K}^\times/(\mathbb{K}^\times)^2$*, where* $(\mathbb{K}^\times)^2$ *denotes the subgroup of squares of* $\mathbb{K}^\times$*.*

The Lie algebras listed above are pairwise non-isomorphic.

The Lie algebras appearing here are described in detail in Table 1 and the basics on Lie algebras can be found in Section 2.

The formalization of this theorem requires several constructions in Lean: first, to introduce all the Lie algebra structures mentioned there ($\mathbb{K}^n$, $\mathfrak{aff}(\mathbb{K})$, $\mathfrak{heis}_3(\mathbb{K})$, etc.) as an `instance` of a typeclass in Lean. We briefly explain the procedure here; for more details, see Section 3. We model each Lie algebra above on $\mathbb{K}^n$ (the n-th cartesian power of $\mathbb{K}$) and explicitly provide the Lie bracket for each one. Part of declaring the Lie algebra instance is to prove in Lean that this bracket indeed satisfies the Lie algebra axioms. After this is done, we show in Section 4 that given a solvable Lie algebra of dimension ≤ 3, there exists a Lie algebra isomorphism to one of the Lie algebras listed above. This is done by using bases of the Lie algebras (as vector spaces). The last (but not least!) part is to show that the defined instances are pairwise non-isomorphic. This is done by formalizing *invariants* of Lie algebras, that is, properties that remain invariant under isomorphisms. For instance, isomorphic Lie algebras are of the same dimension, just as vector spaces. In addition, we show in Lean that their commutator ideals must have the same dimension. As a consequence, an abelian and a non-abelian Lie algebra cannot be isomorphic; in particular, the two Lie algebras in Theorem 1 (ii) are not. More involved invariants were formalized and used to distinguish the Lie algebras in Theorem 1 (iii). A detailed description of this process is presented in Section 4, and the full Lean code is available on Github[3].

Section 5 contains the auxiliary material formalized, consisting on many basic results on vector spaces and linear maps — along with new results and API on top of the already formalized linear algebra and Lie theory in mathlib — with the goal of eventually contributing them back to the library. In addition, we provide results on (solvable) Lie algebras that we plan to contribute to mathlib. A few of them are particularly remarkable:

- the formalization of the semidirect product of Lie algebras,
- writing the Lie algebras in Theorem 1 as semidirect products of smaller pieces, in particular showing that they are all *almost abelian* (see Section 5.5 for the precise definition),
- the proof that a Lie algebra is solvable if a quotient by some solvable ideal is solvable.

One of the frequent lessons in formalization of mathematics is that writing good definitions and theorem statements is just as hard as writing proofs. When formalizing a classification, care must be taken when selecting the representatives for the isomorphism classes and when stating the theorems about isomorphisms,

[3] Repository: https://github.com/LieLean/LowDimSolvClassification.

non-isomorphisms, and characterizations of the cases. Since our project aspires to all of this, it may serve as a reference point for designing further classification projects in mathematics.

Development information on the project is given in Section 6, including the link to our formalization repository. Finally, in Section 7, we comment on future work we plan to approach.

2 Background

2.1 Mathematical Preliminaries

We begin with the mathematical definition of a Lie algebra as it is often found in textbooks.

Definition 1. *A vector space* L *over a field* $\mathbb{K}$ *together with an operation* $[\cdot,\cdot] : L \times L \to L$ *is called a* Lie algebra *over* $\mathbb{K}$ *if the following axioms are satisfied:*

(i) $[\cdot,\cdot] : L \times L \to L$ *is bilinear,*
(ii) $[x, x] = 0$ *for all* $x \in L$*,*
(iii) $[x, [y, z]] + [y, [z, x]] + [z, [x, y]] = 0$ *for all* $x, y, z \in L$*.*

The operation $[\cdot,\cdot] : L \times L \to L$ is called the *Lie bracket* of L. The second condition is called skew-symmetry of the bracket since it implies $[x, y] = -[y, x]$ for all $x, y \in L$. The last condition is known as the *Jacobi identity.*

We note that it is possible to relax some assumptions in the above definition. For example, one may merely assume that $\mathbb{K}$ is a commutative ring instead of a field, as is done in mathlib (see Section 2.2). However, for the purpose of this paper as well as for most applications (in relation to Lie groups or algebraic groups) it suffices to consider Lie algebras over fields.

Abelian Lie algebras. The simplest possible Lie bracket is of course the trivial one, i.e. $[x, y] = 0$ for all $x, y \in L$. If this is the case, the Lie algebra $(L, [\cdot,\cdot])$ is called *abelian.*

Lie subalgebras. A vector subspace $L' \subseteq L$ is called a *Lie subalgebra* of $(L, [\cdot,\cdot])$ if it is closed under the Lie bracket of L, that is $[x, y] \in L'$ for all $x, y \in L'$.

Maps between Lie algebras. Let $(L_1, [\cdot,\cdot]_1)$ and $(L_2, [\cdot,\cdot]_2)$ be Lie algebras over a field $\mathbb{K}$. If $f : L_1 \to L_2$ is a linear map and preserves the Lie bracket, i.e.

$$f([x, y]_1) = [f(x), f(y)]_2 \qquad \forall x, y \in L_1,$$

it is called a *homomorphism* of Lie algebras. As always, an invertible homomorphism is called an *isomorphism.* This will be the notion of equivalence for all classification theorems about Lie algebras.

A linear map $D : L \to L$ from a Lie algebra $(L, [\cdot,\cdot])$ to itself is called a *derivation* if

$$D([x, y]) = [D(x), y] + [x, D(y)] \qquad \forall x, y \in L.$$

The set of all derivations of L is denoted by $\mathrm{Der}(L)$, which is itself a Lie algebra with Lie bracket defined as $[A, B] = AB - BA$, for $A, B \in \mathrm{Der}(L)$.

Ideals. If a vector subspace $I \subseteq L$ is *absorbing*, that is $[x, y] \in I$ for all $x \in L$ and $y \in I$, we say that I is an *ideal* of L. Ideals are to Lie algebras what normal subgroups are to groups. For example, the kernel of a Lie algebra homomorphism is always an ideal. Moreover, if $I \subset L$ is an ideal, then the Lie bracket descends to the (vector space) quotient L/I and turns it into a Lie algebra.

The *center* of L is defined as $\mathfrak{z}(L) = \{x \in L \mid [x, y] = 0 \; \forall y \in L\}$ and is an ideal of L. Clearly, L is abelian if and only if it coincides with its center. A non-abelian Lie algebra L which does not have any ideals other than $\{0\}$ and L itself is called *simple.*

Derived series. For ideals $I, J \subset L$ we declare $[I, J] \subseteq I \cap J$ to be the subspace of L spanned by the set $\{[x, y] \mid x \in I, \; y \in J\}$. The ideal $[L, L]$ is called the *commutator* or *derived subalgebra* of L, and it will be a valuable tool in the proof of the classification theorem. The *derived series* of a Lie algebra is defined as the series of repeated commutators,

$$\mathcal{D}^0(L) := L, \qquad \mathcal{D}^k(L) := [\mathcal{D}^{k-1}(L), \mathcal{D}^{k-1}(L)] \quad \text{for } k \geq 1.$$

Clearly, $\mathcal{D}^0(L) \supseteq \mathcal{D}^1(L) \supseteq \cdots \supseteq \mathcal{D}^k(L) \supseteq \mathcal{D}^{k+1}(L) \supseteq \cdots$. A Lie algebra is called *solvable* if this series terminates eventually, i.e. $\mathcal{D}^k(L) = 0$ for some $k \in \mathbb{N}$. In particular, any abelian Lie algebra is solvable.

It follows from the definitions above that a Lie algebra cannot be both solvable and simple. These two conditions are in a sense complementary for characteristic zero: any Lie algebra can be decomposed as the semidirect product of a solvable and a simple one, as a consequence of Levi's theorem [6]. In dimension at most three, it is well-known that a Lie algebra is either simple or solvable, independently of $\mathbb{K}$.

2.2 Realization in Lean

In what follows, we summarize the existing implementation of the most relevant concepts above in the Lean library *mathlib*. To endow mathematical objects with structure, mathlib makes heavy use of the *typeclass* system on top of Lean's type-theoretic foundations. Roughly, a mathematical object or set is reinterpreted as a type `T : Type*`, and additional structure is encoded as an instance of a typeclass depending on `T`. These instances are usually not named and are automatically inferred when needed. For example, a field $(\mathbb{K}, +, \cdot)$ is formalized as a type `K : Type*` together with an instance of the typeclass `Field K`, which bundles the addition and multiplication together with the proofs of the field axioms.

A *vector space (or module)* V over $\mathbb{K}$ is then understood as a type `V` with instances of the typeclasses `AddCommGroup V` and `Module K V`. On the other hand, it has proved useful to define a *subspace (or submodule)* of V not as a standalone type (since there is no subset relation between types), but as a *structure* `Submodule K V`, which is essentially a bundle of data, consisting of a set of elements of `V` (currently implemented as a *predicate* on `V`) together with the proofs that it contains zero and is closed under addition and scalar multiplication.

```
structure Submodule (K : Type u) (V : Type v)
      [Semiring K] [AddCommMonoid V] [Module K V] : Type v where
  carrier : Set V
  add_mem' {a b : V} : a ∈ self.carrier → b ∈ self.carrier → a + b ∈
  self.carrier
  zero_mem' : 0 ∈ self.carrier
  smul_mem' (c : K) {x : V} : x ∈ self.carrier → c • x ∈ self.carrier
```

Of course any subspace of V is a vector space in its own right – this leads to the use of *type coercions*, which we will briefly discuss at the beginning of Section 5.

A formalization of the *dimension* of a finite dimensional vector space (that is, the rank as a module) is `Module.finrank`, which is a natural number.

Let us turn to some implementation details that are specific to the context of Lie algebras. In mathlib there is a typeclass encoding bracket operations $[\cdot,\cdot]$ without any extra conditions (and motivated from modules of Lie algebras, slightly more general than what is stated above):

```
class Bracket (L M : Type*) where
  bracket : L → M → M
```

In mathlib, a *Lie ring* is an additive group with a compatible bi-additive bracket that is skew-symmetric and satisfies the Jacobi identity, and a Lie algebra is a Lie ring `L` which is also a module over some commutative ring `K` such that the bracket becomes bilinear.

```
class LieRing (L : Type*) extends AddCommGroup L, Bracket L L where [...]
class LieAlgebra (K L : Type*) [CommRing K] [LieRing L] extends Module K
  L where [...]
```

Just as a submodule of a module is a bundled structure in mathlib, the same goes for Lie subalgebras and ideals of a Lie algebra L, which are implemented as `LieSubalgebra K L` and `LieIdeal K L`, respectively.

The current paper deals with particular Lie algebras, namely, the solvable ones. In Lean, the solvability property is given by a typeclass:

```
class LieAlgebra.IsSolvable (L : Type*) [LieRing L] : Prop where
  solvable_int : ∃ k, derivedSeries ℤ L k = ⊥
```

Note that every Lie ring is a Lie algebra over $\mathbb{Z}$, as instantiated in `LieRing.instLieAlgebra`, just like any abelian group is a $\mathbb{Z}$-module. For a Lie algebra over another field, this definition of solvability coincides with the usual one given above, as formalized in the following mathlib theorem:

```
theorem LieAlgebra.isSolvable_iff  (K L : Type*) [CommRing K]
[LieRing L] [LieAlgebra K L] :
IsSolvable L ↔ ∃ (k : ℕ), derivedSeries K L k = ⊥
```

There is a similar typeclass `IsLieAbelian` for the property of being abelian, and the fact that an abelian Lie algebra is solvable manifests as an instance

```
instance LieAlgebra.ofAbelianIsSolvable (L : Type*) [LieRing L]
[IsLieAbelian L] :
IsSolvable L
```

Finally, homomorphisms between Lie algebras L and L' are formalized by the structure `LieHom K L L'`, which may be abbreviated as `L →ₗ⁅K⁆ L'`. This structure is then extended to Lie algebra isomorphisms as `LieEquiv K L L'`, which essentially bundle the underlying homomorphism with its inverse, and is also denoted as `L ≃ₗ⁅K⁆ L'`.

3 The Lie Algebra Instances

In this section we explain how we use the mathlib library to instantiate each Lie algebra appearing in Theorem 1. Even though the theorem requires $\mathbb{K}$ to be a field, the definitions below make also sense for any commutative ring. Declare the following variables:

```
variable (K : Type*) [CommRing K]
```

As introduced in Definition 1, Lie algebras are finite-dimensional vector spaces together with a skew-symmetric bilinear map satisfying the Jacobi condition. Since all vector spaces of the same dimension over a field $\mathbb{K}$ are isomorphic, we may model any n-dimensional Lie algebra over a field $\mathbb{K}$ on the vector space $\mathbb{K}^n$. This could be represented in at least two ways: either as the iterated cartesian product $\mathbb{K} \times \mathbb{K} \times \cdots \times \mathbb{K}$ or as the set $\mathbb{K}^{\{0,\ldots,n-1\}}$ of all possible maps from the finite set of n elements to $\mathbb{K}$.

Since the product is a binary operation and one would have to define `K × (K × (K × ... × K))` recursively, the second option `Fin n → K` turns out to be more practical and scalable. Tuples of elements can then be constructed using vector notation, e.g. for `a b c : K` we have `![a, b, c] : Fin 3 → K`.

It is worth mentioning that the type `Fin n → K` already comes with a `Module K` instance in mathlib, derived from the pointwise structure on $\mathbb{K}$. We may now extend this to a Lie algebra structure.

The Lie algebra $\mathfrak{aff}(\mathbb{K})$. As an example, we describe in detail the set up needed to define the Lie algebra of affinities $\mathfrak{aff}(\mathbb{K})$, the (up to isomorphism) unique non-abelian Lie algebra in dimension two. First, we define `Affine K` as a type synonym in order to avoid conflicts in the instance inference system.

```
namespace LieAlgebra.Dim2
def Affine := Fin 2 → K

instance : LieRing (Affine K) := {
    (inferInstance : AddCommGroup (Fin 2 → K)) with
    bracket := fun l r ↦ ![0, l 0 * r 1 - r 0 * l 1]
    [...] }

instance : LieAlgebra K (Affine K) := {
    (inferInstance : Module K (Fin 2 → K)) with
    lie_smul := [...] }
```

The keyword `inferInstance` helps carrying over the existing instances from `Fin 2 → K`. The omitted parts `[...]` contain the proofs that the bracket is bi-additive, skew-symmetric, Jacobian, and in the last instance compatible with scalar multiplication.

In this way, most of the Lie algebras appearing in Theorem 1 are defined ad hoc. The Lie algebra $\mathfrak{aff}(\mathbb{K})$ is also a special case of the Lie algebra $\mathfrak{aff}(\mathbb{K}^n)$, which we implemented as `LieAlgebra.OfAffineEquiv` in arbitrary dimension (see Section 5.4).

Families in dimension three. Particular attention should be paid to the two one-parameter families L_α and M_δ appearing in Theorem 1. These can be more elegantly subsumed as special cases of a 2-parameter family of Lie algebras, as is done in [4]. We may easily have the type synonym and Lie ring instance depend on the explicit parameters α, β showing up in the Lie bracket:

```
namespace LieAlgebra.Dim3
def Family (_ _ : K) := Fin 3 → K

instance (α β : K) : LieRing (Family K α β) := {
    (inferInstance : AddCommGroup (Fin 3 → K)) with
    bracket := fun l r ↦ ![0, (l 0 * r 2 - l 2 * r 0) * α,
        (l 0 * r 2 - l 2 * r 0) * β + l 0 * r 1 - l 1 * r 0]
    [...] }

instance (α β : K) : LieAlgebra K (Family K α β) := [...]
```

We then set $L_\alpha := F_{\alpha,0}$ and $M_\alpha := F_{\alpha,1}$. Later we show that if $\alpha = \gamma^2\alpha'$ for some $\gamma \in \mathbb{K}^\times$, then $M_\alpha \cong M_{\alpha'}$, thus the isomorphism class $M_{[\alpha]}$, $[\alpha] \in \mathbb{K}^\times/(\mathbb{K}^\times)^2$, is well-defined.

Abelian Lie algebras. The instances for the abelian Lie algebras were constructed a bit differently. We would like to view an arbitrary vector space as an abelian Lie algebra (i.e. with trivial Lie bracket). Clearly it is inadvisible to directly define such a Lie bracket for any type `V` with a `Module K V` instance, since this will lead to conflicts in the instance inference system. Thus we make use of a type synonym

```
namespace LieAlgebra
variable (K : Type*) [Field K] (V : Type*) [AddCommGroup V] [Module K V]

def mkAbelian := V
```

where we set the bracket of any two elements to be zero:

```
instance : Bracket (mkAbelian K V) (mkAbelian K V) where
    bracket := fun _ _ ↦ (0 : V)
```

For the Lie ring and Lie algebra structures, we proceed as above. In this way, for any $\mathbb{K}$-module V, `mkAbelian K V` represents the Lie algebra V with trivial Lie bracket. In order to work with the abelian Lie algebras of dimension ≤ 3, we set

```
abbrev Dim1.Abelian := K
abbrev Dim2.Abelian := mkAbelian K (Fin 2 → K)
abbrev Dim3.Abelian := mkAbelian K (Fin 3 → K)
```

(conveniently, `K` already inherits an abelian Lie algebra structure from its (commutative) algebra structure via the mathlib instance `LieAlgebra.ofAssociativeAlgebra`).

Dim	Notation	Lean name	Non-zero brackets
1	$\mathbb{K}$	`K`	-
2	$\mathbb{K}^2$	`Dim2.Abelian K`	-
	$\mathfrak{aff}(\mathbb{K})$	`Dim2.Affine K`	$[b_0, b_1] = b_1$
3	$\mathbb{K}^3$	`Dim3.Abelian K`	-
	$\mathfrak{heis}_3(\mathbb{K})$	`Dim3.Heisenberg K`	$[b_1, b_2] = b_0$
	$\mathfrak{aff}(\mathbb{K}) \oplus \mathbb{K}$	`Dim3.AffinePlusAbelian K`	$[b_1, b_2] = b_1$
	$\mathfrak{hyp}_3(\mathbb{K})$	`Dim3.Hyperbolic K`	$[b_0, b_1] = b_1$, $[b_0, b_2] = b_2$
	$F_{\alpha,\beta}$, $\alpha \in \mathbb{K}^\times$, $\beta \in \mathbb{K}$	`Dim3.Family K` α β, $\alpha \neq 0$	$[b_0, b_1] = b_2$, $[b_0, b_2] = \alpha b_1 + \beta b_2$
	L_α, $\alpha \in \mathbb{K}^\times$	`Dim3.Family K` α `0`, $\alpha \neq 0$	see above
	$M_{[\alpha]}$, $\alpha \in \mathbb{K}^\times$	`Dim3.Family K` α `1`, $\alpha \neq 0$	see above

Table 1. Notation for low-dimensional Lie algebras.

Summary. For the reader's convenience, in Table 1 we list the labels we used in the Lean code for each Lie algebra mentioned in Theorem 1. In the last line of the table, $[\alpha]$ denotes the class of $\alpha \in \mathbb{K}^\times$ in the quotient $\mathbb{K}^\times/(\mathbb{K}^\times)^2$. We also list the non-zero brackets for a suitable basis (b_i) of the Lie algebra.

4 The Classification Theorem

This section presents the required steps to formalize the proof of Theorem 1. The formalization is divided according to the (finite) dimension of the Lie algebras. As seen in Section 2, if two Lie algebras are isomorphic, then they are isomorphic as vector spaces and thus have the same dimension. This is already formalized in mathlib: the dimension of vector spaces is preserved under linear isomorphism by `LinearEquiv.finrank_eq`, and any isomorphism of Lie algebras is a linear isomorphism by `LieEquiv.coe_toLinearEquiv`.

In order to get the full proof of the theorem, we first focus on showing that the Lie algebras in Section 3 are a set of representatives for the isomorphism classes in the classification – that is, every solvable Lie algebra of dimension ≤ 3 is isomorphic to one of them. In a second stage, we prove that these representatives are pairwise non-equivalent. These two stages are described separately in the following two subsections.

4.1 Establishing Isomorphisms with Representatives

For each $n = 1, 2, 3$, we show that given a solvable Lie algebra of dimension n, there is an isomorphism to one of the Lie algebras from Table 1. The precise statements are as follows (from now on $\mathbb{K}$ is a field).

```
variable {K L : Type*} [Field K] [LieRing L] [LieAlgebra K L]

theorem Dim1.classification (h : Module.finrank K L = 1) :
    Nonempty (L ≃ₗ⁅K⁆ K)

theorem Dim2.classification (h : Module.finrank K L = 2) :
    Nonempty (L ≃ₗ⁅K⁆ (Dim2.Abelian K)) ∨ Nonempty (L ≃ₗ⁅K⁆ (Affine K))

theorem Dim3.classification (h : Module.finrank K L = 3) (hs :
    LieAlgebra.IsSolvable L) :
    Nonempty (L ≃ₗ⁅K⁆ (Dim3.Abelian K)) ∨
    Nonempty (L ≃ₗ⁅K⁆ (Heisenberg K)) ∨
    Nonempty (L ≃ₗ⁅K⁆ (AffinePlusAbelian K)) ∨
    Nonempty (L ≃ₗ⁅K⁆ (Hyperbolic K)) ∨
    (∃ α, α ≠ 0 ∧ Nonempty (L ≃ₗ⁅K⁆ (Family K α 0))) ∨
    (∃ α, α ≠ 0 ∧ Nonempty (L ≃ₗ⁅K⁆ (Family K α 1)))
```

Recall from Table 1 the notation used in Lean code, in comparison to Theorem 1. Notice that the ∨ in the statements is not an exclusive or. The fact that a Lie algebra is isomorphic to only one Lie algebra in Theorem 1 is the subject of the next subsection.

The precise form of these isomorphisms is immaterial, as it depends on a (noncomputable) choice of basis anyway. Therefore we chose to formalize the classifications with `theorem`, which always declares a `Prop`-valued term, instead of declaring a term of `LieEquiv` for each case. The mere *existence* of a term of type `T` can be expressed using the proposition `Nonempty T : Prop`, and through the principle of *proof irrelevance* the term is not remembered by Lean.

The insightful reader will notice that the hypothesis of *solvability* is only present in dimension three. In fact, our theorems include the classification of *all* Lie algebras of dimension ≤ 2 over a field $\mathbb{K}$ – as very well-known, any such Lie algebra is solvable. We obtain this result in Lean as a corollary of our classification. For dimension one, this is immediate from the instance in mathlib `LieAlgebra.ofAbelianIsSolvable`. For dimension two, the proof follows from the latter together with the fact that any Lie algebra having a solvable commutator is solvable, which we formalized as `LieAlgebra.solvable_of_commutator_solvable`.

In order to prove the classification theorems, given a Lie algebra L, we need to provide a Lie algebra isomorphism (`LieEquiv`). For abelian Lie algebras we may choose any basis and use the mathlib definition `Basis.equivFun`, giving a linear isomorphism between a module over $\mathbb{K}$ with a finite basis and the module of functions from its basis to $\mathbb{K}$.

For the non-abelian Lie algebras we construct a basis satisfying special bracket relations. In dimension two, a unique lemma suffices:

```
lemma Dim2.abelian_or_basis (h : Module.finrank K L = 2) :
    IsLieAbelian L ∨ (∃ B : Basis (Fin 2) K L, ⁅B 0, B 1⁆ = B 1)
```

The use of bases in our approach is motivated by the fact that Lie theorists usually define Lie algebras in a concise way by giving the non-zero Lie bracket relations between the basis elements. We believe that this way of definition could be a viable way to go forward in mathlib, possibly together with an automated verification of the Jacobi identity.

With this lemma, the proof of `Dim2.classification` goes as follows:

```
theorem Dim2.classification (h : Module.finrank K L = 2) :
    Nonempty (L ≃ₗ⁅K⁆ (Abelian K)) ∨ Nonempty (L ≃ₗ⁅K⁆ (Affine K)) := by
  obtain (a | ⟨B, pfB⟩) := Dim2.abelianorbasis h
  · left
    /- choose any linear isomorphism f, the bracket condition is then
    trivial -/
    [...]
    exact ⟨{f with [...]}⟩
  · right
    exact ⟨{fun l => ![B.repr l 0, B.repr l 1] with [...]}⟩
```

In the left (abelian) case, we choose some linear isomorphism using existing mathlib definitions, and then show that it (trivially) preserves the bracket; in the right case, we explicitly define the isomorphism by sending an element `x : L` to a vector in `Fin 2 → K` using `B.repr`, which gives the coordinates of `x` in the basis `B` obtained from the lemma above.

The 3-dimensional case is more involved, since now the commutator ideal $[L, L]$ may have dimension 0, 1 or 2. We provide lemmas with bases in each case.

The 0-dimensional commutator case corresponds to the abelian one. When the commutator is of dimension one, two cases need to be considered; for this part we followed mostly the classification in [6]. Under the assumption that the commutator $[L, L]$ is contained in the center $z(L)$, we show that `∃ B : Basis (Fin 3) K L, ⁅B 1, B 2⁆ = B 0 ∧ ⁅B 0, B 1⁆ = 0 ∧ ⁅B 0, B 2⁆ = 0`. On the contrary, if the commutator is not contained in the center we prove `∃ B : Basis (Fin 3) K L, ⁅B 0, B 1⁆ = 0 ∧ ⁅B 0, B 2⁆ = 0 ∧ ⁅B 1, B 2⁆ = B 1`. These two cases correspond to `Heisenberg` and `AffinePlusAbelian`, respectively. Actually, we implement these as *iff* statements, showing that these bases characterize the relation of the commutator and the center when the commutator is 1-dimensional.

The case of commutator of dimension 2 leads to three possible forms of the bracket; for this part, we were guided by the classification in [4]. Here we have

```
lemma Dim3.case2 : Module.finrank K L = 3 ∧ Module.finrank K (commutator
    K L) = 2 ↔
    (∃ B : Basis (Fin 3) K L, ⁅B 0, B 1⁆ =  B 1 ∧ ⁅B 0, B 2⁆ = B 2 ∧ ⁅B
    1, B 2⁆ = 0) ∨
    (∃ B : Basis (Fin 3) K L, ⁅B 0, B 1⁆ = B 2 ∧ ⁅B 1, B 2⁆ = 0 ∧
        (∃ α : K, α ≠ 0 ∧ ⁅B 0, B 2⁆ = α • B 1)) ∨
    (∃ B : Basis (Fin 3) K L, ⁅B 0, B 1⁆ = B 2 ∧ ⁅B 1, B 2⁆ = 0 ∧
        (∃ α : K, α ≠ 0 ∧ ⁅B 0, B 2⁆ = α • B 1 + B 2))
```

The three cases above will correspond to, respectively, the Lie algebras `Hyperbolic K`, `Family K α 0` and `Family K α 1`.

Statements involving bases are the core of the proof of the classification theorem. Once they are established, we proceed as in dimension two, where we define, for each case, an explicit map using `B.repr` and show it is a `LieEquiv`. The proof of these key lemmas for $\dim[L, L] = 2$ motivated most of the general results that were formalized as part of this project. We shall very briefly describe the proof of the lemmas in a general way, since each has its particularities. We start by setting a basis of the commutator ideal and then extend it to a basis of the Lie algebra. This is done because, as can be seen in Table 1, the Lie brackets of some basis elements span the commutator, i.e. the bases of the Lie algebras are *adapted* to the commutator. Finally, we modify the extended set to a basis of the Lie algebra that satisfies the bracket relations of one of the instances.

The procedure of extending a basis is standard in linear algebra. However, in Lean there are several steps to be dealt with before obtaining a basis of the whole space; the subtleties and some of the auxiliary lemmas used are explained in Section 5.1.

4.2 Non-redundancy of the Classification

Here we describe the theorems and tools that allow to show that the Lie algebras in Theorem 1 are pairwise non-isomorphic. As we mentioned before, we can restrict the study to Lie algebras of the same dimension, since different dimension Lie algebras cannot be isomorphic.

In dimension one, there is only one representative, so there is nothing to prove. For dimension two, we proved directly:

```
theorem Dim2.not_iso : IsEmpty (Affine K ≃ₗ⁅K⁆ Abelian K)
```

For dimension 3, we formalized the non-redundancy in several steps. First, we show that if two Lie algebras are isomorphic then their commutator ideals have equal dimension – this is actually for any dimension. This is done in `LieAlgebra.dim_commutator_eq_of_lieEquiv`.

In order to use this result, we characterize the non-abelian Lie algebras of dimension three appearing in Table 1. We prove that such a Lie algebra L:

- is isomorphic to $\mathbb{K}^3$ if and only if it has 0-dimensional commutator (we use a result valid for any dimension, `LieAlgebra.abelian_iff_dim_comm_zero`).
- is isomorphic to $\mathfrak{heis}_3(\mathbb{K})$ if and only if it has 1-dimensional commutator which is contained in the center (`Dim3.heisenberg_iff`).
- is isomorphic to $\mathfrak{aff}(\mathbb{K}) \oplus \mathbb{K}$ if and only if it has 1-dimensional commutator which is not contained in the center (`Dim3.affinePlusAbelian_iff`).
- has commutator of dimension two if and only if it has a basis satisfying particular bracket relations (`Dim3.case2`). We further split this into $\mathfrak{hyp}_3(\mathbb{K})$ and $F_{\alpha,\beta}$ (`Dim3.hyperbolic_iff` and `Dim3.family_iff`).

To conclude that `Heisenberg K` is not isomorphic to `AffinePlusAbelian K`, we use the characterization above and show that any Lie algebra isomorphism (`LieEquiv`) preserves the property of the commutator being contained in the center. Indeed, a Lie algebra satisfying this condition is called *2-step nilpotent*.

The non-isomorphisms of the Lie algebras within the last class requires a bit more of effort. First, we show that `Hyperbolic K` cannot be isomorphic to any Lie algebra in `Family K` α β:

```
theorem Dim3.Family.not_iso_hyperbolic {α β : K} (hα : α ≠ 0) :
    IsEmpty (Family K α β ≃ₗ⁅K⁆ Hyperbolic K)
```

The proof of this theorem uses a more subtle invariant than the 2-step condition. We use the fact that there is an element $e \in \mathfrak{hyp}_3(\mathbb{K})$ whose bracket $\mathrm{ad}(e) := [e, \cdot]$ acts as the identity on the commutator. More precisely, as mentioned above, $\mathfrak{hyp}_3(\mathbb{K})$ admits a basis $\mathcal{B} = \{b_0, b_1, b_2\}$ satisfying the first line of the lemma `Dim3.case2`. With that it is possible to prove in Lean that the commutator of this Lie algebra is spanned by $\{b_1, b_2\}$. In addition, the well-defined endomorphism of the commutator defined as the restriction of $\mathrm{ad}(b_0)$ is the identity map. If a Lie algebra is isomorphic to $\mathfrak{hyp}_3(\mathbb{K})$, then it must contain an element such that the induced endomorphism is also the identity. The proof of `Dim3.Family.not_iso_hyperbolic` shows that `Family K α β` does not possess such an element.

As a last step, we provide criteria to decide when two members of `Family K α β` are isomorphic. This criteria completes the proof of Theorem 1 (see notation in Table 1).

```
theorem Dim3.Family.iso_iff {α α' β β' : K}
(hα : α ≠ 0) (hα' : α' ≠ 0) :
  Nonempty ((Family K α β) ≃ₗ⁅K⁆ Family K α' β') ↔ ∃ (γ : Kˣ),  α = γ
    ^2 * α' ∧ β = γ * β'
```

For this proof, we consider a basis $\mathcal{B} = \{b_0, b_1, b_2\}$ of `Family α β` such that the Lie bracket satisfy $[b_0, b_1] = b_2, [b_1, b_2] = 0, [b_0, b_2] = \alpha b_1 + \beta b_2$. One shows in Lean that the commutator is spanned by b_1, b_2. As done for the hyperbolic, we consider the endomorphism of the commutator induced by taking brackets with b_0. This endomorphism has a matrix, in the basis $\{b_1, b_2\}$, of trace β and determinant $-\alpha$. Therefore, if there is an isomorphism $f : F_{\alpha,\beta} \to F_{\alpha',\beta'}$, then f takes the commutator to the commutator of the image (`LieEquiv.commutator_map`). The image of b_0 by the isomorphism induces a map in the commutator which is a multiple γ of the conjugation of the map induced by b_0 on the domain. Since conjugation preserves trace and determinant, we obtain our result.

We note that the adjoint maps $x \mapsto \mathrm{ad}(x) = [x, \cdot]$ of a Lie algebra are already formalized in mathlib as `LieDerivation.ad`. For the proof of the last theorem, we formalized and used in Lean the restriction of these maps to the commutator. In this way we were able to compute trace and determinants of the 2×2 matrix induced and to show that these were conjugate, up to a multiple.

5 Further Contributions

The formalization of the results in Section 4 required us to implement along the way many auxiliary results about modules, bases, Lie algebras and their substructures. Some are completely new theorems and constructions, other are marginal improvements or adjustments of content already in mathlib. In what follows we give a rough overview of these contributions, including only some selected examples due to the limited scope of this paper.

Many of the following definitions and theorems can and have been stated in high generality, which is one of the design principles of mathlib. For example, vector spaces over fields are just a special case of modules over a ring, but this can be even further generalized to modules over a semiring. This is all encompassed by the typeclass `Module` in mathlib. For the simplicity of exposition, we will state the following theorems with vector spaces and Lie algebras over fields. As we will shortly see, from a working mathematician's and user's perspective it also sometimes makes sense to run contrary to this design philosophy by specializing some definitions to particular cases and giving them new names.

5.1 Linear Algebra Lemmas

The proofs of the classification theorems that we formalized required explicit calculations in finite-dimensional vector spaces on the level of submodules, linear independent sets of vectors, and bases. In mathlib there exist typeclasses for all of these, but stating even mathematically simple statements can quickly become convoluted. For example, let V be a vector space over a field K – that is, `K V : Type*` and there are instances of the typeclasses `Field K`, `AddCommGroup V` and `Module K V`. Recall the definition of `Submodule K V` as a structure type from Section 2.2. A term `p : Submodule K V` corresponds to a vector subspace of V. Trivially, this should be itself a vector space over K. But in order to equip it with a `Module` instance, it first needs to be coerced to a `Type`. This is done by the `Subtype` structure: we obtain a term `↥p : Type*` and a canonical function `Subtype.val : ↥p → V`, and mathlib provides us with an instance of `Module K ↥p`.

This subtlety of type coercions appears all over the place and adds a bit more ballast to the task of formalization, but is ultimately unavoidable. It explains the need to prove mathematically trivial lemmas such as the following two from our project.

```
variable {K L : Type*} [Field K] [AddCommGroup L] [Module K L]

theorem LinearIndependent.iff_in_submodule {S : Type*} (N : Submodule K
    L) {f : S → N} :
    LinearIndependent K f ↔ LinearIndependent K (Subtype.val ∘ f: S → L)

theorem Submodule.linearIndependent_from_ambient {S : Type*} (N :
    Submodule K L) (f : S → L)
        (hs : LinearIndependent K f) (hr : Set.range f ⊆ N) :
    LinearIndependent K (Set.map_into_subtype N f hr)
```

An elementary method in linear algebra is to start with a linearly independent set of vectors, or a basis of some subspace, and then extend it to a basis of the whole vector space. Although there already exist constructions in mathlib that help with this, we felt the need to write some additional API, such as the following that extends a linear independent set of size one less than the rank of the module to a basis.

```
noncomputable def mkFinCons_from_linIndep {n : ℕ} {l : Fin n → L}
        (hs : LinearIndependent K l) (ht : Module.finrank K L = n + 1) :
    Basis (Fin (n + 1)) K L
```

5.2 Lemmas About Lie Algebras

As in the preceding section, some of the lemmas we formalized are of a more technical flavor and some are more mathematically meaningful. One such technical lemma, which also exists under the alias `LieIdeal.coe_map_of_surjective` in mathlib, states that if a Lie algebra homomorphism $f : L \to L'$ is surjective, then the pushforward of an ideal $I \subseteq L$ (i.e. the ideal generated by $f(I)$) is just the image $f(I)$ itself. Because ideals are, in particular, subalgebras, subspaces and subsets, which all correspond to different structure types in mathlib, this statement can be formalized on several levels:

```
variable {K L L': Type*} [Field K] [LieRing L] [LieRing L']
[LieAlgebra K L] [LieAlgebra K L']

theorem LieIdeal.map_eq_image_of_surj {f : L →ₗ⁅K⁆ L'}
        (h : Function.Surjective f) (I : LieIdeal K L) :
    (LieIdeal.map f I).toSubmodule = Submodule.map f.toLinearMap I

theorem LieIdeal.map_eq_image_of_surj' {f : L →ₗ⁅K⁆ L'}
        (h : Function.Surjective f) (I : LieIdeal K L) :
    (LieIdeal.map f I).toLieSubalgebra = LieSubalgebra.map f I

theorem LieIdeal.map_eq_image_of_surj'' {f : L →ₗ⁅K⁆ L'}
        (h : Function.Surjective f) (I : LieIdeal K L) :
    LieIdeal.map f I = f '' I
```

Note that `LieIdeal.map_eq_image_of_surj` already exists in mathlib as `LieIdeal.coe_map_of_surjective`, but having the above alternative versions was very useful to us. For example, it allowed us to construct, starting from an isomorphism $e : L \to L'$ between two Lie algebras, an isomorphism between any ideal $I \subseteq L$ and its image.

```
def LieEquiv.ofIdeals (e : L ≃ₗ⁅K⁆ L') (I : LieIdeal K L) (I' : LieIdeal
    K L')
        (h : LieIdeal.map e.toLieHom I = I') :
    I ≃ₗ⁅K⁆ I'
```

This is analogous to the mathlib theorems `LinearEquiv.ofSubmodules` and `LieEquiv.ofSubalgebras`.

To present another example of coercion between types, consider the derivations of an abelian Lie algebra L. Since the bracket on L is trivial, the derivation condition is vacuous, so every linear endomorphism of L is indeed a derivation. This trivial fact is formalized in the following isomorphism of Lie algebras.

```
def Abelian.DerivationOfLinearMap (K L : Type*) [CommRing K] [LieRing L]
        [LieAlgebra K L] [IsLieAbelian L] :
    End K L ≃ₗ⁅K⁆ LieDerivation K L L
```

Returning to ideals in a Lie algebra, we note the commutator and center ideals were instrumental in the proof of the classification theorems. Even though the commutator ideal is just the first term of the derived series (which is already implemented in mathlib), we deem it worthy of having its own name in Lean. This makes theorem statements and proofs easier to read and think about without introducing additional abstraction. The theorem `LieAlgebra.commutator_eq_span` in turn is vital for the calculational parts of the proofs.

```
abbrev LieAlgebra.commutator : LieIdeal K L :=
  LieAlgebra.derivedSeries K L 1
theorem LieAlgebra.commutator_eq_span :
    (LieAlgebra.commutator K L).toSubmodule =
        Submodule.span K {x : L | ∃ (y : L) (z : L), [y, z] = x}
```

We also needed the fact that commutator and center are preserved under isomorphisms of Lie algebras:

```
def LieEquiv.commutator_equiv (e : L ≃ₗ[K] L') : LieAlgebra.commutator K
    L ≃ₗ[K] LieAlgebra.commutator K L'
theorem LieEquiv.center_map (e : L ≃ₗ[K] L') : LieIdeal.map e
    (LieAlgebra.center K L) = LieAlgebra.center K L'
```

In the first case, the Lie algebra structure of the commutator itself was important, hence the need to define an isomorphism. In the second case, the center is always itself abelian, so there is no information in the Lie algebra structure.

As a concrete interaction between linear algebra concepts and the Lie bracket, there is the elementary consequence of the skew-symmetry of the bracket that two vectors $x, y \in L$ with $[x, y] \neq 0$ are necessarily linearly independent.

```
lemma LieAlgebra.linearIndependent_of_bracket_ne_zero (X Y : L)
   (hXY : [X, Y] ≠ 0) :
    LinearIndependent K ![X, Y]
```

An important fact of a more general interest is that a Lie algebra L is solvable if there exists an ideal $I \subseteq L$ such that both I and the quotient Lie algebra L/I are solvable.

```
theorem LieAlgebra.solvable_of_ideal_and_quot_solvable {I : LieIdeal R L}
        (quotsol : LieAlgebra.IsSolvable (L / I))
      (Isol : LieAlgebra.IsSolvable I) :
    LieAlgebra.IsSolvable L
```

5.3 The Semidirect Product

We turn to a central construction in Lie theory that allows us to define many Lie algebras of interest without resorting to a basis or coordinates. Let $(L, [\cdot,\cdot]_L)$ and $(J, [\cdot,\cdot]_J)$ be two Lie algebras (over the same field) such that L acts on J in the sense of a representation of Lie algebras, that is, we fix a Lie algebra homomorphism $\varphi : L \to \mathrm{Der}(J)$. Then the *semidirect product* $L \ltimes_\varphi J$ is defined as the direct product of vector spaces $L \times J$ together with a Lie bracket given by

$$[(x_1, x_2), (y_1, y_2)] := ([x_1, y_1]_L, [x_2, y_2]_J + \varphi(x_1)y_2 - \varphi(y_1)x_2).$$

This is analogous to group representations and the semidirect product in group theory, which is already formalized in mathlib:

```
structure SemidirectProduct (N G : Type*) [Group N] [Group G]
    (φ : G →* MulAut N) where
    left : N
    right : G
instance {N G : Type*} [Group N] [Group G] {φ : G →* MulAut N} :
    Mul (SemidirectProduct N G φ) where
    mul a b := ⟨a.1 * φ a.2 b.1, a.2 * b.2⟩
```

In our definition of semidirect product of Lie algebras `L J : Type*`, we decided to directly use the product type `L × J`, so we can use its existing `Module` instance.

```
def LieSemidirectProduct {K : Type*} (L J : Type*) [Field K] [LieRing L]
    [LieRing J]
        [LieAlgebra K L] [LieAlgebra K J] (_ : L →ₗ⁅K⁆ LieDerivation K J
    J) :=
    L × J
```

We also set the shorthand notation `L ⋉[φ] J` for `LieSemidirectProduct L J φ`.

```
variable {K L J : Type*} [Field K] [LieRing L] [LieRing J] [LieAlgebra K
    L] [LieAlgebra K J]
    {φ : L →ₗ⁅K⁆ LieDerivation K J J}

instance : AddCommGroup (L ⋉[φ] J) := (inferInstance : AddCommGroup (L ×
     J))
instance : Module K (L ⋉[φ] J) := (inferInstance : Module K (L × J))
instance : Bracket (L ⋉[φ] J) (L ⋉[φ] J) where
    bracket := fun a b ↦ ⟨⁅a.1, b.1⁆, φ a.1 b.2 - φ b.1 a.2 + ⁅a.2,
    b.2⁆⟩
```

Along the way we wrote extensionality and simplification lemmas, as well as the original Lie algebras L and J as subalgebras of $L \ltimes_\varphi J$. In fact, J is even an ideal, but contrary to the direct product, L is generally not.

```
def LieSemidirectProduct.leftSubalgebra : LieSubalgebra K (L ⋉[φ] J)
    := LieHom.range inl
def LieSemidirectProduct.rightIdeal : LieIdeal K (L ⋉[φ] J)
    := LieHom.ker fst
```

Finally, for the trivial representation $\varphi = 0$, the semidirect product just reduces to the direct product:

```
def Prod.toLieSemidirectProduct : (L × J) ≃ₗ⁅K⁆ L ⋉[(0 : L →ₗ⁅K⁆
    LieDerivation K J J)] J
```

The Lie algebras appearing in Theorem 1 can in fact all be written as direct/semidirect products of smaller pieces. We defined the corresponding isomorphisms, and moreover also formalized two general series of Lie algebras, $\mathfrak{aff}(\mathbb{K}^n) = \mathrm{End}(\mathbb{K}^n) \ltimes \mathbb{K}^n$ and $\mathfrak{hyp}_n(\mathbb{K}) = \mathbb{K} \ltimes \mathbb{K}^{n-1}$.

5.4 Series of Lie Algebras

The point of having introduced the semidirect product is that we can now define some general series of Lie algebras. We can already start forming nontrivial semidirect products using the abelian Lie algebras `mkAbelian K V` defined in Section 3.

For example, the *affine group* Aff(V) (`AffineEquiv` in mathlib) on a vector space V is the Lie group of transformations of V that are compositions of invertible linear maps and translations. Its Lie algebra $\mathfrak{aff}(V)$ is isomorphic to the semidirect product $\mathfrak{gl}(V) \ltimes_{\text{Id}} V$, where V has trivial Lie bracket. We can take this as a definition, but first we have to build the homomorphism from $\mathfrak{gl}(V)$ to $\text{Der}(V)$ from the identity map.

```
def ofAffineEquivAux := (Abelian.DerivationOfLinearMap K (mkAbelian K
    V)).toLieHom

abbrev OfAffineEquiv := End K V ⋉[ofAffineEquivAux K V] mkAbelian K V
```

We note that in mathematics the concept of an *affine Lie algebra* is usually related to infinite dimensional Lie algebras, thus distinct from and unrelated to $\mathfrak{aff}(V)$, hence the slightly awkward name `LieAlgebra.OfAffineEquiv`. We also set the notation $\mathfrak{aff}$ for `OfAffineEquiv`.

Another series of solvable Lie algebras appearing in the classification are the ones that are associated to real hyperbolic spaces via the Iwasawa decomposition. They are denoted by $\mathfrak{hyp}_n(\mathbb{K})$, and are isomorphic to the semidirect product $\mathbb{K} \ltimes_\varphi \mathbb{K}^{n-1}$, where $\mathbb{K}$ and $\mathbb{K}^{n-1}$ are abelian and $\varphi(a) = a \cdot \text{Id}$. The implementation in Lean is as follows.

```
def RealHyperbolicAux : K →ₗ[K] LieDerivation K L L
 := LieHom.comp (Abelian.DerivationOfLinearMap K L)
 (LieHom.smulRight (LinearMap.id : End K L))

abbrev RealHyperbolic := K ⋉[RealHyperbolicAux K V] (mkAbelian K V)
```

We also registered the notation $\mathfrak{hyp}$ for `RealHyperbolic`.

5.5 Almost Abelian Lie Algebras

An interesting class of Lie algebras is that of *almost abelian* ones. We call a Lie algebra L almost abelian if L contains an abelian ideal I of codimension one, that is $\dim L/I = 1$. In this case all of the Lie bracket information can be encoded in a single linear endomorphism of I, which makes almost abelian Lie algebras very pleasant objects of study. We formalized the definition (at least for finite-dimensional Lie algebras):

```
variable (K L : Type*) [Field K] [LieRing L] [LieAlgebra K L]
def LieAlgebra.IsAlmostAbelian :
    Prop :=    ∃ I : LieIdeal K L, IsLieAbelian I ∧ Module.finrank K L =
    Module.finrank K I + 1
```

A semidirect product of the form $\mathbb{K} \ltimes_\varphi L$, where L is abelian, is clearly almost abelian.

```
theorem LieSemidirectProduct.isAlmostAbelian {φ : K →ₗ[K] LieDerivation
    K L L}
        [IsLieAbelian L] :
    LieAlgebra.IsAlmostAbelian K (K ⋉[φ] L)
```

Together with the formalized isomorphisms between the low-dimensional Lie algebras in the classification and semidirect products of this form, one may conclude that every solvable Lie algebra of dimension at most three over a field is almost abelian.

In the converse direction, we also formalized the theorem that if a (not necessarily abelian) Lie algebra L has a codimension one ideal I, it is isomorphic to a semidirect product $\mathbb{K} \ltimes_\varphi I$.

```
theorem LieAlgebra.semidirectProduct_of_codim_one_ideal (I : LieIdeal K L)
        (hdim : Module.finrank K L = Module.finrank K I + 1) :
    ∃ φ : K →ₗ[K] LieDerivation K I I, Nonempty (L ≃ₗ[K] K ⋉[φ] I)
```

Expressing the Lie algebras in Theorem 1 as the semidirect products mentioned above allowed us to prove in Lean the very well-known fact that every 3-dimensional Lie algebra is almost abelian.

6 Development

Our development is based on Lean 4 `v4.19.0` and the mathlib4 release tagged with this version number (commit `c44e0c8`), and can be accessed on https://github.com/LieLean/LowDimSolvClassification.

We have decided to work on top of Lie algebras as currently defined in mathlib. As a result of our restriction to low dimensional Lie algebras, we have benefited from the results around finite bases for vector spaces. We have made use of classical axioms through the development, either in direct form or by using mathlib results that make use of these axioms. In particular, we found ourselves needing to choose elements for extending existing linear independent sets and bases, often leading to `noncomputable` definitions. One such example is `LinearIndependent.extend_fin_succ_fun`, where we use `Classical.choose`.

The tactic `module`[4] was useful in certain cases for discharging proofs of Lie algebra equalities, although in some cases we found ourselves needing to apply commutation to Lie atoms of the form `[x, y]` before applying the tactic. To get around this restriction, we created a modified version of `module`, which we call `simplify_lie`, and adds additional support to atoms of the form `[x,y]`. This tactic will perform rewriting of Lie equalities (`lie_add`, `add_lie`, `lie_smul`, `smul_lie`, `lie_neg`, `neg_lie`, `sub_lie` and `lie_sub`), and then proceed with a `match_scalars` modification that will keep lists of items consisting of two forms: either of the

[4] mathlib4 PR #16593: https://github.com/leanprover-community/mathlib4/pull/16593.

form `[x,y]`, or of the regular form `x`, where `x` and `y` represent expressions that are considered atoms. When forming the equations to be solved, this modified `match_scalars` will match `[x, y]` to both `[x, y]` and `[y, x]` (and keep the fact that it goes in negative form) by using a modified version of `AtomM`. In practice, however, we did not find this modification very useful, and we hoped to define an improved tactic that could handle other Lie equations (such as Lie associativity) by finding appropriate normal forms. After the first draft version of this article, we found an open PR[5] on mathlib which introduces a tactic for Lie algebras. It is based on Lyndon words for building the normal forms, and the tactic seems to handle all the equations we wanted to handle. We plan to make use of this tactic in the future.

We plan to contribute all definitions and theorems to mathlib that are of general purpose. These will be broken up into several small pull requests, beginning with API/elementary results for linear algebra and Lie algebras, and then moving on to new constructions, like the semidirect product and special Lie algebras.

The following is a short description for the main files in the development:

- `Classification1.lean`, `Classification2.lean`, `Classification3.lean`: these are the main files introducing the classification theorems for each dimension.
- `GeneralResults.lean`: lemmas about vector spaces and Lie algebras in general dimension.
- `LemmasDim3.lean`: particular lemmas needed in the proof, related to dimension 3.
- `InstancesConstructions.lean`, `InstancesLowDim.lean`: definitions of Lie algebras (general constructions and low dimensional instances used in the classification).
- `Semidirect.lean`: introduces the semidirect product of Lie algebras.
- `QuotientSolvable.lean`: the proof that a Lie algebra is solvable if a quotient by some solvable ideal is solvable.
- `Tactics.lean`: implements the `simplify_lie` tactic based on Macbeth's `module` and Carneiro's `AtomM`.

7 Future Work

The formalization of Theorem 1 led to the mechanization of several well-known results in Lie theory, many of which could potentially be added to mathlib. However, there is still a lot of work to be done.

Looking ahead, we see two promising directions for future work. One is to extend the classification to solvable Lie algebras of dimension ≥ 4. Whenever possible, we have stated theorems and lemmas in a way that applies to arbitrary finite dimension. However, the main classification proofs in this paper rely on

[5] mathlib4 PR #22196: https://github.com/leanprover-community/mathlib4/pull/22196

ad hoc analysis of specific bases by dimension. So far, moving to higher dimensions would require new adapted bases and a case-by-case analysis. It would be interesting to find proof strategies that allow reusing lower-dimensional results in higher-dimensional cases. We believe that the implementation of semidirect products may be helpful in this regard. In fact, any solvable Lie algebra of dimension n is a semidirect product of the field of scalars and a solvable Lie algebra of dimension $n-1$.

Another direction is to complete the picture in dimension three by formalising a classification of simple Lie algebras. In characteristic zero, this is definitely doable. However, in positive characteristic, the choice of the classification theorem to be formalized must be made carefully, as different theorems may yield multiple non-isomorphic classes depending on the characteristic [2,6,16].

Acknowledgments. This project was supported by the Estonian Research Council grant no. PSG749 and the Icelandic Research Fund grant no. 28684-053. V. del Barco is supported by FAPESP grant 2023/15089-9. G. Infanti was supported by an undergraduate fellowship PICME-CNPQ. P. Schwahn is supported by the FAPESP grant 2024/08127-4.

References

1. Beck, R.E., Kolman, B.: Construction of Nilpotent Lie Algebras over Arbitrary Fields. In: Wang, P.S. (ed.) Proceedings of the 1981 ACM Symposium on Symbolic and Algebraic Computation. pp. 169–174. ACM, New York (1981). https://doi.org/10.1145/800206.806390
2. Fowler-Wright, A.: The Classification of Three-dimensional Lie Algebras. Thesis, The University of Warwick, Mathematics Institute (2014)
3. Gong, M.P.: Classification of Nilpotent Lie Algebras of Dimension 7 (over Algebraically Closed Fields and $\mathbb{R}$). Ph.D. thesis, University of Waterloo (Canada) (1998), proQuest LLC, Ann Arbor, MI
4. de Graaf, W.A.: Classification of solvable Lie algebras. Exp. Math. **14**(1), 15–25 (2005). https://doi.org/10.1080/10586458.2005.10128911, https://eudml.org/doc/55967
5. Harper, S., Wu, P.: Classifying the groups of order *pq* in Lean (2025), https://arxiv.org/abs/2501.09769
6. Jacobson, N.: Lie algebras. Dover Publications, Inc., New York (1979), republication of the 1962 original.
7. Morozov, V.V.: Classification of nilpotent Lie algebras of dimension six. Izv. Vyssh. Uchebn. Zaved., Mat. **1958**(4(5)), 161–171 (1958)
8. de Moura, L., Ullrich, S.: The Lean 4 Theorem Prover and Programming Language. In: Automated Deduction – CADE 28. p. 625–635. Springer-Verlag, Berlin, Heidelberg (2021). https://doi.org/10.1007/978-3-030-79876-5_37
9. Nash, O.: Formalising Lie algebras. In: Proceedings of the 11th ACM SIGPLAN International Conference on Certified Programs and Proofs. p. 239–250. CPP 2022, Association for Computing Machinery, New York, NY, USA (2022). https://doi.org/10.1145/3497775.3503672
10. Nash, O.: Engel's Theorem in Mathlib. J. Automat. Reason. **67**(2), 18 (2023). https://doi.org/10.1007/s10817-023-09668-0

11. Nielsen, O.A.: Unitary representations and coadjoint orbits of low-dimensional nilpotent Lie groups, Queen's Pap. Pure Appl. Math., vol. 63. Queen's University, Kingston, Ontario (1983)
12. Patera, J., Zassenhaus, H.: Solvable Lie algebras of dimension ≤4 over perfect fields. Linear Algebra Appl. **142**, 1–17 (1990). https://doi.org/10.1016/0024-3795(90)90251-7
13. Schmoetten, R., Fleuriot, J.D.: Constructing the Lie Algebra of Smooth Vector Fields on a Lie Group in Isabelle/HOL. J. Automat. Reason. **69**(3), 18 (2025). https://doi.org/10.1007/s10817-025-09724-x
14. Shedler, G.S.: On the Classification of Nilpotent Lie Algebras of Dimension Six. Master's thesis, Tufts University (1964)
15. Skjelbred, T., Sund, T.: Sur la classification des algèbres de Lie nilpotentes. C. R. Acad. Sci., Paris, Sér. A **286**, 241–242 (1978)
16. Strade, H.: Simple Lie algebras over fields of positive characteristic. I: Structure theory, De Gruyter Expo. Math., vol. 38. Berlin: de Gruyter (2004)
17. The mathlib Community: The Lean mathematical library. In: Proceedings of the 9th ACM SIGPLAN International Conference on Certified Programs and Proofs. p. 367–381. CPP 2020, Association for Computing Machinery, New York, NY, USA (2020). https://doi.org/10.1145/3372885.3373824
18. Vergne, M.: Variété des Algèbres de Lie Nilpotentes. Thèse de 3ème cycle, Université de Paris (1966)

Certified Algorithms for Numerical Semigroups in Rocq

Massimo Bartoletti, Stefano Bonzio, and Marco Ferrara(✉)

Università degli Studi di Cagliari, Cagliari, Italy
{bart,stefano.bonzio}@unica.it, ferraramarco22@gmail.com

Abstract. A numerical semigroup is a co-finite submonoid of the monoid of non-negative integers under addition. Many properties of numerical semigroups rely on some fundamental invariants, such as, among others, the set of gaps (and its cardinality), the Apéry set or the Frobenius number. Algorithms for calculating invariants are currently based on computational tools, such as GAP, which lack proofs (either formal or informal) of their correctness. In this paper we introduce a Rocq formalization of numerical semigroups. Given the semigroup generators, we provide certified algorithms for computing some of the fundamental invariants: the set of gaps, of small elements, the Apéry set, the multiplicity, the conductor and the Frobenius number. To the best of our knowledge this is the first formalization of numerical semigroups in any proof assistant.

Keywords: Numerical semigroups · Coq/Rocq · Verified theory formalization.

1 Introduction

A numerical semigroup is a co-finite additive submonoid of the monoid of the natural numbers $\mathbb{N}$. The main algebraic reason for the investigation of this class of structures traces back to the so-called "Frobenius problem", namely finding the largest $b \in \mathbb{N}$ such that a Diophantine equation $a_1x_1 + \cdots + a_nx_n = b$, with $a_1, \ldots, a_n$ coprime natural numbers, has no positive integer solution [11]. Nowadays numerical semigroups play a key role in commutative algebra and algebraic geometry. For example, they provide much information about rings of coordinates originated from algebras of polynomials over a field [2], and (free) numerical semigroups are associated to singularities of certain planar curves [10,5]. More recently, numerical semigroups have also been fruitfully applied to cryptography and coding theory [8].

Given a numerical semigroup M, the (finite) set $\mathbb{N} \setminus M$ is called the set of *gaps* of M; every numerical semigroup is univocally determined by the set of its gaps. Moreover, every numerical semigroup is finitely generated [1, Proposition 3]. One of the advantages of computer-aided approaches to algebraic structures, in general, relies on the possibility of producing (counter)examples on whose basis conjectures can be formulated, checked or disproved: since numerical semigroups are finitely generated, examples can be obtained by algorithms that produce

V. de Paiva and P. Koepke (Eds.): CICM 2025, LNAI 16136, pp. 340–356, 2026.
https://doi.org/10.1007/978-3-032-07021-0_19

a numerical semigroup starting from a (finite) set of generators. One natural way to do that—which we implement in Rocq—is by calculating the set of gaps starting from the generators. The inverse problem, namely to compute a (finite) set of generators starting from a given numerical semigroup, turns out to be interesting as well. To this end, we will focus on computing the Apéry set of a numerical semigroup, which is an invariant carrying more information than the set of minimal generators [1].

The study of numerical semigroups, as well as the current development of the related theory, strongly relies on the aid of computational tools: the most popular of which, in the algebraic community, is the GAP [9] package numericalsgps [7]. Algorithmic methods are widely adopted in the theory of numerical semigroups (see, e.g., [4,12,13]): for example, the work [6] studies various algorithms for generalized numerical semigroups. However, the existing literature lacks, on the one side, formal proofs of the correctness of the developed algorithms and, on the other, the implementation of certified algorithms via the use of proof assistants. The main motivation of our work is to fill this gap by introducing the first (to the best of our knowledge) formalization of numerical semigroups in a proof assistant. More specifically, we develop certified algorithms in Rocq that compute:

1. the multiplicity of a numerical semigroup (Section 2.1);
2. the Apéry set of a numerical semigroup (Section 2.2);
3. a numerical semigroup from a (finite) set of generators (Section 3).

Besides mechanically proving the correctness for these algorithms in Rocq, we provide in the paper informal sketches of our proof strategies. Throughout the paper we provide (`links`) to the Rocq sources of our formalization. The code was developed and tested using Rocq version 8.20.

2 Computing Numerical Semigroups Invariants

The standard definition of numerical semigroup given before, albeit elegant, is not practical from a computational perspective, since it does not provide a finite representation that can be fed as input to an algorithm. To define a numerical semigroup M in Rocq, we then rely on the finite set $\mathbb{N} \setminus M$ of *gaps* of M, which we represent as the list of its elements and refer to as $\boldsymbol{g}_M$; we additionally require this list to be ordered and duplicate-free, so to ensure that each numerical semigroup has a unique representation.

Notation. We introduce some notation that will be used throughout the paper. We denote the empty list by $[]$, and the list constructed by appending a head element h to a tail $\boldsymbol{t}$ as $h :: \boldsymbol{t}$ (note that $h \in \mathbb{N}$, while $\boldsymbol{t}$ is a list of natural numbers). E.g., the expression $0 :: (1 :: (2 :: []))$ stands for the list of the first three natural numbers. For brevity, we will often write such list as $[0; 1; 2]$. As usual, the concatenation of two lists is denoted by juxtaposition: for example,

$[0; 1; 2]\,[5; 4; 8] = [0; 1; 2; 5; 4; 8]$. Given a list $\boldsymbol{s}$ and $k, i \in \mathbb{N}$, we write $[k]^i$ for the list made of the element k repeated i times, $\boldsymbol{s}_i$ for the i-th element of $\boldsymbol{s}$ (starting from zero), and $|\boldsymbol{s}|_{\geq i}$ for the number of elements in $\boldsymbol{s}$ that are greater than or equal to i (in particular, $|\boldsymbol{s}|_{\geq 0}$ is the length of $\boldsymbol{s}$, abbreviated as $|\boldsymbol{s}|$). We denote by $\mathbb{L}$ the set of lists of natural numbers, by $\mathbb{L}_{<}$ the subset of $\mathbb{L}$ containing only the lists that are duplicate-free and sorted in ascending order, and by $\mathbb{L}^m_{\geq}$ the subset containing only the lists that are sorted in descending order and whose elements are less than or equal to the natural number m. Note that $\boldsymbol{g}_M \in \mathbb{L}_{<}$.

The standard literature on numerical semigroups [1,14] is obviously based on classical logic, thus the excluded middle law for the membership relation tells us that in a numerical semigroup M, for all $x \in \mathbb{N}$ either $x \in M$ or $x \notin M$. Even though excluded middle could be integrated in Rocq by explicitly assuming the classical axiom, this is not really necessary: it suffices to assume decidability for numerical semigroup membership only. Actually, the definition of numerical semigroups via the list of gaps already includes this hypothesis, since list membership is decidable. In general, our whole implementation does not introduce any additional axioms beyond Rocq's base logic.

We now recap some key invariants associated to a numerical semigroup M:

- ***multiplicity***: the minimum non-zero element of M;
- ***Frobenius number***: the maximum element of $\mathbb{Z} \setminus M$;
- ***conductor***: the successor of the Frobenius number;
- ***small elements***: the elements of M less than or equal to the conductor;
- ***Apéry set***: given an $n \in \mathbb{N}$, they are the elements of M such that $x - n \notin M$.

We define algorithms for computing all of these invariants, given the gaps list $\boldsymbol{g}_M$ representing a numerical semigroup M. Some of these algorithms are relatively simple and are briefly explained here, while the others are examined in greater depth in the rest of the paper. We implement the conductor as follows: if the list of gaps $\boldsymbol{g}_M$ is not empty then the conductor is the maximum element of $\boldsymbol{g}_M$ plus one; otherwise, the conductor is 0. In our Rocq implementation we preferred not to work with integers but only with natural numbers; for this reason, we do not explicitly provide a function calculating the Frobenius number. Note, however, that all the relevant results relying on the Frobenius (see e.g. [14]) can also be expressed via the conductor. We compute the small elements of M as the list obtained by only keeping the elements that belong to M in the sequence of natural numbers between 0 and the conductor.

We say that a numerical semigroup M is ***generated*** by a set $A \subseteq \mathbb{N}$ if every element of M can be written as a linear combination of elements of A, i.e. for all $d \in M$ there exist $a_1, \ldots a_n \in A$ and $\lambda_1, \ldots, \lambda_n \in \mathbb{N}$ such that $d = \sum_{i=1}^{n} \lambda_i a_i$. Every numerical semigroup is generated by a *finite* set [1, Proposition 3].

2.1 Computing the Multiplicity

We compute the multiplicity by searching for the smallest natural number, starting from 1, that does *not* belong to the gaps list. To this purpose, we introduce a function f_1 that, taken as input a list $\boldsymbol{s}$, gives as output the smallest integer greater than the last consecutive integers in $\boldsymbol{s}$. For example, $f_1([1;2;5]) = 3$. Technically, it is convenient to parameterise f_x over an arbitrary $x \in \mathbb{N}$, so that $f_x(\boldsymbol{s})$ outputs x for any list whose first element is different from x, and $n+1$ for any list of the form $[x; x+1; \ldots; x+n, y]$ with $y \neq x + (n+1)$.

Definition 1. (`find_gap`) *For all* $x \in \mathbb{N}$, *let* $f_x\colon \mathbb{L} \to \mathbb{N}$ *be defined recursively as follows:*

$$f_x([\,]) = x \qquad f_x(x :: \boldsymbol{t}) = f_{x+1}(\boldsymbol{t}) \qquad f_x(h :: \boldsymbol{t}) = x \quad \textit{if } h \neq x.$$

For example, we have that $f_1([1;2;3;7]) = f_2([2;3;7]) = f_3([3;7]) = f_4([7]) = 4$.

Theorem 1 states that f_1 gives the multiplicity of M. For example, consider the numerical semigroup M whose list of gaps is $\boldsymbol{g}_M = [1;2;3;5;6;9;13]$. The multiplicity of M is $f_1([1;2;3;5;6;9;13]) = 4$.

Theorem 1. (`multiplicity_min`) *Let* M *be a numerical semigroup represented by the gaps list* $\boldsymbol{g}_M$. *Then,* $f_1(\boldsymbol{g}_M)$ *is the multiplicity of* M.

Proof. We have to show that $f_1(\boldsymbol{g}_M)$ is the minimum non-zero element of M. We start by proving that $f_1(\boldsymbol{g}_M) \neq 0$. This is a special case of the lemma:

$$\forall x \in \mathbb{N},\ \ \forall \boldsymbol{s} \in \mathbb{L},\ \ x \leq f_x(\boldsymbol{s}). \qquad (\texttt{find\_gap\_le})$$

We prove this by induction on the structure of $\boldsymbol{s}$. For the base case $\boldsymbol{s} = [\,]$, we have that $f_x(\boldsymbol{s}) = x \geq x$. For the inductive case, let $\boldsymbol{s} = h :: \boldsymbol{t}$. There are two subcases. If $h \neq x$, then $f_x(h :: \boldsymbol{t}) = x \geq x$. Otherwise, if $h = x$, then $f_x(h :: \boldsymbol{t}) = f_{x+1}(\boldsymbol{t})$ and by inductive hypothesis we have $x \leq x+1 \leq f_{x+1}(\boldsymbol{t})$. ◇

By applying (`find_gap_le`) for $\boldsymbol{s} = \boldsymbol{g}_M$ and $x = 1$, we obtain $f_1(\boldsymbol{g}_M) \neq 0$.

We now prove that $f_1(\boldsymbol{g}_M) \in M$, i.e. $f_1(\boldsymbol{g}_M) \notin \boldsymbol{g}_M$. This is a special case of a more general auxiliary result:

$$\forall x \in \mathbb{N},\ \ \forall \boldsymbol{s} \in \mathbb{L}_<,\ \ |\boldsymbol{s}|_{\geq x} = |\boldsymbol{s}| \ \to\ f_x(\boldsymbol{s}) \notin \boldsymbol{s}. \qquad (\texttt{find\_gap\_notin})$$

We prove this by induction on the structure of $\boldsymbol{s}$. For the base case $\boldsymbol{s} = [\,]$, the thesis holds trivially. For the inductive case $\boldsymbol{s} = h :: \boldsymbol{t}$, there are two subcases:

- $h = x$. Then, $f_x(h :: \boldsymbol{t}) = f_{x+1}(\boldsymbol{t})$. Suppose by contradiction that $f_{x+1}(\boldsymbol{t}) \in h :: \boldsymbol{t}$. If $f_{x+1}(\boldsymbol{t}) = h$ then by (`find_gap_le`) we have $x + 1 \leq f_{x+1}(\boldsymbol{t}) = h = x$—contradiction. Thus, we must have $f_{x+1}(\boldsymbol{t}) \in \boldsymbol{t}$. Note that every element of $\boldsymbol{t}$ is greater than or equal to $x+1$, since $h :: \boldsymbol{t}$ is sorted and duplicate-free, and $h = x$. Therefore, by the inductive hypothesis it follows that $f_{x+1}(\boldsymbol{t}) \notin \boldsymbol{t}$—contradiction.
- $h \neq x$. Then, $f_x(h :: \boldsymbol{t}) = x$. Assume by contradiction that $x \in h :: \boldsymbol{t}$. Then we must have $x \in \boldsymbol{t}$. By hypothesis, every element of $h :: \boldsymbol{t}$ is greater than or equal to x, hence $h \geq x$. Moreover, since $h :: \boldsymbol{t}$ is ordered and duplicate-free, and since $x \in \boldsymbol{t}$, we have that $h < x$—contradiction. ◇

We now apply (`find_gap_notin`) on $\boldsymbol{s} = \boldsymbol{g}_M$ and $x = 1$. Indeed, $\boldsymbol{g}_M \in \mathbb{L}_<$ and its elements are greater than or equal to 1, hence $|\boldsymbol{g}_M|_{\geq 1} = |\boldsymbol{g}_M|$. Therefore, $f_1(\boldsymbol{g}_M) \notin \boldsymbol{g}_M$, which means that $f_1(\boldsymbol{g}_M) \in M$.

To conclude, we have to show that $f_1(\boldsymbol{g}_M)$ is the minimum non-zero element of M, i.e. for all $n \in M \setminus \{0\}$, it must be $f_1(\boldsymbol{g}_M) \leq n$. Again, we obtain this as a special case of a more general lemma:

$$\forall x, n \in \mathbb{N},\ \ \forall \boldsymbol{s} \in \mathbb{L}_<,\ \ x \leq n < f_x(\boldsymbol{s}) \rightarrow n \in \boldsymbol{s}. \qquad (\texttt{find\_gap\_le\_lt\_in})$$

We prove this by induction on the structure of $\boldsymbol{s}$. For the base case $\boldsymbol{s} = []$, we have that $f_x(\boldsymbol{s}) = x$ and there is no such n. For the inductive case, let $\boldsymbol{s} = h :: \boldsymbol{t}$ and let n such that $x \leq n < f_x(h :: \boldsymbol{t})$. If $h = n$, the thesis $n \in h :: \boldsymbol{t}$ holds trivially. Otherwise, if $h \neq n$, there are two subcases. If $h \neq x$ then $f_x(h :: \boldsymbol{t}) = x$ and the thesis holds trivially since the hypothesis $x \leq n < x$ is false. Otherwise, if $h = x$, then $f_x(h :: \boldsymbol{t}) = f_{x+1}(\boldsymbol{t})$. Since $x \neq n$, then $x + 1 \leq n < f_{x+1}(\boldsymbol{t})$, and so $n \in t$ follows by the inductive hypothesis. ◇

We now apply (`find_gap_le_lt_in`) with $\boldsymbol{s} = \boldsymbol{g}_M$ and $x = 1$. The hypothesis $n \in M \setminus \{0\}$ means that $n \notin \boldsymbol{g}_M$, hence by the contrapositive we obtain that $1 \not\leq n$ or $n \not< f_1(\boldsymbol{g}_M)$. The first disjunct is impossible since $n \neq 0$, hence it must be $n \geq f_1(\boldsymbol{g}_M)$—which gives the thesis. □

2.2 Computing the Apéry Set

We present two algorithms for computing the Apéry set of a numerical semigroup M given the list of its gaps $\boldsymbol{g}_M$. Moreover, we provide a formalization of a key theoretical result, i.e. that the Apéry set of M is a generator of M (Theorem 4).

Recall that the Apéry set of a numerical semigroup M w.r.t. n is defined as:

$$\{\, x \in M \mid x - n \notin M \,\},$$

where $x - n$ is the difference in $\mathbb{Z}$. In particular, if $x < n$ then $x - n$ is negative and so it does not belong to M. Since we prefer our Rocq formalization to work with natural numbers only, we instead use truncated subtraction, i.e. $x - n = 0$ when $x < n$, and thus we would have $x - n = 0 \in M$. In order to reflect this difference, we amend the definition of Apéry set as follows.

$$\{\, x \in M \mid n \leq x \ \rightarrow\ x - n \notin M \,\}. \tag{1}$$

As for the other invariants, we represent the Apéry set as a list of natural numbers. Definition 2 gives an algorithm to compute this list from the list of gaps $\boldsymbol{g}_M$ representing M. Theorem 2 establishes the correctness of this algorithm.

Definition 2. (apery) *Let $\boldsymbol{g} \in \mathbb{L}$ and $n \in \mathbb{N}$. Let $\boldsymbol{s} = [0; \ldots; n-1]$, and let $\boldsymbol{t}$ be the list obtained by adding n to every element of $\boldsymbol{g}$. We define $\mathsf{Ap}(\boldsymbol{g}, n)$ as the list obtained by removing the elements in $\boldsymbol{g}$ from the list $\boldsymbol{s}\,\boldsymbol{t}$.*

Theorem 2. (**apery_spec**) *Let M be a numerical semigroup with gaps list $\boldsymbol{g}_M$ and let $n \in \mathbb{N}$. Then, $\mathsf{Ap}(\boldsymbol{g}_M, n)$ coincides with the Apéry set of M with respect to n.*

Proof. Let $x \in \mathsf{Ap}(\boldsymbol{g}_M, n)$. By Definition 2, we have $x \notin \boldsymbol{g}_M$ and $x \in \boldsymbol{s}\,\boldsymbol{t}$, where $\boldsymbol{s} = [0; \ldots; n-1]$ and $\boldsymbol{t}$ is obtained by adding n to every element of $\boldsymbol{g}_M$. If $x \in \boldsymbol{s}$ then $x < n$, and so the implication in (1) holds trivially. If $x \in \boldsymbol{t}$ then $x = y + n$ with $y \in \boldsymbol{g}_M$. Hence, $x - n = y \notin M$ since $\boldsymbol{g}_M$ is the list of gaps, and again the condition in (1) is true. Suppose now that $x \in \{\, x \in M \mid n \leq x \to x - n \notin M \,\}$. If $n \leq x$ then $x - n \notin M$, and thus $x - n \in \boldsymbol{g}_M$. We can write x as $x = (x-n)+n$, and thus $x \in \boldsymbol{t}$. Otherwise, if $x < n$, then clearly $x \in \boldsymbol{s}$. □

Example 1. Let $\boldsymbol{g}_M = [1; 2; 3; 5; 6; 9; 13]$ be the gaps list representing the numerical semigroup M generated by $\{4; 7; 10\}$. Following Definition 2, for $n = 4$ we have $\boldsymbol{s} = [0; 1; 2; 3]$ and $\boldsymbol{t} = [5; 6; 7; 9; 10; 13; 17]$. By removing the elements of $\boldsymbol{g}_M$ from the list $\boldsymbol{s}\,\boldsymbol{t}$, we obtain $\mathsf{Ap}(\boldsymbol{g}_M, n) = [0; 7; 10; 17]$. ◇

We present in Definition 3 an alternative algorithm for computing the Apéry set in the special case $n \in M \setminus \{0\}$. Theorem 3 proves the correctness of this algorithm.

Definition 3. (**apery_2**) *Let $\boldsymbol{s} \in \mathbb{L}$ and let $n, a \in \mathbb{N}$. We define the function $\mathrm{fm}_{\boldsymbol{s}}(n, a)$ as follows:*

- *$\mathrm{fm}_{\boldsymbol{s}}(n, a)$ is the first element x in $\boldsymbol{s}$ such that $x \equiv_n a$, if such element exists;*
- *otherwise, $\mathrm{fm}_{\boldsymbol{s}}(n, a)$ is the smallest natural number x that is greater than the last element of $\boldsymbol{s}$ and such that $x \equiv_n a$.*

We define the list $\mathsf{Ap2}(\boldsymbol{s}, n)$ as $[\mathrm{fm}_{\boldsymbol{s}}(n, 0); \ldots; \mathrm{fm}_{\boldsymbol{s}}(n, n-1)]$.

Theorem 3. (**apery_2_correct**) *Let M be a numerical semigroup and let $n \in M \setminus \{0\}$. Let $\boldsymbol{s}$ be the list of small elements of M. Then $\mathsf{Ap2}(\boldsymbol{s}, n)$ coincides with the Apéry set of M with respect to n.*

Clearly $\mathrm{fm}_M(n, a)$ is the smallest element x of M such that $x \equiv_n a$. Thus, Theorem 3 follows by the next theoretical lemma.

Lemma 1. (**apery_spec_2**) *Let M be a numerical semigroup and let $n \in M \setminus \{0\}$. For all $i = 0, \ldots, n-1$ let $w(i)$ be the smallest element of M such that $w(i) \equiv_n i$. Then the Apéry set of M with respect to n is equal to the set:*

$$\{\, w(0), \ldots, w(n-1) \,\}.$$

We do not present the proof of this lemma here, since it is essentially a formalization of the (informal) proof given in [1].

Example 2. Using this second algorithm, we compute the Apéry set relative to 4 of the same numerical semigroup M presented in Example 1. Given the list of gaps $\boldsymbol{g}_M = [1; 2; 3; 5; 6; 9; 13]$, the list of small elements of M is $\boldsymbol{s} =$

$[0; 4; 7; 8; 10; 11; 12; 14]$. The smallest element of $\boldsymbol{s}$ congruent to 0 modulo 4 is $\mathrm{fm}_{\boldsymbol{s}}(4, 0) = 0$. Similarly, we have $\mathrm{fm}_{\boldsymbol{s}}(4, 2) = 10$ and $\mathrm{fm}_{\boldsymbol{s}}(4, 3) = 7$. No element of $\boldsymbol{s}$ is congruent to 1 modulo 4, and the smallest natural number after 14 that satisfies such property is $\mathrm{fm}_{\boldsymbol{s}}(4, 1) = 17$. Thus, $\mathsf{Ap2}(\boldsymbol{s}, 4) = [0; 17; 10; 7]$.

Theorem 4. (**`apery_generates`**) *Let M be a numerical semigroup with gaps list $\boldsymbol{g}_M$ and let $n \in M \setminus \{0\}$. For all $a \in M$ there exists a unique $(k, w) \in \mathbb{N} \times \mathsf{Ap}(\boldsymbol{g}_M, n)$ such that $a = kn + w$.*

It follows from Theorem 4 that $\mathsf{Ap}(\boldsymbol{g}_M, n) \cup \{n\}$ is a (finite) set of generators for M.

2.3 Equivalent Definitions

We recall in Theorem 5 some equivalent definitions of numerical semigroups (see [1, Proposition 1] and its proof). For the reader's convenience we include (part of) the proof adapted to our Rocq formalization of numerical semigroups.

Theorem 5. (**`numerical_semigroup_2`**) *Let M be an additive submonoid of $\mathbb{N}$ with a decidable membership predicate. Then, the following statements are equivalent:*

1. *M is a numerical semigroup (i.e., $\mathbb{N} \setminus M$ is finite);*
2. *$1 \in G$, where G is the additive subgroup of $\mathbb{Z}$ generated by M;*
3. *there exists an element $a \in M$ such that $a + 1 \in M$.*

Proof. $(2 \Leftrightarrow 3)$ easily follows from the fact that $G = \{x - y \mid x, y \in M\}$.
$(1 \Rightarrow 3)$. If M is a numerical semigroup with conductor c, then $c, c+1 \in M$.
$(3 \Rightarrow 1)$. It is easy to prove (see [1, Proposition 1]) that for every $n \in \mathbb{N}$, if $n \geq (a-1)(a+1)$ then $n \in M$. This can be used to build a gaps list for M. Indeed, let $\boldsymbol{s}$ be the list of natural numbers from 0 to $(a-1)(a+1)-1$, and let $\boldsymbol{g}$ be the list obtained by removing from $\boldsymbol{s}$ the elements that are in M. Then, $\boldsymbol{g}$ is sorted in ascending order, it has no duplicates, and contains exactly the elements that are not in M. Thus, M together with $\boldsymbol{g}$ is a numerical semigroup. □

Remark. Note that the proof of $(3 \Rightarrow 1)$ is constructive: it not only provides a proof that a numerical semigroup on M exists, but also outputs that numerical semigroup (by computing its list of gaps $\boldsymbol{g}$). The decidability of the membership of M is needed in order to construct the list $\boldsymbol{g}$. More precisely, in order to filter out from $\boldsymbol{s}$ the elements not belonging to M, we need an algorithm that computes whether a natural number belongs to M or not. Observe also that condition 3 in the above proposition is much easier to implement in Rocq than condition 2, as it does not require introducing $\mathbb{Z}$ nor any of its (additive) subgroups.

3 Computing a Numerical Semigroup from its Generators

In this section we present an algorithm that takes as input a list $\boldsymbol{a}$, and gives as output the numerical semigroup M generated by $\boldsymbol{a}$, represented by its gaps list $\boldsymbol{g}_M$. Our algorithm works as follows:

1. we start by giving an algorithm that generates *multiplicity index lists*, which encode all (and only) the linear combinations of elements in $\boldsymbol{a}$ (Section 3.1);
2. based on this algorithm, we show how to obtain the actual linear combinations of elements of $\boldsymbol{a}$ (Section 3.2);
3. we compute lists $\boldsymbol{s}$ of increasing length containing the $|\boldsymbol{s}|$ smallest elements of M (Section 3.3);
4. we stop when a list $\boldsymbol{s}$ contains m consecutive natural numbers, where m is the minimum non-zero element of $\boldsymbol{a}$;
5. the list of small elements is the list formed by the element of $\boldsymbol{s}$ up to c, where c is the first of the m consecutive elements of $\boldsymbol{s}$ found in the previous step;
6. finally, we compute the list $\boldsymbol{g}_M$ of gaps by removing the small elements from the list $[0; \ldots ; c]$.

3.1 Generating Multiplicity Index Lists

Let $\boldsymbol{a}$ be a list of generators. Any linear combination of $\boldsymbol{a}$ can be represented as a multiset of elements in $\boldsymbol{a}$ (thus, not mentioning the coefficients $\lambda_i \in \mathbb{N}$). For example, given $\boldsymbol{a} = [4; 7; 10]$, we can represent $45 = 2 \cdot 4 + 1 \cdot 7 + 3 \cdot 10$ as the multiset $\{4, 4, 7, 10, 10, 10\}$, namely 45 is the sum of its elements. This multiset, in turn, can be represented as a list $\boldsymbol{s}$ whose elements are *indices* of elements in $\boldsymbol{a}$: each index i is repeated as many times as the number of occurrences of $\boldsymbol{a}_i$ in the multiset. In our example, the index 0 (corresponding to the generator 4) is repeated 2 times, and so on. In order to have a *unique* representation for each linear combination, we require the list $\boldsymbol{s}$ to be sorted in decreasing order. Therefore, in the previous example, we encode 45 as $\boldsymbol{s} = [2; 2; 2; 1; 0; 0]$.

Thus, generating linear combinations of $\boldsymbol{a}$ is equivalent to generating decreasing lists of natural numbers less than $|\boldsymbol{a}|$, i.e. lists in the set $\mathbb{L}^m_{\geq}$ where $m = |\boldsymbol{a}| - 1$. Such generator is given by the algorithm genL_m (Definition 5), which takes as input a natural number n, and gives as output the n-th multiplicity index list. This is done recursively, by calling the function next_m (Definition 4) on the list obtained at step $n - 1$. The main results in this section are Theorems 6 and 7, which show that genL_m generates all, and only, the lists in $\mathbb{L}^m_{\geq}$.

Definition 4. (**next**) *For all $m \in \mathbb{N}$, we define the function $\mathsf{next}_m \colon \mathbb{L} \to \mathbb{L}$ by the following inference rules:*

$$\mathsf{next}_m([\,]) = [0] \qquad \mathsf{next}_m(h :: \boldsymbol{t}) = (h+1) :: \boldsymbol{t} \ \ \text{if } h < m$$

$$\frac{\mathsf{next}_m(\boldsymbol{t}) = [\,]}{\mathsf{next}_m(h :: \boldsymbol{t}) = [\,]} \ \text{if } h \geq m \qquad \frac{\mathsf{next}_m(\boldsymbol{t}) = x :: \boldsymbol{t}'}{\mathsf{next}_m(h :: \boldsymbol{t}) = x :: x :: \boldsymbol{t}'} \ \text{if } h \geq m.$$

E.g., we have the following derivation, proving that $\mathsf{next}_3([3;3;1;0]) = [2;2;2;0]$:

$$\dfrac{\dfrac{\overline{\mathsf{next}_3(1;0) = [2;0]}}{\mathsf{next}_3([3;1;0]) = [2;2;0]}}{\mathsf{next}_3([3;3;1;0]) = [2;2;2;0]}$$

Note that $\mathsf{next}_m(\boldsymbol{t})$ cannot be the empty list, and so the third rule is never used. However, it is still needed to provide a correct definition of next in Rocq.

Intuitively, $\mathsf{next}_m(\boldsymbol{s})$ searches the leftmost value in $\boldsymbol{s}$ that is (strictly) less than m, increases that value by one, and changes all the elements at its left to that same (increased) value. If all the elements in the list are greater than or equal to m, it adds a new 0 element at the end of the list, and sets all the other elements to 0. For example, given $m = 3$, we have the following mappings:

$$[3;3;1] \xmapsto{\mathsf{next}_3} [2;2;2] \xmapsto{\mathsf{next}_3} [3;2;2] \xmapsto{\mathsf{next}_3} [3;3;2] \xmapsto{\mathsf{next}_3} [3;3;3] \xmapsto{\mathsf{next}_3} [0;0;0;0].$$

This intuition is formalized by the following lemma.

Lemma 2. (next_repeat) *For all* $\boldsymbol{s} \in \mathbb{L}$ *and all* m, n, k *in* $\mathbb{N}$ *with* $k < m$*:*

$$\mathsf{next}_m([m]^n\,(k :: \boldsymbol{s})) = [k+1]^{n+1}\,\boldsymbol{s}.$$

Proof. By induction on n. For the base case $n = 0$, since $k < m$, by the second inference rule in Definition 4 we have that:

$$\mathsf{next}_m([m]^0\,(k :: \boldsymbol{s})) \;=\; \mathsf{next}_m(k :: \boldsymbol{s}) \;=\; (k+1) :: \boldsymbol{s} \;=\; [k+1]^1\,\boldsymbol{s}.$$

For the inductive case, let the induction hypothesis be:

$$\mathsf{next}_m([m]^n\,(k :: \boldsymbol{s})) \;=\; [k+1]^{n+1}\,\boldsymbol{s} \;=\; (k+1) :: [k+1]^n\,\boldsymbol{s}. \tag{2}$$

Then, by the fourth inference rule in Definition 4 we have that:

$$\begin{aligned}\mathsf{next}_m([m]^{n+1}\,(k :: \boldsymbol{s})) &= \mathsf{next}_m(m :: ([m]^n\,(k :: \boldsymbol{s}))) && \text{since } [m]^{n+1} = m :: [m]^n \\ &= (k+1) :: (k+1) :: [k+1]^n\,\boldsymbol{s} && \text{by (2)} \\ &= [k+1]^{n+2}\,\boldsymbol{s}\end{aligned}$$

□

We can now proceed to define our list generating algorithm as the iteration of the function next_m, starting from the empty list.

Definition 5. (lgen) *For all* $m \in \mathbb{N}$*, we define* $\mathsf{genL}_m : \mathbb{N} \to \mathbb{L}$ *as follows:*

$$\mathsf{genL}_m(0) = [\,] \qquad \mathsf{genL}_m(x+1) = \mathsf{next}_m(\mathsf{genL}_m(x)).$$

For illustration, we tabulate below the first 12 values of genL_2:

$\mathsf{genL}_2(0) = [\,]$	$\mathsf{genL}_2(1) = [0]$	$\mathsf{genL}_2(2) = [1]$	$\mathsf{genL}_2(3) = [2]$
$\mathsf{genL}_2(4) = [0;0]$	$\mathsf{genL}_2(5) = [1;0]$	$\mathsf{genL}_2(6) = [2;0]$	$\mathsf{genL}_2(7) = [1;1]$
$\mathsf{genL}_2(8) = [2;1]$	$\mathsf{genL}_2(9) = [2;2]$	$\mathsf{genL}_2(10) = [0;0;0]$	$\mathsf{genL}_2(11) = [1;0;0]$

We now prove that genL_m generates exactly the lists in $\mathbb{L}^m_{\geq}$.

Theorem 6. (lgen_correct) *For all* $m \in \mathbb{N}$, $\mathrm{Im}(\mathsf{genL}_m) \subseteq \mathbb{L}^m_{\geq}$.

Proof. This is a direct consequence of the auxiliary result:

$$\forall \boldsymbol{s} \in \mathbb{L}^m_{\geq},\ \ \mathsf{next}_m(\boldsymbol{s}) \in \mathbb{L}^m_{\geq}. \qquad \text{(gelist\_next)}$$

We prove it by induction on $\boldsymbol{s}$. For the base case $\boldsymbol{s} = []$, we have $\mathsf{next}_m(\boldsymbol{s}) = [0] \in \mathbb{L}^m_{\geq}$. For the inductive case, let $\boldsymbol{s} = h :: \boldsymbol{t}$ be such that $\boldsymbol{s} \in \mathbb{L}^m_{\geq}$. Then also $\boldsymbol{t} \in \mathbb{L}^m_{\geq}$ and thus, by the inductive hypothesis, $\mathsf{next}_m(\boldsymbol{t}) \in \mathbb{L}^m_{\geq}$.

We have two cases. If $h < m$, then $\mathsf{next}(h :: \boldsymbol{t}) = (h+1) :: \boldsymbol{t}$, which is in $\mathbb{L}^m_{\geq}$ since $h :: \boldsymbol{t} \in \mathbb{L}^m_{\geq}$ and $h + 1 \leq m$. If $h = m$, then $\mathsf{next}(h :: \boldsymbol{t}) = x :: x :: \boldsymbol{t}'$, where $x :: \boldsymbol{t}' = \mathsf{next}(\boldsymbol{t})$. Since $\mathsf{next}(\boldsymbol{t}) \in \mathbb{L}^m_{\geq}$, we conclude that $\mathsf{next}(h :: \boldsymbol{t}) \in \mathbb{L}^m_{\geq}$. □

Proving the other inclusion, stated by Theorem 7, is more complex. Indeed, the idea is to prove this theorem by induction, but a simple induction on the list structure does not work, since we cannot easily derive that a list $h :: \boldsymbol{t}$ belongs to $\mathrm{Im}(\mathsf{genL}_m)$ if its tail $\boldsymbol{t}$ does. We first state the theorem, and then present the intuitions, definitions and results that are needed for its proof.

Theorem 7. (lgen_complete) *For all* $m \in \mathbb{N}$, $\mathbb{L}^m_{\geq} \subseteq \mathrm{Im}(\mathsf{genL}_m)$.

To prove Theorem 7, we first define an operator that gives a lexicographic ordering between the lists generated by genL_m. This ordering will then be exploited in our inductive proof. Formally, for all $n \in \mathbb{N}$, we define the operator $|\cdot|_{\geq 0,\ldots,n} : \mathbb{L} \to \mathbb{N}^{n+1}$ as follows:

$$|\boldsymbol{s}|_{\geq 0,\ldots,n} \quad \triangleq \quad \left(|\boldsymbol{s}|_{\geq 0}, \ldots, |\boldsymbol{s}|_{\geq n}\right).$$

Note that the order in which genL_m generates lists corresponds to the lexicographic order associated with $|\boldsymbol{s}|_{\geq 0,\ldots,m}$, as exemplified by the following table:

$\boldsymbol{s}$	$\lvert\boldsymbol{s}\rvert_{\geq 0}$	$\lvert\boldsymbol{s}\rvert_{\geq 1}$	$\lvert\boldsymbol{s}\rvert_{\geq 2}$	$\lvert\boldsymbol{s}\rvert_{\geq 3}$
$\mathsf{genL}_3(x) = [3;3;2;0]$	4	3	3	2
$\mathsf{genL}_3(x+1) = [3;3;3;0]$	4	3	3	3
$\mathsf{genL}_3(x+2) = [1;1;1;1]$	4	4	0	0
$\mathsf{genL}_3(x+3) = [2;1;1;1]$	4	4	1	0

Following this intuition, we prove that if all the lists $\boldsymbol{s}$ with given values for $|\boldsymbol{s}|_{\geq 0}, \ldots, |\boldsymbol{s}|_{\geq n}$ are generated, then all the lists with the same given values, except for $|\boldsymbol{s}|_{\geq n}$, which is increased by one, are generated. This is expressed by the following definition and by Lemma 3.

Definition 6. (le_length_eq_lgen) *For all* $m, n \in \mathbb{N}$ *and* $k \in \mathbb{N}^{n+1}$ *we define the proposition* $A^m_n(k)$ *as follows:*

$$A^m_n(k) \quad \triangleq \quad \forall \boldsymbol{s} \in \mathbb{L}^m_{\geq},\ \ |\boldsymbol{s}|_{\geq 0,\ldots,n} = k \to \boldsymbol{s} \in \mathrm{Im}(\mathsf{genL}_m).$$

Moreover, we define $S_k = (k_0, \ldots, k_{n-1}, k_n + 1)$.

Lemma 3. (`le_length_eq_impl`) *For all $m, n \in \mathbb{N}$ and $k \in \mathbb{N}^{m-n+1}$, if $A^m_{m-n}(k)$ holds then $A^m_{m-n}(S_k)$ holds.*

As a preliminary, we prove a special case.

Lemma 4. (`le_length_0_lgen`) *Let $m, n \in N$ and $k \in \mathbb{N}^{n+1}$ be such that $n \leq m$ and $A^m_n(k)$ holds. If $|\boldsymbol{s}|_{\geq 0,\dots,n} = S_k$ and $|\boldsymbol{s}|_{\geq n+1} = 0$ then $\boldsymbol{s} \in \mathrm{Im}(\mathsf{genL}_m)$.*

Proof. Since $\boldsymbol{s}$ is sorted and $|\boldsymbol{s}|_{\geq n+1} = 0$, all the elements of $\boldsymbol{s}$ up to the position $|\boldsymbol{s}|_{\geq n} = k_n + 1$, and not more, are equal to n; that is, $\boldsymbol{s} = [n]^{k_n+1}\,\boldsymbol{t}$, where the elements of $\boldsymbol{t}$ are less than n. There are two cases:

- If $n \neq 0$, let $\boldsymbol{s}' = [m]^{k_n}\,(n-1) :: \boldsymbol{t}$. The list $\boldsymbol{s}'$ satisfies the hypothesis of $A^m_n(k)$, and thus it belongs to $\mathrm{Im}(\mathsf{genL}_m)$. By Lemma 2, $\mathsf{next}_m(\boldsymbol{s}') = \boldsymbol{s}$.
- If $n = 0$ then $\boldsymbol{s} = [0]^{k_0+1}$, which is the successor of the list $[m]^{k_0}$. This list belongs to $\mathrm{Im}(\mathsf{genL}_m)$ because it satisfies the hypothesis of $A^m_0(k)$. □

Proof (Lemma 3). By induction on n. For the base case $n = 0$, let $\boldsymbol{s}$ satisfy the hypothesis of $A^m_m(S_k)$. In particular $|\boldsymbol{s}|_{\geq m+1} = 0$, since the elements of $\boldsymbol{s}$ are all less than or equal to m. We conclude by Lemma 4.

For the inductive case, let $a = m - n - 1$. The inductive hypothesis is:

$$\forall k \in \mathbb{N}^{a+2},\ \ A^m_{a+1}(k) \rightarrow A^m_{a+1}(S_k). \tag{3}$$

Let $k \in \mathbb{N}^{a+1}$ and let $\boldsymbol{s}$ be a list that satisfies the hypothesis of $A^m_a(S_k)$. Let $x = |\boldsymbol{s}|_{\geq a+1}$. We prove by induction on x that $\boldsymbol{s} \in \mathrm{Im}(\mathsf{genL}_m)$. If $x = 0$ we conclude by Lemma 4.

The inductive hypothesis is the following: for every $k \in \mathbb{N}^{a+1}$ and for every list $\boldsymbol{s}$ that satisfies the hypothesis of $A^m_a(S_k)$ and such that $|\boldsymbol{s}|_{\geq a+1} = x$, we have that $\boldsymbol{s} \in \mathrm{Im}(\mathsf{genL}_m)$. Let $k \in \mathbb{N}^{a+1}$ and let $\boldsymbol{s}$ be a list that satisfies the hypothesis of $A^m_a(S_k)$ and such that $|\boldsymbol{s}|_{\geq a+1} = x + 1$. Let $k' = (k_0, \dots, k_a, x)$. By inductive hypothesis on x, the proposition $A^m_{a+1}(k')$ holds. Thus, by 3 we deduce that $A^m_{a+1}(S_{k'})$ holds. The list $\boldsymbol{s}$ satisfies the hypothesis of $A^m_{a+1}(S_{k'})$, hence $\boldsymbol{s} \in \mathrm{Im}(\mathsf{genL}_m)$. □

Proof (Theorem 7). Let $\boldsymbol{s} \in \mathbb{L}^m_{\geq}$. We prove that $\boldsymbol{s} \in \mathsf{genL}_m$ by induction on the length of $\boldsymbol{s}$. For the base case, if $|\boldsymbol{s}| = 0$ then $\boldsymbol{s} = [] = \mathsf{genL}_m 0$. Suppose that every list of length k belongs to $\mathrm{Im}(\mathsf{genL}_m)$. Then, equivalently, the proposition $A^m_0(k)$ holds. Thus, by Lemma 3, the proposition $A^m_0(S_k) = A^m_0(k+1)$ holds, which is equivalent to: every list of length $k+1$ belongs to $\mathrm{Im}(\mathsf{genL}_m)$. □

3.2 From Multiplicity Index Lists to Linear Combinations

We now apply our genL_m algorithm to obtain all the linear combinations of the (list of) generators $\boldsymbol{a}$ of a numerical semigroup. We do this by introducing in Definition 7 a function $\mathsf{genM}_{\boldsymbol{a}} : \mathbb{N} \rightarrow \mathbb{N}$ that generates the linear combinations of $\boldsymbol{a}$. Namely, $\mathsf{genM}_{\boldsymbol{a}}(n)$ is the linear combination of elements of $\boldsymbol{a}$ corresponding to the list $\mathsf{genL}_m(n)$, where m is the bound on the indices of the multiplicity index lists. We will prove in Theorem 8 that $\mathsf{genM}_{\boldsymbol{a}}$ iteratively generates all the linear combinations of elements of $\boldsymbol{a}$, and thus all possible elements of the submonoid of $\mathbb{N}$ generated by $\boldsymbol{a}$.

Definition 7. (**mgen**) *For all* $\boldsymbol{a} \in \mathbb{L}$, *we define* $\mathsf{genM}_{\boldsymbol{a}} : \mathbb{N} \to \mathbb{N}$ *as:*

$$\mathsf{genM}_{\boldsymbol{a}}(n) \;=\; \sum_{i \in \mathsf{genL}_{|\boldsymbol{a}|-1}(n)} \boldsymbol{a}_i.$$

E.g., recalling the tabulation of genL_2 at page 9, for $\boldsymbol{a} = [4; 7; 10]$, we have:

$$\mathsf{genM}_{\boldsymbol{a}}(3) = \sum_{i \in \mathsf{genL}_2(3)} \boldsymbol{a}_i = \sum_{i \in [2]} \boldsymbol{a}_i = \boldsymbol{a}_2 = 10$$

$$\mathsf{genM}_{\boldsymbol{a}}(4) = \sum_{i \in \mathsf{genL}_2(4)} \boldsymbol{a}_i = \sum_{i \in [0;0]} \boldsymbol{a}_i = \boldsymbol{a}_0 + \boldsymbol{a}_0 = 4 + 4 = 8$$

which shows that $\mathsf{genM}_{\boldsymbol{a}}$ is *not* monotonic, i.e. $n \leq n' \not\to \mathsf{genM}_{\boldsymbol{a}}(n) \leq \mathsf{genM}_{\boldsymbol{a}}(n')$.

Theorem 8. (**mgen_complete**) *Let* M *be the submonoid of* $\mathbb{N}$ *generated by* $\boldsymbol{a} \in \mathbb{L}$, *where* $0 \notin \boldsymbol{a} \neq [\,]$. *Then* $M \subseteq \mathrm{Im}(\mathsf{genM}_{\boldsymbol{a}})$.

Proof. Let $d \in M$. Since M is generated by $\boldsymbol{a}$, its element d can be written as a linear combination of $\boldsymbol{a}$, i.e., there exist $\lambda_1, \ldots, \lambda_n \in \mathbb{N}$ and $x_1, \ldots, x_n \in \boldsymbol{a}$ such that $d = \sum_1^n \lambda_i x_i$. For $i \in \{1, \ldots, n\}$, let p_i be the index of x_i in $\boldsymbol{a}$, starting from 0. Let $\boldsymbol{s}$ be the list obtained by sorting the list $[p_1]^{\lambda_1} \ldots [p_n]^{\lambda_n}$ in descending order. Let $m = |\boldsymbol{a}| - 1$. Since $\boldsymbol{s} \in \mathbb{L}^m_{\geq}$, by Theorem 7 there exists $k \in \mathbb{N}$ such that $\mathsf{genL}_m(k) = \boldsymbol{s}$. From the definition of $\boldsymbol{s}$ it follows that

$$\mathsf{genM}_{\boldsymbol{a}}(k) \;=\; \sum_{i \in \boldsymbol{s}} \boldsymbol{a}_i \;=\; d. \qquad \square$$

Since $\mathsf{genM}_{\boldsymbol{a}}$ does not generate the elements of M in ascending order, we cannot just obtain the small elements of M by applying $\mathsf{genM}_{\boldsymbol{a}}$ until finding the conductor. Still, our algorithm $\mathsf{genM}_{\boldsymbol{a}}$ satisfies the following property: there exist certain numbers n (and they are infinite) such that, when the algorithm has generated n, we know that all possible linear combinations $d \leq n$ have already been generated. Thus, we just need to run the algorithm until one of those numbers that is greater than or equal to the conductor has been generated.

3.3 From Linear Combinations to Small Elements

We present our algorithm to compute the list of small elements of a numerical semigroup in Algorithm 1. For simplicity, there we rely on pseudocode; see (**small_els**) for our actual Rocq implementation. Even if Rocq's underlying language is functional, we adopt imperative pseudocode, as it may be easier to understand for most readers. The main difference with the actual code is the use of while loops, which are in fact implemented as recursive calls.

Algorithm 1 Algorithm for computing the small elements given the generators

```
function CONSECUTIVE-VALUES(s, m, l)                          ▷ Search a subsequence of length m
    next ← 0;   count ← 0;   i ← 0;
    while i < |s| do
        if s_i = next then count ← count + 1;
        else (if s_i ≤ l then count ← 1 else return −1;)
        if count = m then return i + 1 − m;   ▷ Index of 1st element of subsequence
        next ← s_i + 1;   i ← i + 1;
    return −1;

function SMALL-ELEMENTS(a, n)
    se = [];   l ← [];   m ← min a;   i ← 1;
    while i < n do
        while |l| < i do
            se ← (∑_{j∈l} a_j) :: se;
            l ← next_{|a|−1}(l);
        se ← (i · m) :: se;
        l ← next_{|a|−1}(l);
        se ← SORT(se);                                        ▷ Sort in ascending order
        se ← RMDUPS(se);                                      ▷ Remove duplicates
        p ← CONSECUTIVE-VALUES(se, m, i · m);
        if p ≥ 0 then return TAKE(se, p + 1);                 ▷ Prefix of se of length p + 1
        i ← i + 1;
```

The function CONSECUTIVE-VALUES$(\boldsymbol{s}, m, l)$ (**`find_seq`**) returns the index of the first element $x \leq l$ in $\boldsymbol{s}$ such that there is a sequence of m consecutive natural numbers starting from x in $\boldsymbol{s}$. The return value -1 means that no such sequence exists.

Let $\boldsymbol{a} \in \mathbb{L}$ with $0 \notin \boldsymbol{a} \neq []$ be the generator of the numerical semigroup M. The function SMALL-ELEMENTS starts with an empty list $\boldsymbol{se}$ and with $i = 1$. In each iteration inside the outer **while** loop, we add the element $\mathsf{genM}_{\boldsymbol{a}}(j)$ to the list $\boldsymbol{se}$, for every $j \in \mathbb{N}$ such that $|\mathsf{genL}_{|\boldsymbol{a}|-1}(j)| = i - 1$ and for the smallest $j \in \mathbb{N}$ such that $|\mathsf{genL}_{|\boldsymbol{a}|-1}(j)| = i$. In particular, this last element is equal to $i \cdot m$, where $m = \min \boldsymbol{a}$. Next, we sort $\boldsymbol{se}$ in ascending order and we remove any duplicates from it. Lastly, we apply the function CONSECUTIVE-VALUES to the list $\boldsymbol{se}$. If the error value -1 is returned, we proceed with another iteration. Otherwise, let p be the returned value. The main function SMALL-ELEMENTS returns the list made of the first $p+1$ elements of $\boldsymbol{se}$.

Example 3. We illustrate Algorithm 1 through an example with $\boldsymbol{a} = [4; 7; 10]$. At the 3rd iteration of the outer **while** loop, $\boldsymbol{se} = [0; 4; 7; 8; 10; 11; 14; 17; 20]$. Since there are no 4 consecutive elements in this list, we proceed with another iteration. At the 4th iteration, $\boldsymbol{se} = [0; 4; 7; 8; 10; 11; 12; 14; 15; 16; 17; 18; 20; 21; 24; 27; 30]$. The number 14 is the first of a sequence of 4 consecutive numbers in $\boldsymbol{se}$, and $14 \leq 16 = i \cdot m$. Thus, the list of small elements is $[0; 4; 7; 8; 10; 11; 12; 14]$. Consequently, the list of gaps is $[1; 2; 3; 5; 6; 9; 13]$. ◇

We now prove the correctness of the algorithm, namely that the prefix of $\boldsymbol{se}$ of length $p+1$ is the list of small elements of M. Clearly, $\boldsymbol{se} \subseteq M$, since every element added to $\boldsymbol{se}$ during the execution of the algorithm is a sum of elements in $\boldsymbol{a}$. Next, every natural number x greater than or equal to $\boldsymbol{se}_p$ belongs to M. Indeed, x can be obtained by adding m multiple times to one of $c, \ldots, c+m-1$. Since $c, \ldots, c+m-1$ are in $\boldsymbol{se}$ and thus in M, and since $m \in M$, also $x \in M$. Moreover, c is the smallest element of M with this property, since $c-1 \notin M$ (otherwise, Consecutive-Values would have returned the position of $c-1$ instead of the position of c).

Finally, we have to prove that every element of M that is smaller than $\boldsymbol{se}_p$ is in $\boldsymbol{se}$. This is a consequence of the following theorem.

Theorem 9. (`mgen_complete_lt`) *Let* $\boldsymbol{a} \in \mathbb{L}$ *be such that* $0 \notin \boldsymbol{a} \neq []$ *and let* M *be the submonoid of* $\mathbb{N}$ *generated by* $\boldsymbol{a}$. *Let* $k \in \mathbb{N}$ *and let* $x \in M$ *be such that* $x < |\mathsf{genL}_{|\boldsymbol{a}|-1}(k)| \cdot \min \boldsymbol{a}$. *Then there exists* $n < k$ *such that* $\mathsf{genM}_{\boldsymbol{a}}(n) = x$.

The theorem above states that all the elements of M that are less than $|\mathsf{genM}_{\boldsymbol{a}}(k)| \cdot \min \boldsymbol{a}$ are generated before the k-th iteration of $\mathsf{genM}_{\boldsymbol{a}}$. In other words, after generating k elements of M with $\mathsf{genM}_{\boldsymbol{a}}$, we are sure that no elements of M smaller than $|\mathsf{genM}_{\boldsymbol{a}}(k)| \cdot m$ have been forgotten.

For example, recalling the enumeration of genL_2 at page 9, we have that $\mathsf{genL}_2(5) = [1;0]$, and thus, for $\boldsymbol{a} = [4;7;10]$:

$$|\mathsf{genM}_{\boldsymbol{a}}(5)| \cdot \min \boldsymbol{a} \;=\; |[1;0]| \cdot \min[4;7;10] \;=\; 2 \cdot 4 = 8.$$

Every list generated for $n \geq 5$ has at least length 2, and thus the corresponding linear combination is greater than or equal to 8. This means that every number smaller than 8 that is in M is necessarily included in the set:

$$\left\{\mathsf{genM}_{\boldsymbol{a}}(i) \,\middle|\, 0 \leq i < 5\right\} = \{\, 0, 4, 7, 10, 8 \,\}.$$

Proof (Theorem 9). The proof relies on two auxiliary facts. First, we prove that:

$$\mathsf{genM}_{\boldsymbol{a}}(k) \geq |\mathsf{genL}_{|\boldsymbol{a}|-1}(k)| \cdot \min \boldsymbol{a}. \qquad (\texttt{nth\_limit\_le\_mgen})$$

This holds because the term $\mathsf{genM}_{\boldsymbol{a}}(k)$ is the sum of $|\mathsf{genL}_{|\boldsymbol{a}|-1}(k)|$ elements, each of which is greater than or equal to $\min \boldsymbol{a}$. ◇

Second, we prove that:

$$\forall m, n, k \in \mathbb{N},\ n \leq k \rightarrow |\mathsf{genL}_m(n)| \leq |\mathsf{genL}_m(k)|. \qquad (\texttt{length\_lgen\_le})$$

This is a direct consequence of the following auxiliary result:

$$\forall \boldsymbol{s} \in \mathbb{L},\ |\mathsf{next}_m(\boldsymbol{s})| \in \{|\boldsymbol{s}|, |\boldsymbol{s}|+1\}. \qquad (\texttt{length\_next})$$

We prove it by induction on $\boldsymbol{s}$. For the base case, if $\boldsymbol{s} = []$, then $|\mathsf{next}_m(\boldsymbol{s})| = |[0]| = |\boldsymbol{s}| + 1$. For the inductive case, let $\boldsymbol{s} = h :: \boldsymbol{t}$. We have two subcases. If $h < m$, then $|\mathsf{next}_m(h :: \boldsymbol{t})| = |(h+1) :: \boldsymbol{t}| = |h :: \boldsymbol{t}|$. Otherwise, if $h \geq m$, then

$\mathsf{next}_m(h :: \boldsymbol{t}) = x :: x :: \boldsymbol{t}'$, where $x :: \boldsymbol{t}' = \mathsf{next}_m(\boldsymbol{t})$. By the induction hypothesis, $|x :: \boldsymbol{t}'| = |\mathsf{next}_m(\boldsymbol{t})| \in \{|\boldsymbol{t}|, |\boldsymbol{t}| + 1\}$. Therefore:

$$|\mathsf{next}_m(\boldsymbol{s})| = |x :: x :: \boldsymbol{t}'| = 1 + |x :: \boldsymbol{t}'| \in 1 + \{|\boldsymbol{t}|, |\boldsymbol{t}| + 1\} = \{|\boldsymbol{s}|, |\boldsymbol{s}| + 1\}. \quad \diamond$$

We can now prove Theorem 9. By Theorem 8, there exists $n \in \mathbb{N}$ such that $\mathsf{genM}_{\boldsymbol{a}}(n) = x$. Suppose by contradiction that $k \leq n$. Let $m = |\boldsymbol{a}| - 1$. Then, by (**length_lgen_le**) and (**nth_limit_le_mgen**) we have

$$x < |\mathsf{genL}_m(k)| \cdot \min \boldsymbol{a} \leq |\mathsf{genL}_m(n)| \cdot \min \boldsymbol{a} \leq \mathsf{genM}_{\boldsymbol{a}}(n) = x,$$

that is, $x < x$—contradiction. □

4 Conclusions

The present paper provides a first formalization of numerical semigroups in a proof assistant, more precisely Rocq. In particular, we implemented certified algorithms to compute relevant invariants of a numerical semigroup, e.g. its Apéry sets, the small elements, the list of gaps, the multiplicity and the conductor. Although much more has to be done, this work provides a necessary basis for any further implementation of certified algorithms (and proofs) for numerical semigroups. Our formalization is public and counts $\sim$ 3000 lines of Rocq code.

One of the main advantages of using Rocq over other proof assistants is the ability to extract certified C code, which can be integrated into GAP [9]. Indeed, although the functions in the numericalsgps package [7] are currently implemented in the GAP language, the GAP system provides a native C API for performance-critical components. Doing so would make fundamental functions in the numericalsgps package—such as computing the set of gaps, of small elements, the Apéry set, the multiplicity, the conductor and the Frobenius number—certifiably correct. An overhead is that the other functions in the package which depend on these primitives should be adapted to use the new certified implementations, written in Rocq and extracted to C.

While developing our formalization in Rocq, we noted that it is not always convenient to have a perfect match between a mathematical theory and its formalization in a proof assistant. For instance, in informal mathematics we use $\mathbb{N}$ and $\mathbb{Z}$ interchangeably, while this cannot be easily done in Rocq. For this reason we only work with $\mathbb{N}$, and this choice entails more adaptations, like the definition of Apéry set (1). Another difference between the informal theory of numerical semigroups and our implementation is that we use lists to represent finite sets.

An algorithm, different from ours, that computes the gaps of a numerical semigroup from a (finite) set of generators is introduced in [6] in the more general framework of generalized numerical semigroups. More specifically, the algorithm computes the Frobenius number F at first, and then, for every $0 \leq n \leq F$, it checks whether n can be written as linear combination of the generators. These tasks can be seen as instances of the "Frobenius problem", or "money-changing problem", which seeks for non-negative integer solutions to $x_1 a_1 + \cdots + x_n a_n = m$, where a_i and m are positive integers (see [11]), for whose solution several algorithms can be applied [3]. It is worth noticing that since the mentioned procedure requires to check whether each number between 0 and F is a linear combination (of the generators) or not, it makes sense to tackle the "reverse" problem, namely to generate every linear combination instead, which is the first step of our algorithm.

Although the efficiency of our algorithm was not investigated here, its formal proof of correctness is relevant not only intrinsically but also as a benchmark for more efficient algorithms (to be developed in the future), whose correctness can be established by proving their equivalence to our algorithm.

Acknowledgements. Work partially supported by the projects: SERICS (PE00000014) under the MUR National Recovery and Resilience Plan funded by the European Union – NextGenerationEU; PRIN 2022 PNRR project DeLiCE (F53D23009130001); the project MAPS (grant number F73C23001550007) funded by the Fondazione di Sardegna; the StartUp project "GraphNet" funded by the University of Cagliari.

We also gratefully acknowledges also the support of the INDAM GNSAGA (Gruppo Nazionale per le Strutture Algebriche, Geometriche e loro Applicazioni).

Disclosure of Interests. The authors have no competing interests to declare that are relevant to the content of this article.

References

1. Assi, A., D'Anna, M., García-Sànchez, P.A.: Numerical Semigroups and Applications. Springer (2020). https://doi.org/10.1007/97
2. Barucci, V.: Decompositions of ideals into irreducible ideals in numerical semigroups. Journal of Commutative Algebra **2**(3) (2010). https://doi.org/10.1216/JCA-2010-2-3-281
3. Beihoffer, D., Hendry, J., Nijenhuis, A., Wagon, S.: Faster algorithms for Frobenius numbers. The Electronic Journal of Combinatorics **12** (2005). https://doi.org/10.37236/1924
4. Blanco, V., García-Sánchez, P.A., Puerto, J.: Counting numerical semigroups with short generating functions. International Journal of Algebra and Computation **21**(07), 1217–1235 (2011). https://doi.org/10.1142/S0218196711006911
5. Campillo, A., Delgado, F., Gusein-Zade, S.M.: On generators of the semigroup of a plane curve singularity. Journal of the London Mathematical Society **60**(2), 420–430 (10 1999). https://doi.org/10.1112/S0024610799007917
6. Cisto, C., Delgado, M., García-Sánchez, P.A.: Algorithms for generalized numerical semigroups. Journal of Algebra and Its Applications **20**(05) (2021). https://doi.org/10.1142/S0219498821500791
7. Delgado, M., García-Sánchez, P.A., Morais, J.: Numericalsgps, a package for numerical semigroups, version 1.4.0 (2024), refereed gap package, https://gap-packages.github.io/numericalsgps
8. Delgado, M., Farrán, J.I., García-Sánchez, P.A., Llena, D.: On the weight hierarchy of codes coming from semigroups with two generators. IEEE Transactions on Information Theory **60**(1), 282–295 (2014). https://doi.org/10.1109/TIT.2013.2285217

9. The GAP Group: GAP – Groups, Algorithms, and Programming, Version 4.14.0 (2024), https://www.gap-system.org
10. García, A.: Semigroups associated to singular points of plane curves. Journal für die reine und angewandte Mathematik **336**, 165–184 (1982). https://doi.org/10.1515/crll.1982.336.165
11. Ramírez Alfonsín, J.L.: The Diophantine Frobenius Problem. Oxford University Press (2005). https://doi.org/10.1093/acprof:oso/9780198568209.001.0001
12. Rosales, J.C., García-Sánchez, P.A., García-García, J.I., Jiménez Madrid, J.A.: The oversemigroups of a numerical semigroup. Semigroup Forum **67**(1), 145–158 (2003). https://doi.org/10.1007/s00233-002-0007-3
13. Rosales, J.C., García-Sánchez, P.A., García-García, J.I., Jiménez-Madrid, J.A.: Fundamental gaps in numerical semigroups. Journal of Pure and Applied Algebra **189**(1), 301–313 (2004). https://doi.org/10.1016/j.jpaa.2003.10.024
14. Rosales, J.C., García-Sánchez, P.A.: Numerical Semigroups. Springer (2009). https://doi.org/10.1007/978-1-4419-0160-6

Formalizing the Solow Model in ℕaproche

Peter Koepke[1](✉) and Patrick Schäfer[2]

[1] University of Bonn, Bonn, Germany
koepke@math.uni-bonn.de
[2] University of Cologne, Cologne, Germany
patrick.schaefer@wiso.uni-koeln.de

Abstract. In 1956, Robert M. Solow published a mathematical theory which describes capital accumulation, technological advancements, and population growth. The Solow model is widely used in economics. In this paper we describe a formalization of the model in the ℕaproche proof assistant. The formalization also encompasses mathematical foundations from real analysis. This is the first formalization of an economic model which is also readable like an ordinary mathematical text.

Introduction

We present a natural language formalization of the Solow growth model, a cornerstone of macroeconomic theory, using the ℕaproche proof system. The formalization also includes necessary mathematical foundations, such as concepts of continuity, derivatives, the mean value theorem, the inverse function theorem, and the exponential function. This formalization was the main part of the Bachelor project of the second author.

The Solow model is widely used in economics. It describes how capital accumulation, technological advancements, and population growth are linked with economic output. In 2018 Paul Romer received the Nobel Memorial Prize in Economic Sciences for his work on endogenous growth theory, which is a direct extension of the Solow model [13]. Daron Acemoglu, who won the 2024 Nobel-prize, frequently builds on the model [1].

The ℕaproche formalization of the Solow model consists of a collection of LaTeX documents with the extension `.ftl.tex`, which are compiled into a single, unified PDF file (`solow_main.ftl.pdf`). Both the source files and the compiled PDF are available for download from the ℕaproche homepage[1]. The formalization can be inspected and immediately proof-checked by loading it into the Isabelle proof environment which contains a ℕaproche component. Its pdf-output looks similar to ordinary texts in mathematical economics.

The Solow model formalization is one of the largest formalizations in ℕaproche so far. It amounts to 70 typeset pages consisting of strictly formal ℕaproche text on a light-grey background and other descriptive text. The mathematical foundations comprise most of the content. The Solow formalization is testing the limits

[1] `https://naproche.github.io/formalizations.html`

V. de Paiva and P. Koepke (Eds.): CICM 2025, LNAI 16136, pp. 357–370, 2026.
https://doi.org/10.1007/978-3-032-07021-0_20

of the Naproche system: slight variations in the formalization may significantly alter the prover tasks that have to be solved in the checking process and often may make them too time-consuming or even unsolvable for the utilized automated theorem prover (E prover). Checking the complete Solow formalization takes about 9 hours on a standard consumer laptop.

There have been previous computer-checked formalizations of economic theories, such as the *Formal Mathematical Reasoning in Economics* Project [12]. Theorems about voting systems such as Arrow's impossibility theorem and the Gibbard-Satterthwaite theorem have been formalized using the theorem provers Mizar and Isabelle/HOL [17]. Furthermore, Kaliszyk and Parsert [10] formalize the first welfare theorem, and Ahmed et al. [2] formalize the First Order Condition in HOL-Light.

Those formalizations, however, are predominantly focused on microeconomics which studies individual firm behaviour, specific markets, and agents. Macroeconomics in contrast is the discussion of economic variables such as inflation, unemployment rates, GDP, or economic growth. Macroeconomic models provide a mathematical framework to explain empirical findings about these variables. These models usually employ mathematical tools and creating the tools necessary for the Solow growth model provides a library that can aid further macroeconomic formalizations in Naproche. A special focus is placed on readability and intuitiveness in the presentation of the model.

This paper is structured as follows: The first section recalls the Naproche system. The second section introduces the Solow model and highlights concepts employed in the model. The third section discusses the formalization of mathematical foundations such as continuity and differentiation rules. The fourth section contains an excerpt from the Solow model-formalization, which brings many of the before mentioned mathematical concepts together. We also comment on some technical details which were necessary to make the formalization go through. The fifth section briefly reflects on the done work.

1 Naproche

Naproche stands for "Natural Proof Checking" and is a natural proof assistant that aligns closely with the mathematical vernacular language. The system is designed to bridge the gap between human-readable mathematical texts and formal proof verification. This involves supporting common grammatical conventions, symbolic expressions, and familiar text structures such as definition-theorem-proof formats and also allows proofs to consist of some natural argumentative phrases for various proof tactics, such as "We can show that ... ". Naproche is a long-term exploratory project to see whether (controlled) natural language can be used in formal mathematics, instead of computer language which is hardly palatable by ordinary mathematicians and deviates from traditional mathematical practices.

Naproche combines techniques of computer linguistics with strong automated theorem proving (ATP) in first-order logic. The natural language is processed by a combinator-based parser and translated into annotated first-order statements. A reasoner module turns these statements into prover tasks. Some simple tasks are directly discharged by the reasoner. Others are translated into the standard prover language TPTP and given to an ATP to be solved within a time limit. Prover tasks are also generated for checking that (parts of) formulas are reasonable: to use a term like $\frac{s}{t}$ in analysis requires to prove that $t \neq 0$. Equational reasoning may also be delegated to an in-built term rewriter. In total, the Solow formalization produced several thousand prover tasks.

The Naproche initiative stems from two long-term projects aiming towards naturalness in mathematical proofs: the Evidence Algorithm (EA) and System for Automated Deduction (SAD) at the universities of Kyiv and Paris, and the original Naproche project at Bonn [5,4].

Naproche extends the ForTheL language, originally part of SAD, and embeds it into LaTeX, enabling mathematical typesetting while enhancing proof-checking efficiency and variety [6]. In 2018, Naproche got integrated into the Isabelle Prover IDE, where one can interactively edit and run formalizations. Importantly, Naproche is not based upon the Isabelle logic or libraries but converts the controlled natural language input into an internal first-order format. The first-order proof tasks are generated and discharged by Naproche itself or ATPs provided by Isabelle. We hope that in the future we use experiences from Naproche formalizations like the present one to build natural language interfaces for strong systems like Isabelle/HOL and Lean.

Naproche is a bundled component in Isabelle 2024, immediately accessible after downloading and unpacking the Isabelle distribution. It checks ForTheL-files with `.ftl` or `.ftl.tex` extensions. The `.ftl.tex` extension allows formalizations to be compiled by pdfLaTeX into a well readable pdf, looking much like regular mathematical texts.

2 The Solow Model

The Solow growth model was introduced by Robert M. Solow [16] and aims to explain several consistent patterns in economic data, which seem to hold in the long term and which were later summarized in six "stylized" facts named after Nicholas Kaldor [9]:

- G1 Continued growth in the aggregate volume of production, i.e. in the long term economies seem to grow.
- G2 A continued increase in the amount of capital per worker, meaning that each employee manages more and more capital.
- G3 A steady rate of profit on capital, i.e. when you invest money, the average return you get on it when discounting inflation, seems to be quite constant over time.
- G4 Steady capital-output ratios over long periods, which implies the near-identity in the percentage rates of growth of production and of the capital stock.
- G5 A steady share of profits (and of wages) in societies and periods in which the share of investment in output is constant.

G6 There are appreciable differences in the rate of growth of labour productivity and of total output in different societies.

The model economy contains the following main variables:

- The capital K, which is the value of the sum of all machinery used in the economy to produce new goods.
- The labour supply L, which is the total number of hours the sum of all workers are working.
- The technology level A, which represents a measure of how productive the time of the labourers spend working is.
- The output level Y, which is interpretable as a nations GDP.

Larger A could be caused by better machinery or more efficient production processes or better skilled labourers. The analysis of Romer [13] differentiates between productivity gains caused by capital improvements and those gained through higher human capital and the respective consequences thereof. Formally we define K, L, A, and Y as differentiable maps from $\mathbb{R}$ to $\mathbb{R}_{>0}$, where the value $K(t)$ is understood as a nations capital at the point in time t. We assume fixed growth rates for L and A, i.e. $\hat{L}(t) = \frac{\mathrm{D}L(t)}{L(t)} = gL \geq 0$ and $\hat{A}(t) = gA \geq 0$. Additional variables in the model, which are also defined as differentiable maps from $\mathbb{R}$ to $\mathbb{R}_{>0}$, are:

- Capital per efficiency unit labour k, which is defined as $k = (K/(A \cdot L))$.
- Interest rates r.
- Wages w.

Next we introduce axioms that define how these variables are related to each other.

Capital Accumulation The model contains a fixed – i.e. not time-dependent – savings rate $s \in (0,1)$ and a fixed depreciation rate $\delta \in (0,1)$. In discrete time one can interpret s as the fraction of the output that is invested in increasing the capital stock in each period and δ as the reduction of capital due to depreciation from period to period. In continuous time we represent this relationship in Naproche-code in the following way:

Axiom (capital accumulation).

$$\partial K(t) = (s \cdot Y(t)) - (\delta \cdot K(t))$$

$\partial K(t)$ is defined as a real number equal to the slope of the function K in t, while $\mathrm{D}K$ is a function, which is equal to $\partial K(t)$ in every point t (for more information consult section 3, Differentiation).

Production Function A production function f links capital, labour, and technology to an output level Y, which can either be consumed or used as capital.

Signature. A production function is a strictly convex differentiable real map.
Let f denote a production function.

Axiom (constant returns to scale).

$$Y = ((A \cdot L) \cdot (f \circ k)).$$

The Firm's Maximization Problem A firm aims to realize a maximum of profits, i.e.

$$\max_{K_t, L_t} A_t L_t f(k_t) - r_t K_t - w_t L_t.$$

This is total output minus the capital ($r_t K_t$) and labour ($w_t L_t$) costs. The firm chooses its capital and labour demand such that it maximizes profits. Here we will just focus on maximizing profits by capital in line with the Kaldor's facts stated above. Profits depending upon the capital stock are denoted by $\Pi(x) = A_t L_t f\left(\frac{x}{A_t L_t}\right) - r_t x - w_t L_t$ or in our notation[2]:

Definition (def Pi).

$$\Pi_{A,L,f,r,w,t} = (\mathrm{f}_{A(t) \cdot L(t) \cdot \_+0} \circ (f \circ \mathrm{f}_{1/(A(t) \cdot L(t)) \cdot \_+0}) + (-\mathrm{f}_{r(t) \cdot \_+w(t) \cdot L(t)})).$$

After having introduced sufficient conditions on f, we show that Π always has a maximum. We first show that Π is strictly convex by calculating the derivative $\mathrm{D}\Pi = \mathrm{f}_{1 \cdot \_+-r(t)} \circ (\mathrm{D}f \circ \mathrm{f}_{1/(A(t) \cdot L(t)) \cdot \_+0})$ and proving that $\partial \mathrm{D}\Pi(x) < 0$ for every real number x. Next we can show with the intermediate value theorem that there exists a positive real number ξ such that $\mathrm{D}\Pi(\xi) = 0$ by showing $\mathrm{D}\Pi(\omega) < 0 < \mathrm{D}\Pi(0)$ for some positive ω. From the mathematical foundations we then know that these are sufficient conditions for a local as well as global maximum.

We postulate that the implicit firm would set K to maximize their profits.

Axiom (profit maximizing K). $K(t)$ is a maximum of $\Pi_{A,L,f,r,w,t}$.

Steady State The steady state in the Solow model is defined by constant capital per efficiency unit labour, i.e. $\partial k(t) = 0$. This constant level is denoted by κ. To prove the existence of such a value we first show that

Proposition (derivative k). Let Y be an output level and K be a capital stock and L be a labor amount and A be an efficiency level. k is differentiable in t and

$$\partial k(t) = (s \cdot f(k(t))) - ((\delta + (gA + gL)) \cdot k(t)).$$

Then we define a function $\Delta(x) = (s \cdot f(x)) - ((\delta + (gA + gL)) \cdot x)$ such that

[2] For comment on the function notation, see section 3 under Continuity.

Definition (Delta).

$$\Delta_{s,f,\delta,gA,gL} = (\mathrm{f}_{s\cdot\_+0} \circ f + (-\mathrm{f}_{\delta+(gA+gL)\cdot\_+0})).$$

We prove that $\Delta_{s,f,\delta,gA,gL} \circ k = \mathrm{D}k$. Then we show that $\Delta(0) > 0$ and that there exists a positive real number ξ such that $\Delta(\xi) < 0$. By the intermediate value theorem, there exists then a $\kappa \in (0, \xi)$ such that $\Delta(\kappa) = 0$. The Kaldor Facts are – except for G6 – thought of as steady state facts. Therefore as a last axiom we state that the economy is in a steady state, i.e.

Axiom (steady state). $\partial k(t) = 0$.

Kaldor's Facts We formally prove the Kaldor's facts in the model, and we also get an explanation, why they ought to be true.

- G1 Constant output growth rates: $(\widehat{Y/L})(t) = gA$.
  Innovations drive economic growth.
- G2 Increased amount of capital per worker: $\hat{K}(t) = gA + gL$.
  Capital keeping up with the growth of workers and innovation.
- G3 Constant return on capital: $r(t) = \partial f(\kappa)$.
  Steady state interest rates are equal to the marginal productivity of capital.
- G4 Stable capital-output ratios: $\frac{K(t)}{Y(t)} = \frac{\kappa}{f(\kappa)}$.
- G5 Stable share of profits of output: $\frac{r(t) \cdot K(t)}{Y(t)} = \frac{\partial f(\kappa) \cdot \kappa}{f(\kappa)}$.
- G6 Different growth rates can be interpreted as countries being differently far away from the steady state capital accumulation. The lower the capital amount of a country is, the larger is its growth rates from catching up. The following proposition shows that capital per efficiency unit of labor, k, tends to return to its steady-state level over time. When k is below its steady-state value, it grows, while if k is above steady-state, it declines.

  Proposition (off steady state). Let x be positive.
  (If $x < \kappa$ then $\Delta_{s,f,\delta,gA,gL}(x) > 0$) and if $x > \kappa$ then $\Delta_{s,f,\delta,gA,gL}(x) < 0$.

  Since output is positively related to k, increases in k lead to higher-than-steady-state growth rates, while decreases in k result in slower-than-steady-state growth rates.

3 Mathematical Foundations

We base the formalization of the mathematical concepts upon Koepke, Marcol, and Schäfer [11], importing concepts such as the real numbers, $\leq$ and $<$, and upper and lower bounds.

Continuity For the formalization of the Solow growth model we need the ability to join two functions together to create a new function such as $(f \cdot g), (f/g), (f+g), (-f)$ and linear functions $\mathrm{f}_{a\cdot\_+b}(x) := ax + b$. Having defined metrics and absolute values, we define continuity, where $d_{\mathbb{R}}$ represents the Euclidean norm ($d_{\mathbb{R}}(x,y) := |x-y|$) and a real map is a map from $\mathbb{R}$ to $\mathbb{R}$:

Let a, b, x, y denote real numbers. Let δ, ε denote positive real numbers. Let f, g denote real maps.

Definition (def domain restrictor). A domain restrictor for ε and f around a and y is a positive real number δ such that for all $x \in \mathbb{R} \setminus \{a\}$ if $d_{\mathbb{R}}(x,a) < \delta$ then $d_{\mathbb{R}}(f(x), y) < \varepsilon$.

Definition. $\lim_{x \to a} f(x)$ is a real number y such that for every positive real number ε there exists a domain restrictor for ε and f around a and y.

Definition. f is continuous in a iff $\lim_{x \to a} f(x) = f(a)$.

Definition. f is continuous iff for every real number a f is continuous in a.

We introduce a domain restrictor as a Skolem function, which splits the usual definition of continuity into two steps as otherwise its complexity overwhelms the ATP. We show that linear functions are continuous and that adding and multiplying continuous functions preserves continuity.

Differentiation

Let a, b denote real numbers. Let f, g denote real maps.

Definition (def diffquot). $\frac{\Delta f}{\Delta a}$ is a real map such that $\frac{\Delta f}{\Delta a}(x) = \frac{f(x)-f(a)}{x-a}$ for all $x \in \mathbb{R} \setminus \{a\}$.

Definition. f is differentiable in a iff there exists a real number y such that $\lim_{x \to a} \frac{\Delta f}{\Delta a}(x) = y$.

Definition. f is differentiable iff for every real number a f is differentiable in a.

Definition. Assume f is differentiable in a. The derivative of f in a is a real number y such that $\lim_{x \to a} \frac{\Delta f}{\Delta a}(x) = y$.

Let $\partial f(x)$ stand for the derivative of f in x.

Definition. Let f be differentiable. The derivative of f is a real map d such that for every real number x $d(x)$ is equal to the derivative of f in x.

Let $\mathrm{D}f$ stand for the derivative of f.

Lemma (deriv and derivin). Let f be differentiable. $\mathrm{D}f(a) = \partial f(a)$.

Furthermore we prove the differentiation rules $\mathrm{Df}_{a\cdot\_+b} = \mathrm{f}_{0\cdot\_+a}$, $\mathrm{D}(f+g) = (\mathrm{D}f + \mathrm{D}g)$, $\mathrm{D}(-f) = (-\mathrm{D}f)$, $\mathrm{D}(f \cdot g) = ((\mathrm{D}f \cdot g) + (f \cdot \mathrm{D}g))$, and $\mathrm{D}(f \circ g) = ((\mathrm{D}f \circ g) \cdot \mathrm{D}g)$.

Local Functions This serves as a preparation of the goal of proving the inverse function theorem and the proof that $\frac{\partial \ln(x)}{\partial x} = 1/x$ for any $x > 0$. Nearly every macroeconomic model has some agent who maximizes their utility or some firm that maximizes its profits. All those models require taking the derivative of a given utility or production function, and the most common variations of these are the Cobb-Douglas production functions

$$F(K, L) = K^{\alpha} L^{1-\alpha}$$

for $\alpha \in (0, 1)$, which are also often used in the Solow model, and the isoelastic utility function

$$u(c) = \begin{cases} \frac{c^{1-\eta}-1}{1-\eta} & : \eta \geq 0,\ \eta \neq 1 \\ \ln(c) & : \eta = 1 \end{cases}$$

where η is a constant.

When formalizing the differentiation rules for the logarithm and the power function, we are faced with the problem that those functions are only defined on the positive real numbers and not for all real numbers. To apply the concepts of differentiability and continuity to functions that are only defined on a subset of the reals, we introduce the concepts of local continuity and local differentiability. We say that for some subset S of the real numbers, $f : S \to \mathbb{R}$ is locally differentiable in some $a \in S$ if and only if for any real map g such that $g \upharpoonright S = f$, g is differentiable in a. We call such a real map g a real map extension of f. To seamlessly switch between partial functions and their respective real map extensions, we prove two theorems:

1. Every real map extension of a partial function has the same derivative if the partial function is locally differentiable.

   Theorem (lemma differentiation extension). Let S be a subset of $\mathbb{R}$ and g be a real map on S. Assume a is an element of S and g is locally differentiable in a. Let f be a real map extension of g. Then f is differentiable in a and $\partial f(a) = \partial_{\ell} g(a)$.

   $\partial_{\ell} g(a)$ is defined as the derivative of the 'canonical' real map extension of g, which is just zero wherever g is not defined.
2. If there exists a real map extension that is differentiable and the partial function has an open domain, then the partial function is locally differentiable.

Theorem (open set differentiation extension). Let E be an open neighbourhood of a. Let g be a real map on E. Let f be a real map extension of g such that f is differentiable in a. Then g is locally differentiable in a and $\partial_\ell g(a) = \partial f(a)$.

Extrema and Mean Value Theorem In the Solow model firms will maximize their profits. Therefore it is crucial to introduce extrema as well as necessary and sufficient conditions for extrema. We first show the extreme value theorem.

Definition. A maximum domain restrictor for f around ξ is a positive real number δ such that for all $x \in B_\delta(\xi)$ $f(x) \leq f(\xi)$.

Definition. A local maximum of f is a real number ξ such that there exists a positive real number δ such that δ is a maximum domain restrictor for f around ξ.

Theorem (derivative of maximum). Let ξ be a local maximum of f. Let f be differentiable in ξ. Then $\partial f(\xi) = 0$.

The term $[a, b]_{CI}$ refers to the closed interval between a and b, where the CI is added for extra clarity for the ATP.

Theorem (extreme value theorem). Let f be continuous and $a < b$. $f[[a, b]_{CI}]$ is a subset of $\mathbb{R}$ and there exists a $c \in [a, b]_{CI}$ such that $f(c)$ is an upper bound of $f[[a, b]_{CI}]$.

$\vdots$

Theorem (sufficient condition local maximum). Let f be differentiable and $\partial f(\xi) = 0$. Let $\mathrm{D}f$ be differentiable in ξ and $\partial \mathrm{D}f(\xi) < 0$. Then ξ is a local maximum of f.

Inverse Function Theorem

Theorem (inverse function theorem). Let f be continuously differentiable and $\partial f(a) \neq 0$. Then there exists an open neighbourhood E of a such that f is strictly monotone on E and $(f \upharpoonright E)^{-1}$ is a real map on $f[E]$ and $(f \upharpoonright E)^{-1}$ is locally differentiable in $f(a)$ and $\partial_\ell(f \upharpoonright E)^{-1}(f(a)) = 1/\partial f(a)$.

We include "f is strictly monotone on E and $(f \upharpoonright E)^{-1}$ is a real map on $f[E]$ and $(f \upharpoonright E)^{-1}$ is locally differentiable in $f(a)$", because the type parsing would otherwise not recognize $\partial_\ell(f \upharpoonright E)^{-1}(f(a)) = 1/\partial f(a)$ as a valid formulation. In order to make this a bit neater, we introduce the concept of a locally inverse function:

Definition. A locally inverse function to f in a is a real map g such that for some open neighbourhood E of a
$f \restriction E$ is injective and $g \restriction f[E] = (f \restriction E)^{-1}$.

Corollary (inverse function theorem II). Let f be continuously differentiable and $\partial f(a) \neq 0$. Let g be a locally inverse function to f in a. Then g is differentiable in $f(a)$ and $\partial g(f(a)) = 1/\partial f(a)$.

Exponential Function and Logarithm Next we introduce the exponential function $\exp(x)$ as well as a^x, the logarithm, and the power function, and show what their respective derivatives are. We also show common calculation rules for exponents and logarithms. exp is introduced axiomatically:

Signature (natural exponential function). exp is a real map such that $\mathrm{D}\exp = \exp$.

Axiom (exp of 0). $\exp(x) = 1$ iff $x = 0$.

Axiom (exp calculation axiom). $\exp(a + b) = \exp(a) \cdot \exp(b)$.

We show that exp is injective and its range is the positive real numbers. This allows to define ln as the inverse of exp and we show some calculation rules for logarithms like $\ln(xy) = \ln x + \ln y$.

Definition (exponential function). Let a be positive. $\exp_a = \exp \circ \mathrm{f}_{\ln(a)\cdot\_+0}$.

⋮

Definition (power function). $\mathrm{pow}_a = ((\exp \circ \mathrm{f}_{a\cdot\_+0}) \circ \ln) \restriction \mathrm{dom}(\ln)$.

⋮

Proposition (equivalence of exponential and power function). Let b be a positive real number. $\mathrm{pow}_a(b) = \exp_b(a)$.

In `100_theorems.ftl.tex` x^n was defined recursively as $x^{n-1} \cdot x$ with $x^0 = 1$ for any natural number n. We show that our exponentiation is an extension of this definition.

We also present some differentiation rules: The derivative of $\ln(x)$ is $1/x$, which we show using the inverse function theorem. The derivative of the exponential function has already been shown above, and the derivative of the power function is proven by demonstrating that $(\exp \circ (\mathrm{f}_{a\cdot\_+0} \circ ext|_{\ln}))$ is a real map extension of pow_a, and taking the derivative thereof. By the open set differentiation extension theorem (mentioned under 'Local Functions' theorem 2.), its derivative is also the derivative of pow_a.

We also introduce (f/g), where g is a real map with positive range, and demonstrate its differentiability.

Theorem (derivative of a fraction). Let f, g be differentiable in a. Then (f/g) is differentiable in a and

$$\partial(f/g)(a) = \frac{(\partial f(a) \cdot g(a)) - (f(a) \cdot \partial g(a))}{(g(a))^2}.$$

4 Proving the Kaldor Facts in the Solow Model

The Solow model is economically justified since it satisfies the Kaldor facts. In our formalization we give formal proofs for all the facts. Let us for example consider the proof of G3:

[timelimit 10]

Proposition (G3). Let Y be an output level and K be a capital stock and L be a labor amount and A be an efficiency level. Let s be a savings rate and f be a production function and δ be a depreciation rate and gA be an efficiency growth rate and gL be a labor growth rate and w be a wage and k be a capital per efficiency unit labor.

$$r(t) = \partial f(\kappa).$$

Proof. Take $\Pi = \Pi_{A,L,f,r,w,t}$.[prover vampire]
Let us show that $\partial\Pi(K(t)) = 0$. $K(t)$ is the maximum of Π (by profit maximizing K). $\partial\Pi(K(t)) = 0$ (by derivative of maximum). Indeed $K(t)$ is a local maximum of Π (by maximum is local maximum). End.
(1) For any real number x $\mathrm{D}\Pi(x) = \partial f\left(\frac{x}{A(t) \cdot L(t)}\right) - r(t)$ (by derivative profit function).
(2) $\frac{K(t)}{A(t) \cdot L(t)} = k(t)$ (by lemma k).
(3) $k(t) = \kappa$ (by lemma kappa).[prover eprover]
$\mathrm{D}\Pi(K(t)). = \partial f\left(\frac{K(t)}{A(t) \cdot L(t)}\right) - r(t)$ (by 1)
$. = \partial f(k(t)) - r(t)$ (by 2)
$. = \partial f(\kappa) - r(t)$ (by 3).
Thus $r(t) = \partial f(\kappa)$. □

The example illustrates some difficulties of the checking process and ways to mitigate them. Experience and ample trial and error is required to make Naproche formalizations go through. Careful wording of premisses and assumptions influences the proof search of the ATP. The sequence of superposition steps in the E theorem prover is determined by certain heuristics which are chosen according to structural and statistical properties of the prover input [14,15]. Let us comment on a few details:

- Because every single statement is handed over to the ATPs, the verification process is very slow. Since it is a very long document, it is split into several chapters. The following table shows the runtime of each section on a mid-range consumer laptop. Running the entire code takes about 9 hours.

Files	Minutes
`100_theorems.ftl.tex`	~ 30
`0preparation.ftl.tex`	~ 5
`1metrics.ftl.tex`	~ 15
`2continuity.ftl.tex`	~ 60
`3differentiation.ftl.tex`	~ 30
`4locality.ftl.tex`	~ 150
`5extrema.ftl.tex`	~ 150
`6inverse.ftl.tex`	~ 90
`7exponential.ftl.tex`	~ 30
`8solow.ftl.tex`	~ 30
$\sum$	~ 560

- ATP proof searches are restricted by wall clock timeouts, which depend significantly on a system's speed and state. Changing the timeout from the standard of 3 seconds to 10, 20, or more seconds can be done by inserting `[timelimit X]` commands. The timeouts in this formalization are chosen such that the proof runs through on a mid-range consumer laptop. Making the code run on a different laptop may require increasing the timeout or, in very stubborn cases, adding additional proof steps. Sometimes, changing the ATP by inserting `[prover vampire]`, for example may prove helpful as well.
- Although ℕaproche formalizations appear natural, the specific formulation of assumptions and claims may be crucial for efficient proof checking. Logically equivalent but different formulations may lead to different proof tasks some of which may even be unsolvable by the ATPs. For the above proof it was necessary to restate the specifications of Y, K, L, A, s, f, δ, gA, gL, w, and k thus making them easier accessible to the prover.
- ℕaproche often encounters difficulties in checking algebraic identities, since the ATP attempts to prove them from basic axioms instead of more efficient term manipulations. For such situations ℕaproche contains a term rewriting mechanism, which is a lexicographically weighted rewriting algorithm as described in Harrison [8] and was implemented by Steffen Frerix [7]. Equation checking by term rewriting is invoked by using '. =' instead of the ordinary equality symbol '='. After the equation, one has to provide all the definitions, lemmata, and axioms necessary to rewrite the left-hand side to the right-hand side. In the above proposition, we add "(by 1)", for example. If a necessary premise is omitted, the reasoner will certainly fail – unlike general purpose ATPs, it does not try to fill gaps on its own. It is also possible to provide no references at all. In that case, the reasoner will try to identify and extract the relevant information from the context and work with that. This will, however, very likely be unsuccessful, especially if the document is

of any significant length. The mechanism transforms lemmata, definitions, and axioms into rewriting rules according to which it transforms the left and right-hand sides of the equation into lexicographic normal forms. When this is done, it compares the left and right-hand side normal forms, and if it finds one normal form on both sides, it has verified the equation. The reasoner will, however, only find normal forms up to some depth. So having intermediary steps is crucial for the successful verification of an equation, as the reasoner can be overwhelmed when too many steps are necessary to get from one side to the other.

Conclusion

We have carried out the first formalization of the Solow growth model using the Naproche proof assistant. Whilst formalizing a central macroeconomic model we have also built a foundational library of real analysis within the Naproche system, including concepts such as continuity, differentiation, the inverse function theorem and the intermediate value theorems.

The resulting formalization is human-readable, integrated into LaTeX, and spans 70 pages of verified mathematics[3]. By translating key economic principles into formal, machine-checkable statements, we contribute to the growing body of formally verified economics and provide a template for future macroeconomic formalizations such as the Ramsey-model, any neoclassical DSGE, and even the latest HANK models (see for example [3]). These models represent the development of macroeconomic theory from the Solow model until today and could be formalized based upon the same concepts although further concepts like integrals and random variables would have to be introduced.

Using the formalized facts from real analysis, one could continue to formalize modifications of the Solow model and other macroeconomic models. The Naproche proof system allows such formalizations to be carried out in a readable and natural mathematical language.

References

1. Acemoglu, D.: Technical Change, Inequality, and the Labor Market. Journal of economic literature **40**(1), 7–72 (2002)
2. Ahmed, A., Hasan, O., Awwad, F., Bastaki, N.: Formalization of Cost and Utility in Microeconomics. Energies **13**(3) (2020). https://doi.org/10.3390/en13030712, https://www.mdpi.com/1996-1073/13/3/712
3. Broer, T., Harbo Hansen, N.J., Krusell, P., Öberg, E.: The New Keynesian Transmission Mechanism: A Heterogeneous-Agent Perspective. The Review of Economic Studies **87**(1), 77–101 (2020)
4. Cramer, M.: The Naproche System: Proof-Checking Mathematical Texts in Controlled Natural Language. Sprache und Datenverarbeitung. International Journal for Language Data Processing **2014**(1-2) (May 2016)

[3] Both the source files and the compiled PDF are available for download from the Naproche homepage: https://naproche.github.io/formalizations.html

5. Cramer, M., Koepke, P., Kühlwein, D., Schröder, B.: The Naproche System. Calculemus, Emerging Trend Paper (2009)
6. De Lon, A., Koepke, P., Lorenzen, A., Marti, A., Schütz, M., Wenzel, M.: The Isabelle/Naproche Natural Language Proof Assistant. In: Platzer, A., Sutcliffe, G. (eds.) Automated Deduction – CADE 28. pp. 614–624. Springer International Publishing, Cham (2021). https://doi.org/https://doi.org/10.1007/978-3-030-79876-5_36
7. Frerix, S.: Text-Oriented Formalization Methods. Master's thesis, University of Bonn (2018)
8. Harrison, J.: Handbook of Practical Logic and Automated Reasoning. Cambridge University Press, Cambridge, 1 edn. (2009)
9. Kaldor, N.: Capital Accumulation and Economic Growth. In: The Theory of Capital, pp. 177–222. International Economic Association Series, Palgrave Macmillan UK, London (1961)
10. Kaliszyk, C., Parsert, J.: Formal Microeconomic Foundations and the First Welfare Theorem. In: Proceedings of the 7th ACM SIGPLAN International Conference on Certified Programs and Proofs. p. 91–101. CPP 2018, Association for Computing Machinery, New York, NY, USA (2018). https://doi.org/10.1145/3167100, https://doi.org/10.1145/3167100
11. Koepke, P., Marcol, M., Schäfer, P.: Formalizing Sets, Numbers, and Some "Wiedijk Theorems" in Naproche (2023), https://europroofnet.github.io/cambridge-2023
12. Lange, C., Rowat, C., Kerber, M.: The ForMaRE Project – Formal Mathematical Reasoning in Economics. In: Carette, J., Aspinall, D., Lange, C., Sojka, P., Windsteiger, W. (eds.) Intelligent Computer Mathematics. pp. 330–334. Springer Berlin Heidelberg, Berlin, Heidelberg (2013)
13. Romer, P.M.: Endogenous Technological Change. Journal of Political Economy **98**(5, Part 2), S71–S102 (1990)
14. Schulz, S.: E – A Brainiac Theorem Prover. Ai Communications **15**(2-3), 111–126 (2002)
15. Schulz, S., Cruanes, S., Vukmirović, P.: Faster, Higher, Stronger: E 2.3. In: International Conference on Automated Deduction. pp. 495–507. Springer (2019)
16. Solow, R.M.: A Contribution to the Theory of Economic Growth. The Quarterly Journal of Economics **70**(1), 65–94 (1956)
17. Wiedijk, F.: Formalizing Arrow's Theorem. Sādhanā **34**(1), 193–220 (2009). https://doi.org/10.1007/s12046-009-0005-1, https://doi.org/10.1007/s12046-009-0005-1

Formalizing MLTL Formula Progression in Isabelle/HOL

Katherine Kosaian[1](✉), Zili Wang[2], Elizabeth Sloan[2], and Kristin Yvonne Rozier[2]

[1] University of Iowa, Iowa City, IA 52242 USA
katherine-kosaian@uiowa.edu
[2] Iowa State University, Ames, IA 50011 USA
{ziliw1,elisloan,kyrozier}@iastate.edu

Abstract. *Mission-time Linear Temporal Logic (MLTL)* is rapidly increasing in popularity as a specification logic, e.g., for runtime verification and model checking, driving a need for a trustworthy tool base. We formalize the syntax and semantics of MLTL and a library of key properties. We then formalize the algorithm and correctness theorems for MLTL *formula progression*, an algorithm to help decide the satisfiability of an MLTL formula along a given trace, identifying and fixing several errors and gaps in the source material. As a main motivation for our work is *tool validation*, we ensure the executability of our algorithms.

Keywords: Mission-time Linear Temporal Logic (MLTL) · Formula progression · Theorem proving · Modal logic · Runtime verification

1 Introduction

Mission-time Linear Temporal Logic (MLTL) [53,33] adds discrete, closed-interval, natural number bounds to the temporal operators of linear temporal logic (LTL), providing a finite-trace specification logic that captures many common requirements of, e.g., embedded systems. MLTL is a widely-used subset of Signal Temporal Logic (STL) [38] and Metric Temporal Logic (MTL) [2] (see [44]).

Labeled timelines are common representations of requirements for operational concepts of unmanned aircraft systems (UAS) and other aerospace systems. Due to its intuitive expressiveness of finite timeline properties, MLTL has seen wide adoption as a specification logic in this context. After an extensive survey of verification tools and their associated specification languages, NASA's Lunar Gateway Vehicle System Manager (VSM) team selected MLTL to formalize their English Assume-Guarantee Contract requirements [13,14,15]. The VSM team is also running R2U2 [24], a runtime verification engine that natively reasons over MLTL for on-board operational verification and on-ground timeline verification. NASA previously used MLTL to specify fault disambiguation protocols embedded in the knee of Robonaut2 on the International Space Station [27], for runtime requirements of NASA's S1000 octocopter [35] in the Autonomy Operating System

V. de Paiva and P. Koepke (Eds.): CICM 2025, LNAI 16136, pp. 371–391, 2026.
https://doi.org/10.1007/978-3-032-07021-0_21

(AOS) for UAS [34], and to specify system health management properties of the Swift UAS [64,53,18,58] and the DragonEye UAS [64,63]. MLTL was the specification logic of choice for a UAS Traffic Management (UTM) system [9], an open-source UAS [25], and a high-altitude balloon [36]. JAXA used MLTL for specification of a resource-limited autonomous satellite mission [43]. Other space systems with MLTL specifications include a CubeSat communications system [37], a sounding rocket [23], the CySat-I satellite's autonomous fault recovery system [6], and a case study on small satellites and landers [57].

Many formal methods tools natively analyze MLTL specifications. MLTL was first named as the input logic to the Realizable Responsive Unobtrusive Unit (R2U2) [53,61,24]. The Formal Requirements Elicitation Tool (FRET) provides a GUI with color-coded segments of structured natural language to help system designers write better MLTL specifications [20,40,5]. The WEST tool [16] provides a GUI to interactively validate MLTL specifications via regular expressions and sets of satisfying and falsifying traces. The model checker NUXMV accepts a subset of MLTL for use in symbolic model checking, where the G and F operators of an `LTLSPEC` can have integer bounds [28].[1] Ogma is a command-line tool to produce monitoring applications from MLTL formulas [49,47,48]. As MLTL represents a common core of logics used for runtime monitoring, it was featured in the 2018 Runtime Verification Benchmark Competition [60,1]. We closely examine MLTL *formula progression* [32], an algorithm submitted to generate MLTL benchmarks in that competition; later, the Formula PROGression Generator tool (FPROGG) used formula progression to create an (unverified) automated MLTL benchmark generation tool [55]. Intuitively, formula progression aims to help decide the satisfiability of an input MLTL formula φ along an input trace π.

Despite the rapid emergence of tools that analyze MLTL specifications, there is a shortage of provably correct formal foundations from which to validate and verify those tools and their algorithms. We have SAT solvers for MLTL that work through translations to other logics, which rely on pencil-and-paper proofs and experimental validation [33]. The MLTL MAX-SAT algorithm and implementation also relies on hand-proofs and experimental demonstrations of consistency [22]. In contrast, LTL has benefited from multiple mechanized formalizations, including a library [67] and a sizable collection of verified results [65,68,66,62,17] in Isabelle/HOL. Formula progression has even been verified for the 3-valued variant LTL3 [4]. LTL is also formalized in Coq [12] and in PVS, where a library has been developed to facilitate modeling and verification for systems using LTL [39,51]. Similarly, MTL is formalized in PVS; this was used to verify a translation from a structured natural language to MTL [11,69].[2] A Coq formalization of MTL was used to generate OCaml code implementing a past-time MTL monitoring engine [10]. VeriMon [8], a monitoring tool for metric first-order temporal logic (MFOTL), was developed and formally verified in Isabelle/HOL; Isabelle's code export generates OCaml code for the tool. Similarly, Vydra [52], a monitoring tool for metric dynamic logic (MDL), is formalized in Isabelle/HOL. Notably,

[1] Note that bounds cannot be placed on the Until or Release operators of NUXMV.

[2] The library contains some relevant notions for MLTL, but is not specialized to MLTL.

these logics and their associated algorithms can be quite intricate. For example, in the case of Metric Interval Temporal Logic (MITL), recent work [54] found that the original semantics was incorrectly specified; the authors correct some of the original algorithms and use formalization in PVS for extra trustworthiness.

The time has come to formalize MLTL. We formalize MLTL syntax and semantics in the theorem prover Isabelle/HOL [41,45] and develop a formal library of key MLTL properties, including dualities, an NNF transformation, and custom induction rules in Sect. 2. We verify formula progression [32] in Sect. 3, fixing errors in the original proofs; our formalization is *executable* and can be exported to code in SML, OCaml, Haskell, or Scala. Sect. 4 details formalization challenges and insights. Our code is ≈ 3300 lines and is available on Isabelle/HOL's Archive of Formal Proofs [29,30]. Sect. 5 concludes with a high-level discussion of impact and future directions.

2 Encoding MLTL in Isabelle/HOL

We overview MLTL syntax and semantics before turning to our formalization. Let $\mathtt{AP}$ be a finite set of atomic propositions. The grammar for MLTL [33,53] is:

$$\varphi, \psi ::= \text{True} \mid \text{False} \mid p \mid \neg\varphi \mid \varphi \wedge \psi \mid \varphi \vee \psi$$
$$\mid \mathtt{F}_{[a,b]}\varphi \mid \mathtt{G}_{[a,b]}\varphi \mid \varphi \mathtt{U}_{[a,b]}\psi \mid \varphi \mathtt{R}_{[a,b]}\psi,$$

where $p \in \mathtt{AP}$, and $a, b \in \mathbb{N}$ with $0 \leq a \leq b$.

The temporal operators $\mathtt{F}, \mathtt{G}, \mathtt{U}, \mathtt{R}$ are commonly referred to as "Future," (see, e.g., [50,70,59]) "Globally," "Until," and "Release," respectively.[3] We use the above grammar to match the algorithms we wanted to formalize, particularly formula progression [33] and MLTL-to-regular expressions [16]. If a development wants additional operators (such as a Next operator or a variant of Until), they can be defined with abbreviations, or by creating an expanded version of our syntax.

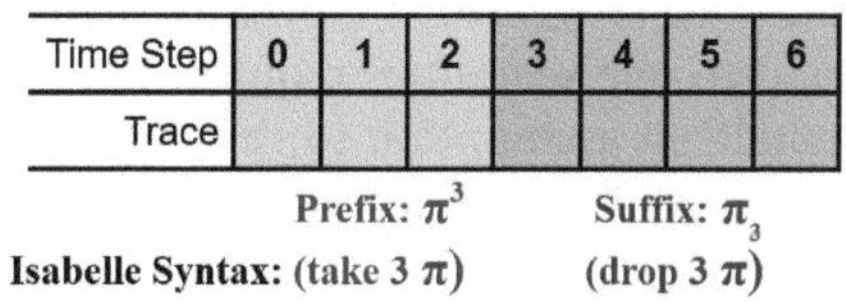

Fig. 1. Prefix and suffix notation for traces.

A *trace* π is a finite sequence of sets of atomic propositions $\pi[0], \ldots, \pi[n]$ where $\pi[i] \subseteq \mathtt{AP}$ for all $i \in \{0, \ldots, n\}$. Each $\pi[i]$ is called a *state* of the trace π and represents the set of atomic propositions that are true at time i. The length of π is denoted by $|\pi|$. We also use the following notation [33,32]: π^k denotes the prefix of trace π from 0 to $k-1$, i.e., $\pi^k = \pi[0], \pi[1], \ldots, \pi[k-1]$, and π_k is the suffix of π from k onwards, i.e., $\pi_k = \pi[k], \pi[i+1], \ldots, \pi[n]$. For easy reference, we visually summarize this notation in Fig. 1.

Trace π satisfies formula φ iff $\pi \models \varphi$, where $\models$ is defined inductively [16]:

[3] The literature often uses ◇ and □ for Future and Globally. We use $\mathtt{F}$ and $\mathtt{G}$ to match the other temporal operators. Future is also called "Finally" or "Eventually" [33,16].

$\pi \models p$ iff $p \in \pi[0]$

$\pi \models \neg\varphi$ iff $\pi \not\models \varphi$

$\pi \models \varphi \wedge \psi$ iff $\pi \models \varphi$ and $\pi \models \psi$

$\pi \models \varphi \vee \psi$ iff $\pi \models \varphi$ or $\pi \models \psi$

$\pi \models \mathtt{F}_{[a,b]}\ \varphi$ iff $|\pi| > a$ and $\exists i \in [a,b].\pi_i \models \varphi$

$\pi \models \mathtt{G}_{[a,b]}\ \varphi$ iff $|\pi| \leq a$ or $\forall i \in [a,b]\ \pi_i \models \varphi$

$\pi \models \varphi\ \mathtt{U}_{[a,b]}\ \psi$ iff $|\pi| > a$ and $\exists i \in [a,b].\pi_i \models \psi$ and $\forall j \in [a, i-1]\ \pi_j \models \varphi$

$\pi \models \varphi\ \mathtt{R}_{[a,b]}\ \psi$ iff $|\pi| \leq a$ or $(\forall i \in [a,b]\ \pi_i \models \psi)$
or $(\exists j \in [a,b].\pi_j \models \varphi$ and $\forall k \in [a,j]\ \pi_k \models \psi)$

Sect. 2.1 presents our formal syntax, Sect. 2.2 overviews our formalization of the semantics, and Sect. 2.3, Sect. 2.4 present verified basic properties and useful functions, respectively. Our development imports only the standard HOL library, but we drew some inspiration from the Isabelle/HOL LTL formalization [67].

2.1 Syntax

In Isabelle/HOL, we formalize the grammar for MLTL formulas in the `mltl` datatype, with syntactic sugar for pretty printing. The atomic formulas are $\mathtt{True}_m$, $\mathtt{False}_m$, and atomic propositions $\mathtt{Prop}_m$ which take a variable with arbitrary type `'a` as an argument (the arbitrary type provides flexibility). The logical connectives are $\mathtt{Not}_m$ ($\neg$), $\mathtt{And}_m$ ($\wedge$), and $\mathtt{Or}_m$ ($\vee$). Lastly, the temporal operators are $\mathtt{F}_m$ (Future), $\mathtt{G}_m$ (Globally), $\mathtt{U}_m$ (Until), and $\mathtt{R}_m$ (Release), each taking an interval $[a, b]$ of two naturals for the associated time bounds. For the syntactic sugar, we mirror the operator precedence in the prior LTL formalization [67].

Notably, our syntax does not include the standard well-definedness assumption on intervals for temporal operators. For instance, our *syntax* allows the formula "$\mathtt{F}_m\ [5,3]\ \mathtt{True}_m$", even though this is not a well-defined formula in MLTL. Instead, our *semantics* requires that these intervals have well-defined bounds; we include an assumption to this effect in our correctness theorems when necessary.

2.2 Semantics

As MLTL traces are finite, we encode them as lists of sets of variables of arbitrary type (in Isabelle/HOL, this is type `'a set list`). For example, given two Boolean variables p and q, the list $[\{p\}, \{p, q\}]$ represents a trace of length two where p is true and q is false at time 0 and both p and q are true at time 1.

We formalize MLTL semantics in `semantics_mltl`, which takes a trace π and an MLTL formula φ and returns true if $\pi \models \varphi$ and false otherwise. Our formal definition mirrors the mathematical one, while making certain implicit assumptions explicit. For example, for atomic propositions, we explicitly ensure that if $\pi \models \mathtt{Prop}_m\ \mathtt{p}$ holds, then π is nonempty (for well-definedness). Additionally, for the temporal operators, we explicitly ensure that the associated time bounds are well-defined (i.e, $\mathtt{a} \leq \mathtt{b}$). We give the formal semantics for a representative subset of operators ($\mathtt{Prop}_m$, $\mathtt{And}_m$, and $\mathtt{U}_m$); the full semantics can be found in our code.

```
fun semantics_mltl::"['a set list, 'a mltl] ⇒ bool" where
"π ⊨m Propm (q) = (π ≠ [] ∧ q ∈ (π ! 0))"
| "π ⊨m φ Andm ψ = (π ⊨m φ ∧ π ⊨m ψ)"
| "π ⊨m (φ Um [a, b] ψ) =  (a ≤ b ∧ length π > a ∧
      (∃i::nat. (i ≥ a ∧ i ≤ b) ∧ ((drop i π) ⊨m ψ
        ∧ (∀j. j ≥ a ∧ j<i ⟶ (drop j π) ⊨m φ))))"
```

Here, for *Prop*$_m$, we check that the atomic proposition *q* is in the set of atomic propositions at the initial timestep (in Isabelle/HOL, this is π ! 0, as ! is the operator to access list elements). For *And_mltl*, we check that trace π satisfies both subformulas φ, ψ. For U_m, we check a≤b for well-definedness, and then we check that there exists an *i* between a and b where ψ is satisfied, (i.e. *drop i* π $\models \psi$), and where φ is satisfied at all timesteps up to *i* (i.e., *drop j* $\pi \models \varphi$ for all *j* between a and *i-1*).

Formalizing MLTL semantics helps to clarify the differences between MLTL and closely-related logics, and we envision formalizing bridges between MLTL and related logics as an important topic for future work. Perhaps the most closely-related is MTL-over-naturals [44]. Unlike MTL-over-naturals, MLTL traces are finite and MLTL intervals are finite, closed, and unitless (generic). The semantics of Until is also different for MTL-over-naturals.[4] Note that other variants of MTL, such as Metric Interval Temporal Logic (MITL) [3] treat the temporal operator intervals as continuous (rather than discrete) intervals that may be open-ended over real numbers (not integers), and even prohibit singular time intervals of the form $[a, a]$. Bounded LTL (BLTL) [26] and LTL$_f$ [19] both reason over finite traces like MLTL, but share syntax with LTL; they have (unspecified) finite bounds on the time domain rather than intervals on each temporal operator and keep the X operator (LTL$_f$ adds a weak next operator as well).

2.3 Properties

To increase the usability of our formal semantics, we verify various essential properties. We aim to establish a reusable formalized library of MLTL properties.

In Isabelle/HOL, we formally define the *semantic equivalence* of MLTL formulas in `semantic_equiv`, which tests if φ and ψ are equivalent by checking if their semantics match on all traces π:

```
definition semantic_equiv::"'a mltl⇒'a mltl⇒bool" ("_ ≡m _" [80,80]80)
  where "semantic_equiv φ ψ = (∀π. (π ⊨m φ) = (π ⊨m ψ))"
```

We then consider properties involving relationships between operators. While we define each core temporal operator (F, G, U, R) in terms of its *mathematical* definition, a common alternative approach (see, e.g., [33,59,22]) is to formally define all MLTL operators via a functionally complete set, like $\{\neg, \wedge, \mathtt{U}\}$ [33], and then derive the standard mathematical definitions. To establish that our encoding matches this alternative approach, we verify key equivalences between

[4] In MTL-over-naturals, $\pi \models \varphi\ \mathtt{U}_{[a,b]}\psi$ iff $|\pi| > a$ and $\exists i \in [a,\ b], i < |\pi|$ s.t. $\pi[i] \models \psi$ and **for all** $j < i$ (including $j < a$), $\pi[j] \models \varphi$.

operators. Many of these prove easily with Isabelle/HOL's built-in automation tactics. For example, we establish that Future can be rewritten with Until in the lemma *future_as_until* by showing that $\texttt{F}_{[a,b]}\varphi$ is equivalent to True $\texttt{U}_{[a,b]}\varphi$, and we establish the duality of Future and Globally (i.e., that $\texttt{G}_{[a,b]}\varphi$ is equivalent to $\neg\texttt{F}_{[a,b]}\neg\varphi$) in *globally_future_dual*. In Isabelle/HOL, we have:

```
lemma future_as_until: assumes "a ≤ b"
  shows "F_m [a,b] φ ≡_m True_m U_m [a,b] φ"

lemma globally_future_dual: assumes "a ≤ b"
  shows "G_m [a,b] φ ≡_m Not_m (F_m [a,b] (Not_m φ))"
```

We also prove the duality of U and R, i.e., that $\varphi\ \texttt{R}_{[a,b]}\psi$ is equivalent to $\neg(\neg\varphi\ \texttt{U}_{[a,b]}\neg\psi)$, in the following lemma:

```
lemma release_until_dual:   assumes "a≤b"
  shows "φ R_m [a,b] ψ ≡_m Not_m ((Not_m φ) U_m [a,b] (Not_m ψ))"
```

This proof is not immediately resolved by Isabelle's automation; we follow a proof sketch from the literature [16] which splits the biconditional into two implications. In each direction, the proof considers three cases: ① when the length of the trace is less than a, ② when ψ is satisfied for all timesteps in the interval $[a, b]$, and ③ when some timestep in $[a, b]$ does not satisfy ψ. In the forward direction of ③, we found an error in the source material [16], which incorrectly reduces the subgoal of showing that $\forall s \in [a, b].(\pi_s \models \psi \vee (\exists t \in [a, s-1].\ \pi_t \models \varphi))$ to showing that $\forall s \in [a, b].(\exists t \in [a, s-1].\ \pi_t \models \varphi)$. Fortunately, Sledgehammer [46] directly proves the desired subgoal.

These duality lemmas, with DeMorgan's laws for $\wedge$ and $\vee$, are sufficient to establish that any well-defined MLTL formula can be rewritten using only $\{\neg, \wedge, \texttt{U}\}$, which is defined in the literature [33] as the Backus Naur Form (BNF) for MLTL. To make use of BNF, we verify a custom induction rule, *bnf_induct*; when this rule applies, it considerably reduces the number of cases compared to the default structural induction rule for MLTL (which cases on each operator):

```
lemma bnf_induct[case_names WellDef PProp True False Prop Not And Until]:
  assumes WellDef: "intervals_welldef η"
  and PProp: "(⋀ η φ. (η ≡_m φ ⟶ 𝒫 η = 𝒫 φ))" and True: "𝒫 True_m"
  and False: "𝒫 False_m" and Prop: "⋀ p. 𝒫 (Prop_m (p))"
  and Not: "⋀ η φ. ⟦η = Not_m φ; 𝒫 φ⟧ ⟹ 𝒫 η"
  and And: "⋀η φ ψ.  ⟦η = φ And_m ψ; 𝒫 φ; 𝒫 ψ⟧ ⟹ 𝒫 η"
  and Until:"⋀η φ ψ a b. ⟦η = φ U_m [a,b] ψ; 𝒫 φ; 𝒫 ψ⟧ ⟹ 𝒫 η"
  shows "𝒫 η"
```

To use *bnf_induct* to prove a property $\mathcal{P}$ of an MLTL formula η, we must prove not only the structural induction cases (covering formulas of the shape True_m, False_m, Prop_m, $\mathit{Not}_m\ \varphi$, $\varphi\ \mathit{And}_m\ \psi$, and $\varphi\ \mathit{U}_m\,[a,b]\ \psi$ in *True*, *False*, *Prop*, *Not*, *And*, and *Until*, respectively) but also two additional properties. First, we must show that $\mathcal{P}$ is invariant on semantically equivalent formulas: i.e., for semantically equivalent η and φ, $\mathcal{P}$ holds on η if and only if $\mathcal{P}$ holds on φ (as in *bnf_induct*'s assumption *PProp*). Second, if η contains any temporal operators, then their corresponding time intervals should be well-defined; for example, if η is "*True*$_m$ *U*$_m$*[a,b] False*$_m$", then a $\leq$ b. This is stipulated in *WellDef* in **bnf_induct**, where *intervals_welldef* formalizes the well-definedness property.

We prove a number of additional useful basic properties, like distributivity for U and R over $\wedge$ and $\vee$; Isabelle's automation makes most of these easy.

2.4 Useful Functions and Custom Induction Rules

We augment our MLTL library with some useful functions on MLTL formulas. First, *convert_nnf* uses the operator duality properties to convert an MLTL formula to its negation normal form (NNF), where negations are only in front of atomic propositions. We prove that *convert_nnf* preserves the semantics of the input formula, and that it is idempotent:

```
lemma convert_nnf_preserves_semantics:
  assumes "intervals_welldef φ" shows "φ ≡m (convert_nnf φ)"

lemma convert_nnf_convert_nnf:
  shows "convert_nnf (convert_nnf φ) = convert_nnf φ"
```

The proofs of these two lemmas work by induction on the *depth* of the formula; accordingly, we formalize **depth_mltl**, a depth function for MLTL formulas. We also define a function, *nnf_subformulas*, to compute the set of subformulas of an MLTL formula, and prove (by induction on formula depth) that any subformula of a formula in NNF is itself in NNF:

```
lemma nnf_subformulas:
  assumes "φ = convert_nnf init_φ" and "ψ ∈ subformulas φ"
  shows "∃ init_ψ. ψ = convert_nnf init_ψ"
```

Using these functions and properties, we establish the following custom induction rule, *nnf_induct*, as another useful tool for proving properties about MLTL formulas. In contrast to **bnf_induct**, which reduces the number of inductive cases, *nnf_induct* limits the Not case to negations of atomic propositions (in case *Not_Prop*). Happily, *nnf_induct* imposes no requirements on the desired property $\mathcal{P}$ (as opposed to **bnf_induct**, which requires $\mathcal{P}$ to be invariant on semantically equivalent formulas). However, *nnf_induct* does require that the input formula η is in NNF (in assumption *nnf*). Fortunately, as MLTL formulas can be efficiently converted to NNF [16], this is easily satisfied.

```
lemma nnf_induct[case_names nnf True False Prop And Or Final
                 Global Until Release NotProp]:
  assumes nnf: "∃φ. η = convert_nnf φ" and True: "P Truem"
  and False: "P Falsem" and Prop: "⋀ p. P (Propm (p))"
  and And: "⋀η φ ψ. ⟦η = φ Andm ψ; P φ; P ψ⟧ ⟹ P η"
  and Or: "⋀η φ ψ. ⟦η = φ Orm ψ;P φ; P ψ⟧ ⟹ P η"
  and Final: "⋀η φ  a b. ⟦η = Fm[a,b] φ; P φ⟧ ⟹ P η"
  and Global: "⋀η φ  a b. ⟦η = Gm[a,b] φ; P φ⟧ ⟹ P η"
```

```
and Until: "⋀η φ ψ a b. ⟦η = φ U_m [a,b] ψ; P φ; P ψ⟧ ⟹ P η"
and Release: "⋀η φ ψ a b. ⟦η = φ R_m [a,b] ψ; P φ; P ψ⟧ ⟹ P η"
and Not_Prop: "⋀ η p. η = Not_m (Prop_m (p)) ⟹ P η"
shows "P η"
```

Finally, we formalize the *computation length* (complen) of an MLTL formula. This is recursively defined as follows, for $p \in \mathtt{AP}$ and MLTL formulas φ, ψ [16]:

$$\mathtt{complen}(p) = \mathtt{complen}(\neg p) = 1,$$
$$\mathtt{complen}(\varphi \wedge \psi) = \mathtt{complen}(\varphi \vee \psi) = \max(\mathtt{complen}(\varphi), \mathtt{complen}(\psi)),$$
$$\mathtt{complen}(\mathtt{G}_{[a,b]}\varphi) = \mathtt{complen}(\mathtt{F}_{[a,b]}\varphi) = b + \mathtt{complen}(\varphi),$$
$$\mathtt{complen}(\varphi\ \mathtt{U}_{[a,b]}\ \psi) = \mathtt{complen}(\varphi\ \mathtt{R}_{[a,b]}\ \psi) = b + \max(\mathtt{complen}(\varphi) - 1, \mathtt{complen}(\psi))$$

We formalize this in *complen_mltl*, which maps an MLTL formula to a natural number. The formal definition mirrors the mathematical definition, modulo syntax changes, except that we define the computation length of *True_mltl* and *False_mltl* (to be 1); these definitions were missing in the literature [16]. We present a few representative cases; the full definition is in our code.

```
fun complen_mltl::"'a mltl ⇒ nat" where "complen_mltl Prop_m (p) = 1"
|"complen_mltl (φ And_m ψ)=max (complen_mltl φ) (complen_mltl ψ)"
|"complen_mltl (φ U_m [a,b] ψ)=b+max (complen_mltl φ-1) (complen_mltl ψ)"
```

Computation length is a slightly optimized version of an earlier and closely-related[5] notion of the *worst-case propagation delay (wpd)* of a formula. Wpd was introduced in the context of runtime verification [27, Definition 5] and was designed to give the maximum number of timesteps an observer needs to *wait from the current timestep* to decide the satisfaction of an MLTL formula so that the decision will not change with further information. For example, if we try to evaluate the satisfaction of $\mathtt{F}_{[0,2]}p$ on a trace of length 2, then it is possible that further information could change the verdict; e.g., $\mathtt{F}_{[0,2]}p$ is false on $[\{\},\{\}]$ but true on $[\{\},\{\},\{p\}]$. However, after $\mathtt{complen}(\mathtt{F}_{[0,2]}p) = 3$ timesteps, the value of p in subsequent timesteps will not change whether the trace satisfies $\mathtt{F}_{[0,2]}p$. In particular, the R2U2 tool [27], which checks the satisfaction of MLTL formulas on traces, does not return an answer until it is certain that the answer will not change with further information. In this context, the wpd of the formula captures the duration of the worst possible delay of an answer from the current time.

Interestingly, though it is not mentioned in the source material [32], computation length plays a key role in the formal proofs of the formula progression algorithm. We now turn to our formalization of formula progression; computation length's role therein will be discussed in Sect. 3.4.

[5] Computation length and wpd are very similar, but computation length includes a -1 term in the Until and Release cases which is not present in wpd (this is a small optimization). The other difference is that the computation length of atomic propositions is defined to be 1 but the wpd of atomic propositions is 0; this difference is purely cosmetic, as wpd captures the delay *from the current timestep* (as is standard in runtime verification) while computation length captures the total delay.

3 Formula Progression

Formula progression represents a straightforward and generally easy-to-implement algorithm to evaluate if a temporal trace satisfies a given formula. It is used in many contexts (e.g. satisfiability solving, validation, runtime verification, and benchmark generation). It dates back to the 1990's [7] and has been developed for various temporal logics including MTL [31], LTL_f [42], and MLTL [32].

We formalize MLTL formula progression and its associated correctness theorems [32]. While we mostly follow the original paper [32] that developed the algorithm, we found and fixed several errors in the top-level correctness results. In particular, the source material states three key theorems (and a corollary); Fig. 2 overviews our changes to these top-level results. We now discuss the formula progression algorithm and each main result, with an emphasis on our modifications.

Statement	Additions / Modifications	Lines (Source)	LOC (Isabelle)
Theorem 1: *decomposition* $\mathbf{prog}(\varphi, \pi) = \mathbf{prog}(\mathbf{prog}(\varphi, \pi^k), \pi_k)$	*Filled in* previously elided proof of the following: $\text{prog}(\text{prog}(\varphi, \pi^k), \pi[k]) = \text{prog}(\phi, \pi^{k+1})$	6	~135
Theorem 2: *satisfiability preserving* $\pi \models \varphi \leftrightarrow \pi_k \models \mathbf{prog}(\varphi, \pi^k)$	*Modified* assumption on k from: $1 \leq k \leq \|\pi\|$ to $1 \leq k < \|\pi\|$	5	~750
Theorem 3: *correctness* $\pi \models \varphi \leftrightarrow (\mathbf{prog}(\varphi, \pi) \equiv \mathbf{True})$	*Added* key assumption on computation length: $\text{complen}(\varphi) \leq \|\pi\|$	6	~1000
Corollary 1: *trace extension* $\pi \models \varphi \rightarrow \pi @ \zeta \models \varphi$	*Added* key assumption on computation length: $\text{complen}(\varphi) \leq \|\pi\|$	3	~15

Fig. 2. We summarize our modifications to the top-level formula progression results, comparing the number of lines in the proof sketches [32] with the LOC in Isabelle/HOL. Our formal proof of Theorem 3 required identifying and formalizing properties of computation length (not present in the source material), and we count these in the LOC.

3.1 Encoding the Formula Progression Algorithm

Formula progression takes an MLTL formula and steps through a trace; at each timestep, the input formula is partially evaluated and transformed into a simplified formula which, under some unrestrictive conditions, is logically equivalent.

As MLTL is an inherently bounded logic, it is well-suited for formula progression (one can easily predetermine how many timesteps are needed to transform a formula into True or False), and the definitions for MLTL formula progression [32, Definition 1] are straightforward to formalize. For a trace π of length greater than 1, $\text{prog}(\varphi, \pi)$ is defined as $\text{prog}(\text{prog}(\varphi, \pi[0]), \pi_1)$. Formally:

```
fun formula_progression:: "'a mltl ⇒ 'a set list ⇒ 'a mltl"
```

```
where "formula_progression φ π = (if length π = 0 then φ
else if length π = 1 then (formula_progression_len1 φ (π!0))
else formula_progression (formula_progression_len1 φ (π!0)) (drop 1 π))"
```

This function takes an MLTL formula φ and a trace π and cases on $|\pi|$. If π is empty, it returns φ; if π has length 1, it calls *formula_progression_len1*, a helper function which handles formula progression on traces of length 1. When π has length longer than 1, it evaluates $\text{prog}(\varphi, \pi[0])$ as *formula_progression_len1 φ (π!0)* and passes the result to *formula_progression* on *drop 1 π* (which is π_1).

The helper function *formula_progression_len1* cases on the structure of the input formula, closely following the associated mathematical definitions [32, Definition 1]. As a representative example, we show one of the most complicated cases, for formulas of shape $\varphi\ U_{[a,b]}\ \psi$; the full function is in our code. Here,

$$\texttt{prog}(\varphi\ U_{[a,b]}\ \psi, \pi) = \begin{cases} \varphi\ U_{[a-1,b-1]}\ \psi & \text{if } 0 < a \leq b \\ \texttt{prog}(\psi, \pi)\ \vee (\texttt{prog}(\varphi, \pi)\ \wedge \varphi\ U_{[0,b-1]}\ \psi) & \text{if } 0 = a < b \\ \texttt{prog}(\psi, \pi) & \text{if } 0 = a = b. \end{cases}$$

This is encoded in Isabelle/HOL as follows:

```
formula_progression_len1 (φ U_m [a,b] ψ) tr_entry =
(if (0<a ∧ a≤b) then (φ U_m [(a-1), (b-1)] ψ) else (if (0=a ∧ a<b)
  then ((formula_progression_len1 ψ tr_entry) Or_m
    ((formula_progression_len1 φ tr_entry) And_m (φ U_m [0, (b-1)] ψ)))
  else (formula_progression_len1 ψ tr_entry)))"
```

As our functions are executable, we can use the **value** command (invoking Isabelle's code generator [21]) to evaluate formula progression. For example, running formula progression on the formula $\texttt{G}_{[0,2]}p$ and the trace $[\{p\}, \{p\}, \{\}]$ yields $\neg((\neg\text{True}) \vee ((\neg\text{True}) \vee (\neg\text{False})))$, which is logically equivalent to False. Note that the algorithm *is not guaranteed* to produce an output in simplest form.

3.2 Verifying Theorem 1: Decomposition

The first key theorem for formula progression informally states that performing formula progression along a trace can be split into first performing formula progression on the prefix, and then on the suffix, of the trace. Mathematically, this is $\texttt{prog}(\varphi, \pi) = \texttt{prog}(\texttt{prog}(\varphi, \pi^k), \pi_k)$ for $1 \leq k \leq$ `length` π. In Isabelle/HOL, we prove the following, where "*take k π*" is π^k and "*drop k π*" is π_k (see Fig. 1).

```
theorem formula_progression_decomposition:
assumes "k ≥ 1" and "k ≤ length π"
shows "formula_progression (formula_progression φ (take k π)) (drop k π)
      = formula_progression φ π"
```

Our formal proof follows the sketch in the original paper [32] relatively closely. We found it effective to split out the following identity into a separate helper lemma: $\text{prog}(\text{prog}(\varphi, \pi^k), \pi[k]) = \text{prog}(\varphi, \pi^{k+1})$. Although the source states that this property holds by definition, our proof required induction on k. This highlights the role of formalization, which necessitates making all handwaving rigorous. Even so, Theorem 1 was the easiest of the three top-level theorems to prove; requiring just ~135 LOC (compared to 6 lines of proof in the source material).

3.3 Verifying Theorem 2: Satisfiability Preservation

The second key theorem states that (in most cases) π satisfies φ iff the suffix of π satisfies the formula progression of φ on the prefix of π. Mathematically, this is $\pi \models \varphi$ iff $\pi_k \models \text{prog}(\varphi, \pi^k)$; the source material [32] stated this theorem for $1 \leq k \leq \text{length } \pi$, but our formal statement is for $1 \leq k < \text{length } \pi$:

```
theorem satisfiability_preservation:
assumes "k ≥ 1" and "k < length π" and "intervals_welldef φ"
shows "drop k π ⊨m (formula_progression φ (take k π)) ⟷ π ⊨m φ"
```

In addition to altering the bound on **k**, we assume (in **intervals_welldef** φ) that all temporal operators have well-defined timebounds (cross-reference Sect. 2.1). This well-definedness assumption is implicitly present in the source material. The altered bound, however, is *mathematically necessary* for the correctness of the result and was overlooked in the source material. We uncovered this when formalizing the base case. The source material inducts on k and claims the base case ($k = 1$) by induction without providing details. The issue here is related to *end-of-trace behavior*. If both $k = 1$ and $|\pi| = 1$, Theorem 2 would claim $\pi \models \varphi \longleftrightarrow [] \models \texttt{prog}(\varphi, \pi)$, and this does not hold in general.

Specifically, consider a formula of the shape $\texttt{G}_{[0,b]}p$ for $b > 0$ with trace $\pi = [\{p\}]$ of length 1. If we allow $k = 1$, then we would want to establish $\pi \models \texttt{G}_{[0,b]}p \longleftrightarrow \pi_1 \models \texttt{prog}(\texttt{G}_{[0,b]}\varphi, \pi^1)$. We have that $\pi_1 = []$ and $\pi^1 = \pi$, so this becomes $\pi \models \texttt{G}_{[0,b]}p \longleftrightarrow [] \models \texttt{prog}(\texttt{G}_{[0,b]}p, \pi)$. Then using the semantics of MLTL on the LHS, $\pi \models \texttt{G}_{[0,b]}p$ reduces to $\forall i \in [0, b].\ \pi_i \models p$, which further reduces to $\forall i \in [0, b].(\pi_i \neq [] \wedge p \in \pi_i[0])$. However, this is *false* because $\pi_1 = []$.

Applying the definition of formula progression to the RHS, we have:

$$\begin{aligned}\texttt{prog}(\texttt{G}_{[0,b]}p, \pi) &= \neg\texttt{prog}(\texttt{F}_{[0,b]}\neg p, \pi) = \neg(\neg\texttt{prog}(p, \pi) \vee \texttt{F}_{[0,b-1]}\neg p) \\ &= \neg(\neg true \vee \texttt{F}_{[0,b-1]}\neg p) = \neg\texttt{F}_{[0,b-1]}\neg p = \texttt{G}_{[0,b-1]}p\end{aligned}$$

Thus, the RHS becomes $[] \models \texttt{G}_{[0,b-1]}p$; using the semantics of MLTL this is $|[]| \leq 0 \vee (\forall i \in [0, b-1].\ []_i \models p)$, which is *true* because the left disjunct is true.

Modifying the statement of Theorem 2 to insist $k < |\pi|$ instead of $k \leq |\pi|$ removes this issue (because, for $k = 1$, the traces π must have length at least 2). Further, and crucially, we are still able to use the modified version of Theorem 2 in the proofs of Theorem 3 and the top-level corollary.

3.4 Verifying Theorem 3 and Corollary 1: Correctness

The third key theorem for formula progression informally states that, for a sufficiently long input trace π, and for a well-defined input formula φ, π models formula φ if and only if the formula progression of φ over π is logically equivalent to True. More precisely, we require (in the first assumption) that all intervals in φ are well-defined, and we require (in the second assumption) that the length of π is at least the *computation length* of the formula (cross-reference Sect. 2.4, [16]). In Isabelle, we have the following theorem, where `semantic_equiv` encodes logical equivalence of two MLTL formulas (cross-reference Sect. 2.4):

```
theorem formula_progression_correctness:
  assumes "intervals_welldef φ" and "length π ≥ complen_mltl φ"
  shows "((formula_progression φ π) ≡m True_mltl) ⟷ π ⊨m φ"
```

Here, the assumption that the length of π is at least the computation length of φ is *mathematically crucial* for the theorem's correctness. Notably, this was missing in the corresponding theorem in the original source [32, Theorem 3]; identifying it is a contribution of our work. Note that this does not affect the practicality of formula progression; in practice, traces are typically long streams of data, so it is not too restrictive to assume that a trace is sufficiently long.

We identified this assumption when attempting to prove the base case of Theorem 3. The source material states that this is by structural induction and omits all mathematical details. When initially attempting to formalize the base case *without this critical assumption*, we quickly ran into issues in the `Or_mltl` case. We were trying to prove that $(\pi \models \varphi \vee \psi) \longleftrightarrow (\text{prog}(\varphi \vee \psi, \pi) \equiv \text{True})$ for a trace π of length 1, given that $(\pi \models \varphi) \longleftrightarrow (\text{prog}(\varphi, \pi) \equiv \text{True})$ and $(\pi \models \psi) \longleftrightarrow (\text{prog}(\psi, \pi) \equiv \text{True})$. Because $\text{prog}(\varphi \vee \psi, \pi)$ is defined as $\text{prog}(\varphi, \pi) \vee \text{prog}(\psi, \pi)$ when π has length 1, and using that $\pi \models \varphi \vee \psi \longleftrightarrow (\pi \models \varphi \vee \pi \models \psi)$, our goal becomes $(\pi \models \varphi \vee \pi \models \psi) \longleftrightarrow ((\text{prog}(\varphi, \pi) \vee \text{prog}(\varphi, \pi)) \equiv \text{True})$. Then, using our inductive hypotheses, we incur the goal: $(\text{prog}(\psi, \pi) \equiv \text{True} \vee \text{prog}(\varphi, \pi) \equiv \text{True}) \longleftrightarrow ((\text{prog}(\varphi, \pi) \vee \text{prog}(\psi, \pi)) \equiv \text{True})$. This does not hold; $\text{prog}(\varphi, \pi) \vee \text{prog}(\psi, \pi)$ can be logically equivalent to True without either $\text{prog}(\varphi, \pi)$ or $\text{prog}(\psi, \pi)$ being logically equivalent to True; all that is required is that $\text{prog}(\varphi, \pi)$ must hold in any states where $\text{prog}(\psi, \pi)$ is false and vice-versa.

By adding the assumption on the computation length, the base case of the formula progression theorem inherits the (structurally strong) assumption that 1 is greater than or equal to the computation length of the input formula φ. This assumption is strong enough to establish that the formula progression of φ on any trace of length 1 is either globally true or globally false. This solves the above issue in the `Or_mltl` case, since $\text{prog}(\varphi, \pi)$ and $\text{prog}(\psi, \pi)$ are now globally either True or False, we can conclude $(\text{prog}(\psi, \pi) = \text{True} \vee \text{prog}(\varphi, \pi) = \text{True}) \longleftrightarrow ((\text{prog}(\varphi, \pi) \vee \text{prog}(\psi, \pi)) = \text{True})$. We establish this useful property of the computation length in the following key lemma:

```
lemma complen_bounded_by_1:
assumes "intervals_welldef φ" and "1 ≥ complen_mltl φ"
shows "(∀η. semantics_mltl η (formula_progression_len1 φ (π!0)) = True)
   ∨ (∀η. semantics_mltl η (formula_progression_len1 φ (π!0)) = False)"
```

This lemma is sufficient to prove our strengthened base case; however, we also need to ensure that the strengthened base case is *usable* in the proof of

Theorem 3. This requires several additional properties of the computation length. In particular, we establish the following two crucial properties:

```
lemma complen_one_implies_one:
assumes "intervals_welldef φ" and "complen_mltl φ = 1"
shows "complen_mltl (formula_progression φ π) = 1"

lemma formula_progression_decreases_complen:
assumes "intervals_welldef φ"
shows "complen_mltl φ = 1 ∨ complen_mltl (formula_progression φ π) = 1
∨ complen_mltl (formula_progression φ π) ≤ complen_mltl φ - (length π)"
```

The first lemma proves that (for φ with well-defined intervals), if the computation length of φ is 1, then the computation length of prog(φ π) is also 1; i.e., formula progression does not increase the computation length for formulas that already have the minimum computation length. The second key lemma establishes that performing formula progression on a formula φ over a trace π usually decreases computation length proportionally to the length of π. More precisely, either the computation length of φ equals 1 (i.e., is already minimal), or the computation length of prog(φ, π) equals 1 (i.e., is minimal), or the computation length of prog(φ, π) is less than or equal to the computation length of φ minus $|\pi|$ (i.e., the computation length of the progression is decreased by $|\pi|$).

Both lemmas are used in the proof of Theorem 3 to establish that complen prog$(\varphi, (\pi^{\text{length } \pi-1})) \leq$ length$(\pi_{\text{ length } \pi-1})$, which is equivalent to complen prog$(\varphi, (\pi^{\text{length } \pi-1})) \leq 1$. This then allows us to use the base case of Theorem 3 with the formula prog$(\varphi, (\pi^{\text{length } \pi-1}))$ and the trace $\pi_{\text{ length } \pi-1}$ to prove that prog(prog$(\varphi, (\pi^{\text{length } \pi-1}), \pi_{\text{ length } \pi-1}))$ = True is equal to $\pi_{\text{ length } \pi-1} \models$ prog$(\varphi, (\pi^{\text{length } \pi-1}))$. Then, following the source material [32], we can conclude that ① prog(prog $(\varphi, (\pi^{\text{length } \pi-1}), \pi_{\text{ length } \pi-1}))$ = prog(φ, π) using Theorem 1 and ② $\pi_{\text{ length } \pi-1} \models$ prog$(\varphi, (\pi^{\text{length } \pi-1}))$ iff $\pi \models \varphi$ using Theorem 2. Putting these pieces together closes the proof.

In total, *formula_progression_correctness* took ≈ 1000 lines of code to formalize (this includes about 800 lines for establishing the necessary properties of the computation length), as compared to 6 lines in the original source material.

Putting the three key theorems together, we achieve the following top-level corollary, which informally states that, for a well-defined MLTL formula φ and a sufficiently long trace π, if $\pi \models \varphi$, then any trace whose prefix is π also models φ. Formally, we prove the following result in Isabelle/HOL, where @ is Isabelle/HOL's syntax for appending lists.

```
corollary trace_append: fixes φ::"'a mltl"
  assumes "intervals_welldef φ" and "length π ≥ complen_mltl φ"
  and "π ⊨m φ" shows "(π @ ζ) ⊨m φ"
```

The source material [32, Corollary 1] had stated this corollary without the key assumption on the length of the trace, but that is incorrect. Consider the following example. We know that $[\{2\}] \models G_{[1,3]}$False, as the length of $[\{2\}]$ is ≤ 1 (cross-reference Sect. 2, MLTL semantics). Then, without the assumption that the length of $[\{2\}]$ must be greater than or equal to the computation length of $G_{[1,3]}$False, which is 4, we could obtain, for example, $[\{2\}, \{3\}, \{4\}, \{2, 3\}] \models G_{[1,3]}$False, which contradicts MLTL semantics. Fortunately, after adding in the necessary assumption, the (formal) proof of the corollary is quite straightforward and follows the proof in the source material [32].

Further, we realized that we could go a step further and formalize that if a sufficiently long trace π does not satisfy φ, then prog(φ, π) is logically equivalent to False. Though the proof of this exactly mirrors the proof of Theorem 3, it is not immediately implied by Theorem 3.[6] Together with Theorem 3, we obtain that for sufficiently long π, prog(φ π) is logically equivalent to True or False:[7]

```
lemma formula_progression_true_or_false:
fixes φ::"'a mltl" assumes "intervals_welldef φ"
  and "length π ≥ complen_mltl φ" and "ψ = (formula_progression φ π)"
shows "(ψ ≡m False_mltl) ∨ (ψ ≡m True_mltl)"
```

We also use our alternate version of Theorem 3 to prove the inverse of the top-level corollary, strengthening it to an if-and-only-if statement:

```
corollary trace_append_iff:
assumes "intervals_welldef φ" and "length π ≥ complen_mltl φ"
shows "π ⊨m φ ⟷ (∀ζ. (π @ ζ) ⊨m φ)"
```

This says that for a long enough trace π, extending π with additional states (in ζ) does not affect the satisfaction of φ. This formalizes the intuition for computation length—timesteps beyond the computation length of a formula do not affect the satisfaction of that formula. Retrospectively, a bonus of our formalization is that it nicely integrates various related MLTL concepts (like formula progression and computation length) in a centralized and easily extensible library.

4 Challenges and Insights

We view our formalization as emblematic of the potential benefits of formalizing source material that heavily relies on intuition. The mathematical intuition for formula progression for MLTL is clear because of its boundedness. Accordingly, the original source material elided many important details (possibly in light of space constraints), which introduced bugs. In particular, the base cases of Theorem 2 and Theorem 3 were claimed to hold by structural induction; mathematically, this seems quite intuitive. However, formalization found that the base cases needed modifications, which propagated into the top-level results.

A main creative challenge was identifying the necessary assumptions to add to the base cases. These needed to walk a fine line: they must be strong enough to prove the base cases but weak enough that they can still be used to prove the top-level results. They should also maintain formula progression's practicality.

[6] Assuming that $\pi \not\models \varphi$, Theorem 3 yields that prog(φ, π) is not semantically equivalent to True, which does not necessitate that prog(φ, π) is equivalent to False.

[7] Lemma *complen_bounded_by_1* is actually a special case of this.

We found that it was useful to keep the high-level context in mind throughout our formalization; we frequently switched back and forth between working on a base case and using that base case to prove the overall desired result.

Similarly, only by analyzing the top-level corollary did we identify the main necessary assumption for Theorem 3 (that $\texttt{length}\ \pi \geq \texttt{complen\_mltl}\ \varphi$). We found it intuitive that this assumption establishes the corollary and that it does not affect practicality (traces in real-world systems tend to be long). Interestingly, we were initially unsure whether it was strong enough to fix the proof of Theorem 3. Establishing this required identifying and proving various key properties of the computation length (see Sect. 3), which show that formula progression tends to decrease computation length. Initially, we stated these in a series of (unproven) lemmas that we *wanted*; we were pleased when we later found they all held.

Another key challenge relates to end-of-trace behavior. We noticed this especially in Theorem 2; the behavior of the empty trace caused issues in the theorem as originally stated. In practice, MLTL traces are usually long, and we suspect that this makes it easy to overlook edge cases involving the empty trace. Also, MLTL end-of-trace behavior can be unintuitive; for example, $[] \models G_{[0,0]}\mathrm{False}$ according to MLTL semantics, because Globally is satisfied if the length of the trace is less than or equal to the lower bound on its associated interval. Fortunately, formalization is excellent at making unintuitive edge cases precise.

Finally, we comment on our choice of theorem prover. As mentioned previously (see Sect. 2.1), we do not include the well-definedness assumptions on intervals within our MLTL syntax; this is in fact a consequence of using a theorem prover that is based on simple types (with dependent types, one could directly embed these well-definedness assumptions within the formal MLTL syntax). In Isabelle/HOL, there are various ways that one could ensure that these assumptions hold, including (for example) with the use of a locale; our choice, as previously explained, is to add the well-definedness conditions explicitly in the theorem statements. In any case, this does not pose any real restriction, and overall, we greatly benefited from the use of Isabelle/HOL. Throughout our work, we particularly appreciated Sledgehammer's automation [46] and Isabelle/HOL's built-in support for unrolling definitions and functions; the latter was extremely helpful in a number of structural induction proofs that reduced into detailed casework.

5 Conclusion and Future Work

We formalize MLTL syntax and semantics and develop a library of useful properties, including dualities, an NNF transformation, and custom induction rules. We also verify MLTL formula progression [32], which necessitated fixing errors in the correctness proofs. In the process, we develop the foundational notion of *computation length* [16]. The literature on computation length and its earlier counterpart, worst-case propagation delay [27], is piecemeal; we contribute a centralized body of verified computation length lemmas. Our work can facilitate future MLTL formalizations or serve as a reference point for theoretical work.

A natural next step is to further develop our library, e.g. by verifying more on computation length and related results involving worst-case propagation delay, e.g. [73, Lemma 4]. More broadly, we envision a suite of verified MLTL algorithms that can be developed into tools or used for tool validation. We have already leveraged our formalization of MLTL to verify the MLTL to regular expressions algorithm [72] and validate the WEST tool [71], and (separately) to formalize some new theoretical results for MLTL [56]. As our formula progression algorithm is executable, it could be used to validate the FPROGG tool [55]. Finally, it would be valuable to bridge our work with formalizations of related logics; we are particularly interested in connecting MLTL to VeriMon [8] and Vydra [52].

Acknowledgments. This material is based upon work supported by a National Science Foundation Graduate Research Fellowship under Grant No. 2024364991, NSF CAREER Award CNS-1552934 and CCRI-2016592, and by the Iowa State Bridging the Divide Grant. Thank you to Dmitriy Traytel for useful discussions on MLTL and related work. Thanks also to Alec Rosentrater and to various anonymous reviewers for useful comments on the paper.

Disclosure of Interests. The authors have no competing interests to declare that are relevant to the content of this article.

References

1. 2018 Runtime Verification Benchmark Competition. https://www.rv-competition.org/2018-2/
2. Alur, R., Henzinger, T.A.: Real-time logics: complexity and expressiveness. In: LICS. pp. 390–401. IEEE (1990)
3. Alur, R., Feder, T., Henzinger, T.A.: The benefits of relaxing punctuality. In: Logrippo, L. (ed.) PODC. pp. 139–152. ACM (1991). https://doi.org/10.1145/112600.112613, https://doi.org/10.1145/112600.112613
4. Amjad, R., van Glabbeek, R., O'Connor, L.: Definitive set semantics for LTL3. Archive of Formal Proofs (August 2024), https://isa-afp.org/entries/LTL3_Semantics.html, Formal proof development
5. Anastasia Mavridou: Capturing and analyzing requirements with FRET. Presentation, NFM, https://github.com/NASA-SW-VnV/fret, NASA, Pasadena, California, USA (May 2022)
6. Aurandt, A., Jones, P., Rozier, K.Y.: Runtime verification triggers real-time, autonomous fault recovery on the CySat-I. In: NFM. LNCS, vol. 13260. Springer, Cham, Caltech, California, USA (May 2022). https://doi.org/10.1007/978-3-031-06773-0_45
7. Bacchus, F., Kabanza, F.: Planning for temporally extended goals. In: Clancey, W.J., Weld, D.S. (eds.) AAAI. pp. 1215–1222. AAAI Press / The MIT Press (1996), http://www.aaai.org/Library/AAAI/1996/aaai96-180.php
8. Basin, D.A., Dardinier, T., Hauser, N., Heimes, L., y Munive, J.J.H., Kaletsch, N., Krstic, S., Marsicano, E., Raszyk, M., Schneider, J., Tirore, D.L., Traytel, D., Zingg, S.: VeriMon: A formally verified monitoring tool. In: Seidl, H., Liu, Z., Pasareanu, C.S. (eds.) ICTAC. LNCS, vol. 13572, pp. 1–6. Springer (2022). https://doi.org/10.1007/978-3-031-17715-6_1, https://doi.org/10.1007/978-3-031-17715-6_1

9. Cauwels, M., Hammer, A., Hertz, B., Jones, P., Rozier, K.Y.: Integrating runtime verification into an automated UAS traffic management system. In: Proceedings of DETECT: international workshop on moDeling, vErification and Testing of dEpendable CriTical systems. CCIS, Springer, L'Aquila, Italy (September 2020). https://doi.org/10.1007/978-3-030-59155-7_26
10. Chattopadhyay, A., Mamouras, K.: A verified online monitor for metric temporal logic with quantitative semantics. In: Deshmukh, J., Ničković, D. (eds.) RV. pp. 383–403. Springer International Publishing, Cham (2020)
11. Conrad, E., Titolo, L., Giannakopoulou, D., Pressburger, T., Dutle, A.: A compositional proof framework for FRETish requirements. In: Popescu, A., Zdancewic, S. (eds.) CPP. pp. 68–81. ACM (2022). https://doi.org/10.1145/3497775.3503685, https://doi.org/10.1145/3497775.3503685
12. Coupet-Grimal, S.: An axiomatization of linear temporal logic in the calculus of inductive constructions. J. Log. Comput. **13**(6), 801–813 (2003). https://doi.org/10.1093/LOGCOM/13.6.801, https://doi.org/10.1093/logcom/13.6.801
13. Dabney, J.B., Badger, J.M., Rajagopal, P.: Adding a verification view for an autonomous real-time system architecture. In: Proceedings of SciTech Forum. p. Online. 2021-0566, AIAA (January 2021). https://doi.org/https://doi.org/10.2514/6.2021-0566
14. Dabney, J.B.: Using assume-guarantee contracts in autonomous spacecraft. Flight Software Workshop (FSW) Online: https://www.youtube.com/watch?v=zrtyiyNf674 (February 2021)
15. Dabney, J.B., Rajagopal, P., Badger, J.M.: Using assume-guarantee contracts for developmental verification of autonomous spacecraft. Flight Software Workshop (FSW) Online: https://www.youtube.com/watch?v=HFnn6TzblPg (February 2022)
16. Elwing, J., Gamboa-Guzman, L., Sorkin, J., Travesset, C., Wang, Z., Rozier, K.Y.: Mission-time LTL (MLTL) formula validation via regular expressions. In: Herber, P., Wijs, A. (eds.) iFM. LNCS, vol. 14300, pp. 279–301. Springer (2023). https://doi.org/10.1007/978-3-031-47705-8_15, https://doi.org/10.1007/978-3-031-47705-8_15
17. Esparza, J., Lammich, P., Neumann, R., Nipkow, T., Schimpf, A., Smaus, J.G.: A fully verified executable LTL model checker. Archive of Formal Proofs (May 2014), https://isa-afp.org/entries/CAVA_LTL_Modelchecker.html, Formal proof development
18. Geist, J., Rozier, K.Y., Schumann, J.: Runtime Observer Pairs and Bayesian Network Reasoners On-board FPGAs: Flight-Certifiable System Health Management for Embedded Systems. In: RV. vol. 8734, pp. 215–230. Springer-Verlag (September 2014)
19. Giacomo, G.D., Vardi, M.Y.: Linear temporal logic and linear dynamic logic on finite traces. In: Rossi, F. (ed.) IJCAI. pp. 854–860. IJCAI/AAAI (2013), http://www.aaai.org/ocs/index.php/IJCAI/IJCAI13/paper/view/6997
20. Giannakopoulou, D., Mavridou, A., Rhein, J., Pressburger, T., Schumann, J., Shi, N.: Formal requirements elicitation with FRET. In: International Working Conference on Requirements Engineering: Foundation for Software Quality (REFSQ-2020). No. ARC-E-DAA-TN77785 (2020)
21. Haftmann, F.: Code generation from Isabelle/HOL theories. https://isabelle.in.tum.de/doc/codegen.pdf (2024), tutorial, with contributions from Lukas Bulwahn and Tobias Nipkow

22. Hariharan, G., Jones, P.H., Rozier, K.Y., Wongpiromsarn, T.: Maximum satisfiability of Mission-time Linear Temporal Logic. In: Petrucci, L., Sproston, J. (eds.) FORMATS. LNCS, vol. 14138, pp. 86–104. Springer (2023). https://doi.org/10.1007/978-3-031-42626-1_6, https://doi.org/10.1007/978-3-031-42626-1_6
23. Hertz, B., Luppen, Z., Rozier, K.Y.: Integrating runtime verification into a sounding rocket control system. In: NFM (May 2021), available online at http://temporallogic.org/research/NFM21/
24. Johannsen, C., Jones, P., Kempa, B., Rozier, K.Y., Zhang, P.: R2U2 version 3.0: Re-imagining a toolchain for specification, resource estimation, and optimized observer generation for runtime verification in hardware and software. In: Enea, C., Lal, A. (eds.) CAV. pp. 483–497. Springer Nature Switzerland, Cham (2023)
25. Johannsen, C., Anderson, M., Burken, W., Diersen, E., Edgren, J., Glick, C., Jou, S., Kumar, A., Levandowski, J., Moyer, E., Roquet, T., VandeLoo, A., Rozier, K.Y.: OpenUAS Version 1.0. IEEE, Athens, Greece (Virtual) (June 2021)
26. Kamide, N.: Bounded linear-time temporal logic: A proof-theoretic investigation. Ann. Pure Appl. Log. **163**(4), 439–466 (2012). https://doi.org/10.1016/J.APAL.2011.12.002, https://doi.org/10.1016/j.apal.2011.12.002
27. Kempa, B., Zhang, P., Jones, P.H., Zambreno, J., Rozier, K.Y.: Embedding Online Runtime Verification for Fault Disambiguation on Robonaut2. In: FORMATS. pp. 196–214. LNCS, Springer, Vienna, Austria (September 2020), http://research.temporallogic.org/papers/KZJZR20.pdf
28. Kessler, F.B.: nuXmv 1.1.0 (2016-05-10) Release Notes. https://es-static.fbk.eu/tools/nuxmv/downloads/NEWS.txt (2016)
29. Kosaian, K., Wang, Z., Sloan, E.: Mission-time Linear Temporal Logic. Archive of Formal Proofs (January 2025), https://isa-afp.org/entries/Mission_Time_LTL.html, Formal proof development
30. Kosaian, K., Wang, Z., Sloan, E.: Mission-time Linear Temporal Logic formula progression. Archive of Formal Proofs (July 2025), https://isa-afp.org/entries/Mission_Time_LTL_Formula_Progression.html, Formal proof development
31. de Leng, D., Heintz, F.: Approximate stream reasoning with metric temporal logic under uncertainty. In: AAAI. pp. 2760–2767. AAAI Press (2019). https://doi.org/10.1609/AAAI.V33I01.33012760, https://doi.org/10.1609/aaai.v33i01.33012760
32. Li, J., Rozier, K.Y.: MLTL benchmark generation via formula progression. In: Colombo, C., Leucker, M. (eds.) RV. LNCS, vol. 11237, pp. 426–433. Springer (2018). https://doi.org/10.1007/978-3-030-03769-7_25, https://doi.org/10.1007/978-3-030-03769-7_25
33. Li, J., Vardi, M.Y., Rozier, K.Y.: Satisfiability checking for Mission-time LTL. In: CAV. LNCS, Springer, New York, NY, USA (July 2019)
34. Lowry, M., Bajwa, A.: Autonomy Operating System (AOS) for UAVs. Proposal Presentation, NASA Ames Research Center, Moffett Field, California (June 2015)
35. Lowry, M., Bajwa, A., Quach, P., Karsai, G., Rozier, K.Y., Rayadurgam, S.: Autonomy Operating System for UAVs. Online: https://nari.arc.nasa.gov/sites/default/files/attachments/15%29%20Mike%20Lowry%20SAEApril19-2017.Final_.pdf (April 2017)
36. Luppen, Z., Jacks, M., Baughman, N., Hertz, B., Cutler, J., Lee, D.Y., Rozier, K.Y.: Elucidation and analysis of specification patterns in aerospace system telemetry. In: NFM. LNCS, vol. 13260. Springer, Cham, Caltech, California, USA (May 2022). https://doi.org/10.1007/978-3-031-06773-0_28
37. Luppen, Z.A., Lee, D.Y., Rozier, K.Y.: A case study in formal specification and runtime verification of a CubeSat communications system. In: SciTech. AIAA, Nashville, TN, USA (January 2021)

38. Maler, O., Nickovic, D.: Monitoring temporal properties of continuous signals. In: Formal Techniques, Modelling and Analysis of Timed and Fault-Tolerant Systems, pp. 152–166. Springer (2004)
39. NASA: PVS library: LTL module. https://github.com/nasa/pvslib/tree/master/LTL (nd)
40. NASA Technology Transfer Program: FRET : Formal Requirements Elicitation Tool (ARC-18066-1). Online: https://software.nasa.gov/software/ARC-18066-1 (2024)
41. Nipkow, T., Paulson, L.C., Wenzel, M.: Isabelle/HOL - A Proof Assistant for Higher-Order Logic, LNCS, vol. 2283. Springer (2002). https://doi.org/10.1007/3-540-45949-9
42. Niu, T., Xu, Y., Xiao, S., Xiao, L., Huang, Y., Li, J.: LTL_f satisfiability checking via formula progression. In: Chang, S. (ed.) SEKE. pp. 357–362. KSI Research Inc. (2023). https://doi.org/10.18293/SEKE2023-143, https://doi.org/10.18293/SEKE2023-143
43. Okubo, N.: Using R2U2 in JAXA program. Electronic correspondence (November–December 2020), correspondance
44. Ouaknine, J., Worrell, J.: Some recent results in metric temporal logic. In: Cassez, F., Jard, C. (eds.) Formal Modeling and Analysis of Timed Systems. pp. 1–13. Springer Berlin Heidelberg, Berlin, Heidelberg (2008)
45. Paulson, L.C.: The foundation of a generic theorem prover. J. Autom. Reason. **5**(3), 363–397 (1989). https://doi.org/10.1007/BF00248324
46. Paulson, L.C., Blanchette, J.C.: Three years of experience with Sledgehammer, a practical link between automatic and interactive theorem provers. In: Sutcliffe, G., Schulz, S., Ternovska, E. (eds.) IWIL. EPiC Series in Computing, vol. 2, pp. 1–11. EasyChair (2010). https://doi.org/10.29007/36DT
47. Perez, I.: Runtime verification with Ogma. In: Invited Talk to University of California (2023)
48. Perez, I., Goodloe, A.: Ogma. https://github.com/nasa/ogma (2021)
49. Perez, I., Mavridou, A., Pressburger, T., Goodloe, A., Giannakopoulou, D.: Automated translation of natural language requirements to runtime monitors. In: Fisman, D., Rosu, G. (eds.) TACAS. pp. 387–395. Springer International Publishing, Cham (2022)
50. Pnueli, A.: The temporal logic of programs. In: FOCS, Proc. 18th IEEE Symp. pp. 46–57 (1977)
51. Pnueli, A., Arons, T.: TLPVS: A PVS-based LTL verification system. In: Dershowitz, N. (ed.) Verification: Theory and Practice, Essays Dedicated to Zohar Manna on the Occasion of His 64th Birthday. LNCS, vol. 2772, pp. 598–625. Springer (2003). https://doi.org/10.1007/978-3-540-39910-0_26, https://doi.org/10.1007/978-3-540-39910-0_26
52. Raszyk, M., Basin, D.A., Traytel, D.: Multi-head monitoring of metric dynamic logic. In: Hung, D.V., Sokolsky, O. (eds.) ATVA. LNCS, vol. 12302, pp. 233–250. Springer (2020). https://doi.org/10.1007/978-3-030-59152-6_13, https://doi.org/10.1007/978-3-030-59152-6_13
53. Reinbacher, T., Rozier, K.Y., Schumann, J.: Temporal-logic based runtime observer pairs for system health management of real-time systems. In: TACAS. LNCS, vol. 8413, pp. 357–372. Springer-Verlag (April 2014)
54. Roohi, N., Viswanathan, M.: Revisiting MITL to fix decision procedures. In: Dillig, I., Palsberg, J. (eds.) VMCAI. LNCS, vol. 10747, pp. 474–494. Springer (2018). https://doi.org/10.1007/978-3-319-73721-8_22, https://doi.org/10.1007/978-3-319-73721-8_22

55. Rosentrater, A., Rozier, K.Y.: FPROGG: A formula progression-based MLTL benchmark generator. To appear (2025)
56. Rosentrater, A., Wang, Z., Kosaian, K., Rozier, K.Y.: Language partitioning for Mission-Time Linear Temporal Logic. In: Dutle, A., Humphrey, L.R., Titolo, L. (eds.) NFM. LNCS, vol. 15682, pp. 313–332. Springer (2025). https://doi.org/10.1007/978-3-031-93706-4_18, https://doi.org/10.1007/978-3-031-93706-4_18
57. Rozier, K.Y.: R2U2 in space: System and software health management for small satellites. In: Spacecraft Flight Software Workshop (FSW) (December 2016), https://www.youtube.com/watch?v=OAgQFuEGSi8, https://www.youtube.com/watch?v=OAgQFuEGSi8
58. Rozier, K.Y., Schumann, J., Ippolito, C.: Intelligent Hardware-Enabled Sensor and Software Safety and Health Management for Autonomous UAS. Technical Memorandum NASA/TM-2015-218817, NASA, NASA Ames Research Center, Moffett Field, CA 94035, USA (May 2015)
59. Rozier, K.Y.: Linear temporal logic Symbolic Model Checking. Computer Science Review Journal **5**(2), 163–203 (May 2011). https://doi.org/doi:10.1016/j.cosrev.2010.06.002, http://dx.doi.org/10.1016/j.cosrev.2010.06.002
60. Rozier, K.Y.: On the evaluation and comparison of runtime verification tools for hardware and cyber-physical systems. In: RV-CUBES. vol. 3, pp. 123–137. Kalpa Publications, Seattle, WA, USA (September 2017). https://doi.org/10.29007/pld3, https://easychair.org/publications/paper/877G
61. Rozier, K.Y., Schumann, J.: R2U2: Tool Overview. In: RV-CUBES. vol. 3, pp. 138–156. Kalpa Publications, Seattle, WA, USA (September 2017), https://easychair.org/publications/paper/Vncw
62. Schimpf, A., Lammich, P.: Converting linear-time temporal logic to generalized Büchi automata. Archive of Formal Proofs (May 2014), https://isa-afp.org/entries/LTL_to_GBA.html, Formal proof development
63. Schumann, J., Moosbrugger, P., Rozier, K.Y.: Runtime analysis with R2U2: A tool exhibition report. In: RV. Springer-Verlag, Madrid, Spain (September 2016)
64. Schumann, J., Rozier, K.Y., Reinbacher, T., Mengshoel, O.J., Mbaya, T., Ippolito, C.: Towards real-time, on-board, hardware-supported sensor and software health management for unmanned aerial systems. IJPHM **6**(1), 1–27 (June 2015)
65. Seidl, B., Sickert, S.: A compositional and unified translation of LTL into ω-automata. Archive of Formal Proofs (April 2019), https://isa-afp.org/entries/LTL_Master_Theorem.html, Formal proof development
66. Sickert, S.: Converting linear temporal logic to deterministic (generalized) Rabin automata. Archive of Formal Proofs (September 2015), https://isa-afp.org/entries/LTL_to_DRA.html, Formal proof development
67. Sickert, S.: Linear temporal logic. Archive of Formal Proofs (March 2016), https://isa-afp.org/entries/LTL.html, Formal proof development
68. Sickert, S.: An efficient normalisation procedure for linear temporal logic: Isabelle/HOL formalisation. Archive of Formal Proofs (May 2020), https://isa-afp.org/entries/LTL_Normal_Form.html, Formal proof development
69. Titolo, L., Conrad, E., Giannakopoulou, D., Pressburger, T., Dutle, A.: FRET Proof Framework. https://lauratitolo.github.io/project/fret-proof-framework/ (2022)
70. Vardi, M.Y.: From Church and Prior to PSL. In: 25 Years of Model Checking: History, Achievements, Perspectives, pp. 150–171. Springer (2008)
71. Wang, Z., Gamboa-Guzman, L.P., Rozier, K.Y.: WEST: Interactive validation of Mission-time Linear Temporal Logic (MLTL) (2024), https://temporallogic.org/research/WEST/

72. Wang, Z., Kosaian, K., Rozier, K.: Formally verifying a transformation from MLTL formulas to regular expressions, accepted to TACAS 2025, preprint available at: https://arxiv.org/abs/2501.17444
73. Zhang, P., Aurandt, A.A., Dureja, R., Jones, P.H., Rozier, K.Y.: Model predictive runtime verification for cyber-physical systems with real-time deadlines. In: Petrucci, L., Sproston, J. (eds.) FORMATS. LNCS, vol. 14138, pp. 158–180. Springer (2023). https://doi.org/10.1007/978-3-031-42626-1_10, https://doi.org/10.1007/978-3-031-42626-1_10

Formalising Fairness in the Assignment Problem with Ordinal Preferences in Isabelle/HOL

Duc Minh Do[1](✉) and Christine Rizkallah[2]

[1] University of New South Wales, Sydney, New South Wales, Australia
duc_minh.do@unsw.edu.au
[2] The University of Melbourne, Melbourne, Victoria, Australia
christine.rizkallah@unimelb.edu.au

Abstract. Social choice theory is a multidisciplinary research area that studies collective decision-making based on individual preferences. A central problem in this domain is the fair assignment of indivisible resources, which arises in applications such as organ matching, school admissions, and job placements. Notions of fairness, such as proportionality and envy-freeness, are well-established; they are sometimes unattainable, particularly in the discrete setting, where resources cannot be divided. We present a mechanised formalisation of key fairness concepts for the assignment problem under ordinal preferences using the Isabelle/HOL theorem prover. Our development captures both discrete and fractional assignment settings and formalises the responsive set extension, which is a central concept for lifting preferences over resources to preferences over sets of resources, enabling the comparison of allocations under ordinal preferences. We formalise multiple fairness notions—including stochastic dominance (SD) proportionality and envy-freeness, as well as their relaxed variants—and we formally verify relationships between these notions. The formalisation builds on existing verified results in social choice theory and closes gaps found in pen-and-paper proofs.

Keywords: Social choice theory · Fairness · Interactive theorem proving

1 Introduction

Social choice theory is a multidisciplinary field that studies how individual preferences can be aggregated into collective decisions. It draws on ideas from economics, mathematics, political science, computer science, and philosophy. Despite its broad scope, problems in social choice theory share the following central question: how can individual preferences be combined into decisions that best reflect society's interests as a whole? A well-studied subarea of social choice theory is *voting theory*. Voting theory examines how to aggregate individual preferences over candidates into a collective outcome, such as a single winning candidate, a set of winning candidates, or a ranked list of the candidates [33]. It addresses fundamental questions about different voting systems, exploring how different

V. de Paiva and P. Koepke (Eds.): CICM 2025, LNAI 16136, pp. 392–411, 2026.
https://doi.org/10.1007/978-3-032-07021-0_22

voting mechanisms can produce different societal outcomes from the same list of individual preferences. Foundational results in this area, such as Arrow's impossibility theorem [2], the Condorcet Paradox [21], and the Gibbard–Satterthwaite theorem [38], highlight the inherent limitations of designing voting mechanisms that meet a small set of intuitive and seemingly reasonable criteria.

Another key subarea–central to this work–is the *assignment problem*, which involves allocating resources to individuals based on their preferences. This problem is also known as the *house allocation problem* and as the *two-sided matching with one-sided preferences* [5]. Here, the main challenge is to allocate a limited set of resources to individuals in a way that respects various levels of fairness and efficiency criteria. As such, this problem is sometimes also referred to as the *fair allocation problem* [12].

There are two main settings in which this problem is studied, based on whether or not the resources are divisible. In the case when the resources are divisible, the problem can be framed as a *fractional assignment* problem, where each individual receives a proportion of each resource. In the case when resources are indivisible, solutions typically involve either *discrete assignments*—where individuals receive whole resources—or *randomised assignments*—where individuals are assigned probabilities over whether or not they are allocated each resource [1].

Fairness in the assignment problem has real-world applications such as CPU time allocation, school admissions, job placements, public housing, and allocating organs to patients. Equitable resource allocation is critical in such scenarios. This underscores the importance of rigorously defining and reasoning about fairness.

Two of the most fundamental and widely studied notions of fairness are *envy-freeness* [19], and *proportionality* (only defined in the fractional and the randomised setting) [29,16]. Envy-freeness requires that no individual prefers another individual's allocation to their own. Proportionality imposes a minimal requirement on each individual's allocation, requiring that each individual's allocation be at least as good as the uniform distribution of resources to individuals [37,9].

While desirable, these fairness criteria are sometimes impossible to achieve in practice, especially in the discrete setting with indivisible resources [1,3]. As a result, researchers study weaker variants such as *weak envy-freeness*, *weak proportionality*, and *proportionality up to a fixed number* of resources [9,15].

As many of the foundational results in social choice theory are impossibility theorems and due to the field's amenability to satisfying desired axiomatic properties, there is a strong motivation for researchers to use theorem provers as a tool to aid the research process [4]. There has been an extensive line of work in verifying existing social choice theoretic results in proof assistants [27,32,31,35]. Beyond verifying existing results, theorem provers and SAT solvers have also enabled researchers to quickly discover new theorems and insights in the field [7,13,14,8]. Recent efforts have also focused on formalising core concepts in social choice theory, establishing a reusable foundation for future mechanisation efforts in this field [36,34,18]. Although important concepts in randomised social choice, such as stochastic dominance and utility functions, have been formalised in Isabelle/HOL, to the best of our knowledge, there is no general formalisation of the assignment problem or its associated fairness criteria.

This paper describes an Isabelle/HOL formalisation of the assignment problem that relates various notions of fairness in the *fractional/randomised* and *discrete* settings, and provides formal proofs of known relationships between these notions [6]. In particular, we define envy-freeness and proportionality using the stochastic dominance (SD) relation and using utility functions to compare allocations. For the discrete case, we also formalise the established notion of a responsive set extension (RS) relation, which lifts ordinal preferences over resources to preferences over sets of resources [6].

Developing a formalisation of the assignment problem establishes a theoretical foundation that enables verifying relationships between existing notions of fairness. While we verified most of the pen-and-paper results [6] relating these notions, one relationship between two notions of fairness turned out to be incorrect. For this notion, we provide a formalised counter-example.

We start by presenting some background on the theoretical foundations of the assignment problem and its fairness definitions, followed by an explanation of their mechanised counterparts in Isabelle/HOL. The formalisation is publicly available [17].

2 Preliminaries

This section introduces some background that is necessary for understanding our development. We begin by defining the assignment problem in both its fractional and discrete settings, followed by a presentation of the key fairness notions that we formalise. Our definitions and proofs follow existing pen-and-paper results [6].

The Assignment Problem. The assignment problem is typically defined as a triple $(N, O, \mathcal{R})$, where $N = \{a_1, a_2, \ldots, a_n\}$ is a finite set of agents, $O = \{o_1, o_2, \ldots, o_m\}$ is a finite set of objects, and $\mathcal{R} = \{R_1, R_2, \ldots, R_n\}$ is a profile of ordinal preference relations—one for each agent. Each relation R_i is a weak total preorder over O, representing the preferences of agent i. An assignment p is typically represented as an $n \times m$ matrix, where entry $p[i, j]$ indicates the fraction (or probability) that object o_j is allocated to agent a_i. In the randomised setting, these entries are real numbers in [0, 1]. A common assumption in this setting is that there is only one occurrence of each object, thus, the sum of the probabilities of receiving a particular object over all agents must sum to one: $\sum_{i=1}^{n} p[i, j] = 1$, for all $j \in \{1...m\}$. In the discrete setting, with indivisible objects, the definition of an allocation is similar to that of the randomised setting, but with the added restriction that entries have to be either 0 or 1, depending on whether an agent receives a given object in full. To accommodate scenarios where agents may receive multiple objects, we relax the usual assumption that each agent's allocation is a lottery (i.e., sums to 1). Instead, we allow each agent's total allocation to sum to a fixed constant, which is shared across agents. This enables the use of the stochastic dominance even in scenarios when allocations are not lotteries.

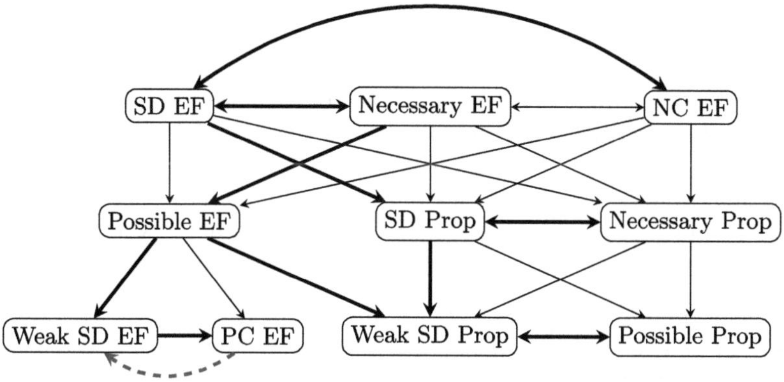

Fig. 1: Logical relationships between fairness notions as presented in prior work [6]. Envy-freeness is abbreviated EF, proportionality is abbreviated Prop, arrows indicate implication, and bidirectional arrows indicate equivalence. We use a dotted arrow to identify the implication we disproved and use bold to identify relationships that are verified directly; the remaining arrows are verified as corollaries.

Fairness Notions. As discussed earlier, various existing notions of fairness are studied in the literature. These notions form a hierarchy of fairness concepts [6], presented in Figure 1, that we formalise and verify in this paper.

SD Based. First, let's consider the two key notions of fairness based on the probabilistic *stochastic dominance* (SD) relation which compares preference allocations. An allocation satisfies *SD envy-freeness* (SD EF) if every agent prefers their allocation to that of any other agent under the SD relation. A weaker variant of this notion is *weak SD envy-freeness* (Weak SD EF), satisfied when no agent prefers other agents' allocation to their own. The second notion is *SD proportionality* (SD Prop), which is satisfied if every agent prefers their allocation to the uniform allocation of objects to agents. There is also a weaker variant of this notion, *weak SD proportionality* (Weak SD Prop), of which an assignment satisfies when no agent prefers the uniform allocation to their own.

Utility-Based Variants. We also formalise *utility-based* variants of each of these two fairness notions: *necessary fairness* holds if the fairness notion is satisfied for all utility functions that are consistent with each agent's ordinal preferences. Meanwhile, *possible fairness* holds if there exists at least one utility function for which the fairness notion is satisfied. The notion of *necessary fairness* includes both *necessary envy-freeness* (Necessary EF) and *necessary proportionality* (Necessary Prop), and the notion *possible fairness* includes both *possible envy-freeness* (Possible EF) and *possible proportionality* (Possible Prop).

Responsive Set Extension Variants. In the discrete setting, where allocations are sets rather than distributions, we lift preferences over individual objects to preferences over sets using the *responsive set extension* [10]. Given a preference relation

R over objects, an agent prefers a set A to a set B if there exists an injection $f : B \rightarrow A$ such that for all $x \in B$, $f(x)$ is preferred to x under R. This provides a principled way to compare their allocated set of indivisible objects using only ordinal information. This lifting is used to define two additional fairness notions that have been studied in the discrete setting [10]. In particular, *necessary completion envy-freeness* (NC EF) which holds when agents prefer their allocations to other allocations under all completions of the responsive set extension, and *possible completion envy-freeness* (PC EF), which holds when there exists a completion of the responsive set extension under which the fairness notion holds.

The definitions of NC EF and PC EF are underspecified in the pen-and-paper work [6]. As we will see later on, we explore two possible interpretations of these definitions, one that equates NC EF and PC EF, and the other, presented in Figure 1, enables PC EF to be trivially satisfied, leading to a simple counterexample demonstrating PC EF but not Weak SD EF. It remains open whether there are alternative interpretations of these definitions that preserve equivalence between Weak SD EF and PC EF while not equating PC EF and NC EF.

Overview of Isabelle/HOL. Before we delve into the formalisation, we start by introducing some Isabelle/HOL concepts and notation.

Types and Notation. To mechanise the setting of the assignment problem, we use Isabelle/HOL as our tool of development.

In Isabelle/HOL, each term has a type, and types in Isabelle/HOL are polymorphic, which allows us to reason about properties in multiple type classes at a time. Take the type $'a\ list$, which describes a list whose elements are of any type $'a$. We can define a function *rev* to reverse this list, and prove that $rev\ (rev\ l) = l$, which means reversing a list twice will obtain the original list. Since the property holds for a generic list, we can be sure that the property also holds for a list of numbers or a list of functions of the same type.

Isabelle/HOL's type constructors are expressive enough for our formalisation purposes. Some type constructors used in this formalisation are $'a\ set$ to describe a generic set, $'a \Rightarrow 'b$ to describe a function type with one input, $'a \Rightarrow 'b \Rightarrow 'c$ to describe a (curried) function that takes two arguments, and $'a\ relation$ to describe a predicate that takes a pair of values of type $'a$ and returns a boolean.

We use the infix notation $x \preceq [R]\, y$ to mean $R\, x\, y$, and $x \succeq [R]\, y$ to mean $R\, y\, x$.

Locales. In Isabelle/HOL, locales are a module system that enables describing complex theoretical structures and dependencies. Each locale defines a new context, with a fixed set of constants and/or assumptions. A theorem that holds within the context of a locale is true under the set of introduced variables and assumptions of the locale. New locales can be defined as extensions of existing locales by importing the assumptions and variables from existing locales and adding new variables or assumptions. This creates a hierarchy of locale dependencies that inherit theorems from the parent locales. We can use the Isabelle/HOL keyword *sublocale* to demonstrate locale dependency and enable the reuse of theorems proven in the context of existing locales.

Some locales we formalise and use throughout our mechanised proofs are the *random-assignment* and *discrete-assignment* locales, which describe the fractional/random assignment setting and the discrete assignment setting, respectively. In our formalisation, we also reuse locales from the Randomised Social Choice AFP entry [18]. Namely, the *pref-profile-wf* locale that defines a preference profile of agents, and the *vnm-utility* locale that introduces the von Neumann-Morgenstein utility function.

3 Formalising the Assignment Problem and Fairness

We start with the formalisation of the assignment problem. We follow the standard pen-and-paper definitions [6]. Figure 2 presents the Isabelle/HOL locales that underpin our formalisation of the assignment problem. These locales encode preference profiles and allocations, and the assignment problem in a modular and extensible way, supporting both the randomised (and fractional) and discrete settings.

We reuse the locale *pref-profile-wf* from the Randomised Social Choice AFP entry [18]. This locale defines a well-formed preference profile over a finite set of agents and a finite set of alternatives. Each agent is associated with a total preorder over the alternatives, representing their (possibly non-strict) ordinal preferences.

On pen-and-paper [6], an assignment p is represented as an $n \times m$ matrix, where n is the number of agents and m is the number of alternatives, and where each entry $p[i][j]$ is the probability that alternative j is assigned to agent i, or the fraction of j assigned to i in the divisible resource setting [6]. Instead, in our formalism, we weave out concepts, first defining an allocation as a function operating on a set of alternatives that maps each alternative to a real number. Then, we define an assignment p that maps each agent in the set of agents to an allocation over the set of alternatives. This structure accommodates both randomised (fractional) and discrete assignments, allowing us to capture general settings in a unified formalism, separating assumptions so our theorems are more general, and with the discrete setting defined as a special case of a more general setting.

The locale *random-allocation* encodes the constraints of a valid allocation to a single agent: the set of alternatives is finite, undefined alternatives are assigned zero weight, and all values lie within the range $[0, 1]$. The *random-assignment* locale lifts this to multiple agents, ensuring that each agent receives a valid allocation. Unlike the assumption that each agent receives a lottery (i.e., a probability distribution summing to 1), we allow for general allocations where each agent's total mass is constant across all agents $\exists c.\ \forall i \in agents.\ \sum_{j \in alts} p\ i\ j = c$. This is because we are also interested in the discrete setting, and in that setting the lottery assumption has the direct consequence that the expectation of the number of objects an agent can receive is exactly 1. This generalisation per-

```
type_synonym (α, β) pref-profile = α ⇒ β relation

locale pref-profile-wf =
  fixes agents :: α set  and alts :: β set  and R :: (α, β) pref-profile
  assumes nonempty_agents: agents ≠ {}
  assumes nonempty_alts: alts ≠ {}
  assumes prefs_wf: ∀ i ∈ agents. finite-total-preorder-on alts (R i)
  assumes prefs_undefined: ∀ i ∉ agents. ¬ R i x y

type_synonym β allocation = β ⇒ real

locale random-allocation =
  fixes alts :: β set and  h :: β allocation
  assumes finite_alts: finite alts
  assumes undefined_alts: j ∉ alts ⟶ h j = 0
  assumes prob: ∀j ∈ alts. (0 ≤ h j ∧ h j ≤ 1)

type_synonym (α, β) assignment = α ⇒ β allocation

locale random-assignment =
  fixes agents :: α set and alts :: β set and R :: (α, β) pref-profile
  assumes pref-profile-wf agents alts R
  fixes p :: (α, β)assignment
  assumes random_alloc: ∀i ∈ agents. random-allocation alts (p i)
  assumes undefined_agent: ∀j. i ∉ agents ⟶ p i j = 0
  assumes stochastic: ∀j ∈ alts. (∑ i∈agents. p i j) = 1
  assumes sum_prob_equal_agents: ∃c :: real. ∀ i ∈ agents. (∑ j ∈ alts. p i j) = c
  assumes fin: finite agents

locale discrete_allocation = random-allocation +
  assumes disc: ∀i ∈ alts. h i = 0 ∨ h i = 1

locale discrete_assignment = random-assignment +
  assumes discr: ∀i ∈ agents. discrete_allocation alts ((p :: (α, β) assignment) i)

definition allocated-alts :: β allocation ⇒ β set ⇒ β set where
  allocated-alts p alts = {x. x ∈ alts ∧ p x ≠ 0}
```

Fig. 2: Locales: preference profiles, allocations, and assignments

mits a wider class of fair allocation scenarios while preserving compatibility with fairness criteria based on stochastic dominance. The *discrete-allocation* locale restricts *random-allocation* to binary values 0 or 1 representing full resource ownership. This constraint is propagated to the *discrete-assignment* locale that defines discrete assignments across agents. Additionally, the function *allocated-alts* allows us to interprete allocations as sets of alternatives. These definitions support reasoning about indivisible goods in the discrete setting.

Figure 2 also includes the definition of a helper function *allocated-alts*, which extracts the set of alternatives that is allocated to an agent from their allocation function. As we will see shortly, this function is essential for defining fairness notions that are based on the responsive set extension.

Our layered structure of locales and functions provides a shared foundation for stating fairness properties and verifying their relationships in both the randomised and the discrete setting. It promotes reuse and compositional reasoning in subsequent proofs about the formalisation.

Formalizing Fairness. We now introduce the formalisation of ten fairness notions in the assignment problem, capturing both strong and relaxed variants of two core concepts: proportionality and envy-freeness. These fairness notions are expressed using three key mathematical tools: stochastic dominance (SD), utility functions, and the responsive set extension. Figure 3 presents our formal definitions of the ten different notions of fairness, and the remainder of this section elaborates on these formal definitions. The final two definitions are ambiguous on pen-and-paper, and we discuss how we resolve the ambiguity in our formalism.

We represent all notions of fairness as a predicate over a given assignment that holds when the assignment is considered fair according to the respective fairness definition. The most prominent notions of fairness in the randomised setting are based on stochastic dominance (SD). Stochastic dominance provides a way to compare allocations when agents' preferences are represented as ordinal relations. An agent *SD-prefers* one allocation to another if, for every alternative j, the first allocation provides the agent with at least as many alternatives that are at least as good as j as in the second allocation. We extend the classic definition of SD to allow allocations that are not necessarily lotteries, i.e., not summing to 1, by introducing a custom relation $SDA(R)$. In the definition of proportionality, the function *pmf-like-set* constructs an assignment formed of the uniform allocation (similar to a uniform distribution), where each agent receives an equal share of the alternatives.

Using this extended definition, we define the following four notions of fairness: *SD-proportional*: where each agent SD-prefers their allocation to the uniform allocation, *weak-SD-proportional*, where no agent strictly SD-prefers the uniform allocation over their own, *SD-envyfreeness*, where each agent SD-prefers their allocation to every other agent's allocation, and *weak-SD-envyfreeness*, where no agent strictly SD-prefers another agent's allocation to their own.

We also formalise fairness based on von Neumann–Morgenstern utility functions consistent with each agent's ordinal preferences. These enable defining alternative notions of fairness based on expected utility over allocations. Let

```
definition
  SDA :: β relation ⇒ (β allocation) relation where
  p ≿[SDA(R)] q ≡
    ∀x. R x x ⟶ (∑i∈{y. R y y ∧ y ≿[R] x}. p i) ≥ (∑i∈{y. R y y ∧ y ≿[R] x}. q i)

 locale vnm-utility = finite-total-preorder-on S R +
  fixes u :: 'a ⇒ real
  assumes utility_le_iff: x ∈ S ⟹ y ∈ S ⟹ u x ≤ u y ⟷ x ≾[R] y

definition RS :: β relation ⇒(β set) relation  where
  p ≿[RS(P)] q ≡ ∃ f :: (β ⇒ β). (inj_on f q ∧ f ‘ q ⊆ p ∧ (∀(x:: β)∈q. f x ≿[P] x))

definition SD-proportional :: (α, β) assignment ⇒ bool where
  SD-proportional A ≡ ∀i ∈ agents. A i ≿[SDA(R i)] pmf-like-set alts

definition weak-SD-proportional :: (α, β) assignment ⇒ bool where
  weak-SD-proportional A ≡ ∀i ∈ agents. ¬(pmf-like-set alts ≿[SDA(R i)] A i)

definition possible-proportional :: (α, β) assignment ⇒ bool where
  possible-proportional A ≡
    ∀i ∈ agents. ∃u :: (β ⇒ real).
      vnm-utility alts (R i) u ∧ sum-utility u alts (A i) ≥ sum u alts / (card agents)

definition necessary-proportional :: (α, β) assignment ⇒ bool where
  necessary-proportional A ≡
    ∀i ∈ agents. ∀u :: (β ⇒ real).
      vnm-utility alts (R i) u ⟶ sum-utility u alts (A i) ≥ sum u alts /(card agents)

definition SD-envyfreeness :: (α, β) assignment ⇒ bool where
  SD-envyfreeness A ≡ ∀i ∃ agents. ∀j ∈ agents. A i ≿[SDA(R i)] A j

definition weak_SD-envyfreeness :: (α, β) assignment ⇒ bool where
  weak_SD-envyfreeness A ≡ ∀i ∈ agents. ∀j ∈ agents. ¬ (A j ≿[SDA(R i)] A i)

definition possible-envyfreeness :: (α, β) assignment ⇒ bool where
  possible-envyfreeness A ≡
   ∀i ∈ agents. ∃u :: (β ⇒ real).
   ∀j ∈ agents. vnm-utility alts (R i) u ∧ sum-utility u alts (A i) ≥ sum-utility u alts (A j)

definition necessary-envyfreeness :: (α, β) assignment ⇒ bool where
  necessary-envyfreeness A ≡
   ∀i ∈ agents. ∀ u :: (β ⇒ real).
   ∀j ∈ agents. vnm-utility alts (R i) u ⟶ sum-utility u alts (A i) ≥ sum-utility u alts (A j)

definition possible-completion-envyfreeness :: (α, β) assignment ⇒ bool where
  possible-completion-envyfreeness A ≡
  ∀i ∈ agents. (∃P :: β set ⇒ β set ⇒ bool.
                        (∀s1 s2.  s2 ≿[RS(R i)] s1 ⟶ s2 ≿[P] s1) ∧
                        (∀j ∈ agents. allocated-alts (A i) alts ≿[P] allocated-alts (A j) alts))

definition necessary-completion-envyfreeness :: (α, β) assignment ⇒ bool where
  necessary-completion-envyfreeness A ≡
    ∀i ∈ agents. ∀P :: β set ⇒ β set ⇒ bool.
       (∀s1 s2.  s2 ≿[RS(R i)] s1 ⟶ s2 ≿[P] s1) ⟶
    (∀j ∈ agents. allocated-alts (A i) alts ≿[P] allocated-alts (A j) alts)
```

Fig. 3: Formal definitions of fairness and underlying formal definitions

sum-utility u alts p be defined as the sum of an agent's utility for a given allocation p over alternatives *alts* using the utility function u, $\sum_{j \in alts}(u\ i) * (p\ i)$. The *vnm-utility* locale [18], presented in Figure 3 for convenience, provides the condition under which a utility function is a von Neumann–Morgenstern utility.

With these utility definitions, we are ready to present four more notions of fairness: *necessary-proportional*: each agent prefers their allocation at least as much as the uniform allocation using any possible utility function consistent with an agent's preferences, *possible-proportional*: there exists such a utility function for each agent, *necessary-envyfreeness*: for all consistent utility functions, agents prefer their allocation to any other agent's allocation, and *possible-envyfreeness*: for each agent, there exists a utility function under which they prefer their allocation.

In the discrete setting, we use the *responsive set extension* (RS) to lift preferences over alternatives to preferences over sets. As defined in Figure 3, given a preference relation R, an agent i prefers set A to B under RS if there exists an injection $f : B \rightarrow A$ such that $f(x) \succeq_i x$ for all $x \in B$.

Using this definition, we can introduce two fairness notions in the discrete setting.

We note two important clarifications regarding our formalisation of *completion-based* fairness notions. First, although our definitions are inspired by Bouveret and Lemaître [10], we allow weak (non-strict) preferences, supporting indifference, whereas their original formulation assumes strict preference. The paper we are formalising [6], refers to the original definitions [10] but is also inconsistent with the original notions in that it defines fairness under weak preferences. Second, the definition of a relation *consistent with the responsive set extension* is ambiguous in prior work. In particular, Aziz et al. [6] use this terminology but do not specify whether consistency should be interpreted as refinement (implication) or as equivalence. The original paper [10], defines a refinement R_0 of a relation R as satisfying $R \subseteq R_0$, i.e., implication. In contrast, Aziz et al. [6] use the term *consistent* elsewhere in their article to describe equivalence (bi-implication) with respect to utility functions. To maintain compatibility with the intended refinement-based semantics of the responsive set extension, we adopt the implication interpretation: we require that the completion relation P refines RS(R), not that it is logically equivalent to it.

In fact, we first interpreted the definition with equivalence as the relation. The statement "a relation consistent with the responsive set extension of the preference relation of the agent" is formalised as $\forall s1\ s2.\ s2 \succeq [RS(R\ i)]s1 \longleftrightarrow s2 \succeq [P]s1$.

definition *possible-completion-envyfreeness* :: (α, β) *assignment* $\Rightarrow$ *bool* **where**
possible-completion-envyfreeness A ≡ ∀i ∈ agents. (∃P :: *β set* ⇒ *β set* ⇒ *bool*.
(∀s1 s2. s1 ⪰[*RS*(R i)] s2 ⟷ s1 ⪰[P] s2) ∧
(∀j ∈ agents. *allocated-alts* (A i) alts ⪰[P] *allocated-alts* (A j) alts))

definition *necessary-completion-envyfreeness* :: (α, β) *assignment* $\Rightarrow$ *bool* **where**
necessary-completion-envyfreeness A ≡ ∀i ∈ agents. ∀P :: *β set* ⇒ *β set* ⇒ *bool*.
(∀s1 s2. s1 ⪰[*RS*(R i)] s2 ⟷ s1 ⪰[P] s2) ⟶
(∀j ∈ agents. *allocated-alts* (A i) alts ⪰[P] *allocated-alts* (A j) alts)

However, once the definition has been formalised, we could see that the definitions of *necessary-completion-envyfreeness* and *possible-completion-envyfreeness* would be equivalent using equivalence rather than refinement. Given an agent i and preference profile R, the one and only P relation that satisfies formula

$$\forall\ s_1\ s_2. s_1 \succeq [RS(R\ i)] s_2 \longleftrightarrow s1 \succeq [P] s2$$

is in fact the relation $RS(R\ i)$ itself. Hence, both definitions now collapse into:

∀i, j ∈ agents. *allocated-alts* (A i) alts $\succeq [RS(\text{R i})]$ *allocated-alts* (A j) alts

This would not be sensible if we are trying to have definitions that follow the hierarchical structure presented in Figure 1. We hence use the definitions that rely the refinement relation instead, as shown in Figure 3.

4 Verification

We verify relationships between the different fairness notions that we formalised, following the original pen-and-paper results. The key results of interest [6] are Theorems 2 and 3, which capture equivalences and implications among the various notions of fairness, respectively. Note that we disproved one of these results in the original paper, in particular, Equation 3b. In particular, they state the following:

$$\textit{weak-SD-proportional} \longleftrightarrow \textit{possible-proportional} \tag{1}$$

$$\textit{SD-proportional} \longleftrightarrow \textit{necessary-proportional} \tag{2}$$

$$\textit{weak-SD-envyfreeness} \longrightarrow \textit{possible-completion-envyfreeness} \tag{3a}$$

$$\textit{weak-SD-envyfreeness} \not\longleftarrow \textit{possible-completion-envyfreeness} \tag{3b}$$

$$\textit{SD-envyfreeness} \longleftrightarrow \textit{necessary-envyfreeness} \tag{4a}$$

$$\textit{necessary-envyfreeness} \longleftrightarrow \textit{necessary-completion-envyfreeness} \tag{4b}$$

$$\textit{SD-envyfreeness} \longrightarrow \textit{SD-proportional} \tag{5}$$

$$\textit{SD-proportional} \longrightarrow \textit{weak-SD-proportional} \tag{6}$$

$$\textit{possible-envyfreeness} \longrightarrow \textit{SD-proportional} \tag{7}$$

$$\textit{possible-envyfreeness} \longrightarrow \textit{weak-SD-envyfreeness} \tag{8}$$

We also prove the following simple fact in order to complete the relationships described in Figure 1:

$$\textit{necessary-envyfreeness} \longrightarrow \textit{possible-envyfreeness} \tag{9}$$

For convenience, we sometimes refer to the fairness properties to mean the property applied to a given assignment. To facilitate verification, we classify the theorems into two categories: those applicable in the randomised setting and those specific to the discrete setting. Among these eleven relationships, three involve discrete notions—namely, those based on possible and necessary completion envy-freeness. We formalise and verify these properties separately within the appropriate locales: *random-assignment* for the randomised setting and *discrete-assignment* for the discrete setting. We prove that *discrete-assignment* is a sublocale of *random-assignment*, enabling the reuse of theorems that are proven in the random setting within the discrete setting. This hierarchy ensures modularity and avoids duplicating proofs when fairness notions coincide across settings.

The fairness notions rely on the three important concepts: our extended definition of stochastic dominance, the utility function, and the responsive set extension. We divide the fairness notions into three further categories, based on which notion they refer to.

As such, once we have established the relationships between these three further notions, the equivalences and the implications among the remaining fairness notions will follow directly.

We then state our most important theorem, which lays the foundation for the relationship between fairness notions. The theorem states that the three statements below are equivalent (given two assignments p and q, and a particular agent i). The paper [6] denotes the allocation of agent i in assignment p and q as $p(i)$ and $q(i)$, respectively. They also use $\succeq_i^{SD}$ to describe the stochastic dominance relation, $\succeq_i^{RS}$ to describe the relation using the responsive set extension, both of which with regard to agent i's preference profile. The set $\mathcal{U}_i$ is the set of all utility functions that are consistent with the preference relation of agent i. In the discrete setting, $u_i(p\,i)$ is defined as the sum of agent i's valuation of the allocation [6]. However, in the context of the randomised or the fractional setting, it is more appropriate to interpret utility as a weighted sum of the agent's valuation over alternatives, where the weights correspond to the probabilities (in the random setting) or fractions (in the fractional setting) of receiving each alternative. This is the interpretation we adopt in our formalisation and verification. The equivalent statements are:

$$p\,i \succeq_i^{SD} q\,i \tag{i}$$

$$\forall u_i \in \mathcal{U}_i.\ u_i(p\,i) \geq u_i(q\,i) \tag{ii}$$

$$p\,i \succeq_i^{RS} q\,i \tag{iii}$$

In our verification effort, to prove the equivalence of these three statements, we prove the following: (i) and (ii) are equivalent, (iii) implies (ii), and (i) implies (iii). In particular, the equivalence of (i) and (ii) will be proven in the random setting, which is the locale *random-assignment*. The theorems relating (iii) to (ii), and (i) to (iii) are proven in the discrete setting (*discrete-assignment* locale). We also establish the relationship that *discrete-assignment* is a **sublocale** of *random-assignment*, which will allow us to reuse the theorem about the equivalence of (i) and (ii) in the discrete setting, so that we can claim that the three definitions are equivalent in the discrete setting.

The equivalence of (i) and (ii) is a classic result in social choice theory, and there have been both pen-and-paper proofs [11] and mechanised proofs [18]. Recall, though, that in this formalisation we generalise the notion of SD.

For the forward direction, we first prove an important fact that for each agent with a total transitive order on the set of alternatives, there exists an increasing ordering of the set of alternatives (a sequence where each element is preferred to the previous element). Given a set of alternatives, let the ordering on the alternatives be $a_1, a_2, ..., a_m$, where a_i is preferred to a_j for any $i \geq j$. To prove that (extended) stochastic dominance indeed implies the property of every utility function, we assume that we have two allocations p and q where $p \succeq [SDA(R)]q$, and R is an arbitrary preference relation on the set of alternatives. We thus have $a_j \succeq [R]a_i$ for any $j \geq i$. We then show that, for any agents i, assuming we have any arbitrary utility function u consistent with R (denoting $p\,j$ and $q\,j$ as the fractions/probability of alternative j in each allocations): $\sum_{j \in alts} u\,j\,(p\,j) \geq \sum_{j\,\in\,alts} u\,j\,(q\,j)$ is equivalent to $\sum_{j \in alts} u\,j\,(p\,j - q\,j) \geq 0$. The proof follows by using the Abel's summation technique [30], where summations can be rearranged as follows:

$$\sum_{j \in alts} u\,j(p\,j - q\,j) = u\,a_1(\sum_{i=1}^{m} p\,a_i - q\,a_i) + \sum_{i=2}^{m}((u\,a_i - u\,a_{i-1})(\sum_{k=i}^{m} p\,a_k - q\,a_k))$$

This is where we use our assumptions. Firstly, our original assumption for the assignment problem, where the sums of fractions in an allocation are constant across agents, makes the first summand on the right-hand side zero (note that the sequence $a_1, a_2, ..., a_m$ contains all and only the alternatives in our original set of alternatives). Regarding the second summand, we resort to the definition of our (extended) stochastic dominance to prove that each term in the summand is nonnegative, or we are proving: $\forall i \in \{2, .., m\}.(u\,a_i - u\,a_{i-1})(\sum_{k=i}^{m} p\,a_k - q\,a_k) \geq 0$ The definition can be summarised as $p \succeq [SDA(R)]q$ iff for each alternative o, the total fraction of alternatives that is at least as preferred as o (with respect to the preference relation R) in p is more than in q. For each i, either i is the smallest index j that a_j is at least as preferred to as a_i, or there is an index $k < i$ such that $a_k \succeq [R]a_i$. The first case implies that the second factor in (1) is nonnegative, and according to the consistency of the utility function with the preference relation, the first factor is also nonnegative, hence, we must have the product in (1) nonnegative. For the second case, since there is an index $k < i$ such that $a_k \succeq [R]a_i$, $u\,a_k \geq u\,a_i$ by the consistency of utility functions. We also have that $u\,a_i \geq u\,a_k$ according to the fact that $a_i \succeq [R]a_k$ for any $i \geq k$. Thus $u\,a_k = u\,a_i$, following the fact that the utilities of all alternatives from a_k leading up to a_{i-1} are all equal to $u\,a_i$. As a result, the first factor is 0 in the second case, which proved our theorem in the forward direction.

For the backward direction, we assume that with any utility function consistent with the preference relation R, the weighted sum of utility in p is greater than or equal to the weighted sum of utility in q. To prove that $p \succeq [SDA(R)]q$, we prove using its definition that for any alternative o, the sum of fractions allocated to alternatives that are at least as preferred as o is larger in p than in q. Fixing an arbitrary x, we prove that the sum of fractions allocated to alternatives that are at least as preferred as x is larger in p: $\sum_{y \succeq [R] x} p\,y \geq \sum_{y \succeq [R] x} q\,y$. The utility function assumption implies $\sum_{j \in alts} u\,j\,(p\,j) \geq \sum_{j\ \in\ alts} u\,j\,(q\,j)$. We would like to pick a utility function that, when substituted in $\sum_{j \in alts} u\,j\,(p\,j)$, will give us $\sum_{y \succeq [R] x} p(y)$. One intuitive indicator function to consider is the function that returns 1 if the input alternative is strictly preferred to x, and returns 0 otherwise. We call this function g. However, since the value of the utility function is the same for all inputs preferred to x, this is not a von Neumann-Morgenstein utility function. We need to add a function to g (possibly a utility function) to ensure it satisfies the von Neumann-Morgenstein utility function assumption. Our candidate function is another indicator-like function. This function takes an alternative k, and returns the number of alternatives that are at most as preferred as k. It is trivial to notice that this is indeed a utility function, call this function f, and adding f to g creates a utility function. However, we just want to use g to reach our conclusion; thus, we want to eliminate the dependency of whether g satisfies the desired condition on f. Notice that $g + \epsilon * f$ is a utility function for any $\epsilon > 0$. Substitute this into (2) gives us:

$$\sum_{j \in alts} (g\,j + \epsilon * f\,j)(p\,j - q\,j) \geq 0 \longleftrightarrow$$

$$\sum_{j \in alts} g\,j(p\,j - q\,j) + \epsilon * (\sum_{j \in alts} f\,j\,(p\,j - q\,j)) \geq 0$$

Knowing that ϵ can be arbitrarily small and the inequality above is true for all $\epsilon > 0$, we can prove $\sum_{j \in alts} g\,j\,(p\,j - q\,j) \geq 0$. And according to our observation of the definition of g, this is actually equivalent to (2). Hence, we have proven both directions of the theorem relating (i) $\Leftrightarrow$ (ii).

Moving on to the relationships: (iii) $\Rightarrow$ (ii) and (i) $\Rightarrow$ (iii), in the discrete setting. Proving (iii) $\Rightarrow$ (ii) is rather trivial; all that remains is a matter of how to interpret allocations as sets of alternatives. Assuming that $p \succeq [RS(R)]q$, where p and q are two allocations, and R is our preference relation, we want to prove that for any utility function u consistent with R, the weighted sum of utility in p is larger than that in q. From the definition of responsive set extension, there must be a total injective mapping f from q to p such that $f(x) \succeq [R]x$ for any $x \in q$. With our assumption that the sum of proportions for all agents is equal, the sum of proportions in p and in q is equal. Since in the discrete setting, all allocations are 0 or 1, which translates to the set of alternatives with proportions being 1. As a result, the mapping f above is not just injective but also bijective, which means it is a one-to-one mapping, where each element in the domain is preferred to its image under the mapping f. With this observation, the total utility of allocation p must be larger than or equal to q according to the consistency of utility functions with the preference relation

Now we prove (i) $\Rightarrow$ (iii), assuming that we have $p \succeq [SDA(R)]q$, where p and q are allocations which can both be either interpreted as a function or a set of alternatives, and R is the preference relation, we prove that $p \succeq [RS(R)]q$. One thing to note is that, since we are also interpreting p and q as sets, (extended) stochastic dominance now means that for any alternative x, the number of alternatives that are at least as preferred to x in p is more than that in q.

To prove the responsive set property, we need to show that there exists an injection from q to p, mapping an element in q to a more preferred element in p. Interpreting this as a matching in a graph[6] where the set of vertices is $p \cup q$, we want to find a matching that covers all vertices in q.

We refer to Hall's marriage theorem to prove this result [23,24], and we rely on a prior formalisation of this theorem in Isabelle/HOL [26,25]. The theorem (in its graph-theoretic formulation) state that given a bipartite graph $G = (X, Y, E)$ with bipartite sets X and Y, there is a X-perfect matching (a matching that covers all vertices in X) if and only if for all subsets W of X, the number of elements that are adjacent to W (elements in Y that are adjacent to at least an element in W) is at least as large as the number of elements in W. To use this theorem, we need to prove that for any subset $t \subseteq q$, the number of elements in p that are at least as preferred as some elements in t is at least the cardinality of t. Since the preference relation is total and transitive on the set of alternatives, it is also total and transitive on any subsets of the set of alternatives, namely t, p and q. We also establish that there is a minimal element a in t. Since a is the minimal element in t, and $t \subseteq q$, it is a subset of the set containing all elements that are at least as preferred to a in q. This subset then has smaller cardinality than the set containing all elements that are at least as preferred to a in p, according to (extended) stochastic dominance. The set containing all elements in p that are at least as preferred to a, is then a subset of the set containing all elements in p that are at least as preferred to an element in t. As a result, we must have that the number of elements in p that is at least as preferred to an element in t is at least as large as the number of elements in t, hence there exists such a matching. In our proof, the observation is that the matching is the relation $\succeq [R]$, where an element (alternative) a is adjacent to an element b iff $a \succeq [R] b$. Since (i) $\Leftrightarrow$ (ii), (iii) $\Rightarrow$ (ii), and (i) $\Rightarrow$ (iii), we can conclude that the three statements are equivalent in the discrete setting.

One more important result remains before we investigate relationships between fairness notions. We prove that a *weaker* version of (extended) stochastic dominance would be equivalent to a weakened notion for utility functions. We prove that an allocation q not strictly *SD preferred* to another allocation p is equivalent to the fact that there exists a utility function that makes the weighted sum of the utility of alternatives in p is larger than or equal to the weighted sum of the utility of alternatives in q. Here, q is strictly SD preferred to p means $q \succeq [SDA(R)] p \wedge \neg p \succeq [SDA(R)] q$. What we need to prove is:

$$\neg p \succeq [SDA(R)] q \longleftrightarrow \exists u. u \in \mathcal{U} \wedge \sum_{j \in alts} (u\, j)\, (p\, j) \geq \sum_{j \in alts} (u\, j)\, (q\, j)$$

Here, $\mathcal{U}$ is the set of all utility functions that are consistent with the preference relation R. This equivalence is already formalised and proved in the work [18], our proof adopts this proof, with some minor modifications taking into account our weakened assumption that the allocations are not necessarily lotteries.

Relationships between fairness notions. With our new definition in contrast to the original definition by [6], a modification to the equivalence is needed, where instead of an Equivalence (3a, 3b) as per the pen-and-paper proof, only Implication (3a) from *weak-SD-envyfreeness* to *possible-completion-envyfreeness* holds. We have a counterexample showing that *possible-completion-envyfreeness* does not imply *weak-SD-envyfreeness* that is formalised in Isabelle/HOL. It remains to be seen whether an alternative definition of *possible-completion-envyfreeness* implies *weak-SD-envyfreeness* while retaining the current relationships with other notions of fairness.

With the equivalence in the previous section about stochastic dominance and utility functions, Equivalence (2) and the equivalence of *SD-envyfreeness* and *necessary-envyfreeness* in Equivalence (4a) conveniently follow. The equivalence of *necessary-envyfreeness* and *necessary-completion-envyfreeness* in Equivalence (4b), and Implication (3a) follow from the equivalence between the stochastic dominance relation and the responsive set extension relation. Equivalence (1) follows from the equivalence of (i) and (ii).

The implication of *possible-envyfreeness* for *possible-proportionality* and the implication of *necessary-envy-freeness* for *necessary-proportionality* follows directly from the observation that if an agents value their allocations at least as much as other agents, then they must value their allocations at least as much as the equal share allocation (or average share allocation). Combine this with Equivalences (2), (4a), (4b), we should obtain Implications (5) and (7). Implication (6) is rather trivial, as the latter definition is a weaker variant of the former one. Implications (8) also follows from the equivalence of (i) and (ii).

5 Related Work

The formalisation and verification of foundational results in social choice theory using proof assistants has received increasing attention in the formal methods community. Much of the existing work focuses on voting systems, particularly formalising classical impossibility theorems and properties of collective decision-making rules or on certifying voting mechanisms.

Among the most well-known results, Arrow's impossibility theorem [2] has been formalised multiple times. Notably, Nipkow [32,31] and Gammie [20] each provided formalisations in Isabelle/HOL, while Wiedijk formalised the theorem in Mizar [41]. Gammie's formalisation further extends to incorporate May's majority decision theorem [28] and Sen's liberal paradox [40]. May's theorem has also been formalised independently by Li [27] in the Roqc Prover (formerly Coq). Nipkow's Isabelle/HOL formalisation [32] also includes a proof of the Gibbard–Satterthwaite theorem [22,39], another cornerstone result in voting theory. While these efforts have significantly contributed to the reliable formalisation of classical results in social choice theory, their primary focus is on the aggregation of preferences to select a winning candidate or to generate a collective ranking. In contrast, our work addresses a distinct branch of social choice theory: the fair allocation of indivisible goods, which focuses on distributing resources across individuals under ordinal preferences.

In the domain of resource allocation, there has been some foundational formalisation work. Parsert and Kaliszyk [36] as well as Eberl [18] have independently formalised the von Neumann–Morgenstern (vNM) utility function in Isabelle/HOL. Eberl's work on formalising randomised social choice further includes the notions of preference profiles, lottery-based social choice functions, and a notion of stochastic dominance for random assignments. These formalised concepts provide a critical basis for reasoning about randomised outcomes in collective decision-making.

Our work builds directly on Eberl's formalisation, reusing the definitions of preference profiles and utility function to formalise the assignment problem setting, with a generalisation of Eberl's stochastic dominance definition to account for the discrete setting of the assignment problem.

This is the first formalisation of the assignment problem along with associated fairness notions such as SD-proportionality and SD-envy-freeness. The formalisation verifies known relationships between these notions and formally refutes one pen-and-paper relationship that was thought to be true [6]. Similar to the pen-and-paper proofs, our proofs rely on Hall's theorem [23]. Our formalisation relies on an existing Isabelle/HOL formalisation of this theorem [26].

6 Conclusion

We presented a formalisation of the assignment problem in Isabelle/HOL, covering both the fractional (randomised) and discrete settings. Our formalisation defines the core structure of assignment problems, introduces multiple notions of fairness across these settings, and provides formal proofs about how they relate.

References

1. Amanatidis, G., Aziz, H., Birmpas, G., Filos-Ratsikas, A., Li, B., Moulin, H., Voudouris, A.A., Wu, X.: Fair division of indivisible goods: Recent progress and open questions. Artif. Intell. **322**(C) (Sep 2023). https://doi.org/10.1016/j.artint.2023.103965, `https://doi.org/10.1016/j.artint.2023.103965`
2. Arrow, K.J.: Social Choice and Individual Values. Yale University Press (2012), `http://www.jstor.org/stable/j.ctt1nqb90`
3. Aziz, H.: Developments in multi-agent fair allocation. In: The Thirty-Fourth AAAI Conference on Artificial Intelligence, AAAI 2020, The Thirty-Second Innovative Applications of Artificial Intelligence Conference, IAAI 2020, The Tenth AAAI Symposium on Educational Advances in Artificial Intelligence, EAAI 2020, New York, NY, USA, February 7-12, 2020. pp. 13563–13568. AAAI Press (2020). https://doi.org/10.1609/AAAI.V34I09.7082, `https://doi.org/10.1609/aaai.v34i09.7082`
4. Aziz, H., Brandt, F., Elkind, E., Skowron, P.: Computational social choice: The first ten years and beyond. In: Steffen, B., Woeginger, G.J. (eds.) Computing and

Software Science - State of the Art and Perspectives, Lecture Notes in Computer Science, vol. 10000, pp. 48–65. Springer (2019). https://doi.org/10.1007/978-3-319-91908-9_4, https://doi.org/10.1007/978-3-319-91908-9_4

5. Aziz, H., Brandt, F., Stursberg, P.: On popular random assignments. In: Vöcking, B. (ed.) Algorithmic Game Theory. pp. 183–194. Springer Berlin Heidelberg, Berlin, Heidelberg (2013)
6. Aziz, H., Gaspers, S., Mackenzie, S., Walsh, T.: Fair assignment of indivisible objects under ordinal preferences. Artificial Intelligence **227**, 71–92 (2015). https://doi.org/https://doi.org/10.1016/j.artint.2015.06.002, https://www.sciencedirect.com/science/article/pii/S0004370215000880
7. Aziz, H., Luo, P., Rizkallah, C.: Incompatibility of efficiency and strategyproofness in the random assignment setting with indifferences. Economics Letters **160**, 46–49 (2017). https://doi.org/https://doi.org/10.1016/j.econlet.2017.08.010, https://www.sciencedirect.com/science/article/pii/S0165176517303336
8. Aziz, H., Luo, P., Rizkallah, C.: Rank maximal equal contribution: A probabilistic social choice function. In: McIlraith, S.A., Weinberger, K.Q. (eds.) Proceedings of the Thirty-Second AAAI Conference on Artificial Intelligence, (AAAI-18), the 30th innovative Applications of Artificial Intelligence (IAAI-18), and the 8th AAAI Symposium on Educational Advances in Artificial Intelligence (EAAI-18), New Orleans, Louisiana, USA, February 2-7, 2018. pp. 910–916. AAAI Press (2018). https://doi.org/10.1609/AAAI.V32I1.11448, https://doi.org/10.1609/aaai.v32i1.11448
9. Bogomolnaia, A., Moulin, H.: A new solution to the random assignment problem. J. Econ. Theory **100**(2), 295–328 (2001). https://doi.org/10.1006/JETH.2000.2710, https://doi.org/10.1006/jeth.2000.2710
10. Bouveret, S., Endriss, U., Lang, J.: Fair division under ordinal preferences: Computing envy-free allocations of indivisible goods. In: Coelho, H., Studer, R., Wooldridge, M.J. (eds.) ECAI 2010 - 19th European Conference on Artificial Intelligence, Lisbon, Portugal, August 16-20, 2010, Proceedings. Frontiers in Artificial Intelligence and Applications, vol. 215, pp. 387–392. IOS Press (2010). https://doi.org/10.3233/978-1-60750-606-5-387, https://doi.org/10.3233/978-1-60750-606-5-387
11. Brandl, F., Brandt, F., Eberl, M., Geist, C.: Proving the incompatibility of efficiency and strategyproofness via SMT solving. J. ACM **65**(2), 6:1–6:28 (2018). https://doi.org/10.1145/3125642, https://doi.org/10.1145/3125642
12. Brandt, F., Conitzer, V., Endriss, U., Lang, J., Procaccia, A.D.: Handbook of Computational Social Choice. Cambridge University Press, USA, 1st edn. (2016)
13. Brandt, F., Geist, C.: Finding strategyproof social choice functions via SAT solving. J. Artif. Intell. Res. **55**, 565–602 (2016). https://doi.org/10.1613/JAIR.4959, https://doi.org/10.1613/jair.4959
14. Brandt, F., Geist, C., Peters, D.: Optimal bounds for the no-show paradox via SAT solving. Math. Soc. Sci. **90**, 18–27 (2017). https://doi.org/10.1016/J.MATHSOCSCI.2016.09.003, https://doi.org/10.1016/j.mathsocsci.2016.09.003
15. Caragiannis, I., Gravin, N., Huang, X.: Envy-freeness up to any item with high nash welfare: The virtue of donating items. In: Karlin, A.R., Immorlica, N., Johari, R. (eds.) Proceedings of the 2019 ACM Conference on Economics and Computation, EC 2019, Phoenix, AZ, USA, June 24-28, 2019. pp. 527–545. ACM (2019). https://doi.org/10.1145/3328526.3329574, https://doi.org/10.1145/3328526.3329574

16. Chakraborty, M., Segal-Halevi, E., Suksompong, W.: Weighted fairness notions for indivisible items revisited. ACM Transactions on Economics and Computation **12**(3) (Sep 2024). https://doi.org/10.1145/3665799, https://doi.org/10.1145/3665799
17. Do, D.M., Rizkallah, C.: Formalising fairness in the assignment problem with ordinal preferences in isabelle/hol (artefact), https://github.com/crizkallah/crizkallah.github.io/blob/master/formalisations/Fairness_Fractional_Assignment.thy, last accessed July 2025
18. Eberl, M.: Randomised social choice theory. Archive of Formal Proofs (May 2016), https://isa-afp.org/entries/Randomised_Social_Choice.html, Formal proof development
19. Endriss, U.: Lecture notes on fair division. CoRR **abs/1806.04234** (2018), http://arxiv.org/abs/1806.04234
20. Gammie, P.: Some classical results in social choice theory. Archive of Formal Proofs (November 2008), https://isa-afp.org/entries/SenSocialChoice.html, Formal proof development
21. Gehrlein, W.V.: Condorcet's paradox. Theory and Decision **15**(2), 161–197 (1983). https://doi.org/10.1007/BF00143070, https://doi.org/10.1007/BF00143070
22. Gibbard, A.: Manipulation of voting schemes: A general result. Econometrica **41**(4), 587–601 (1973), http://www.jstor.org/stable/1914083
23. Hall, P.: On representatives of subsets. Classic Papers in Combinatorics pp. 58–62 (1987)
24. Halmos, P.R., Vaughan, H.E.: The marriage problem. In: Classic Papers in Combinatorics, pp. 146–147. Springer (2009)
25. Jiang, D., Nipkow, T.: Hall's marriage theorem. Archive of Formal Proofs (December 2010), https://isa-afp.org/entries/Marriage.html, Formal proof development
26. Jiang, D., Nipkow, T.: Proof pearl: The marriage theorem. In: Jouannaud, J., Shao, Z. (eds.) Proceedings of the First International Conference on Certified Programs and Proofs CPP 2011, Kenting, Taiwan, December 7-9, 2011. Lecture Notes in Computer Science, vol. 7086, pp. 394–399. Springer (2011). https://doi.org/10.1007/978-3-642-25379-9_28, https://doi.org/10.1007/978-3-642-25379-9_28
27. Li, K.H.: Formalizing May's theorem. CoRR **abs/2210.05342** (2022). https://doi.org/10.48550/ARXIV.2210.05342, https://doi.org/10.48550/arXiv.2210.05342
28. May, K.O.: A set of independent necessary and sufficient conditions for simple majority decision. Econometrica **20**(4), 680–684 (1952). https://doi.org/10.2307/1907651
29. Mishra, S., Padala, M., Gujar, S.: Fair allocation of goods and chores - tutorial and survey of recent results. CoRR **abs/2307.10985** (2023). https://doi.org/10.48550/ARXIV.2307.10985, https://doi.org/10.48550/arXiv.2307.10985
30. Niculescu, C.P., Stănescu, M.M.: A note on abel's partial summation formula. Aequationes mathematicae **91**, 1009–1024 (2017)
31. Nipkow, T.: Arrow and Gibbard-Satterthwaite. Archive of Formal Proofs (September 2008), https://isa-afp.org/entries/ArrowImpossibilityGS.html, Formal proof development
32. Nipkow, T.: Social choice theory in HOL. Journal of Automated Reasoning **43**(3), 289–304 (2009). https://doi.org/10.1007/S10817-009-9147-4, https://doi.org/10.1007/s10817-009-9147-4

33. Pacuit, E.: Voting Methods. In: Zalta, E.N., Nodelman, U. (eds.) The Stanford Encyclopedia of Philosophy. Metaphysics Research Lab, Stanford University, Summer 2024 edn. (2024)
34. Parsert, J., Kaliszyk, C.: Microeconomics and the first welfare theorem. Archive of Formal Proofs (September 2017), `https://isa-afp.org/entries/First_Welfare_Theorem.html`, Formal proof development
35. Parsert, J., Kaliszyk, C.: Towards formal foundations for game theory. In: Avigad, J., Mahboubi, A. (eds.) Interactive Theorem Proving (ITP). Lecture Notes in Computer Science, vol. 10895, pp. 495–503. Springer (2018). https://doi.org/10.1007/978-3-319-94821-8_29, `https://doi.org/10.1007/978-3-319-94821-8_29`
36. Parsert, J., Kaliszyk, C.: Von-neumann-morgenstern utility theorem. Archive of Formal Proofs (July 2018), `https://isa-afp.org/entries/Neumann_Morgenstern_Utility.html`, Formal proof development
37. Pruhs, K., Woeginger, G.J.: Divorcing made easy. In: Kranakis, E., Krizanc, D., Luccio, F.L. (eds.) Fun with Algorithms - 6th International Conference, FUN 2012, Venice, Italy, June 4-6, 2012. Proceedings. Lecture Notes in Computer Science, vol. 7288, pp. 305–314. Springer (2012). https://doi.org/10.1007/978-3-642-30347-0_30, `https://doi.org/10.1007/978-3-642-30347-0_30`
38. Satterthwaite, M.A.: Strategy-proofness and Arrow's conditions: Existence and correspondence theorems for voting procedures and social welfare functions. Journal of Economic Theory **10**(2), 187–217 (1975). https://doi.org/https://doi.org/10.1016/0022-0531(75)90050-2, `https://www.sciencedirect.com/science/article/pii/0022053175900502`
39. Satterthwaite, M.A.: Strategy-proofness and arrow's conditions: Existence and correspondence theorems for voting procedures and social welfare functions. Journal of Economic Theory **10**(2), 187–217 (1975). https://doi.org/https://doi.org/10.1016/0022-0531(75)90050-2, `https://www.sciencedirect.com/science/article/pii/0022053175900502`
40. Sen, A.K.: The impossibility of a paretian liberal. Journal of Political Economy **78**(1), 152–157 (1970)
41. Wiedijk, F.: Formalizing arrow's theorem. Sadhana **34**(1), 193–220 (2009)

A PVS Library on the Infinitude of Primes

Bruno Berto de Oliveira Ribeiro[1](✉), Mariano M. Moscato[2](✉), Thaynara Arielly de Lima[3](✉), and Mauricio Ayala-Rincón[1](✉)

[1] Universidade de Brasília, Exact Sciences Institute, Brasília D.F., Brazil
ayala@unb.br, bruno.berto@aluno.unb.br
[2] Analytical Mechanics Associates Inc., Hampton, VA, U.S.A.
mariano.m.moscato@nasa.gov
[3] Universidade Federal de Goiás, Institute of Mathematics and Statistics, Goiânia, Brazil
thaynaradelima@ufg.br

Abstract. This paper discusses the formalization in PVS of diverse proofs of the infinitude of primes. These proofs are developed using techniques from various areas of mathematics, including set theory, algebra, analysis, number theory, and topology. The availability of such a variety of proofs is helpful as a didactic resource, aiming to encourage mathematicians working in different areas to adopt interactive theorem provers as one of their everyday tools. The presented collection of formalizations follows the proofs selected by Erdös, Aigner, and Ziegler in their famous work "Proofs from THE BOOK," namely those based on Fermat numbers, Mersenne numbers and algebraic structures, topological properties, and the analysis of harmonic series. The paper discusses the differences between informal proofs and mechanical formalization, highlighting the usefulness of distinguishing features of PVS to guide and facilitate the presented mechanization.

Keywords: Primes, Fermat Numbers, Mersenne Numbers, Harmonic Series, Theorem Proving, Algebraic Formalizations, PVS.

1 Introduction

Euclid's proof of the infinitude of primes [4] is a classic and highly illustrative result. As the concept of primality is typically presented in introductory math courses, this proof offers an excellent example of approaching problems involving infinity. Over the years, many mathematicians, such as Paul Erdös, have provided new proofs of this result, each drawing from different areas of mathematics. These proofs are not only valuable for showcasing the tools offered by such diverse fields, but they also serve as a reminder that mathematics is a profoundly interconnected discipline, where concepts and techniques from diverse branches often come together to solve fundamental problems.

V. de Paiva and P. Koepke (Eds.): CICM 2025, LNAI 16136, pp. 412–430, 2026.
https://doi.org/10.1007/978-3-032-07021-0_23

In the context of formalizing mathematical knowledge, proof assistants offer invaluable tools to ensure rigor and correctness. They provide a structured and reliable approach to formalizing and verifying logical reasoning, ensuring that the proof is free of errors, ambiguities, and gaps. This work presents five alternative proofs of the infinitude of primes using the Prototype Verification System (PVS) [25]. These formalizations explore various proof techniques derived from different areas of mathematics, including algebra, number theory, topology, and analysis. Each proof is constructed carefully to ensure logical consistency and rigor. The proofs are derived from those in "Proofs from THE BOOK" by Martin Aigner and Günter Ziegler [1], which offer six different proofs. Euclid's classical proof, the first in the mentioned book, is omitted here as it is already part of the NASA PVS Libraries, *NASALib*[1]. The presented mechanization relies on results from diverse libraries, including those from NASALib and the PVS prelude. NASALib offers valuable abstractions for mathematical structures, including sets, groups, and Cartesian products.

Notably, this work does not assume the infinitude of primes beforehand, as circular reasoning is not accepted by proof assistants such as PVS. This kind of circularity can arise inadvertently in manual theorem proving when using a result much stronger than necessary. A notable example is the use of the Gödel Completeness Theorem [17] to prove the Compactness Theorem. In "Proofs from THE BOOK," notation such as $p_1, p_2, p_3, \ldots$ is used for prime enumeration, but notice that this type of notation assumes the infinitude of primes beforehand.

One key aspect of this study is the identification and correction of notational errors and *informalities* in "Proofs from THE BOOK." PVS's robust type system helped to highlight and address these flaws, ensuring the proofs are precise and rigorous. Moreover, this work emphasizes the educational value of using PVS to formalize mathematical proofs. By breaking down the proofs into step-by-step procedures, this work not only demonstrates various formal proof techniques but also serves as a pedagogical resource. It offers readers the opportunity to learn how to structure and validate proofs within a proof assistant, fostering a deeper understanding of formal methods in mathematics. Thus, the mechanization of these proofs serves both as a study of mathematical reasoning and as a guide to using proof assistants effectively in diverse mathematical contexts.

1.1 Related Work

A significant number of the needed theorems for fields such as algebra, number theory, analysis, and topology are already available as PVS formalizations in NASALib [7,18,22]. These theorems were imported when the code was initially set up, which significantly streamlined the work. This allows for a solid foundation, avoiding the need to prove basic results and instead focusing on more advanced or specific aspects of the problem at hand.

Euclid's classic proof of the infinitude of primes has been formalized in various proof assistants, each presenting different approaches. One notable collection of

[1] `https://github.com/nasa/pvslib/blob/master/numbers/infinite_primes.pvs`.

such formalizations can be found in the "Formalizing 100 Theorems" project [30], which references formalizations on eleven different proof assistants. The usual strategies employed in these formalizations often revolve around two key techniques. One approach uses the product of primes plus one variant of Euclid's proof, as seen in proofs formalized in systems like Naproche [20] and the NASALib itself. The other approach employs a factorial plus one method, which is used in the Isabelle/HOL and Coq proofs.

In addition to the classical Euclid's proof of the infinitude of primes, other proofs have been developed using different proof assistants, such as those found in Isabelle. Such proofs are Fürstenberg's topological proof [12] and another involving the zeta function [11]. The former formalization imports the Isabelle HOL theories for reals, number theory, and analysis, and in addition to the formalization of Fürstenberg's proof, includes also proof of properties of Fürstenberg's topology. However, the topology-based proof of the infinitude of primes is elementary to formalize, as it relies on fewer mathematical structures compared to other proofs in "Proofs from THE BOOK" ("THE BOOK," for short). Indeed, Fürstenberg's proof requires essentially few basic notions of topological spaces, set theory, and number theory, leaving less room for alternative approaches. As a result, the existing formalizations differ primarily in how they are handled by different proof assistants, rather than in the structure of the proof itself. For didactic matters, the current formalization of Fürstenberg's proof imports the topology library and the minimum necessary notions from NASALib. On the other hand, the proof using the zeta function employs the Euler Product and the Cauchy Equality. It is presented in "THE BOOK," and also covered in the current formalization. The formalization in [11] presents a significant divergence regarding "THE BOOK." It employs a more complex approach that utilizes the analytic continuation of the zeta function and then leverages the divergence at $s = 1$ to prove the infinitude of primes. In contrast, the current formalization follows a pedagogical approach, also importing the minimum necessary PVS libraries on series and reals. However, some non-trivial results assumed in "THE BOOK," such as the Cauchy Equality, were mechanized to obtain a complete formalization of this proof.

While the primary focus of this paper is on the infinitude of primes, the first topic of "THE BOOK," it is also worth noting that there are other formalizations in "THE BOOK" beyond this first topic. These include proofs of the irrationality of certain numbers [26] and Fermat's two-square theorem [8].

1.2 Main Contributions

The main contributions of this work are:

- The formalization in PVS of five additional proofs for the infinitude of primes, which can be presented as applications of the results from various NASALib's libraries, such as `ints`, `algebra`, `analysis`, and `topology`.
- The discussion and formalization of omitted details in "THE BOOK."

- A new approach for the standard prime factorization theorem in NASALib and general structure specification.
- Several improvements in the **algebra** library, such as the $\mathbb{Z}/p\mathbb{Z}$ coset manipulation and type-checking related problems.
- Minor improvements in the manipulation of integer expressions in PVS, especially related to the *gcd* function.

1.3 Organization

Section 2 sketches the informal proofs that guide the formalization presented in this paper. Section 3 discusses aspects of the formalizations, focusing on the two more interesting proofs in terms of the usage of distinguishing typing features provided by PVS and the level of difficulty involved in their mechanical verification. Section 4 concludes the paper by providing some final remarks, also providing quantitative data, and discussing possible lines of future work. The paper includes hyperlinks to specific points of the formalization using the symbol. The complete formalization is available at `https://github.com/nasa/pvslib/tree/master/ints/inf_primes`. An extended version of this work includes more detailed information on the proofs and the PVS formalization [24].

2 Brief Description of the Informal Proofs

This section provides a brief description of the proofs addressed in the presented formalization. In the following, the set of prime numbers is denoted by $\mathbb{P}$.

2.1 Fermat Numbers

The second proof detailed in [1] uses number theory [19]. More precisely, it uses the infinitude of the Fermat numbers [27]. The Fermat numbers are of the form:

$$F_n = 2^{2^n} + 1, \text{ where } n \in \mathbb{Z}_{\geq 0}.$$

The main idea guiding the proof is to show that Fermat numbers are pairwise relatively prime. In other words, each Fermat number must have at least one distinct prime divisor. Since it is possible to find infinitely many Fermat numbers, it follows that there must be infinitely many prime numbers. Since NASALib and the PVS prelude provide a strong set of theorems in number theory, this proof turned out to be one of the shortest.

2.2 Mersenne Numbers

The third proof uses the Mersenne numbers [27], which are defined as $M_n = 2^n - 1$, $n \in \mathbb{Z}_{\geq 0}$. In this proof, n is restricted to the set of prime numbers and is denoted by p. The main idea of the proof is to show that there exists a prime divisor q of M_p such that q is greater than p. If there were finite primes, there must exist a maximum prime p_{max}. This is a contradiction since one can find a greater prime in the set of divisors of $M_{p_{max}}$.

The approach followed in "Proofs from THE BOOK" is based on abstract algebra, the application of Lagrange's Theorem [21], and the fact that $\mathbb{Z}_q \setminus \{0\}$ is a group under multiplication. The proof is structured as described below.

1. Let p be an arbitrary prime and q be one prime factor of $M_p = 2^p - 1$. Notice that q must be odd since $2^p - 1$ is odd.
2. Since q divides $2^p - 1$, this implies that $2^p \equiv 1 (\mathrm{mod}\ q)$. The number p is a prime; thus, it must be the order of the element $\overline{2}$ in $\mathbb{Z}_q \setminus \{0\}$. Otherwise, there would be $r \in \mathbb{N}, 1 < r < p$, which divides p.
3. An element $\overline{a} \in \mathbb{Z}_q \setminus \{0\}$ of order n generates a subgroup $\langle \overline{a} \rangle = \{\overline{a}^i : i \in \mathbb{Z}_{\geq 0}\}$ with cardinality $|\langle \overline{a} \rangle| = n$. By applying Lagrange's Theorem, $|\langle \overline{2} \rangle| = p$ divides $|\mathbb{Z}_q \setminus \{0\}| = q - 1$.
4. Assume there exists a maximum prime p_{max}. Thus, there exists $q \in \mathbb{P}$ such that $p_{max} \mid q - 1$. Consequently, $p_{max} \leq q - 1$, and $p_{max} < q$, which is a contradiction. Therefore, there are infinitely many primes.

2.3 Euler Product Formula and Cauchy Equality

The structure of the manual proof can be divided into the following steps.

1. Let $\pi(n)$ be the prime-counting function that counts the number of prime numbers smaller than or equal to n. Suppose there exists an enumeration of $\mathbb{P}$ in increasing order.
2. The harmonic numbers can be underestimated with natural logarithms as
$$\log(n) \leq H_n = 1 + \frac{1}{2} + \frac{1}{3} + \cdots + \frac{1}{n}.$$
3. The product of a geometric series of inverse prime numbers less than or equal to n is equal to another series that contains every $\frac{1}{k}$ from $H_n = 1 + \frac{1}{2} + \ldots + \frac{1}{n}$:
$$H_n \leq \prod_{i=1}^{\pi(n)} \sum_{k=0}^{\infty} \frac{1}{p_i^k} = \sum_{\substack{k \in \mathbb{Z}_{>0}, \\ k=1 \ \vee \ \exists p \in \mathbb{P}, \\ (p \leq n \ \wedge \ p \mid k)}} \frac{1}{k}.$$
4. For each prime number p_i, the geometric series $\sum_{k=0}^{\infty} \frac{1}{p_i^k}$ converges to $\frac{p_i}{p_i - 1}$. Also, $p_i \geq i + 1$, which implies that $\frac{p_i}{p_i - 1} \leq \frac{i+1}{i}$. Consequently,
$$\prod_{i=1}^{\pi(n)} \sum_{k=0}^{\infty} \frac{1}{p_i^k} = \prod_{i=1}^{\pi(n)} \frac{p_i}{p_i - 1} \leq \prod_{i=1}^{\pi(n)} \frac{i+1}{i} = \pi(n) + 1.$$
5. By arranging inequalities, $\log(n) \leq \pi(n) + 1$. Since the natural logarithmic function is strictly increasing, the sequence generated by the π function diverges, which means that $\mathbb{P}$ is infinite.

2.4 Fürstenberg's Topological Proof

Hillel Fürstenberg introduced this elegant proof as a 12-line note in the section on Mathematical Notes of the American Mathematical Monthly in 1995 [15]. This non-traditional approach builds a topology [23] on integer numbers. The structure of this proof can be divided into the following parts.

1. Define the family of sets $N_{a,b} = \{a + bn : n \in \mathbb{Z}, b > 0\}$, where $a \in \mathbb{Z}, b \in \mathbb{Z}^+$.
2. A set $O \subseteq \mathbb{Z}$ is called *open* whether $O = \emptyset$ or for every element $a \in O$, there exists some $b \in \mathbb{Z}, b > 0$ with $N_{a,b} \subseteq O$. As usual in topology, a *closed* set is defined as the complement of an open set in $\mathbb{Z}$.
3. By definition, the union of two open sets $O_1 \cup O_2$ is another open set. Also, the intersection of two open sets is also an open set: if $a \in O_1 \cap O_2$, thus there exist $b_1 > 0$ and $b_2 > 0$, such that $N_{a,b_1} \subseteq O_1$ and $N_{a,b_2} \subseteq O_2$; consequently, $N_{a,b_1 b_2} \subseteq O_1 \cap O_2$. Therefore, such open sets induce a well-defined topology.
4. For any $a, b \in \mathbb{Z}$, $b > 0$, $N_{a,b}$ is open. Also, notice that $N_{a,b} = \mathbb{Z} \setminus \bigcup_{i=1}^{b-1} N_{a+i,b}$. Since $N_{a,b}$ is the complement of the open set $\bigcup_{i=1}^{b-1} N_{a+i,b}$, thus $N_{a,b}$ is a closed set.
5. If O is a nonempty open set then O is infinite, since $N_{a,b} \subseteq O$ for some $b > 0$.
6. Every $n \in \mathbb{Z} \setminus \{-1, 1\}$ has a prime divisor p, which implies that $n \in N_{0,p}$. Consequently, $\mathbb{Z} \setminus \{-1, 1\} = \bigcup_{p \in \mathbb{P}} N_{0,p}$.
7. If $\mathbb{P}$ is finite, then $\mathbb{Z} \setminus \{-1, 1\}$ is a closed set since it is a finite union of closed sets, as pointed out above. Consequently, $\{-1, 1\}$ is an open set, which is a contradiction since all open sets in this topology are infinite.

2.5 Prime Reciprocal Harmonic Series

Paul Erdös originally proved the sixth and last proof in the 20th century [13] and can be viewed as inspired by the proof found in Section 2.3. The main idea is to consider another series of reciprocal numbers, but instead of using the positive integers, the prime numbers are used, i.e., $\sum_{i=1}^{n} \frac{1}{p_i}$. As a finite summation of numbers converges, if this series diverges, the set of primes must be infinite.

In this proof, the set of primes is divided into two types: the *Small* primes, which are smaller or equal to a prime p_k, and *Big* primes, the remaining ones. From this classification, other sets are defined: $N(n)$, the set of positive numbers less than or equal to n; $N_s(n, k)$, the numbers from $N(n)$ with only *Small* prime divisors; $N_b(n, k)$ the numbers from $N(n)$ with at least one *Big* prime divisor. It can be shown that $N(n) = N_s(n, k) \cup N_b(n, k)$.

1. Consider a prime enumeration p_i and suppose that the series $\sum_{i=1}^{N} \frac{1}{p_i}$ converges. Therefore exists a κ such that $\sum_{i=\kappa+1}^{\infty} \frac{1}{p_i} < \frac{1}{2}$.
2. Define $N_{div}(d, n)$ the subset of $N(n)$ whose elements are multiples of $d \in \mathbb{N}, d \geq 1$. It can be proven that $|N_{div}(d, n)| = \lfloor \frac{|N(n)|}{d} \rfloor = \lfloor \frac{n}{d} \rfloor$. Noticing that $N_b(n, k)$ is the union of all $N_{div}(p_i, n)$, where $i > k$, one can estimate the size of $N_b(n, \kappa)$ by:

$$|N_b(n, \kappa)| \leq \sum_{i=\kappa+1}^{\infty} \left\lfloor \frac{n}{p_i} \right\rfloor \leq \sum_{i=\kappa+1}^{\infty} \frac{n}{p_i} < \frac{n}{2}.$$

3. An element $m \in N_s(n,k)$ can be written as $m = a \cdot b$, where $a, b \in N_s(n,k)$, a is a square-free part of m, and b is a perfect square of an element of $N_s(n,k)$. From this observation, two other sets are defined: $S_{free}(n,k)$, composed of all elements a, and $S_{div}(n,k)$, composed of all elements b. With these considerations, the size of $N_s(n,k)$ is estimated:

$$|N_s(n,k)| \leq |S_{free}(n,k) \times S_{div}(n,k)| = |S_{free}(n,k)| \cdot |S_{div}(n,k)|.$$

4. Since $m = a \cdot b$ for all $m \in N_s(n,k)$, the number of elements of $S_{div}(n,k)$ can be estimated by setting $a = 1$ and using the definition of b, i.e. $b = r^2$ for $r \in N_s(n,k)$. Finding the size of $S_{div}(n,k)$ turns into a problem of counting the number of valid $m = r^2$. Noticing that $N_s(n,k) \subseteq N(n)$, one can establish: $|S_{div}(n,k)| \leq \sqrt{|N_s(n,k)|} \leq \sqrt{|N(n)|} = \sqrt{n}$.
5. An element of $S_{free}(n,k)$ is of the form $m = p_1^{\epsilon_1} \cdot p_2^{\epsilon_2} \cdots p_k^{\epsilon_k}$, where $\epsilon_i \in \{0,1\}$. Consequently, $|S_{free}(n,k)| \leq 2^k$.
6. Since $N(n) = N_s(n,k) \cup N_b(n,k)$, for every k, one concludes that:

$$|N(n)| \leq |N_s(n,\kappa)| + |N_b(n,\kappa)| < 2^{\kappa}\sqrt{n} + \frac{n}{2}.$$

7. In particular, if $n = 2^{2\kappa+2}$ then $|N(n)| < 2^{2\kappa+2} = n$, which is a contradiction, since $|N(n)| = n$. Therefore, the original consideration of the convergence of a series of prime reciprocals must be false. That is only possible if there are infinitely many primes.

3 Description of the Formalization

Only the formalizations of the proofs based on Mersenne Numbers and on the Euler Product Formula are discussed here, as they required significantly more effort than the traditional proofs. The formalization based on the Harmonic Prime Reciprocal Series presented the most significant divergences from the informal proof. On the contrary, it was possible to develop a formalization fairly close to the manual proofs for the ones based on Fermat Numbers and Fürstenberg's topological arguments.

Before diving into the details, it is worth noticing the main building blocks on which this effort is founded. In addition to the PVS prelude and basic NASALib libraries such as `set` and `structures`, the presented formalization leverages specialized results from the NASALib libraries `algebra`, `topology`, `series`, and `analysis`. Notably, the concepts of topological spaces and relations between open and closed sets were taken from the library `topology`. Some properties about limits and integrals were imported from the `analysis` library. The `series` library provides properties about the convergence of (infinite) series. Finally, from the `algebra` library, results related to (finite) groups and cosets were used. As an original contribution to these libraries, several results were added, such as a reformulation of the Fundamental Theorem of Arithmetic and a version of the Cauchy Product Theorem, among others.

3.1 Mersenne Numbers

The first design decision addressed how to specify the multiplicative group $\mathbb{Z}_p \setminus \{\overline{0}\}$, where p is a prime number. Although there is a specification for the ring $\mathbb{Z}/n\mathbb{Z}$, there exists no direct implementation for the multiplicative group $\mathbb{Z}/n\mathbb{Z} \setminus \{n\mathbb{Z}\}$. The group-related theorems that were applied belong to theories that rely on the following assumption: the set of all elements of an abstract type `T` must satisfy a group predicate. In other words, the importation of these theories introduces a *Type Correctness Condition* (TCC) automatically generated by the system, which is a proof obligation for checking whether the type `T` consists of a complete set of elements forming a group. This is not a direct application of the lemma `Zp_prime_is_field`, already in NASALib, stating that $\mathbb{Z}/p\mathbb{Z}$ is a field when p is a prime number and thus, that $\mathbb{Z}/p\mathbb{Z} \setminus \{p\mathbb{Z}\}$ forms a group under multiplication. Indeed, the specification of `field` in the theory `field_def`, from a division ring, gives the flexibility of considering the set of cosets of $n\mathbb{Z}$ in $\mathbb{Z}$ as a parameter in the lemma `Zp_prime_is_field`, without excluding the identity for addition $n\mathbb{Z}$. To use the results in theory `finite_groups`, it was necessary to specify the type `nz_coset(n)` and then prove that it satisfies the group properties when n is a prime number. Roughly, it could be done by using the lemma `Zp_prime_is_field` combined with enough expansions of the definition of `group?[nz_coset(n)](Z(n))` in the lemma `nz_prime_is_group`.

Still, some TCCs appeared during the manipulation of elements of type `nz_coset(p)`; for this reason, additional utility lemmas were proved and separated in the `ring_zn_extra.pvs` file, as they could be used in more general situations. The content of this file ranges from lemmas of equivalence of the operations in $\mathbb{Z}_n$ and $\mathbb{Z}/n\mathbb{Z}$ to some direct ring properties, such as product and summation closure, and the characteristic of the ring $\mathbb{Z}_p$ being p.

It is worth mentioning that some type-related proofs can be avoided; instead of using generic definitions such as the power function specified in the group file, it is possible to define a specialized function for handling this new `nz_coset` type. This could be done by forcing the type to be `nz_coset` instead of the PVS-deduced coset type. For example, the signature of the power function was restricted to $pow : \mathbb{Z}/p\mathbb{Z} \setminus \{p\mathbb{Z}\} \times \mathbb{Z}_{\geq 0} \rightarrow \mathbb{Z}/p\mathbb{Z} \setminus \{p\mathbb{Z}\}$ instead of using the more general version $pow : \mathbb{Z}/p\mathbb{Z} \times \mathbb{Z}_{\geq 0} \rightarrow \mathbb{Z}/p\mathbb{Z}$.

After the explanation of these preliminaries, the actual proof of the infinitude of prime numbers can be finally discussed.

Lemma 1. *If d is a divisor of M_p where $p \in \mathbb{P}$, then d is odd.*

Proof. Since p is a prime number, $p \geq 2$, implying that $M_p = 2 \cdot 2^{p-1} - 1$ is odd. Suppose that d is even. Since it is a divisor of M_p,

$$M_p = d \cdot k_1, k_1 \in \mathbb{Z}.$$

By the evenness of d

$$M_p = 2 \cdot k_2 \cdot k_1, k_2 \in \mathbb{Z}.$$

This is a contradiction since M_p is odd.

Lemma 2. *Let $q, p \in \mathbb{P}$, where q is a divisor of M_p, then*

$$(2 + q\mathbb{Z})^{q-1} = 1 + q\mathbb{Z}.$$

Proof. By Lemma 1, q is an odd number since q is a prime $q \geq 3$. By Fermat's Little Theorem,

$$2^{q-1} \equiv 1 (\text{mod } q), \text{ which implies that } (2 + q\mathbb{Z})^{q-1} = 1 + q\mathbb{Z}.$$

The last equation comes from the ring isomorphism $\mathbb{Z}/n\mathbb{Z} \cong \mathbb{Z}_n$.

In the PVS specification, the equivalence in the modular arithmetic formulation and quotient ring formulation was proved directly. It was also necessary to adapt Fermat's Little Theorem to the requirements in the proof: it was specified in the $a^p \equiv a \pmod p$ form, not in the $a^{p-1} \equiv 1 \pmod p$ form.

Lemma 3. *Let $q, p \in \mathbb{P}$, where q is a divisor of M_p, then*

$$(2 + q\mathbb{Z})^p = 1 + q\mathbb{Z}.$$

Proof. Since q divides M_p,

$$M_p \equiv 0 \pmod q, \text{ which implies}$$

$$2^p - 1 \equiv 0 \pmod q, \text{ which is equivalent to}$$

$$2^p \equiv 1 \pmod q.$$

Using the isomorphism $\mathbb{Z}/n\mathbb{Z} \cong \mathbb{Z}_n$.

$$(2 + q\mathbb{Z})^p = 1 + q\mathbb{Z}.$$

Theorem 1. *There are infinitely many primes.*

Proof. Suppose there exists a finite number of prime numbers; then there should exist a maximum prime p_{max}. Let $q \in \mathbb{P}$ be the divisor of $M_{p_{max}}$. Using Lemma 3,

$$(2 + q\mathbb{Z})^{p_{max}} = 1 + q\mathbb{Z}.$$

In particular, from the definition of order, it follows that $ord(2 + q\mathbb{Z}) \mid p_{max}$, but that is only possible if $ord(2+q\mathbb{Z}) = 1$ or $ord(2+q\mathbb{Z}) = p_{max}$. If $ord(2+q\mathbb{Z}) = 1$, then $2 + q\mathbb{Z} = 1 + q\mathbb{Z}$, which is not possible since $q > 1$. Therefore, it must be the case that $ord(2 + q\mathbb{Z}) = p_{max}$.

Using Lemma 2,

$$(2 + q\mathbb{Z})^{q-1} = 1 + q\mathbb{Z}.$$

Again, by the definition of order, $ord(2 + q\mathbb{Z}) \mid q - 1$ and $p_{max} \mid q - 1$. Since a divisor is smaller than or equal to the number it divides, $p_{max} \leq q - 1$. More specifically, $p_{max} < q$. Therefore, q is a prime greater than the maximum prime, a contradiction.

It turns out that Lagrange's Theorem was not necessary. In fact, if it had been used, it would have been necessary to prove additional lemmas on group orders; however, these proofs can be quite tedious. Instead, the following classical theorem was used: if an element a from a group G satisfies $a^n = 1$ for some integer n, then $ord(a)$ divides n.

Related to TCCs, since the definition of structures in the NASALib's algebra library, such as rings, is built upon groups, and these in turn are based on monoids (and so on), type dependencies become an exhaustive issue. The problem arises because they require a significant number of TCCs. If such structures are imported naively, each new algebraic structure used in a proof could generate around five new TCCs. Consequently, there is room for improvement in the algebra library from various angles, such as through new utility theorems, new proof strategies (conservative extensions of the proof calculus provided by PVS), and possibly type judgments, which provide more information to the type checker. Nevertheless, the algebra library contains many powerful theorems, including classic group and ring theory results, such as Lagrange's Theorem, Sylow's Theorems, and many others, which facilitated the presented work.

3.2 Formalization Based on Euler Product Formula and Cauchy Equality

The fourth proof in "THE BOOK" relies on analytic number theory [3]. As a side effect of Euler's Formula [14], proved in the 18th century by Leonhard Euler, this proof has a deep connection to the Riemann zeta function [28]. The key idea is to demonstrate that the zeta function can be factored into a product over prime numbers. With this connection, the estimation for the number of primes can be as large as desired, confirming that primes are indeed infinite.

The Riemann-zeta function is defined as:

$$\zeta(s) = \sum_{n=1}^{\infty} \frac{1}{n^s} \quad \text{for } s \in \mathbb{C}, \quad \text{Re}(s) > 1.$$

Euler's product formula, on the other hand, relates the primes as follows:

$$\zeta(s) = \prod_{p \text{ prime}} \left(1 - \frac{1}{p^s}\right)^{-1} \text{for } s \in \mathbb{C}, \quad \text{Re}(s) > 1.$$

Notice that, from the definition of the zeta function, s must have a real part greater than one. It turns out that this Euler product also works for $s = 1$, but the zeta function at this value tends to infinity, something that should not happen if there are finite primes.

In particular, it is possible to estimate the prime-counting function by the product of the primes according to the Euler formula, which by itself can be bounded using the natural logarithm function in the following way:

$$\log(n) \leq \prod_{p \text{ prime}} \left(1 - \frac{1}{p}\right)^{-1} \leq \pi(n) + 1.$$

where $\log(n)$ is the natural logarithm function and $\pi(n)$ is the function that counts the number of prime numbers less than or equal to a given number n.

As is typical in traditional number theory proofs, this proof heavily relies on concepts from analysis, such as limits and series, which are addressed in the NASALib Analysis library [18].

3.2.1 Prime Enumeration The notation $\mathbb{P} = \{p_1, p_2, p_3, \ldots\}$ in [1] has the problem of assuming that the set of prime numbers $\mathbb{P}$ is infinite beforehand, and the sequence should be undefined otherwise. For simplicity, in the specification, the starting index is zero, and undefined cases are set to zero. This means that if the prime numbers have an end at the nth value, then $p_i = 0$ for $i \geq n$. Therefore, $p_0 = 2 \quad p_1 = 3 \quad p_2 = 5$. The proper definition of the prime sequence is given by a function $\rho : \mathbb{Z}_{\geq 0} \to \mathbb{Z}_{\geq 0}$. It remains to prove that for a subset of the domain, $S \subseteq \mathbb{Z}_{\geq 0}$, this function is an enumeration. For this purpose, some necessary properties are inductively formalized, such as:

1. $\rho(i+1) > \rho(i) \lor \rho(i+1) = 0$;
2. $\forall \rho(i), \rho(j) \in \mathbb{P}, \rho(i) = \rho(j) \Rightarrow i = j$;
3. $\forall p \in \mathbb{P}, \exists i \in \mathbb{Z}_{\geq 0}, \rho(i) = p$;
4. Let $i, n \in \mathbb{Z}_{\geq 0}$, $i < \pi(n) \Rightarrow \rho(i) \in \mathbb{P}$.

The ρ function is indeed an enumeration for a subset of the domain. If there are infinitely many primes, all primes will appear in ascending order in the domain $\mathbb{Z}_{\geq 0}$. Otherwise, for the domain $S = \{n \in \mathbb{Z}_{\geq 0} : n < \pi(p_{max})\}$, all primes will also appear in ascending order, and in its complement, $\mathbb{Z}_{\geq 0} \setminus S$, the function will be zero.

In the following proofs, it will be necessary to use the Fundamental Theorem of Arithmetic [16]. This theorem is in NASALib, but specified generically: any natural greater than one can be written as a product of a non-decreasing sequence of primes, for example, $360 = 2 \cdot 2 \cdot 2 \cdot 3 \cdot 3 \cdot 5$. For the current purposes, a specialized version of this theorem is used, stating that any natural number greater than one can be written as a product of an increasing sequence of powers of primes, for instance, $360 = 2^3 \cdot 3^2 \cdot 5$.

Because a prime enumeration was already specified, it can be used to specify the prime powers in sorted form. Still, knowing beforehand that there are infinitely many primes, one should be tempted to describe the Fundamental Theorem as the existence of the infinite product, with large enough terms having exponent zero, such as $360 = \rho(0)^3 \cdot \rho(1)^2 \cdot \rho(2)^1 \cdot \rho(3)^0 \cdot \rho(4)^0 \ldots$. However, this would lead to the same mistake of circularly assuming that there are infinitely many primes. Therefore, a new version of the Fundamental Theorem was formalized.

Given a family of sets $E_p = \{n \in \mathbb{Z} : \exists k \in \mathbb{Z}_{\geq 0}, n = p^k\}$, where $p \in \mathbb{P}$, the set D_n can be defined as the finite Cartesian product shown below.

$$D_n = \bigtimes_{i=0}^{\pi(n)-1} E_{\rho(i)}.$$

Thus, the Fundamental Theorem can be rewritten as the existence of a unique element $(\rho(0)^{\epsilon_0}, \rho(1)^{\epsilon_1}, \ldots, \rho(\pi(n)-1)^{\epsilon_{\pi(n)-1}}) \in D_n$, such that the product of its entries equals n for every $n \in \mathbb{Z}, n > 1$; i.e.,

$$n = \prod_{i=0}^{\pi(n)-1} \rho(i)^{\epsilon_i}.$$

Since the greatest prime divisor of a number is the number itself, the upper limit of the product, $\pi(n) - 1$, guarantees that all prime divisors will appear in the product.

It is worth mentioning that the definition of prime enumeration and prime factorization is reused for the formalization based on prime reciprocal series (Subsection 2.5); because of that, these proofs, alongside another general purpose ρ function manipulation, were separated to a new file called **`prime_enum`**. Additionally, using this new framework for the proof of the Fundamental Theorem of Arithmetic, the application of lemmas related to integers was useful. Among these lemmas, some properties related to the *gcd* function were recently added to NASALib in the file `number_util.pvs`.

3.2.2 A Few Inequalities For the completion of the proof, a few inequalities must be proven, starting from a classic one.

Lemma 4. $\forall n \in \mathbb{Z}_{\geq 0}, \log(n) \leq H_n$.

Despite being well known, this inequality was not stated in NASALib, but all its prerequisites had already been proven in the **`analysis`** library. This made its assisted proof relatively easy. The only minor problem was a TCC related to the integrability of each integral expression required in the proof; as the summation is applied over slices of the larger integral, it was necessary to ensure that everything is indeed integrable. However, lemmas for these steps were also in the files defining the logarithmic function and integral operations.

The next inequality uses two definitions of functions. At first glance, the defined functions appear to be different, but they are actually equivalent. Let $n \in \mathbb{Z}_{\geq 0}, n \geq 2$; the functions ξ and μ are defined as:

$$\xi(n) = \prod_{i=0}^{\pi(n)-1} \sum_{k=0}^{\infty} \frac{1}{\rho(i)^k} \qquad \text{and} \qquad \mu(n) = \sum_{\substack{k \in \mathbb{Z}_{>0}, \\ k=1 \ \vee\ \exists p \in \mathbb{P}, \\ (p \leq n \ \wedge\ p|k)}} \frac{1}{k}.$$

One thing to notice is that in ξ, there are divisions by $\rho(i)$, which can have zero value if one tries to use a nonexistent prime number, but as the product is taken from $i = 0$ to $i = \pi(n) - 1$, using property 4, all $\rho(i)$ values are primes. Even though it is not completely obvious, these two functions are indeed the same. Some non-trivial lemmas must be proven first to formalize this fact.

Given the Cauchy product [10], the product of two convergent series is another series.

$$\left(\sum_{n=0}^{\infty} a_i\right) \cdot \left(\sum_{n=0}^{\infty} b_i\right) = \sum_{n=0}^{\infty}\sum_{k=0}^{n} a_{n-k}b_k. \tag{1}$$

This formula has the restriction of one of the series being absolutely convergent, but the series in the formalization is defined over positive numbers, making this restriction trivially valid. The last series in the formula can be flattened in such a way that it maintains its convergence, but to prove this, first, two other functions are defined. Let $n \in \mathbb{Z}_{\geq 0}$, the functions θ and τ are defined as:

$$\theta(n) = max\left(\left\{k \in \mathbb{Z}_{\geq 0} : \frac{k(k+1)}{2} \leq n\right\}\right) \quad \text{and} \quad \tau(n) = n - \frac{\theta(n)(\theta(n)+1)}{2}$$

Corollary 1. *Let $n, k \in \mathbb{Z}_{\geq 0}, 0 \leq k \leq n$, then $\theta(\frac{n(n+1)}{2} + k) = n$ and $\tau(\frac{n(n+1)}{2} + k) = k$.*

Lemma 5. *Let $n, k \in \mathbb{Z}_{\geq 0}, 0 \leq k \leq n$, then*
$$\sum_{k=0}^{n} a_{n-k}b_k = \sum_{k=\frac{n(n+1)}{2}}^{\frac{n(n+1)}{2}+n} a_{(\theta(k)-\tau(k))} \cdot b_{\tau(k)}.$$

Lemma 6. *Let $N \in \mathbb{Z}_{\geq 0}$, then*
$$\sum_{n=0}^{N}\sum_{k=0}^{n} a_{n-k}b_k = \sum_{n=0}^{\frac{N(N+1)}{2}+N} a_{(\theta(k)-\tau(k))} \cdot b_{\tau(k)}.$$

The next theorem requires formalizing one more lemma.

Lemma 7. *Let $n \in \mathbb{Z}_{\geq 0}$, there exist $m, r \in \mathbb{Z}_{\geq 0}$, with $r \leq m$, and $n = \frac{m\cdot(m+1)}{2} + r$.*

Now, the flattened version of the series is shown to be equal to the original series.

Theorem 2. *Let a_n and b_n be positive sequences and $\sum_{n=0}^{\infty}\sum_{k=0}^{n} a_{n-k}b_k$ convergent. Then $\sum_{n=0}^{\infty}\sum_{k=0}^{n} a_{n-k}b_k = \sum_{k=0}^{\infty} a_{(\theta(k)-\tau(k))} \cdot b_{\tau(k)}$.*

Since there was no previous specification of the Cauchy product in PVS, its formalization was essential to obtain a complete theory.

The series flattening process was generalized for the product of more series.

Lemma 8. *Let $n \in \mathbb{Z}_{>0}$, then*
$$\prod_{i=0}^{n-1}\sum_{k=0}^{\infty} a_i(k) = \sum_{\substack{k, j_l \in \mathbb{Z}_{\geq 0} \\ j_0+j_1+\ldots+j_{n-1}=k}} \prod_{i=0}^{n-1} a_i(j_i).$$

The equality of functions ξ and μ, used in the informal proof, can be obtained using Lemma 8 and the Fundamental Theorem of Arithmetic. However, in PVS, as this property was only needed in the next lemma, it was faster to associate each term directly in the next proof instead of stating this equality as a lemma.

Lemma 9. *Let $n \in \mathbb{Z}_{>0}$, $H_n \leq \mu(n)$.*

Proof. From the definition of the μ function, and since it is an absolutely convergent series, if for every $\frac{1}{k}$, $1 < k \leq n$, there exists a prime $p \mid k$, $p \leq n$, the series can be ordered as:

$$\mu(n) = \sum_{k=1}^{n} \frac{1}{k} + \sum_{\substack{k \in \mathbb{Z}_{>n}, \\ k=1 \vee \exists p \in \mathbb{P}, \\ (p \leq n \wedge p|k)}} \frac{1}{k}.$$

Which trivially results in $H_n \leq \mu(n)$. To conclude, since $1 < k \leq n$ and a divisor is less than or equal to the number it divides, all prime divisors of k satisfy the inequality $p \leq k$. Therefore, the maximal prime divisor of k, say p, is such that $p \leq n$.

For the PVS formalization, such a series rearrangement needed to be expressed in a more explicit form; for that reason, a theory called `sequence_extra` was included, in which a constructive specification of the function that orders by common summed values is given.

Lemma 10. *Let* $n, i \in \mathbb{Z}_{\geq 0}$, *for* $i < \pi(n)$, $\frac{\rho(i)}{\rho(i)-1} \leq \frac{i+2}{i+1}$.

Proof. Notice that $\frac{\rho(i)}{\rho(i)-1} \leq \frac{i+2}{i+1} \iff 1+\frac{1}{\rho(i)-1} \leq 1+\frac{1}{i+1} \iff i+1 \leq \rho(i)-1$ $\iff i+2 \leq \rho(i)$.

This is proved by induction. For $i = 0$, $0+2 \leq 2$; for $i > 0$, by i.h., $i+1 \leq \rho(i-1)$, which implies that $i+2 \leq \rho(i-1)+1$. By the property 4, $\rho(i) \neq 0$, and using Lemma 1, it can be shown that $\rho(i-1) < \rho(i)$. Since $\rho(i-1)$ is an integer, $\rho(i-1)+1 \leq \rho(i)$; therefore, $i+2 \leq \rho(i)$.

Lemma 11. $\xi(n) \leq \pi(n)+1$.

Theorem 3. *There are infinitely many primes.*

Proof. By composing the inequalities from Lemmas 4, 11 and 9, one obtains $\log(n) \leq \xi(n) = \mu(n) \leq \pi(n)+1$. Since the logarithm is a strictly increasing function, there is no maximum $\pi(n)$ value.

4 Conclusion and Future Work

One of the goals of the presented PVS library is to demonstrate to mathematicians the potential of interactive theorem provers in formalizing complex mathematical concepts, showing that substantial and technically intricate proofs can be rigorously verified using computer software. The complete formalization of distinct proofs of the infinitude of primes from the renowned book "Proofs from THE BOOK" contributed significantly to the development of a rich and mathematically diverse library to attract the interest of researchers from various branches of mathematics. This represents a significant step forward regarding other libraries intended for algebraists and computer scientists (e.g., [2,5–7]). Table 1 shows a quantitative overview of the formalization effort.

Table 1: Quantitative data.

<table>
<tr><th rowspan="2">PVS theory</th><th rowspan="2">Form.</th><th rowspan="2">TCCs</th><th rowspan="2">Spec. Size .pvs lines</th><th rowspan="2">Proof Comm. .prf lines</th><th colspan="6">Main Dependencies</th></tr>
<tr><th>Prime enum</th><th>Cauchy Product</th><th>series</th><th>Topology (NASA Lib)</th><th>Algebra (NASA Lib)</th><th>Num. Theory Extra</th></tr>
<tr><td>Fermat</td><td>17</td><td>8</td><td>75</td><td>981</td><td></td><td></td><td></td><td></td><td></td><td>✔</td></tr>
<tr><td>Mersenne</td><td>28</td><td>17</td><td>112</td><td>2568</td><td></td><td></td><td></td><td></td><td>✔</td><td>✔</td></tr>
<tr><td>Euler</td><td>39</td><td>28</td><td>112</td><td>3408</td><td>✔</td><td>✔</td><td>✔</td><td></td><td></td><td>✔</td></tr>
<tr><td>Fürstenberg</td><td>19</td><td>2</td><td>115</td><td>1822</td><td></td><td></td><td></td><td>✔</td><td></td><td>✔</td></tr>
<tr><td>Erdös</td><td>71</td><td>35</td><td>273</td><td>8117</td><td>✔</td><td></td><td>✔</td><td></td><td></td><td>✔</td></tr>
<tr><th colspan="11">Additional Theories Quantitative Data</th></tr>
<tr><th colspan="3">PVS theory</th><th colspan="2">Formulas</th><th colspan="2">TCCs</th><th colspan="2">Specification size</th><th colspan="2">Proof commands</th></tr>
<tr><td colspan="3">Primes enumeration</td><td colspan="2">65</td><td colspan="2">37</td><td colspan="2">212</td><td colspan="2">4574</td></tr>
<tr><td colspan="3">Cauchy product formula</td><td colspan="2">21</td><td colspan="2">10</td><td colspan="2">111</td><td colspan="2">2302</td></tr>
<tr><td colspan="3">Series extra</td><td colspan="2">23</td><td colspan="2">8</td><td colspan="2">109</td><td colspan="2">1610</td></tr>
<tr><td colspan="3">Others</td><td colspan="2">89</td><td colspan="2">51</td><td colspan="2">419</td><td colspan="2">5125</td></tr>
</table>

This work highlights essential differences between the original proofs and their mechanically checked counterparts. One of these differences is the way in which primes are initially enumerated in the pen and paper proofs, where no consideration is given regarding the possibility of the existence of a maximum number of primes. To address such an imprecision, an enumeration function was defined in PVS, avoiding the initial implicit assumption on the infinitude of primes, and thus ensuring a rigorous foundation for the required adaptation of the Fundamental Theorem of Arithmetic. This result can be found in the file `prime_enum`. Furthermore, the rich typing system supported by PVS played a crucial role in highlighting the importance of distinguishing between the different algebraic structures at play. In particular, for the proof based on Mersenne numbers, the type system helped clarify the relationships between the different structures involved. Also, although Lagrange's theorem is not used, the formalization leveraged a result about group orders, proving that the order of any group element satisfying a particular condition divides a given integer.

Another key difference between the proofs in "THE BOOK" and their formalizations arises when the Cauchy product is used to prove the Euler product. In "THE BOOK," the connection between the Euler product and the harmonic series is somewhat informal, which necessitated improving the rigor of the proof as part of the formalization effort. Since the Cauchy product was not included in NASALib, its incorporation benefits both the analysis and the Series library.

Additionally, the characteristic PVS features and existing PVS libraries were crucial in guiding the formalization effort, particularly in handling aspects of topology and number theory. Fürstenberger's topological proof was straightforward due to the well-established PVS topology library, part of NASALib. Similarly, the proof using Fermat numbers benefited from the comprehensive number theory library in the PVS prelude. All that, conjugated with the typing system and the ability to define custom functions, made it possible to address the nuances of the infinitude of primes and formalize the proofs in a rigorous and structured manner. It also allowed addressing the omissions and imprecision in the original proofs and facilitated discovering simpler proof alternatives.

The proof using Fermat numbers (2.1) in "THE BOOK," shows that any two Fermat numbers are relatively prime, basically proving by induction that the recursive relation $\prod_{k=0}^{n-1} F_k = F_n - 2$ holds. Then, the number 1 is the only common divisor of two different Fermat numbers, since any Fermat number is odd. From that, it is concluded that there must be infinitely many primes, since there are infinitely many Fermat numbers. The last consequence is assumed without proof. Although it is intuitive, it is not completely trivial. Indeed, its proof has at least the same level of difficulty as the verification of the previous recursive relation. The mechanization allowed addressing various similar omissions, and provided a clear insight that the proofs of intuitive observations are not necessarily minor parts of the proving process. For the specific previously discussed consequence, for each Fermat number k, it was considered the minimum prime divisor of k (and formally proved that such a minimum exists). Then, an injective function was built from the set of natural numbers to the set of minimum primes that divide Fermat numbers. Since this subset of prime numbers is infinite, the set of prime numbers itself is infinite. Table 2 summarizes some relevant differences between the proof in "THE BOOK" and the mechanized proofs.

Further expansions of the library can include proofs uncovered in "Proofs from THE BOOK," particularly those exploring other branches of mathematics or offering alternative perspectives on well-known approaches. One area of interest is the formalization of a geometry-related proof of the infinitude of primes, such as the one given in [9], which would broaden the scope of the library beyond number theory, analysis, topology, and algebra. Additionally, incorporating more advanced results in number theory, such as Dirichlet's Theorem on primes in arithmetic progressions, would be a valuable addition. More in general, a key focus will also be to improve the level of automation in the PVS proofs. For instance, leveraging algebraic manipulations for structures other than number fields, which is currently highly automated through the Manip package [29]. This is particularly useful in streamlining the process of formalizing pen-and-paper proofs without obscuring essential mathematical reasoning steps.

Acknowledgments. This work was partially supported by the NASA's System Wide Safety Project via RSES 80LARC23DA003; the Brazilian Research Council CNPq via UG 409003/21-2 and RG 313290/21-0; and the Goiás Research Foundation FAPEG, RG 202310267000223.

Disclosure of Interests. The authors have no competing interests to declare that are relevant to the content of this article.

Table 2: Relevant differences between "Proofs from THE BOOK" on the infinitude of primes and their PVS formalization.

Proofs	"THE BOOK"	Formalization
Fermat numbers (Sec. 2.1)	Assumption of the infinitude of Fermat numbers implies the infinitude of primes, without a formal proof.	Build an injection from the infinite set of Fermat numbers to the set of minimal primes dividing each Fermat number.
Mersenne Numbers (Secs. 2.2 and 3.1)	Assumption of isomorphisms between algebraic structures.	Specification of particular types from cosets for applying results from NASALib regarding finite groups. Explicit proofs of properties and relations between modular arithmetic and quotient rings.
	Application of Lagrange's Theorem.	Application of an algebraic lemma that considers the divisor of the order of an element, instead of using Lagrange's Theorem.
Euler product (Secs. 2.3 and 3.2)	Informal usage of series of primes of the form $p_1, p_2 \ldots,$ without explicitly considering the possibility of finitude.	Construction of an enumeration function of $\mathbb{P} \cup \{0\}$ avoiding the implicit assumption of the infinitude of primes. Alternative version of the Fundamental Theorem of Arithmetic, making explicit the power of each prime in the decomposition.
	Implicit usage of the Cauchy product formula.	Formalization of the Cauchy product.
Fürstenberg (Sec. 2.4)	Minor omissions when proving properties on the Cardinality of open and closed sets in the topological space built on sets $N_{a,b}$.	Mechanized manipulation of different types of sets and formalizations of properties of the topological space using basic notions of the PVS set and topology theories.
Prime reciprocal series (Sec. 2.5)	Informal usage of notation $p_1, p_2, \ldots$ for $\mathbb{P}$.	Use of an explicit enumeration function. Further consideration on sets specified in terms of prime enumeration.

References

1. Aigner, M., Ziegler, G.M.: Proofs from THE BOOK. Berlin. Germany **1**(2), 12 (1999). https://doi.org/10.1007/978-3-662-57265-8
2. Almeida, A.A., Oliveira, A.C.R., Ramos, T.M.F., de Moura, F.L.C., Ayala-Rincón, M.: The Computational Relevance of Formal Logic Through Formal Proofs. In: Dongol, B., Petre, L., Smith, G. (eds.) Formal Methods Teaching - Third International Workshop and Tutorial, FMTea 2019, Held as Part of the Third World Congress on Formal Methods, FM 2019, Porto, Portugal, October 7, 2019, Proceedings. Lecture Notes in Computer Science, vol. 11758, pp. 81–96. Springer (2019). https://doi.org/10.1007/978-3-030-32441-4_6
3. Apostol, T.M.: Introduction to analytic number theory. Springer Science & Business Media (2013). https://doi.org/10.1007/978-1-4757-5579-4
4. Artmann, B.: Euclid—the creation of mathematics. Springer Science & Business Media (2012). https://doi.org/10.1007/978-1-4612-1412-0
5. Ayala-Rincón, M., De Moura, F.L.: Applied logic for computer scientists: computational deduction and formal proofs. Springer (2017). https://doi.org/10.1007/978-3-319-51653-0
6. Ayala-Rincón, M., de Lima, T.A.: Teaching Interactive Proofs to Mathematicians. In: Quaresma, P., Neuper, W., Marcos, J. (eds.) Proceedings 9th International Workshop on Theorem Proving Components for Educational Software, ThEdu@IJCAR 2020, Paris, France, 29th June 2020. EPTCS, vol. 328, pp. 1–17 (2020). https://doi.org/10.4204/EPTCS.328.1
7. Ayala-Rincón, M., de Lima, T.A., Avelar, A.B., Galdino, A.L.: Formalization of Algebraic Theorems in PVS (Invited Talk). In: Piskac, R., Voronkov, A. (eds.) LPAR 2023: Proceedings of 24th International Conference on Logic for Programming, Artificial Intelligence and Reasoning, Manizales, Colombia, 4-9th June 2023. EPiC Series in Computing, vol. 94, pp. 1–10. EasyChair (2023). https://doi.org/10.29007/7JBV
8. Bortin, M.: From THE BOOK: Two Squares via Involutions. Archive of Formal Proofs (August 2022), https://isa-afp.org/entries/Involutions2Squares.html
9. de Castro, D.: Infinitude of primes: Euclid's proof using angles between lattice vectors. Elemente der Mathematik **76**(1), 28–32 (2021). https://doi.org/10.4171/EM/425
10. Cauchy, A.L.: Cours d'analyse de L'Ecole Polytechnique. Oeuvres Complètes 2, t–3 (1821), https://doi.org/10.1017/CBO9780511702525
11. Eberl, M.: The Hurwitz and Riemann ζ Functions. Arch. Formal Proofs (2017), https://www.isa-afp.org/entries/Zeta_Function.html
12. Eberl, M.: Furstenberg's topology and his proof of the infinitude of primes. Archive of Formal Proofs (2020), https://isa-afp.org/entries/Furstenberg_Topology.html
13. Erdös, P.: Uber die Reihe $\Sigma\, 1/p$. Mathematica, Zutphen B **7**, 1–2 (1938)
14. Euler), L.E.L.: Introductio in analysin infinitorum, vol. tomus primus. Marcum-Michaelem Bousquet & Socies, Lausanne (1748)
15. Furstenberg, H.: On the infinitude of primes. Amer. Math. Monthly **62**(5), 353 (1955). https://doi.org/10.1080/00029890.1955.11988641, note in *Mathematical Notes*, pages 349-353
16. Gauss, C.F.: Disquisitiones arithmeticae. Springer-Verlag, English edn. (1986). https://doi.org/10.1007/978-1-4939-7560-0

17. Gödel, K.: Über Formal Unentscheidbare Sätze der Principia Mathematica Und Verwandter Systeme I. Monatshefte für Mathematik **38**(1), 173–198 (1931)
18. Gottliebsen, H., Hardy, R., Lightfoot, O., Martin, U.: Applications of real number theorem proving in PVS. Formal Aspects Comput. **25**(6), 993–1016 (2013). https://doi.org/10.1007/S00165-012-0232-9
19. Hua, L.K.: Introduction to number theory. Springer Science & Business Media (2012)
20. Koepke, P., Marcol, M., Schäfer, P.: Formalizing Sets and Numbers, and some of Wiedijk's "100 Theorems" in Naproche (2023), https://naproche.github.io/100_theorems.ftl.pdf, naproche repository document
21. de Lagrange, J.L.: Réflexions sur la résolution algébrique des équations. Prussian Academy (1770)
22. Lester, D.R.: Topology in PVS: continuous mathematics with applications. In: Proceedings of the second workshop on Automated formal methods AFM. pp. 11–20. ACM (2007). https://doi.org/https://doi.org/10.1145/1345169.1345171
23. Mendelson, B.: Introduction to topology. Dover Publications, third edn. (1990)
24. de Oliveira Ribeiro, B.B.: PVS formalization of proofs of the infinitude of primes (2025), Bachelor's thesis, Universidade de Brasília. https://bdm.unb.br/handle/10483/41607
25. Owre, S., Rushby, J.M., Shankar, N.: PVS: A prototype verification system. In: Proceedings 11th International Conference on Automated Deduction CADE-11. Lecture Notes in Computer Science, vol. 607, pp. 748–752. Springer (1992). https://doi.org/10.1007/3-540-55602-8_217
26. Paulson, L.C.: Irrational numbers from THE BOOK. Archive of Formal Proofs (2022), https://isa-afp.org/entries/Irrationals_From_THEBOOK.html
27. Robinson, R.M.: Mersenne and Fermat numbers. Proceedings of the American Mathematical Society **5**(5), 842–846 (1954)
28. Titchmarsh, E.C.: The theory of the Riemann Zeta-function. The Clarendon Press Oxford University Press (1986)
29. Vito, B.L.D.: Manip User's Guide. NASA Langley Research Center (2012), https://pvs.csl.sri.com/doc/manip-guide.pdf
30. Wiedijk, F.: Formalizing 100 Theorems (Formal proof–getting started) (Web page, last visited February 2023), https://www.cs.ru.nl/~freek/100/

Vector Graphics through Category Theory

Davi Sales Barreira[1] (✉), Henrique Borges Carvalho[1], Alexandre Rademaker[1], and Asla Medeiros e Sá[2], and Flávio Codeço Coelho[1]

[1] EMAp, Fundação Getúlio Vargas, Rio de Janeiro, Brazil
davisbarreira@gmail.com
[2] IMPA Tech, Rio de Janeiro, Brazil

Abstract. This paper introduces a novel approach to vector graphics drawing by formalizing it within Category Theory (CT). Using the *categorical programming* paradigm, CT abstractions are interpreted as design patterns within Functional Programming (FP), bridging theoretical formalism and practical implementation. Building on Yorgey's work, we represent diagrams as lists of graphical primitives, serving as a *normal form* for vector graphics. Diagrams are manipulated via graphical transformations (e.g., translation, rotation, scaling, color change) and list concatenation, which are modeled as an endofunctor F. This enables the construction of a free monad $\mathbb{T} \cong$ `Free F` as a way to accumulate operations into expression trees lazily. We formalize graphical marks as abstractions over diagrams via slice categories, and vector graphics as values of the free monad $\mathbb{T}$ over marks. Lastly, we introduce *graphic expressions* as a way to leverage F-algebras and F-coalgebras to construct complex graphics systematically. A prototype implementation in Lean demonstrates the applicability of our theory in a programming language based on dependent types, illustrating how categorical programming bridges the gap between mathematical abstraction and practical programming. An implementation in Julia is presented elsewhere.

Keywords: Vector Graphics; Category Theory; Diagrams; Functional Programming; Lean

1 Introduction

In recent years, Category Theory has found applications in a wide range of disciplines, including chemistry, biology, natural language processing, and database theory, among others [6]. Such widespread applications gave rise to Applied Category Theory (ACT) as a distinct field. [3]

The most influential application of Category Theory has been in programming, especially within Functional Programming. Orchard [12] states that the application of CT to programming can be divided into two distinct approaches, namely *categorical programming* and *categorical semantics*.

[3] The first conference named Applied Category Theory Conference took place in 2018.

V. de Paiva and P. Koepke (Eds.): CICM 2025, LNAI 16136, pp. 431–446, 2026.
https://doi.org/10.1007/978-3-032-07021-0_24

Categorical semantics formally interprets programming languages through the structures of Category Theory, as a means to define the precise meaning of programs and their components. In this approach, one commonly interprets types of the programming language as objects in a category, while functions or transformations between types are represented as morphisms. Employing this abstraction provides a more rigorous and principled approach to studying programming constructions, enabling formal proofs of properties such as code correctness and equivalence.

Categorical programming, on the other hand, uses categorical concepts as design patterns for organizing and structuring programs. Rather than using Category Theory to define the program's semantics rigorously, one uses categorical constructions, such as functors and monads, as tools for creating precise abstractions and designing modular, composable code. Thus, categorical programming can be used even within programming languages that are far removed from the Functional Programming paradigm.

By integrating category-theoretic principles, both approaches offer powerful ways to model, structure, and reason about software. Categorical semantics provides a foundational understanding, while categorical programming applies these abstract concepts in more practical ways. Together, they bring the clarity and rigor of Category Theory into the realm of programming.

In this paper, we explore how categorical programming can be used to formalize the vector graphics drawing process. Our work builds upon the foundation laid out by Yorgey [19], who demonstrated how monoids could be used to structure diagrams. We extend this approach by introducing the concepts of graphical marks and graphic expressions, which ease the construction of complex graphics.[4]

This work not only provides a theoretical foundation for vector graphics but also demonstrates how categorical programming can serve as a bridge between mathematical abstraction and practical implementation.[5] The ideas in this paper have also been used to develop the data visualization library `Vizagrams.jl` [2], which is implemented in the `Julia` programming language.

Our presentation is organized as follows. We start by introducing the basic concepts of Category Theory that will be used within our formulation (Section 2). Then, we present the formalization of the vector graphics drawing process starting from the graphical primitives, followed by lists of graphical primitives, tree expressions, and graphical marks (Section 3). With vector graphics properly defined, we introduce graphic expressions and demonstrate how they systematize the construction of vector graphics as a split-apply-combine process (Section 4). In Section 5, we made some additional considerations about our ongoing implementation in the Lean programming language with a preliminary example of a simple plot.

[4] This work is based on the first author's PhD thesis [3].

[5] The code for this paper is available at `https://github.com/arademaker/vizagrams`

2 Brief Introduction to Category Theory

In this section, we provide a brief overview of key selected concepts from Category Theory that underpin our theoretical framework. Furthermore, we show how these concepts can serve as valuable *design patterns* for constructing graphics. This section is to be used mainly as a reference, and is not intended to be a comprehensive introduction to Category Theory. The reader not acquainted with Category Theory is encouraged to read [10], where CT is properly introduced and connected to Functional Programming.

2.1 Categories, Functors and Natural Transformations

A **category** $\mathcal{C} = \langle \mathrm{Ob}_{\mathcal{C}}, \mathrm{Mor}_{\mathcal{C}} \rangle$ consists of a class of objects $\mathrm{Ob}_{\mathcal{C}}$ and a class of morphisms $\mathrm{Mor}_{\mathcal{C}}$ satisfying the following properties:

- Every morphism $f \in \mathrm{Mor}_{\mathcal{C}}$ is associated to two objects $A, B \in \mathrm{Ob}_{\mathcal{C}}$ where $dom(f) = A$ is called the domain of f and $cod(f) = B$ is the codomain. We denote the collection of morphisms going from A to B by $\mathrm{Mor}_{\mathcal{C}}(A, B)$, and an individual morphism $f \in \mathrm{Mor}_{\mathcal{C}}(A, B)$ by $f : A \to B$;
- Every object $A \in \mathrm{Ob}_{\mathcal{C}}$ has a morphism $id_A \in \mathrm{Mor}_{\mathcal{C}}(A, A)$ called the identity.
- For any two morphisms $f : A \to B$ and $g : B \to C$, there exists a third morphism called the *composite* of g after f denoted by $(g \circ f) : A \to C$.
- The composition operator $\circ$ must be:
  - **Unital**: given $f : A \to B$, then $f \circ id_A = f$ and $id_B \circ f = f$.
  - **Associative**: given $f : A \to B$, $g : B \to C$ and $h : C \to D$, $h \circ (g \circ f) = (h \circ g) \circ f$.

An example is the category **Set**, where the objects are sets, the morphisms are functions, and the composition $\circ$ is functional composition, i.e., $g \circ f = g(f)$.

A **functor** $F : \mathcal{C} \to \mathcal{D}$ maps objects in $\mathcal{C}$ to objects in $\mathcal{D}$, and morphisms in $\mathcal{C}$ to morphisms in $\mathcal{D}$ while preserving the structure in the categories. In other words, given $f : A \to B \in \mathrm{Mor}_{\mathcal{C}}$, then $FA \in \mathrm{Ob}_{\mathcal{D}}$, $FB \in \mathrm{Ob}_{\mathcal{D}}$ and $Ff : FA \to FB \in \mathrm{Mor}_{\mathcal{D}}$. The preservation of structure means that identities in $\mathcal{C}$ are taken to identities in $\mathcal{D}$, i.e. $Fid_A = id_{FA}$, and associativity in $\mathcal{C}$ is preserved, i.e. for $g \circ f$ in $\mathcal{C}$ then $F(g \circ f) = Fg \circ Ff$ in $\mathcal{D}$.

Similar to morphisms, functors can be composed and we also have an identity functor $Id : \mathcal{C} \to \mathcal{C}$ which simply takes the objects and morphisms to themselves. Moreover, if a functor has the same category for domain and co-domain, we call it an endofunctor.

A **natural transformation** $\alpha : F \to G$, where $F, G : \mathcal{C} \to \mathcal{D}$ are functors, is such that:

- For all $A \in \mathcal{C}$, there exists $\alpha_A : FA \to GA \in Mor_{\mathcal{D}}(FA, GA)$;
- (Naturality) For all $f \in Mor_{\mathcal{C}}(A, B)$, then $\alpha_B \circ F(f) = G(f) \circ \alpha_A$.

Given two categories $\mathcal{C}$ and $\mathcal{D}$, we can define the category of functors, denoted by $[\mathcal{C}, \mathcal{D}]$. In this category, the objects are functors, e.g., $F : \mathcal{C} \to \mathcal{D}$. The morphisms are the natural transformations, where natural transformations can be composed by $(\beta \circ \alpha)_A = \beta_A \circ \alpha_A$, for every object $A \in \mathrm{Ob}_{\mathcal{C}}$.

2.2 Monoids and Monads

A **monoid** over a set A is a triple $(A, \oplus, e)$ where $e \in A$ is the neutral element and $\oplus$ is an associative binary operation that takes two values of A and returns another value in A. There are several possible monoids over the same set, for example $(\mathbb{Z}, +, 0)$ and $(\mathbb{Z}, *, 1)$.

For any given set A, one can construct what is known as a *free monoid*, denoted by $([A], \circ, [\,])$, where $[A]$ represent lists of elements of A, $\circ$ stands for list concatenation and $[\,]$ is the empty list. The *free monoid* is the most "general" monoid one can construct over a given set, in the sense that for any function $f : A \to M$ and monoid $(M, \oplus, e_M)$, we can extend f uniquely into a monoid homomorphism $\overline{f} : ([A], \circ, [\,]) \to (M, \oplus, e_M)$.

The monoid definition above is the set-theoretic definition. In the language of categories, a monoid in the category **Set** is a triple (M, μ, η), where $M \in \text{Ob}_{\mathbf{Set}}$, $\mu : M \times M \to M$ and $\eta : 1 \to M$ are two morphisms in **Set** satisfying the associativity and unitality properties. η is akin to the neutral element, and μ is akin to the binary operator. Note that 1 is the terminal object in **Set**, i.e., a singleton set.

We can use this categorical construction to generalize the concept of a monoid to categories other than **Set**, which takes us to the definition of a monad.

A **monad** is a monoid in the category of endofunctors $[\mathcal{C}, \mathcal{C}]$, where the triple (T, μ, η) consists in a functor $T : \mathcal{C} \to \mathcal{C}$, and two natural transformations $\mu : T \circ T \to T$ and $\eta : 1 \to T$.

Similar to how a free monoid is the most general monoid constructed over a given set, a *free monad* is the most general monad constructed over a given endofunctor. In Functional Programming, free monads can be used to model embedded Domain-Specific Languages, as they allow for the separation of syntax from interpretation [16].

Monads induce a category called *Kleisli category*. Such a category is of special interest in Functional Programming, where it is used to model computational effects. Let (T, μ, η) be a monad over a category $\mathcal{C}$. The Kleisli category is the category $\mathcal{C}_T$, where:

- $\text{Ob}_{\mathcal{C}_T} = \text{Ob}_{\mathcal{C}}$;
- $\text{Mor}_{\mathcal{C}_T}(A, B) = \text{Mor}_{\mathcal{C}}(A, TB)$;
- the composition of morphisms in $\mathcal{C}_T$ is given by:

$$g \circ_T f := \mu_C \circ Tg \circ f,$$

  with $f : A \to TB$ and $g : B \to TC$ as morphisms in $\mathcal{C}$;
- the identity morphism of an object A in $\mathcal{C}_T$ is $\eta : A \to TA$.

In summary, the Kleisli category is defined in such a way that two morphisms $f : A \to TB$ and $g : B \to TC$ can be composed using $g \circ_T f : A \to TC$.

2.3 Algebras and Coalgebras

The idea of creating expressions and evaluating them is formalized through the definition of F-algebras. An F**-algebra** consists in a tuple (A, alg), where

$F : \mathcal{C} \to \mathcal{C}$ is an endofunctor, $A \in \text{Ob}_{\mathcal{C}}$ and $alg : FA \to A$. The endofunctor F is used to construct the algebraic expressions, while the alg function is used to evaluate the expression.

The dual of an F-algebra is an **F-coalgebra**. It consists of a tuple $(A, coalg)$ where $coalg : A \to FA$. While an algebra evaluates expressions, a coalgebra produces expressions.

For a fixed endofunctor, we can define a category of F-algebras, where the objects are the F-algebras (i.e., tuples (A, alg)), and the morphisms are homomorphisms between F-algebras. Analogously, one can also define a category of F-coalgebras.

For some functors, the F-algebra category has an initial object, for which the algebra function is called *catamorphism*. Similarly, the F-coalgebra category can have a terminal object where the coalgebra function is called *anamorphism*. These two concepts are used within Functional Programming as a means to formalize recursions [18]. An example of the use of F-algebras and F-coalgebras within FP is described in [15].

2.4 Slice Categories

Given an existing category $\mathcal{C}$, there are several ways to construct new categories from it. One of the most useful constructions is the so-called **slice category**. A slice category $\mathcal{C}/S$ is a category where, given a fixed object $S \in \text{Ob}_{\mathcal{C}}$, the objects of $\mathcal{C}/S$ are tuples (A, f) such that $A \in \text{Ob}_{\mathcal{C}}$ and $f : A \to S$.

In $\mathcal{C}/S$, a morphism $\phi_{A,B} : (A, f) \to (B, g)$ is a $\phi \in \text{Mor(A,B)}_{\mathcal{C}}$, such that $f = g \circ \phi$. In other words, a morphism $\phi_{A,B}$ is equivalent to a morphism ϕ in the category $\mathcal{C}$, such that going from A to S through f is the same as going to B through ϕ and then from B to S through g.

Slice categories will be utilized in our framework to model categories of graphical marks.

2.5 Categorical Programming

Categorical programming consists of using CT formalism to structure programs [12]. To do so, we must interpret programs as a category. A common approach involves interpreting data types (e.g. `Int`, `String`, `Float`) as sets and programming functions as mathematical functions, so that we can consider ourselves to be working within **Set** [10].

Once we have established that types are sets and functions are morphisms, we can begin to incorporate other concepts from category theory (CT). For example, an endofunctor F : **Set** $\to$ **Set** can be modeled as a parametric type `F (A : Type)` coupled with a `map : (A → B) → F A → F B` function. The `map` function takes a function `f : A → B` and a value of `F A` and returns a value of type `F B`. Note that the map captures the functor behavior of lifting functions, but not the covariant behavior and the identity laws. In other words, it is up to the programmer to ensure that `map` respects the functor laws.

In Functional Programming, this coupling of `map` with the parametric type `F` is done via type classes. One defines a type class `Functor` with a `map` function as the constraint. A type `F` can be made into an instance of the `Functor` class by providing an implementation of the `map` function. This allows `map` to be used as an ad-hoc polymorphic function, i.e., a function that behaves differently depending on the type of the input.

Type classes can also be used to model other categorical concepts, such as monoids and monads. Similar to how it works for functors, the classes are defined with the required functions as constraints. Yet, it is up to the programmer to ensure that the functions satisfy the monoid or monad laws. For a more complete treatment of the topic, see [10].

3 Vector Graphics through Category Theory

A graphic is a visual presentation on some surface, such as a piece of paper or a computer screen [14]. A computer graphic is any computational representation of a visual presentation, be it static, animated, or interactive. Every computer graphic, in the final analysis, is a raster graphic, i.e., a matrix of colored pixels.

A **vector graphic** is a scalable computer graphic representation consisting of collections of geometric shapes [8], where the rasterization process consists of drawing each shape on top of the other. At its core, vector graphics differ from raster graphics in that they can be composed and transformed using geometric and style transformations.

There are several vector graphics formats, such as SVG [7], PDF [4], PostScript [1], and others. Each format implements its graphical primitives, and each of these primitives has a representation as a raster graphic; that is, there is a *raster* function that converts a primitive into a raster graphic.

In this section, we formalize the concept of vector graphics within the context of Category Theory. Our framework is based on the work of Yorgey [19]. As such, we begin with the concept of graphical primitives and their associated transformations, gradually building up to the idea of vector graphics.

3.1 Graphic Primitives

Graphical primitives, or simply primitives, consist of a set of fundamental shapes with known, parameterized representations, such as circles, rectangles, polygons, and Bézier curves, for which a known rasterization process exists. Primitives can be transformed by applying graphical transformations, which include geometric transformations such as translation, rotation, and uniform scaling, as well as style transformations like changes in color and opacity.

Computationally, primitives can be modeled as a type `Prim` containing two fields: `geom` for geometric attributes, and `style` for style attributes. Geometric attributes are invariant under style transformations, while style attributes are invariant under geometric transformations.

```
structure Prim where
    geom : Geom
    s : Style
```

Similarly, we can define a type `G` for geometric transformations, a type `S` for style transformations, and a type `H := G × S` for graphical transformations. Note that both geometric and style transformations have identity transformations, which makes `(G, identity)` isomorphic to `G` and `(identity, S)` isomorphic to `S`.

For our framework to be consistent, we require that the set of primitives be closed under the application of graphical transformations, i.e., for any primitive `p : Prim` and graphical transformation `g : H`, the result of applying `g` to `p` must again be of type `Prim`. Thus, we restrict the geometric transformations to translations, rotations, and uniform scaling. When it comes to style transformations, we do not impose any restrictions, as all primitives share the style attributes.

3.2 Diagrams

Yorgey [19] defines **diagrams** as ordered lists of primitives, where the order in the list defines the order for rendering. In other words, diagrams are values of type `List Prim`, which represent lists of primitives. Lists can be treated as a free monoid `(List Prim,++, [])`, where `++` is list concatenation.

A graphical transformation `g` can be applied to a diagram by applying it to each element in the diagram. This is done using the `map` function, which comes from the fact that `List` is a functor (the type `List T` implements the `Functor` class in Lean):

```
[p1, p2, p3].map g == [g p1,g p2, g p3]
```

An ordered list of primitives can be thought of as the *normal form* of a vector graphic. Here we use the term *normal form* in the context of lambda calculus, in which it refers to an expression that cannot be further reduced via β-reduction. The idea is that an ordered list of primitives is the simplest form of a vector graphic, in the sense that it cannot be simplified any further.

3.3 Expression Trees via Free Monads

Working directly with a list of primitives as a representation for vector graphics might lead to inefficiency when constructing complex graphics [19]. Hence, Yorgey [19] proposes the use of *monoidal trees*, a polymorphic data structure where the leaves contain monoidal structures.

Instead of monoidal trees, we use *free monads*, which is a concept from Category Theory commonly used in Functional Programming to build embedded domain-specific languages. Free monads formalize the idea of expression trees, i.e., binary trees where each branch contains an operation and each leaf contains an operand. An area where such trees are found is in Constructive Solid Geometry (CSG), where they are used to represent geometric shapes by placing primitive shapes in the leaves, and Boolean operations or geometric transformations in branches [13].

Akin to CSG, the idea is to represent vector graphics using trees where the branches contain either graphical transformations or diagram concatenation, and the leaves contain lists of primitives. While using a list of primitives directly requires eager evaluation, expression trees provide a lazy data structure that stores these operations inside the tree structure, which can then be evaluated only in the rendering process.

As stated, this tree structure can be given a formal interpretation within Category Theory via free monads. While a free monoid is defined over a given set (e.g. `List Prim`), a free monad is defined over an endofunctor F. This endofunctor F is used to represent the branch operations of the tree, which in our case are:

- `comp`: Constructor representing diagram composition.
- `act`: Constructor representing the (lazy) application of a graphical transformation (of type H). The application is lazy in the sense that the transformation is not immediately performed, but rather stored in the expression tree to be evaluated later when the diagram is flattened into a list of primitives.

Computationally, we define F as follows:

```
inductive F (α : Type) where
  | comp : α → α → F α
  | act : H → α → F α

instance : Functor F where
  map f a := match a with
    | F.comp x y => F.comp (f x) (f y)
    | F.act h x => F.act h (f x)
```

The free monad is the structure that enables us to compose the nodes (values of type `F`) into tree expressions. We define the free monad as an inductive type with constructors `pure`, `comp`, and `act`.

```
inductive 𝕋 (α : Type) where
  | pure : α → 𝕋 α
  | comp : 𝕋 α → 𝕋 α → 𝕋 α
  | act  : H → 𝕋 α → 𝕋 α
```

Since $\mathbb{T}$ is a monad, it means that $\mathbb{T}$ is a functor together with the natural transformations η and μ representing the unit and multiplication of the monad, respectively. In Functional Programming, it is more common to use the terms `pure` and `bind`, where `pure` is equivalent to the η natural transformation, and `bind` is a variation of μ combined with `map`.

```
def 𝕋.map (f : α → β) (a : 𝕋 α) : 𝕋 β :=
  match a with
  | 𝕋.pure x => 𝕋.pure (f x)
  | 𝕋.comp x y => 𝕋.comp (𝕋.map f x) (𝕋.map f y)
  | 𝕋.act h x => 𝕋.act h (𝕋.map f x)

instance : Functor 𝕋 where
```

```
  map := 𝕋.map

def η : α → 𝕋 α := fun a => 𝕋.pure a

def μ : 𝕋 (𝕋 α) → 𝕋 α
  | 𝕋.pure x => x
  | 𝕋.comp x y => 𝕋.comp (μ x) (μ y)
  | 𝕋.act h x =>
    match x with
      | 𝕋.act h' y => 𝕋.act (h * h') (μ y)
      | a => μ a

def freebind : (𝕋 α) → (α → 𝕋 β) → (𝕋 β) :=
  fun ma f => (μ ∘ (𝕋.map f)) ma

instance : Monad 𝕋 where
  pure := η
  bind := freebind
```

Therefore, the $\mathbb{T}$ `(List Prim)` type represents a tree structure where the nodes have diagrams and the branches either `comp` or `act`.

For this representation to be useful, we need to be able to evaluate the tree structure into a value of type `List Prim`. This is done by defining an $\mathbb{T}$-algebra that evaluates the tree structure into a value of type `List Prim`.

```
def alg : 𝕋 (List Prim) → List Prim
  | 𝕋.pure x => x
  | 𝕋.comp x y => (alg x) ⊕ (alg y)
  | 𝕋.act h x => map h (alg x)
```

3.4 Graphical Marks

The concept of a graphical mark is common in the data visualization literature, where it refers to graphical primitives used to represent data [11]. For example, in a bar chart, rectangle bars are graphical marks, while in a scatter plot, circles are. A related concept is that of glyphs, which is used to denote collections of graphical primitives [5]. An example of this is a boxplot, where the box and whiskers are graphical primitives, and the whole box is a glyph.

Instead of dealing with both concepts separately, we propose a unified definition by collapsing the concepts of glyphs and graphical marks. Through a bit of abstraction, we can think of a graphical mark as any type that can be turned into a diagram. In more precise terms, we define **graphical mark** as a tuple $(\mathtt{A}, \theta_{\mathtt{A}})$, where `A` is a type and $\theta_{\mathtt{A}}$ is a function $\theta_{\mathtt{A}} : \mathtt{A} \rightarrow \mathbb{T}\mathtt{List\ Prim}$. We could have used `List Prim` as the codomain of $\theta_{\mathtt{A}}$ instead of $\mathbb{T}$`List Prim`, since both are valid representations for diagrams. Yet, the latter will have a clearer categorical interpretation, and thus we adopt it.

Note that our new definition covers both primitives and glyphs, as both can be interpreted as marks. Observe that any primitive `p : Prim` can be interpreted as a mark ($\texttt{Prim}, \theta_{\texttt{Prim}}$), where $\theta_{\texttt{Prim}}(\texttt{p}) := \eta(\texttt{List p})$. Analogously, any glyph (collection of primitives) can be interpreted as a mark ($\texttt{List Prim}, \eta$).

Within the categorical programming framework, such a definition can be implemented through the concept of type classes:

```
class MarkInterface (a : Type) where
    θ : a -> 𝕋 (List Prim)
```

This means that any type `A` belonging to a `MarkInterface` has a function θ that turns values of type `A` into a tree of diagrams.

Note that, in this construction, `MarkInterface` is a type class, and not a type. We can make it into a type by encapsulating it into a type `Mark`.

```
structure Mark where
  {T : Type}
  [inst : MarkInterface T]
  val : T

def Mark.θ : Mark → 𝕋 (List Prim) := fun m => m.inst.θ m.val
```

Together with type `Mark`, we define the `Mark.`θ function, which uses the θ corresponding to the type `T` encapsulated.

3.5 Vector Graphics as Free Monads over Marks

With the concept of graphical marks firmly established, we can now use them to construct vector graphics. We define **vector graphics** as values of type $\mathbb{T}$ `Mark`, in other words, a tree expression where the leaves are marks.

We can flatten a tree expression of type $\mathbb{T}$ `Mark` into a value of type `List Prim` using $alg \circ \mu \circ \mathbb{T}\theta$. In other words, first we map the θ function to the leaves of the tree, which returns a tree of tree expressions, i.e., a value of type $\mathbb{T}$ $\mathbb{T}$ `(List Prim)`. Then, we use our μ to obtain a value of type $\mathbb{T}$ `[Prim]`. Finally, we use the `alg` function to evaluate the tree expression into a value of type `List Prim`. In Lean, this is implemented as:

```
def flatten (t : 𝕋 Mark) : List Prim := alg (μ ((𝕋.map Mark.θ) t))
```

In summary, users can define graphical marks to represent semantically meaningful objects, which can then be combined just like any other graphical primitives, thus constructing vector graphics.

3.6 Building Marks from Other Marks

Our construction suggests that if we want to define a mark, we must pick a type and a function that turns this type into a `[Prim]`. This works fine for simple marks where one can easily describe them by combining primitives, but as marks become more complex, this can become too cumbersome. Alternatively, a more effective strategy would be to use predefined marks to construct new ones, thereby increasing complexity incrementally. In other words, we need to find a way to define a graphical mark $(\mathtt{A}, \theta_{\mathtt{A}})$ where instead of implementing $\theta_{\mathtt{A}} : \mathtt{A} \to \mathtt{[Prim]}$, we can implement a function $\zeta_{\mathtt{A}} : \mathtt{A} \to \mathbb{T}\mathtt{Mark}$ and derive $\theta_{\mathtt{A}}$ "for free".

Thankfully, this is quite easy to do. We just need to compose the $\zeta : \mathtt{A} \to \mathbb{T}\mathtt{Mark}$ with our $\mathtt{flatten} : \mathbb{T}\mathtt{Mark} \to \mathtt{[Prim]}$ function:

$$\theta_{\mathtt{A}} := \mathtt{flatten} \circ \zeta_{\mathtt{A}}.$$

In programming languages where types are not enforced, one must be careful not to create circular (non-terminating) constructions. For example, if we define ζ_A returning a tree with a mark B and ζ_B returning a tree with a mark A, then when we try to compute θ_A, we will fall into a non-terminating loop. In languages like Haskell and Lean, this circularity is not allowed, as the compiler will verify if the output type for ζ is indeed a mark.

3.7 Category of Marks

We have shown that it is possible to build marks from previously defined marks via the ζ function, which can be used to derive the appropriate θ function. This derivation of θ from ζ has a category-theoretic origin, which can be used to formalize our construction rigorously.

First, recall that our tree constructor $\mathbb{T}$ is modeled as a free monad $(\mathbb{T}, \eta, \mu)$ over the category **Set**. Thus, we can define the Kleisli Category $\mathbf{Set}_{\mathbb{T}}$, where $\mathrm{Ob}_{\mathbf{Set}_{\mathbb{T}}} = \mathrm{Ob}_{\mathbf{Set}}$, $\mathrm{Mor}_{\mathbf{Set}_{\mathbb{T}}}(A, B) = \mathrm{Mor}_{\mathbf{Set}}(A, \mathbb{T}B)$, and composition is given by:

$$g \circ_{\mathbb{T}} f := \mu_C \circ \mathbb{T}g \circ f,$$

with $f : A \to \mathbb{T}B$ and $g : B \to \mathbb{T}C$.

From $\mathbf{Set}_{\mathbb{T}}$, we construct the slice category $\mathbf{Set}_{\mathbb{T}}/\mathtt{[Prim]}$, in which an object is a pair (A, θ_A) with $\theta_A \in \mathrm{Mor}_{\mathbf{Set}_{\mathbb{T}}}(A, \mathtt{[Prim]})$, and a morphism between (A, θ_A) and (B, θ_B) is equivalent to a function $\zeta_A \in \mathrm{Mor}_{\mathbf{Set}_{\mathbb{T}}}(A, B)$, such that:

$$\theta_A = \theta_B \circ_{\mathbb{T}} \zeta_A = \mu_B \circ \mathbb{T}\theta_B \circ \zeta_A.$$

Thus, the $\mathbf{Set}_{\mathbb{T}}/\mathtt{[Prim]}$ category very closely resembles how we are modelling marks, yet it still misses some critical points.

In $\mathbf{Set}_{\mathbb{T}}/\mathtt{[Prim]}$, every set (type) is an object, which is not true for marks, since only types that are instances of `MarkInterface` are valid. Moreover, for any mark type A, there must exist only a single function (morphism) $\theta_{\mathtt{A}}$ taking A to $\mathbb{T}\mathtt{[Prim]}$, otherwise, this would imply that the same mark could be drawn differently, which is again not true in $\mathbf{Set}_{\mathbb{T}}/\mathtt{[Prim]}$. In summary, we need smaller category.

To address these constraints, we pose the existence of a **category of marks**, denoted by $\mathcal{M}$. This category is constructed as a *thin* subcategory of $\mathbf{Set}_{\mathbb{T}}/\mathtt{[Prim]}$, where only types that are instances of `MarkInterface` are objects. Furthermore, the fact that $\mathcal{M}$ is thin implies that at most one morphism exists between any two objects. This captures the principle that each mark type must be associated with a unique morphism θ. Another consequence of this definition is that the ζ

functions are also unique. This uniqueness of morphisms is what ensures that our system of graphical marks is consistent, in the sense that a mark cannot be drawn in more than one distinct way.

4 Graphic Expressions

We have seen how vector graphics can be constructed by composing graphical marks and applying transformations to them. Complex graphics usually involve multiple transformations and compositions, and it is often helpful to reason about them in a structured way. For this reason, we introduce the concept of graphic expressions, which provide a formal way to describe the construction of a graphic.

A **graphic expression** is a triple $(expr, alg, coalg)$, where:

$$\sum_{coalg}^{alg} expr \cong \begin{bmatrix} expr : D \to \mathbb{T}\texttt{Mark} \\ alg : [\mathbb{T}\texttt{Mark}] \to \mathbb{T}\texttt{Mark} \\ coalg : D \to [D] \end{bmatrix}$$

In categorical terms, alg is an F-algebra and $coalg$ is an F-coalgebra where F is the list functor $\texttt{[ ]} : \mathbf{Set} \to \mathbf{Set}$.

The intuition behind the definition of graphic expressions is that they are akin to the *split-apply-combine* pattern [17], a common approach in data science for transforming datasets from one configuration to another. In the *split-apply-combine*, the data is split into chunks, each chunk is processed by an *apply* function, and the results are then combined back into a single result. In the graphic expression, the *expr* is a function that emulates the *apply* step, which, in our case, takes a value of type `D` and produces a vector graphic (a $\mathbb{T}$ `Mark`). The *coalg* is the function that takes the values of the type `D` and turns it into a list of subsets of `D`, thus emulating the *split* step. Lastly, the *alg* is the reducing function that takes a list of vector graphics and combines them into a single vector graphic, thus emulating the *combine* step. This process is illustrated in Figure 1.

Graphic expressions are similar to the recursion structure known in Functional Programming as hylomorphism [9], with the difference that it includes *expr* as a separate function mapping between distinct types. Thus, a graphic expression is evaluated by the following formula:

$$\left(\sum_{coalg}^{alg} expr \right) = alg \circ \texttt{map}(expr) \circ coalg$$

In other words, a graphic expression is itself a function from a type `D` to a graphic $\mathbb{T}$ `Mark`, which applies the `coalg` followed by the `expr` via the `map` operator for the list functor, and then the `alg`.

Depending on the desired graphic, one may combine summands to produce sequences of splits and combinations. For example:

$$\sum_{coalg_2}^{alg_2} \sum_{coalg_1}^{alg_1} expr = alg_2 \circ \texttt{map} \left(\sum_{coalg_1}^{alg_1} expr \right) \circ coalg_2.$$

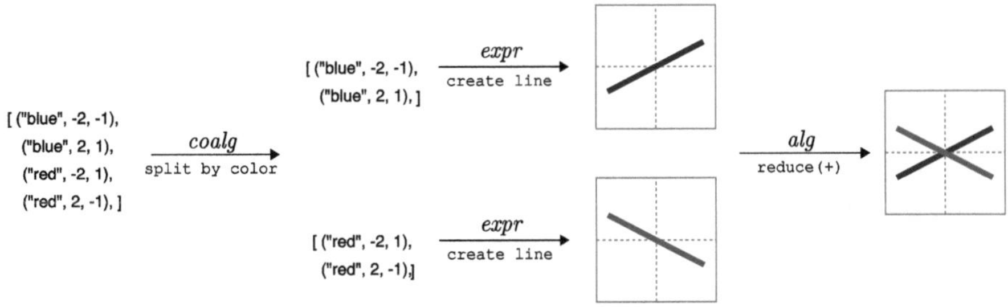

Fig. 1: Illustration exemplifying a graphic expression. The input is a list of tuples, shown on the left. This list is split into two subsets by the coalgebra, giving a list of list of tuples. The expression function is applied to each subset, producing lines with different colors. The algebra combines these lines using the diagram composition operator (+), thus producing the final graphic where both lines are visible. The final graphic is shown on the right.

Within Lean, this can be implemented as follows:

```
structure GraphicExpression (D : Type) :=
    expr : D → 𝕋 Mark
    alg : List (𝕋 Mark) → 𝕋 Mark
    coalg : D → List D

def GraphicExpression.eval {D : Type} (ge : GraphicExpression D) : D → 𝕋
      Mark :=
  fun d => ge.alg (List.map ge.expr (ge.coalg d))
```

5 Implementation

Our implementation uses two Lean libraries. We use `Mathlib` to handle matrix and vector operations. In particular, we define the types `Mat2` and `Vec2` to represent 2×2 matrices and 2-dimensional vectors, respectively:

```
abbrev Vec2 := Fin 2 → Float
abbrev Mat2 := Matrix (Fin 2) (Fin 2) Float
```

We define the class `AffineMapLike`, which provides a general interface for affine transformations over arbitrary types:

```
class AffineMapLike (G : Type) (V : Type) where
  eval : G → V → V
  compose : G → G → G
```

Types that implement this class can be evaluated on vectors and composed as affine maps. For instance, we define a structure `Mat2Vec2`, which is a tuple of `Mat2` and `Vec2`, and we provide an instance of `AffineMapLike` for it.

We also depend on `ProofWidgets` for serializing SVG elements and interacting with VSCode's *InfoView* to render the diagrams. To accomplish this, we define a function that converts our primitives (`Prim`) into `ProofWidgets.Element` structures:

```
def draw (t : 𝕋 Mark): ProofWidgets.Html
```

Figure 2 shows an example of how our implementation can be used to render a figure by applying the concepts introduced earlier in this article.

```
def data: List Float := [1.0, 2.3, 0.7, 3.1, 0.3]

def barPolygon (h: Float) (w: Float := 0.8) : Prim :=
  let pts: Array Vec2 :=
    #[![0, 0], ![w, 0], ![w, h], ![0, h]]
  NewPolygon pts {fillColor := Color.mk (3*h/2) (2*h/3) (h/5)}

def coalgbar (t : List Float) : List ( List Float ) :=
  t.map (fun x => [x])


def barExpr : List Float → 𝕋 Mark
  | [h] => 𝕋.pure (barPolygon h)
  | _ => 𝕋.pure Nil.mk


def algBar (t :List (𝕋 Mark)) : 𝕋 Mark :=
  match t with
    | x :: xs => List.foldl (• →[0.5] •) x xs
    | [] => 𝕋.pure Nil.mk

def bars : GraphicExpression (List Float):= {
  expr := barExpr
  coalg := coalgbar
  alg:= algBar
}

#html draw ( bars.eval data )
```

Fig. 2: Example of a complete Lean code for a preliminary plotting.

We use a `List Float` to represent the dataset and generate a simple figure resembling a bar chart, although without axes, legends, and other standard graphical components.

To achieve this, we define a function that maps each data value to a graphical mark (in this case, a colored bar encoded as a `Prim`). Since `Prim` is a special case of `Mark`, this function is used in the `expr` component of a `GraphicExpression`.

Finally, we use the `draw` function to convert a value of type 𝕋 `Mark` into a `ProofWidgets.Element`, which is then rendered in Visual Studio Code.

6 Conclusion

One of the strengths of Category Theory is its capacity to model a wide range of abstractions, making it well-suited for formalizing applied domains. Once a field is expressed categorically, the categorical programming paradigm provides a systematic path from theory to implementation. In this paper, we formalized the process of drawing vector graphics, and by leveraging categorical programming, we translated this abstract formalism into code.

Our formalization took a constructive approach, starting from graphical primitives, then lists of graphical primitives, and finally, graphical marks, culminating in vector graphics as expressions of graphical marks. Each component was interpreted within the context of Category Theory, along with its corresponding programming interpretation. We then showed how this construction could be interpreted as a *thin* subcategory of $\mathbf{Set}_{\mathbb{T}}/\texttt{[Prim]}$, where $\mathbf{Set}_{\mathbb{T}}$ is the Kleisli Category of the free monad $\mathbb{T}$ over the category of sets.

To construct complex graphics, we introduced graphic expressions as a concept similar to the split-apply-combine process. Again, Category Theory was used to provide a formal foundation to this concept. The split and combine processes were formalized as F-algebras and F-coalgebras, respectively, where the endofunctor F used was the list functor.

This formalism was then implemented as a Lean library, serving as a proof of concept for the categorical approach to vector graphics. In the Julia programming language, the Vizagrams.jl [2] package also implemented these ideas, thus demonstrating the usefulness of the categorical formalism. Often, the conceptual theory of an application diverges significantly from its actual implementation, making it challenging for developers other than the original ones to implement it in different programming languages, or even in the same language.

References

1. Adobe Systems Inc, C.: PostScript language reference. Addison-Wesley Longman Publishing Co., Inc. (1999)
2. Barreira, D.S.: davibarreira/vizagrams.jl: v0.2.3 (Aug 2024). https://doi.org/10.5281/zenodo.13331908
3. Barreira, D.S.: Data Visualization from a Category Theory Perspective. Ph.D. thesis, Fundação Getulio Vargas (2025), https://hdl.handle.net/10438/36341, phD thesis
4. Bienz, T., Cohn, R., Adobe Systems (Mountain View, C.: Portable document format reference manual. Citeseer (1993)
5. Borgo, R., Kehrer, J., Chung, D.H., Maguire, E., Laramee, R.S., Hauser, H., Ward, M., Chen, M.: Glyph-based visualization: Foundations, design guidelines, techniques and applications. In: Eurographics (state of the art reports). pp. 39–63 (2013)
6. Bradley, T.D.: What is applied category theory? arXiv preprint arXiv:1809.05923 (2018)
7. Dengler, P., Grasso, A., Lilley, C., McCormack, C., Schepers, D., Watt, J.: Scalable vector graphics (svg) 1.1 (2011)
8. Eisenberg, J.D., Bellamy-Royds, A.: SVG essentials: Producing scalable vector graphics with XML. " O'Reilly Media, Inc." (2014)
9. Meijer, E., Fokkinga, M., Paterson, R.: Functional programming with bananas, lenses, envelopes and barbed wire. In: Conference on functional programming languages and computer architecture. pp. 124–144. Springer (1991)
10. Milewski, B.: Category theory for programmers. Blurb (2018)

11. Munzner, T.: Visualization analysis and design. CRC press (2014)
12. Orchard, D.: Programming contextual computations. Tech. rep., University of Cambridge, Computer Laboratory (2014)
13. Requicha, A.G.: Representations for rigid solids: Theory, methods, and systems. ACM Computing Surveys (CSUR) **12**(4), 437–464 (1980)
14. Salomon, D.: The computer graphics manual. Springer Science & Business Media (2011)
15. Slodičák, V., Macko, P.: Some new approaches in functional programming using algebras and coalgebras. Electronic Notes in Theoretical Computer Science **279**(3), 41–62 (2011)
16. Swierstra, W.: Data types à la carte. Journal of Functional Programming **18**(4), 423–436 (2008). https://doi.org/10.1017/S0956796808006758
17. Wickham, H.: The split-apply-combine strategy for data analysis. Journal of statistical software **40**, 1–29 (2011)
18. Yang, Z., Wu, N.: Fantastic morphisms and where to find them: A guide to recursion schemes. In: International Conference on Mathematics of Program Construction. pp. 222–267. Springer (2022)
19. Yorgey, B.A.: Monoids: theme and variations (functional pearl). ACM SIGPLAN Notices **47**(12), 105–116 (2012)

A Lean-based Language for Teaching Proof in High School

Frédéric Tran Minh(✉)[1], Laure Gonnord[1], and Julien Narboux[2]

[1] Grenoble INP - LCIS, UGA, Valence, France
{frederic.tran-minh,laure.gonnord}@lcis.grenoble-inp.fr
[2] IRIF - CNRS - Université Paris Cité Inria, Paris, France
narboux@irif.fr

Abstract. Now pervasive in many mathematics and computer science research domains, proof assistants have recently gained importance in education, mostly during the college years. In this article, we propose a new learning environment as a layer above the Lean proof assistant, specifically targeting high-school level proofs. Drawing inspiration from coherent logic and adaptations of proof assistants for teaching, such as Lean-Verbose and Coq Waterproof, along with our own experience using proof assistants in higher education, we designed Yalep, a declarative controlled natural language, with a minimal number of syntactic constructions, which favors forward-chaining of facts. Yalep provides convenience for type theory hiding, and functions defined on type subsets. This paper presents the design choices and implementation of these features.

1 Introduction

Proof assistants are software that help users construct formal proofs and verify their correctness. Proof assistants are used more and more for teaching proof and proving[1] in higher education, but their use in high school is still limited. In [37], we presented a survey of the use of proof assistants for teaching, and we showed that most of the work is done in the context of higher education. Very few works are done in the context of high school. TPE [32], EasyProve [25], and Edukera [28] have been partly designed for high school. As these tools provide mainly a point-and-click user interface, the design of the input language was not crucial. Sylvie Boldo *et al.* also designed a set of exercises for high-school students about divisibility using the Coq/Rocq proof assistant and tested it with three high-school students [5].

[1] Mathematics didactics distinguishes between proof and proving [34]. Proving is the process, proof is the concept. Yalep aims to support the teaching of both: what is a proof (which, as opposed to a simple convincing argument, can be checked mechanically), and also how to produce a proof (by training students). For the sake of concision, in the paper we wrote "teaching proof" to mean "teaching proof and proving".

V. de Paiva and P. Koepke (Eds.): CICM 2025, LNAI 16136, pp. 447–467, 2026.
https://doi.org/10.1007/978-3-032-07021-0_25

In this paper, we present the prototype of a tool called Yalep[2] for teaching proof in high school using a proof assistant. Our work is inspired by Lean-Verbose [24], Coq Waterproof [43] and Isabelle Proof Buddy [18], which are layers above a proof assistant for use in higher education. Other ingredients for the design include our personal empirical experience with proof assistants in research and/or higher education, as well as coherent logic. The main goal of Yalep is to provide an environment for learning proof using a minimal language that is close to the language used in high school.

The context of the design of Yalep is the French educational system, in which all coauthors of this paper are involved. We chose to address high-school students because we all encountered difficulties in our undergraduate courses when it came to writing proofs.[3] Addressing high-school proofs requires us to develop a system that is easy to use, targeting students and teachers without a background in computer science or logic. Despite the fact that a few design choices may be specific to the French context, we strongly believe that many ideas presented in the paper could be used in other countries where proof is part of the curriculum.

In Section 2, we draw on the particularities of the high-school teaching context to set out the requirements for our tool. In Section 3, we describe the main characteristics and the design of our language. We then dive into more implementation details. Section 4 describes how Yalep renders the type-theoretical foundations of the proof assistant as invisible as possible. Section 5 focuses on how it represents functions whose domain and co-domain are type subsets. Section 6 presents a didactic progression to validate our tool.

2 Requirements Geared Towards High School

Our ambition for Yalep is to provide an ecosystem that helps high-school students understand the notion of mathematical proofs. This section provides a specification for Yalep, along with the limitations of existing approaches.

Language design Usually, and notably in the French educational system, high-school students are not familiar with logic and formal proofs, and very few of them are familiar with programming languages. Wemmenhove [42] thus points out that the steep learning curve of the syntax of an educative proving tool is one major difficulty for students (and also math teachers). Conversely, existing approaches using point-and-click user interfaces (such as Edukera), despite their "intuitive" interface, have shown their limits in terms of efficiency in the long term: some skills required for paper-and-pencil proofs may in fact be hidden in the graphical interface [3,19]. We aim to design a language "natural enough"

[2] Yet Another Learning Environment for Proof.

[3] Moreover, Villani (field medallist) and Torossian wrote in 2018 a report about teaching mathematics (https://www.education.gouv.fr/21-mesures-pour-l-enseignement-des-mathematiques-3242) which advocates to give more room to proof in high school.

so it can be read by high-school students without prior training or executing the proof script in a proof assistant, and as uncluttered as possible without generating ambiguity, so students can use it while focusing on proof rather than syntax.

We thus propose the following language requirements:

RL1 A declarative style for the proofs resembling what we could expect a high-school student to write.
RL2 A restricted formal textual language: very few keywords, no synonyms (different keywords referring to the same proof action, like obtain/fix for eliminating existential).
RL3 No overloaded keywords (a same keyword referring to separate proof actions depending on the context, like "let $x := 0$" / "let $x \in \mathbb{R}$")
RL4 Syntactic sugar to hide the mathematical notations that are out of the scope of high-school curriculum: for instance, avoid the $\forall$ symbol.

Expressivity and automation With a focus on high-school curriculum, the topics covered by our proposal have to include at least: elementary number theory, elementary numeric and literal computations, numeric functions (composition, variations), numeric sequences, limits, and derivatives. In addition, our solution should enable some (restricted) kind of automation, to transparently enable the computer check to "skip" parts of the proofs that would not have been justified by students.

This variety of topics gives the following requirements:

RA1 The technological choices should make it possible to consider extensions to many secondary education subjects without too much development;
RA2 All proof steps for which the teacher considers that no justification is needed should be accepted silently;
RA3 All proof steps for which the teacher expects a proof should be rejected when submitted without a sub-proof;
RA4 The level of justification required should be configurable by the teacher.

Assistance The tool should assist the student in the process of writing a proof, more specifically, the learning environment should:

RH1 display the current proof state, making explicit the known statements and the current goal at a given point of a proof;
RH2 provide constant feedback to the student about the correctness of the proof steps;
RH3 provide relevant explanations in case of errors;
RH4 help the student with the formal "rhetorical" part of the proof, providing help with proof by cases/induction;
RH5 provide help for the "creative" part of the proof.

2.1 The choice of Lean

Proof assistants, unlike (fully automatic) provers, offer facilities to adapt the automation level to topics or users' skills. Their interaction features also enable a constant display of the proof state (requirement RH1).

Among the available proof assistants, we chose Lean, which provides the following relevant features:

- A particularly flexible parser and delaborator (pretty printer), which is convenient to implement a controlled natural language (referred to as CNL in the rest of the paper) [24];
- A large and unified mathematical library for having solid foundations without reinventing the wheel;
- Lean4Web[4] runs Lean in a web browser, enabling easy usage in class;
- A Lean module enables to interact with JavaScript/React widgets hosted in a Visual Studio extension [26], which we exploit for some graphical display and point-and-click interaction.

The work described in this paper could also be carried out using Rocq. We could quite easily adapt Coq Waterproof to fit our design goals, and use Jscoq for the web interface, as it also allows some interactivity [13]. Jscoq runs the proof assistant on the client side, which allows dealing with many students with a modest server.

3 Yalep, a Tiny Controlled Language for Forward Reasoning

Our proposition, Yalep, constructed as a layer over Lean, aims at describing a set of statements followed by their proof.[5] In order to give a taste of it, we depict in Figure 1 a simple running example for the current section.

3.1 A "pseudo-natural" declarative language with very few variants

A proof exercise in Yalep is composed of a statement (under the form of Assumptions followed by a Conclusion), and its Proof. The syntax for proofs is inspired by coherent logic [33], a subset of first-order logic that is as expressive as first-order logic and has good meta-theoretical properties.

A proof (that can be hierarchical) is composed of a list of *facts*, delimited using the connector ◆. It ends with the □ connector. Proofs are mandatorily expressed using *forward reasoning*.

Assumptions and proof statements are not mandatorily labeled. This brings the user scripts closer to traditional pen-and-paper practice, where assumptions

[4] https://github.com/leanprover-community/lean4web

[5] Its grammar, intentionally restricted, is available in BNF format in the project repository hosted at https://gricad-gitlab.univ-grenoble-alpes.fr/yalep/Yalep as well as other examples in English and in French.

[6] In the Yalep language, `integer` qualifies an element of $\mathbb{Z}$.

```
Theorem product_even "5. Proving (for all ...)"
  Conclusion: for all integer n, for all integer b, if n is even then n*b is even
Proof
  let n be an integer
  let b be an integer
  assume n is even
  • there exists an integer k such that n = 2*k
  obtain such k
  • n*b = 2*(k*b)
  • there exists an integer q such that n*b = 2*q
  • n*b is even
□

Theorem nn1even "7. Using (... or ...) : proof by cases"
    Assumptions: (forall integer n, n is even or n is odd)
    Conclusion: for all integer n, n*(n+1) is even
Proof
    let n be an integer
    • n is even or n is odd
    • if n is even then n*(n+1) is even
      proof
        assume n is even
        • n*(n+1) is even by product_even
      □
    • if n is odd then n*(n+1) is even
      proof
        assume n is odd
        • n+1 is even
        • n*(n+1) is even by product_even
      □
    • n*(n+1) is even
□
```

Fig. 1: A taste of Yalep proofs.[6]

are generally only named when they represent key facts or as abbreviations to avoid copying long statements (Requirement RL1).

To meet the requirements of the French high-school curriculum, statements and facts are expressed in plain English (or French) using verbal formulations that correspond to the usual symbols (e.g., logical symbols $\wedge, \vee, \forall, \exists, \Longrightarrow, \Longleftrightarrow$, and number set notations $\mathbb{N}$, $\mathbb{Z}$, $\mathbb{Q}$, $\mathbb{R}$) to which pupils are not yet supposed to be exposed, depending on their grade level (RL4). Our tool also extends the relative quantification (like $\forall x > 0, \ldots$) already available out of the box in proof assistants, to tactic constructs (such as `let x>0;let n be an integer`, etc.) (RL1).

Predicates can be written in sentential form, such as `n is odd` in Figure 1.

Additionally, to fulfill requirement RL2, and unlike other CNL, we chose to provide, if possible, a unique syntactical construct for each proof action. As an example, our language does not allow writing "let $x \in \mathbb{R}$ such that $x + 2 > 0$", since the same semantics can be achieved using `let x∈ℝ, assume x+2>0`.

In our language, we do not allow imperative commands such as "Unfold the definition of ..." or "Let's rewrite the goal" that are often used in proof assistants. As an example, in Figure 1, the fact `• n is even or n is odd` has to be stated instead of saying "apply assumption 1 to n" as possible in Lean Verbose/Coq Waterproof.

In the following sections, we will explain the underlying choices behind this syntax and the automation.

3.2 A language based on forward chaining

Backward reasoning consists of proof steps (or tactics in a proof assistant) modifying the goal or creating new goals, whereas forward chaining corresponds to proof steps acting on the assumptions, or deducing new facts from assumptions in the context.

In usual mathematical practice, as well as in proof assistant scripts, steps of both kinds are freely mixed. Occurrences of backward reasoning are usually explicitly introduced, for instance, with "since ... it suffices to prove that ...". However, since proof beginners tend to confuse necessary and sufficient conditions, some teachers try to stick to forward reasoning, at least as far as the written trace of the proof is concerned. In the proof search phase, however, backward chaining is frequently used orally.

This analysis led us to propose a rather constrained language that "syntactically avoids" backward reasoning in final proofs; whereas it enables "proof holes" to mimic the "bottom to top" blackboard usage, frequently used by teachers. As an example, case disjunction is not triggered by an a priori announcement like "Let's discuss whether n is even or n is odd". Instead, the user has to state (and possibly prove) three facts: `◆ P ⟹ R`; `◆ Q ⟹ R` and `◆ R`.

Mixing backward and forward Our language discards as many backward tactics as possible. However, two of them must remain to maintain expressivity, namely `let` and `assume`, corresponding respectively to the introduction rules of the connectors $\forall$ and $\Longrightarrow$.[7] Since they introduce a new object or hypothesis into the context, and consequently modify the goal, they have no forward equivalent.[8]

Discussion From the pedagogical perspective, favoring forward chaining has the following advantages:[9]

- It restricts the number of commands (RL2): instead of learning a list of tactics (one per backward chaining command), students only learn the sole forward chaining command, `◆`, that inserts a new fact in the proof context.
- Students have to explicitly announce new facts (RL1): for instance, to prove R by using the assumption P or Q, they should explicitly announce (and prove) `◆ P ⟹ R` and `◆ Q ⟹ R` (like a pen and paper proof). The counterpart here is that the proof assistant does not help/assist the user in the task of discovering new goals.
- Forward facts can be written in any order, provided that they are provable in the context at the moment they are needed. The drawback here is that it may favor "unstructured proofs". In backward automated proofs, only "opened" sub-goals can be proven.

---

[7] In fact, these two constructions are the same in proof assistants implementing the type-theory paradigm of "propositions as types".

[8] This ability to introduce $\forall$ and $\Rightarrow$ and to create sub-proofs distinguishes our language from flat two-column proofs [16].

[9] As an illustrative comparison, we provide, in the project documentation, two variants of an inductive proof that every natural number is either even or odd.

- Forward tactics do not modify the main goal; instead, they make an accumulation of facts in the current context. Each fact can be justified by a "sub-proof". This is the analogue of sub-goal creation in backward chaining.

3.3 Implicit proof actions

Yalep also provides additional features so to fulfill requirement RA2:
- It implicitly introduces or eliminates some of the logic connectors.
- Connectors ◎ and ◆ allow to structure proofs and trigger parametrized automation.

Implicit versus explicit connectors Table 1 depicts usual logic connectors' usage in Yalep. The indication "(silent)" means that:
- if the connector appears in the goal, the presence of the premises in the context is enough to state a new fact introducing the connector.
- if the connector appears in a hypothesis, one can state a new fact following from the elimination of the connector, without justifying anything.

Table 1: Implicit or explicit introduction or elimination of connectors in Yalep

Connector	Appears in goal	Appears in assumption
`P and Q`	(silent)	(silent)
`P or Q`	(silent)	(silent)
$P \Longrightarrow Q$	`assume P`	(silent)
$\forall x \in E, P(x)$	`let x ∈ E`	(silent)
$\exists x \in E, P(x)$	(silent)	`obtain such x`
$P \Longleftrightarrow Q$	(silent)	(silent)

As on paper proofs, dealing with conjunction is completely implicit, and introduction of existential is implicit ($\exists x \in E, P(x)$ needs no justification as long as the context contains $a \in E$ and a proof of $P(a)$). For disjunction, usually, on paper, the introduction rule is implicit, but the elimination of disjunction (reasoning by cases) often is explicit. We decided to make both implicit, which contributes to reducing the language.[10]

Finally, similarly to coherent logic [33], we allow the implicit combination of universal quantifier and implication. For example, if a fact of the form $\forall \overline{x}, H_1(\overline{x}) \wedge \ldots \wedge H_n(\overline{x}) \Rightarrow Q(\overline{x})$ is known and facts $H_1(\overline{a}), \ldots, H_n(\overline{a})$ are in the context, one can conclude $Q(\overline{a})$ without any explicit justification.

The introductions of the universal quantifier and implication need to remain explicit, as they are usually explicit in paper proofs, and rendering the introduction of the universal quantifier implicit would require automatic naming. One could decide to introduce implicitly x when the goal is $\forall x, P(x)$ and x is available.

[10] More precisely, case disjunction is implicit but not automatic; if `P or Q` lies in the context, it is up to the user to decide whether to create or not and prove new facts `◆ P ⟹ R` and `◆ Q ⟹ R` so that subsequent fact `◆ R` can be asserted without further explicit justification.

But that would introduce confusion between the name of the bound variable and the name of the arbitrary variable, and the system would assist the student too much.

The rule for eliminating the existential quantifier needs to be explicit, because it introduces a new object. Precisely, it is often a pedagogical objective to expect from the student a proper naming of the newly introduced free variable, not necessarily named after the bounded variable, especially if a same existential definition is used twice and they should choose two different names (as in "assume that m and n are even. Obtain k and k' such that...").

Solving facts As we give priority to forward chaining, the syntactic construction to create a new fact (•) has a central role. The user can then solve this subgoal in three different ways:

- either opening a whole nested sub-proof by the construct (`proof` ... □).
- either by using one of the two provided types of explicit short justifications, those that relate to a statement or a fact (we use the keyword `since` as in `since x > 0`) and those that relate to a statement or a fact name (we use the keyword `by` as in `by triangle inequality`).
- either silently, with no justification at all, by relying on the automation.

We provide a syntactic construction (◎) that is similar to Lean (`calc`) or Lean Verbose (`Calc`) or Waterproof (`&`) tactics. It enables chaining several relational propositions by transitivity.[11]

Unlike Lean Verbose (that uses the current computation to solve the current goal), our (◎) keeps the pure forward chaining style, and introduces a new fact independently of the current goal. It even feeds the context with intermediate calculations. For example:

◎ `x` $\leqslant$ `y`	will add three new facts to the context: $x \leqslant y$, $y < z$
_ $<$ `z`	and $x < z$.

Discussion Let us firstly remark that all the (silent) in Table 1 demonstrate the minimal need for additional syntax (Requirement RL2).

Making elimination implicit also enables a step towards coherent logic [33], in which proofs are of coarser granularity than those in, for instance, natural deduction.[12] As a simple example, $A \wedge B \wedge C$ is automatically split onto $\{A, B, C\}$ as soon as it enters the context, which saves the double elimination of $\wedge$.

Some teachers may find the implicit elimination of connectors $\forall$, $\Longrightarrow$, $\Longleftrightarrow$, or $\vee$ too permissive (RA3). This advocates for a (yet to be developed) "à la carte" justification, according to some teacher-based parametrization (RA4), because it depends on the contextual "base of knowledge".

---

[11] The term is somewhat mathematically abusive since we allow combining different relations, e.g. $x \leqslant y \wedge y < z \Longrightarrow x < z$.

[12] This approach tending to enlarge proof granularity [29] is similar to assertion level proofs [17], implemented in Tutch [1] or Omega [31,2].

3.4 User interface, interaction and automation

Proof automation In this section, we consider the choices toward the objective of requirement RA2. The design choice is to rely on Lean powerful tactics, instead of relying on a general-purpose prover (like Lurch [8], Naproche). We think that this choice will facilitate the fulfillment of requirement RA3, and produce relevant feedback.

Our tool provides different kinds of automation that are triggered silently, which include:

- Elimination of connectors such as `and`, `or`, $\Longrightarrow$ (already discussed in the previous section).
- Termination of unfinished proofs (from the proof assistant point of view, but that should "look finished" for the user). It is generally triggered by the end-of-proof or end-of-sub-proof token , but can be called by other tactics. The implementation of the tactic itself is an ordered collection of trial and error attempts, using connector introduction, basic properties of operators (commutativity, associativity) or "trivial" lemmas (such as $x > 0 \Rightarrow x \geqslant 0$), and the Lean tactic for solving tautologies.[13]
- Justification of numerical facts: whenever a stated fact is left unjustified, it triggers native Lean tactics performing numerical computations and applying lemmas from the math Lean library targeting the high-school topics.
- Proof of legality of a function application: it derives facts from assumptions and membership class inference. (see Section 5)

Some other automation tactics are triggered by some idioms of our language. For instance, on Figure 1, `n is odd` is elaborated into a library definition, and `by product_even` has the effect of trying to prove the statement using the provided predicate. Other similar behaviors are linked to `since` or `by induction`.

User interface and facilitation The user already benefits from the native real-time display of the "proof state" (current assumptions and goal) provided by the Lean Proof assistant, customized thanks to the configurability of the pretty printer.

Considering that in the research phase of a proof, a student is frequently led to conduct backward reasoning, either orally or in draft form, we propose a point-and-click user-friendly way to trigger "backward-style" actions, which insert text into the proof script in our forward style.

The integration of interface buttons via JavaScript widgets hosted in a Visual Code extension communicating with the Lean Server is made possible by the Lean ProofWidgets layer [26]. For instance:

- when selecting the goal, the system displays a button to insert an appropriate "tactic" introducing the main connector.
- when selecting an assumption in the proof state, a button is displayed to insert a tactic eliminating the main connector of the assumption.

[13] This implies that Yalep is not suitable for teaching the fine-grained rules of logic. Many other tools are available for this purpose [14,12,27,38,36,23,20,35,22,40,39,41], see [37] for further details.

In our example, starting with the incomplete proof on the left of Figure 2, clicking on `n is even or n is odd` will expand the hole ? with the proof displayed on the right-hand side.

```
• n is even or n is odd
?
```

```
• n is even or n is odd
• if n is even then n*(n+1) is even
   proof
     assume n is even
     ?
   □
• if n is odd then n*(n+1) is even
   -- similar
```

Fig. 2: Backward reasoning using proof widgets.

4 Hiding Types from High-school Students

In type theory — which constitutes the basis of proof assistants such as Rocq or Lean — each object x comes with a type T, and the judgement $x : T$ is not a proposition; in contrast, usual educational presentation of mathematics relies on set theory, where all objects are un-typed sets, and when x and T are two sets, the proposition $x \in T$ can be proved or disproved. In contrast, Yalep allows to state and prove $\sqrt{2} \notin \mathbb{Q}$.[14] Without any additional interface, students would have to grasp the subtle nuance between $x : \mathbb{R}$ and $x \in \mathbb{R}^+$; the tight seal between types would lead to weird considerations when mixing different types of numbers, e.g., $((2 : \mathbb{N}) > 0)$ could be rejected when $((2 : \mathbb{R}) > 0)$ is expected ; functions defined between types do not model accurately usual high-school functions defined between sets as they would have to be "type-partial" (see next section).

Yalep avoids any type manipulation. On the cosmetic side, we exploit the Lean ability to implicitly infer any type ascription, either in statements ($\forall x \in E, P(x)$ elaborates as $\forall x : T, x \in E \implies P(x)$), in tactics (`let x ∈ E` will elaborate as `let x:T \ assume x ∈ E`) or in theorem statements (`Theorem test (...) Assumptions: (x ∈ E) (...)` will elaborate as `theorem test (x:T) (h : x ∈ E) (...)`). In each case, the type ascription $x : T$ does not appear explicitly, replaced by a set-based predicate ($x \in E$).

On the theoretical side, one step towards hiding types is to consider several types as subsets of a unique type. The special case of number types is essential. Proof assistants like Lean, Rocq, usually represent sets of numbers ($\mathbb{N}$, $\mathbb{Z}$, $\mathbb{Q}$, $\mathbb{R}$) as "hermetic" types, resulting from their construction. T. Portet and Y. Bertot presented a formalization of numbers where the only number type to be considered is the `Real` type [4]. In their proposition, $\mathbb{N}$ is considered as an inductive predicate over `Real`, which allows to keep native inductive proofs and to recover recursive sequence definitions by means of an additional layer. Since the stability of operations over $\mathbb{N}$ becomes propositional ($(x + y \in \mathbb{N})$ is a statement to be

[14] Two different proofs of this statement are available in the project repository.

proved, whereas the judgement $(x + y : \text{Nat})$ was definitional), automatic proof of such statements is triggered by a type class inference mechanism.

Yalep implements some of the above ideas, taking into account the requirements for high-school proofs. We keep the idea of a unique number type, of which $\mathbb{N}$, $\mathbb{Z}$, $\mathbb{Q}$, $\mathbb{R}$ are subsets, and the solution of using class inference to facilitate automation triggering. However, we do not define $\mathbb{N}$ inductively. Rather, for any types T and E, provided there exists an injective mapping $c : E \to T$, we define the set of objects of type E with ${}^{s}E := \{x : T \mid \exists y : E, x = c(y)\}$. For numbers, we denote our reference type by `Number` (presently an alias of `Real` but it may evolve to the type `Complex` in the future).

This simpler representation has the advantage of applying directly and in the same manner to $\mathbb{N}$, $\mathbb{Z}$, $\mathbb{Q}$ and $\mathbb{R}$, with the adaptation of the library theorems specific to number type being reduced to a matter of coercions. However, inductive proofs and recursive functions are not native in Yalep and require intermediate lemmas. In addition, we are not aiming at preserving computability, whereas it is an objective of Portet and Bertot's work.

5 Partial Functions in Yalep

In proof assistants based on type theory (Lean, Rocq, ...), functions are total over a type (let's say "type-total"): they must be defined at any point of the domain type. In mathematics education, functions are total over a set (let's say "set-total"). A set being a predicate on a type, these functions would have to be represented in type theory as "type-partial".

Various approaches have been proposed to handle this situation.

Mathlib for Lean or Math Components for Rocq give a default value (e.g., 0) to functions where they are not defined, and subject associated theorems to assumptions that guarantee that function arguments belong to their domain. For example, in Lean's Mathlib, the inverse of $(0 : \mathbb{Q})$ is defined to be 0, but the predicate $a \cdot a^{-1} = 1$ will only hold if $a \neq 0$. Other ways of dealing with this issue include attaching a proof obligation to each relation involving terms that may be undefined [32] (implemented in TPE), or simulating a logic of partial terms with partial setoids and formalizing "directed quasi equalities", then automating their proofs [9].[15] In this last paper, Sacerdoti-Coen and Zoli specify that they do not consider the Rocq type theoretic approach (also possible in Lean) to encode the function domain into the type because it makes visible that a proof term is an argument of the function. We propose exploring this approach anyway, but hiding the proof term in suitable syntactic sugar with automation.

Considering that students are usually supposed to verify that a term is defined *before* writing it, and that set-theoretic presentation of a function is a triple $f := (D, F, G)$ encoding the domain D, the co-domain F, and the graph $G \subseteq D \times F$, we aim at obtaining a Lean formalization of a type-partial function $f \in F^D$, that,

[15] A synthetic presentation can also be found in C. Paulin's lecture https://www.lri.fr/~paulin/LASER/coq-slides4.pdf

associated with suitable automation and syntactic sugar, satisfies the following conditions:

PF1 The internal representation of f contains its domain and co-domain, and should expose them whenever it is required;
PF2 To write the term $f(x)$ the context must contain a proof of $x \in D$, should it be proven silently or by the user;
PF3 The internal representation of f contains a proof of $\forall x \in D, f(x) \in F$;
PF4 Usual notations for function application and definition are preserved (RL4).

The rest of the section is devoted to the design of our library for partial functions.

5.1 A first proposition: functions between subtypes associated to sets

Consider a set D and a set F of elements of respective types α and β, and that we want to model a map from D to F. The sub-type associated to `D:Set α`, denoted $\uparrow D$, is the type $\sum_{x:\alpha}(x \in D)$ of dependent pairs `⟨x:α,hx: x ∈ D⟩`. As $\uparrow D$ is a type, as well as $\uparrow F$, we can consider the type-total function $f : \uparrow D \to \uparrow F$ which embeds all the required information. This representation satisfies PF1, PF2 and PF3 and also, on the developer side:

(a) eases the definition of a function $f \in F^D$ such that $\forall x \in D, f(x) = \dots$ (provided a proof that $\forall x \in D, f(x) \in F$). Example:
`def f:↑[2;+∞[→↑[3;+∞[:=fun ⟨x,(hx:x⩾2)⟩=>⟨x^2,((by nlinarith):(x^2 ⩾ 3))⟩` creates the square function f from $[2;+\infty[$ to $[3;+\infty[$;
(b) eases the definition of a function application expression $f(x)$, provided a proof that $x \in D$ is given.
Example: `(f ⟨3,(by norm_num:(2:Real)⩽3)⟩).val` would mean $f(3)$;
(c) allows $f(x)$ to be definitionaly equal to its expression (e.g. x^2) (their equality does not require any proof). Example: Lean would automatically unify the previous expression with 3^2.

Let's now examine (a) and (b) from the student side: the examples above show that the underlying formalization has to be encapsulated to satisfy PF4. Regarding (b): each time the user wants to apply f to some $x : \alpha$, she has to express `f ⟨x,hx: x ∈ D⟩`, that is, prove that $x \in D$, which is tedious in practice (even if it has been proved once, it must be repeated each time); additionally the notation is heavy. Thus, we combine this formalization with:

- A tactic that automates the proof of $x \in D$. It calls the Lean tactic `assumption`, so that proving the fact once is enough for all occurrences of $f(x)$. It will also attempt to perform basic numerical calculations, as well as class inferences, to determine membership in a subset of numbers.
- Some syntactic sugar to hide the original notation. We take advantage of the fact that, while proof assistants use the `f x` notation for function application, the usual mathematical notation is $f(x)$. So, parsing `f(x)` will discharge the

proof goal $hx: x \in D$ and then expand to `f ⟨x,hx⟩`.[16] Note that to avoid parsing conflicts, we chose to use here a special Unicode pair of parentheses.

Regarding (a), to define a new function, the user has to prove that $f(x) \in F$ provided that $x \in D$. To avoid this, we provide a tactic automating this task and some syntactic sugar to create a new function while triggering the tactic. In Yalep, our previous function then becomes:

```
let's define the function f from [2;+∞[ to [3;+∞[ that maps x to x^2
```

5.2 A second formalization for partial functions

The previous formalization still has a few drawbacks:

- `f : ↑D → ↑F` is a type ascription. Type manipulation is exposed to the user.
- Given `f : ↑D → ↑F` and `g : ↑D' → ↑F'`, f and g have distinct types, thus homogeneous equality $f = g$ does not typecheck, even if $D = D'$ and $F = F'$ propositionally (it does not make sense to prove or disprove it).[17] For example, suppose that for $f : D \to F$ we denote by f' the derivative of f, whose domain is $D'_f := \{x \in D \mid f \text{ is derivable at } x\}$. Then it is not possible to define the set of functions $\{f : D \to F \mid D'_f = D \text{ and } f = f'\}$.

To tackle this, we bundle the function domain, co-domain, and a type-total function into a structure (`Map` α β). Any function from a set of elements of type α to a set of elements of type β would have type (`Map` α β).

```
structure Map (α β : Type)  [i:Inhabited β]  where
  func : α  → β
  domain : Set α
  codomain : Set β
  prop : ∀ x ∈ domain, func x ∈ codomain
  prop_out : ∀ x:α,  x ∉ domain →  func x = i.default
```

For instance, two functions $g : [1,2] \times \mathbb{Q}^+ \to \mathbb{Z}$ and $h : \mathbb{N} \times \mathbb{Q}^- \to [0;+\infty[$ would have the same type `Map (Number × Number) Number`.

The main drawback of this structure is the absence of automatic proof obligations when applying a function. We restore these proof obligations by defining two mutually reciprocal functions σ and ζ, allowing to switch from one representation to another. Then, applying and defining a function within the second representation reduces to the same activities as within the first one:

- *Applying a function:* σ maps (`u : Map` α β) to $[\sigma(u) : \uparrow(u.domain) \to \uparrow(u.codomain)]$ well-defined by: $\forall \langle x,h\rangle \in \uparrow(u.domain), \sigma(u)\langle x,h\rangle = \langle \text{func}(u)(x), \text{prop}(u)(h)\rangle$.

[16] `f ⟨x,hx⟩` being a pair ⟨`y:`β`,hy: y ∈ F`⟩, the macro $f(x)$ also silently applies the projection `Subtype.val := fun ⟨y,hy⟩ => y` when needed, to avoid students manipulating directly objects of sub-type $\uparrow F$.

[17] It might have been worth considering heterogeneous equality here, but we did not investigate further since it might have led to considering two different equalities, and run into complications about congruence closure [30].

Applying u to x means applying $\sigma(u)$ to $\langle x, h : x \in D\rangle$, thus the operation generates the obligation to prove $x \in D$. The user oriented macro $u(\cdot)$ expands just like $\sigma(u)(\cdot)$.

- *Defining a function:* Conversely, ζ maps a function $f : \uparrow D \to \uparrow F$ to a structure $\zeta(f)$ of type `Map` α β, defined by:
  - domain$(\zeta(f)) = D$ and codomain$(\zeta(f)) = F$
  - $\forall x, \text{func}(\zeta(f))(x) = \begin{cases} \text{Subtype.val}\,(f\langle x, h_x\rangle)^{18} & \text{if } (h_x : x \in D) \\ b \text{ (an arbitrary fixed value of type } \beta) & \text{if } (h_x : x \notin D) \end{cases}$
  - proofs of prop$(\zeta(f))$ and prop_out$(\zeta(f))$ are straightforward.

Like in the first formalization, a specific syntax allows to define a new application $u := \zeta(f)$ where f is built as described in §5.1. But two technical difficulties arise: first, `if x ∈ D...` blocks automatic unification and forces a call to the tactic `apply dif_pos` judiciously placed in the appropriate tactics.[19] Second, the statement `u∈F^D`, which means `u.domain=D and u.codomain=F`, is propositional (rather than definitional): once again, a tactic has to be triggered to use it when needed.

In our solution, a macro providing an interface for function definition also automatically generates, for each defined function, two lemmas that help tactics to unify `u(x)` with its expression, and `u.domain` and `u.codomain` with concrete values to which they may be propositionally equal.

For instance, the last example of section 5.1 generates:[18]

- `f.def:      ∀x∈[2;+∞[,  ((sigma f) ⟨x, ...⟩).val = x^2`
- `f.domains: f ∈ [3;+∞[^[2;+∞[`

5.3 Consequences

Defining function properties Each definition of a property of a function may require its own automation. Once again, we hide the automation in the syntax.

For example, defining the syntax "f is increasing on D'" requires proving that $D' \subseteq D$. If not, in the term `∀x∈D',∀y∈D', x⩽y⟹f(x)⩽f(y)`, the automation associated to `f(x)` will not be able to deduce that $x \in D$ from $x \in D'$.

The need of contextual connectors (and , ⟹) As pointed out by Wiedijk [45], when elaborating $P \implies Q$ or (P and Q), the automation will be stuck if elaborating Q requires a proof of P. For example, to be able to elaborate statements like $\forall x,\ x \neq 0 \longrightarrow f(x) \neq 0$ or $\forall x \in \mathbb{R}, x^2 + 1 \neq 0$ and $f\left(x^2 + 1\right) > 0$, the automation hidden in $f(\cdot)$ should access respectively proofs that $x \neq 0$ and $x^2 + 1 \neq 0$. For that reason, we redefine the implication $P \implies Q$ as $\forall (h : P),\ Q$ and the conjunction (P and Q) to mean $\exists (h : P),\ Q$.

[18] `Subtype.val` is the projection `fun ⟨y,hy⟩ => y`. When `z:↑F`, `z.val` is syntactic sugar for `Subtype.val z`.

[19] The decision procedure generated by `if x ∈ D` would demand that proposition `x ∈ D` is decidable, which is not the case in general, except in classical logic, at the cost of marking definition `noncomputable`.

6 Validation

During the design of Yalep, we also developed a pedagogical progression intended for tenth-graders. Its goal is to introduce the main proof structures gradually, without emphasizing formal logic. Our running example 1 is part of this progression: it illustrates two exercises designed respectively to present the introduction of quantifier ∀ and the elimination of connector or (proof by cases). The whole progression culminates in the classical proof of irrationality of $\sqrt{2}$ (as integer parity and this particular proof are parts of the French high-school curriculum). This proof is the classical proof used as an example and will allow the reader to compare with other proof assistants [31,32,44]. To demonstrate the readability and accessibility of Yalep, we also reproduced the so-called informal proof proposed by Barendregt in the first chapter of [44], which is based on the fact that there is no infinite descending sequence of natural numbers.[20]

In June 2025, the tool was tested during a 6-hour workshop at IRIF[21] spread over a week, with tenth-grade students. Students engaged enthusiastically in the proof tasks and the goals of supporting an introduction to proof course at the high-school level, while leaving plenty of autonomy were achieved. We felt that students really grasped the main ideas about proof, but were often hampered by their weaknesses in literal arithmetic. However, the main technical limitations we encountered were the current inability to configure the scope of the automation – some incoherently ordered proof steps have sometimes been validated simply because the tool could prove them to be true – and the lack of optimization leading to poor responsiveness for an interactive tool on ageing machines.

7 Related work

TPE [32] is a complete environment geared towards teaching proof. Proof steps are checked with Otter. Since it only provides a "point-and-click" end-user interaction mode, there is no need for defining and parsing an input language.

As for minimality, the syntax of Tutch [1] is close to Yalep's since the tool was conceived with the same objective in mind. However, the tool does not seem to handle any other theory than natural numbers, logic, and lists.

Lean Verbose [24] and Coq Waterproof [43], respectively based on proof assistants Lean and Rocq, provide other controlled natural languages (CNL) with comprehensive libraries. They both propose teacher configuration and help commands. Coq Waterproof also presents a proof/HTML mixed document interface. Both adapt the language to make the transfer to paper proof effective, but none of them tries to restrict the language to a minimal set of constructs. Figure 3

[20] The detailed progression as well as all mentioned proof scripts — solutions to exercises in the progression, the standard proof and the Barendregt proof of irrationality of $\sqrt{2}$ — are available in the project repository.

[21] a French computer science research lab in Paris

shows a comparison between Lean Verbose and Yalep based on a proof of the squeeze theorem.

```
Example "The squeeze theorem. (Lean Verbose)"
 Given: (u v w:ℕ→ℝ) (ℓ:ℝ)
 Assume: (hu:u converges to ℓ)
         (hw:w converges to ℓ)
         (h :∀n,u n⩽v n) (h':∀n,v n⩽ w n)
 Conclusion: v converges to ℓ
Proof:
 Let's prove that ∀ε>0, ∃N,∀n⩾N,|v n-ℓ|⩽ε
 Fix ε>0
 Since u converges to ℓ and ε>0 we get n₁
  such that h₁:∀n⩾n₁,|u n-ℓ|⩽ε
 Since w converges to ℓ and ε > 0 we get n₂
  such that h₂:∀n⩾n₂,|w n-ℓ|⩽ε
 Let's prove that max n₁ n₂ works:
  ∀n⩾max n₁ n₂,|v n-ℓ|⩽ε
 Fix n⩾max n₁ n₂
 Since n⩾max n₁ n₂ we get
  (hn₁: n⩾n₁) and (hn₂: n⩾n₂)
 Since ∀n⩾n₁, |u n-ℓ|⩽ε and n⩾n₁ we get
  (hn₁ℓ:-ε⩽u n-ℓ) and (hn₁d:u n-ℓ⩽ε)
 Since ∀n⩾n₂,|w n-ℓ|⩽ε and n⩾n₂ we get
  (hn₂l:-ε⩽w n-ℓ) and (hn₂d:w n-ℓ⩽ε)
 Let's prove that |v n-ℓ|⩽ε
 Let's first prove that -ε⩽v n-ℓ
 Calc -ε⩽u n-ℓ by assumption
    _  ⩽v n-ℓ since u n⩽v n
 Let's now prove that v n-ℓ⩽ε
 Calc v n-ℓ⩽w n-ℓ since v n⩽w n
    _      ⩽ε      by assumption
 QED
```

```
Theorem squeeze "The squeeze theorem (Yalep)"
 Assumptions:
  (u∈ℝ^ℕ)(v∈ℝ^ℕ)(w∈ℝ^ℕ)(ℓ∈ℝ)
  (u converges to ℓ)(w converges to ℓ)
  (for all natural n,u(n)⩽v(n))
  (for all natural n,v(n)⩽w(n))
  Conclusion: (v converges to ℓ)
Proof
 let ε > 0
 ◆ there exists a natural n₁ such that
   for all natural n,if n⩾n₁ then |u(n)-ℓ|⩽ε
 obtain such n₁
 ◆ there exists a natural n₂ such that
   for all natural n,if n⩾n₂ then |w(n)-ℓ|⩽ε
 obtain such n₂
 define n₀:=max n₁ n₂
 ◆ for all natural n,if n⩾n₀ then |v(n)-ℓ|⩽ε
  proof
   let n be a natural
   assume n⩾ n₀
   ◆ |u(n)-ℓ|⩽ε since n⩾n₁
   ◆ |w(n)-ℓ|⩽ε since n⩾n₂
   ◎ -ε⩽u(n)-ℓ
     _ ⩽v(n)-ℓ
   ◎ v(n)-ℓ⩽w(n)-ℓ
     _   ⩽ ε
   ◆ |v(n)-ℓ|⩽ε
  □
□
```

Fig. 3: Comparison of LeanVerbose and Yalep for the squeeze theorem. The proof in Lean Verbose is extracted from [24]. In the header, when data are defined by a type ascription in Lean Verbose (`ℓ:ℝ`), the same is obtained by a predicate in Yalep (`ℓ∈ℝ`)(for that reason it appears in the section 'Assumptions'). The type ascription (`ℓ:Number`) exists in the underlying Lean representation but is implicitly inferred. Lean Verbose expects a precise justification of each fact, expressed in a rich syntax, whereas Yalep allows it to be omitted. In Lean Verbose, some specific syntax is dedicated to backward introduction of existential quantifier and conjunction, as a few (respectively `Let's prove that ... works` and `Let's first prove ...`)

Diproche [7] also proposes a CNL geared towards education. The most advanced student error diagnosis technology we know of is "antiATP" technology.[22] As the verification engine is specially tailored to enable better control over feedback, Diproche does not rely on an existing and maintained comprehensive library. As a consequence, available topics, currently limited to elementary number theory, set theory, and geometry, may be difficult to extend. On the interaction side, Diproche does not display the proof state.

[22] Carl calls the principle of "buggy rules" antiATP, which consists of adding students' frequent errors as lemmas and checking whether automation solves the goal. See also [6,37] for details.

Proof Buddy [18] uses the declarative language of Isar but is geared towards learning logic, leaving the rules of meta-logic apparent.

While proposing a non-ambiguous syntax with minimal redundancy, Yalep does not aim at recognizing proofs nor statements expressed in natural language nor distinguishing ambiguities that arise from such a language, like in [46]. As ambiguities of natural language are additional hurdles to learning proof [10,11,15], we propose to separate the learning of logic from the acculturation to mathematical style. Our goal is hence very different from that of Naproche [21], or even Diproche, which uses the same syntax for the introduction of variables/assumptions and the elimination of the existential quantifier.

Finally, to our knowledge, none of the cited tools, based or not on type theory, claim to make proofs involving functions defined on subsets of $\mathbb{R}$ accessible to high-school students.[23]

Other comparisons of Yalep with Lean Verbose, Coq Waterproof, and Diproche are available in the Yalep repository.

8 Conclusion and Future Work

We have presented Yalep, a Lean-based prototype of a pedagogical environment for high-school students to learn the concept of proof using a proof assistant. Yalep's input language for proofs is inspired by coherent logic, and designed to favor forward chaining of facts.

In addition to text-based proof writing, Yalep provides point-and-click helpers and controlled automation. It also offers a formalization of the notion of function (from sets to sets), and an ambient type `Number` that prevents explicit type coercion. All these features were developed with ease of use for high-school students in mind, as well as similarity to pen-and-paper proofs, and were tested by tenth-grade students.

Yalep has several limitations: automation can be slow, especially when it fails to prove the statement proposed by the student; and it is sometimes too powerful in automatically proving statements that the teacher would require a justification for. Moreover, our formalization of numbers is not geared toward computations.

In the future, we plan to work on improving the automation to make it more configurable by the teacher. Our next goal is to improve the feedback given to the students (including error messages) beyond the success/failure diagnostic. We will also evaluate the pedagogical impact of our tool (using students/teachers surveys, pre- and post-tests, analysis of student productions), in collaboration with maths teachers and experts in math education.

Acknowledgments This work is partially funded by the ANR Project APPAM ANR-23-CE38-0009-01. Yalep front-end is inspired by Lean Verbose and even

[23] At the time of submitting the paper, Massot informed us that he tweaked Lean Verbose to make type number coercions transparent to the student and provided a convincing proof that $\sqrt{2} \notin \mathbb{Q}$. Due to time constraints, we could not investigate deeply.

relies on some pieces of its code, specifically: parts of its parser for theorem headers and the 'Calc' environment, and some helper functions.

References

1. Abel, A., Chang, B.Y.E., Pfenning, F.: Human-Readable Machine-Verifiable Proofs for Teaching Constructive Logic. In: Workshop Proof Transformation and Presentation and Proof Complexities (PTP'01) (2001), https://www.cs.cmu.edu/~fp/papers/ptp01.pdf
2. Autexier, S.: The CoRe Calculus. In: Hutchison, D., Kanade, T., Kittler, J., Kleinberg, J.M., Mattern, F., Mitchell, J.C., Naor, M., Nierstrasz, O., Pandu Rangan, C., Steffen, B., Sudan, M., Terzopoulos, D., Tygar, D., Vardi, M.Y., Weikum, G., Nieuwenhuis, R. (eds.) Automated Deduction – CADE-20, vol. 3632, pp. 84–98. Springer Berlin Heidelberg, Berlin, Heidelberg (2005). https://doi.org/10.1007/11532231_7
3. Bartzia, E., Meyer, A., Narboux, J.: Proof assistants for undergraduate mathematics and computer science education: elements of a priori analysis. In: Trigueros, M. (ed.) INDRUM 2022: Fourth conference of the International Network for Didactic Research in University Mathematics. pp. 253–262. Reinhard Hochmuth, Hanovre, Germany (Oct 2022), https://hal.science/hal-03648357
4. Bertot, Y., Portet, T.: Chassez le naturel dans la formalisation des mathématiques. In: 36es Journées Francophones des Langages Applicatifs (JFLA 2025). Roiffé, France (Jan 2025), https://inria.hal.science/hal-04757635
5. Boldo, S., Clément, F., Hamelin, D., Mayero, M., Rousselin, P.: Teaching divisibility and binomials with coq. In: Proceedings of 13th International Workshop on Theorem proving components for Educational software (ThEdu'24). vol. 419, p. 124–139. Open Publishing Association (May 2025). https://doi.org/10.4204/eptcs.419.8, http://dx.doi.org/10.4204/EPTCS.419.8
6. Carl, M.: Using Automated Theorem Provers for Mistake Diagnosis in the Didactics of Mathematics. CoRR **abs/2002.05083**(arXiv:2002.05083) (feb 2020). https://doi.org/10.48550/arxiv.2002.05083, https://arxiv.org/abs/2002.05083
7. Carl, M., Lorenzen, H., Schmitz, M.: Natural Language Proof Checking in Introduction to Proof Classes – First Experiences with Diproche. In: Proceedings of the International Workshop on Theorem Proving Components for Educational Software (Th'Edu) 2021. vol. 354, pp. 59–70 (Feb 2022). https://doi.org/10.4204/EPTCS.354.5
8. Carter, N.C., Monks, K.G.: Lurch: A Word Processor that Can Grade Students' Proofs. In: Lange, C., Aspinall, D., Carette, J., Davenport, J., Kohlhase, A., Kohlhase, M., Libbrecht, P., Quaresma, P., Rabe, F., Sojka, P., Whiteside, I., Windsteiger, W. (eds.) Joint Proceedings of the MathUI, OpenMath, PLMMS and ThEdu Workshops and Work in Progress at the Conference on Intelligent Computer Mathematics 2013. No. 1010 in CEUR Workshop Proceedings, Aachen (2013), http://ceur-ws.org/Vol-1010/paper-04.pdf
9. Coen, C.S., Zoli, E.: A Note on Formalising Undefined Terms in Real Analysis. In: Proceedings of International Workshop on Proof Assistants and Types in Education (PATE07) (2007), https://www.cs.unibo.it/~sacerdot/PAPERS/pate07.pdf
10. Durand-Guerrier, V., Njomgang-Ngansop, J.: Questions de logique et de langage à la transition secondaire - supérieur. L'exemple de la négation. In: Kuzniak Alain & Sokhna Mohamed (ed.) Actes du Colloque Espace Mathématique Francophone. pp. 1033–1047. No. numéro spécial, Dakar, Senegal (Apr 2009), https://hal.science/hal-00804096

11. Edmonds-Wathen, C., Trinick, T., Durand-Guerrier, V.: Impact of Differing Grammatical Structures in Mathematics Teaching and Learning, pp. 23–46. Springer International Publishing, Cham (2016). https://doi.org/10.1007/978-3-319-14511-2_2, https://doi.org/10.1007/978-3-319-14511-2_2
12. Ehle, A., Hundeshagen, N., Lange, M.: The Sequent Calculus Trainer with Automated Reasoning - Helping Students to Find Proofs. In: Proceedings of 6th International Workshop on Theorem proving components for Educational software (ThEdu'17). vol. 267, pp. 19–37 (Mar 2018). https://doi.org/10.4204/EPTCS.267.2, http://arxiv.org/abs/1803.01467v1
13. Gallego Arias, E.J., Pin, B., Jouvelot, P.: jsCoq: Towards Hybrid Theorem Proving Interfaces. In: Proceedings of 5th International Workshop on Theorem proving components for Educational software (ThEdu'16). vol. 239, pp. 15–27 (Jan 2017). https://doi.org/10.4204/EPTCS.239.2
14. Gasquet, O., Schwarzentruber, F., Strecker, M.: Panda: A Proof Assistant in Natural Deduction for All. A Gentzen Style Proof Assistant for Undergraduate Students. In: Blackburn, P., van Ditmarsch, H., Manzano, M., Soler-Toscano, F. (eds.) Tools for Teaching Logic - Third International Congress, TICTTL 2011, Salamanca, Spain, June 1-4, 2011. Proceedings. Lecture Notes in Computer Science, vol. 6680, pp. 85–92. Springer (2011). https://doi.org/10.1007/978-3-642-21350-2_11
15. Hache, C., Mesnil, Z.: Outils logiques pour analyser les formulations des preuves dans des manuels de lycée. In: Séminaire national de didactique des mathématiques de l'ARDM. Paris, France (Nov 2019), https://hal.science/hal-03257750
16. Herbst, P.G.: Establishing a custom of proving in american school geometry: Evolution of the two-column proof in the early twentieth century. Educational Studies in Mathematics **49**(3), 283–312 (2002). https://doi.org/10.1023/A:1020264906740
17. Huang, X.: Reconstruction Proofs at the Assertion Level. In: Proceedings of the 12th International Conference on Automated Deduction. p. 738–752. CADE-12, Springer-Verlag, Berlin, Heidelberg (1994)
18. Karsten, N., Jacobsen, F.K., Eiken, K.J., Nestmann, U., Villadsen, J.: ProofBuddy: A Proof Assistant for Learning and Monitoring. In: Proceedings Twelfth International Workshop on Trends in Functional Programming in Education. vol. 382, pp. 1–21 (Aug 2023). https://doi.org/10.4204/EPTCS.382.1
19. Kerjean, M., Leroux, F., Massot, P., Mayero, M., Mesnil, Z., Modeste, S., Narboux, J., Rousselin, P.: Utilisation des assistants de preuves pour l'enseignement en L1 - Retours d'expériences. Gazette Société Mathématique de France (Aug 2022), https://hal.science/hal-03979238
20. Korkut, J.: A Proof Tree Builder for Sequent Calculus and Hoare Logic. In: Proceedings ThEdu'22. vol. 375, pp. 54–62 (2023). https://doi.org/10.4204/EPTCS.375.5, http://arxiv.org/abs/2303.05865v1
21. Kühlwein, D., Cramer, M., Koepke, P., Schröder, B.: The Naproche System. In: Calculemus Emerging Trends 2009 (joint with CICM'09) (july 2009)
22. Leach-Krouse, G.: Carnap: An Open Framework for Formal Reasoning in the Browser. In: Proceedings 6th International Workshop on Theorem proving components for Educational software, ThEdu@CADE 2017. vol. 267, pp. 70–88 (Mar 2018). https://doi.org/10.4204/EPTCS.267.5
23. Machın, B., Sierra, L.: Yoda: A Simple Tool for Natural Deduction (2011), http://logicae.usal.es/TICTTL/actas/MachinSierra.pdf
24. Massot, P.: Teaching Mathematics Using Lean and Controlled Natural Language. In: Bertot, Y., Kutsia, T., Norrish, M. (eds.) 15th International Conference on Interactive Theorem Proving (ITP 2024). Leibniz International Proceedings in Informatics

(LIPIcs), vol. 309, pp. 27:1–27:19. Schloss Dagstuhl – Leibniz-Zentrum für Informatik, Dagstuhl, Germany (2024). https://doi.org/10.4230/LIPIcs.ITP.2024.27
25. Materzok, M.: Easyprove: A Tool for Teaching Precise Reasoning. In: Proceedings of the Fourth International Conference on Tools for Teaching Logic (TTL2015). M. Antonia Huertas, João Marcos, María Manzano, Sophie Pinchinat, François Schwarzentruber, Rennes, France (June 2015), https://arxiv.org/abs/1507.03675
26. Nawrocki, W., Ayers, E.W., Ebner, G.: An Extensible User Interface for Lean 4. In: Naumowicz, A., Thiemann, R. (eds.) 14th International Conference on Interactive Theorem Proving (ITP 2023). Leibniz International Proceedings in Informatics (LIPIcs), vol. 268, pp. 24:1–24:20. Schloss Dagstuhl – Leibniz-Zentrum für Informatik, Dagstuhl, Germany (2023). https://doi.org/10.4230/LIPIcs.ITP.2023.24, https://drops.dagstuhl.de/entities/document/10.4230/LIPIcs.ITP.2023.24
27. Perháč, J., Novotný, S., Chodarev, S., Kristensen, J.T., Tveito, L., Shturmov, O., Thomsen, M.K.: OnlineProver: Experience with a Visualisation Tool for Teaching Formal Proofs. In: Proceedings of 13th International Workshop on Theorem proving components for Educational software (ThEdu'24) (2024). https://doi.org/10.5324/nikt.6205
28. Rognier, B., Duhamel, G.: Présentation de la plateforme Edukera. In: Signoles, J. (ed.) Vingt-septièmes Journées Francophones des Langages Applicatifs (JFLA 2016). Saint-Malo, France (Jan 2016), https://hal.science/hal-01333606
29. Schiller, M.R.G.: Granularity Analysis for Mathematical Proofs. Topics in Cognitive Science **5**(2), 251–269 (Apr 2013). https://doi.org/10.1111/tops.12012
30. Selsam, D., Moura, L.: Congruence Closure in Intensional Type Theory. In: Proceedings of the 8th International Joint Conference on Automated Reasoning - Volume 9706. p. 99–115. Springer-Verlag, Berlin, Heidelberg (2016). https://doi.org/10.1007/978-3-319-40229-1_8, https://doi.org/10.1007/978-3-319-40229-1_8
31. Siekmann, J., Benzmüller, C., Fiedler, A., Meier, A., Normann, I., Pollet, M.: Proof Development in OMEGA: The Irrationality of Square Root of 2. pp. 271–314 (Jan 2003)
32. Sommer, R., Nuckols, G.: A Proof Environment for Teaching Mathematics. Journal of Automated Reasoning **32**, 227–258 (2004). https://doi.org/10.1023/B:JARS.0000044825.55318.95
33. Stojanovic, S., Narboux, J., Bezem, M., Janicic, P.: A Vernacular for Coherent Logic. In: Lecture Notes in Computer Science. Lecture Notes in Computer Science, vol. 8543, p. 16. Springer, Coimbra, Portugal (Jul 2014). https://doi.org/10.1007/978-3-319-08434-3_28, https://inria.hal.science/hal-00983975
34. Stylianides, G.J., Stylianides, A.J., Moutsios-Rentzos, A.: Proof and proving in school and university mathematics education research: a systematic review. ZDM – Mathematics Education **56**(1), 47–59 (Feb 2024). https://doi.org/10.1007/s11858-023-01518-y, https://link.springer.com/10.1007/s11858-023-01518-y
35. Tao, T.: QED - an interactive textbook. https://teorth.github.io/QED/ (2018)
36. Thompson, D., Seligman, J.: Teaching natural deduction in the right order with natural deduction planner. IfCoLog Journal of Logics and their Applications **4**(1), 193–219 (January 2017)
37. Tran Minh, F., Gonnord, L., Narboux, J.: Proof Assistants for Teaching: a Survey. In: Proceedings of 13th International Workshop on Theorem proving components for Educational software (ThEdu'24). vol. 419, p. 1–27. Open Publishing Association (May 2025). https://doi.org/10.4204/eptcs.419.1, http://dx.doi.org/10.4204/EPTCS.419.1
38. Vasconcelos, D.R.: ANITA: Analytic Tableau Proof Assistant. Electronic Proceedings in Theoretical Computer Science **375**, 38–53 (2023). https://doi.org/10.4204/EPTCS.375.4, http://arxiv.org/abs/2303.05864v1, in Post-Proceedings ThEdu'22

39. Villadsen, J., Jacobsen, F.K.: Using Isabelle in Two Courses on Logic and Automated Reasoning. In: Ferreira, J.F., Mendes, A., Menghi, C. (eds.) Formal Methods Teaching. pp. 117–132. Springer International Publishing, Cham (2021). https://doi.org/10.1007/978-3-030-91550-6-9
40. Villadsen, J., Jensen, A.B., Schlichtkrull, A.: NaDeA: A Natural Deduction Assistant with a Formalization in Isabelle. In: Proceedings of the Fourth International Conference on Tools for Teaching Logic (TTL2015) (Jul 2015). https://doi.org/10.48550/arXiv.1507.04002
41. Villadsen, J.: Minimal Sequent Calculus for Teaching First-Order Logic: Lessons Learned. In: Proceedings of 13th International Workshop on Theorem proving components for Educational software (ThEdu'24). vol. 419, p. 75–89. Open Publishing Association (May 2025). https://doi.org/10.4204/eptcs.419.5, http://dx.doi.org/10.4204/EPTCS.419.5
42. Wemmenhove, A.: Waterproof: Transforming a proof assistant into an educational tool. Ph.D. thesis, Mathematics and Computer Science (Mar 2025)
43. Wemmenhove, J., Arends, D., Beurskens, T., Bhaid, M., McCarren, S., Moraal, J., Rivera Garrido, D., Tuin, D., Vassallo, M., Wils, P., Portegies, J.: Waterproof: Educational Software for Learning How to Write Mathematical Proofs. In: Proceedings ThEdu'23. vol. 400, p. 96–119. Open Publishing Association (Apr 2024). https://doi.org/10.4204/eptcs.400.7
44. Wiedijk, F.: The Seventeen Provers of the World. Springer, Berlin, Heidelberg (2006)
45. Wiedijk, F., Zwanenburg, J.: First Order Logic with Domain Conditions. In: Goos, G., Hartmanis, J., Van Leeuwen, J., Basin, D., Wolff, B. (eds.) Theorem Proving in Higher Order Logics, vol. 2758, pp. 221–237. Springer Berlin Heidelberg, Berlin, Heidelberg (2003). https://doi.org/10.1007/10930755_15
46. Xie, L., Hui, Z., Cao, Q.: A Natural Formalized Proof Language. In: Chin, W.N., Xu, Z. (eds.) Theoretical Aspects of Software Engineering. pp. 446–464. Springer Nature Switzerland (2024). https://doi.org/10.1007/978-3-031-64626-3_26

[illegible]
[illegible] Formal Proofs [illegible]
[illegible] (2020) [illegible]
[illegible]

[illegible] Natural [illegible] Learning [illegible]
[illegible] natural [illegible]
[illegible] educational [illegible]
[illegible]

[illegible]

[illegible] Chen, [illegible] Trends in [illegible] (eds.) [illegible]
[illegible]
[illegible]

Author Index

A

Alidra, Abdelghani 258
Ayala-Rincón, Mauricio 113, 412

B

Baanen, Anne 51
Ballard, Matthew Robert 51
Barreira, Davi Sales 431
Bartoletti, Massimo 340
Baumgartner, Alexander 133
Bonzio, Stefano 340
Brown, Chad E. 3, 71

C

Carvalho, Henrique Borges 431
Chen, Bryan Gin–ge 51
Coelho, Flávio Codeço 431
Commelin, Johan 51

D

de Lima, Thaynara Arielly 113, 412
de Oliveira Ribeiro, Bruno Berto 412
del Barco, Viviana 317
Do, Duc Minh 392

E

Ehling, Georg 113

F

Ferrara, Marco 340

G

Gonnord, Laure 447

H

Hajdu, Márton 21
Heule, Marijn 29
Horowitz, Lucy 279
Hozzová, Petra 21
Huch, Fabian 91

I

Infanti, Gustavo 317

K

Kaliszyk, Cezary 3, 71
Kamareddine, Fairouz 171
Karatarakis, Michail 279
Kelber, Josefin 191
Koepke, Peter 357
Kohlhase, Michael 191, 208, 222
Kosaian, Katherine 371
Kovács, Laura 21
Kutsia, Temur 113, 133

M

Mackey, Ethan 29
Medeiros e Sá, Asla 431
Moscato, Mariano M. 412

N

Nantes-Sobrinho, Daniele 133
Narboux, Julien 447

P

Pathak, Shashank 152

Q

Qian, Long 29

R

Rabe, Florian 222, 240
Rademaker, Alexandre 431
Ren, Xuandi 279
Rivas, Exequiel 317
Rizkallah, Christine 392
Rothgang, Michael 51
Rozier, Kristin Yvonne 371

V. de Paiva and P. Koepke (Eds.): CICM 2025, LNAI 16136, pp. 469–470, 2026.
https://doi.org/10.1007/978-3-032-07021-0

S
Sacerdoti Coen, Claudio 258
Sanchez Ocegueda, Alejandro 279
Schaefer, Jan Frederik 191, 208
Schäfer, Patrick 357
Schmidt-Schauß, Manfred 133
Schütz, Marcel 191, 222
Schwahn, Paul 317
Shan, Ruocheng 300
Sloan, Elizabeth 371
Subercaseaux, Bernardo 29
Suda, Martin 3

T
Testa, Damiano 51
Tran Minh, Frédéric 447

U
Urban, Josef 3, 71

V
Voronkov, Andrei 21
Vrečar, Luka 171

W
Wagner, Eva Maria 21
Wang, Zili 371
Wells, Joe 171

Y
Youssef, Abdou 300

Z
Žilinčík, Richard Steven 21

MIX
Papier aus verantwortungsvollen Quellen
Paper from responsible sources
FSC® C105338

If you have any concerns about our products,
you can contact us on
ProductSafety@springernature.com

In case Publisher is established outside the EU,
the EU authorized representative is:
Springer Nature Customer Service Center GmbH
Europaplatz 3, 69115 Heidelberg, Germany

Printed by Libri Plureos GmbH
in Hamburg, Germany